T0354768

# TRUE LOVE

## CHRONICLE OF AN EX-WHITE WITCH

## PAULA GILBERT

authorHOUSE®

*AuthorHouse™*
*1663 Liberty Drive*
*Bloomington, IN 47403*
*www.authorhouse.com*
*Phone: 1 (800) 839-8640*

*Published by AuthorHouse  09/18/2019*

*ISBN: 978-1-5246-8855-4 (sc)*
*ISBN: 978-1-5246-8856-1 (e)*

*Library of Congress Control Number: 2017909384*

*Print information available on the last page.*

*Print information available on the last page.*

*The names in this book have been changed to protect the identity of all those involved.*

*All scriptures taken from the KJV (King James Version) of the Bible; public domain*

Due to the explicit nature of subjects discussed in these pages, this book is not suitable for children or possibly teens, and may even disturb some Christians. Please use discretion.

# Preface

WHEN I, THE AUTHOR, FIRST published this book in its original form under a different name in 2000, it did not get a warm reception from the close community of Christian friends and mentors I was involved with at the time. This was due to its explicit content, which many felt was not healthy for me to dwell on, or for others to learn about. Admittedly, upon reading it through again nearly seventeen years later, I realize that it could have done without a few things. I was certainly younger in my Christian walk, both spiritually *and* doctrinally. After taking this book out of print shortly after its publication (or at least, I *assumed* it had been taken out of print, when for some reason, it wasn't), I never thought I would touch it again. But the Lord had other plans; hence this revised, newer version. In retrospect, I realize now that I never wrote this book for Christians to begin with. I wrote it for those who would understand my journey because they perhaps were undergoing a similar one themselves. This book was meant to be an evangelical outreach for the lost, downtrodden, and hurting, as well as those seeking the supernatural. Therefore, Christians, please be warned that for the renewed mind, a graphic account of my life could stir up memories you have long since put to death. For this reason, I suggest you pray to ensure you should read such a book. To further explain my intentions: the literary pursuit of this autobiography is for readers to live life in my shoes beginning at an early age; observing my thought patterns, emotions and behavior, as well as the experiences that impact the paths I choose to take. I feel this is really the most effective way for me to communicate how a person comes to such conclusions as I did, and how the supernatural realm seeks to influence each one of us on a frequent basis—for good, or bad.

# Contents

**TRUE LOVE**

By night on my bed
I sought him whom my soul loveth:
I sought him, but I found him not.

(Song of Solomon 3:1)

# I.

## THE SPIRIT WORLD

I OPENED MY EYES, SUDDENLY awakened out of a deep sleep—again. My heart started pounding as that familiar feeling of dread washed over me. Looking up then, I sensed something watching me. And there it was. A black mass—much like a cloud suspended from the ceiling of my dark room—hovered above my head. Then came the cold, rushing in as if someone had just opened the door to a walk-in freezer.

The evil was here, arriving in its usual way. It infiltrated every molecule of ¹air, smothering me until I was paralyzed with fear. It pressed its way into my room, into my mind, and into my body. Like before, it pounced on me, pinning me down to my bed so that I couldn't move. I gasped for air, my tongue frozen, my lips quivering in an attempt to scream. No. It wouldn't let me. I thought in my mind that I needed to get up—to run, but every nerve in my body was rendered inactive.

Then somehow, after what seemed like eternity, I was up and bolting out of my bedroom to find safety in the protection of my mother and father, climbing into bed between the two of them. As I struggled to relay to them this terrifying experience, they calmly informed me that I was having another bad dream.

Another bad dream... though I would come to them many times during my childhood, insisting that this thing—whatever it was—had entered my room again. No, a bad dream was when I saw the dark cloaked figures locking me in a cage and slowly lowering me into fire, only to awake with relief to the shadows of a quiet bedroom and the

1

familiar scent of home. Bad dreams don't happen when your eyes are open and you are fully awake.

The supernatural world I'd come to know at times frightened me, at times intrigued me. When it frightened me, I'd sputter out a Hail Mary or grope for my rosary, thinking the touch of the beads in my hand would somehow make that world disappear. I'd envision in my head at night that I was climbing [2]ladders, each one ascending in the clouds to a higher level where the evil beings could not reach me. I climbed as quickly as I could, knowing that they were trying desperately to grab me and pull me back down so that they could devour me. I was climbing up to where God was.

Everything I did involved running from them, even during the day when the birds chirped and the sun shone bright. I'd run as fast as I could to wash my hands or exit a room, knowing they were right there behind me, ready to kill. It was almost like a game, where if I didn't do something in a certain amount of time, I lost—and the price for losing was my life. I would suffer torment at their hands. So I told myself whenever the fear pierced my mind that I had to hurry—I had to run quick before *it* or *them* got me.

For some reason, the evil was attracted to me like a magnet, manifesting itself through others who seemed to have no motive for the terrible way they treated me. Kids I didn't know physically abused me: strangling me, punching me dead-on in the face, hunting me down on the playground every recess to beat me up...

I walked around in a daze, feeling alienated and alone. Like a paper cup blowing in the wind, it seemed I had no control over what happened to me. I felt somehow I was an adult trapped in a child's body, able to discern things that other children could not. Yet at the same time, I didn't understand what it was that I was discerning. I just knew there was something out there—a whole different world consisting of evil.

At times, however, this other world carried me away into a fairy tale that somehow made me feel at home. It beckoned to me softly, promising me comfort in my loneliness. When other children mocked me because of my rather large bucked teeth, glasses, and weight problem, or when I gazed out the window to watch below as they played their two-faced games, feeling unattached but happy to be estranged from their juvenile power trips which invariably ended with the stronger personality dominating over the weak; I went to my other world, where I was understood—and welcomed. I didn't really have to try to go there, for it seemed I was magically transported without any effort on my part. And though I couldn't see the beings in this other world, I felt them. They were watching me. They were all around me, enveloping me in a haze of enchantment. Yet, there was a sinister presence here too, though not to the degree that I'd felt it at other times. This presence thrilled me, as I began to sense something hidden in its grasp that I had yet to discover.

"Tell me, Daddy, about hypnotism again," I would plead, feeling a rush of excitement in my veins.

My father, I knew, also explored this other world, because he talked of these strange powers he'd possessed before. He told me how he put people in a trance, as if they were asleep, and then he made them bark like dogs and walk around the room without them knowing it. Even when they didn't believe him, he proved them wrong. They woke up afterward, clueless as to what had taken place, while observers relayed to them everything they had done.

He said he'd read books on animal hypnotism as well. He talked about a spot on a dog's head where if you touched it just the right way, you could put the dog in a total trance.

I asked him to hypnotize me, but he refused, telling me he hadn't done it in a long time and he wasn't sure he'd be able to wake me up. He said I might wander out into the street, then, and get hit by a car.

We were very close, my father and I; sometimes closer than he and my mother, it seemed. I was deeply influenced by him in many ways, especially when it came to reading. His love for books was immense, and his thirst for worldly knowledge unquenchable. In his library, a room that conveyed to me mystery as well as great wisdom, he sat scanning through countless books and jotting down notes in the back. Or he wrote poetry pondering his spiritual existence. I, too, began cultivating these same areas of interest, often reading or writing alongside him in our quiet sanctuary.

The mystery in that room was the Pandora's Box I was forbidden to open: the tempting fruit resting on the top shelves, out of my reach but within full view. "Daddy, what's that book?" I'd ask again for the fifth time, aching to touch it, to look through it, to read just a few words…

"Reincarnation. Your mother says it's evil, so you can't look at it," he'd answer the same as last time.

Once, however, I succeeded in getting him to tell me more when I asked him what *reincarnation* meant. He explained to me it was about people living more than one life, which made me knit my brows together as I groped for the mentality to understand his reply. I vaguely remember him refuting my mother's opinion on the book, which made me then question why I couldn't look at it. He gently answered, "You're too young to understand."

In the bottom cupboards, stacked amidst scuba diving and treasure hunting magazines, I discovered lust one day: periodicals with nude pictures and letters from readers giving graphic details of their sexual experiences. I read about men and women, men and men, women and women, groups of both men and women, and even women with *animals*. How did I instinctively know that these magazines were forbidden—that I should not be reading them? But yet I watched my father go into the bathroom sometimes with one wrapped inside his newspaper.

Of course, my cousin *Dr. Matt* played a part in my early exposure to sex, as well. At age four, I lie down on the operating table so he could "examine" me with a cigarette lighter. I went upstairs where my parents were having a big party and told my mom. I don't think she really believed me. She told my aunt about it, and of course, Matt claimed I was lying. The incident was brushed aside, and the party continued.

By the age of seven, I was already fully aware of certain sexual mysteries that most seven-year-olds are not. Another secret I stumbled upon in my father's library.

Ah, but there were other mysteries, these being of a more sinister kind! The authentic Japanese suit of armor lurking in the corner seemed to be watching my every move. Though no eyes inhabited the large holes beneath the helmet, others shared my convictions upon standing in its presence. My cousins, when visiting from out of town, would plead not to have to sleep in the library, as they thought it was haunted.

The wire-haired mustache attached below the nose of the armor's face piece served only to make it look more alive. One could easily envision a very small, very evil looking man behind the disguise; anxious to attack his prey. Perched atop the helmet was a rather peculiar ornament: a gold rabbit with large ears, one of which had broken and was glued on rather sloppily. Though one would expect the armor to be similar to that of the thick medieval mail, it was actually rather soft and pliable. I found out later that it came with an old piece of parchment on which was scribbled the history of its wearer. A Japanese translator could read only parts of it since the language was very old, but told my father that apparently it had been worn by a young girl who murdered her family and then committed suicide. At least, that's what I was told. A sword was also included with the armor, and I wondered if it had been the very weapon she'd used for the massacre.

And then there was the Egyptian death mask which captivated my father when he purchased it from the man running an ad in the *Trader's Weekly*. It seemed so frightening, yet so esoteric at the same time. I recall carefully removing it from its box on the shelf in the library closet, as if not to disturb its ancient sleep. My friends all commented on how eerie it looked. Though it was only a replication of a mummy's head, there seemed to be a strange power emanating from it. I liked to think it was the real thing because it looked very old and cracked.

Ghosts were a popular subject with my father: ghosts and mysterious women. He had books on ghosts, and he wrote of them in his poetry. One poem in particular I remember was about a haunted New England town in which he met the ghost of a fair maiden whose life had tragically been taken. They strolled together hand in hand, as he pondered that [3]"perhaps fate meant that our lives should intertwine." But then the cathedral bell tolled, and they had to say good-bye, though he vowed that he would return to the enchanted town.

In another poem, while walking down the street, he opened a [4]"cryptic door" to a bar penetrated with evil. An exotic belly dancer swayed and gyrated to a strange beat. She was bewitching and alluring, and seemed to be in a hypnotic trance as she performed her dance of the veils. Then once again, time slipped away. The clock on the wall told him he had to go, and he exited through the door with remorse. Perhaps he wrote the poem about my mother, who was taking belly-dancing lessons at the time. As for the previous poem, the three of us had also visited a

New England town on one of our vacations. It seemed either my father created fictitious scenarios in which the main characters were actually he and my mother—a role playing of sorts—or he wrote of supposed past life experiences.

I remember dramatizing these poems on tape with him, using music and other sound effects. His words came to life then, placing me in the midst of haunting romantic encounters with people from another time. They struck a chord deep within me as they communicated the unbearable ache in a lover's soul upon separation from his mate. It was then, I believe, that I developed an unconscious recognition of the incredible strength, power, and mystery of love.

Other subjects my father touched upon were: mind control/mental powers, psychic phenomenon, transcendental meditation, divination, sex magic, magic potions, voodoo spells, and astral projection.

At fifteen, he astral projected one afternoon, meaning: his soul left his body. His experience was not a pleasant one. He told me of how he floated upward to look down upon his body, and then drifted into an icy cold darkness from which emerged the loudest, most evil laugh he'd ever heard. It scared him so bad that he snapped back into his body. He jerked himself up off the bed and proceeded to check the house thoroughly inside and out. Apparently, the voice had sounded so real and so loud that he thought perhaps a man had entered the premises to frighten him.

After hearing of my father's astral projection experience, I viewed a TV horror show about a woman lifting up, up, traveling to another state of consciousness as she imagined herself in an elevator. I remember lying in bed after watching it that night, praying with all my might that I wouldn't leave my body as the elevator seemed to appear in my mind against my will, wanting me to ascend with it.

Following my father's purchase of the Egyptian death mask, a Saturday morning thriller about mummies caught my interest. The part that always stuck out the most in my memory after watching it was the ritualistic dancing and burial rites the Egyptians performed after mummification of their dead. They danced around in a frenzy of evil, spellbound and seemingly intoxicated with lust.

One of my favorite kid's movies was *Witch Hill*. It was about children possessing psychic powers. Because I had been exposed to the supernatural at such an early age, I was well able to relate to these children.

In school, I was always elected to play the witch during recess; everyone said I did such a good job. I soon found myself playing it at home, too, when I tired of reading and didn't want to join in the cruel games of the neighborhood kids. I'd gallop on the front lawn with a broom, pretending I had a pet dragon following close behind.

My father and I frequently visited the bookstore. On one of our trips, during which we ate at our favorite Greek restaurant beforehand and then browsed for what seemed like hours among paperbacks, hardcovers, and magazines, I spotted a book about a young teenage witch. To my delight, my father bought it for me. Though I was a very good reader for my age, I had trouble understanding the story due to the long, complicated words. However, I would often get it out and skim through some of the magic potions, then stare intently at the cover, wishing I could be a witch like the girl in the picture. She looked friendly. That's because she was a *good* witch. It seemed very glamorous to me.

The next-door neighbor and I invented a game we played quite often. Since we both had crushes on various men from our favorite TV shows, we'd pretend that their ghost was present in the room with us. We'd decide which male characters we wanted to follow us around that day, and then [5]talk to them as if they were actually there, floating through the air though we couldn't see them.

One day, while alone in the house, we asked the ghosts to knock on the wall to prove that they were in the room with us. To our surprise and fright, a loud knock sounded on the wall several times. Each of us jumped, then quickly assumed that the other had done it. We asked once more, watching one another to be sure. Again, the knock sounded. We screamed, tearing out of the house as fast as we could. It occurred to us that perhaps my brother had caused the spooky knocks. However, we spotted him down by the lake and realized that he could not possibly have sounded a knock from inside the living room wall if he'd been outside, especially when we lived in a brick house. Had my next-door neighbor managed to knock without me seeing it?

While growing up, my father instructed me not to dabble in the Occult. He warned me to stay away from such things as Ouija boards, telling me I would be playing with the Devil if I did such things.

I told him about a game my friends and I had played, called Bloody Mary, where the object was to see the Devil's mistress by standing in a dark room with no windows and staring into a mirror chanting "Bloody Mary" ten times until a small, red dot appeared in the center of the mirror and grew into a picture of her. He became very stern with me, telling me not to mess around anymore with that game. A rumor had been going around that one girl, after summoning Bloody Mary, was then chased by her and scratched badly in the face with her long, red fingernails until the girl jumped into a body of water: the only way to repel the evil mistress.

Though my father commanded me not to play with the Occult, his warnings didn't hold much weight for me. I saw that he had dabbled in it while growing up, and apparently still held an interest in it judging from the large collection of books he possessed on the subject.

It wasn't long before a Ouija board was introduced to me by a friend. We played it at her house once, and I remember feeling really strange about it for some reason. Then she brought it over one night to a small slumber party I was having. I told myself it was just a game and nothing to be afraid of, with neat pictures of a sun and moon, and some letters and numbers… how could such a thing be evil?

After we woke up the next morning, we pulled the shades and closed my bedroom door as Katy told us we needed to be quiet and concentrate in order to [6]contact the spirits. Gathering around the game, we put our fingers on the plastic dome shaped marker and began asking it questions, while the marker glided across the board to spell out the answers. I was a little skeptical, since it seemed perhaps my friends might have been moving the marker on their own accord. Then Katy suggested we ask it whose presence was in the room with us. We all agreed excitedly. The room grew very still as we waited for a reply, each of us holding our breath in frightened anticipation. Somebody then said something about making the spirits angry, and it was during this time that my brother Jim, who'd been lingering outside in the hallway for an opportunity to frighten us, decided to cease the moment. While we awaited the spirit's reply, he groaned in a deep voice, pushing open the bedroom door. Needless to say, we screamed at the top of our lungs and ran out of the room as fast as our feet could carry us! Apparently, my mother, who'd been cooking breakfast downstairs, put him up to it. She said she wanted to teach us a lesson about playing around with those kinds of things.

As if that wasn't enough torment for the day, Jim had to top it off by frightening me again when I went into my room later to grab a pair of socks so I could go sledding. As I rummaged through the drawer, he pulled on a string he had rigged up to a few things on my shelf, and I looked up to see my [7]Mrs. Beasley doll along with an ice cream cone candle and something else come plummeting down right on top of me. I decided after that day that I'd had enough of the Ouija board for a while.

* * *

My father talked to me occasionally about spiritual things, especially where evil was concerned. He said that [8]hovering all around me in the air, though I couldn't see them, were demons trying to attack me. They wanted to get me angry like they did him. Sometimes, when he combed his hair and the comb suddenly flew out of his hand, he told me it was because they had made it happen so that he would get angry and cuss. But also around me were angels, he said, who were constantly fighting with the demons to protect me. This was a comforting thought after imagining ugly, evil demons ready to pounce on me.

I was sure I'd seen angels on at least two occasions. Once at my grandmother's house, I'd been lying in bed in the small back room with a curtain drawn over the doorway. I looked up to see a bright form floating over the top of the curtain rod and into the room. It seemed to have a face and was gazing at me intently. That's all I can recall. Another time, I was out playing down the block near the house on the corner. I'd never been to the house before. Then a man, I believe, asked me if I wanted to come into the yard. A girl and I went, though I don't recall who she was. I felt very good about the whole thing. We entered the screened-in porch and sat down on the couch, noticing some neat games to play. I was intrigued by one in particular: [9]Chinese Checkers. I kept gazing at the colorful star shape, which consisted of two overlapping triangles more commonly known as the Star of David, a familiar symbol in Judaism. It held a certain fascination for me. Everything seemed really different, though I wasn't sure why. Somehow I felt safe in that place on the screened-in porch, as if my father had just wrapped his arms around me to shelter me from harm. The young man, who appeared to have been dressed in white, had long since gone though we hadn't seen him leave at all. The girl and I ventured back out onto the sidewalk shortly after that.

One of the most profound stories my father ever relayed to me was about a little boy sitting on the beach with a bucket, absorbed in trying to empty the entire ocean into the small bucket. But try as he might, he couldn't. It would fill up, and he'd dump it in the sand, then go and get another bucketful. Each time he did this, it seemed he hadn't made any progress at all. The ocean was still large and full, though he'd made many trips back and forth by now. As he continued to do this, an angel suddenly appeared in the form of a young man, and asked the boy what he was doing.

"Why, I'm trying to empty the ocean into this bucket," he replied, "but it's not working. The more water I put in here, the more seems to be out there again."

"Just as you cannot possibly empty all of this water into your little bucket, so neither can you know all of the ways of God, for it is a mystery," said the angel, and then vanished from the boy's sight.

My father expounded on this story by explaining that the ocean was all of the knowledge and mystery of God, while the bucket was our small, finite mind. "Just as I can read and read all the books I want until the day I die, but still never acquire all of the knowledge that is to be had."

But what of God? We went to a Catholic church here and there, though I didn't know what on earth it meant to be a *Catholic*. I used to comment to people that I was "a Catholic and a Christian," to which my mother and father would chuckle because I knew not what either meant. They were terms I'd heard *them* use before.

The particular church we went to seemed dark and cold to me, though I wasn't sure why. Not like the dark, cold presence that sometimes bothered me at night—yet not warm, not friendly. I felt God was stern and hard to follow or comprehend. At times he seemed even boring, as I'd try and keep from falling asleep in the middle of the service while the priest droned on and on in a monotone voice, quoting the Bible. I grew tired of sitting, kneeling, standing, sitting, kneeling, standing every few minutes.

Nor did I understand why we had to eat that yummy little round piece of bread, though I looked forward to it. And it seemed the priest always had such a deep scowl on his face: the same scowl Sister Landers kept on her face continually. She was my Catholic schoolteacher, and she was very mean. She constantly picked on me, especially when I asked questions about the Bible in class. It seemed ever since I told her my dad said there was going to be a rapture and she denied it, she had a grudge against me.

It was my mom's idea to put me in Catholic school after our next-door neighbor enrolled her daughter. And since whatever Suzan did I had to do, I ended up going there in third grade. I remember thinking to myself that it was even worse than regular school. The kids seemed even meaner. They swore more, they acted up in class more... and the nuns were scary because they yelled a lot and never smiled or made me feel comfortable. I finally told my father that I didn't want to go back there for fourth grade, and he talked my mother into letting me attend public school once more while Suzan continued on to fifth grade.

Dad was already starting to have doubts about Catholicism, claiming they always wanted a lot of money and that seemed to be it. He stopped going to Catholic church after a while, and we just kind of stayed home on Sundays and ate donuts and drank coffee with lots of cream and sugar.

I believed in God, though I didn't know much about him. During Christmas once I gift-wrapped a box for Jesus. When asked what was in it, I told my parents it contained all of my love for him.

A plastic plaque hung on my bedroom wall of Jesus nailed to the cross. I used to lie in bed and stare at it for a long time. I'd think to myself, *Father, Son and Holy Ghost*, shivering a little when I got to the *Ghost* part. It frightened me that there was a ghost involved with God. I didn't get it. What kind of ghost was he—mean or nice? And why was

Jesus hurting? Why did he have to hang there with nails in his hands and feet? What was the purpose? It seemed strange to me. Strange and unnecessary.

\* \* \*

At a time in my life when I didn't have many friends, my father was the best friend I had. He constantly encouraged me in everything I did. When I wrote, he commented on how smart and creative I was. When I sang, (as my dream was to become a singer), he told me I had a beautiful voice. But most of all, he always reassured me that I was a very intelligent girl and mature beyond my years. He said I knew better than to waste my time with children who enjoyed being cruel and manipulative. He liked the fact that I spent my time reading and writing instead of getting involved in their little power struggles.

My brother Jim, on the other hand, told me I was a freak because I spent all of my time reading instead of playing with the other kids like a normal child would do. He was constantly putting me down and I didn't know why. One day he even told me to jump down the stairs and kill myself, much to my shock and disbelief that my own brother could say such a thing. Again, it was that evil cloud that seemed to hover over me wherever I went and whatever I did, bringing with it a wave of people who seemed to hate me for no tangible reason.

And then something weird began to happen. Dad just wasn't the same anymore. He started to turn on me, picking on me for the least little thing. If I wiped off the table after dinner, he'd get down on his hands and knees in the sunlight for the next ten minutes and check for crumbs before I could go outside and play. If he found even one little crumb, he'd yell at me for a long time. And when I came back in from playing two hours later, he'd bring up the crumb again, yelling at me some more. If I did things on accident, like spill pop, he'd accuse me of doing it on purpose. And if I tried to explain, he'd curse at me and tell me I was lying. My heart sank within me as I groped to understand what was happening to my father. He used to love me…

I hated coming home from school anymore because he was waiting for me: sitting in the living room ready to talk to me about the end of the world and *Armageddon.* Before I could even go upstairs and get changed into my shorts, he'd make me sit down while he told me horror stories of nuclear bombs going off and people's eyes melting out of their heads. By the time he was through, I felt sick to my stomach and very depressed. I hated that book and record he'd bought from the ad on TV. It made him crazy somehow.

He and my mom argued over his decision to buy gas masks and all kinds of dried food and supplies to store away for when the end of the world came. He even had a place picked out on the map for us where we'd go when all of this took place. I didn't know what *Armageddon* was. All I knew was that I hated it.

One day I came home from school to find a note from my mom explaining that I had to eat dinner by myself because she took my dad to the hospital. It was nothing serious, she assured me in the note. He'd gotten a little sick during the night and would be home soon.

But he never came home. He stayed in the hospital for weeks and weeks, telling us he just wanted to die. My mom explained to me that he'd had an *aneurysm,* where a blood vessel in his head broke and that's why he kept having terrible headaches all these years. When I went to visit him, he didn't know who I was. He kicked the covers off of him and laughed as I winced at the sight of his naked body, while my mom scolded him for doing so in front of his daughter. It really hurt me to see him that way.

There was a small ray of hope, however, when his condition began improving. He regained his memory, recognizing family members once more, and was able to make small talk with them.

Then on Father's Day, just as I'd finished making him a card because we were getting ready to go visit him, we got the call that his condition had worsened and we should come immediately. My mom wasn't feeling good, so she had Suzan's mother drive us to the hospital. I guess she was really nervous and frightened after the telephone call. When we arrived, my two brothers, Jim and Stephen, came to greet us with sympathy written all over their faces.

"Where's Dad?" I asked, pushing past them as they tried to restrain me. And then I saw the door of his room, closed and with a blue tag hanging from the knob.

That's when the nurse's words echoed in my head like the distant sound of gunshots: "I'm sorry, but your father is no longer with us. He... passed away today."

"*Noooo!*" I screamed. "How could you leave us alone?! *Noooo!*" I was only thirteen! I was too young to be without a dad! The room was spinning around, and I felt I was going to throw up. I flung myself into a nearby chair, breaking the armrest. Bursting into tears then, I picked up the wooden piece and hurled it down the hall.

An Indian family in the room across from my dad's heard all of the mourning going on between my mother, brothers and I, and came out to console us. "We'll pray for you," they said sympathetically.

"Don't bother—he's *already dead!*" I hissed vehemently. I hated God at that minute for what he did to my father. It was all his fault.

The day of the funeral, I came home and began trimming the weeds, numb from all the pain I'd suffered the past week. My father had been asking me to trim the weeds for a while.

After his burial, we all stood around on the porch talking about him—about how he was doing and where he was. My Godmother assured me he was probably up in Heaven looking down upon us. Just then, a tiny bird suddenly fluttered over to where we were standing and rested on each of our shoulders for a brief moment.

"That's Paul right there!" exclaimed my Godmother, as I watched the bird fly off, my heart pounding. "It's a sign that he's okay."

I wondered then, if perhaps the bird really *had* been my father, alive from the dead. And at that moment, in my heart, I believed it was.

\* \* \*

The following year I met a girl in my French class named Robin. She began telling me about the ghost that lived in her house. She said it sometimes turned on the television at night while they were sleeping, or made the rocking chair rock by itself. They heard cupboards opening and pots and pans banging when the house was quiet. She told me that she thought it was a good ghost because it never really did anything to hurt them.

Sometime after that, she invited me to spend the night. I'd forgotten all about the poltergeist as we played video games at the arcade, joked and laughed, and talked about the teenage crushes in our lives thus far.

At dinnertime, Robin mentioned the ghost once more. She told me not to worry if it woke me up during the night. I didn't pay much attention to her warning, though. Somehow I wasn't afraid. Upon leaving the dinner table, the topic of ghosts disappeared from my mind altogether as we occupied ourselves with activities. Then, before I knew it, the night escaped us and it was time for bed. Worn out, we instantly fell asleep.

But sometime during the night I awoke, as at other times, sensing an evil presence. I turned onto my side, attempting to ignore it as the dog groaned, crawling under the bed. Seconds later, a single bolt of thunder and a flash of lightning rendered me fully awake. I knew for certain that the room was occupied by something other than just the three of us. My heart beat faster as I dreaded what was to follow.

Just then, a loud creak sounded in the floorboard next to the bed, inches away from me. At that exact moment, a freezing chill raced up the length of my arm, which was dangling over the side of the mattress, as if icy cold fingers had suddenly touched it. I jerked it inside the covers, panicking. A thought popped into my head, though I knew it wasn't my thought. *"I'm cooold,"* it said.

I'm not sure if I was testing the whole experience to measure its validity or merely feeding my curiosity, because I answered back mentally, *Well, get under the covers.*

A couple of seconds went by. I waited, wondering if this was really happening. Maybe it was nothing but my imagination. Suddenly, the bed covers shifted ever so slightly and I felt a light weight over my feet, as if someone had placed a pillow over top of them! The terror I felt was mixed with amazement. I was talking to a real ghost, and it had climbed in bed with me! Perhaps this entity was someone whom I'd known previously in my life, now attempting to inform me of his or her whereabouts. My deceased father? My grandmother?

All at once, the bed started shaking, actually lifting *some inches* off the floor. I felt my heart leap into my throat. I could hardly believe this was happening! It didn't seem possible. I managed to croak out Robin's name as she lie sleeping beside me. But calling her name did no good. Neither did shaking her. She seemed under a spell, a [10]Sleeping Beauty unable to awake, as if something prevented her from doing so. A few moments later, the bed ceased shaking.

*Who are you?* I communicated once again via the thought process. Then, *Why are you bothering me? I've done nothing to you.*

All was quiet, though I didn't wait long for a reply. Somewhere deep inside me, I knew [11]I shouldn't be trying to communicate with this thing or being—whatever it was.

*Go away!* I commanded, ending all further contact with it. I began fervently praying the best I knew how, whispering [12]Our Fathers and Hail Marys repeatedly, the covers pulled up over my head as if they could somehow shield me from this spooky presence. The next thing I knew, it was morning. As I awoke to a light filled room, the incident seemed a shadow of reality. I told Robin about it. She was hardly surprised.

She mentioned to me that she awoke once to an elf-like figure standing beside her bed with hooves for hands, just like in [13]*Amityville Horror*. Thinking it was her brother wearing a Halloween mask, she yelled at him to go away. However, he wouldn't leave. She continued to yell and he continued to stand there silently. Finally, she kicked at him, her foot going right through the image. He slumped to the floor, disappearing into thin air. Somehow, this didn't give me a good feeling. In fact, it scared me to death.

Her family then confirmed to me over breakfast that all of what Robin said was true, and just as in the case of my own personal encounters with the spirit world, they professed that they'd grown used to it.

About a month or so after my visit to Robin's house, the strange experiences in my own house intensified. All by myself one night as I talked on the phone, a moaning noise broke forth from somewhere upstairs. This was clearly not the wind blowing: it sounded like a woman's voice. I started toward the stairway. The moans seemed to be coming from the vicinity of Jim's room. I didn't dare venture any further, but begged my friend to stay on the line with me until my mother came home. He declined, having a good laugh about my *imagination*. I was left with no choice but to drown out the sound with the television. I huddled on the sofa with my back flat against the wall and a butcher knife in my hand until my mother arrived home.

Another evening while home alone, I decided to do laundry. I started down the stairway to the basement, which admittedly wasn't my favorite place to begin with. Jim had commented that he felt eyes watching him whenever he was down there, and my friends said our basement was spooky. Just as I reached the bottom of the staircase and was about to turn the corner, I discovered a crow perched on the clothesline. For some reason, I felt a terrible evil associated with this dark winged creature. Its presence greatly frightened me. But I rationalized that it was only a bird and made my way toward the washer and dryer, whistling as I went to ease the fear.

The bird immediately chased after me, as if intent on pecking the flesh off my back. The loud, fluttering sound of its wings grew closer as it gained on me. I let out a loud cry of panic and ran toward the stairs again. Sensing my desire to escape, it flew ahead of me and blocked the basement door, planting itself on the railing and staring at me with its beady eyes. I rationalized that this was only a frightened bird acting on instinct and attempted to ignore its threats, whistling as I turned and approached the washer and dryer once more. The fluttering grew loud behind my back again, and I felt at any moment that the crow would rip my skin apart with its razor-sharp beak.

By this time, I was so scared that I started crying. I huddled in the corner with my arms over my head like I did in school during tornado drills. The crow positioned itself on the clothesline where it could guard its prisoner. Hours seemed to pass before my mom came home. I heard the buzzing of the alarm system and then the door to the kitchen open upstairs. I yelled for her to help me, explaining that a bird had me trapped. She came down with a broomstick and chased it out the garage door.

Then there were times that I heard knocks inside the wall of my bedroom accompanied by scratching noises. Though my mother told me it was probably just mice, I was not persuaded. I doubted that a tiny mouse could make such a loud noise—especially a knocking noise. It would literally have to body slam itself against the wall, and even then, it could never duplicate the sound of knuckles hitting plaster.

Besides, when games flew out of my bedroom closet and crashed to the floor on more than one occasion, no mouse could be blamed.

Robin mentioned that ghosts have been known to follow people home. Her sister agreed, commenting that this was often the case whenever the person had an interest in the supernatural. I was beginning to think that perhaps their mischievous poltergeist had decided to pack its bags and move in with me.

## II. LIKE FATHER, LIKE DAUGHTER

NINTH GRADE MARKED A TURNING point in my life. Thanks to my mother and father's generous contribution, I said good-bye to bucked teeth forever. Two years of braces along with months of wearing *headgear* to bed finally paid off. Next, my mother bought me contact lenses. I felt like a new person. I'd even slimmed down a bit, cutting back on my eating.

My interests were changing rapidly: in clothes, in music, and in friends. For the first time in my life, I was discovering recognition. It felt good to be liked by other peers for a change. It also felt good to be noticed by members of the opposite sex—namely one in particular: Keith Sandor. He was like a Greek god to me—only Italian. He had dark eyes, dark hair, and the kind of tan that lasts all year round. His physique was in buff condition, due to the fact that he lifted weights. Since my father had at one time been a body builder, I immediately liked this about Keith.

But unfortunately, I wasn't the only one to observe him. He spent his time in class flirting with several girls who fluttered around him like little birds. So naturally, when he took notice of my existence, I was shocked. Small talk turned into him asking me for my phone number, and before long, we were having two and three-hour conversations about everything from school to the recent death of our fathers. Because his dad had died also, I felt a common bond with him: a bond of pain and sorrow.

It was a dream come true for me to have this incredibly gorgeous guy actually interested in what I had to say. I began to consider him my best friend. Never before had I been on such a deep level with a male, except for my father. Keith made me feel important, attractive, and intelligent all at the same time. There was only one small problem: he had a girlfriend. Her name was Melony, and they'd been together for a few years. When I questioned him as to whether she would get mad that we were constantly on the phone with one another, he replied, "Who cares? I can talk to you if I want."

This flattered me. The fact that he was interested enough in me to cause a possible problem in their relationship said a lot for our friendship. Maybe there was even a chance he liked me for more than a friend. We continued our frequent phone conversations, and sometimes he even came over or I went to his house. Girls who before had thought of me as a social outcast suddenly acknowledged me because Keith and I were good friends. And then, to my surprise, he asked me out to a movie. It seemed from the way he'd been flirting around with me on the phone that it would be somewhat of a date. I was so excited.

He picked me up in his van, which had curtains over the windows. When I got in, I noticed he'd purchased some wine, which gave me sort of an uneasy feeling. I'd never drank before, except to have a couple sips of my father's [15]Cold Duck whenever he allowed it. He asked me then if I wanted to try some. I decided I did. I wanted him to like me—I wanted more than anything for him to be mine. Thinking the wine would help loosen things up a bit, I told myself I'd just have a *little*. By the time we got to the movie theater, I was floating on air. Noticing I was somewhat intoxicated, Keith asked if I was okay. I told him I thought we should just skip the movie and hang out and talk. I was feeling quite frivolous now.

The next thing I knew, my hopes were coming true and he was making a move to kiss me. It had been a long time since I'd kissed anyone. A real long time. It felt so good to have this man I was helplessly infatuated with return my affection. However, I had no idea that it would go so far so fast. Within minutes, I was on the foldout bed in the back of the van with the curtains drawn; feeling unattached as I stared up at the ceiling with glazed eyes, the quick and painful loss of my virginity taking place. Afterward, Keith asked if I was okay while I shook my head yes, in shock over what had just happened. I'd expected it to be so much more. Why did the movies make it seem so enjoyable?

When the wine started wearing off, he drove me home. I went upstairs to the bathroom, surprised to discover I was [16]bleeding. No one had ever told me about that. Or if they had, I'd forgotten. I felt then, that a very special piece of me had been taken, and I wasn't exactly sure why. On the one hand, I was happy Keith liked me. On the other, I was depressed. But I told myself that now he would break up with Melony and finally be mine.

To my dismay, however, he didn't care to discuss that night with me when next we talked. He asked me once more if I was alright, and then just kind of blew it off as if it never happened. I felt used. Cheap. I hated myself for letting him into my secret places—my inner parts—because he'd only stolen from me, never having any intention of leaving Melony.

Still, I tried not to believe it. I didn't want to believe it had all been for nothing. He had to have *some* feelings for me to go that far. It must have meant something to him like it did to me. Couldn't he feel how special it was? Not the act itself so much, but the invisible bond that somehow tied us together now.

\* \* \*

One day I was browsing through the library in our house, which I hadn't been able to frequent since the death of my father. It was painful for me, because I imagined him standing there with a book in his hand or sitting at his desk writing poetry. Sometimes I expected him to suddenly appear, as if he'd only been on a long vacation. The reality of his death still hadn't sunk in for me. It was hard to grasp the fact that I would never see him again.

[14]I found a slim book about magic experiments and mind power wedged between some other books. When I opened it up, I noticed a creased chart inside, and unfolded it to discover columns of tiny pictures such as hearts and skulls. Next to the pictures were statements like those found in fortune cookies. As I began to read the forward to the book, I discovered that it was a divining oracle, adapted from ancient Egyptian times.

The instructions talked of using it every third full moon, or something to that effect, with a feather dipped in blood as the writing utensil. Seeing as I was in desperate need of answers to my obsession with Keith, and seeing as it wasn't the third full moon and I didn't have a feather dipped in blood, I merely used an ink pen. I concentrated really hard on my question, making a series of random dots as fast as I could like the oracle required, then went back and counted their pattern afterward to match it with the corresponding picture and answer.

Eventually, since the answers I received were ambiguous to me, I figured I should add a little blood. I smeared some on the paper from a small cut I had, hoping this would empower the oracle to be more specific. Though I don't recall exactly what the reply was once I did this, I know it must have appealed to me in some way because I continued to use the oracle for other questions as well. Spotting it in my room one day, my mother took it and hid it because she said it was evil. However, I found it in her nightstand drawer and began using it again. She gave up on retrieving it after that.

My friend Shelly left her Ouija board in my room. I hadn't played around with one in a long time: not since the [17]Mrs. Beasley/ice cream cone incident. But we'd been trying to contact the entity in my house. A few of us thought maybe the Egyptian death mask was haunted. So we brought it upstairs, whipping out Shelly's Ouija board and asking the spirit to reveal itself. Nothing much happened that night.

Then I brought home my date one evening. We were hanging out in my room when he commented on the Ouija board. I explained that my friends and I had attempted to contact the spirit that occupied my house to see whether it was a good or evil one. When I briefed him on some of the eerie experiences that took place, he suggested we contact it once more. Both of us were intoxicated and feeling brave. We laid out the board and touched our fingers to the glass dome marker.

"Spirit, if you're in here, then reveal yourself," he commanded now. I noticed him moving the marker on his own strength and told him to cut it out. "This is *stupid*," he protested, pushing the board away in disgust. "There isn't any ghost in here. You're making it up."

"I'm not kidding you, William! There *is* a ghost. He makes games fly out of the closet and stuff." At that precise moment, as if on cue, a board game shot out of the closet at us. We shrieked, terrified, and bolted out of the room and down the stairs as fast as our legs could go.

As we stood in the kitchen now, catching our breath, he accused me of rigging the whole incident. How? I didn't have any string in my hand, and no one was home but us. I assured him that I did no such thing.

I continued to see Keith. One night after turning up my stereo, latching my door, and stuffing my bed to make it look as if I was sleeping in it, I climbed through my bedroom window and onto the garage roof, jumping off into Keith and his friend Justin's arms. My mother had forbidden me to go out with him because it was too late, but he only called once in a while, so I had to cease the opportunity while I could. I still felt that attachment to him— that soul tie because we'd become one flesh.

All three of us drove around in the van for hours, drinking until right before sunrise. I was happy that Keith wanted me for more than a friend again, as his actions displayed. The two of us made out in the back while Justin drove.

I returned home drunk and stumbling all over the place to find my mother waiting for me with swollen eyes from crying all night; she'd broken through the chain lock on my door after rationalizing that I couldn't possibly be sleeping with the music blaring full blast like it was. She warned me that she'd better never see Keith around me anymore. I felt so guilty that she'd waited up worrying about me the whole night that I didn't argue with her decision.

September rolled around and school started again. It was my first year of high school, and a lot of changes were taking place for me. Keith had dropped out in ninth grade, so I no longer saw him in school. When I'd attended the junior high near his house, he'd been up there almost every day, roaming the halls during classes and stopping to wave at me now and then.

Over Christmas break, he telephoned to wish me a Merry Christmas. I was excited to hear from him. Though months had passed by, the bond still existed, refusing to be broken that easily. In my heart, I kept liking him. In my mind, I kept thinking we could still have something together. He'd mentioned on several occasions that he'd been considering breaking up with Melony because he was growing tired of her. Though he'd been saying that ever since we first met, I hoped this time he meant it. He told me to tell my mother Merry Christmas, and that he was sorry for going against her wishes the night he helped me sneak out the window. She seemed somewhat appeased by his apology.

On Christmas Day, he called me from his friend's house to ask me if I could go to the movies. My mother agreed to let me as long as I wouldn't be out too late. Jim, who'd been listening on the line unbeknownst to me, commented that it sounded as if they were having a party over at his friend's. He told me I better watch out because they might have plans to rape me. I thought that was the most ludicrous thing I'd ever heard, and reminded him that he didn't know Keith like I did. I wondered where he'd come up with such a notion.

In the truck, with Justin driving and Keith sitting next to me, I blabbed on happily about school and what I'd gotten for Christmas, etc., etc. Keith informed me then that instead of going to the movies, we were going to watch some movies at his friend Vince's house. Vince's parents were gone on vacation, and we'd have the house to ourselves. I felt a little uneasy, but agreed.

We arrived at Vince's, and I waved a hello as Keith introduced us. I knew somewhat of him already; he'd dated one of the girls I took a class with in junior high.

Keith told me to have a seat, so I plopped down in the recliner while he went into the kitchen to get me a beer. At least, I thought he was getting me a beer. He came back into the living room a few minutes later carrying a large mug full of whiskey. I was hesitant as he handed it to me.

"Well, what are you waiting for? Drink up!"

"I don't know..." I told him, "I've never had whiskey before. I don't want to get too drunk..."

"Come on, it's good. And don't worry—it'll wear off by the time I take you home."

I started to put the mug to my lips, then stopped, noticing what appeared to be a tiny purple sweet tart dissolving in the alcohol. At first, I thought I was seeing things. But upon closer examination, a strange feeling suddenly clutched at my heart.

"What's this purple thing floating in here?"

"What purple thing? There's no purple thing."

24

"Yes there is! What is it, Keith?"

"Oh, alright. It's just one of those Little Dot sweet tarts," he laughed. "I just wanted to see what you'd say. I know how you are about mixing drugs with alcohol."

I'd told him before about the article in the paper my mom read to me: a young girl at a party got really drunk and then took some drugs. She went into a coma and hadn't snapped out of it yet.

"Come on, drink it. I was only joking," he prodded. Still hesitating, I gave him a searching look now, pondering whether or not to believe him. "Come on, Paula... don't you trust me? I would never hurt you," he assured me, giving me a long, luscious look with those flirting brown eyes of his.

*Of course not! Keith would never hurt me—he's my friend. What am I thinking?* The foreboding feeling I had suddenly seemed absurd. It was quickly drowned out in the noisy din of my rationale. With that, I took large sips, puckering my face as I tried to endure the bitter taste of the whiskey.

I woke up on the floor in front of the TV, a snarling dog (which seemed more like a miniature monster) ready to bite my lip off. His growl echoed in my head, a thousand times amplified. I shrieked in terror as Keith laughed, calling the dog away from me. Disoriented, I looked up to see the three of them sitting in chairs watching me with amusement: Keith, Justin, and their friend Vince. They all seemed so big sitting in their chairs, and I felt so small, like [18]Alice in Wonderland. Everything looked kind of round and elongated, as if I were peering through a fish bowl.

I must have blacked out again, because I now found myself alone in the living room with just Keith. I recall trying to explain to him that I loved him as he was leaving to go to the store. I reminded him of that special night we shared. He responded with apathy, pushing me aside roughly.

"Don't you care? Please... I love you!" I slurred, feeling as if I was floating on air. I wrapped my arms around him. He tried pulling away. "Keith! What's wrong? Don't you care about me?"

A raging storm clouded his face then, a side of him I'd never seen before. It frightened me, yet I was so numb and rubbery that it didn't seem to matter. "*Alright*, is that what you want?" he growled. He picked me up roughly, carrying me into the bedroom while making vulgar sexual remarks.

"Nooo..." I sobbed. "No, Keith. Don't."

He stopped. "Alright then, shut up!" Stomping out of the room, he left for the store while I lie on the floor crying.

\* \* \*

The light was so bright it seemed to burn into my skin. I stirred, opening my eyes and lifting my head up to see Vince smiling down at me. I was lying in bed with him, though fully clothed. He was not fully clothed.

*What's happening?* I felt so strange waking up to find myself someplace different again. *How did I get in bed with this guy?* "Where's Keith?" I asked.

"They left."

My heart sank with these words as I felt the pain of abandonment.

"He... left?" *Keith left me here—alone?*

Bending over now, he stroked my hair, kissing me on the forehead. "Yeah. Don't worry about Keith. He doesn't care about you. But I do."

I felt rejected, and sooo weak. A million thoughts raced full speed ahead like a freight train. I couldn't catch them. *My mother... how will I get ho—*

"You're so beautiful," he whispered.

Just the words I needed to hear, but coming from a total stranger. How could Keith not care? I'd given him a piece of myself, both physically and spiritually. How could it be—after all we'd been through?

The TV was on. Some old comedy show. [19]*I Love Lucy?*

\* \* \*

Cold. My eyes opened to feel that uncomfortable blast of icy wind common for December. Slowly I came to, noticing the window was open above me. I was lying across someone's lap, and I could hear Keith's voice.

26

*Keith... he's back.*

We were moving. We were in the truck. The music on the radio seemed distant. He spoke once more. "She's waking up. Hey, Paula, you awake?"

Eyes slowly opening, trying to focus... his zipper was down. *No...* Fading out again...

\* \* \*

Pain. Keith grabbed me by my chest and pulled me out of the truck. How could he hurt me like this? How could he? Justin came around the side of the truck to help him. They were dragging me somewhere... A trailer. Somebody mentioned a trailer, though I couldn't see. My eyes rolled back in my head as once more I struggled to keep them focused. For some reason, I wanted to laugh, though inside I was crying. I could feel my lips breaking out into a huge, stupid grin; and then I was laughing against my will in the shadows of a trailer somewhere, feeling like I was in a tin can. I could hear Keith and Justin talking, but I didn't know where they were. Their voices were muffled.

Lying on the damp, hard floor, women's musk cologne filled my nostrils—a Christmas present from my mom that I'd worn especially for Keith. I gazed up at him now—at his long, rubbery, distorted face. He was sneering at me.

\* \* \*

The bumpy road brought me back to consciousness. Once more, the icy cold air from the window whipped over my skin.

"Man, we can't bring her home like this," Justin protested. "What's her mom gonna say?"

"Let's just drop her off in a ditch somewhere," Keith replied to my horror. His words sliced me deep inside as I tried to grasp how he could do such a thing. A thought of being found dead in a ditch like other women on the news crossed my mind. Fear clutched at my heart, though it was quickly diminished by numbness. I wanted to protest, to stand up for myself. But I felt I was just a tiny person living in a thick layer of blubber they call flesh.

So tiny.

So far away… was I even attached to my body?

Surrounded by cold, wet snow now, I heard the truck drive off. I was not in a ditch, but in a snow bank next to my garage. I lie there for a while, hearing them pass by the house once more and slow down a little. Then the sound of the motor faded off and I was left alone, the thick silence of the early morning and the hot, bright floodlight overhead seeming to stand out above everything else at that moment.

I managed to make my way into the garage and up the steps into the kitchen, attempting to shut off the alarm system as my fingers struggled to find the right numbers. Mom was hurrying toward me from the living room.

* * *

"Paula…" Someone was gently shaking me. "Paula!"

"Huh?" I opened my eyes, straining to see my mother standing over me. I was in bed, and it was daytime.

"*Who* put something in your drink?" she asked me now.

"Huh? What are you talking about?" Everything was cloudy. My head felt clogged.

"You said that somebody put something in your drink," she answered firmly. I struggled to think, then. "Don't you remember? You were with Keith last night."

It took me weeks to piece it all together: the truck, a camera flash, Keith's face hovering over me…

My mom said I'd come in the door, and after mumbling about them putting something in my drink, I fell in her arms and passed out. I would never know if I was fully raped or not, because all I could remember were bits and pieces of things. My mom wanted me to go to a doctor to see, but I refused. She wanted me to press charges, but once again, I refused. I wanted to sink back into my safe little world of repressed memories—to pretend it never happened. I suppose in my heart I knew that I'd been somewhat responsible by sleeping with Keith in the first place. Not to mention, I didn't feel like dealing with the pain and emotional baggage that would have followed.

He was the only man besides my father to show me any attention. I knew that since he'd started doing cocaine and other drugs, he'd changed for the worst. I tried holding on to what we once had—our talks on the phone, him meeting me after school to hang out and talk and listen to music... all of the good memories.

About a month or so later, I called him to tell him I forgave him and still loved him. I begged him to meet me somewhere and talk about what had happened because I knew he wasn't himself. He laughed, telling me I was crazy and that he hadn't done anything wrong. He made me feel like it was all my fault.

Then my friend Sybil happened to get her hair cut by Melony one day. To my dismay, she brought up the rape incident, and Melony told her that she'd already heard about it from Keith. She said I made the whole thing up and she was going to come after me. As if I hadn't suffered enough trauma already! I was devastated that she actually thought I could make up such a story—and fearful. Sybil informed me then, of Melony's undefeated boxing record.

I felt so alone, so horrified by my whole life at that point that I wished I was never born. That's when I decided the best thing to do was escape reality by running away to some place where I could start all over again. Some place where nobody knew anything about me and where Melony would not be able to find me. I mentioned to Shelly that I was running away, and she tried talking me out of it. When I wouldn't be persuaded, she decided to go with me. Why not? she thought. Shelly loved adventures.

A boisterous, bubbly blond, she was the life of the party, though a few times, her life almost resulted in death for all of us. When going somewhere with her, I quickly learned to expect the unexpected. If I wasn't stuck in the back seat of her car, climbing the windows to get out while she did donuts at 45 miles per hour in the middle of a main road, plastered out of her mind; then I was stuck in the back seat of her car while she decided to do some last-minute toilet papering to an old boyfriend's house, a cop car pulling into the street to head us off before we could make our get-away. Yes, Shelly loved adventures.

I was relieved to have her as a road-side companion, because the fact of the matter was, I had not the slightest idea where to go, or how to get there with no transportation and no money. And looking back now, I see she really cared about me; she didn't want me going off by myself into the cruel world.

She called up Dayne, then, and asked him to go with us. He was our best friend, after all, and he had a car (well, his dad's car, but he drove it all the time since his dad had another one). He refused the invitation, so she gave him a guilt trip about letting the two of us—two helpless women—go off by ourselves without any transportation and God knew what out there in the world. Being the nice guy that he was, he finally agreed to go with us. Shelly had always been good at persuading people, and I was glad.

Besides, running away didn't sound like too bad of an idea to Dayne the more he thought about it. He longed to be free to live the gay lifestyle he wanted with no restrictions. I think he kind of envisioned himself as the homosexual guy in that Bronx Rhythm song:

> *"I'll pack up my bags and go far away,*
> *Cuz they don't understand I'm in love with a man."*

Ever since he came out of the closet, his parents gave him a hard time. He felt like a freak, he said. Why couldn't they just understand? But deep down, he seemed unsure of the choice he'd made, even discouraging me when I questioned my own sexuality once.

Oddly enough, when I accompanied him to the gay bars on occasion, I got hit on more by men there than I did at the straight bars. As I came to know some of them, they confided in me that they hated themselves and their lifestyle. One even broke down and cried, [20]burdened with immense guilt. Perhaps there were deep rooted issues—skeletons in the closet for some of these men—like molestation, ritual abuse, or other traumatic occurrences. Clearly though, their flesh was warring against their conscience.

Dayne had his first homosexual encounter with a really strange guy I'd known ever since sixth grade camp. His name was Brandon Erins, and my fondest recollection of him was when he sat down at the lunch table one day in ninth grade and told everyone what they had to eat for dinner the night before. Skeptical of his supposed *psychic powers,* I defiantly challenged him to tell me what *I* had for dinner.

"Hot dogs," he answered, smiling.

"What—did you look in my window or something while I was eating?!" I asked, amazed.

"No. I told you, I'm psychic," he responded rather matter-of-factly.

Though for a day or so I was inclined to believe him, I soon dismissed the incident from my mind, preoccupied with other matters more important to a ninth grader about to attend high school.

After meeting Dayne my second semester of tenth grade, he and I soon became best friends, to which he then confided in me of his sexual preference. That's when he told me about Brandon—how Brandon was mysterious and had some kind of power over him. He said there was something about the way he looked at him with those dark eyes of his that made him go crazy with lust.

I kind of laughed, because the way I remembered Brandon from sixth grade camp, he was the social outcast, sort of like me. He just seemed like an average kid—and quiet. I had trouble picturing him as some sexual swami. Not that he hadn't gained a few friends and gotten better looking through the years as we all had, but still… power? Come on, Dayne, we're talking about Brandon Erins here!

Later that year, I found out from Sybil (who was also head over heels for Brandon—she had no idea he was gay), that he was involved in witchcraft: [21]*Wicca,* to be exact. I'd never heard of Wicca until Sybil explained it was a huge sect of witches, almost like a religion in and of itself. Some people, she explained, couldn't participate in actual covens because there simply weren't any in the area. So they offered correspondence courses through the mail, as Brandon was taking, in order to become one of them.

Dayne had his own deck of tarot cards that Brandon helped him pick out. One time, he did a reading for me. The cards predicted that a man with dark hair and dark eyes was going to come along and entrance me with his power. I didn't know who that was, especially when the guy I was hooked on at the time of the reading had blond hair and blue eyes.

Anyway, Brandon ended up dumping Dayne, which I found hard to believe because Dayne was so cute, and eventually moved to Pennsylvania. After a while, I forgot all about him. Dayne *tried* to forget all about him. He was on the rebound now, searching for another homosexual relationship. Meanwhile, Shelly was helplessly infatuated with him. She didn't know he was gay. For a long time, nobody in our circle of friends knew but me. I'd sworn to keep it a secret, and I did.

Besides Shelly, I think all of us girls had a slight crush on Dayne: Sybil, Jamie, Stacie, and me. We all agreed he was adorable: very attractive, very nice, a good sense of humor... the good ol' American *boy next door*. He didn't really act effeminate or anything—at least, not until he hung around the bars habitually and developed a new nature. Even then, he wasn't totally fem like some of them I came to know, but it was clear to see that he'd picked up their mannerisms.

I suppose I always hoped I could somehow change him back into liking members of the opposite sex once more, though in college he confessed his attraction to a woman, even dating her for a few months. Afterwards, he came to the conclusion that he was bisexual.

Despite his claim of only being attracted to one woman, I am pretty sure he was attracted to more than one: he just chose to override it. I speculate that on the college campus, however, he'd probably been surrounded by heterosexuals leading normal lifestyles, thus it was easier to fall into their pattern and date a woman. It is very easy to become a product of one's environment.

So here we were: the gay, the rape victim, and the party animal; on our way to Florida where we could all change our identities and start over. No one knew us there. We could be anything we wanted to be. Erase the past. Create the future.

Dayne had supposedly picked us up "for school" in his maroon [22]Monarch. My mom was sleeping, and I had my things sitting out in the garage ready to go. We loaded them in the trunk and he and Shelly and I were off, grandiose notions of camping out on the beach until we found a place to live, and partying every weekend with no curfew, filling our heads.

Shelly brought along some gold jewelry, hoping to get a lot of money for it. Unfortunately, we weren't aware of the fact that pawn shops paid according to the weight of the gold and not its worth. We left the state with practically nothing, disillusioned and guilty. But we remained hopeful despite the uncomfortable gnawing in all our hearts.

Traveling onward, we stopped at a shopping mall and a restaurant, taking in the sights as we chattered excitedly about what we'd do once we arrived in Florida.

However, before we could leave Ohio, a sudden CLUMP CLUMP CLUMPing noise indicated that the [23]Monarch Butterfly would soon be landing. Sure enough, we pulled over to the side of the road to discover we'd blown a tire. And with insufficient funds to repair it, Dayne made the decision to call his father, despite my whining and complaining. I knew there was nothing else we could really do. We had a car full of stuff and hitchhiking hardly seemed the solution, even if we didn't have the stuff with us. But I didn't want to go back to my depressing life, and I especially didn't want to face our angry parents.

Dayne's dad ended up footing the bill for our stay in the plush hotel conveniently located nearby, where Dayne and Shelly swam in the pool and soaked in the [24]Jacuzzi. I stayed in the room in bed, sulking over how nothing ever turned out right. [25]I was Eor the depressed donkey, Dayne was Christopher Robin, and Shelly was Tigger.

The next morning we left for home, me crammed in the back seat amidst a heaping pile of junk, staring glumly out the window, tears dripping down my face; while the two of them laughed and sang theme songs from [26]*Happy Days* and [27]*The Brady Bunch*. They didn't understand… I had nothing to go back to.

We eventually had to reimburse Dayne's dad for the money he footed toward our little adventure, and he gave us a big lecture to boot when we arrived at his house. My mom came to get me there, not saying a whole lot. I remember I apologized to her once more when we got home, and she changed the subject, offering me some of my favorite yogurt raisins.

She didn't really care to go into it. I mean, she was happy to have me home again—she'd been worried sick—but as usual, everything was surface talk. I suppose now that she probably sympathized with me due to my father's death and the recent rape incident, and so decided not to give me a hard time. I went to bed exhausted and relieved, though still broken inside.

The three years of high school marked a drastic change in my life. After Keith, I'd somehow managed to wind up with three relationships almost back-to-back in which my boyfriends turned out to be closet homosexuals. Needless to say, this made a definite impact on my self-esteem as I began wondering what was wrong with me that I attracted these kinds of men. Although Dayne was gay, I wasn't meeting these men through him. Rather, they seemed led to me for some strange reason.

I met the first guy, Cory, through my friend's youth group at church, even before I'd met Dayne. We only dated for about two months and we never slept together or anything. He was just the new wave guy at school. I liked him because he was really unique: two-toned hair, earrings, tight pleather pants that revealed long, slender legs…

He was a singer in a band with an awesome record collection to boot. He'd constantly tell me I was beautiful, giving me longing stares that stirred passion in me to a degree I'd never felt. And he liked me because he was in love with Sylvia Houston-Von and thought I looked like her, (during her *Let's Make Contact* days my hair was cut very similar and I'd lost a ton of weight), and because I was new wave like him.

I guess I was really naive. As I already mentioned, I hadn't yet befriended Dayne, so I'd never met a gay guy before. I had no idea what singled them out oftentimes. I was pretty much clueless about homosexuality. I didn't even know what [28]*sodomy* meant. But if I had been knowledgeable, I wouldn't have missed the signs—the flashing neon signs—that Cory gave off. The high voice (I guess I assumed he was still going through puberty, a late bloomer or something), the feminine gestures and motions with his wrists (I thought he was just dramatic since he was really into drama class), the wiggly butt walk (I might have concluded he was hyperactive, I don't know). All of this just went right over my gullible little head; I was so infatuated with the guy.

Then one day he wrote me a letter and poured his heart out to me about how he was *bisexual*. I'd never heard the word before—it sounded like some Geometry term to me—so he had to explain that it meant he was attracted to both sexes. I stared at him in bewilderment. Was he *kidding*? This kind of stuff only happened in movies, right? I guess

I'd forgotten all about the porno magazines I'd read and the kind of relationships those people had. Why me? I thought.

I didn't understand at the time, that just like a good majority of bands the new wave music movement ushered in, Cory was following in their footsteps of homosexuality, femininity, and [29]cross dressing. There was a spirit behind this secular movement.

A few months later, Cory moved away. He'd confided in more than a few people about his sexual preference, and it wasn't long before the whole school knew. I guess it happened wherever he went. He said his parents kept moving around just as soon as the schools and community found out about their effeminate son. This time, however, they'd been more reluctant to move. So he persuaded them by threatening suicide: he drank some bleach and had to have his stomach pumped. They moved shortly after that.

About a year or so later, I met Michael. My friend Maggie, (who at the time took great advantage of the Day-Glo fashion trend, and was very patient with me when she had to sit in my room enduring my Angry Samosas album while I tried covering my zit for an hour), introduced me to him. He managed the movie theater where she worked.

Michael was a strange guy: a mixture of middle-upper class meets rebellion. A few years older than me, he was an intellectual type who talked rather formal, swearing only on occasion, as opposed to me. He wore slacks, dress shirts, and a long, black wool coat; his blond hair kept short and neat. Though he really didn't look the part, he hung out at all the underground bars and listened to the underground music. He took me to places I'd never heard of—little gothic dives tucked away in various coves of the city. His whole appeal was the fact that he was so mysterious. He rarely talked about himself; I knew only bits and pieces. It really didn't matter though. He had money, and he always supplied me with alcohol, introducing me to the pure pleasure of gin.

But pure it was not, as I found myself participating in X-rated photography which Michael claimed was art. Unlike when Keith had snapped pictures of me against my will that horrible Christmas Night, this time, I posed willingly for Michael. *Why not?* I thought. I really didn't care about myself anyway. It seemed if someone wanted to admire my body, then they were admiring me. That's what I'd always wanted, after all: to be admired by a man. It wasn't until later that I regretted my actions.

And then Michael confessed to me that he was bisexual, asking me to move in with him and some others who apparently shared his sexual preference. I suppose my first clue should have been the fact that he was a ballet dancer from New York who wished he had my feet. He used to take my foot in his hand and stare at the way it naturally curved, explaining that he was jealous of women because they had such beautiful arches. Apparently arches were very important to ballet dancers.

My third relationship with a closet homosexual was longer and more painful. I met Ryan through my friend Stacie and her sister Jamie. He told them that he had the hots for me, and they relayed the news. All of us had been chumming around for a few weeks, so I'd gotten a chance to know him a little bit prior to hearing about his attraction to me. Though he was the total opposite of anything I was looking for in a man, the fact was, I was lonely. And he grew on me.

He was tall and stocky with wavy, short brown hair. He dressed preppie for the most part: in golf shirts, jeans, and tennis shoes. His voice was very deep—something I liked about him. He had big brown eyes that knew just the right look to give in order to get me to either melt like butter or break down and cry out of pity for him. He also had a good sense of humor, always making me laugh. That was something I rarely did seeing as I was the Queen of Depression.

I'd met a guy at a teen nightclub about a year before who'd influenced me a great deal in the punk rock arena. Fresh out of Baltimore, Maryland, where apparently the punk rock/hardcore scene flourished, Rob supplied me with underground music and colorful stories about he and his old girlfriends. They slept all day and prowled all night dressed in mohawks and black clothing with outlandish vampire style makeup; snorting coke, drinking, dropping acid, and having sex.

The guy was a complete doll: blond haired, blue eyed, and slender. He wore black high tops or combat boots, faded jeans and muscle shirts, and a small stud or hoop in one ear—still unique looking, but a lot more masculine than Cory. He was a charmer, luring me away with his sexy voice and provoking stares. I think I was just so elated that someone so cool could be interested in me. Little did I know that like his divorced father, he was a lady-killer: a chip off the old block. I only heard from him whenever he tired of his five or ten other giddy teenage girlfriends. He constantly rotated us for variety.

I think he thought of girls as a kind of [30]Whitman's Sampler: if he tired of the creams, he simply stuck them back in the box half-eaten and moved to the caramels or to the raspberry cordials. And I went along with it, available at his beck and call. I suppose I thought he was *making me into a woman* or something. At any rate, it seemed he helped me discover an identity for myself. I was stronger now—tough as nails. With my mohawk and combat boots, my black slips and army jackets, I was saying, *Don't touch me* on the outside. But yet on the inside, *Please touch me. I'm hurting.*

Still, I liked my new image. It felt good. I'd put on my hardcore records and scream out the lyrics: *suicide and pain and kill and hate and death and sex and drugs and destruction and rape and murder and abuse.* It was my life. It was reality. And I was a realist. Why hide behind a Buffy mask and tell people everything's okay, a tennis racquet in my hand and a date with Skip the Meathead? No, I didn't want to cover up anything. The fact was: I was a depressed person. I hated myself, and I hated my life.

I was glad that Ryan liked the real me, mohawk and all—the raw pain I projected, the beauty of ugliness. If he could appreciate me the way I looked, then I figured I didn't have a problem with the way *he* looked.

Life was improving. I had a new used [31]Korg keyboard, a full carton of Carlsboro Light cigarettes my mom bought me before leaving on vacation to Costa Rica (she couldn't really argue with me smoking when she smoked), and a big brick house all to myself. My New Year's Eve party was only a day away. Jamie and I sat in my room now, cranking out the jams.

Slender, pale, and tomboyish like me, Jamie dressed in a yellow and green striped man's long-sleeved shirt, an old faded pair of [32]Levi's, and some motorcycle boots. Her hair was shaved an eighth of an inch short around her whole head, except for a long strand of bangs in the front that stuck straight up, coming to a point at the top like a unicorn horn. It was her own personal "do." I'd never seen another one like it.

At fifteen years old, she was a little powerhouse, strong as an ox. In fact, she probably could have kicked my butt easily. But that was just her hardcore image—she and I were *the tough girls*. Once you got to know her, she was really quite cute and lovable; very sensitive, and in desperate need of affection like everyone else in the scene who'd come from broken homes.

Though I'd originally started hanging around her sister Stacie, Jamie and I ended up being better friends. We had a lot in common. Stacie was more avant-garde/vogue, artistically inclined; and Jamie and I were more punk rock/hardcore, musically inclined. We liked to go places and do things—to explore the awful world we'd been born into. And most of all, to *kick out the jams*. Stacie, on the other hand, was more of a home body. She did a lot of painting, and read a lot of fashion magazines, which ended up paying off for her. Last I heard, she had a great job setting up window displays for a major department store in New York.

Jamie kicked back in one of the wooden chairs we'd brought up from the dining room now, legs crossed guy style and her new bass guitar resting in her lap (Christmas had been good to us). I sat Indian style on the bed with my keyboard, wearing a men's long sleeved black shirt, my Dark Flag army jacket, a pair of jeans, and my combat boots. My large mohawk stuck up about a foot off my head, perfectly even, with one long, pointed strip of bangs known as a *devil lock* hanging down between my eyes. Whaling on the keys, I screamed out lyrics about a stupid punk rock girl with an attitude I'd seen recently at a bar, making up stuff as I went along.

"SHE WAS BETTY HARDCORE, BUT NOT ANYMORE
SHE WAS BETTY HARDCORE, NOW SHE'S BLOOD ON THE FLOOR
ALL THAT'S LEFT IS HER JACKET, ALL GARNISHED WITH CHAINS
SHE WAS BETTY HARDCORE, AND SHE HAD NO BRAINS!"

Jamie followed my lead, plunking away on her bass and backing me up with growls of agreement:

"YEAH, BETTY, THAT OLD BETTY!"

We made The Sex Guns sound like The Boston Harmonic.

Stacie came over the house to have a listen, then. Tall, and slender like her sister, she was a gorgeous girl. No matter what bizarre outfit she dreamed up, she always looked like she'd just stepped off the Paris runway; she could have made a garbage bag look chic. She wore her short, brunette bob either comb teased or pinned back in small sections with tiny barrettes. Five beauty moles sprinkled along her left cheek and the sides of her chin accentuated her fashion model appearance.

The doorbell rang about ten minutes later, just as we'd finished taping our new smash hit. It was Shelly, scuttling up the stairs with her suitcase full of clothes and hurrying into the bathroom to put on her pajamas and overnight cream. "I figured we could have a pajama party," she bubbled over now. "Just us girls."

Then Ryan showed up, immediately going right to the refrigerator to see what we had to eat. We weren't actually going out yet; I was still wrapped up in Rob the punkrocker.

I called Rob earlier to invite him to my party, but he was already going to one at some *girl's* house in Ann Arbor, and they were "dropping acid," he said. Oh well. It felt good, anyway, just to be able to tell him *I* was having a party—to let him know I'd finally graduated from *pseudo punk* to hardcore. I owed it to him—along with Byron and John Hassle, the real punks in high school—for showing me that punk rock wasn't just about putting on some combat boots and buying a bunch of angry sounding records. You had to be corrupt, hateful, profane, slutty, and most of all—rebellious. One didn't *try* to be punk rock/hardcore. Trying was for *pseudos. Wanna-be's.*

So now I was *living* it. I had a bunch of friends, I was putting a band together, and in Windsor, Canada, I was actually famous in my own right. People referred to me as "the hardcore girl from the States that sells her poetry—the one with the cool '*hawk.*'" A couple of girls even took my picture into a salon, requesting their hair be cut like mine.

One night on the street corner there, I got in my first fight with a short little metal chick who'd been teasing me. That was before Jamie showed me how to throw a punch though, so all I knew to do was rip the girl's shirt off and break the gold chain around her neck that her boyfriend bought her. But after that incident, which had been witnessed by half of the punks, goths, and mods, rumors started flying: girls telling other girls at school that if they didn't leave them alone, they'd get *Martyr from the States* after them! I couldn't believe it. For once in my life, I had respect. No one would step on me anymore. I said good-bye to the weak, feeble Paula, and said hello to the tough, punk sex goddess Martyr. *Martyr*, because I was always *dying* for the sake of love.

### Martyr in Windsor

Dayne, Shelly, Stacie, Jamie and I made our Saturday night escape under the tunnel and into the lost city of Windsor: our Mecca that proved the world wasn't flat after all. Things here were different. The punks, mods, and goths (the freaks) hung around in droves together. They had to, because the metal heads and jocks teamed up against them, instigating riots in the streets.

We stepped through the door our Canadian friends now led us to, paying our five-dollar cover fee, and I had a look around the dark little night club. At once, a beautiful, blond headed man with a mohawk came over to me, addressing me by my name *Martyr*.

*He knows who I am. How flattering.*

Smiling, he handed me an offering. It was free, because I was *Martyr*. Wow. Opening the little piece of cellophane, I stared at a tiny purple dot, like a Little Dot sweet tart.

"It's Purple Microdot," he informed me.

I was a little hesitant, suddenly remembering I'd had a run-in with that once before. "Uhhh…"

"*Trust me*, it's mild. You'll love it."

I smiled, thanking him profusely, and stuck it in my mouth. I had to look cool. I was *Martyr*, after all. Gulp. It was now traveling toward my stomach, about to make its way into my bloodstream. *Here's to the element of surprise.* I shrugged and made my way over to the dance floor.

It was about twenty-five or thirty minutes later, in the middle of an extended version of a Tale of Tunes song, that I began to feel the fiery passion of red beneath the glowing rarity of a blue moon; in short, the beautiful color of purple.

"*Get a big kick out of living it up. Do what you want, it's good for you,*" the song advised. The strobe lights were flashing. Wow. The first time I'd seen strobe lights, or at least, noticed them. The extended mix melded into another song now. "*World of chaos. It's a world of chaos. Hey!*"

The beat was incredible. I could feel it coursing through my body like electric waves of sunshine, warming my bones and launching me into sheer ecstasy. Round and round I spun, Stacie and Dayne nearby. I loved the dark little club. I loved the people in black dancing next to me. I loved that gorgeous guy with the mohawk. And I loved... the new me.

One o'clock rolled around and we had to go before we turned into a pumpkin. We said good-bye to the Windsor natives and stepped out the door of time to board our mother's ship.

Taking a little stroll down the steep sidewalk, I stopped alongside the black wrought iron railing to gaze down at the building below us. Jamie stood next to me. We peered over at its windows now. A table caught my eye in one of them; a little round table covered with a cloth. In the middle of it sat a candle. *Flicker flicker* flickered the flame, hypnotizing me with its mysterious dance. Suddenly a white haired old woman appeared out of nowhere, staring down at the table. Did she have a crystal ball? As if sensing my presence, she abruptly looked up at me—a sharp, piercing look—staring, staring into my eyes. I felt she knew something about me. *How?* She frightened me, yet...

"Come on, Paula, we've gotta go!" Dayne alias Christopher Columbus urged.

"*Martyr.* The name's *Martyr.*"

"Yeah, yeah. Come on."

I turned to follow my friends, taking one last look at the strange and mysterious woman in the window. "Did you see that lady?" I asked them as we headed to the car, my breath vaporizing in the cold night air.

"What lady?"

"That lady—in the window. She was weird, man. Something was *weird* about that lady... the way she was staring at me."

## Martyr at the Grimstone

The Grimstone was an old punk rock bar down in Detroit. We'd get drunk in the bank parking lot next door and then file inside the historic building to watch people bash into each other at the speed of music and stage dive into the crowd. This was known as *slam dancing,* or *thrashing.* Once in a while, I joined in the fun until all the tall people overlooked my existence and drove me to the floor, stomping on my shoulders. Extreme pain accompanied by claustrophobia, I'd then seek a way out of the Pit, as they appropriately called it. Hmmm… was it the pit of Hell?

I'd seen Suicidal Inclination play there, Dead Nixon, and Harry Ross' outstanding poetry reading: (my man. I thought he was as gorgeous as he was intense).

The show ended and the recorded music came on once more. The Pit Zombies dispersed, revealing a short, skinny, hunched over girl with a major cowlick in her hair who until now, had been hidden. She hobbled along, using the hooked cane in her hand to retrieve empty plastic cups on the floor. There was something strange about the girl. Jamie noticed it as well. The two of us stood against the wall, watching her. She looked a cross between the [33]Hunchback of Notre Dame and a young, haggard *old* witch, if that was possible. Seeming to notice our interest in her, she turned toward us with a partially toothless grin and said rather loudly in a creepy southern drawl, "*Sam Hain's* comin'! *Sam Hain's* comin'!"

[34]Besides being the name of a band, Sam Hain is also, as I would discover later, the favorite holiday of witches and Satanists: The Festival of the Dead, occurring at Halloween.

The girl limped closer now, thrusting her cane out like a weapon to stab the cups, still eyeing us with dark curiosity. "*Sam Hain's* comin'! *Sam Hain's* comin'!" she said again.

"*Alright, alright!*" Jamie growled. "I think we know *Sam Hain's* coming."

* * *

I wrapped my beloved childhood doll, [35]Baby Alive, in a black felt cloak pinned together with a huge rhinestone broach. Then I ratted her hair out, painted her eye lids and lips black, and stuck a cigarette in her open mouth. She was now affectionately nicknamed: Baby *Dead*. Eve laughed as I stuck the sign on the doll while Jamie chortled loudly. Baby Dead stood on the shelf in my room, all ready for the New Year's Eve party.

Soon people began arriving—more people than I'd imagined—and they brought friends I didn't know. So I had a whole house full; a mixed assortment of punks, gays, preps, Shayna B and Sexy popstar look-a-likes… (the Shayna B and Sexy wanna-be's I could have done without. They went upstairs in my bedroom and started playing my keyboard, stealing my Butchermen stickers to top it off. I didn't know who the crud they were—my friend Monica brought them along).

And everyone got blasted. Eve supplied the cocaine, Ryan or someone brought the weed, plus we had plenty of booze on hand. We were heavy into a game of Poker when the ball dropped on Times Square at midnight.

A few minutes prior to that, Stacie, Ryan, and some others had come running down the stairs yelling from fright. I guess they'd been lying on my mom's king-sized bed when they heard the distinctive sound of footsteps creaking across the floor on the other side of the huge room. Either they were joking around, or *it* was back.

On New Year's Day evening when everyone had gone home and I was left all by myself, worn down from the various drugs I'd consumed, I made my way upstairs after examining the house one more time for any traces of a party. The whole bunch of us had spent the day scrubbing puke off the walls and cocaine powder off hand mirrors, vacuuming and dusting, picking up trash—destroying all the evidence against me. Now I was exhausted. It felt kind of like I was coming down with a cold or something.

As I neared the top of the stairs, the density in the atmosphere grew weighty and oppressive. I'd experienced this often enough to know that I wasn't alone again. Something lurked nearby, and this time, I was really spooked. There was no doubt in my mind that whatever it was, it was *completely evil*. I recalled what Ryan, Stacie, and the others had told me about the footsteps in my mom's room. Turning to the right now, I quickly closed her door, hoping to somehow trap the entity inside.

I headed to the left to enter my bedroom, then remembered the woman's voice crying in Jim's room a few years before. I would have to shut *his* door as well. Reluctantly, I made a right again, following the banister around toward his room while singing a Dark Flag song to ease my fear. The evil presence grew stronger the closer I got.

Jim's bedroom door was hard to close. I always had to sort of slam it until I heard a solid click to let me know it had fastened all the way. Grabbing the knob now, I pulled it forcefully toward me. Click. It shut. Good. Everything was okay. I breathed a sigh of relief and started back toward my room.

Suddenly, the latch *un*clicked. I froze, then slowly turned around, afraid to look. The door was open again! Petrified, I fled down the hallway and into my bedroom, slamming my door behind me and locking it. Then I called Ryan and made him talk to me the rest of the night until we both fell asleep on the phone.

When my mom returned from her vacation, I was lying in bed with the flu, sicker than a dog. I hadn't moved in a whole day. Besides her friend posting her on the scores of cars parked in our driveway on New Year's Eve, she'd found beer caps under the couch cushions and some puke on the wall that we'd overlooked. I was busted.

\* \* \*

Her name was Jezebel. She had dark skin, dark eyes, nappy hair, and a little green flowered dress. Dayne found her in one of the drawers in his house. Oh yeah, and she was a doll. A rag doll of some sort, kind of resembling a voodoo doll that you stick pins and needles in when you want to mess with someone really bad. Dayne gave her to Shelly for her birthday or something. She named her [36]Jezebel, and that's when the trouble started. As much as she loved that doll, there was something evil about that little bundle of rags. It reminded me of that song by Suzie and the Bad Sheep that Brandon used to sing to me:

> *"I've got a little dolly all dressed in pretty pins.*
> *And when I stick another one in*
> *You'll feel your head start to spin.*

*Now there's evil all around, do you feel it?*
*When she drains the life from you, do you feel it?"*

Whenever Jezebel was present, which was usually always because Shelly carried her in her purse, bad things happened. We got in arguments, we had car trouble—all sorts of things.

Then one night when Shelly slept over at my house, the two of us were at each other's throat. I didn't like how she went into our fridge, picked up a piece of kielbasa, then decided she didn't want it and threw it back in the container. I didn't like how we had nothing "*good to eat*" and it seemed nothing pleased her that evening.

So as she sat against the wall in my bedroom, giving me that indignant look while the two of us exchanged words, I picked up my mom's lead crystal ashtray and whipped it at her head. Thank God it missed her and hit the wall instead. The thing was so heavy, it didn't even break, but instead chipped the plaster.

"You could have *killed* me," she whispered, frightened.

That's when I realized the extent of my anger, frightening myself as well. I got up off the bed and ran over to her, wrapping my arms around her because she was still alive—and I was so sorry that I'd let the evil get the best of me. She brought up the doll then. "It's Jezebel. I think she doesn't want us to be friends."

"Yeah, ever since you got that doll, nothing but bad luck has come upon us. I think you should get rid of her," I agreed. The next morning, I woke up with a large, red [37]'X' scratched on my neck. I was sure Jezebel did it. That doll hated me.

Then one night, she disappeared while all of us were riding in Dayne's dad's car. Shelly noticed she was missing when we stopped to get gas. A couple of days later, she received a few ransom notes demanding candy, money, etc. if she ever wanted to see Jezebel again. *Of course* Dayne wrote them. However, he claimed he never *stole* Jezebel—that she vanished on her own. Who cared? I was just glad to get rid of that voodoo doll in the green printed dress.

\* \* \*

"Hello, Paula?"

"Yeah? Who's this?"

"This is Brandon. Remember me?"

"Brandon Erins? No way! Where are you, man?"

"I'm in Pennsylvania still. It's great out here. I'm in this coven, and it's really awesome. But I'm calling you because I just got this huge crystal ball, and I saw you in it. You have psychic powers, you know. I'm calling to tell you that you need a crystal ball of your own."

"Huh? Really?"

"Yeah."

"Hmmm. So have you talked to Sybil lately?"

"Uh, yeah. About a month back or so."

"I haven't talked to her in a while. We don't really hang around much anymore."

Sybil and I had been pretty close at one time. We used to talk on the phone for hours on end, and go to the local teen nightclub together. For my 16th birthday party, she came up with the brilliant idea for me to send everyone a list of the record albums I wanted along with their invitation; so each person bought me an album. I cashed in big that year.

"Oh. Well, this crystal ball is sooo awesome, Paula. You would love it. But listen, I've got to go. I just wanted to tell you that, okay?"

"Uh, yeah… okay."

"Remember, *you need a crystal ball.*"

\* \* \*

A few months later, another strange incident occurred in the house. Shelly was in my room talking to Stacie on the phone when I heard a crash and then she screamed. I came running out of the bathroom at the same time that my mom was jogging up the stairs. Both of us hurried into the bedroom to see what was going on. Shelly was pretty shaken up. She claimed that the metal tin containing my father's old drawing pencils, though perfectly stationary on the dresser, had suddenly lifted into the air and sailed toward her before hitting the floor and spilling everywhere.

It seemed my mom never experienced any of these hauntings as my friends and I did. She believed it was my deceased father, warning me to change my evil ways.

Right before I turned eighteen, I moved in with Ryan while Mom was at work one afternoon, leaving her a note that I would contact her after my birthday to let her know of my whereabouts, which I did.

She'd forbidden me to move out, but the two of us were arguing so much over my punk lifestyle—the clothes, the music, the friends—that I couldn't take it anymore. I attempted to have talks with her on several occasions about how I was just being an individual and not purposely trying to hurt her, but it seemed the two of us simply could not communicate. So I wrote her a couple of letters to try and explain; I'd always been better at putting my feelings on paper. After reading the letters, she acted as if everything was alright again. Then about a week later, she flew off the handle once more. This went on continuously.

I even asked her the first time I got a mohawk if it would be alright. She answered, "I don't care. It's *your* hair, honey," in a sarcastic tone. "You're the one that's gonna have to live with it—not me."

For a couple of weeks, I continued to prepare her, telling her I was making a hair appointment and that my friends were giving me a ride to get it done. She seemed okay with it, so I thought everything was fine. Even my friends thought that she was cool for not getting upset. However, right after I got it done, she freaked out. My head wasn't even shaved bald on the sides or anything. It was just cut an eighth of an inch short or so. She laughed along with her friends at first, who were all sitting on the patio when I got home. Then she came up to my room where Stacie, Jamie, and I were hanging out and totally lost it, screaming at the top of her lungs while tears poured out of her eyes.

Not even remotely understanding what it's like to be a mother, I was ticked off at her. This was precisely the thing that bugged me about her: she said one thing and did another. Lies. I couldn't take it anymore. The hypocrisy coupled with her heavy drinking, and Jim's heavy drinking whenever she decided to let him move back in again, was just too much. And since she refused to communicate with me, I felt I had to leave to stay sane. Ryan offered that I could move in with him. He assured me the two of us would have a great time. It seemed like a good idea to me.

His stepmother Lonna owned a house in Pontiac. Lonna was a strange bird. She reminded me of some fictitious character you'd see in a movie. She had a huge beehive hairdo and cat eye glasses like my dad used to wear. All her outfits were from the sixties and seventies: polyester bell bottom pantsuits, long flowery dresses, shirts with huge pointy collars, and big gaudy jewelry—some of which I absolutely loved. Ryan told me she'd been a flower child at one time.

Whenever she came over to visit, she sat in front of the TV for hours watching [38]*The 700 Club* or some other religious station, and eating [39]Kentucky Fried Chicken right out of the bucket. Once in a while, she'd sing along to some of the gospel songs in her southern drawl, chicken crumbs on her lips.

But for the most part, Ryan and I had the house to ourselves. Lonna was a live-in caregiver for a rich person in the suburbs. She spent the majority of her time there unless she had a day off or an errand to run in the immediate area.

The house was a health hazard in every respect. It was infested with cockroaches, probably due to the fact that before I came along, Ryan let the dishes stack up for weeks until they were all the way out on the dining room table. We had no hot water, so we had to boil kettles of water in order to take a bath. When it rained, the ceiling leaked in about ten different places, and pots and pans were set on the floor throughout the house to catch the drips. The upstairs, where my room was, had a bathroom with a broken toilet. Once or twice Ryan and I made the mistake of getting up in the middle of the night and using it, to which we then had to endure the horrible consequences afterward. There was a huge hole in the wall near my bedroom caused by nesting pigeons that had slowly plucked away at the already rotten structure. Rain *poured* in there, so a big bucket had to be emptied continuously.

The room I stayed in had apparently been ransacked by some out of control toddlers. Crayon slashes and scribbles adorned the walls and ceiling as if they'd made a day of their coloring adventure. My friends and I added our own finishing touches of graffiti, each of them leaving a little memento to reflect on whenever they paid a visit. Rob had started the trend.

Once, he came over to teach Jamie some bass lessons. I'd been drinking pretty heavily, and decided I wanted to go downstairs via the outside staircase near my bedroom. I opened the door, and as I took my first step, the staircase crumbled beneath my feet. He grabbed me just in time before I went with it.

Lonna made me take down the shredded black piece of cloth I had hanging from the light fixture in my room. She told Ryan she thought I was in some kind of cult. I didn't understand why a shredded cloth would indicate that I was involved in a cult, but Ryan mentioned that it was the graffiti that also made her suspect: especially the 'KILL' and 'CHARLES MANSON RULES.'

He and I spent most of our time partying. We drank, we snorted big chunks of speed through a straw, we smoked pot—anything we could get our hands on.

Eventually, I pursued my education once more, my mom taking me to the nearby high school to enroll. Though the high school had a bad reputation for gangs and violence, it turned out that my grades improved tremendously while I was there.

The teachers really seemed to care. I found that they didn't intimidate me or make fun of me in front of the rest of the class like at my old high school. Instead, they let me do my own thing, committing themselves to the cause of higher learning rather than how much laughter they could stir up from the rest of the class.

Since security was tight, it was nearly impossible to skip school. Hall monitors were present in every hallway wanting to know where your pass was to be out of class. If you *did* manage to sneak past them and exit out the door, it locked behind you. If you were smart, you put a rock or some other piece of debris in the door to keep it open a crack. And if you were lucky, it was still there when you returned for the next class because they neglected to notice it.

At first, I was extremely lonely. I stood outside by myself at lunch time, smoking cigarettes under the doorway of a bible bookstore that had long since closed down and was now boarded up to discourage vandalism. People walked by and laughed at my punk rock attire: army jackets and long black skirts, fish net stockings, and Egyptian style eye makeup like Liz Taylor wore in the movie [40]*Cleopatra*. Though my mohawk had long since grown out and my hair was just comb teased, they acted as though I was some kind of alien.

Contrary to what society thought, I didn't want to get attention. I was just doing my own thing—trying to find my own niche in life. I didn't want to be picked out of a crowd to be laughed at. I just wanted respect. I preferred it when people didn't give me any special attention— why couldn't they just let me alone and let me *do what I wanted to do?* Who invented the dress code, anyway? Who decided I had to wear high heels with a skirt? Why couldn't I wear combat boots?

I wasn't sure, though, if it was my individual style that bugged these high school students, or my skin color. Perhaps it was a combination of both. I tried smiling at them, saying hello—everything—but with no success. I contributed to the small percentage of Caucasians that attended the school. There were also a handful of Hispanics, a couple of which I became quite fond of because they liked me for who I was. But the majority of students were African-Americans, and though I didn't have a problem with them, many of the females there seemed to have a major problem with me. I was sarcastically referred to as "that *white ho*" etc., etc., while they made crude comments about my appearance.

Soon however, at least where school was concerned, things began looking up for me. I met two other punk rockers, Jonathan and Reese. They had mohawks and dressed in the attire of our favorite underground movie, [41]*A Clockwork Orange*; with long, fake eye-lashes on one of their eyes, thermal underwear wielding an exterior sports cup, derby hats, and canes in their hand. The three of us hung around together between classes and occasionally at lunch.

But after school, I went home to a complete jerk: Ryan. All of a sudden he was treating me rudely, even criticizing the way I dressed after telling me before that he liked it. He wanted me to change and become *normal* like him.

To make matters worse, Lonna's real son Harry, a Vietnam veteran, moved in with us. We couldn't do anything about it since we didn't really pay rent—we only gave Lonna a little money here and there whenever Ryan worked at the party store. So we had no say in the matter. Unfortunately Harry, on top of having severe Nam flashbacks, was a major alcoholic. And when he got drunk, he got very angry at the world; including the people within his immediate surroundings, which now happened to be Ryan and me. Ryan warned me that when he was drunk, you let him have his own way. He told me of the time that Harry was blasting country music on the radio and he went to change the station. Harry pulled out a switchblade and told him he better leave it where it was.

I had trouble sleeping most nights because I feared Harry would sneak up on me. The whole scenario was beginning to remind me of living with Jim all over again. I'd be in my bedroom minding my own business, and Harry would come barging in, wasted out of his mind. He'd start harassing me just like Jim used to do, intimidating and demeaning me.

It gave me the creeps, too, that there was a golf ball sized hole in the ceiling directly overlooking the downstairs bathroom. Ryan stated that Harry probably carved it out so he could be a pervert. From that moment on, I made sure to plug it up with a towel whenever I took a bath. The two doors adjoining the bathroom on either side were raised about an inch and a half off the floor, leaving a nice sized space to peer through. I shoved towels under them as well so no mirrors could be used.

I just felt terribly uneasy with him living there, though Ryan found my fear of Harry quite amusing. When it came to protecting me, he was about as helpful as a spectator in a lion's den.

One evening I was in my room again, headphones on, singing aloud to The Nuns of Grace *Reptilia* EP. Ryan was downstairs talking on the phone. Harry had a friend over, an ex-con who'd recently been released from prison but didn't seem any better for the experience. Like Harry, he too was a hard-core drinker and an ornery man. I heard the two of them calling my name loudly in a snaky sort of tone, and before I could react, it was too late—one had come in the first door of the bedroom, and the other in the adjoining door. They now stood grinning, blocking me in.

Holding their hands over their zippers, they made sexually explicit remarks. Next thing I knew, they were unzipping their pants. Fear gripped me as scenes of what I'd undergone with Keith and his friend flashed through my mind. I screamed out at the top of my lungs to Ryan, the two of them closing in on me, but he wouldn't answer. I could hear him downstairs still talking on the phone—the muffled sound of his low voice and occasional loud laughter. Once more I screamed, and still no reply. Frantic, I searched desperately for a way of escape.

By what seemed like a miracle, Harry suddenly shouted out something unintelligible, whipping his arms over his head for protection as if something was flying through the air at him. I took it he was having a flashback like Ryan told me he sometimes had. My eyes darted around the room then, seizing the opportunity. In his post-war trauma, he'd moved too far away from the door, leaving a large enough opening to where I could get through. Instantly I dashed toward it, swerving around him before he or Pete could stop me, and was out the door and bolting down the stairs to Ryan.

As I stood before him now, yelling at him for not coming to my rescue, he calmly told the person on the other end to hold on a minute and cupped his hand over the receiver. I sputtered out what just happened. A huge grin appeared on his face and he burst out laughing. Picking up the phone once more, he continued his conversation where he'd left off. I was devastated that he could be so heartless and unconcerned. I grabbed a knife from out of the kitchen drawer in case Harry and his buddy came after me again, and left the house to take a walk.

The next time Rob came over to fix our plumbing in the upstairs bathroom, he brought me a crowbar and a better knife. The crowbar always remained close at hand, and I slept with the knife under my mattress, just within arm's reach.

A local biker I'd recently met told me to mention to Harry that I knew a motorcycle gang that lived around the corner, ready to come to my rescue since they were friends of mine. Though I recall mentioning it in a casual way to him, I never had any more problems where he was concerned because I moved out shortly after that.

Ryan had called my mom one night and told her to come and get me; he was kicking me out. We'd been arguing nonstop, and half the time he was gone somewhere and I didn't see him. If he brought me any food or anything, he expected a sexual favor in return. Though I was hurt that he kicked me out, I was relieved to get out of that crummy, run-down house and away from Harry. Mom took me back gladly—and I was glad she did.

I continued to go to the same high school until Jonathan suggested I get another mohawk. I thought it a good idea as well. So Eve, a short, petite cosmetology student with state-of-the-art hair and vintage clothes, broke out the razor and went to town on my head one night; though leaving the sides an eighth of an inch short like the last time.

The next morning my mom lifted the blankets off me to wake me up for school. As she pulled them back from my face, she had another fit when she saw the long, pointed spikes sticking straight up on her daughter's head once more. Needless to say, she wasn't too happy with Eve. She screamed at both of us the whole way to school, even rolling down the window at a stoplight and yelling over to the guy in the car beside us, who was gawking at me, "Yeah, this is my daughter! Isn't she *ugly?*"

*Ouch.* I thought that was a little extreme, and so did Eve. "Oh my gawwwd," she offered from the back seat now, "how bogue, I'm *sure!*"

She was coming to school with me as a guest that day. Unfortunately, as soon as we set foot in the building, the principal pulled us aside, motioning for us to come into his office. He forbid me to go to class because I would be a *distraction* to the students. When I protested that Jonathan also had a mohawk and attended there, he replied that Jonathan was a male and so it was *permissible.* To make matters worse, I accidentally gave him my mom's address instead of Ryan's when he asked where I lived. He happily expelled me because I was *outside of the district.*

The school newspaper staff wrote a tribute to me as a plea for equal rights, which I thought was quite nice. It didn't change matters however, so I said good-bye to my Hispanic brothers and sisters, as well as to Jonathan and Reese. Jonathan and I had a short-lived fling after that, and then I didn't see either one of them until they befriended Jamie about a year and a half later.

I guess I was a glutton for punishment, because I eventually began dating Ryan again right after my graduation. I'd moved in with Rob's ex-girlfriend Kay and her friend Michele, who rented a nice three-bedroom house in a suburb of Detroit. I worked down the street as a barmaid in a small motorcycle/rugby pub. There, I did all the cooking and bartending while the uptight owner sat on a stool all day watching rugby tournaments on television; downing beers and stroking his handlebar mustache.

Ryan had lived with Kay and Michele until he slacked off on the rent and they kicked him out. Now he lived down the street with a hippie biker couple and their kids. As usual, we fought constantly, Kay warning me that he was no good.

And then he started hanging out at an adult bookstore on the corner. He'd met a girl who lived upstairs at the store (her dad owned it) and ended up having his first homosexual encounter with one of her friends. I flipped out when he confessed he was coming out of the closet. Kay told me she'd known all along that he was a flamer; I even remember Ryan mentioning to me before that she'd asked him if he was. I cried and cried, wondering why this had to happen *again*.

Ryan now being my third *surprise* relationship with a homosexual man, or actually my *fourth*, since even Rob claimed that he'd been bisexual for a time in Maryland where it was a *cool thing* to be—I soon thought I would have a nervous breakdown. Jim assured me that there was something wrong with me since I kept dating "*fags*." He said I was probably making them *turn* gay. Needless to say, I became a very angry woman with a very big complex.

It wasn't long before I met more homosexuals—at work, through others—until my entire circle of friends consisted mainly of gays. They affectionately referred to me as their "fag hag:" a term for a straight woman who hangs around a gay man.

On weekends, because they refused to go to straight bars and I had no heterosexual friends who wanted to go either (Jamie and Stacie were pretty much *straight edge*, a punk term meaning they didn't drink or do drugs), I spent my time at gay bars in a drunken stupor watching some of the most gorgeous men in the world make out with each other. Occasionally, they'd get really drunk and open up to me, telling me they didn't want to be gay and making passes at me. I never got hit on to this extent at the heterosexual nightclubs, so it was a real ego boost. I even had sexual relations with two of them. I guess I felt honored to be that special woman to turn a homosexual "straight" again—even if it was only temporary—and in my heart I hoped I could change them all. So with the high-power disco music booming in the background and the smell of vodka in the air, I made out with the attractive ones who came on to me.

Not long after that, I found out that Stacie had hooked up with her female roommate, who'd made a pass at her, and now professed to be *bisexual*. I was devastated. About a year later, Eve followed suit. Her cute vintage look replaced with a butch image, she dropped by one day to tell me she was a lesbian. She tried convincing me that I was a lesbian as well. "I always thought you and Jamie were gay," she informed me.

Weirded out, I questioned my own sexuality then. What made her think I was gay? *Was* I? Strange that I'd had a dream about *her* being gay before, and making a pass at me. Now it had come true—and she was telling me she thought *I* was! No. I didn't care what she said. I was not gay! I told her she thought wrong, because I liked *men*, not women, to which she replied that I ought to *try it*. She went on to say that the first time she'd committed the act, she hadn't liked it either. She'd even gotten sick, throwing up afterward.

"It takes getting used to, that's all," she coaxed.

I assured her that I was not interested in finding out. Although at times I definitely felt something pulling me in that direction (a temptation), and [42]even fantasized about it, I chose not to carry out the urge. There was something extremely dark and forbidden about it, and deep down inside, I knew it was wrong.

The next day, I saw Jamie at the pizzeria our friends owned. I told her Eve was a lesbian, and mentioned that she thought the two of us were, as well.

A scared look swept across her face suddenly. Weakening, she plopped down in one of the chairs. "Oh my God, are you *serious*?" she asked faintly.

\* \* \*

About a year and a half out of high school, I met a really nice man employed in the military through a mutual friend of ours. Craig was a cute skate punk. He liked some of the same music as me, dressed different like me, and most of all, *he wasn't gay!* Though we had nothing much in common as far as hobbies or even communication was concerned, we went out for three years, after which time he found out he was being transferred to a military base in Florida. He stated rather matter-of-factly that in order for us to stay together, we would have to get married. To my disappointment however, he was too macho to officially propose to me, though I begged him to do so.

Before our wedding, I took an AIDS test at the local health department. The waiting period was one of the scariest times in my life. I was so afraid that due to my history of sexual relationships, I'd contracted the deadly disease. As I stood in line to have bloodwork done, I noticed a poster about AIDS hanging on the wall. It pictured a grim reaper with a sickle in his hand and the word *DEATH*. My life flashed before my eyes at that moment, and I remember praying fervently to God to *please let me not have it*—that I wouldn't mess around on Craig anymore.

I'd recently had a fling with Mark, my friend Randy's straight cousin. He too was awaiting the results after I confessed to him that I'd also slept with Randy, whom he knew was gay. And then the results came: I tested negative. Relief flooded over me.

Craig and I said our vows before a judge in a courtroom, forgetting the rings—duh! I wore a black wedding dress during the ceremony to mock the traditional symbol of purity, proudly displaying the fact that I wasn't a virgin while at the same time demonstrating my deep appreciation for the gothic scene; which celebrated death, darkness, solemnity and morbidity. My long, straight hair was pulled back in a black veil, large rhinestone hoop earrings completing the bridal ensemble.

Afterward, we had a big reception at a golf course country club. We stayed at the reception until the very end, despite Craig's constant suggestions that he was tired and we should go back to the hotel. Since I was moving to Florida, it would be the last time I'd see my friends for a while—and I really wasn't looking forward to our wedding night, because as I'd suspected, it was just another night of sex; there'd been nothing special to set it apart from the others.

Craig was a good provider, and like a brother and friend to me. But I really didn't love him because I had no concept of what love was. Still, I wanted to hold on to him for security after the difficult relationships

I'd had. And more than anything, I wanted to leave the state for the purpose of escaping Jim, my abusive brother who'd hit me on more than one occasion.

Once, he'd punched me dead on in the forehead with his fist, leaving a nice sized lump. About a week or so later, I started stuttering and felt slightly disoriented. Another time, I attempted to defend my mom by pointing a kitchen knife at him because he and his friend were drunk and harassing her. He calmly told me to put it away, then followed me into the house, knocking me clear across the kitchen floor and bloodying my nose (it's a little crooked as a result). After trying to strangle me with the phone cord while I attempted to call Jamie and Stacie for help, he left the house. The two of them came rushing over to my rescue when they heard what he'd done.

My mother, however, refused to see the abuse. Despite the large black and blue lump in the middle of my forehead, she claimed Jim didn't punch me but just *slapped* me. When I pointed out that she hadn't been there to see what actually happened, and informed her that the next-door neighbors had witnessed the whole thing (though they refused to get involved), she responded with, "Well, brothers and sisters *fight*, Paula," like it's a normal thing to get beat up by one's own brother.

Regardless of her unwillingness to see, the fact remained: Jim made my life miserable through his drunken abuse and perversity. He even tried pulling me into the shower once with his friend Darryl, while making vulgar sexual suggestions about what Darryl wanted me to do with him. It took all of Jamie's strength to pull me back while I screamed out in terror, the monkey in the middle between their tug-of-war as I feared what would happen if she lost.

And sadly enough, in more recent times, I've given him a hug only to have him get *a little too friendly* with his hands or slip me a tongue in the ear. He has also made several comments on my sexual attractiveness despite the fact that, as he puts it, *I'm his sister.*

While growing up, he always made it a point to degrade me, telling me I'd never amount to anything. When I sang, he told me to give it up because I'd never make it as a singer. When I did my homework, he barged into my room angry and drunk, reminding me that I was nobody and would never go anywhere with my life. He constantly threatened me, and I dreaded whenever my mom went away with her friends and left me alone with him. Darryl would come over and they'd get wasted out of their minds. I was lucky if they entertained themselves with a good fight and left me alone.

Once, after talking of getting guns out of their trucks and blowing each other's heads off, they threw beer bottles at my mom's decorative pictures hanging over the fireplace and shattered the glass. The next morning, I found a note telling me to clean up the mess.

Despite my mom and Stephen's pleas, I refused to invite Jim to my wedding, and forbid anyone to mention it to him. Not only was I afraid of him, but I was afraid of what he'd do to Craig. It seemed whenever I had a boyfriend, he threatened me with *kicking his butt*, to put it mildly. So I wasn't about to invite him to do so at our wedding.

And I hated him for all the things he'd done to me, crushing my self-esteem since I was a small child. He had to be the most evil man I'd ever met. Sometimes I was sure he was the Devil himself.

Looking back, I think the point where he really went off the deep end was the night he took drugs over at his friend's house: a Satanist who once tried poisoning his own mother. I remember Jim running down the street in the dark like a wild animal with my parents chasing him. It seems he either bit, or tried to bite, my mom or dad in the leg. I think it was my dad.

Then one night many years later after I went to pick him up from the bar, he was talking to me when suddenly another voice came out of him—a voice that didn't sound human. I was completely startled and wondered if he was possessed.

Concerning my marriage to Craig, my family members kept their promise to me and said not a word to Jim about the wedding. One day while visiting my mom, he asked where I was. She told him I was married and lived in Florida, explaining why he hadn't been invited. He broke down and cried.

\* \* \*

In spite of the beautiful sunny days, the luscious green palm trees, the splendor of the vast ocean with its sandy white beaches; and all the new restaurants, surf shops and clubs to explore, Florida was a lonely place for me.

Craig and I never got a decent honeymoon; we moved right after our wedding and he was called to sea duty for three weeks immediately upon our arrival.

Sick in bed with the flu, I waited in a temporary housing arrangement for about a week while our co-op was being prepared. But at least all of our stuff had been dropped off by a moving company beforehand and was ready to unpack when I finally received the key.

Crawling with police cars and men in uniform, the fenced-in military base was like a city within a city. It contained its own grocery store, liquor store, mall, bank, etc., and then of course, all the blocks and blocks of homes that make up military housing. Certain sections of the base were comprised of check points requiring that travelers tell the attendant where they were going, or if returning home, where they'd been. I always had to show my military ID card before purchasing anything.

A trip to the grocery exchange meant tipping the bagger at the checkout lane, to which he faithfully carried your groceries out to the car regardless of whether you wanted him to or not.

It wasn't long before I discovered the base liquor store, which quickly became my favorite place. There, I was surrounded by any and every kind of alcoholic beverage I could possibly want—at discount prices.

Our entire living situation was foreign to me. To conserve water, we had rules about when we could wash our car and water our flowers— and it was *required* that we plant flowers in the designated spot beneath our kitchen window. I came home one time after being gone for a few weeks to a small jungle in my front yard: the innocent *little* sunflowers I'd planted beneath the kitchen window now about six feet tall, heads drooped over dismally. It was quite obvious I knew nothing about botany.

My next-door neighbor commented on the *interesting* flowers I'd planted. He jokingly referred to Craig and me as [43]*The Addams Family*. With my all-black attire and pet iguana I walked on a leash, and now the gigantic sunflowers on display, I couldn't say I blamed him. Besides, I kind of liked his term of endearment. I'd always admired [44]Morticia for her gothic beauty, and with the short hair and mustache, I guess Craig *could* have resembled [45]Gomez in a small way—minus the pin striped suit and kisses up and down my arms.

Craig's father moved from Detroit to live with us for a while. He was a cool guy—kind of an old Mexican biker type—but he drank very heavily, always out at the bars. I got up to go to the bathroom early in the morning and stepped in a puddle from where he missed the toilet the night before.

He didn't pay us rent because he didn't work a whole lot, and if he bought any food, it was for himself. Although he'd promised only to stay with us until he found a job and a place of his own, the fact remained that he wasn't really looking that hard; I sensed he was a little too comfortable with his immediate surroundings. Finally, I told him he had to leave. Craig didn't have the heart to do it, and I simply could not take him mooching off us any longer. He ended up finding his own place shortly after that, along with a steady job.

The military wives tried their best to welcome me and make me feel right at home. Still, I just didn't quite fit in with them. They were all older and did things like play flag football or attend tea parties with the captain's wife. I went to a few engagements, but always felt like a misfit hanging out in the background. I clearly did not belong.

I managed to make friends with a few of them who weren't as uptight. The ship doctor's wife, Sharla, came over every now and then and we went shopping or to the military bar. She helped me get our house in order too, putting together the entertainment system and hanging the blinds. I would have been lost without her, since I had no clue how to read those foreign instruction booklets, which always seem to leave out the most important details of assembly (they probably get lost in the translation).

Her daughter Nicki, who was a few years younger than me, soon moved in with Craig and I once Sharla and the doc transferred out of state. She didn't want to leave her boyfriend because they were pretty serious, so we put her up in the spare bedroom and she gave us a little rent money each month.

About five houses down from us lived Jean, her husband, and their kid. Jean attended college. She helped me enroll when I decided to continue my education, familiarizing me with the campus. We carpooled together for a while until I got sick of being late for class because she was always searching for the perfect parking spot. She also helped me select living room furniture, arranging for a friend to haul it back to our house in his truck.

And here and there I baby-sat for Joanie's kids. She was the commanding officer's wife. It made me feel good that she trusted me with her kids even though I dressed sort of unusual. But she seemed open-minded. I had a feeling she used be a flower child or something.

Living with Nicki was awkward. Quiet and reserved, she stayed in her room most of the time. Occasionally she and I went jogging together, but other than that, I rarely saw her. Still, it was the small loss of freedom that I missed: being able to play my keyboard at one or two in the morning or turn on the stereo. I'd always been a late-night person. When other people were going to bed, I was getting my second wind.

Thankfully, whenever Craig returned from sea duty, Nicki always left for a few days to give us some time together, although it really didn't matter anyway. Craig's idea of time together was hanging out in front of the TV, me watching him watch sports. Of course, it had always been like that. Nothing changed just because we were married. But where my friends used to fill the void in our relationship, they no longer could. I was far away from anything familiar to me—and extremely lonely. I wanted to have fun.

Though I started a part time job working at L-Mart in the shoe department, and though studying became my main focus, I couldn't help but miss everyone back home. Craig was away at sea ninety percent of the time and there was no one in my new surroundings I could really connect with. So I drank to kill the loneliness.

Music was such a prevalent thing in Florida, especially at the college where I attended, which seemed like the alternative capital of the world. So many people were in bands, with new ones emerging all the time. I finally decided then, despite Craig's disapproval, to form my own band. It had been a dream of mine for as long as I could remember—Jamie and I never did quite pull it off.

I put an ad in the local paper, receiving a myriad of responses. After a few wasted trips attempting to mesh with people who just weren't on the same wavelength, two roommates I'd recently had phone conversations with seemed fitted to me in both music *and* lifestyle. I decided to make the almost two-hour haul to their apartment so we could jam together.

When I arrived, I was pleased to see that they were around the same age as me, give or take a few years. This meant that they were hip to the music scene and well able to identify with the type of band I had in mind. Their bohemian clothes and furnishings also communicated this to me.

Camron, seventeen and the younger of the two, answered the door. The surprised expression on his face coupled with his rather large, rather shy smile, told me that he also was pleased with what he saw standing before him. Soft spoken and mellow, he was the exact opposite of his roommate Kris, who preferred being in the limelight. His brown hair was short, though unkempt and wavy. His clothes matched his personality: laid back. He wore a stud earring and a beaded necklace. A flannel shirt and baggy pants hung loosely on his skinny frame, big black combat boots completing the ensemble. Because he was so easily approachable, I immediately felt comfortable in my new surroundings. He called Kris now, who was fresh out of the shower, the smell of deodorant soap following him into the living room.

Kris was twenty, just a year younger than me. Like Camron, he kept his wavy, bleach blond hair short and unruly, a black bandanna wrapped around his head just below his bangs. In one of his ears he wore a small silver hoop earring, and his eyes were a gorgeous ocean blue. He smiled at me now. I noticed his teeth were a bit crooked, but his full lips and attractive dimples offset them quite nicely. He was dressed all in black just as I was, though I remember thinking that the fringed loafers on his feet somehow didn't fit in with the rest of his getup. As he shook my hand firmly and uttered a suave hello, introducing himself, I immediately sensed a Don Juan mentality emanating from him, which seemed to warn me to keep my distance. His self-assured air told me he was confident, though perhaps a little too confident. I began studying him closer, however, only to discover by the end of the night that I'd developed an attraction to him. He'd helped me reach this conclusion, simply because he made it quite evident he was attracted to me. His full name was Krisstopher, which I fancied to be rather gothic due to its unique spelling. It had such a nice, romantic ring to it that I preferred not to condense it, and everyone else followed suit after that.

Through with the initial stage of sizing each other up, Krisstopher, Camron, and I went on to talk about music. They mentioned to me that they were renting an office and using it as a practice space. We headed over there to set up my keyboard and jam, where a couple of their friends joined us. Though we ate hamburgers and drank beer more than we played, somehow we made our decision that night to become a band.

And so every weekend I made the two-hour hike to their apartment, which seemed more like minutes when traveling eighty-five miles per hour at the speed of sound in Craig's new [46]Nissan, the stereo system blasting gothic love songs as the love bugs met their death on my windshield.

## III. SOUL MATES

Somehow in the scheme of things, our band became secondary. Surrounded by all the new faces I'd met through Camron and Krisstopher, I seemed to encapsulate some small part of each of them, as they did, me. I spent more time socializing and partying than I did creating music. These were my kind of people. They weren't content living the ordinary life of doldrums. Colorful and spontaneous, they sought, as I did, for something more. Each personality contained a uniqueness not yet corrupted by society's standard of conformity. Each individual possessed a childlike quality that allowed him or her to be free amidst a world of clipped wings.

When Sunday rolled around and I had to leave them and return to the mundane world I came from, I felt I left the realm of color and entered once more into the black and white. The dismal. The reality of life in all its disappointments and boredom.

It meant another week of cold, apathetic people walking around: people who once had dreams themselves but had stamped them underfoot in their attempt to become *grown up* and *mature* and *one of the Joneses*. It was rare even to get a smile out of these kinds of people, due to either their elitist attitude or their jealousy over someone else's expression of freedom. Whatever the reason, I felt virtually alone during the week, and Craig's continued absence, even when present, didn't improve matters any.

Because I longed for conversation and mutual displays of affection, I found myself yearning for the companionship he could not give. Though he was nice enough, he never made an effort to really know me. I continuously vied with the TV for his affection, never winning. It wasn't the act of sex I wanted anymore: it was the intimacy that was supposed to lead up to the act that I craved.

Krisstopher and his friends now filled this void for me. They actually sought to know me: my likes, dislikes, hopes, and dreams. They praised me for my talents. They supported me in my ambitions. Especially Krisstopher.

The two of us talked for hours on end about everything I'd always wanted to talk about with Craig—life. Not just "Hello," "Goodbye," "What's for dinner?" "What's on TV?"—but life. Its let downs, disappointments, achievements, politics, religion, people, etc., etc. I could feel the attraction growing between us as our companionship deepened. He offered excitement—new territory to be explored. I didn't want an ordinary life of grocery shopping, flag football, and finger sandwiches with the ship captain's wife. I felt I was drowning in a cesspool of boredom, starving for attention from a sports-crazed husband whose idea of affection was a five-minute encounter in the bedroom.

Krisstopher made me feel like the woman I never felt like with Craig. He was entertaining and humorous, spontaneous and fun. My senses were overloading from all the attention I was receiving from him and his friends. On the downside, he partied. And partied. And partied—too much. I'd been pretty good about cleaning up my act since I arrived in Florida. After the California acid experience a few years back, I'd vowed never to take it again. I'd even quit smoking—something I'd been wanting to do for a long time, especially after the carbon monoxide poisoning I received from the big green gas heater in our old efficiency apartment about two years prior.

I'd been wondering, back then, why I just couldn't get up out of bed anymore. I was soooo tired, soooo weak. My mom would call at four o'clock in the afternoon and I was still lying there, drifting in and out of sleep. The only time I seemed to revive a little was after a walk to the grocery store with Craig. The brisk air felt incredibly good to breathe in for some reason.

After my mom's next-door neighbor, an elderly woman, died from carbon monoxide poisoning, my mom began to suspect that perhaps I had it as well. She instructed me to call the gas company, though Craig doubted there was a problem. He said he felt fine, probably because he spent ten or eleven hours out of the house each day at work. But I was currently unemployed.

The gasman came out and tagged our heater, confirming my mother's suspicion that it *was* emitting poisonous fumes. Despite this warning label, Craig insisted that it was not giving off carbon monoxide. So I moved back home, and my strength slowly returned. Nevertheless, I continued to smoke, soon discovering that it didn't mix well with the carbon monoxide still present in my lungs.

On college campus, I had to stop every few feet just walking to the next building because I couldn't breathe. Students passed by, giving me strange looks as they watched me clutch my hand to my chest and gasp for air. But no one paused to see if I was okay. I guess they didn't want to be late for their next class. In the end, I was thankful for the experience. It helped me kick my cruddy habit—at least, for a while.

Then eventually, I quit smoking weed. It never really did anything for me, so it wasn't hard to do. But I still drank. Every so often, Sharla and I would go to the bar on base and have a few. I'd get pretty sloshed, and then we'd argue with the Air Force guys about who worked harder: them or the Coast Guard. But I wasn't much of a partier like I used to be. I guess I just grew sick of being sedated all the time. And since Craig was straight edge all the way, I didn't really crave drugs anymore.

In Krisstopher's world, however, partying was a major theme. His sort-of, kind-of girlfriend (whose name also happened to be Jamie) and he were constantly stoned on something. They took shrooms (or poisonous mushrooms), they smoked pot, they tripped on acid, and if none of that was readily available, then they popped pills for motion sickness; which, when one is stationary, give the feeling of being in motion.

It was on a weekend when we were supposedly meeting for band practice, which was turning out to be an excuse these days for getting together with Krisstopher and drinking a few, that I arrived at the apartment to find him diligently making out a shopping list. He asked me if I'd take him to the store to buy a couple of items, namely: gin, vodka, rum, scotch, [47]Southern Comfort, sherbet, orange juice and some fruit. A whole bunch of them were going camping, he said, and would I like to go? He then explained that he was making a concoction which he affectionately entitled: Puke Punch.

At first, I was disappointed that he decided to ditch band practice without telling me. Then I got depressed because Jamie was over, gung-ho about the idea of this brew he was making for their camping experience. I'd hoped the two of us could be alone without her.

He and I took a drive then, and after I saw he wanted to be where the party was, I made up my mind that I'd have to go too if I didn't want Jamie to seduce him. Whenever he got trashed, they ended up sleeping together. This made me insanely jealous, despite the fact that I had a husband.

I'd recently started taking speed again, which Krisstopher gave me one night before a Cowboys and Homos concert. Craig, who'd accompanied us to the show, forbid me to take it. So I popped it in my mouth secretly when he wasn't looking. Later that evening, Krisstopher placed a little cellophane package in my pocket containing a couple more tablets.

I took them the night before, and now I was in a major state of depression accompanied by crankiness from sleep deprivation. I hardly felt like camping, let alone partying. I was crying and I didn't even know why.

I think my body reacted differently to uppers than most people's. Cocaine hardly affected me, except to make me tired and depressed. The only sensation I got off it was the numb, tingly feeling in my gums. Weed made me yawn a lot and forget things, but I never really understood what *high* meant. And now the speed, which had given me somewhat of a warm, fuzzy body buzz and a rapidly beating heart, was making me cry. It seemed I couldn't help it. I lie on the kitchen floor of the apartment, tears streaming down my face while Veg (pronounced like Vegetable) tried cheering me up. He was a friend of ours who'd recently given me a cool skull bracelet belonging to his ex-girlfriend since I was the only one besides her who had a small enough wrist to wear it.

"I'm sorry," I sobbed, "I think it's just the speed I took. I feel so cruddy!"

Then Krisstopher mentioned something about putting LSD in the punch he was making. For sure I didn't want any now. I told him how I swore after a bad trip in California that I'd never take acid again.

"You don't *have* to take any..." he offered.

I recalled the evening the skinhead with the sideburns gave me the tiny slip of paper with the two purple hearts. He quietly held it out for me to grab, looking at me with cold steel eyes, his face expressionless. I'd been to a ton of hardcore shows and seen a ton of skinheads—but this one scared me. Why? I stuck the little piece of paper on my tongue, sucking on it for a while and then swallowing it as Craig had instructed. Prior to that, I'd only taken mescaline, a milder hallucinogenic which came in the form of microdot tablets.

Craig didn't take any acid, seeing as he was in the Coast Guard. Anyhow, he'd quit drugs a long time ago. But his friends consumed more drugs in one sitting than anyone I'd ever seen. They'd pass around a pipe heaped full of marijuana, then when that was finished, they'd snort a couple of lines of speed through a straw. Afterward, they'd have some shrooms and maybe a beer or two. I was surprised they weren't dead—seriously. Not many people's systems could handle all of those toxins at once.

So there we were, in the mountains—literally—way high up, the altitude plugging my eardrums; somewhere in California. We'd driven up, up, up a narrow winding path big enough for only one car as I watched over the side. No guard rails here. If you somehow got off the beaten path, you plunged downward to your death.

There was a party going on. A huge party. Just a bunch of people— mostly punks and metal heads—and some mountains. Huge mountains. As I surveyed my surroundings, I was reminded of that horror flick, *The Mountains Are Watching You*. Even some of the people resembled that bald headed guy in the movie with the gruesome demeanor. Two skins in particular I found to be quite a match. They were really creepy. In fact, they even called themselves *creepers*. They purposely walked around slightly hunched over, their hands hidden behind their backs and their legs taking long, slow strides.

They came over to Craig and his friends and I a few times, grinning fiendishly while informing us in spooky laughing tones, "We're *creeping*. Huh huh huh. We're *creeping*." I remember one of them getting real close to my face, his large eyeballs examining me as he continued smiling rather deviously. I was trying to figure out if he always acted this weird, or if it was just his charade for the evening.

"Yeah, those are the creepers," Craig told me. They crept away while I stared after them for a moment, a puzzled look on my face.

A couple of bands would be playing soon, powered by two huge generators. I soon forgot I'd taken the LSD, overwhelmed by everything and everyone around me. So many people were here, and somehow they all seemed different to me. I looked around at each one of them with interest.

Currently on a plateau, we started climbing a bunch of steep rocks on another mountain to sit down and get a full view of the show. I hated climbing. I hated heights. I followed along fearfully on the rocks behind Craig, groping for a secure spot to station my feet as I struggled to pull myself up to the next one. Suddenly I couldn't feel the rocks beneath my feet anymore. In fact, I couldn't even feel my feet. I stepped into the air now, my body falling, falling...

"*Help meeee!*" I screamed. "I'm *falling!*"

"No you're not. See?" Craig pointed to the rock I was standing on. "You're okay. Trust me," he said calmly.

I struggled to gain my bearings for a moment, looking down at the rock once more to make sure it was still underneath me. I was sure just a minute ago it *hadn't* been.

We climbed considerably high up. It seemed very dangerous. But as we sat down, I looked around me, noticing a bunch of people had done the same thing. I felt more at ease as I observed that none of them seemed concerned about the height. They sat in various spots on the rocks, talking and laughing, drinking and smoking. The stench of beer was strong in the air. I'd never smelled it so strong before.

I caught sight of a longhaired guy sitting near me. He was wearing the most awesome leather jacket I'd ever seen. One sleeve was painted yellow, the other red. The colors were amazingly vivid. On the red sleeve hung a strand of cowbells. The whole thing was decked out in cool metal work and patches, with a large painting on the back. I reached over and tapped him on the shoulder. He turned around.

"Hey, I like your jacket," I told him, smiling.

He broke out in a huge grin from ear to ear, his crimson red lips showing large, white teeth. "Duhhh luhhh uhhh," he replied with a slow, deep mutter. My eyes grew as big as saucers then. I grabbed hold of Craig's arm, tugging on it.

"What?" He turned around to see what I was so excited about. "Oh, that's Deaf Dan. He can't hear you—see?"

The guy was still looking my way, now pointing at his tongue to let me know he couldn't speak. I sighed with relief to know I hadn't just *heard* his words all jumbled up. Reality was quickly turning upside down for me. I wasn't quite sure *what* was real anymore.

I pointed to his jacket then, giving him the thumbs up symbol to let him know I liked it. He smiled and gave me a silent thanks by shaking his head up and down, then turned back around toward his friends. I thought it strange that a deaf guy would be into punk rock since he couldn't hear the music. But Craig informed me that he could feel the vibrations—the beat.

Now the band was starting. From up where we were sitting, I peered down in amazement at the lead singer, who seemed colossal as he stomped around in a blond mohawk, army boots, jeans, and white T-shirt. I was sure he had to be about nine feet tall.

"Man, that guy's a *giant!* Look how tall he is," I commented to Craig.

He smiled. "No he's not. It just *looks* that way right now."

"Huh?"

The band was doing a cover of *Fearful* by Witch's Sabbath. I started to sing along to the words in my mind. *"I wonder if I'm crazy cuz—"*

I stopped abruptly, terrified as the singer snarled backwards, *"Emit eht lla seciov reah I!"*

I tried to hear him forward, but I couldn't. It seemed I could no longer control my mind. I felt a whirring going on in my brain. Then over the backwards lyrics another voice, low and distorted like a warped record growled, "Saaatan!"

I screamed out, clutching my head in my hands. *I'm losing my mind. Oh my God, I'm losing my mind!*

"What?! Babe, what's wrong?" Craig asked, frightened.

"Craig, I'm scared!" I sobbed, tears in my eyes. "Why are the words *backwards?* I feel like I'm going insane!"

"No, Babe. That's just the acid. It's *supposed* to sound like that," he reassured me. "Just go with it. Don't be afraid."

I was horrified that he hadn't bothered to tell me what this stuff was going to be like. How was I ever going to make it through the night? I heard someone say, "You can control it. Just tell yourself you can control it. You're strong." Was it Craig? No, I think it was his friend. It helped me.

*I'm not losing my mind*, I told myself. *I'm not losing my mind.* The music sounded normal again. Everything was going to be okay. I fished around in my jacket pocket for my cigarettes. It seemed my hand sunk down, down, down until I finally grabbed hold of the soft, crinkly package. Pulling one out, I lit it. Uugh! What was that horrible taste?

"You lit the wrong end," Craig informed me. I threw it down beside us and fumbled for another, my fingers too big now to grab one.

POW POW POW!

We both jumped, frightened by the loud sound that pierced the air, drowning out the band for a brief moment. Craig whipped his head around to peer further up the mountain where it came from. "They've got *guns*, man! They're shooting off *guns* up there!"

My heart leaped in my throat. "*What?!* Come on, we gotta get out of here!" I panicked, starting to get up.

"No," he said, pulling me back down again, "don't get up or we'll be more of a target. Just act cool. People are out of their freakin' minds tonight."

I sat frozen as more shots were fired, other people around us getting antsy as well. Then the shooting stopped.

The bands ended shortly after that, and Craig and his friends helped me maneuver my way back down the mountain. The feeling in my feet returned, but I was rubbery all over, and everything I touched was rubbery too.

Some people Craig hadn't seen in a while came over to talk to him as we all stood around in the dark. A couple of small fires were crackling here and there, providing minimal light. I watched in horror while the creepers stood directly in the middle of one, laughing as the flames licked their ankles. I waited for screams of pain to indicate their flesh was burning. Nothing. Nothing but laughter. How?

"Man, those guys are *nuts!*" Craig exclaimed, spotting them now. "I'd hate to be *them* in the morning."

*Would* they be burnt? Or wouldn't they?

About eleven hours later, back at his sister's house with Craig sound asleep, I lie in the dark as shapes became robot men marching toward me to attack; their bodies square and circular and triangular. I closed my eyes, a million images flashing in my mind. My heart beat terribly fast; speeding up, slowing down. Then it seemed to stop for a moment. I gasped for air, sure I was having a heart attack. I was sweating profusely, and I remember saying to God then, "If you just let me live, I swear I'll never take acid again."

When Craig awoke the next morning, I started yelling at him for falling asleep when I almost died. Then I started yelling at him because I'd taken the acid. "I'll *never* take that stuff again!" I snarled, both angry and cranky from lack of sleep.

"Yeah, Martyr, you don't *have* to take any acid if you don't want to," Jamie said now, echoing Krisstopher.

I watched her as she laughed and joked and scurried around the apartment, helping him plan this awesome camping experience. He liked her because she knew how to have fun. She had no cares, no worries, no fears, it seemed. They were so much alike. What was I doing here? And yet, I'd come out of my shell so much since I'd met these guys. I'd made so many new friends. Man, I didn't want to be a bore. And I especially didn't want to lose Krisstopher to Jamie's partying schemes. I was clearly falling for him, though married.

During the week, while I worked and went to school, the two of them did fun stuff like visit thrift stores and buy weird clothes, then go out in a field somewhere and pick wild mushrooms poisonous enough to make them hallucinate and trip out, but not poisonous enough to kill.

This was an extremely dangerous thing to do, for it was of the utmost importance that one had a knowledge of which mushrooms were deadly. Apparently Jamie, (or *Rabie* as they'd affectionately nicknamed her), knew the difference. I guess she'd read a book on it or something. Still, I wondered how they could take such a chance. But then again, I suppose it wasn't much different than taking some drug somebody got off the street when you had no idea where it originally came from and just *who* put *what* in it. Either way it was Russian roulette.

The next morning, we all headed over to the campgrounds. Since I was the oldest in the group, they elected me to sign for a site. There were thirteen of us: Veg and Raoul, Tim and Garrett, Camron and Misty (whom he was seeing at the time), Jasmine (Misty's sister) and her boyfriend, Jasmine's two friends Gabriella and Steve, Krisstopher, Rabie and me.

I was extremely worried we would be checked for alcohol or drugs or something. I'd already instructed everyone not to carry along any bottles or cans if they were bringing anything in. Krisstopher had the Puke Punch in a huge five-gallon container. He'd added five hits of acid to it just before we left, along with the sherbet and fruit that now complimented the five-blend alcoholic brew. Storing it in the back seat with our gear and a bunch of other stuff made it less noticeable. To my relief, we got in really easy. They just asked for my ID and didn't bother checking anything. I guess they weren't allowed to.

Now I was faced with the decision: to have some punch or not. It sat on the picnic table, looking pretty inviting—and harmless—a bright pink color with soft clouds of orange sherbet, plump grapes, and other fruit. Krisstopher assured me that if I did have some, I probably wouldn't get much acid anyway, since there were only five hits floating around: a hit to a gallon. I made up my mind to try it. Scooping some of it into my paper cup, I drank it down fast. It was really good. So I had some more. And some more.

A bunch of us took a hike then, splitting up and taking a couple of different trails. It rained for a short time, then the sun came out for the rest of the day. We lost Krisstopher. He'd wandered off by himself. Raoul informed me that he'd spotted him swimming down by the river.

Raoul was a really laid-back Puerto Rican guy who loved the band Jean's Habit. He was quite lovable with his short, curly hair, somewhat chubby body, and thick accent. Lately he wore really weird knee-highs with his shorts and loafers, apparently on some kick or another. The black and white striped ones were my favorite. But today he had on a pair that were sheer white with a checked pattern, like *women's* knee-highs.

We went off to the springs, where families of people were swimming and eyeballing our group with curiosity. I found Krisstopher. He'd rented a canoe and went on a voyage, where he saw some skeleton men in another canoe following him. I was amazed. The only drug vision I'd had remotely close to that were the robot men, and I thought *they* were scary. I couldn't imagine seeing skeletons chasing me in a canoe! He didn't seem frightened, though. He said it was all part of taking the acid—the visuals. The California trip had been somewhat visual, but not really.

As I saw how much fun everyone was having, I started to get bummed that I wasn't getting any hallucinations. I wasn't getting anything at all. Rabie was frying. Everybody else was either frying or drunk.

Garrett, a hippie-looking guy who was another friend of Jasmine's and Misty's, walked with me back to the site as I complained, "Man, everybody else is frying. I want to fry. I don't feel a—"

The trees came to life then, with eyes and arms like an enchanted forest in a [48]Disney movie.

"Wow!" I breathed.

"What?"

"I think I'm frying."

"Cool."

Raoul trailed behind us with a big thick branch of wood he used as a staff, or cane. He looked like some distinguished old wizard to me as he shuffled along, poking things with it. So we deemed him Raoul the Wizard.

All of us that were frying danced and shouted through the emerald green forest while those who'd gotten the brunt of the alcohol rather than the LSD just kind of chilled out in a drunken stupor. Tim, a short little guy with an alternative bob haircut, smoked a joint with Veg and then they climbed some trees, jumping down when we least expected it.

I was beginning to see that they were right: LSD wasn't bad after all. Raoul and Krisstopher said you hardly ever got a bad hit. This trip was really cool. I felt so spiritual. Why? I wasn't sure. Suddenly everything around me was magical, like I was rediscovering the spirit world. Everything had some kind of deep meaning behind it. It seemed I gained an inner awareness of myself and others which was not possible otherwise. I discerned what they were thinking and how they were feeling, [49]as if spiritual power had suddenly been granted to me. It was simply incredible. If only life could be like this all the time!

My senses were sharpened beyond belief. I could see a tiny ant from ten feet away. I could hear a conversation from sixty feet away, or if many were going on, I could tune in to whichever one I wanted and hear it perfectly. Smelling was magnified tremendously—even the smells one doesn't normally zero in on, like the smell of someone's skin or the smell of dirt. And touching things was wonderful. Every bump, every crevice, was intensified. Soft was softer. Hard was harder. Sometimes though, things felt really rubbery.

I liked how I perceived myself on LSD. I wasn't self-conscious anymore, but confident. I could concentrate on the good things about me instead of the flaws. I was prettier when I looked in the mirror; my eyes were bluer, my teeth were whiter. Even my body looked better. I felt like a goddess. For once in my life, I was happy to be me.

I sat down on a grassy hill now with Garrett. He and I were really bonding for some reason. It appeared as if we were on the same trip.

"I can't believe it," I laughed.

"What?" he asked.

"How ironic that here I am, the wife of somebody in the Coast Guard, tripping out on drugs while my husband's out busting people in Haiti right now for drugs."

He smiled. Then we both laughed.

"Oh, man. What am I going to *do?*" I asked. The debate was taking place within me: Craig vs. Krisstopher. Guilt and passion were synonymous this day.

Krisstopher and I hadn't even gotten together. In fact, he'd been with Rabie last night while Raoul and I camped out in the living room, talking half the night before finally falling asleep. I was thankful Raoul stayed awake with me until the speed finally wore off or I would have been all alone—going out of my mind while I sought to go to sleep and couldn't.

I liked how Krisstopher kept staring at me now that I was hanging out with Garrett. He'd been off on his own practically since we'd gotten to the site—or Rabie was with him. So I played it cool, just sort of hooking up with Garrett somehow. Ever since we'd come back from the springs, he stayed faithfully by my side. I'd never met him before. In fact, I had to keep asking him what his name was because I kept forgetting. But like I mentioned earlier, we seemed to be on the same trip, though Craig had told me once that no one has the same trip. How is it then that he and I heard the same noise at the same time, which sent the two of us running off in total fright while everyone else stared after us, perplexed? They hadn't heard it.

We were still hanging out on the hill talking when Rabie or someone told me that the park rangers wanted to speak to the person responsible for the site, which happened to be me. Apparently they'd found open alcohol. By this time, I was frying so hard I could barely talk. I told Krisstopher, "I can't talk, man. I can't even *think* straight."

"Just be cool. Answer yes and no. You don't have to talk a lot."

Garrett trudged along beside me, a comfort somehow since I found the khaki ranger outfits with the badges to be quite intimidating.

"Are you the person in charge here?" one of the rangers asked, eyeing me suspiciously. With his western style hat and sunglasses, he resembled one of the members of Cowboys and Homos. I hoped he couldn't see that my pupils were as large as frying pans, a sure sign of drug use.

"Yes," I answered.

"You've got open alcohol in the car. Is this your car?" He pointed to Craig's [50]Nissan.

"Yes."

On the floor in the back were some beer cans and an empty bottle of [51]Jack Daniels. I stared at them in horror. How could this be happening? No one brought alcohol in besides us… did they?

"I didn't bring those!" I declared, both shocked and angry.

"Those are Veg and Tim's," Krisstopher told the rangers.

I turned to yell at Veg and Tim now, who were standing nearby. "I told you guys not to bring anything in here with you! I can't believe you—now you got *me* in trouble."

To my relief, they admitted to bringing in the alcohol and the rangers expelled them from the site, letting me and everyone else off the hook. We were then warned to quiet down a little since this was a family campground and people didn't appreciate our noise.

After that, Gabriella's boyfriend Steve took charge, telling us we better shut up and settle down. He was an older guy—probably in his thirties—and kind of redneck looking. In fact, I think he really *had* a red neck. It appeared that way to me, anyway. He was angry and drunk, and I instinctively cowered at the tone of his voice. He reminded me of Jim. We stood by his cooler, where he had [52]Cokes and [53]Mountain Dews. I asked him if I could have a pop. He sneered at me, hating the way I said *pop* instead of soda.

"You're from Detroit, aren't you?" he snarled. "Cuz they all say *pop* there." He acted like it was a federal offense. I stayed out of his way the rest of the night, not wanting a Jim flashback. When it got dark, he left to get Veg and Tim, bringing them into the site once more.

We spent the rest of the evening listening to industrial music and staring up at the stars. Raoul had quite an industrial music collection. I hadn't even heard of half the stuff until he played it for me. Like everything else, it was a new experience.

The next morning we drove away in formation, our little caravan blasting The Malones: *Tina My Punk Rock Girl*, while families paused from eating breakfast around the fire to stare at us, food still in their mouths.

Krisstopher asked me later that day why I'd hung around Garrett the whole time. He stated that he thought Garrett had the hots for me. I knew then that he was jealous. I mentioned how he'd spent a lot of time with Rabie as well, though he swore to me they hadn't done anything when they'd both slept in Steve's van the night before. Steve and Gabriella had pitched a tent, as had some of the others. Raoul and I also ended up crashing in a tent, purely for sleeping purposes. Tim came along later and sacked out beside us.

77

It wasn't long before Krisstopher and I dropped all subtlety and made our desire for one another crystal clear. Though I half-fought it for a while, at least in the physical sense, I eventually gave in to the temptation and [54]committed adultery with him. Craig was still away at sea—he had been for nearly three months now. Afterward, I found myself amidst the immense guilt wondering what I should do.

* * *

Krisstopher was dabbling in the Occult, especially since Camron had so many books on it. We'd recently stopped in at one of the metaphysical stores so I could purchase some tarot cards after he'd told me about them. An Egyptian deck caught my eye. I recalled a psychic lunch monitor in high school telling me that I'd been Egyptian royalty in another life. Maybe the dramatic eyeliner gave her a clue?

I'd recently gotten a tattoo on my shoulder of Anubis, the jackal god of the [55]Underworld. It seemed very spiritual to me since I remembered reading somewhere about the [56]ancient knowledge the Egyptians possessed. Anubis held the ankh in his hand, which symbolized the key to eternal life. That was my favorite part of the whole tattoo. Later in Humanities class in college, I discovered that Anubis was Osirus' helper. He weighed the soul to a feather before it could pass on to the Underworld. If it was as light as a feather, it could pass on to the next life. If it failed to be equal in weight, it was then eaten by a female crocodile, according to ancient myth.

A few years before, a college professor recommended a book on [57]past lives, or reincarnation. I found the book absolutely fascinating, and remembered my father had kept a book dealing with the subject in his library.

The tarot cards I'd purchased told me that Krisstopher was my soul mate, reincarnated from another life. His significator cards were the Prince—and more frequently the Knight—of Swords. These aggressive suit cards demonstrated how he'd rushed into my life with great strength and boldness to sweep me off my feet and cause dissention between my husband and me.

Prior to that, I'd read a book on soul mates that made me anticipate the union two people could share which extended far beyond the flesh. It was a deeper tie involving the senses and the souls of the lovers—the very cores of their personas—and I wanted it. I'd never experienced anything but sex with a man. I needed something more spiritual. I needed someone to want a deeper part of me.

Apparently there were different types of soul mates: those who were *karmic*, (such as friends or lovers with which there existed previously unsettled relationships, like premature deaths or karmic debts to which you owed them restitution for wronging them in some way (or vice versa) before you could part forever); and [58]*eternal* soul mates, (those whom you would be with forever once you worked out your unresolved karma together).

The cards seemed to be pointing to the fact that Craig and I had unresolved karma to work out. Shortly after that, I dreamed we had been together in another life, but he'd been brutally murdered so that we could not say good-bye to each other. Our souls then could not rest until we were united once again. But now it was time to say good-bye, because a higher form of soul mate had come along: Krisstopher.

For days, I weighed everything out. What would happen if I left Craig? Though the cards pointed to the fact that Krisstopher was indeed my soul mate, I couldn't help but feel a nagging doubt in the back of my mind: a doubt that he was serious enough to have an actual long-term relationship. He'd return to Rabie whenever Craig came home, which made me feel like he didn't value our relationship enough to wait for me, and I just felt there was some apathy on his part, though I wasn't quite sure why. I wondered if he was mature enough to take care of me, to support me, to stay with me if I went through with my decision to leave Craig. After all, this was no small matter. I was far away from home, in another state with people I barely knew. I'd have to leave most of my possessions behind, like furniture I'd bought with the money my family gave us for our wedding. I'd even have to drop out of college after my mom just paid to have me return once more because I'd no longer have a car to get to classes.

Yet, there was a sense of excitement about living on the edge and doing things on the spur of the moment. Krisstopher was much like me in this respect, I discovered. Neither one of us really thought things through before we did them.

The notion of hurting Craig made me cringe. What would he do? What would all his friends on the ship say—those I'd come to know so well? Reality slapped me in the face once more. I got a terrible, awful, sinking feeling in my gut. But what was I to do—miss my chance at having the kind of spiritual love I'd always dreamed about? I tried picturing the rest of my life spent with a man who didn't know how to communicate to me or make me feel like something other than part of the furniture, and it was more than I could bear. No, I deserved better. My life had been pretty crummy thus far, and I knew there had to be more out there for me. Life had to contain more than this—it just *had* to!

For weeks I mulled everything over. My days were spent going to college and working part time in the shoe department at L-Mart. My nights were spent drinking heavily—usually a whole bottle of [59]Kahlua with crème or several tall glasses of rum and [60]Coke; reading tarot cards while listening to spiritual music about love and mystery and magic. The exotic vocals of Peter Morphine and the mesmerizing fretless riffs of Hong Kong's ex-bass player transported me on *Dali's Llama* to another realm.

I'd burn incense, turn the lights down, and open the sacred, carved wooden box, the intoxicating smell of patchouli filling my nostrils as I carefully lifted the cards out of the perfumed cloth I'd wrapped them in to consecrate them. Patchouli was a longtime favorite of Egyptians, who recognized it as a type of aphrodisiac. Its fragrance spoke to me of magic and lust... and dirt. Spreading the cards on the bed then, I'd stare at their detailed pictures in a drunken stupor. They seemed as keys unlocking doors I had yet to enter. Doors of secrets. Doors of love.

Yet something unexplainable was happening to me, especially at college, a place where my mind and thinking faculties played a vital role. I found myself unable to function at times, as if a force would suddenly come upon me and I'd be thrown into a whirlpool of confusion. I often forgot where my room was, arriving ten and fifteen minutes late although I'd been going to the class consecutively. Once I forgot my own age, telling someone I was a year younger. When I realized my error and corrected myself, they stared at me as if I was crazy not to know how old

I was. Of course, forgetting how old you are isn't really that big of a deal and can happen to anybody, especially as the years tick on and people no longer want to keep track. But still, I somehow felt crazy. Disoriented. My mind was cluttered.

Bad luck followed me like a storm cloud, hovering indefinitely above my head. I tripped over desks and chairs to the dismay of other students. My backpack strap caught on the doorknob while I walked, violently jerking me backward. People stared at me as if I had a real problem, which made me more timid and self-conscious. I developed a nervous shake in class, my head even twitching every now and then as if it had a mind of its own. Once I left campus, however, I was fine.

Though a few of these incidents might have been explained as life's most embarrassing moments, I felt (perhaps on an unconscious level) that they were warning signals of some kind.

\* \* \*

Worms. Big, thick night crawlers. Someone had spotted one in the bedroom under the glow of the purple light. A whole bunch of us were gathered in the apartment; I think we'd just come back from [61]*The Rocky Horror Picture Show*. I came out of the bathroom to see Veg, a girl named Jade, Rabie, Raoul, and Krisstopher scooping up the worms.

"They're all over—look at them all!" somebody commented now.

"Where in the pit of Hell did they come from? There's no way they came up out of the carpeting."

We all wondered at their appearance. The doors and windows had been closed, and they couldn't possibly have squeezed through both floorboard and carpeting.

"Man, this is like some kind of *bad omen* or something."

\* \* \*

I was mad at Krisstopher. We were supposed to fry together, but by the time I got off work and arrived at his apartment, he was sleeping from partying all night and day—probably with Rabie.

"Can't you just wait until another time and I'll fry with you?" he asked groggily as I sat on his bed now. "I'm just sooo tired. I've got to get some sleep."

"No, man. I can't wait. I've been looking forward to this all day. Just give me the acid and I'll fry by myself, alright?"

He told me maybe he'd join me later, but I knew he was crashed out for the night. So I set out for the land of adventure by myself. A nocturnal adventure. I turned off the lights in the living room, except for the red light, and spread out my tarot cards on the floor. But seeing as it was too dim to read them, I abandoned divining, concentrating instead on the red light. The window caught my attention now, as Peter Morphine of Bow House sang in the background. A breeze was blowing through the screen, lifting the curtains in a mysterious, flowing motion. That's when I felt him.

Who was he? I don't know. I could only see him in my mind's eye. He was dressed in black—a cloak, to be exact. I couldn't make out his face, though his short dark hair resembled Andrew William Elder's from The Nuns of Grace. As he appeared via the living room window now, standing in the bloody red shadows, he carried with him on the wind a certain promise of pleasure amidst the pain. Yes, he was a vampire. *Sky clad*, as the Wiccans refer to it, I performed a brief ritual. Why? I don't know. It seemed the appropriate thing to do. And then he was gone.

A little chilly, I crept into the bedroom walk-in closet to grab something of Krisstopher's to keep me warm. As I flicked on the light and reached for a sweater on the shelf, a large, beady-eyed rat with fangs glared at me. Jerking my hand back, I let out a shriek and ran into the living room. Just a hallucination. But I'd wait awhile to get the sweater.

\* \* \*

I was anxious for Krisstopher to call. We were going to get together later that evening. The phone rang and I bolted into the kitchen. "Hello?" I asked excitedly.

"Meet me in Christmas," he answered now in his usual suave tone.

"Huh?"

"*Christmas*. Meet me in Christmas."

"Krisstopher, what are you talking about? What do you mean, *Christmas?*"

"It's a place. And that's all I'm telling you. I'll be there tonight at eight—with Lucy." Lucy was a code name for LSD.

"But how am I going to find—"

"You'll find it. I know you will."

"But how? Krisstopher, this is ridi—"

"Get a map or something. I'll be at the gas station waiting for you."

"*What* gas station?"

"You'll see it when you get there."

"But how are you getting there without a car? Is someone dropping you off?"

"No. Don't worry about it. I'm going to hitchhike."

"*Hitchhike!* That could take *forever*—and it's dangerous. Krisstopher, I don't think this is a good—"

"Don't *worry*, I'll be there at eight. See you tonight. Bye." He hung up, leaving me standing in the middle of the kitchen, perturbed at his little riddle. He knew I was bad with directions—how was I supposed to find this place? Obviously he was trying hard to impress me. A little *too* hard, I thought. But I attempted to find humor and espionage in this enigma rather than view it in a negative way. After all, he was my soul mate. *Something* good had to come out of all this.

I called up Jean to see if she knew anything about Christmas. She mentioned that she'd heard of it but wasn't sure of its location. Apparently it was a small town (population of about 250 or something) that sold Christmas ornaments year-round. At her suggestion, I called Joanie, who had a map. She told me to come over and she'd help chart a way for me to get there. She was true to her word.

The drive took about an hour and a half. I arrived a little before eight, spotting the gas station Krisstopher was talking about. It was the only one in town, located just past the sign which simply read:

CHRISTMAS

The station was comprised of a few old-fashioned pumps and a small convenience store. I pulled in and kept the car running for about ten or so minutes, then shut it off when he still hadn't come. Another ten minutes went by. Then twenty. I began to grow worried. What if he couldn't make it because no one picked him up? The man and young girl inside the store were eyeing me suspiciously. I thought they would soon call the cops, thinking I was casing the place or something.

My worry turned into anger now as I glanced at the time once more. Nine o'clock. I'd been waiting one hour. How could he make me drive all the way out here and then not show? That was it. I started the car again. Maybe I'd see him on the way back home, still trying to bum a ride. No, maybe I wouldn't bother looking. The whole thing was probably a big joke.

I flipped the car into reverse and took my foot off the brake. Suddenly, bright colored lights flashed in my rearview mirror as a police car pulled in behind me.

"I don't believe it. They called the cops!" I grumbled aloud, fear washing over me.

At that point in my life, I didn't like cops. They made me nervous. In the past, they harassed me for no reason simply because of the way I looked. They'd catch sight of my mohawk or gothic attire and immediately turn on their lights, motioning for me to pull over while coming up with some petty excuse for having me do so. Or at least, it seemed petty at the time. I realize now that I probably *did* look suspicious—and wearing a dinner fork around my wrist *could* be considered a weapon when crossing the border to Canada. But I thought they ought to be picking on someone who was *really* causing problems. Only once or twice had I actually met some friendly cops that didn't have attitudes.

I continued staring in the rearview mirror now as my mind raced. Registration. Proof of insurance. Were they in the glove compartment? Yeah, that's where they were.

The passenger side door on the cop car opened, and to my surprise, Krisstopher climbed out. "See you later. Thanks again for the ride," he said casually, waving to the cop.

Relief flooded over me as I watched the police car pull away, my mouth hanging open in awe. Krisstopher approached the car, peering through the window at me with a big smirk on his face. He was clad in an army jacket with black, plastic spiders attached to the shoulders.

Strapped across his chest was an old canteen containing God only knew what. A black scarf was tied around his forehead hippie style, and his eyes were saturated in black eyeliner, giving him a gothic football player look. He climbed in the car.

"Hey, love," he said with an English accent, turning to kiss me. "Were you scared I wouldn't show?"

He then told me of his hitchhiking adventures. Someone had dropped him off halfway. Traipsing through a field, he'd just downed two hits of acid marinating in orange juice and tossed the bottle alongside the road when the cop pulled up next to him. He thought he was toast, especially since he had vodka and OJ in the canteen and another four hits of acid stuffed in his underwear. The cop asked him where he was headed, warning him that he was in the midst of KKK territory and they didn't appreciate people of his fashion couture. He then told him to get in and he'd drive him the rest of the way to Christmas. It was about a half-hour ride in which he had to maintain a conversation with the officer while trying to keep Lucy from introducing herself. She refused to keep silent any longer as they arrived at the gas station, not a moment too soon where he was concerned.

"Did you like those flashing lights?" he laughed now. "I asked him to turn them on just to scare you."

"Yeah, well you did a good job! I thought I was history."

I drove us back to my house while he placed a hit in my mouth. Yuck. Bitter. Another cop car began following us then. I tried ditching him on back roads, but he stayed close on my tail. Finally, Krisstopher instructed me to pull into a convenience store and to our relief, he kept going.

I was grateful when we finally entered the base, safe from the perils of driving while flying. I couldn't wait to get out from behind the wheel and bust loose. Nicki was staying at her boyfriend's, so we had the house to ourselves. As we turned on my street, Jean passed us in her car, slowing down to wave while staring over at Krisstopher.

"Great. Now the military wives are going to know you spent the night," I mumbled. Thoughts of what they'd think accompanied with worry that it might get back to Craig tortured my mind. I shook them off, the drug helping to ease the guilt for now. "Oh well. Who cares *what* they think?!"

## The Goth of Romance

The night was a black raven that took me in its wings. The love I wanted so desperately to feel… was it here now? Krisstopher crooned closeness, cradling me in his coffin.

Another hit and a half each. A couple of drinks. A hundred love songs. And I spilled my soul.

Yet it was all so bestial.

When the raven dropped me off on the edge of the morning, the construction workers pounded on the walls; their low voices grumbling, their tinny rock music blaring on their toy radio. An addition to the back porch. We left the shades pulled in our little world.

My mom called long distance. Yes, your daughter's fine. She has a man over and she's cheating on her husband. If only you knew… Idle chit chat. Hide the guilt. Hide the reality. Sweep them both under the carpet.

Stepping outside now, the sun burned our eyes. We went on a forty-five-minute quest for a Coney dog, finally locating a dive somewhere that had the goods. Three Stakes blared on the car stereo… Trint Razor really knew how to put my feelings into words—something about being *crucified for his lover.*

Then I had to go deal with shoes in the world of L Mart. Krisstopher said, "Don't fret: just be happy and sing a little shoe song."

I left him home sleeping beautifully. My soul mate.

## THE BOOK OF SHADOWS

"You can come with me to the forest, where magic and adventure abound, or you can stay here with Craig. The choice is yours," Krisstopher told me one morning as I sat fidgeting in bed with my guilt and indecision.

I made up my mind to leave Craig. It was undoubtedly easier to make the decision while hanging out with Lucy. She helped talk me into it—or at least, told me what I wanted to hear. So it was, after inviting her in for a cup of tea one night, she lent me her ear—and her frivolous mind.

As usual, Krisstopher was already fast asleep, tired of talking with her. I, on the other hand, urged her to stay just a little while longer. As the sun rose and the apartment complex slowly came to life with the sound of birds chirping and people starting their cars to leave for work, I shook the sleeping prince gently, anxious to share the good news; he'd been telling me for days that I needed to make a decision. He wouldn't budge.

I stood in the middle of the room looking around, a fingertip pressed against my lips; deep in thought. Presently, he got up out of bed on his own accord and paced back and forth, as if in a trance.

"Krisstopher, wake up!" I shouted.

"Huh?"

He blinked, looking around the room and then back at me.

"You were sleepwalking."

"Oh."

Excitement welled up within me once more. "Guess what? I decided I want to go to the forest. I'm leaving Craig."

He stared at me blankly, scratching his head while I waited for a reply.

"Well?"

"Okay," he mumbled groggily, then flung himself down on the bed again, instantly asleep.

Somehow I wasn't expecting such an apathetic reaction to a decision that would affect the rest of my life, as well as the lives of those close to me. For a moment, anger seethed within me. It quickly turned into doubt mixed with last minute reserve. I shook it off, reminding myself that Krisstopher was virtually unconscious and my timing was bad.

It seemed he did a lot of sleeping even after that day, however, as if he'd fallen into a massive state of depression. I wondered if he *also* was having second thoughts, but he assured me he wasn't. He said he was just tired. Even Jasmine and Camron noticed his odd sleeping spells.

I couldn't help but somehow feel that this whole thing had been a game for him—*a frolic in the forest* of sorts in which he never really thought I'd end up leaving Craig. Perhaps the reality that he'd stolen someone's wife was finally hitting him. Of course, I *allowed* myself to be stolen.

It was time to break the news to Craig. His ship had docked a few days before, but I hadn't bothered to pick him up as I'd been sedated and still undecided. I called him now from Krisstopher's apartment. He was happy to hear from me—and worried. One of his crewmembers had given him a ride home, and he wondered where I was.

I explained that I'd been hanging out with Krisstopher and the band, and that I needed to come home and talk to him because I had some bad news to tell him. At first he thought I wrecked the car, which made me feel terrible because that would have been light in comparison to what I was about to drop on him. It pained me at my heart that he had no idea what his wife had been doing while he was away. Not that he was Mr. Innocent himself. I'd heard stories about how he and the guys on the ship would go to bars (though Craig didn't drink) and rate the women on a scale from one to ten. And I had a feeling that he'd been slightly unfaithful to me, or at least wanted to, when he'd gone back for a visit to California once to see his friends and met a girl there that he constantly talked about. That had been before we were married though.

I drove home to tell him the news. It happened to be his birthday. I explained that I was in love with Krisstopher and wanted a divorce. He asked me if I'd cheated on him. I told him yes. Stunned, he stood there for a moment, not saying a word. Suddenly, realization gave way to anger and he ripped one of the storage closet doors off its hinges. That was the first time I ever saw him get violent.

He told me he'd had a feeling I liked Krisstopher ever since we drove back to Michigan earlier that summer to see my family. I'd played a tape of Krisstopher's old mosh band over and over on the car ride there. I guess I talked a lot about him too.

His anger changed to a plea now as he offered that we could go for marriage counseling. He begged me not to leave him, sobbing like a baby. I guess I never knew he loved me that much. I tried explaining to him that we just weren't meant to be—we weren't compatible. He was a *karmic* soul mate. I reminded him how his mom used to do tarot cards and how I was reading them now. (As a matter of fact, she had forecasted something bad about our relationship when she did a spread for me once). I reassured him that someone else would come along who was better suited to him.

As I collected my things together, he flung himself on the bed, violently crying. Every vein in his body bulged out in torment. My heart sank within me then, as I watched the fruit of my actions. Still, I remembered that something more spiritual awaited me. I owed it to myself to find out what it was.

Within the same week that I left Craig, his mother was shot in the chest and killed when a man broke into her home to steal her television set. A year and a half prior, his sister whom we'd stayed with in California, was shot and killed. The police suspected it was drug related since she'd been a dealer. The only family Craig had left now was a heroin addict for a brother and an alcoholic father who'd never been anything but a roommate to him. The guilt I felt was unbearable, so I made sure to sedate it with more drugs and alcohol.

A few weeks before Halloween, he called over to Krisstopher's apartment and asked to speak to me. He was having a big Halloween party, he said, and I was invited. His band was playing. Band? I asked. Yes, he'd taken up bass guitar. He then informed me that he also drank now. My heart hurt. I knew he wanted desperately to be the Krisstopher I was attracted to. The Krisstopher that rode in on a party animal and captured his wife, whisking her off to *Never Never* Land, that forbidden place. I declined his invitation. And my heart still hurt.

"Uhh... hi Mom. How're you doing? Good, good. Well... I have something to tell you. I think you better sit down for this one. Yeah. Well I uh... left Craig."

* * *

We finally resumed the band thing once again, making an effort to write new material and practice diligently. Camron, however, was busy doing his own thing. When practice time rolled around, he was always out somewhere dropping acid or over at his girlfriend's. We sensed he just wasn't as serious about playing as we were, probably because his musical style deferred somewhat from ours. My ad had originally stated I wanted to play *diverse* kinds of music. However, my dark record collection was growing on Krisstopher, and we were progressively leaning toward the gothic sound. Camron, on the other hand, preferred the psychedelic sixties and folk/alternative sound. So we put an ad out in the paper for another guitar player, and after a few mismatches, finally found someone who fit our repertoire.

Barry was a good guitarist, though a little on the egotistical side. He lived with his girlfriend Carry in an apartment just down the street from us. The two of them seemed as opposite a couple as any could be. He was loud and outspoken. She was quiet and reserved. He partied a lot. She studied a lot, since she was in college. He was the [62]Big Bad Wolf, out stalking all the [63]Little Red Riding Hoods of the world.

One night, much to my surprise, Carry opened up to me when the two of us were alone. She told me that she knew Barry was unfaithful to her, though since he'd given her herpes, she felt she had no choice but to stay with him because no other man would want her after learning of her [64]incurable disease. I tried to encourage her the best I could by telling her that if a man really loved her, he would not care, though in my heart I doubted the validity of my own words.

Somehow we got on the subject of witchcraft then, and she told me about how she'd seen a bunch of spirits once, like dead bodies, bursting up through the floor tiles. Apparently she went into some kind of trance during this time, in which she said Barry had to break open one of his protective crystals to absorb the apparition. She denied being on any drugs, but claimed she merely had psychic-type abilities to sense evil. I found this extremely interesting.

I myself had been in a sort of trance once when I lived with Craig before our marriage, though not a visual trance. After taking mescaline one night, I'd put on some Bow House and stood up to dance in the bedroom of our efficiency apartment. As the music consumed me, I danced round and round and round, faster and faster and faster. I felt as if I was flying. My friend Charles, who had not taken any drugs, said that my eyes got really wide and I started turning counterclockwise. He said he felt some really intense energy and it scared him. Later, I discovered that spinning counterclockwise is a practice in witchcraft known as *widdershins*. Since it goes against the universal flow of things, it is used to invoke negative energy (or stir up evil spirits). Incidentally, one of the songs I was dancing to contained a prayer recited backwards.

After about a month or two, Barry started blowing off band practice. He wouldn't return our calls, either. Unfortunately, he still had one of Krisstopher's bass guitars and a microphone stand. When we went over there one day and asked Carry about it, she claimed they weren't there—that he'd loaned them to a friend or something. We looked in the band room but couldn't find them. Conveniently, Barry wasn't home. Krisstopher suspected he probably had the stuff in the trunk of his car and was riding around with it.

So once again, we had no choice but to look for another guitar player, this time suffering the loss of some band equipment.

\* \* \*

I had one of those freaky dreams—the kind that bordered on being frightening, yet always had some weird element in them to keep them from becoming a total nightmare. Like the old *Outer Zone* episodes. They couldn't really be classified in the same category as say, the Saturday morning horror flicks, yet there was always some aspect of horror they possessed. I suppose these kinds of dreams could be labeled *psycho science fiction dreams*, kind of like my whole relationship with Krisstopher: it was *scary* because I never knew what to expect, yet it kept me coming back for more thrills and chills. And spills.

I lie in bed now, my heart beating a little faster than normal, as the dream had startled me awake. It was still fresh in my mind: a line of cars sat waiting to cross over a bridge. I was in the ⁶⁵Nissan, also waiting. Traffic was horrendously backed up. And then I noticed it. A fire. Its fierce flames cackled and danced until they devoured the bridge, severing it in half. Suddenly cars dropped off one by one into the water far below. My car was next. I screamed now as it approached the edge and began tilting downward, then over, falling... falling... splash! I hit the water, which wasn't as far as I thought. That's when I woke up.

As was customary procedure with my soul mate and me, bizarre dreams were always grounds for discussion. After all, they could hold some spiritual meaning we didn't dare overlook.

We took our time getting out of bed each morning anyway, talking and laughing and snuggling up together. It was a ritual for us. And of course, that's when bizarre dreams, if any, were shared and contemplated. This morning, I told him I'd had a weird dream about a bridge. A kind of scary dream.

"No way! I had a dream about a bridge too," he responded with interest.

"Really?" I relayed to him the line of cars, the fire, and then the cars falling off into the water.

"*I was on that same bridge!*" he replied in awe. "In another car, but I don't remember who I was with. I saw the cars falling off into the water."

Both of us were sure this was some kind of spiritual sign that we were connected. I'd never shared the same dream with anyone before, but after hearing of all the supernatural encounters in other's lives, I knew it to be probable. Not only probable, but almost *expected*.

Why not? After all, wasn't this part of the territory that went along with being soul mates? The déjà vu, the ESP—all of the paranormal experiences?

* * *

Purple Flying Saucer. I stared at the tiny square of paper in the palm of my hand. It was indeed a cute little purple flying saucer someone had printed on it. We hadn't fried in a while. I sure hoped it would be a live one. There was nothing worse than getting myself psyched up for a good LSD experience, only to discover I'd gotten a dead hit. Better that I didn't get any and just *jones* for some than get a bum hit.

Some guy with a plaid shirt had scored for us. I don't remember how we knew him. He drove us to the nearest party store so Krisstopher and I could get some orange juice, which activated the strychnine quicker because of the vitamin C. We downed a couple of bottles and he dropped us back off at the apartment.

"Man, I can't believe it. This is a bum hit. I thought this stuff was supposed to be good!" I snarled, both depressed and angry at the same time. I'd been wandering around aimlessly, waiting for the drug to kick in. But nearly an hour had lapsed, and neither one of us felt a thing. Disappointed, I headed toward the bathroom. "I'm taking a bath," I grumbled. I really wanted to step outside my mind tonight. I didn't feel like dealing with reality. The last of my hope faded now as I felt nothing but the same old me.

The doorbell rang and Krisstopher answered it. "Jade and Blake are here!" he called.

"Well, tell them I'm taking a bath," I snapped, closing the door.

Jade was this really beautiful, really petite girl with long, bright red hair and green eyes. She always dressed unique. One time, she wore a cool black and white print mini skirt with strange symbols on it, along with some green tights and tall, purple suede boots. I liked how she had her own style. You really couldn't classify her as anything. She'd given Krisstopher a book on white magic to read. He'd then shown it to me, raving about how excellent it was. I was now in the process of looking it over, and found I was definitely developing an interest in witchcraft because of it.

Blake was Jade's sort of pale, dark haired boyfriend of a few years, whom she'd met in a club or something. He was real nice, and kind of normal looking—though she told me the first time she'd noticed him on the dance floor, he was goth all the way. Then as they started dating, he just sort of mellowed out. She wasn't sure why. I think she liked his goth look better.

I didn't know either of them very well. Apparently Krisstopher met them through Rabie or Jasmine. In any case, we didn't see them a whole lot.

The tub filled up and I shut off the water. The steam felt good against my face. I watched it rise, mixing with the cool air. In the bedroom, I could hear Krisstopher's bass thunking away. I sank further into the water, eyeing my feet as they stuck out. I guessed I liked them after all. So what if they were wide? They looked pretty good. I even liked my legs. *Thunk Thunk Thunk Thunk Thunk* continued Krisstopher's bass, while I continued admiring my more despised body parts. After soaking for about twenty minutes or so, I sat up, pulling the plug on the drain.

That's when I noticed [66]Johnny Walker Red, the old statue on the back of our toilet that my parents received for display when they owned a liquor store. Was he staring at me with evil intent, or was it just the lighting in here? He seemed especially colorful tonight in his black knickers and red overcoat with tails, his top hat perched high on his head and a hooked walking cane clasped in his hand. I could swear he'd even turned a little to face me now, and his sadistic smile and beady eyes let me know he was up to no good. Strange, but I hadn't noticed him looking that animated before. Maybe...

I glanced around the bathroom. Nope, everything else appeared normal. Still a bum hit. I made a mental note to tell Krisstopher about our bizarre little friend.

Drying off with a towel, I slipped into my black dress with the skull and dagger print and my black tights, then closed the lid on the toilet and sat down. Krisstopher was *really jamming*. Definitely in rare form tonight. It seemed his bass was alive, making noises like a little pet monster.

AAAARGH! GGRRRRRRRR! HOWWWWWWLL!

*Brrrrr,* I shivered, my feet cold against the floor. Really cold. I glanced down at them. BLAAAM! A hand violently burst out of the tile, cracking it open as the earth caved in around it. It was followed by a head. I let out a short, sharp scream and darted out into the shadows of the bedroom where Krisstopher sat, back against the wall, still creating supernatural sounds. His favorite black scarf was tied around his forehead and his hair and fingernails were pure white under the glow of the purple fluorescent light. He strummed his bass as if in a trance.

"Krisstopher, I think the acid is—" I started, then stopped as he turned slowly and sneered at me, his lips and bleach white teeth hovering in the air while the rest of his face melted.

The Purple Flying Saucer was taking off after all.

For just a moment, I was really frightened. I'd never had a hit so intense. So morbid. Not since the double hearts in California with Craig's friends; and even that, though scary, was no comparison visually.

I hurried into the living room to collect my sanity, surprised to see Jade and Blake kicking back, listening to Devotion and Missiles. I'd forgotten all about them. Jade sat facing the other way, twenty or so little eyes blinking at me through the back of her red hair. As I approached the couch, the eyeballs stared in different directions while I gasped in horror. She turned around then to greet me. *They're not real,* I reminded myself, regaining my composure to sit down beside her.

Unlike the freaky, scary atmosphere the bedroom offered, the living room was an enchanted forest. Birds chirped and I could smell fragrant pine trees. The vocals of Nathan Hash skated through the air. Clean and resilient, they floated along, knowing no bounds. In fact, there were no bounds. The entire living room was open and free, no longer confined by walls.

Jade's dress was yellow—*really* yellow. We had a nice talk about that for a few moments, and then we were quiet. Good, I didn't feel like talking.

"*Sooo,* Krisstopher told us you guys took some acid," she mentioned casually.

"Uh huh."

She babbled on now, telling me about a small *monkey* that appeared to her one night although she wasn't on any drugs. She said she was able to alter her state of mind without drugs. Anyway, she kept referring back to this monkey in her bedroom, and I didn't understand what she was getting at. I sat perplexed as to why she was telling me this particular bit of information at a time when she knew I was tripping out. I remember saying all the necessary "Really?s" and "Oh wow!s"— when in actuality I was a million miles away from our conversation.

I started to notice as I sat beside her, however, that her ears were growing unusually pointy. I glanced over at Blake, who was sitting on the floor next to the stereo. His ears were pointy too. All at once, I realized they'd turned into elves. I became frightened again, though I wasn't sure why. It wasn't like I'd never hallucinated before (though not to the extent that I was tonight, as I mentioned earlier). But I sensed something deeper here than just mere hallucinations. Something… something… evil?

I tried adjusting to the elves sitting before me. If I hadn't known better, I would have thought the two to be changelings who were now manifesting their true form to me.

Somehow I ended up on the floor next to Blake. I think Jade was just getting too intense for me and my mind couldn't handle it. So I concentrated instead on *The Opposing Forces in Your Flower Bed*. What did that song mean, anyway?

And then I wound up back on the couch again while Jade told me nonchalantly how she once made a girl hurt herself using mind power. My dad had books on mind power, so I was already somewhat acquainted with it. She shared with me about how easy it was to do, although she said it wasn't good to use it for bad things. "I sense that you've got it too," she informed me, "and you just need to *know* you've got it."

The two of us were alone. Blake had gone into the other room to see Krisstopher. She made a comment now about me being *tuned in*, then proceeded to bring up the topic of soul mates. "Soul mates can have a lot of power—a lot of energy together."

"Yeah, like Krisstopher and me. We're soul mates. I wanna get more into magic power with him."

She sighed. "I thought Blake and I were soul mates too. He seemed really tuned in at first. But it's like, now he's *clueless*. He doesn't know how to please me. He doesn't try to use his *mind*. To *concentrate*. I'm trying to teach him, but he just doesn't seem to get it. Sex can be *powerful* if you have the right person."

I wasn't sure why again, but I was starting to feel really uncomfortable around Jade.

"Come on, let's go out in my car where we can talk in private," she said, getting up off the couch. I really didn't want to leave the forest. I felt safe here. But I put on my [67] Doc Martens and leather jacket and followed her reluctantly out the door.

In her car, I felt confined. Cramped. It wasn't a good scene at all. We stared for a couple of minutes straight ahead through the windshield. As if by magic, a beast suddenly appeared in front of the shrubs.

"Do you see that?" I asked excitedly.

The beast was glowing—greenish white, and his form was much like a lion. Yet he had some kind of spike or something on his head, and he looked mythical. My dad had an incense burner like this once.

"What? Oh, you mean that over there?" she replied, pointing directly at it.

"Yeah…" I droned off, surprised that she could see it without drugs.

"Yeah. It's there. See, I don't need drugs to see it. I told you."

When I turned from looking at her in amazement, the beast was gone. A plastic garbage bag lie in its place, blowing slightly in the wind. "Oh… it was just a garbage bag," I said, rather doubtful.

"No. It really *was* there, because *I* saw it too," she reassured me.

We were quiet for a few moments. The beast, though only a hallucination, seemed so real: like he was there all along and had just chosen to manifest himself to me at that particular moment. Seeing him frightened me—an inner fright that I couldn't explain.

"I know where that's from!" I blurted out suddenly as I recollected where I'd seen the beast-like image. The Heckling Jackals had passed out stickers once after their show. The bass player walked up to me where I was seated at a table with a few other people and handed me a sticker. Nobody else at the table got one. I felt privileged, like he'd chosen me out of them all for some reason. Maybe he just remembered me from the time I'd talked to the lead singer downstairs at the Swine Factory. At any rate, I peered at the sticker anxiously.

A lion-like beast with a pitchfork was standing on a highway, his form glowing against the black night. Below him was written something like:

IT WAS REALLY THERE, WASN'T IT? I KNOW WHAT I SAW STANDING IN THE ROAD THAT NIGHT...

That had been so long ago, I'd nearly forgotten. As I relayed the story to Jade, she didn't seem surprised in the least.

She started telling me about a man she once knew who was in a powerful coven. A Satanist who said he was her soul mate. She told him to prove it. So he made an apparition of one of her favorite singers appear on the wall, as if she were watching a movie through a projector. She was still doubtful, however, thinking that a magician would have no problem creating such an illusion.

Even though I would have been convinced by this, she told him she wanted more proof. Something a little more personal, I suppose. So he told her to imagine she was walking along a beach by the ocean, and to bend down and pick up a stone. He gave her a week to picture the stone perfectly in her mind: the size, the shape, the texture, the color...

After one week he knocked on the door. When she opened it, he held the exact same stone in his hand.

My heart burned within me as I heard of her experience. I wanted that kind of spiritual power with someone. Though it was somewhat scary, it was also incredible. I was jealous that she'd experienced such a tie with a man. I wished with every bone in my body that I could find that kind of soul mate. Was it Krisstopher?

A click sounded, jolting me out of my thoughts now as she locked the car doors. I suddenly felt trapped like a helpless animal. Why was she locking the doors, anyway?

"I don't want Blake to come and disturb us," she explained soothingly, sensing my suspicion. But the uneasiness I'd felt with her in the living room returned. Little beads of sweat broke out on my forehead as claustrophobia set in. I squirmed nervously, wanting out of the car.

Licking my dry lips, I looked around, wondering if she had the only control to the locks.

Suddenly Blake was tapping on the driver side window, peering in at us with curiosity. Relief swept over me. Jade sputtered out some insult directed toward him and rolled the window down halfway. "Leave us alone! We're trying to have a *private* conversation," she snarled.

"I was just wondering where you were," he replied, glancing over at me.

"Yeah, we really *should* be getting back inside. I want to see what Krisstopher's doing," I said rather loudly, making a motion toward the door handle.

She unlocked the doors then, and I got out. The cool night air never felt so good. As Blake walked up ahead of us, she made me promise not to tell anyone—not even Krisstopher—what we'd discussed, though I detected more of a *warning* in her voice than anything. I assured her that I wouldn't, but I didn't see what the big deal was.

After they left, however, I couldn't help but tell Krisstopher the amazing tales she'd relayed to me. I especially wanted to communicate to him the fact that he and I could have the kind of power she was referring to since we were soul mates. He seemed unenthusiastic, telling me that if I promised not to tell, I shouldn't have: it was only supposed to be between her and me. When I mentioned that she freaked me out—that she said she knew how to hurt people, he didn't give much of a reply. He seemed completely unable to grasp any kind of spiritual enlightenment from what we'd discussed, or to offer any consolation to me in my fear.

The next afternoon, Jade and Blake dropped by again to see if we wanted to go to the motorcycle shop with them. Jade wanted to buy something—a wallet, I believe. The minute she set foot in our apartment and looked me straight in the eye, I felt naked before her—like she knew I'd broken our promise.

She kept eyeing me the whole afternoon, and her eyes looked especially weird. She was wearing purple contact lenses, which stood out in contrast to her long red hair, giving her an almost supernatural appearance.

While steering the car, she glanced through the rear-view mirror at me. As my gaze met hers, she popped in a cassette of My Days With

The Happy Death Klan and cranked up the stereo. For the first time, I heard the sampled lyrics as she sang along, "This is the Devil. This is the Devil," while the female chorus chimed in, *"Saaaaatan—our god, our master."*

\* \* \*

Krisstopher lost his job when the waterbed company went out of business. Shortly after that, we received an eviction notice. Camron had been staying at Jasmine's, who was now his girlfriend, and therefore felt he didn't need to pay his half of the rent. Krisstopher didn't have enough to cover it all, and I had to quit my L-Mart job after being offered the position of assistant manager of the shoe department because it was too far away without transportation.

Craig found out we had no food and were raiding the dumpsters at Dippin' Donuts. Despite all I'd done to him, he came over with eighty-five dollars' worth of groceries for us. This made me feel even worse.

The two of us had a long talk, during which time he confessed that he needed to change some things about himself, like his pride and his lack of communication. He also confessed that I'd been right about the girl in California—he *had* found her attractive, even kissing her. I then confessed to him that I'd cheated on him with Mark. Still, I would not be persuaded to go back to him, convinced I'd fulfilled my karma where he was concerned. Now I was on to bigger and better things—spiritual things.

A couple of times Rabie took us shopping with her. She'd take along a large carryall purse, sticking it in the front of the cart and holding her grocery list over it. Then we'd point to what we wanted and she'd shove it in the purse. At first, I felt horribly guilty about this. But since we were broke and she got away with it so easily, I began to get used to it.

On the day we were to be evicted, Jasmine agreed to let us move in with her and Camron after Krisstopher begged her. Camron had been dating Jasmine's sister Misty up until recently.

Misty was really strange. I couldn't figure her out. When I first met her, her mind was always in the gutter, focused on sex. But sometime after I began seeing Krisstopher, she totally changed. We found her paintings hanging out to dry on Jasmine's front porch, portraying the Devil and evil.

She and Jasmine used to live together until she started staying with their grandparents, who were said to be *religious.* They agreed to help her get back on her feet financially if she changed her lifestyle. So now she was talking about God all the time. I don't really remember what she was saying, just that she constantly talked about religion.

Jasmine had a drawer full of cassette tapes in the living room. Misty opened it one day and started pointing out all the bands that were, as she put it, *"of the Devil."* I was sure she'd taken one trip too many and never returned.

Two days before we moved to Jasmine's, my pet iguana Thor got loose from the bush where he'd been sun bathing. I put a magic spell out for him to return to me, and just as we'd packed the rest of our stuff and were getting ready to leave, I found him in the exact same spot where I'd originally tied him. He was basking in the sun once more with a look of contentment on his face. I picked him up and kissed him, happy he was back. It wasn't that he tried to run from me—only that he liked to explore. That's just how iguanas were. They instinctively looked for the tallest tree so they could climb all the way to the top. Then they forgot how to get down once they were up there. But most of them had no problem with being held. In fact, one of their favorite spots was perched atop a head where they felt safe up high or cuddled against a neck where it was warm.

When I'd first relocated to Krisstopher's apartment, Thor had to make himself understood right away. Hellcat, the stray that had followed Krisstopher home one night, noticed him hanging on the curtain and crept over to take a look. She twitched her tail back and forth for the longest time while he eyed her cautiously with one eyeball. Then she made her move, batting a paw at his long tail. CRACK! He whipped her in the face with it, sending her reeling backward. She got the message, and they pretty much existed in harmony after that.

We called him Thor the Party Animal. Krisstopher found a little plastic top hat in a bag of crafts and we glued a tiny yellow plume on it. This became known as his party hat. An elastic strap secured it snugly on his head. He'd lay stretched out on the back of the couch with the hat on, looking like a little old green man. While we pointed and laughed, he stared at us, not at all amused. Then after about five or ten minutes, when he could bear it no longer, he rubbed his head against the couch and shook it off.

Hellcat, strangely enough, was about the coolest cat I ever knew. Generally I didn't get along with cats. They were usually really snotty or mean to me. But Hellcat was different. She was down to earth. When we moved into Jasmine's, we brought her along too. Jasmine already had four of her kittens running around. She'd taken them just as soon as they were able to walk with ease.

The night Hellcat birthed them in Krisstopher's bedroom, a bunch of us just sat and watched in awe. It felt like we were in an episode of [68]National Geographic or something. After the kittens came out, along with the stewed tomato looking stuff, Hellcat picked up the black one between her teeth and put it down by itself, far away from the rest of the litter.

"Well, that's bogue! She's deserting her baby," I said, disgusted. So I carried it back over to the others and set it down again. She picked it up and marched across the room with it, this time placing it even further away as if to tell us something. "Why is she doing that? There's nothing wrong with that cat," I told them all.

We picked it up, examining it carefully. We couldn't see anything wrong with it. It wasn't dead or anything, and it didn't look defective in any way. Somebody else laid it back with its brothers and sisters then. Tired of arguing with us, Hellcat gave up on ditching it and let it remain with the rest of the litter. However, we discovered as the misfit kitty began to grow that it was somewhat mentally slow. Interesting how its mother had perceived this without any outward indication.

At Jasmine's, Hellcat acted like she didn't even know her own kitties. She was even somewhat rude to them. Apparently their two-month separation from her had caused a breach in the maternal instinct.

Jasmine's apartment was extremely small. The four of us were crammed in there like sardines in a can. We could sense that she didn't exactly like the idea of us living there, especially since we weren't rushing out to find jobs. After about a month, however, we were both employed. I was hired at a soft serve yogurt shop, and shortly after that, Krisstopher began working midnights at a gas station.

At the yogurt shop, I met a girl who was a friend of one of the employees. She had a strange tattoo on her hand—a symbol of some kind. When I asked her what it was, she explained that it was a branding from the satanic coven she used to be in. She told me that she used to put spells out on people—like the time she caused a girl at school's face to break out really bad.

Her male friend and I and another guy went out behind the strip mall where the yogurt shop was located one night. They wanted me to do a tarot reading for them. I had just laid out the cards and was in the middle of the reading when two policemen showed up out of nowhere, forbidding me to continue. They said what I was doing was illegal, though I didn't understand why. Apparently I did not have a business license to do such things, even though I wasn't charging money for it. They warned me to pack up my cards and get out of there.

Though both employed, neither Krisstopher nor I got paid right away since they held back our paychecks for two weeks, so we continued to eat out of dumpsters, day-old donuts being our main course, aside from somebody's leftover pizza, too.

Camron quit his job at the steakhouse, so he and Jasmine were living off of her salary. Occasionally they even resorted to dumpster runs like we did, usually if she spent all her money on marijuana and rent.

If we couldn't find any donuts in the dumpster at Dippin' Donuts, we'd sometimes knock on the back door of the kitchen and ask the guys when they were going to be throwing some out. That was always a risky situation though, because we never knew what cruel joke they were bound to play on a few degenerate punks waiting for a square meal. I recall Jasmine enjoying her cream donut one day, only to stop chewing suddenly and yell out, "Gross!" We watched as she picked out a cigarette butt and held it up for display. Apparently someone had used the donut as a make-shift ashtray.

Krisstopher and I held a yard sale to get some money. We had a few things we didn't really need anymore, so we were hoping to get some drugs and food out of the deal. Unfortunately it didn't go over too well. Only a few people bothered to stop and look. Towards the late afternoon,

Thor escaped again. This time he didn't return. I was immensely sad for days. My tarot cards said he'd found death—eaten by something—perhaps the large possum that lived under the porch and consumed all of the cat food. I put out a spell then, that he would return to me in the form of another animal.

When Halloween arrived, which happened to be mine and Krisstopher's favorite holiday, I hocked my gold wedding band and my stereo so we could have money to buy alcohol. I received all of about forty-five dollars out of the deal: enough to buy some food and a bottle of [69]Captain Morgan's Spiced Rum.

Later at a party, someone stole the rum as soon as I opened it and set it down on the counter. We left shortly after that while I complained of still being sober, and of the audacity some people had to steal from others, which of course was ridiculous because I was only reaping what I had sowed.

To appease me, Krisstopher and a friend stole a case of beer from a nearby grocery store, running like crazy the five or six blocks to get it back to Jasmine's after being sighted by a cashier. Somehow it wasn't enjoyable though, and I ended up going to bed after having two cans or so.

> [70]"It's not hard to steal
> I do it all the time
> Just walk out the door
> When you don't want to buy."
>
> —Jean's Habit

Not long after that, Krisstopher began stealing from the gas station. At first it was a pack of cigarettes here and there. But then he started helping himself to the food, running up a tab that kept getting bigger and bigger—a tab he never quite paid in full.

Some nights, I'd wait in the parking lot across the street until the owner left and he was all alone. He'd flash the overhead lights to let me know it was safe to come, and I'd bike over to the station to keep him company on the midnight shift. We'd eat our fill of sub sandwiches and snacks, and smoke cigarettes until morning came and his shift ended, even taking a carton of cigarettes home with us.

It was on those nights that we played a little game of ESP to pass the time. He'd draw various shapes on paper, then stare at one of them, mentally projecting its identity to me while I attempted to home in on his thought waves. Or we'd try and guess which brand of cigarettes or pop the other was about to choose. Always, the results were amazingly accurate. It was plain to see that Krisstopher and I possessed psychic powers. After Brandon Erins and other psychics I'd run across, I had no trouble believing in such powers.

I remembered the lady I'd met a few years back in the meat department at Mather's while working the seafood section. She'd also claimed to be psychic. To prove her power to me, she predicted a couple of times who was on the phone before I even answered it. And I certainly would never forget the day she warned me to *be careful* as I was leaving work, to which I then pulled out of the parking lot ten minutes later and got into an accident. It was weird, though, how I'd sensed something threatening in her warning.

\* \* \*

I called my mom from the gas station one night to tell her where Krisstopher and I were now living. We talked for a few minutes, and then I mentioned that I was getting into witchcraft—carrying on where Dad had left off in his spirituality. To my surprise, she told me that witchcraft was evil.

"But Mom, the pentagrams are *right side up,* not upside down."

"I don't care, honey. Didn't your father tell you not to mess around with the Occult?"

"Yeah, but this is different. This is *white* magic, not black magic."

"It doesn't matter, Paula. I'm telling you, stay away from that stuff."

Mom. I knew she meant well, but nonetheless, she was wrong.

\* \* \*

Finally our paychecks came. We went on a grocery-shopping spree and then bought some party necessities like alcohol and marijuana. I'd started smoking weed again since Jasmine, Camron, and Krisstopher baked out a lot. I even got high for the first time: a happy, spaced out feeling. Now I knew what everyone meant when they talked of being high. Still, I preferred acid much better.

Krisstopher and I agreed that we should give Jasmine some money for rent. The following morning, however, she woke us up to tell us we had to get out that day because her landlord would be paying a visit and she wasn't supposed to have people living with her. We had a feeling she was just tired of us staying there, especially since she didn't kick Camron out.

Krisstopher searched around frantically for someone we could stay with. Finally Roy, a guy we barely knew who worked at a music store in Orlando, told us we could stay with his mom and sister and him for one week only. We knew we wouldn't be able to save for an apartment in time, not to mention our jobs were not conveniently located. This left us two choices: fall back on our parents or live in the streets. Since we had things like our band equipment and my family heirlooms, we couldn't rough it without losing them. And neither of us dared to sell our instruments since we eventually hoped to make a living performing music.

I mentioned to Krisstopher that since my mom was still in shock about my separation from Craig, the last thing I wanted to do was ask her if we could move in with her. He agreed, feeling uncomfortable where she was concerned anyway since he was a major factor involved in the break up. We decided the best thing to do would be to talk to *his* mom, Sharon.

Sharon lived in a senior citizen's complex in New Hampshire due to her rare disease, which limited her ability to care for herself. Confined to a wheel chair, she had a personal nurse, Helen, who took care of her during the day; and a cook who came during the evening to provide dinner for her. She agreed to let us stay with her, but only for a few weeks since her rent was state funded and she wasn't supposed to have anyone living there. Krisstopher figured we'd be able to stay with friends of his later if we had to.

In the meantime, we hauled our things over to Roy's mother's. We'd booked a bus for New England to leave in a week. The bus allowed for one carry-on item each and a few suitcases to store below. We decided Krisstopher's bass and my [71]Yamaha keyboard would be our carry-on items; the rest of our equipment and clothes going below. Though I'd had to beg Craig to give me the [72]Yamaha since he'd bought it for my birthday, he refused to give me the keyboard amp he'd recently purchased to go with it, so we didn't have much else in the way of band gear except for my [73]Korg, some headphones, and some effects pedals. Krisstopher had to sell his bass amp because it was too big to take with us. Blain, one of his old band members, bought it.

I'd met Blain briefly a few months back when I did a tarot reading for him concerning an old girlfriend. He informed me that the reading came true. He then mentioned that his mother, who'd recently answered the door when we went to his house to discuss the amp, referred to Krisstopher and I as "the Devil and his mistress." I was shocked and perplexed that she would say such a thing. Blain explained that she was very religious and thought we were evil. Krisstopher and I had a good laugh about her being *mental*.

* * *

At Roy's, we were crammed in his tiny, dark bedroom with black walls. His huge waterbed with black satin sheets took up almost the whole room as it was, not to mention our clothes and miscellaneous stuff crammed in the corner or shoved in his small closet. A lot of our bigger items were in boxes on the screened-in porch.

Somewhere running around the room was the tiny lizard I'd found stuck to the pavement when we left Jasmine's, nearly frozen to death after a slight frost. I'd transferred some of my healing energy into him via the thought process, then breathed on him and lifted him up to the sun, calling on Ra the Egyptian sun god. After a little bit, he sprang back to life, his large dewlap below his neck no longer swollen but safely tucked inside once more. Then I'd insisted on bringing him to Roy's. But housed in a shallow box with no lid, Ra the anole lizard soon made his escape. Unlike Thor, who liked to be free to explore, Ra escaped for the mere reason that he was afraid.

It was rare to find anoles that weren't timid of humans. Though they were common in Florida, often basking in the sun right on your front door step, they bolted as soon as they caught sight of you. The more unfortunate ones who found their way inside houses often met their death after crawling up into the refrigerator motor to keep warm, or from starvation.

The walls in Roy's room were covered with posters of all my favorite gothic/alternative bands making religious statements. One of them displayed a picture of Jesus and two women—all naked. Another, a large cross with an 'X' through it. Other posters depicted zombie/vampire portrayals as the band members dressed all in black and wore white face paint, heavy black eye makeup, and blood red or black lipstick. For the most part, I was oblivious to their meaning. I looked at them, but somehow didn't really comprehend them. The [74]cross with an 'X' through it seemed like some mysterious symbol. I wondered what it signified.

Roy was undoubtedly the palest au naturale goth I'd ever met, with thin red lips and dark eyes that sunk back slightly in his head. Tall and incredibly skeletal, he had short, dark hair which was thinning at the top. He didn't talk a whole lot, and if he did manage to say something, it was usually profound.

He himself admitted to being a vampire, or bloodsucker. He told us he loved to bite his girlfriends during sexual intercourse until he broke the skin and drank their blood. Proudly, he displayed his sharp incisors. He delighted in giving and receiving pain, he said, because it gave him a sexual rush. I found Roy's preferences very bizarre, though not necessarily repulsive. Whatever worked for him, I thought. Besides, I didn't picture that he actually drew *that* much blood. I half-wondered if he was exaggerating.

He got some acid for us but told us not to take it when he wasn't home, probably because he didn't want us freaking out in his house. However, we couldn't wait. He went away one night and we knew he wouldn't return until the morning. It was then that we took it. We went out for a walk around nine or so, sticking the little pieces of paper in our mouths and letting them dissolve on our tongues. The strong bitter taste let us know that we hadn't been gypped of strychnine.

Our plan was to get back into the house and sneak away safely to Roy's bedroom just before we peaked and began our little trip to Wonderland. However, as we stepped into the living room, Roy's mother suddenly appeared in the hallway. She was a heavy woman with long, grayish blond hair. We hadn't really conversed much with her before, but it was plain to see that tonight she was in a talkative mood. We ended up sitting down on the sofa while she stood before us, jabbering on vivaciously.

As the drug kicked in, it seemed she became even more animated on purpose. We began to think she was messing with our heads, somehow aware of the fact that we'd taken LSD. The two of us watched in horror as every few moments she lifted her already short yellow house dress to reveal her large underwear, then continued chatting as if it was a normal gesture to make when emphasizing one's point. In her hand, she held some huge bras she'd just gotten fresh out of the dryer. She twirled them around, and I remember thinking I could not bear much more of her bizarre visual aids.

When next I checked into the conversation, she was discussing her daughter's rebelliousness. We commented here and there, Krisstopher more so than me since I was doing all I could just to stay focused as the rat poisoning struggled to unleash itself in a major way.

Eons passed by and we finally made it into Roy's bedroom, shutting the door on reality. I gave a sigh of relief and threw myself down on the waterbed as Krisstopher slid a Priesthood video into the VCR. He sat on the edge of the bed with his face up close to the TV, forgetting all about me as he watched and listened, entranced. The video showed footage of the band live in concert, and every once in a while it flashed some images of fire across the screen. It wasn't doing a thing for me. I was in the mood to hear something more mysterious and spiritual, like one of my favorite goth bands doing a love song.

"This is boring, Krisstopher. Can't we find something else to watch?" I asked.

"Huh?" He pulled himself out of his trance to look at me.

"Can we put in another tape?"

He rummaged around on the dresser, discovering a Devotion and Missiles video. "Hey, it's Devotion and Missiles—*The Spooky Aquarium.* You want to watch this?"

"Yeah, okay!" I said excitedly.

Nathan's vocals whispered and dripped invitingly like sweet honey on the wind. I watched as the band performed in fuzzy fly costumes. The video kept switching back and forth to the flies, then to a scene having to do with the song. At the end of one of the songs, it showed a car pulling up with the band members inside. As Nathan leaned out the window, waving at me now, he suddenly turned into a monkey.

"Did you *see* that?! He just turned into a monkey!" I told Krisstopher.

"Huh?"

"Rewind that again. I want to see if it's still there."

He stopped the tape, rewinding it to the spot where the car first pulled up. It happened again.

"Oh, that must be part of the video," I said. Or was it?

Pretty soon I got up to go to the bathroom, not wanting to leave our little Den of Security and enter the Hallway of Realism again. I was afraid I'd run into Roy's mother, but Krisstopher assured me that she and her daughter were fast asleep by now.

The bathroom smelled of soapy fresh bath water. I glanced at the tub where Roy's mother had taken a bath earlier. Right before our walk she'd been running the bath water, and at that time I'd noticed a mysteriously inscribed coin on the ledge of the tub. Coupled with the running water, it reminded me of a money spell I'd seen in one of our witchcraft books.

Old coins and silver coins were used to attain money once they were imbued with magic power. For a moment, I'd wondered if perhaps Roy's mother was a witch herself.

After all, Roy had told me that his deceased father, a painter whose pieces I admired for their dark innuendoes, had at one time been a Christian until a large stone from the lawn of a church had been rocketed by a lawn mower into his eye; rendering him partially blind. His paintings were never the same after that. Nor was his faith in God. Roy mentioned something about him being angry with God and departing from the Christian religion. He died an unhappy man, though I can't remember what killed him.

Perhaps in his anger, I thought, as Roy had conveyed the story to me, he decided to join sides with the Devil; becoming some sort of Satanist or black magician. His wife could have then followed in his footsteps. Ahh, but this was all just an analytical mind at work. Who knew what really happened? Although some of his later pictures did give me a sense of uneasiness...

But now as I stood in the bathroom, I noticed that the coin on the tub ledge was gone. In its place was a dollar bill. I studied it for a moment, wondering why it was just lying there. Surely money spells produced more than that! Still, it struck me as strange. I went back into the bedroom and told Krisstopher. He shrugged, saying someone probably just forgot and left it there. Nonetheless, I instructed him not to take it, just in case Roy's mom was testing us to see if we would steal it.

A little while later, Krisstopher went to the bathroom. When he returned, I asked him if the dollar bill was still there. He said it was gone, though I hadn't heard anyone get up to use the bathroom.

I did my first candle spell in Roy's room. It was a spell for Craig to find another woman more suited to him: somebody who had more in common with him. I empowered a small sachet full of herbs for love. Meeting with him one last time, I gave him the sachet and told him to keep it with him, explaining what I'd done. He agreed to put it in his car in the glove compartment, since he spent a lot of time driving.

Later, he told me that shortly after I'd given him the sachet, he met a woman who loved sports—especially baseball, which was his ultimate favorite. He seemed very happy with her, telling me they were even considering marriage just as soon as our divorce went through.

* * *

One night when I didn't go to work with Krisstopher but stayed home and slept, a rather bizarre man came into the gas station. Somehow he and the man got on the topic of spirituality, to which Krisstopher told him he used witchcraft as a means of bringing about requests or desires in his life. The man then suggested that he make a box which he called a 'God Box,' and write down all of his concerns and requests on paper, putting them in the box when he finished. He told him to concentrate on God as he did this, or something weird to that effect.

When I asked him what else they talked about, and what the man was like, etc. etc., he could not tell me. He said he didn't really remember—that they talked about a lot of things, and that the God Box was the thing that stuck out most in his mind. He kept saying that the man was really bizarre, but in a good way—that he had a good feeling about him. It was then that he and I followed the man's suggestion and each made our own God Box.

* * *

The day came for Krisstopher and me to leave. We were waiting for Rabie to pick us up and take us to the bus station. On the bed in Roy's room, I skimmed through a goth magazine, spotting a brief article on one of my favorite male vocalists. It stated that he was married: now a heterosexual and a Christian.

"What?! A *Christian!*" I laughed. "Is this some kind of joke?" I didn't get it. What was he talking about? I showed the article to Krisstopher and he shrugged. Then we went to thank Roy's family once again for letting us crash there. Roy had already left for work or something.

Rabie arrived and we loaded our boxes in the car. Her dad said we could store our stuff in their garage for a while until we got settled.

It didn't really sink in that we were leaving until we got to the bus station, where we were forced to say our good-byes.

I felt sorry that things turned out the way they did for Rabie and Krisstopher. I mean, I was happy for me but sad for her. I'd even apologized once for breaking them up as I tried communicating my feelings to her in an honest way. "Krisstopher's my soul mate, Rabie. I hope you understand. You'll meet yours one day."

Oddly enough, we'd always gotten along with each other despite our previous vying for Krisstopher's attention and the separation that occurred between them. The only time we ever experienced problems was when she got drunk. Her true feelings showed then—her jealousy, her rage, her pain. Yet even in those periodic displays of emotion, no fights ever broke out between us.

112

But now, I could see that this was painful for both of them. They'd been close friends as well as lovers for a long time before I entered the picture. I watched with mixed emotions as they hugged each other tightly.

We promised to write her just as soon as we could and send money so she could UPS our stuff to us. She drove away while I smiled sadly, waving my last good-bye. I'd miss Rabie. I'd miss everyone. We hadn't even gotten a chance to say good-bye to Camron, Jasmine, Misty, Raoul, Veg or Garrett. (Tim had already split for California months before). I knew Krisstopher was probably feeling the impact of it all worse than I was, since they were initially his friends. He sat quietly for a long time, not saying a word.

\* \* \*

Sharon's cook, David, picked us up at the bus station on the outskirts of New Hampshire. It was a cold, snowy night—a rude awakening after living in the sun and fun of Florida. David spent the car ride filling Krisstopher in on the condition of his mother while I sat in the back quietly looking out the window as we passed small towns asleep beneath a blanket of snow. I was a stranger in a strange land. Uneasiness gnawed away at me as I wondered what lie ahead for me here in Krisstopher's hometown. Exhaustion set in while I pondered everything that had happened so far: my separation from Craig, moving now for the fourth time since then; the small electrical fire that broke out on the bus ride from New York, causing us to frantically grab our instruments and scramble off the bus…

I just wanted to sleep. Would we ever find a place to settle down in? I wondered.

Meeting Krisstopher's mother Sharon was a strange and uncomfortable situation for me. She sat in the middle of the living room in her wheelchair, a fairly young woman in her late thirties, skinny and pale, with brown hair cropped close to her neck, and bangs. Her brown eyes, though wide open, were unable to see me hovering over her; she was completely blind. When she spoke, her voice was slow and distorted, making it hard for me to understand her. I struggled to interpret her words, Krisstopher often translating them for me. The rare disease, which attacks the cerebellum, had slowed down the motor action in her brain and paralyzed her muscles. Her hands remained perpetually bent at the wrist, and often her arms flailed out violently beyond her control. She was unable to go to the bathroom by herself during the day because she needed help unfastening and pulling down her pants as well as lifting herself onto the toilet. When alone at night, she simply had to make do.

Her apartment was small; consisting of a living room, a tiny kitchen, a bathroom and a back bedroom. I glanced around, picturing all of us trying to coexist there peacefully. Krisstopher pointed to a small bed where we'd be sleeping. It was situated against the wall facing the kitchen, a bookshelf beside it. We set our luggage down nearby, and he propped his bass up in the corner. My two keyboards went in Sharon's closet in the back bedroom for lack of space.

That night I didn't sleep much at all. Sharon wheeled around the apartment, moaning and grunting. She bumped into things, and every once in a while I heard something crash to the floor. Krisstopher got up a few times to make sure she was alright. I sensed his helplessness and depression over the whole situation.

I awoke the next morning to a boisterous voice, thick with the New England dialect that pronounces the 'R's like 'A's on most every word, although the accent varies from person to person. Strange that Krisstopher spent most of his life in New England, yet hadn't developed the dialect.

Helen was a cheerful woman in her early forties with short, curly brown hair. She hustled and bustled about, cleaning the apartment and getting Sharon bathed and dressed as she did every weekday morning.

"Helen, this is my girlfriend Martyr," Krisstopher told her.

"Hello Mahta. Pleased ta meet ya."

A door-to-door food service came in the afternoon to give Sharon her lunch. When Helen finished feeding her, she cleaned up, took her to the bathroom, and then left for the day to attend to her other clients. At that time, Sharon usually listened to the TV until David came over in the evening to cook dinner for her.

Now that we were in a little bigger a space than Roy's bedroom, I could lay out my tarot cards once more and divine. I did this the second night we were there, anxious to pick up where I'd left off in spiritual matters. The book I'd been reading on white magic and Dianic worship (one I'd gotten from Camron), instructed that the neophyte beginning his or her spiritual journey into magic power should first construct a pentagram corresponding to the Roman god and triune goddess and their related aspects of nature, as well as the five senses.

When I relayed to Krisstopher that the book said we should call on the names of deities, he advised that perhaps we shouldn't pray to things we knew nothing about. I argued that the book said they were good deities—gods and goddesses of nature. He still seemed apprehensive.

But it was there in Sharon's bedroom floor that I erected my first pentagram, drawing invisible lines of energy and placing colored candles correlating to each deity's character in the five points of the star. I then said my [75]alignments and incantations to become one with these higher forces, declaring and invoking their power by honoring their name. Next, I [76]stated my need, visualizing it coming to pass, and [77]considered it done by the final statement, [78]"So mote it be." Finally, I collected my magic circle of protection that was supposed to keep any evil forces from entering in, and thought about the spell no more as it was now manifesting itself in the spiritual realm, soon to be followed in the physical.

Sharon seemed pretty open minded to witchcraft. When Krisstopher had been a child, she'd befriended a witch. The two of us found some incense oils and a small pewter wizard necklace in her room, things she'd kept from that time period. She told us we could wear the necklace. It seemed that maybe even the witch had given it to her, but I'm not certain. At any rate, Krisstopher and I desired to contact her old friend, but Sharon didn't know where she was now.

One of Krisstopher's strangest and most prominent childhood memories, he said, was waking up every morning to black wallpaper with white skeletons on it. He couldn't believe his mom put that kind of wallpaper in her child's room.

"Cool, man. You're lucky you had such a cool mom when you were growing up," I told him.

"Yeah..." he drifted off, smiling faintly as he was transported back to that room—back to the skeletons staring at him. But I had a feeling by the look in his eyes that it somehow wasn't so cool. It seemed both to shock and sadden him as he recalled it to mind. He had mentioned that it was rather dismal to stare at day in and day out—especially through the eyes of a very small child. Children, as we know, are easily frightened. Noises scare them. Strange things scare them. The dark often scares them. I suppose that having the temporary fears of Halloween last year-round in your bedroom would not be pleasant.

It was after I'd construed the invisible pentagram in Sharon's room that it seemed she changed for the worst. She screamed off and on of something attacking her. She flailed and kicked and cried while Krisstopher tried desperately to figure out what she thought was attacking her. We knew she didn't like his small lizard that stayed in the aquarium out in the living room. Apparently she thought it was crawling on her because she felt things touching her. Krisstopher assured her that it remained securely behind glass, covered by a metal screen.

"I think she's having some kind of mental hallucination—probably from her medication," he reasoned.

\* \* \*

In the woods near the apartment complex one winter day, we cast a spell for money. We were told we couldn't eat much of Sharon's food since the state supplied it according to her medical expense budget. Fortunately, we'd gotten a few canned food handouts at a local church, and Helen also brought over a couple of things for us.

Here and there David and his boyfriend Scott had us over for dinner. Aside from the wonderful gourmet food David whipped up, I looked forward to the cocktails. They had the largest selection of alcoholic beverages I'd seen in a long time. We always ended up getting smashed and playing board games all night—at least until Krisstopher and I broke out in our usual argument.

So in the arena of food, we weren't quite starving like we had been for a while in Florida. Still, we were completely broke and knew we could not thrive long in this condition. We needed money in order to start off on the right foot since we had no jobs and no transportation.

The nearest town was about twenty miles away. We hitchhiked a couple of times in the freezing cold, Krisstopher putting in an application at the smokehouse where he'd cooked before. We weren't quite sure how both of us were going to work when we lived so far away, especially if we had different schedules. The thought of hitchhiking alone in a strange place didn't appeal to me. We knew, too, that we couldn't stay at his mom's much longer. Which one of his friends would put us up for a while with no rent money, and for how long?

Krisstopher had mentioned on at least two occasions that perhaps I should move back to my mom's since he couldn't really take care of me. However, by the tone of his voice and the look on his face, I knew it was an excuse to get rid of me.

He'd fallen into a massive state of depression upon our arrival there. He spent every day sleeping in late and then going next door to play video games with Sharon's friend Peter until six or seven in the evening, leaving me to take care of Sharon once Helen left. Sometimes he'd come home even later and I'd be in bed already. I could tell he was beginning to think he'd made a mistake, as was I. But when he tried to coax me into moving back with my mom, I stated firmly, "Oh no you don't! I left my husband for you. I left everything for you. You're not getting rid of me that easily."

All along, I'd been denying the terrible gut feeling going on inside me. Reality was setting in. I'd made my choice to go with Krisstopher, and although Craig hadn't been the best companion in the world, at least I could count on him to a considerable extent. He had proven his love to me by purchasing food for me in my infidelity, admitting his faults to me with willingness to change, and offering to go to marriage counseling.

Krisstopher, on the other hand, was not who I thought he was. It had been at the Halloween party in Florida when I really discovered this. I'd walked into the kitchen to find him flirting with another woman already, and it hadn't even been a month since I'd left Craig! I was devastated. When I questioned him about it, he told me that he didn't want to be chained down. He said "love was like an open football field," whatever *that* meant. I was totally floored by his remarks.

What happened to all his promises? He told me we were going to the forest together. He said he'd take care of me. I'd left my whole life behind for him: my husband, my house, my car, my job, my schooling...

I felt sick. I couldn't go back to my mom's by myself and tell her Krisstopher didn't want me now. Anger seethed within me as I realized he'd lied to me all along, never thinking I'd actually leave Craig; thinking he'd just have a little fling with a married woman, sort of like a trophy to add to his collection. He'd wanted me only until responsibility entered the picture. That's how it was with all of his relationships, whether family, friends, or girlfriends. Once he had to become responsible for someone or something, he found it easier just to hit the road.

And now here we were, falling apart before we even began. I was stuck in some rinky-dink place in the mountains, far from anything familiar to me. There was nothing to cling to now *except* him. I wasn't about to let him ditch me for some hippie love theory he hid behind to support his irresponsibility.

Then a tarot spread I did in the living room floor one afternoon seemed to indicate that at some time in the future, Krisstopher would be tempted by another soul mate: The Queen of Pentacles, who also had some occult knowledge but was an extremely evil woman. Knowing his weakness for women, I somehow doubted that if and when he ran into this Queen, he'd be able to pass the spiritual trial. When I told him of this, he assured me that there was no one around who fit such a description.

\* \* \*

Krisstopher's closest friend, Chris Renhardt (or Renny—to avoid the confusion of two Chris's since everyone there still called Krisstopher Kris), invited us over to see his pad. He and his girlfriend shared an upper apartment overlooking a small tourist town surrounded by mountains; famous for its skiing.

Talkative and easy-going, Renny sat us down at the kitchen table and passed a bowl around (or a small pipe filled with marijuana). We had a couple of beers while he and Krisstopher laughed about old times and their close calls with nearly getting busted by the cops. I studied him from across the table now.

Around our age, he had blue eyes and short, sandy blond hair beneath a baseball hat. He'd grown a small, thin mustache that he kept neatly trimmed, and when he smiled, I noticed he had even, white teeth. From what I could gather, he was pretty athletic; into skateboarding, snowboarding, and skiing. He made it a point to include me in the conversation, which I liked. I listened to him talk about how he wanted to attend a gourmet cooking school in Colorado, then slowly faded out the conversation as the street below caught my interest.

Through the window I watched large snowflakes fall softly, covering the town in dazzling white. A girl trudged through the small drifts, making her way toward the shops.

"Thaa's Mikal," Renny announced, pointing down at her.

"Isn't that your old girlfriend, Kris?" Troy, the other guy that was with us, asked.

"Yeah," Krisstopher answered, watching her.

I recognized her then as the girl we'd met the other night on our way to the store to get cigarettes. She'd been leaving her studio: a space she rented where she kept all her paintings. I'd seen one of them she'd done for Krisstopher while they were going out. Huge and obscure, it hung above our bed in Sharon's apartment, an unpleasant reminder for me of their four-year relationship.

Krisstopher had introduced us that night, but she looked different today, which explained why I didn't recognize her at first. Her more stylish leather was replaced by a biker leather, and her trendier boots by combat boots. I had to admit she looked better this way, though jealousy burned within me, coupled with worry. When I'd first seen her, I'd thought she didn't look a match for Krisstopher. Though she was pretty, it didn't appear they had much in common. Today, however, I changed my mind.

"She must be going to wuhk. She wuhks at Deadquartas now," Renny told him. "She's still going out with Duhk."

Dirk was one of Krisstopher's old band buddies. He'd been the drummer in their thrash metal days. When Krisstopher broke it off with Mikal and moved to Florida, she'd hooked up with him.

However, she still kept in touch with Krisstopher because she was good friends with his mom. She took Sharon shopping and out to eat a lot, as well as helped her run errands. I read letters she wrote him in Florida, keeping him posted on her condition.

As I came to know and observe Mikal, I was convinced that deep down inside, she still loved Krisstopher. He'd been the one to break it off with her. Still, she faithfully took care of Sharon while he was miles away. I think she always hoped he would grow up a little, come back, and realize that she was the perfect woman for him; especially because she cared so much for his mother.

While they'd gone out, she'd written him so many cards and love letters—it was plain to see she'd been head over heels for him. He told me she always bought stuff for him and did little things for him, though it seems I recall him mentioning that it smothered him after a while. Perhaps she'd catered to him too much—the mistake I was now making.

It seemed Krisstopher preferred women who gave him a challenge. Women who, like him, played mind games. He'd told me, too, that Mikal never partied or went out to the bars, and hated when he did. He grew tired of arguing about his lifestyle with her. It was plain to see they were from two different worlds. So he broke up with her and moved to Florida soon after that to be a cook in his friend's new restaurant, though eventually the restaurant closed down and he ended up working in a waterbed warehouse.

Unlike many old girlfriends, Mikal was always civil to me whenever we ran into each other. However, I sensed an underlying coldness despite her good manners.

"Yeah, why don't you guys plan on headin' ovuh to Felician and Klay's place latuh?" Renny offered now. "The *old gang* will be thaa pahtyin'."

Felician was another one of Krisstopher's old girlfriends. I'd seen a picture of her in Florida when she'd written him a letter, including one of her poems and the photo. Like me, she wrote a lot of poetry. It was pretty good stuff. The more I got to know her, the more I realized that her tough girl act was a mask she hid behind. Inside was a hurting woman who had a lot of problems to work through. She'd had a pretty rough life, and I recognized her pain, though it might have been a different kind than mine. Pain came in all forms, but it was still pain.

She stared at me as we walked into her apartment and sat down. *Everyone* was staring—checking out Krisstopher's new girlfriend—measuring me mentally and physically to see if I had what it took to become one of them.

They seemed a different breed than Krisstopher's friends in Florida. Instead of displaying their attitudes externally, through clothing, they displayed them internally; their whole presence proved to be quite intimidating. They were harder to get to know, like they hid themselves behind a wall. Probably because most of them had grown up roughing it, children of alcoholics and drug addicts, themselves learning substance abuse at an early age. They were street smart, cautious of everyone. I sensed their guard was up now. Coolly they observed me as I sat on the couch next to Krisstopher, feeling awkward and alone. Maybe because they had a little clique going and I was a newcomer on the scene. Nobody liked to be the newcomer. It was a hated experience. It made me feel really insecure.

Someone suggested we all go sledding—probably Renny. I didn't have my [79]Docs on, so his girlfriend Samantha (or Sam for short), leant me a pair of her boots to wear. They were more for fashion than anything however, and after sledding down the hill once, I spent a good forty-five minutes or so trying to get back *up* the hill since I had no traction to help me climb. I was embarrassed that everyone else had already been up and down the hill again fifty times over.

"Hav'n a little trouble thaa, Mahta?" they'd call as they breezed by on sled.

It amazed me that these people could drink and smoke so much (both weed and cigarettes), and yet be so athletic. I was completely out of breath.

"Ya *still* try'n to get up the hill, Mahta?" Renny laughed, dashing past me with ease. Exhausted, I finally swallowed my pride and let Sam pull me to the top, cursing all the while under my breath that I hadn't worn my [80]Doc Martens. She suggested we go back to the apartment and get warm.

"Good idea," I agreed, my teeth chattering. "I hate cold weather." Clad in my biker leather, a thin spandex top, a tie-dye mini skirt, and black leotard tights, I was literally shaking, the cold blowing right through to my bones. My fingers and toes were stinging. I could barely move them.

I watched as Felician got whaled in the eye with a solid packed slush ball, falling over backwards in pain and lying on the ground for a good two minutes or so. She handled it well, managing a laugh and a "You guys coulda blinded me. Be more caahful." Then she picked herself up and dusted off her snowmobile pants, her eye red and watering.

I sensed you had to possess a certain kind of mindset to be accepted in this group: a tough, read-between-the-lines mentality. Emotionally weak people were not tolerated, nor were clueless people. Though everyone pretty much kept to the surface here, refusing to say how they really felt, you had to have an understanding that went beyond superficiality in order to perceive how this worked. The object was to act really hard-nosed and noncommittal while still managing to have a good time. Individual strength was evaluated by how much pain you could take without letting it show. And respect followed suit to the degree that you passed the test.

At parties, card games were for those who knew how to play. If you were only out to kill time, forget it—go drink on the couch and leave the table. I somehow felt inadequate as I quietly made this assessment one night, my cards in hand while I struggled to remember if Aces were high or low. Their stern looks and annoyed tones were the only clues I needed. The hand ended and I folded, getting up from my chair. I wanted desperately to cling to Krisstopher, the only sense of familiarity I knew, but he was *skillfully* playing. So I went over and sat on the couch beside Sam.

We were at Derek's apartment. An upstairs bachelor type efficiency, it contained a little kitchen complete with a bar, a living room, and a back bedroom and bathroom. Krisstopher and I and Renny had dropped some acid a little while ago. I sat drinking a beer now, waiting for it to kick in.

"Yeah, *I* used to dress like that when I was in New Yohk," Sam suddenly commented, referring to the red and black laced bustier I now wore with my tight spandex pants. My friend Randy stole it from a prostitute who'd lived with his boyfriend. "But nobody dresses like that around heeya. It's just not appropriate."

I gave her a strange look, wondering just what she was getting at, then shrugged. "I don't care. I *like* dressing like this," I replied, not meaning to sound snotty, but just to let her know I wasn't interested in fitting in with the Joneses.

The people there were labeled *Granolas,* or *Dead Heads:* laid back hippie naturalist mountain folk who liked to party and smoke massive amounts of weed. Their attire consisted mainly of plaid shirts and sweaters, jeans, hiking boots, beaded necklaces, and tukes or baseball caps.

I was starting to get bionic ears now as the LSD finally took effect. I excused myself to go to the bathroom, where I could plainly hear Felician and Sam all the way out in the living room as they discussed Derek's new girlfriend who was standing in the small kitchen, calling her *clueless.*

"Yeah, but Mahta's cool."

"Yeah, she's cool."

As I got up off the toilet seat, pulling up my tights and spandex pants, sudden dizziness washed over me accompanied by a hot flash and then the immediate urge to throw up. I hunched over the porcelain bowl and puked, then waited for a while, still feeling like I was going to be sick. Finally, I stuck my finger down my throat to help it along. Felician knocked on the door.

"Mahta, you alright?"

"Yeah, I was just pukn', that's all."

She opened the door and I instantly made myself better, wanting to be tough like her.

"Ya sure ya alright?"

I stared in the toilet at the maroon colored liquid that resembled fruit punch.

"Yeah... but what did I drink that was red?"

* * *

Sharon mentioned something about an investment account for Krisstopher. Apparently information had come in the mail recently regarding the status of it. The head caregiver Matti told her it was probably nothing: just some small account his grandfather opened for him before his death which probably hadn't accrued much at all.

She'd advised Sharon not to even bother mentioning it to Krisstopher. However, Helen thought he had a right to know so he could at least check into it.

He retrieved the letter from Matti, seemingly upon her disapproval. The small account turned out to be worth seven thousand dollars. Immediately we recalled our spell for money, thoroughly convinced that witchcraft worked.

Within a week, Krisstopher had access to the money. He set out first to buy a car, purchasing a used red [81]Volvo Stationwagon from a private owner. As he was driving home with the car, he picked up a hitchhiker: some young kid who needed to get to Vermont. The kid informed him that Slaying Her was playing in concert that evening at the high school, so Krisstopher agreed to take him, picking Troy and I up first.

We headed to Vermont, Krisstopher clad in his brand-new leather he'd picked up earlier that day, and me in my old one that Jamie's boyfriend Andy had done awesome artwork on. At my request, he'd painted MARTYR across the back, which when one peered closely at the letters, discovered they were all pictures in and of themselves. There was a picture of Jesus on the cross, a wizard looking in a crystal ball, an anarchy sign, and a bunch of other stuff, including something X-rated that blended in so well I didn't notice it until someone pointed it out to me. I constantly received comments on how unique the jacket was. Similar to Deaf Dan's, I'd painted one of the sleeves yellow; the other orange. I'd also hung bells on the sleeve, though mine were jingle bells instead of cowbells, consecrated to ward off evil.

While purchasing his leather, Krisstopher had picked up a little gift for me: a tiny, flat, turquoise stone for my nose, since I'd had it pierced the time Craig and I went back to Michigan to visit.

On the way to the concert, we stopped at what appeared to be a farmhouse somewhere out in the boonies. The hitchhiker kid knew a hippie guy there who had some weed for sale. Krisstopher purchased one hundred and fifty dollars' worth, and we spent a good ten minutes stuffing the bags down the inside backs of the front seats, which happened to have some convenient holes in the upholstery perfect for hiding these types of things.

The rest of the night proved interesting. The high school was the only sign of life in the small town, which appeared deserted since everything else was closed and no one occupied the streets. As we got out of the car, we felt the heavy vibration of drums coming from inside the building.

Rather than pay cover at the door, we entered in through the second-floor window; another one of Krisstopher's spontaneous ideas. He forgot to take into consideration the fact that I wasn't a good climber. After much difficulty I made it inside, though I don't remember how.

It seemed only fifty or so people showed up for the concert, the majority of them being longhaired metal heads. I spent the remainder of the evening quietly taking in my new surroundings. The white flashing strobe lights gave everything a weird, slow motion effect. I noticed that the band's stage props, once inverted crosses, were now right side up.

A really tall, big boned metal head with long blond hair stood nearby, his arms folded as he watched the band. Every once in a while I could feel him staring at me. Something was bizarre about him. Hmmm... what was it?

I listened to the deep growls of the singer, the eerie wailing of guitar and sinister thumping of bass, and the fast frenzied drums that shook the gymnasium.

Next thing I knew, we were sitting at the kitchen table in some goth girl's house, an old chipped crystal ball the centerpiece. I discovered it belonged to the girl's grandmother. Near the fridge, a picture of Jesus Christ hung on the wall. I stared at it curiously for a few moments.

The girl, who was dressed in flowing black garbs with short, bleach blond hair, spent most of her time on the phone talking to her friend. I didn't know why, but I got bad vibes from her. She had an attitude problem, it seemed.

We hung out long enough to smoke a few bowls and then left the state of Vermont, saying good-bye to our roadside companion.

* * *

Mud season was beginning soon. That meant a lack of tourists now that winter was nearing an end. Most places had to lay off employees during this time, or at least cut their hours in half. Where would we get full time jobs?

Admittedly, we weren't searching too hard. Why bother? We had Krisstopher's nice little inheritance to live on and a two-month supply of weed. Life was grand. We'd smoke out in Sharon's bedroom, then he and Troy and I would go for a ride, our red [82]Volvo navigating the winding back roads in a winter wonderland. Shimmery, glimmery, snow-bedazzled.

Let me explain Troy. He was... as *troy* as a Troy could be. Short, wavy brown hair. Brown eyes. Casual dresser. Thin. Somewhat nervous at times. Quiet. A wayfarer. Occasionally he lived with his sister in town. But usually and almost always he was somewhere else—wherever the party was. He'd work once in a while—temp work, when they called him. But more oft than not he lived off the fat of other people's land. Ah, but we ourselves were not foreign to such a thing, either.

I'd first met Troy, believe it or not, in Florida, where he'd hitched all the way there just to see Krisstopher. It got old after a while though, when Krisstopher had to keep buying him food, beverages, and party necessities; as well as put him up for shelter on a continual basis. He'd been staying at the [83]YMCA prior to that until some of the other roomies there stole a bunch of his stuff. Krisstopher finally had to break the news to him that he couldn't afford to support him any longer. Eventually he hitched back to New Hampshire.

Today we were hanging out in the living room at his sister's place, TV on with the sound turned down and music jamming. He'd actually bought us a case of beer to make up for all those times Krisstopher helped him out.

For a while, he'd stopped partying completely. I think he'd mentioned something about being *born again*, whatever *that* meant.

He sat on the couch beside me talking about his bizarre experience in jail. "I'm dead serious, Martyr. I found God when I was in jail. It's like, he heard me. I was feeling really depressed. Really alone, y'know? And he heard me. I just *knew* he was there."

"That's cool. Hey—I believe you," I told him, grinning. But that was about the end of that. He never spoke of God again.

Later, Krisstopher and I had a good laugh about it. How weird man. How absolutely *weird*. But that was Troy for you. Somehow he was a necessary ingredient in Krisstopher's clan of friends. Spice of life, I guess.

Matti figured now that we had money, it was time for us to move on. So she gave us two weeks to be out of Sharon's place.

I really didn't want to live in New Hampshire anymore. There was really nowhere to play once we got a band going, unless of course, we played for free at somebody's party. And it was just too barren to suit me. No clubs... only one cool clothing store—and not even the type of clothing I wore—more like Dead Head flower child stuff. I was starting to get a little homesick, too.

I mentioned to Krisstopher the myriad of possibilities that lie waiting for us back in Michigan. My mom had already agreed to let us move in with her for a while until we got jobs (I'd briefed her on Krisstopher's inheritance and promised to give her some money for rent). To my relief, he thought it sounded like a good idea. So we said our good-byes to Sharon. He gave her some money to cover rent, though probably not enough since we'd stayed there about three months.

We packed up our newly acquired band equipment: a big [84]Marshall amp, two [85]Peavey multi-directional mics with stands, a used four track from Dirk, and a stage monitor. Then, having paid our good-bye party dues to various members of the *old gang*, we headed out for Michigan.

Soho, an old-time anole lizard veteran that had survived for years in the aquarium at Sharon's, came along for the ride. Our new boom box/CD player located in the back seat provided adequate theme music for the traveling companions.

Both of us were keen on the idea of another new adventure. When things got stale, our motto: bail. It was what both of us had done best in our lives thus far. I suppose it was a safety outlet—a way to deal with pain. Just block it out. Just run.

A journal entry I'd written as a teenager the time I ran away:

WE HAD THIS DREAM THAT WE COULD RUN
FROM THE WORLD WE LIVED IN TO A BETTER
PLACE.

WE THOUGHT WE COULD CHANGE EVERYTHING
WE HATED ABOUT OURSELVES AND BECOME
INDEPENDENT.

Soho, who'd been hanging out on the dashboard by the heater, decided he wanted to crawl up inside the dashboard where it was nice n' cozy and warm. We'd taken him out of the aquarium because it was cold and he had no hot rock to sustain his body temperature.

But we had an understanding with him—kind of like a psychic link. We knew he'd realize he was missed and come out sooner or later. And he did. Unfortunately, it was in the middle of the night when we were tucked away safely in bed at my mom's in Michigan, the temperature outside about twenty degrees.

We woke the next day to discover his little frozen body on the floor beneath the dashboard. I cried and cried while my mom's friend Don tried to revive him by soaking him in warm water mixed with salt, some home remedy he'd heard of that he probably made up just for my benefit. I appreciated his effort. However, Soho could not be revived. Not like Ra. So we stuck him in a little cardboard box and buried him in the backyard, conducting an authentic lizard funeral complete with Wiccan blessings.

To cheer me up, Krisstopher bought me another iguana. I immediately grew attached to it upon holding it at the pet store. The guy who worked there said it was a male iguana. So I named it Zain, after a tarot card: *The Lovers*, which pictured a man and woman romantically involved. This was one of my favorite cards, though it represented temptation: when one chose vice over virtue.

Zain was the Hebrew letter corresponding to the card. It was also the name of Liza the Black Witch's kid—Liza was yet another old girlfriend of Krisstopher's who apparently provided much supernatural entertainment for him throughout their relationship. So anyway, I thought the name Zain sounded really cool. It just had a nice ring to it.

I could tell my mom was happy to have me back. Especially when she'd told me an iguana would never set foot in her house (I'd wanted one ever since I was a kid). Zain was not only setting foot in her house, but he was *uncaged*, at that. He basically had free roam of Jim's old bedroom where Krisstopher and I now resided, and sometimes even the living room downstairs as long as he was chaperoned. He'd hang out on her curtains for hours, climbing to the top where no one could disturb him.

I worked on potty training him, providing a box with dirt and some humorous visual examples for him to observe of me squatting down over the box, making appropriate 'bathroom' noises and then saying, "Potty. Potty." Of course, Krisstopher found this quite amusing, but I didn't care. The iguana manual said it could be done. It was rare. But it could be done. Not that it recommended using *visual and audio* aids, but hey, everyone had their own method of teaching.

About two and a half feet long including his tail, I soon discovered Zain had a personality of his own, highly protective of me. I'd recently made him my *animal familiar,* as the witchcraft books stated it was a good idea to have one. According to the books, an [86]animal familiar, such as a black cat, shares a special psychic link with you and the spirit world. It helps aid you in spiritual endeavors as you combine its power with yours.

Following their advice, I consecrated Zain to the deities, tracing invisible pentagrams over him while chanting certain incantations. When I did any kind of reading—whether tarot, rune, I Ching or crystal ball—I invited him to join in for the purpose of intensifying the magic power. Witches keep an account of their various spells, incantations, etc., commonly known as the *Book of Shadows.* Krisstopher and I bought hard cover journals and adapted this suggestion.

Spells for love. Spells for money. Spells for cleansing and purification. You name it: it was in my Book of Shadows. I'd made a careful and diligent search of anything that could possibly aid me at all and listed it within the pages.

Then Krisstopher and I were rummaging through some of my dad's books in the library when I discovered a dictionary of satanic terms and practices. *Why did Dad have this?* I wondered. *He wasn't a Satan worshiper!* Upon opening the dictionary, my face paled when I discovered all of the deities I prayed to listed within its pages: Kernunnos, Pan, Isis, Osirus, Thoth, Diana, Hecate, etc., etc.

"What a lie!" I snarled as I showed the book to Krisstopher. "They don't know what they're talking about!" But inside me, a small fear began to grow.

Shortly after that, I read that Christians took [87]Kernunnos or Pan, the god of the pagans—a gentle, beautiful goat god of nature—and made him into their horned Devil, Satan. Convinced of this argument, I resumed praying to the *gentle, beautiful goat god,* as well as to all the other deities supposedly labeled *satanic.*

Krisstopher was the first to get a job, working at a music and movie store about ten minutes away from the house. One day, he came home and told me about a black witch who also worked there. She was heavily into voodoo, and claimed to have tombstones by her bed and huge altars set up in her room. I sensed he was intrigued by her from the way he constantly talked about her. This worried me a great deal. Then he mentioned another woman: one of the assistant managers whom he recently discovered had the hots for him. I grew insanely jealous, asking him not to tell me these things. But it seemed my request was forever slipping his mind.

In the meantime, we'd put a music ad out in a local newspaper, *Urban News.* After a few unlikely candidates and a couple of short-lived band members, we met up with two amazing guys: pieces that fit perfectly in our gothic puzzle. We now had the ultimate band. After a couple of shaky practices, we somehow launched into an orbit of celestial perfection—music to all our ears. It was very simple. We were meant to be.

> **All things positive have come our way**
> **So mote it be, now let them stay.**

THE ACE OF SPADES

*You opened the door...*
*To my heart*
*I beheld your eyes as they were moonbeams*
*Dancing*
*In my soul*

MY OLD PAL JAMIE CALLED me in the morning before band practice. She was working on an assignment for her photography class at college, and wanted to know if I'd come along with her to Ann Arbor later that day.

"I'm filming this guy who's just really *different*. You've gotta meet him to know what I'm talking about. He's punk and he's an um... heroin addict. He gave me permission to take pictures of him shooting up and stuff. I don't really feel comfortable going by myself—and Andy's at work."

The hour-long car ride went fast as we briefed each other on the latest. She and I had always been close, but when I'd moved in with Ryan's ex-roommates, we'd slowly drifted apart. Since then, she'd become close to Jonathan and Reese, my punk friends from high school, as well as to a myriad of other people she'd met through the scene. With my moving from state to state, and with the band and everything else going on in my life, we didn't talk that much anymore.

She was still seeing Andy, her first real love whom she'd been dating for four years or so. I filled her in on Krisstopher and I—how I left Craig and moved in with him, and all our adventures from that time up until

131

now. She already knew the story somewhat from our conversation a couple of summers ago when I'd been up to visit with Craig, stopping in at the pizzeria to see her and some other friends. They'd heard all about Krisstopher then, and how I was considering leaving my husband for him.

She soon pulled into a subdivision and we parked in front of a nice-sized brick home. Gathering together her camera and some other stuff while I carried her tripod and Zain on my shoulder, the two of us then followed the little walkway to the front entrance marked by double doors. Immediately upon ringing the bell, we heard the sharp yelping of a small dog. One of the doors swung open.

Every mental image I'd construed of the man Jamie described to me now melted away into oblivion as I stood mesmerized by his extraordinary beauty. For a minute, I was totally speechless.

His hair was deep pink—almost fuchsia—and a little wavy, falling just below the shoulders. He stood before us dressed in black, his eyes darting from me to Jamie and then back to me again, where they remained fixed for a few moments. Black shining eyes they were, like precious stones casting rays of light, invisible yet somehow visible as they pierced me deep within. His large nose, beautifully crafted upon his face, was adorned with small studs and rings, a hoop joining together the two nostrils. Big boned, it stood out like a majestic tower against his olive colored skin. Small yet full lips turned up ever so slightly at the corners upon seeing us as he nodded a hello.

We stood in the foyer now. I glanced down at his skinny legs, clothed in black jeans and swallowed up in a pair of full calve motorcycle boots. As our gaze locked again, something manifested itself. Something totally foreign to me. A power—a vibe so strong that it pulled me like a magnet. The weight of it left me giddy. No one ever looked at me like this before. It seemed he was mentally picking me apart piece by piece, eyeballs probing every sinew as he gently separated flesh from bone. Instantly an invisible lasso tightened around me. This man standing before me had somehow hooked my heart. Or was it my soul? This... spiritual... *connection*—what was it?

I'd never seen anyone like him. Nor had I ever fallen in love at first sight before—until now. His aura both frightened and amazed me. Yet there was something so familiar about it all. I found myself strolling through the unexpected doorway of another déjà vu dreamscape.

*Think. Fathom. Who is he and where have I—*

"War, this is Paula—uh—Martyr. Martyr, this is War."

"Don't I know ya from somewhere?" he asked me now, eyes searching my face once more.

He echoed my thoughts. How did he *know?*

His voice was unique: low but not deep, nasally yet possessing a certain seductive appeal.

"I was just thinking the same thing," I replied, surprised. We exchanged information on schools, hangouts, etc., then concluded we'd never met before.

"You just *look* familiar," he said again.

A thought crept into my mind then. *"He's your eternal soul mate,"* it seemed to say.

"Fairy, shut up!" he shouted at his dog for the fifth time, then motioned for us to follow him up the stairs. "Come on, let's go to my room."

*Fairy. An odd name for a dog,* I thought as I trailed behind him and Jamie.

He walked with an attitude. An air of confidence. Not too much, but just enough to win my respect and admiration. The small mutt growled at me and continued barking.

Jamie set up her tripod while I looked around the room: a desk with books and a computer facing the wall, a long table piled with junk, a dresser, a bed with old striped sheets... and some normal posters. It hardly fit his image. I found out, then, that it used to be his brother's room; his brother was a dermatologist who now lived out of state. That explained all the college-looking stuff. Apparently War moved a lot, and he was just crashing here at his parents' temporarily.

He sat on the bed, lighting up a cigarette while Jamie focused her camera. I plopped down Indian-style on the floor. My eyes were suddenly drawn to a pack of matches not far away on the blue shag carpeting. Crawling over to it, I picked it up to examine the cover, recognizing it to be one of the suit cards—*The Princess of Pentacles*—from the tarot deck. Pentacles, or pentagrams, were often representative of the magic arts—*the Craft*, as some refer to it. This particular card depicted a woman skilled in the area of the Occult, possessing spiritual powers. I glanced at War now, who was staring at me with those interrogating eyes of his.

"Martyr's in a band," Jamie offered.

"Oh yeah? What kinda music is it?" he asked me.

"Uh, it's gothic music. I play keyboards and sing, and my boyfriend Krisstopher plays bass and sings."

"That's cool. Yeah, I'm mostly into punk music myself."

Jamie snapped pictures as we talked, instructing him to act natural. Presently he lit up a joint, and after taking a couple of hits, offered it to her. She declined. He then passed it to me.

His arms were covered with various tattoos. And just below the knuckles of both hands, I noticed tattooed words on his fingers in faded black ink. HATE caught my eye. Somehow it hardly seemed fitting for him. He was a punk, yet without the offensive attitude typical of the whole punk rock genre.

In punk rock, one supposedly retaliates against the social system that has come to be; goes against the norm of a certain dress code, a certain socially acceptable behavior, a certain conformity society has deemed necessary and proper. Yet most punks are the epitome of what they struggle to escape, wallowing in hypocrisy, themselves *a chip off the old block of* society on a smaller scale. They merely succeed in setting up their own clique—a *"subculture within a culture,"* as someone had stated. Instead of being one of the Joneses, they're one of the [88]*Sids*, embracing a different set of ideals backed by the same prejudices: *You're not cool enough, punk enough, knowledgeable enough—or you simply don't have the right look about you—to hang with us.*

Hopefully one eventually awakes to this discovery, disillusioned by the several million cans of super hold hairspray for his mohawk and the spikes meant to keep people away when in actuality he is screaming for closeness. The dogma then embraced is: *Why? What for?* This usually emerges after he realizes he has no true friends and his life is just a superficial lie. He's been *in the scene* for fifteen years or more, like a hamster running in place on a wheel in a cage: getting older, doing the same thing… getting older, doing the same thing.

But War was a little different in some respects. His friends were not chosen by any personal caste system. He embraced them all with the same acceptance, no matter what they looked like. And he was too loving to be hateful. Too social to be antisocial.

I sat on the floor still, a little dreamy from the bud. Pentagrams were the reoccurring theme in my head now. Princess. *Pentagrams*. Romance. Soul mates. *Pentagrams*. I decided to bait the hook then, to see where War stood when it came to pentagrams, or magic powers. I mentioned something about white witchcraft. He didn't flinch. He didn't react either way. Finally, after further discussion of my spiritual endeavors, he stated that he didn't believe in *that crap*—that it was all *hokey*.

I tried tying in these remarks with the other messages I seemed to be getting from him: the unspoken signs, the piercing glances, and the invisible connection to which we'd now been polarized. Somehow there was no place for them. I'd read in a book before that real spiritual adepts, or witches, will not profess they are such. They keep all of their occult paraphernalia *hidden*, because it is supposed to be a hidden or *secret* practice.

He suggested we get some more drugs so that Jamie could continue photographing him with new props. I picked up Zain, who'd been climbing around on the table, and we hopped into Jamie's car.

* * *

"Man, I wish he'd hurry up. This is making me *really* uncomfortable," Jamie said, looking around nervously. We were parked in a shabby looking neighborhood with run down houses somewhere just outside of downtown Ypsilanti. War had gone into one of the houses nearly ten minutes ago.

I turned around to check on Zain, who was sprawled out behind me in the back window, a ferret harness I'd converted into a leash fastened around his neck. His mouth was wide open, like he was gasping for air. "I think Zain needs water. He doesn't look so good."

A few minutes passed, and then War came out of the house. I watched him walk toward us, admiring the black T-shirt bandanna he'd wrapped around his head, which gave him a mysterious gypsy look.

With his hair pulled back, I could now see that his ears were covered from lobe to top with various silver studs, hoops, and crosses—both regular and inverted. He got in the front seat and Jamie started the car, ready to put it in drive.

Zain still looked parched, as if his mouth had frozen in an eternal yawn. I'd never seen him do this before. It worried me. "Man, you guys, my iguana *really* needs some water. Where can we get some water—fast?"

War turned around to the back where I was sitting, then opened the car door and stuck his foot out. "I'll be right back," he said.

"Man, what the crud is he doing *now*?" Jamie asked, throwing her hands up in the air.

"I don't know," I said quietly.

He returned a few moments later, carrying a small [89]Dixie Cup in his hand.

"I don't believe it," she laughed. "He went to get you some water."

"Here ya go." He handed the cup to me through the window, then got back in the car. I was surprised that he risked getting caught in a crack house just to get my iguana some water.

"Wow, man. Thanks a lot. You're a sweetheart," I said, thoroughly impressed with his act of chivalry. I held the cup in front of Zain. He jerked his head away from it and closed his mouth suddenly, like he'd been psyching me out all along just to see what I'd do. "Oops. I guess he doesn't need water after all."

"Pull in here," War instructed after a few minutes, motioning to a small dirt parking lot overlooking a river. Jamie abruptly turned in and parked. He took a small pipe from out of his pocket and opened one of the viles containing tiny crack rocks. Crouching down low in the seat, he lit the pipe and took a long drag off it. It didn't faze me. I was too busy thinking of him and me.

Was he my *eternal* soul mate—the highest form of love possible that I'd been searching for, especially since Jade mentioned her experiences to me? I stared out the window at the river, my eyes drawn to the small leafy tree next to it. "I'll be right back," I told them, climbing out of the car to follow the walkway down to the tree. I grabbed a leaf, scratching a rune symbol for love into its surface and empowering it with thoughts of romance while speaking aloud: "If War is the perfect love, then so mote it be. Let the perfect love, according to the free will of the universe, come to me." I let the leaf down into the water, releasing the spell's power, and watched as it was carried away by the stream's current. Then I stood gazing at the bridge for a moment before making my way back to the car.

When Jamie and I left later that day, she commented, "Man, War was *digging* you, Martyr. I've never seen him look at anyone like that before. I could just tell he *really* likes you."

A wonderful feeling sprang up in my heart then, the feeling that arises when you're attracted to someone and you think they might be attracted to you—that tingly euphoria accompanied by nervous excitement.

"You know, you're right—I don't know what it is about him, but I've never met anyone like him before," I said.

She smiled. "See, I *told* you. All the women go crazy for him. He's just got this strange kind of *power* over them. I don't know what it is." She was silent for a moment, then added, "But he was definitely *lovin'* *you*, girl. I could see him checkin' you out."

"You think so?"

"I *know* so."

* * *

I stared at the various drawings on the cards laid out before me. I'd just asked whether or not War was indeed my soul mate. Sitting Indian-style on the floor in the bedroom, Zain perched on the white wooden clothes shoot that led to the basement, one eye watching me intently from the side; I examined now the divine answer.

*The Ace of Swords*, comparable to *Spades* in a traditional deck, was the card signifying War's main character trait. In conjunction with the other cards, it indicated that he had much personal power. He was bold. He caused division. As I began studying the other cards in relation to this one, I saw that War and I had unresolved karma. Our love went back many, many lifetimes—he was definitely a soul mate. The *coins, or pentagrams* in the spread, let me know that he was skilled in the magic arts—more skilled than Krisstopher or I. However, as *The Devil* card appeared, I detected that his power was somewhat negative—*very* negative, actually. It leaned more toward the black arts.

For days I thought about him. It seemed I became conscious of an inward emptiness I'd never felt to this degree before. Now that I knew War was a powerful soul mate of mine, I desired to reach back in time and pull out all the answers to this ancient love of ours—to find out what purpose it had, and if in fact, it was as deep as the soul ties Jade spoke of.

I longed to see him again. When Jamie told me Andy's band was playing at The Whitehouse, an old theater in Ann Arbor that specialized in punk rock shows, I told Krisstopher I wanted to go check them out. My deepest hope was that I'd see War there since it was his stomping ground, as Jamie had relayed to me.

Inside the theater, graffiti covered the white walls. Toward the back, a girl handed out cups of water. *Water?* A lot of younger punks were hanging out; it was an all-ages show. I searched through the crowd for a glimpse of War, but there was no sign of him anywhere. Figured. This mob was probably too juvenile for him.

*Social Derelicts* climbed on stage to play a set. The music raged and Andy fired away on the vocals, his face contorted as he let out an angry scream. Suddenly a crowd of thrashers stormed the Pit while Jamie stood off to the side snapping pictures.

About halfway through the show, I convinced Krisstopher to come out to the car with me. We had some jumbos in the back that we'd gotten from the party store earlier, and I really wanted to get plastered. I was bummed about War.

We sat in the car smoking cigarettes and drinking the [90]Budweisers, which had kept well in the cold. Then somehow we got on the subject of Krisstopher's old girlfriends (I probably introduced the topic), and which one he had the most spiritual relationship with. As I guessed, it was Mikal.

"But *I'm* the most spiritual one out of them all, right?" I asked.

"Uh, yeah."

"Because you know, I'm jealous of the relationship you guys had. I mean, it seems you still might kind of like her," I told him, the beer buzz inciting my honesty all of a sudden.

"We *did* have a pretty special relationship," he admitted.

"Yeah, but now you love *me* more, right?" I prodded.

"Uh huh."

A beige car circled the parking lot then, blaring punk music. It stopped abruptly, and some punks ran toward it shouting, "Hey War!"

My heart skipped a beat at the sound of his name. Again the tingly sensation. *Russshhhh.* "That's War, the guy Jamie took pictures of!" I told Krisstopher excitedly, scrambling out of the car to see him. He followed after me, not quite as excited.

Behind the wheel of his '91 Cavalier, a black T-shirt bandanna wrapped around his head, War looked more beautiful than ever.

"Hi War. Remember me?"

He swung open the door suddenly, one foot on the pavement as he doubled over and started puking violently. Not quite the reception I had in mind. He heaved and heaved, and then it was dry heaves while I watched in horror.

"War, are you *okay?*" I asked, afraid. "Are you sick or something?"

"I'll be alright," he answered, straightening up and wiping his mouth with his sleeve. "Wicked cramps... uuhhh." He was clutching his stomach, muttering some drug terminology.

"Huh?" I asked, not understanding.

"He shot up cocaine," Krisstopher explained, familiar with all that stuff since he used to free base with his mom and her boyfriend.

"Cocaine? I didn't know you could shoot up cocaine."

"Well, yeah Martyr. You can shoot up *anything.*"

War was shaking like a leaf now.

"Are you sure you're alright? I'm worried about you," I told him.

Little beads of sweat broke out on his forehead. "I'm positive, man. I'll be fine," he reassured me.

But as I continued to watch him, a thought suddenly crossed my mind: *War has a deathwish.* Couldn't he see that he was destroying himself? Didn't he care?

"This is my boyfriend Krisstopher. Krisstopher, this is War."

He held out his hand. "How's it goin', dude?"

"Alright," Krisstopher answered, shaking it.

* * *

We were in the bank parking lot across from The Whitehouse. War was one car away from us on the left. I couldn't see him, but I could still hear his music.

"I gotta go to the bathroom," I told Krisstopher, opening the driver's side door. I got out and headed toward the car to the right of us. The jumbo made me relaxed enough to where I was content to go in the great outdoors, apathetic of the fact that people might see me. I squatted down beside the empty car, my back against the cement divider, and started to pee.

A bum appeared seemingly out of nowhere, shuffling over to me with a big grin on his face. "What are you doin'?" he slurred.

"I'm going to the bathroom, okay?" I answered nicely. He edged his way closer, apparently not getting the hint. "I'm trying to go to the bathroom. Now leave me alone!" I said louder, thinking perhaps he hadn't heard me.

"Huh? What are you doin'?" he repeated, taking a few more steps toward me and crouching down with the same stupid grin on his face. He was only about two feet away and I got a bad feeling that he wanted something other than a friendly conversation.

"Krisstopher! Help!"

I heard the car door slam and Krisstopher approached us. "What's going on?" he asked calmly, eyeing the bum.

"I told him I'm going to the bathroom, but he keeps coming closer and closer."

"Listen, creep! Leave her alone! She told you, she's going to the bathroom!" he yelled, kicking the bum smack in the face with his boot.

"Krisstopher, don't hurt him!" I pleaded as he crumpled backward to the ground.

"Nooo, dude! What are ya *doin'*?!" War cried angrily, dashing toward us with an alarmed look on his face. He halted suddenly when he saw the bum picking himself up off the pavement and me unharmed. "Oh dude, that *scared* me! I thought you were kicking *her*."

I melted like butter at that moment. War felt he needed to protect me, though I barely knew him. He'd been ready to defend me, like a knight in shining armor. A valiant prince. The look of fear and anger

I'd seen on his face let me know that he meant it from the heart: his chivalry was not an act.

Even Krisstopher had defended me. I was thankful, though surprised. I guess I was growing so used to his apathy lately. Still, why did it seem that War's concern was genuine where Krisstopher's seemed almost *mechanical?* I couldn't explain it. I just *felt* it somehow.

\* \* \*

Jason was driving. He was a tall, sturdy guy with hazel eyes and shoulder length, bleach blond hair that he wore pulled back with a folded bandanna for a headband, like the guy from Jean's Habit. He worked with Krisstopher at the music store.

The first time I met him, he went with us to get some acid from a friend of his, then gave us a whole bunch of cigarettes on the way home since we were fresh out. After that, the three of us started hanging around together. We liked a lot of the same music, and Jason wanted to learn how to play bass. Krisstopher was going to give him some lessons.

A little bit younger than us, nineteen to be exact, he was a real practical joker. He joked so much that I didn't know when to take him seriously. But he was also fun to be around; easygoing and personable. He was Krisstopher's closest friend besides me since we'd moved to Michigan, and probably mine as well since I'd lost touch with everyone else.

We sat in the back seat of his car now, smoking a bunch of old roaches War had pulled out of his leather jacket. The stubby little joints weren't doing a lot to get me high. By the time Krisstopher passed them to me, the paper was pretty much down to nothing and I burned my lips on the metal clip. But War needed drugs. Jason had agreed to drive him to get some, and we were just along for the ride.

In the passenger seat, War squirmed and fidgeted, constantly on the lookout for cops. "Slow down, dude. The speed limit's thirty-five here," he told Jason nervously. He kept turning his head in every direction as if expecting a secret attack. It reminded me of the first time I really saw him freak out: I think he'd shot up some heroin and then smoked a little crack. We were at his house, and he was standing behind the curtains peeking out the window; telling us *they* were out there. *They* were going to get him. Then he pulled down the shade. Running out of the room, he grabbed a wooden rod—I believe it was a broom handle—and clutched it tightly in his hands, ready for battle.

Jamie kept saying, "*Who's* out there, War? *Who's* going to get you?" She grinned at me then and whispered, "Man, he's freaking out! I wish he'd settle his butt *down*."

I wondered how such a spiritual adept like War could be so afraid, but then I remembered I was not immune to the effects of drugs, either. After all, that was the whole purpose of taking them—to alter one's state of mind. [92]And according to our witchcraft books, if taken in the proper manner, drugs (or *sacred spiritual medicine*) were a useful aid to spiritual awareness, opening one up to the spirit world.

The books stated that the American Indians had often used peyote, a hallucinogenic that produced visions and dreams; while witches used belladonna and hemp to induce astral projection and unleash psychic powers.

Many ancient spells I acquired contained drugs in their formulas. Still, I didn't see why War liked this particular high. It seemed more *de*structive than *con*structive. What on earth could he be learning spiritually from all this paranoia?

On the other hand, weed made me extremely paranoid, yet I liked the way it tuned me in to the spirit world. And though I found acid to be very useful, the hallucinations it caused often scared me half to death.

But as he darted around the room, dodging furniture and dropping to a crawl on the floor, I saw a different side of him. The confident, bold, and powerful War was nowhere to be found. I wanted him back. I liked him better.

"I have to go to the bathroom!" I called from the backseat now. The pressing in my bladder let me know it was urgent.

"You gotta go to the bathroom, Martyr?" Jason echoed loudly, a smirk on his face as he eyed me in the rearview mirror.

"Yeah."

"Alright. I'll get you to a bathroom. Here's one... right..." He slowed down in front of a gas station as if planning to turn in the entrance, then suddenly sped up, passing it by. "Oops, sorry! I forgot to stop," he teased.

I sighed. Couldn't he just be serious for once, especially right now when my bladder depended on it?

Five minutes went by, and I reminded him again. "Jason, I still have to go to the bathroom!"

Another gas station was coming up in the distance. This time, instead of slowing down, he plowed right by it. "Sorry, can't stop there!" he laughed.

"C'mon, Jason! I'm not kidding," I told him angrily. "I really have to go—*now!*" I was no longer in the mood for jokes, seeing as I'd had the unpleasant experience of several bladder infections in the past. I didn't want to risk holding it much longer.

"Pull over *now*, dude! She's gotta go," War commanded. Krisstopher sat in silence.

We turned into a deserted lot somewhere. War got out of the car and pulled back the seat to let me out. Relieved, I crouched down out of sight behind a dumpster and started to go.

"Alright, hurry up. I'm coverin' for ya," a voice said, startling me. I froze, then, as War came and squatted down right next to me practically. The idea of someone I was deeply attracted to watching me go to the bathroom when I barely knew him wasn't exactly comforting.

"Ya done yet?"

"No. I can't go. I'm trying..." I answered.

"C'mon, hurry," he said anxiously, holding his arm out in front of me as if to shield me from something visible only to him. He continued guarding me, peering around nervously in every direction like he'd been doing in the car. "It's still clear," he informed me.

I glanced around, trying to figure out just who he thought would be showing up. Perhaps because of the incident with the bum, he wanted to make sure no one bothered me this time.

"I can't go," I said finally, though my bladder felt like it would burst at any given moment.

We got back in the car. After yelling at Jason about the bladder infection I was probably developing, I winced in pain with every bump we rode over, pondering how War was so attached to me. So... nice. Incredibly nice. A few minutes later, Jason pulled in at a $^{93}$7-Eleven so

I could try again. This time, alone in the privacy of a restroom, I was finally able to go.

*  *  *

In his [94]Cavalier, War followed Krisstopher and me to the gas station near the freeway. We were leaving for home. I hopped out of the car to say good-bye, taking a long look at him as he leaned out the window and stared at me, the moonlight seeming to catch in his black eyes.

"War, please take care of yourself. I'm really worried about you. I care a *lot* for you," I said, pouring out my heart as I hugged him good-bye. My arms around him now, I could smell his leather jacket, and I felt his spikes poke me in the chin. Somehow it felt good though, because they were part of him. I didn't want to let go. I didn't want to say good-bye.

He seemed deeply moved by my words. I could tell by the way he looked at me—a stare that indicated I'd broken down some wall in his heart—some barrier that not many women succeeded in penetrating.

"I'll be alright. Thanks, though," he smiled faintly. It was a quiet, sad smile. A smile meant only for me. "I'll see ya around, okay?"

*  *  *

Our connection grew stronger with each passing day. I did a lot of thinking. Every spare minute was spent seeking out answers to this puzzle. I scryed in my crystal ball. I did countless tarot spreads. The oracles all pointed toward the same thing: War was *the* soul mate. Not just a karmic one like the other men in my life, but the eternal one. He was the power I sought. The love I craved. But there was only one problem: he was dark. He controlled. He divided. He possessed... and he would stop at nothing.

He'd already proven his attachment to me in the short time we were together, stepping onto the scene as if Krisstopher didn't even exist. His boldness was apparent. Again I thought of The Ace of Spades (or Swords) card that signified his personality.

A few weeks had gone by since the last time I saw him. Now Jamie had some bad news: he was moving to New York. She wanted to know if I'd like to come along with her and Andy to say good-bye. My heart hurt. How could he leave me when we'd just met up again in this life? I thought he was my eternal soul mate. I thought we were *connected*.

Andy and Jamie picked me up and we headed to Ann Arbor. Krisstopher had to work that day. I was relieved, because I wanted to be alone with War. To sort out my feelings with him. The car ride was spent telling the two of them about white witchcraft and my eternal tie with War, while they shared with me that they'd been going to church and were getting into Jesus. Jamie told me church was really cool, and she felt a good feeling there. It didn't really faze me. I just kept talking about witchcraft and how spiritual it was. I told them War had magic powers. They didn't say much after that.

We arrived at his house, Fairy barking the whole time until he yelled for her to shut up. As usual, he motioned for us to follow him upstairs, the pesky little mutt racing ahead of us with growls of dislike, which I took to be personally directed toward me.

In his room, we all stood around for a minute, not saying much. Andy went to use the bathroom then, and War put a record on the turntable. *Crackle crackle crackle.* The Mortal Dead song started up, and after a moment, he sang along to the chorus: "I am black as The *Ace of Spades!* Black, black as The *Ace of Spades!*"

I gasped in astonishment. How was he possibly aware that The Ace of Spades was his character card in my tarot spread? He sang it with confidence, like he *knew*. Somehow... he knew.

He and Andy talked about hair dye while I looked around the room, this time noticing a candle on a small table at the head of his bed. The wax had melted and dripped around the outside of the holder. At its base were scattered a few odd-looking gold coins with weird inscriptions on them. Once again, I thought of the spells in my Wiccan book that embraced candles and coins. I wanted desperately to pick up one of the coins and examine what was on it, but knew better. I wasn't supposed to touch another witch's consecrated property for the sake of preserving the energy in it. I hoped War would know that I respected this rule. I was confident that he *would* in fact know, just as he knew other things without me having to say them.

After discussing the leopard spots—the new hairdo he would help Andy create, he then mentioned that he needed to go to the store. I watched him slap on some cologne from a small green bottle on the shelf near the door, smiling to myself because I had a feeling it was for my benefit.

As we all headed outside toward Jamie's car, I wished secretly that War and I could ride alone together. But if Andy was driving, then it wouldn't be possible. Besides, what sense would it be to take two cars? I guessed I was the only romantic in the group.

"Um... Andy, why don't you and Jamie drive together? I'll take *my* car," he suddenly suggested, as if reading my mind. "I wanna be *alone* with Martyr."

My heart skipped a few beats at his remark, while my eyes widened in amazement. How did he *know*? There was no question in my mind now that he had power. Not even Krisstopher and I experienced this frequent of a psychic connection—only once in a while. The tarots and crystal ball were right: War's power was much stronger. I hadn't even begun to realize just *how* strong.

We started off down the road with Andy and Jamie following behind us. I sat quietly in the passenger seat, intoxicated by his presence.

"Sooo, how's it goin'?" he asked, glancing over at me.

*That bandanna. I love that bandanna.* "Fine," I answered a little shyly.

"Ya know, I wanted just you and me to ride together because I wanted to talk to ya about somethin'."

"That's cool, because I need to talk to you too."

"Yeah?" He paused for a moment, switching on the heat. "Ya warm?"

"Yeah, I'm okay. Thanks."

"So... like I was sayin', I have somethin' I need to discuss with ya." Pause. "And ya might find this weird, cuz I know I just met ya and stuff..." he turned to flash me a look with his dark eyes now, "but in case ya haven't noticed—I like you. I mean, I *really* like you."

I could hardly believe what I was hearing. It was true then, he *was* my soul mate. And it was all coming to pass so fast!

146

"I like you too War—"

"And I want ya to be my girlfriend."

*Whoa! I'm going to faint. He wants me to be his girlfriend—his GIRLFRIEND, and I don't even know him. Or do I?*

"And I don't just pick *any* woman, either. I'm real *choosy* about my women. Ya know what I'm sayin'? It takes a certain type of woman to go out with me. She has to be really *special,* if ya know what I mean."

Immediately I thought of the book of matches I'd found in his room with The Princess of Pentacles on the cover: a woman possessing magic powers. This was no ordinary woman. She was a woman who was spiritually aware. And if I'd been searching for my magical prince all along, then it made since that War also searched for his princess. Like mine, his soul longed for that person he had a spiritual link with. This explained why he kept coming back to me throughout many lifetimes. Together, our spiritual energy was more powerful than any lower form of earthly love. After all, we were eternal soul mates, not karmic ones. We'd always desired a higher love that many people didn't know about or care about. They were content to live in mediocrity, unaware of the power that could exist between lovers if only they sought it. But because they settled for the mundane lower form of passion—purely physical— that's exactly what they got.

I could hardly take it all in. I could hardly contain myself. On the one hand, my heart was so happy. I just wanted to be with him— forever. On the other, I knew that it was not possible. First off, there was Krisstopher to think about. And secondly, War was somewhat evil. He had bad karma. He used black powers.

"War... I like you so much. I can't get my mind off you."

"Yeah?" he smiled.

"Yeah. I think I'm falling in love with you." I sighed, looking out the window for a moment, then continued. "I didn't know what it was about you, but I felt something between us the minute we met. And then I did a tarot card spread. My cards told me you and I are soul mates—meaning, we go back many lifetimes together. You've got a lot of spiritual power, but it's *negative*—"

"Man, I don't *understand* what you're talkin' about," he interjected, seemingly frustrated. "I *told* ya, I don't get into that witchcraft stuff. It's bad news."

We pulled into the grocery store parking lot, and I followed him inside, waving to Andy and Jamie as they waited in the car.

"Ya want a beer? Let's get a beer." He walked over to the cooler, grabbing two [95]Budweiser jumbos, and we got in the express lane. "Yeah, let me have a pack of [96]Zig Zag rolling papers," he told the lady cashier.

I handed him some money for my beer, refusing to let him buy it. While she rang us up, I stood there dreamily, mulling over what he'd said. Why wouldn't he just admit to the witchcraft? His name was *War*. I knew it was short for warlock—that piece of spiritual information had already been relayed to me. It wasn't his real name, after all. I'd heard his mom call him *Richard*. Why couldn't he just be honest with me? Everything pointed to his power—the tarots, the crystal ball, the weird signs I kept getting...

Back in the car, he lit a cigarette and we pulled onto the road. "Y'know, I think you could be the one to help me get off heroin," he said, continuing our conversation. "I think you'd be good for me. So I want ya to move to New York with me."

*New York?!* I was quiet for a moment, never expecting such a proposition—especially so soon after we'd met. Part of me was saying, *He doesn't even know me. What on earth is he thinking?* But the other part was both flattered and enraptured by his offer.

Still, squatting in abandoned buildings with some guy I barely knew sounded a little risky to me. He was going there, as he always did, to score drugs. Probably heroin. How was I going to help him kick his habit? And besides, what about Krisstopher?

I took a deep breath, letting it out slowly as I thought of how to respond. "War... I like you so much—please understand. I've never felt like this before about anyone—not even Krisstopher."

I took a good look at him now—at this gorgeous hunk of a man sitting beside me. It was all happening just the way I wanted—the spiritual link—and yet, I couldn't have it because it was somehow all wrong.

"But... your powers are dark," I continued regretfully. "You've got some kind of *bad karma*. And besides that, I left my husband for Krisstopher. He moved all the way here from New Hampshire and we live at my mom's now. I can't just up and leave him when he doesn't know anybody..." Pause. "And—I love him. He's my soul mate also. But I love *you* too. I'm so confused. I don't know what to do." *Am I going to regret this? I'm missing the chance to be with the one I'm supposed to be with. Or am I really supposed to be with him?*

"It's cool—I understand," he assured me as we pulled into the driveway. But I sensed it wasn't over... yet.

As the four of us entered the room again, I took a big swig out of my jumbo and sat down on the floor. He plopped down on the bed, patting the spot beside him. "Martyr, come sit *here*. I want ya to sit by me." I looked at Jamie, who was still standing, and we smiled at each other. Then I got up and went over to the bed. After a few seconds, the phone rang.

"Here, hold this for a minute, will ya? I'll be right back." He handed me some kind of plastic holiday tray heaped full of marijuana.

*Wow. That's a lot of weed.* I stared down at the green mound, noticing a small slip of paper from a fortune cookie placed directly on top. It read:

YOU ARE THE CHOSEN ONE.
YOUR LUCKY NUMBERS ARE:
5, 7, 9, 11, 32

His words echoed in my mind: *"I don't just pick any woman, either. I'm real choosy about my women."*

I continued to stare in astonishment at the slip of paper. *I am the chosen one. I am the chosen one. I am the cho—*

He strode back into the room then, retrieving the tray from out of my hands. After rolling a joint, he hit it and passed it to me. I took a long drag, holding in the hot smoke as it burned my lungs.

Mesmerized, I thought of the fortune I'd just read. There was no way it was just coincidence. First off, there'd be no logical reason for a Chinese fortune to be lying in a pile of weed. And furthermore, it backed up what I thought he'd meant earlier in the car. I was *the* one. Out of all the women he'd been with throughout centuries, I was the chosen match for his soul.

He and Andy went in the bathroom to dye each other's hair, while Jamie and I talked and listened to some of his records. After a while, Bruce showed up. I'd never met him before. He sauntered into the room, uttering a quiet "hello." As I looked him up and down in a stoned stupor, my parched mouth hanging open a little and my contacts sticking to my itching eyeballs, I came to the conclusion that he was *interesting*. Tall and large, he dressed in a black button-down trench coat, baggy black shirt and jeans, and combat boots. In one hand, he clutched a purse, also black. As I stared down at it, I noticed his long, pointy black fingernails. Hmmm… were they press-ons, or homegrown? Part African-American, he had a thick, fuzzy mohawk that resembled an afro—he called it his *frohawk*—and fuzzy sideburns which extended to the middle of his cheeks, coming to a point at the ends.

War lit up another joint now and passed it to him. He took it and sat down on the floor.

"Martyr, Bruce is really into the gothic scene too," Jamie said. She looked over at him. "Martyr's in a band."

"Yeah Martyr, this is the guy I was telling you about," Andy informed me. "You two could probably hook up musically since you like the same kind of stuff."

He'd mentioned earlier that a friend of his was heavily into goth like me, and though he didn't play an instrument, he wouldn't mind singing or something. But no way. Two singers were already *one too many* for my liking without adding another. I doubted Krisstopher wanted to share the spotlight, either.

"Yeah, except we already have two singers," I told Bruce. "I sing, and my boyfriend Krisstopher sings."

He didn't respond, but sat on the floor with his back against the door, quietly taking everything in. He seemed remote, distant—like he preferred hanging out in the shadows rather than talking, at the moment.

My jumbo was nearly gone, and I felt extremely relaxed. Andy's leopard spots were complete, War had a fresh pink dye job, and everyone was just kind of sitting around vegging out. Finally, War suggested we go someplace.

"Where?" Andy asked.

"I don't know. Like, we could take a walk or somethin', just to get out of the house for a while."

"Alright. As long as we're not too long. We have to get going pretty soon."

War slipped on his leather once more. I admired it for the first time. It was one of the coolest I'd ever seen, ranking right up there with Deaf Dan's. The metal work was intricate: rows and rows of carefully placed spikes and studs, all in corresponding patterns. He'd sewn a large piece of leopard skin on one side near the shoulder. I stared at it for a moment, then shifted my gaze to the opposite side, my eyes now resting on the small pin ornament up near the collar. It was The *Ace of Spades!*

We piled in Jamie's car and I sat comatose in the back seat. By this time, I was pretty much unaware of my surroundings, not to mention the fact that I didn't know the city of Ann Arbor too well to begin with. We ended up parking and walking down an incline of some sort. It was dark outside, and I was so stoned I could barely see a thing. War instinctively grabbed my hand, helping me over every rock and piece of debris that crossed our path.

I felt so loved by him then. He was different than the others, though I couldn't really explain how. I just knew I held a special place in his heart, and that his affection and concern were genuine. He felt what I felt. He said what I thought. And he treated me the way I'd always wished a man would treat me. We were one... before being one. I hadn't even been intimate with him yet, and already, on a spiritual level, we were *connected.*

Under some kind of bridge covered with graffiti, the five of us sat down on an embankment near the river. The cement vibrated as cars zoomed overhead. War lit a pipe and passed it to me. I took a hit off it, handing it back to him, and he gave it to Bruce then. Lost in a dream, I hoped I never woke up. I recalled Jamie's words: *"Man, War was digging you, Martyr. I've never seen him look at anyone like that before. I could just tell he really likes you."* And War's: *"...but in case ya haven't noticed—I like you. I mean, I **really** like you."*

And then it seemed we'd only been there for about two seconds when Jamie and Andy mentioned we had to be going because it was getting late. My heart sank. I would never see War again. I wanted desperately for all of time just to stop. He made the excuse that we had to come back to his house and have a piece of his birthday cake. I was glad to stall for another half hour or so.

While everyone stood around in the dining room, a Jewish religious plaque of some kind hanging on the wall, I excused myself to go use the bathroom. I had a real phobia about people hearing me go, and as I mentioned before, especially someone that I absolutely adored, like War. So I figured as long as he was busy talking to Jamie, Andy, and Bruce, I could go in peace.

But as I sat on the toilet seat, I started to feel very uncomfortable, like I'd felt the time he stood guard for me by the dumpster. I didn't know why, but I just sensed he was near the door for some reason. Was he? No... I was probably just being paranoid. Dismissing the thought, I finished going to the bathroom and got up off the toilet seat. Suddenly, I got a strong premonition that he was going to barge in on me, even though I knew I'd locked the door. It was so strong that I hurriedly yanked up my tights and started to pull my skirt back down. As if on cue, the door opened and there he was!

"Oops, sorry!" he said, his eyes scanning my body as I quickly covered myself. He turned around then and walked out, leaving me to wonder, once again, how I knew that was going to happen. I was sure he'd done it purposely. And how did he get in when I'd locked the door?

Back in the dining room, he gave us the number and address to where he'd be staying for a while in New York. I stared down at the piece of paper he handed me. He'd spelled his name wrong. It read:

WOR

When I questioned him on this, thinking maybe he was just wasted or something, he mentioned that it could be spelled either way: W-O-R or W-A-R. I thought to myself that if it stood for *warlock*, then it should be spelled the *right way*.

As we started to leave out the door, I felt I wanted to cry. I hugged him then, and he gently grabbed me by the arms, looking me deep in the eyes. "Martyr, stay with me tonight," he urged quietly.

"I can't, War. Krisstopher's at home waiting for me."

"Come on, please… I'll drive ya home later if ya want."

"I'm sorry, War. I can't. Please don't be mad."

As much as I wanted to, there were a few good reasons why I couldn't: Krisstopher being one of them. I loved him, didn't I? It was hard to tell anymore what I felt. Everything always changed.

\* \* \*

About a week later, Jamie called to tell me she'd developed the pictures she took and wondered if I'd like to come over and see them. So Krisstopher and I went over to her dad's where she was staying. The house held many memories for me. I'd spent a lot of time there. As we sat in the living room, I recalled Stacie's graduation party with a smile.

That was the day I banged up my mom's [97]Oldsmobile on the way to pick up Ryan. It was pouring rain out, and some heavy metal dude on the freeway lost control of his car, slid up the embankment, and came barreling down in front of me, plowing into the front bumper. I felt sorry for him because he had no insurance, and let him go with the promise that he'd get some scrap metal and fix the car for us. Yeah right. I never heard from him again. Naiveté is an ugly lesson to learn, and one that I seemed to flunk over and over.

Jamie pulled out a box crammed full of pictures of War. I scanned through them eagerly while Krisstopher sat quietly beside us. The pictures were excellent. She'd succeeded in capturing the essence of his character. Black and whites of him injecting himself with heroin showed the desperate reality of an addict, while blurred psychedelic photos taken at low shutter speeds depicted his drug-induced euphoria. There was one that I absolutely loved. She showed it to me when Krisstopher got up to go to the bathroom: he was sitting on a metal garbage can in his room, clothed in nothing but a pair of leather briefs and his motorcycle boots. It was the epitome of War. The look in his eye was one of lust mixed with the confident, powerful radiance I'd come to know so well.

"Wow," I breathed.

"You want it?" she whispered.

"Really?" I asked excitedly.

"Yeah. I knew you'd like this one. That's why I waited until Krisstopher was gone." She slipped me the picture and I stuck it carefully in my purse.

When Krisstopher returned, we all went outside for some fresh air. The moon was full. It hung in the sky, a majestic globe representing the triune goddess Diana, a.k.a. Hecate and Selene. I wanted to charge my goddess ring with some of its energy. I lifted my forefinger in the air, pointing directly at it, and began whispering my alignments. A cat meowed suddenly, its shrill voice ripping through the blanket of quietness that had fallen over the subdivision.

"Where'd that come from?" somebody asked. I don't remember if it was Jamie or Krisstopher.

"Over there—in the bushes. See its eyes?"

By the neighbor's house, two small, fiery eyes flashed between the branches of shrubbery.

"It's a black cat," Krisstopher commented.

I fixed my eyes on it for a few moments, falling into a daze. When I shook myself out of it, Krisstopher and Jamie were heading back in the house. The screen door slammed behind them and I was alone. I turned around again to continue where I'd left off with my alignments. The cat meowed louder this time, as if demanding my attention. Something about it frightened me, and I wasn't sure why. I stopped and turned toward it once more.

"MEOWWW!!! MEOWWW!!! MEOWWW!!!" it continued. Then its voice began to change, the pitch lowering and distorting. Finally, the meow changed altogether into the wailing voice of a man. "*I LOVE YOU, MARTYR,*" he droned. "*I LOVE YOU.*"

A chill raced up my spine, accompanied by nervous excitement. War was communicating to me, even though he was in New York! I marveled at the fact that I was experiencing this without the use of any drugs. Jade was right: there *was* power if you found the right soul mate. *Much* power.

On the way home that night, I decided to relay all that I knew to Krisstopher: the tarot card spreads, the fact that War was my soul mate, and the dark power he possessed. I wanted to be completely honest with him—to warn him of the danger that threatened to break up our relationship. I told him, then, that I was sure the cat we'd seen had been War contacting me. To my surprise, he agreed, telling me that he also had gotten a really creepy feeling about the cat to begin with.

Both of us had heard stories about [98]Don Juan, a man who'd supposedly studied, among other things, the art of turning oneself into an animal through the use of magic powers. And our Wiccan books, along with other books we owned, spoke of how one did this by projecting his or her astral energy into a particular form. War had mastered this art. How?

The wizard necklace we'd discovered at Sharon's now served a purpose for me: a reminder of War the sorcerer. War the sage. War... the warlock. I'd consecrated it to the Craft, and it continuously hung around my neck as a symbol of his power.

## VI. TRUE LOVE

Buzzzzzz, Buzzzzzzz, Buzzzzzzz. The sound was almost intolerable, but I couldn't wake myself out of this dream. Buzzzzz, Buzzzzzzz, like a [99]swarm of flies—rattling my skull, vibrating every bone in my body. Even my jaw hurt.

A man's face. Was it War? It seemed to resemble him, but yet... I wasn't sure. Maybe in another life. He was evil. I felt it. Evil seeped out of him and into me. Uhhhhh, if only I could wake up. I tossed restlessly, somehow sore and aching. The man whispered in my ear, but the whispering was more like hissing. Poison venom. What was he saying? Some strange name—foreign sounding. Did it start with a 'B'? I broke free then, jerking upright in bed as the sunlight spilled through the window, nearly blinding me. Yet it was somehow comforting after *that* nightmare.

* * *

Beastulust, our new and improved band, was doing its first gig. Amazing how fast we'd sort of meshed and melded together into a perfect breed of goth.

Hazael was our drummer. His real name was Christopher, thus our guitar player suggested the alias in order to avoid confusion. Thin and lanky, he looked the part of a Michelangelo painting with his long, black, wavy hair and delicate features. Dark, dreamy eyes peered out just above high cheekbones on a satin skinned face. His lips were full and perfectly carved at the peak, or *Cupid's bow*, as it is often referred to. They seldom smiled, as it was just his nature to be grave. Once, he'd posed as Jesus for a clothing ad, lying in a makeshift Mary's arms like the famous Michelangelo's [100]*Pieta*. He did, in fact, resemble a young Jesus as earlier paintings depicted him.

I was amazed at how much his drum playing had improved since the first time I'd heard him. He had a way of knowing precisely what mood we were attempting to convey through our songs. For him, drumming wasn't just keeping a beat: it was a form of artistic expression. His drums were the canvas, his drumsticks the brush.

He was a quiet, reflective person. His recent experiences with a Ouija board sparked an interest in reincarnation. He and his friend Jennifer had summoned up a spirit who'd communicated to them that they all shared past lives together. Apparently the spirit, who called himself Bildad, presently did not occupy a bodily form, though he had previously. Hazael shared with us that Bildad was extremely possessive of he and Jennifer—especially Jennifer, whom he claimed to have had several romantic involvements with in times long past.

He prevented her from entering relationships with other males, causing them to abandon her or scaring them away somehow, often by launching them into confusion or depression. Occasionally, he even took his anger out on her personally, like the time he changed the cold shower water into scalding hot water that could not be adjusted. It seemed he was always doing something to create confusion and chaos. Hazael admitted that at first it was amusing, but now it was taking a more serious turn. Neither one of them knew how to get rid of Bildad the spirit.

I did a crystal ball reading for Hazael at his request. When I finished relaying to him the scenes I saw in the glass, he told me that they confirmed what Bildad had already told he and Jennifer concerning their past lives together.

He brought Jennifer to practice with him one night. Upon meeting her, I sensed something dark and oppressive about her. Granted, she hadn't exactly given me a warm reception to begin with, but that was beside the point. There was just a lot of negative energy coming from her. It seemed her aura was made up of tiny little daggers, stabbing away at anyone she came in contact with.

After practice, she wanted Krisstopher to do a tarot spread for her, so they went upstairs in our bedroom. They returned about forty-five minutes later, and then she asked me if I would do a crystal ball reading for her. I took her upstairs into the room once more.

She and I sat around the cloth-covered table and I lit a candle. For a long time, I peered into the ball but could see nothing. She waited, watching me. I felt a mental block that could not be broken, no matter how hard I tried. Embarrassed, I told her that I wasn't sure what was going on, but that I just could not divine anything for some reason. She told me it was because Bildad was in the room, preventing me from seeing anything. He was blocking my flow.

Try as I might, I could not bring myself to like her. I just knew she was after Krisstopher. I could sense it. She was very chummy with him, but very aloof with me. Krisstopher mentioned later that The Queen of Pentacles came up during one of the tarot spreads he did for her. I would definitely keep a close eye on her now. I could see she was trying to act mysterious and witchy so as to intrigue him.

When I mentioned to Fiend, our guitar player, that Jennifer might be The Queen of Pentacles Krisstopher was going to have his trial with, he told me not to worry.

Fiend was actually *Freddy*. He became Fiend after insisting upon a cool name for himself. Everyone had really unique names but him, he said. *Freddy* just didn't seem to jive with *Hazael, Krisstopher,* and *Martyr*. For some reason, he asked *me* to pick out a name for him. *Fiend* just sort of popped in my head one day, so I looked it up in our dictionary of magic to discover it meant *demon, imp,* or *a mischievous person*. Freddy loved it, immediately adopting it as his new alias. I had to admit, it fit him like a glove. It just had a sinister sound to it, and he was somewhat of a sinister person. He had an air of mystery about him that kept us all wondering.

He was older than us, though he wouldn't say how old. Of medium stature and also thin, he had neck length brown hair that he ratted out for the gothic rock star look. Unlike Hazael, his face was weathered, though not necessarily old looking. Depth of character was etched all over it. One knew by looking at him that he'd lived an eventful life, though just what all it entailed we weren't sure. He usually had a five o'clock shadow, an indication that he hadn't shaved in a couple of days. And he always wore a look of scrutiny—except when he was smiling— his mind probably constantly at work dissecting and bisecting every piece of conversation that went on.

Fiend was an unsolved riddle to all of us in the band. Krisstopher and Hazael looked up to him as a sort of spiritual adept. True, even I felt he qualified in this category. He never spoke of his experiences in great detail, but rather, issued forth spiritual parables every once in a while which kept us contemplating on the nature of his persona. Exactly *who* or *what* was he? We weren't quite sure. We only knew that he greatly admired [101] Aleister Crowley, as well as a few other masters he'd "studied with" that he was rather vague about. *Was he a Wiccan? Some sort of guru? A Satanist?* we all pondered among ourselves after he left practice or before he arrived. Sometimes, we'd call each other on the phone and exchange possible clues: bits and pieces of conversations, dreams, visions...

As a guitar player, Fiend showed exceptional talent. The sounds he created through his effects processor were phenomenal. They reminded me of the supernatural sounds I'd heard coming from Krisstopher's bass the night we'd been beamed aboard the Purple Flying Saucer. He complimented my keyboards quite nicely, knowing when to emerge from the shadows with his song of sorcery, and when to hide again and let me take the lead. With Krisstopher doing radical bass parts that often sounded like guitar because of the high fret, Fiend was quick to play the low end and mimic the bass sound that was lacking. It was amazing how they switched off and on in perfect harmony.

We'd practiced diligently for a few months, and now it was paying off. We were opening up for another band: Polysorbate 60. Drew, our short-lived guitar player before Fiend, was good friends with the band. That's how we got the show. He brought one of the members to a practice session just to introduce us. The kid looked about sixteen or seventeen at the most. The whole time we jammed, he just kept staring at me really freaky with a horrified expression on his face.

Afterward, I found out he'd had a dream about me even before meeting me. In the dream, he'd been running to his mother after something evil was trying to chase him, and then his mother turned around and it was me. I growled, *"I'm not your mother!"* in a really demonic voice or something. Then he woke up.

Though I laughed and tried to make light of the whole thing, it was pretty clear to see that he was hanging onto that dream for all it was worth. He refused to warm up to me in the least. He told Drew he wanted to go home.

We played the show anyway at a little dive bar out in the middle of what seemed to me like nowhere. It was a country type bar, but I guessed even The Sex Guns had to pay their dues to the cowpokes.

Fiend had just given me one of [102]Aleister Crowley's books for some reason, stating that I might find it interesting. We started setting up for the show then. I worked on assembling the huge aluminum keyboard stand I'd borrowed from Hazael's friend, who played keys in a local industrial band Lock Garage. Krisstopher distributed the candles everywhere and lit them. When I got the stand together, he crowned it with the finishing touch: a plastic skull head that lit up and made a spooky noise when I pushed a button. The sound guy came up to us then.

"Are you folks Satan worshipers?" he asked.

We stared at him, surprised by his question. He looked like someone from the Bob Seagull era—you know, kind of like an old hippie rocker—but he talked like country star Wailin' Jimmings. We started laughing then.

"Noooo... what makes you say that?" Krisstopher replied.

"I don't know. You guys just seem kind of evil. I mean, with all this *stuff* here," he pointed to our stage props, "and the way you all are dressed..."

I looked at Krisstopher then and shook my head, thinking to myself that this guy was obviously spiritually deprived—nice, but definitely not enlightened.

After Polysorbate finished their half hour set, we made our big debut in front of about twenty people. The lights dimmed and we embarked on our eerie musical adventure. My [103]Korg decided to bite the dust right then and there, so I gave Fiend a stressed look, motioning for him to fill in the intro part with some sound effects. He got the hint, covering for me, and we launched into the first song. Immediately, everyone started moving forward from the back where they'd been sitting to gather around the stage, their eyes wide as if they were in some sort of hypnotic trance.

*Wow, they love us!* I thought.

It was a rush to know that people actually appreciated our talent. Polysorbate abruptly got up from where they'd been sitting and walked out after our second song like they were utterly appalled.

*They're just jealous*, I told myself.

Later, we saw them at [104]Denny's Restaurant. They didn't say a word to us, and left shortly after we sat down. I felt like the town leper or something.

It turned out my [105]Korg shorted out due to corrosion, as Thor had decided to *relieve himself* on the keys a year and a half prior. However, a brilliant friend of mine took it apart and cleaned it about five years later, after which it worked like new. In the meantime, Hazael's pal from Lock Garage came through again, selling me a [106]Kawaii keyboard for a hundred dollars to replace my dear departed [107]Korg. It was well worth the money and then some, with the absolute ultimate effects.

\* \* \*

**If I'm doing positive magic to harm no one, then why do I feel like I'm going insane? Please help me. I feel I'm losing my mind. What's wrong with me?**

I carefully folded the piece of paper and stuck it inside my God Box. Surely I'd get an answer. As I closed the lid, I realized that I'd neglected to mention the goddess when I'd decorated the outside of the box. I took a marker now, drawing a slash after the word *God*, and wrote

GODDESS

Then I included pentagrams on each of the four sides, empowering them as I drew them.

There was such an unbearable tightness in my head lately. The confusion was greater than ever before. Coupled with a sudden case of severe depression, it was more than I could handle. I felt really afraid. Afraid for myself. I kept getting this picture of me sitting in some mental institution rocking back and forth while staring out the window with a blank expression on my face.

The job I had now wasn't helping matters any. I worked with four mentally handicapped women who lived in an apartment complex nearby. As their personal care worker, it was my responsibility to drive them to and from work, and to run errands; as well as to assist them in budget planning and meal preparation.

Feeling I needed help myself, it was extremely difficult listening to their problems each and every day. They often vented their anger and frustration on me when they felt they needed to lash out at someone. The more I studied their thinking and behavior patterns, I found myself wondering if perhaps I belonged right alongside them. Especially when confusion spells attacked quite often, leaving my head spinning.

One of them said, "Man, what's wrong with you? You're acting *mental* lately." Ironically enough, she was the one I drove to a psychiatrist once a week. A very angry young woman, she was also an epileptic: prone to occasional seizures. When I accepted the job, I was told by my supervisor that I would soon take the necessary health courses to equip me for her seizures. However, she had one in the van while I was driving, leaving me frightened and clueless because I still hadn't attended any courses.

Another one of the women was paralyzed, confined to a wheelchair due to a mild case of cerebral palsy. Overweight, she was heavier than a ton of bricks—all *dead* weight since she could not move the lower half of her body at all—and I had the unpleasant experience of trying to lift her back into her wheelchair when she fell out; a nearly impossible feat. I felt helpless, and very unqualified.

I'd drive her to work in the van, loading her onto the wheelchair ramp and making sure she was fastened securely in place. While I waited for her to finish her shift, I usually had a good three hours of free time on my hands before I was back on the clock again. I spent that time at home scrying in my crystal ball.

I really missed War. I worried about him profusely, knowing he was somewhere shooting up—squatting here and there in abandoned buildings with junkies so he could score. I'd had a dream about him recently, and it scared me: I was calling his name, looking everywhere for him. I wandered over to the ruins of what had once been a great [108]castle. Only the foundation was left now, and even that was crumbling away into nothing. For some reason, my final perception of the dream was the terrible feeling I had that he was dead. Upon waking, however, I remembered it no more until Jason mentioned there was a rumor going around that War had died in New York. Suddenly the dream came flooding back to me. I quickly relayed it to him, frightened that it might be true.

Jamie had also heard the rumor. Both of us were worried. We decided to check on him, calling the number in New York he'd left us. Hopefully he was still there, as he mentioned he'd only be there for a little while.

I asked to speak to him. To our relief, they called him to the phone. I was elated to hear his voice again, though he sounded somewhat detached. He was nice enough, but I'd expected an in-depth discussion as to whether or not I'd perceived the spiritual messages he'd communicated to me. Instead, he kept the conversation rather trivial. Puzzled, I handed the phone to Jamie and she talked to him for a few minutes. Then he let us go, mentioning that he might be moving back to Ann Arbor soon.

His messages continued. My scrying abilities became greatly enhanced almost overnight. I didn't have to use the crystal ball to see him anymore. I saw his name in walls and in carpeting. I saw him in drinking glasses with his bright pink hair, staring at me with those dark eyes. But I'd also witnessed a vision in one of my medium sized crystals that really disturbed me:

A circle of people were standing around, dressed in hooded black cloaks. Two of the figures seemed more prominent than the rest. They caught my attention, so I zeroed in on them. A familiar feeling suddenly washed over me. I could see now that the taller figure was a man, while the shorter was a woman. I looked on in horror as the man held a bloody human body part in his hand—a male procreative body part, to be exact, which he scalped with a knife. He urged the woman to participate, but she refused. I knew then that this had been War and I in another life. We'd been part of a coven together. Even then I'd wanted nothing to do with his evil schemes.

The fact that he was sacrificing such a body part confirmed to me he was highly skilled in the area of sex magic; he'd sacrificed that which he desired to gain. Jamie mentioned there was something about him that women loved. She was right. I felt a sensual energy whenever I was around him that permeated the atmosphere. Never had I felt such a strong aura like this coming from a person, though I'd sensed people's feelings in the past on a smaller scale.

I'd been reading a book on astral projection which raved about the advantage of *astral sex:* when two people's spirits left their fleshly bodies and meshed together on the astral plane. Supposedly one hadn't really lived until he or she experienced this.

And then I'd come across a few other statements, either through books or people, concerning the powerfully incredible arena of sex magic. As Jade had briefly mentioned the intimate experience two soul mates could share, I'd also heard Krisstopher speak of his ex-girlfriend Liza, the black witch. The power between them during sexual relations once made the bed lift up off the floor and float in the air!

I wondered why he and I could not experience such things together. I always felt dull in comparison next to Liza the Enchantress or Mikal the Pure One who never partied yet somehow held a piece of Krisstopher's heart, even though he'd dumped her.

What would it be like to have a man be so intoxicated by my beauty and femininity, my inner essence and spirituality, that he desired only me and me alone? No porn needed to motivate him, as my ex-husband. No other women to compete with as I always felt where Krisstopher was concerned. Just my beloved prince and I. Forever.

War offered a ray of hope that something special could be shared between two people—something comparable to a fairy tale romance that transcended time and space. Though it was a bit murky and frightening, it appealed to me because I knew it to be deeper than anything I'd ever felt before: the greatest intrinsic experience where a member of the opposite sex was concerned. And I had a feeling that he was very much aware of this. He'd obviously taken great pains to pursue these kinds of experiences himself, which told me he was more suited to me than anyone else because at least we were on the same level.

\* \* \*

I folded up the letter now, one of my tears dripping onto the lined paper scented with patchouli oil, and slipped it inside the envelope to mail to War in New York. In it, I'd poured out my heart—nothing short of all I felt for him. The love, the fear, the angst. The intense passion and lust.

He'd lit the fire burning within me—the eternal flame that blazed out of control. It seemed I couldn't get away from him—he was everywhere and in everything. I begged him to stop putting this spell on me, reminding him that I knew he was involved in some kind of black magic because The Devil card kept popping up in my tarot spreads.

'I'VE NEVER FELT LIKE THIS BEFORE ABOUT ANYONE,' I wrote, 'BUT IT HAS GOT TO STOP. PLEASE. I CAN'T TAKE IT ANYMORE. I KNOW YOU'RE MY SOUL MATE, BUT WE CAN'T BE WITH EACH OTHER. I LOVE YOU SO MUCH, BUT YOUR POWER IS EVIL.'

Crying out of helplessness mixed with yearning, I now traced an invisible pentagram over the letter with my finger and stuck it in the mailbox.

\* \* \*

Fiend was emerging from the shadows to play a deeper role in the scheme of things than I'd originally thought. I began discerning that he very much desired me by the looks and comments he directed my way. More signs began pointing to the fact that he possessed spiritual skills further along than those of mine or Krisstopher's.

For instance, once Drew and Krisstopher and I went to a medieval festival after which we were to meet Hazael and Fiend so we could go to a few Detroit bars and promote our band. We returned from the festival, decked out in gothic array and still a little amped from the LSD we'd taken, though it was a weak hit which offered no hallucinations. I

165

telephoned Fiend to find out where and when we'd meet. To my surprise, he told me to tell Krisstopher to change that *God-awful outfit* he had on, though we hadn't seen him at all that day and so wondered how he knew what Krisstopher was wearing.

"You look great, as usual, Martyr," he added, "but that garb Krisstopher has on has to go."

It took us both for a loop, since Krisstopher was wearing some salmon colored jeans with bleach spots and ink pen writing on them, a change from his usual black attire. He'd even asked me earlier that day if they looked okay. *I* thought so, but apparently Fiend didn't. He mentioned something about dressing up to look the part of a gothic band. I changed outfits then, too, replacing the white mini skirt I had on with a black one.

Had Fiend merely taken a chance and called our bluff to see if he could psyche us out? This was entirely possible. Still, judging from the vibes we continually got from him, it seemed more likely that he obtained the knowledge supernaturally.

Hazael was pretty shaken up about a vision he'd had recently while fully awake: Fiend was a very ugly green monster with horns on his head, resembling the Devil himself, and he was smiling deviously. We both agreed that whatever he was involved in was evil, for the most part. Yet it seemed a different kind of evil than what I sensed with War. I often wondered whose was worse. It was hard to tell. All I knew was that Fiend's dark powers did not affect me in the same way. I knew we were connected—that both he and Hazael were also soul mates from past lives, which explained why our band as well as our personalities melded together so nicely. But it was no comparison to the connection that existed between War and me. *Nothing* compared to the way he made me feel. Absolutely nothing.

However, it was interesting that at our second gig my friend Elyse had commented that she could feel the power between Fiend and me. She didn't mention anything about Krisstopher or Hazael, almost as if we two were the main energy conductors in the band—the generators, if you will. I'd said something to her once about his personal magnetism and spiritual background. Apparently she sensed what I was talking about.

I, on the other hand, felt energy from the band as a complete unit. It hovered in the air like ectoplasm, a harmonious hum heard only to those tuned to the frequency.

*"I see your life force, it's fading,* [109]*Emmanuelle!"* I half-sang, half-shouted over the music.

I'd chosen the name Emmanuelle after it popped in my head one day, then arranged the letters to equal the negative vibration fifteen, also equal to The Devil card in the tarot deck. Each letter in the name was assigned a different number containing a specific vibration, which when added, totaled fifteen. I'd written the song about War and his heroin addiction; how it was draining the life out of him as its negative energy coursed through his veins.

*"You're falling, falling. I'm calling, calling!"*

We'd played that October night at a well-known local dive bar in Hamtramck, the Polish offshoot of Detroit. The gig had been a disaster, with the soundman purposely turning down my vocals and making a mess of everything, as well as cutting our set in half.

We knew it was because the headlining band, Kill His Majesty, wanted their friend's band Jerome's Wheel of Fortune to open up for them; though we'd booked the show even before they did. Fiend had a little argument with the bass player over it, and thus Kurt the soundman provided audio mixing at its 'best.' Obviously he sided with Kill His Majesty for reasons beyond my grasp, although I did suspect *somebody* else had a hand in things as well. I didn't know exactly who, but I felt a blocking power—a force of some kind that helped throw a wrench into the whole evening. Jennifer was there. Maybe she and Bildad were raining on our parade.

Afterwards as we were breaking down our set, Kurt came up to me with an evil smile on his face and asked in a kiddy sounding voice, "Oh, are you upset because *Uncle Kurt* messed up your vocals?" I knew for sure then that I hadn't just imagined it: there'd *definitely* been a plot against us.

So as I sat at the table downing rum and [110]Cokes, and [111]Heinekins, I crossed over into the black for just a moment, though others liked to call it *gray* magic. I'd read in [112]Crowley's book that there are times when one has to use a bit of negative power, as if it isn't possible to be completely white. One's lust for power, especially upon discovering he or she has attained that power, inevitably leads to the gray as circumstances present themselves. Sometimes it is merely for purposes of self-defense. Other times it is a means to gain an end.

This would be the first time that I could recall crossing over, though I had a most uneasy feeling accompanying it. I watched the bass player from Kill His Majesty on stage, wearing a black onyx stone around his neck which was often indicative of negative energy. I wondered if he hadn't been the one to put a damper on the evening. After all, he and Fiend had been arguing about us opening for them. Squinting really hard, I imagined with all my might for a moment that he would mess up on the song while my ears listened closely for the result of my effort. Oddly enough, he seemed to be playing everything in key—I could hear nothing out of whack. It was as if a wall was around him and I couldn't touch him.

However, I'd never endeavored to do such things before. Something told me it wasn't quite as easy as I thought. Perhaps that's why black magic required a lot of ritual and sacrifice. The more you did to please the forces of evil, supposedly the more power they granted you. One book I'd recently read discussed the importance of animal sacrifice. Furthermore, the strange invocations it included seemed demonic judging from some of the weird names of the deities mentioned.

After a moment of seething anger, I shrugged off the fact that I was unable to curse the bass player. Anyway, it only heaped bad karma to me in the long run. I reminded myself that I still had power—but just a different kind. After all, people commented that they sensed it.

\* \* \*

I copied a few notes from [113]Crowley's book and gave it back to Fiend, explaining that it was a little too black to suit me. He argued that Crowley had not been a black magician, but I begged to differ. He told me that one of Crowley's organizations, [114]The Golden Dawn, was a highly respected spiritual sect. Maybe, but all I knew was the book wasn't on my most favored reading list. Besides, it seemed highly complicated to me with all the diagrams and hard-to-pronounce names. I preferred to stick to my Wiccan/positive magic books.

I wasn't certain just what I was learning from Fiend as of yet, but I knew that he must have been led in my path for a reason. Surely *something* was evolving out of our connection. After all, we'd been together in another life before. So apparently we had some kind of karma to work out. Most likely he was sent to teach me something, as War was also teaching me. Both of them refused to openly discuss their spiritual backgrounds. This was the sign of a true adept—one who knew better than to blab his experiential knowledge to anyone who came along. Those who were spiritually minded would pick up on it without having to be told.

That would explain why War preferred instead to reveal his true identity to me in other ways—ways more fitting. I recalled all the times he'd spoken aloud my thoughts, or confirmed things that I'd divined. And now that we were apart, he communicated to me through other mediums. Perhaps he was teaching me to sharpen my intuition—to follow my heart despite what the extraneous information seemed to convey. Perhaps I needed only to believe. The black cat lingered in my mind as I recalled his words to me: *"I LOVE YOU, MARTYR."*

The fire burned on, unquenchable.

* * *

I'd been painting another tarot card for my own personal deck when I noticed my crystal ball actually glowing. Crawling over to it, I peered down into its depths.

Fish turning into... [115]aliens. Two aliens stared at me with large, sunken eyes. They were green/brown in color. I sensed they were trying to give me a message of some kind. It seemed they were a higher life form spiritually. Stonehenge seemed to point to UFOs, and so did the legend of Atlantis, a city my father wrote of in his poetry which had mysteriously disappeared like objects crossing the Bermuda Triangle. Perhaps, then, the places and objects entered that other dimension known as the spirit world, and perhaps aliens had something to do with it. As I marveled at the vision, it suddenly vanished, replaced by a wedding.

A wedding? Yes, two people were dressed in white, and I recognized one to be the bride with her flowing white gown. Zeroing in on the vision, I now saw the [116]groom with his long, black hair. He was holding something in his hand. A… [117]chalice, yes, and he wanted the [118]bride to partake of it. As he stared at her, I looked intently into her face. It was then that I felt she was supposed to be me.

\* \* \*

My prince. My beautiful War. A [119]Coke in my hands, lying on the bed listening to The Field of Fallen Angels, I felt him so strongly that I broke down in tears once more. A terrible sadness in my soul. An overwhelming emptiness.

> *"Remember moments past*
> *When I stroked your hair*
> *I am the unblessed living*
> *On promises…"*

*Promises. Yes, War. We must have made them together, and you are determined that I adhere to mine. If only… if only you could be here right now. I wish you could hold me in your arms.*

He frequented my tarot readings quite often lately as the Knight of Pentacles: the man with the magic power—the warlock. I'd even painted my own version of the card: him arrayed in a shining suit of armor, only his dark eyes peering boldly through the helmet. Riding with fury on a large, black horse with flames for a mane. Storming into my life once more, as he'd done countless times in the past.

> *"The sunset in your eyes*
> *The purpose of my life…"*

He was speaking to me now through the song—speaking of our past life together in which he yearned for me to return to him. Death could not part us:

170

*"Come, my princess, rise*
*From your sleep now, rise*
*I am the unblessed hanging*
*On your promises...*
*And you leave*
*To find new highways*
*Another road in time*
*But you'll burn with me."*

No—he wasn't evil! I could help him. I could change him. And then we could finally be together for eternity...

*"Remember moments past*
*When I stroked your hair*
*My eternal place*
*Your shadows of my mind*
*I praise you, lady*
*Because you've changed me."*

—The Field of Fallen Angels

I was gaining a deeper interest in astral projection. As of yet, I hadn't actually done it, though once at Jasmine's I nearly succeeded. I concentrated really hard that night on her ceiling, imagining I needed to reach it. As if by magic, I felt myself begin to levitate upward, a marvelous floating sensation. Suddenly the front door slammed with a bang as Camron entered the apartment, sending me back into my body with a jolt.

I was still a little fearful of it, remembering what my father had told me about his experience. He'd warned me that it was evil, as well as a good way to get a demon inside my body because it could enter in when I was floating around. The books I'd read claimed this wasn't true because one had an astral cord that still attached them to their body and went on for miles before it could actually be broken, thus leaving no vacancy for demons. However, the books also warned that the lower realms were occupied by devious creatures: evil spirits waiting to attack. The astral traveler needed to learn how to raise himself to a higher realm to *escape their danger*. What danger?

In addition to willful astral projection, people supposedly could *involuntarily* leave their bodies; for instance, while asleep. Much like dreaming, they would spontaneously drift into any given set of circumstances and be forced to react. This wasn't necessarily bad—although not as beneficial as having complete control over their course of travel. A second way they could involuntarily project is by another soul pulling them out of their body—a soul already occupying the astral plane. A frightening thought, unless perhaps one was pulled out by the *right* soul. Like War.

I myself preferred the idea of projecting while asleep. It seemed to tie in with what I was reading about dreamwork: having greater control over one's dream life through the use of practical magic.

I placed consecrated crystals under my pillow that I'd empowered with energy to produce spiritual night visions. It was my desire that by doing so, certain people would enter my dreams and I could communicate to them this way: War being first and foremost; and next, Fiend, who always provoked my interest.

\* \* \*

I put a spell out for a new job—*the perfect job according to the free will of all* to come to me. It was time to quit my job as a caregiver—to weed out the negativity in my life. Perhaps then my focus would be clear again. I could no longer handle the emotional baggage I carried for four other people. My own baggage was heavy enough without their extra load. Krisstopher was also tired, as was my mom, of me coming home crying and yelling after being put down and shouted at the entire day by the mentally handicapped women. I obviously needed a less stressful line of employment.

So I applied at the music store. Though Krisstopher no longer worked there (he now worked at a nursery and crafts outlet), at least I'd work with Jason if I got hired. Surrounded by music and one of my best friends all day long sounded like the perfect job to me.

After casting the spell, I saw in my crystal ball a rather blurry picture of a man with short, blond, slicked back hair. A few hours later, I received a phone call from the music store manager. He wanted to interview me. Upon meeting him, I was surprised to discover he had short, blond, slicked back hair; greatly resembling the man I'd seen in the crystal ball. I was hired on the spot.

While training on the cash register at work, I met Ian. He was one of the assistant managers in charge that night. His hair was long and wavy; dark brown. His eyes were also dark and brooding, and he wore a neatly trimmed goatee. A metal head, he was the lead singer in a band: Black Hymn. I instantly became shy and embarrassed upon our introduction.

As a long line of people suddenly gathered at the register, I panicked. Ian came to help me, and it was then that I frantically fumbled to open a roll of quarters, only to have them fly into the air and scatter in three different directions.

"Dude, chill out, would you?" he asked. "It's going to be okay." He showed me how to open quarters by cracking them on the edge of the drawer. Then after the line died down, he squeezed past me to go to the manager's office, gently grabbing me by both hips to get me to move. I felt a surge of passion race through me.

I liked when he opened or closed the store on my shift. He knew I was a witch, and it seemed he was a little intrigued by it. Maybe even creeped, I don't know. When our eyes met sometimes from across the store, me at the register and him at the video counter, he'd mumble, "Saatan!" in a spooky voice. He pretty much teased me about the whole thing, but in a nice way.

\* \* \*

I was sleeping when suddenly I became aware of the fact that I wasn't sleeping anymore. My eyes were still closed, but I could hear Krisstopher snoring beside me. I could feel the glare coming from the light over the anole's aquarium—bright shadows behind my eyelids. Now I was lifting up, up, up... I didn't want to open my eyes for fear I'd ruin the experience.

A vision appeared in my mind. I saw it with the utmost clarity—not only saw it, but *felt* it. Black and white tile floors. White marker cards behind CDs. I was at work. Literally. I *had* to be astral projecting, because the store was deserted just as it would be this time of night. I looked around now. Of all places to be, why was I here? Had someone brought me here? Yes, someone *must* have—but who? Who would bring me to work? Maybe… Ian!

*Ian?* I called now in my mind. No response. *Ian?* Hmmm… was *Fiend* the instigator of this whole thing? Yeah, probably. *Fiend, is that you? Fiend?*

Suddenly I was transported to what felt like another plane of existence. I was in a room, and all around me were large [120]crystals. They projected hues of rainbows, like auras, which wrapped me in waves of splendor. I felt… euphoric, like nothing I'd ever experienced. I wondered for a brief moment if perhaps I was frying on acid. No, of course not—I'd been sleeping before. Anyway, this feeling… no drug compared. My mind struggled to identify it—to put it into words.

And then I was floating. Peacefully floating like a cloud. I stopped. A tunnel appeared before my eyes. Gazing into its darkness, I was drawn like a moth to the light shining at the end of it. [121]A man dressed in white stood there. He *was* the shining light. His hair was semi-long, but I could not discern the color since his whole being was glowing like lightning. [122]He stretched out his arms toward me, as if beckoning for me to come join him.

*War?* I called. Instantly he disappeared and I felt my soul gently return to my body. I opened my eyes to see the room as I'd sensed it earlier: Krisstopher beside me still snoring, and the lizard light glaring.

* * *

The spider on the ceiling. Amazing how he crawled around, seeming to follow me wherever I went. Even more amazing was that I'd just seen a vision of him less than an hour ago in my crystal ball with the word WAR appearing directly above him. Was it… could it be… *War?* Well, if someone told me [123]Don Juan had changed into a black crow, and if War had already changed into a cat, then why not a spider?

Fear washed over me suddenly as I pictured Krisstopher coming in the room and smooshing him with a [124]Kleenex. The astral projection books warned that certain people might spot the *vehicle*, or image you chose to manifest your energy as, and try to hurt you. Not that Krisstopher would know it was War. He'd simply think it was a spider.

"War," I whispered now to the spider, "War, I know it's you. You have to leave the room. Quick—before Krisstopher spots you and kills you." It stopped abruptly, as if listening. "Leave—go on! Please..." I pleaded with it. To my surprise, it started crawling toward the door, then paused again. "Go on! Leave!"

Crawl crawl. Crawl crawl. Crawl. Crawl crawl crawl. Out the door and into the hallway.

* * *

Krisstopher was in the shower. I sat on the bedroom floor with my cards spread out in front of me, Zain watching from his usual roost on the clothes shoot. Suddenly he cracked his tail indignantly. I looked up from the reading I was doing to stare at him curiously. He appeared upset for some reason. His dewlap was puffed out and he was bobbing his head up and down.

"What is it, Zain?" I asked. "What's wrong?"

Arching his back like a cat prepared to attack, he stiffened his tail into a whip. CRAACK! it went again. I watched as he moved his head around in circles, seeming to follow something with his eyes—something that only *he* could see.

With a jump, he was off of the clothes shoot and onto the floor. He marched right for me, gazing upward, still pursuing whatever he saw with his eyes. Round and round went his head like he was following loops in the air. With another jump he was in my lap, climbing onto my sweater. It appeared from the direction he was looking that the invisible substance was now hovering just above my head. He pulled himself onto my shoulder, trying to reach it, while I sat very still, unsure of what to do. The substance must have moved then, because he crawled down from my shoulder and back onto the floor.

Cracking his tail again, he chased it around the room. Toward the bed. Toward the dresser. Toward the TV. Finally, bolting at the door, he stopped abruptly right on the threshold and stared out into the hallway for a few moments. It was gone.

I gave a sigh of relief as he turned and began calmly making his way toward the clothes shoot once more, as proud as a cat who'd just rid the house of a mouse. Yet, I detected a terror in his eyes. A terror I'd never seen before. Something had been in the room, and my animal familiar had protected me. *What or who* was it? Somebody astral projecting? Fiend? War? Whatever it was, Zain didn't like it.

"Good boy, Zainy," I told him now, petting him on the head. "That's a good boy." For the first time in a long time, I felt afraid. And I wasn't sure why.

\* \* \*

Pathworking: a process of traveling spheres and paths on the tree of life in order to advance spiritually. Every traveler must endure trials—testing in order to perfect his or her soul. Every traveler must experience certain paths in order to reach the next level, and certain spheres before moving to the next plain of existence in the spirit realm. Krisstopher bought me a book recently that explained this journey in detail, as well as instructed the neophyte on how to accomplish it with greater ease.

I lie in bed, my eyes closed, inhaling the aroma of ylang ylang incense that this particular path I was traveling called for. Various crystals and stones surrounded my body to help empower my journey. I finished my breathing and chakra exercises.

Then, with intense concentration, I imagined the old tree deep in the heart of a tropical forest, next to a babbling brook. It was a big [125]tree, and within the hollow of its trunk a door suddenly appeared. Stepping through it, I found myself inside the tree, in a dark little room with a hard, earthen floor. Directly in the middle of the room stood a [126]table. And on the table, I noticed a [127]big, black, leather bound book collecting dust. I knew I would soon have to open the book and read it. Walking over to it, I touched the cover with curiosity.

*Leviathan*, the giant [128]snake that lived in the tree, whispered that before I could read it, I needed to gain the wisdom necessary to understand its contents. [129]This wisdom, he said, could only be gained by allowing him to bite me.

*Bite* me? No, I wasn't ready for that yet.

\* \* \*

Another crystal ball vision that really disturbed me: I saw Zain lying on his hot rock on the clothes shoot. [130]Next, I saw a streak of what appeared to be smoke, which quickly turned into a miniature sized War, drifting through the air and right into his body, where he disappeared. Had War entered Zain? I didn't quite understand what the vision meant.

\* \* \*

Jason called me one afternoon to ask if Krisstopher and I wanted to go to the Reptile Haus, a nightclub in Ypsilanti. He said he could get some acid, and that maybe we'd be able to talk to the owner about playing there. Bruce with the frohawk was coming along. Apparently Jason and he had been friends for a while. "Oh yeah, I guess *War's* back in town," he mentioned toward the end of our conversation. My heart skipped a beat.

"Really? Do you think he might be there?"

"I don't know...I guess he hangs out at The Burning Flame a lot, which is right next to there. But I doubt it. I really don't think he's into the nightclub scene." Still, I had hope.

We picked Bruce up at his house and grabbed something to eat. Unlike the first time I'd met him at War's, he was the master of conversation tonight. He sat staring at me across the table in the restaurant, jabbering on and on. I marveled at the change in his mood.

This time he dressed like he was having a slight beatnik attack, kind of like when I had my Stacie Hicks/gypsy attacks (Stacie was a hippie Wiccan singer who dressed in long, flowing outfits). He'd grown a slight goatee, and he had on a little reggae beanie cap and a bunch of necklaces. I noticed a few cool medallions with weird symbols on them and asked where he got them. He told me that a guy at the Darkroom made them. I decided I wanted the guy to make me one with a big pentagram on it and some other Wiccan stuff.

We took the acid and headed over to the Reptile Haus. The parking lot was pretty vacant since it was still early, so we stood around for a few minutes and talked. Jason introduced us to the DJ, who was heading inside with a box of records. Then he pointed to a sign picturing a flickering flame and we followed him inside a door directly beneath a striped awning.

We were now in The Burning Flame. A small bar room, it was cluttered with pictures on every square inch of wall and little tables crammed together. The biggest focal point in the place was the actual bar itself, behind which glistened rows of bottles guaranteed to please any palate and temporarily cure any wound. I was presently experiencing a happy, racy feeling as the LSD kicked in. It was going to be a mild hit.

Jason approached the bar, where his sister Jane sat beside a guy in a black tuke, light blue down ski vest and dirty hiking boots. As I walked past them in search of the rest room, I suddenly heard War's unmistakable voice say hello to me. Stopping in my tracks, I peered around anxiously to see where it was coming from. To my surprise, he was the guy in the ski vest next to Jane. I hadn't recognized him without his usual punk rock attire.

He mentioned he'd just gotten off work at his uncle's factory. I was glad he was working. When I asked where his leather was, he told me he traded it in New York for some crack. I didn't know why, but I felt a small loss when I realized I would never see that awesome jacket again. Maybe because it was a part of him I'd come to know and love. It fit his image so perfectly.

"Man, you spent so much *time* on that," I said, disappointment in my voice.

"Yeah, I know," he agreed a little sadly. "But I can always make another one."

As we talked some more, I tried playing it cool, acting nonchalant. But inside, I wanted desperately just to ditch everyone else and hang out with him the rest of the night. Jane and I chatted briefly for a moment, and then I told War we were going to the Reptile Haus. He mentioned something about being barred from there. I was bummed.

* * *

Techno-house music boomed. The dance floor shook as alternative club goers spun and gyrated to the beat. A mirrored disco ball hung from the ceiling, surrounding them with prisms of colored light. I followed Jason, Bruce, and Krisstopher to the back of the club. We were going to play pool.

The green felt table looked incredibly green. Choosing the shortest, lightest stick I could find, I chalked up, all the while thinking to myself that I hated playing pool in public. I wasn't very good at it, and I hated when people stood around and watched me. But nobody was paying attention. We were at the furthest table in the back. Somebody else was playing at the next table over, but luckily they were minding their own business. Besides, with a few drinks in me I wouldn't care who watched. Except...

War! My eyes spotted him wandering around near the front of the bar. They must have let him in after all. He glanced over at me and made his way to the first pool table where apparently he knew someone playing.

"Your turn, Martyr."

"Huh? Oh!" I moved into position, eyeing War again before making my shot. Good. He had his head turned the other way. Oops. Missed.

The black walls were covered with really weird paintings: faces... eyeballs... strange winged creatures... I dug them.

War was looking my way again. I continued to play it cool, laughing and shooting pool like it was no big deal. I even managed to get a couple of balls in the pocket. The alcohol must have been kicking in. It was hard to tell with the adrenaline rush I had from the acid. I didn't want to get too drunk, because then it made for a weird trip. System shock set in whenever that happened, and my body felt like a car: stopping, accelerating, slowing down... stopping, accelerating, slowing down... I couldn't really enjoy hallucinations then either, because the alcohol canceled them out. Except for in the case of the Puke Punch. That had been a major exception.

But this was another non-visual hit we'd taken anyway. I could tell because my senses were sharpened, enhancing my inner awareness of things, but everything looked pretty much the same unless I really concentrated. With this kind of hit, I always had to dig deeper if I wanted to experience anything. Coupled with magic powers, however, it made for an interesting adventure. Not too heavy so that I couldn't control myself, but more focused to where I could scry or tune in on things with a little added spiritual boost than if I had just been completely straight.

Our fascination with pool soon ended. Jason and Bruce sat down at a cocktail table near the front while Krisstopher and I went off to explore. We ended up in another room furnished with an old couch and matching chair. Plopping down on the couch, which was broken in quite nicely, we admired the staircase directly in front of us leading to a closed off room. It reminded us both of something out of a horror flick, with its old chipped wooden banister and carpeted stairs. I thought it to be rather romantic in the gothic sense as I pictured a whole scenario in my mind involving the staircase.

"Can't you just picture Dracula walking down those steps right now, his satin cape flowing behind him?" I asked Krisstopher.

"Yeah!" he said, getting up to play the part. He started up the stairs.

Just then War entered the room, taking my breath away. "Heyyyy, what are ya guys doin'?"

"We're just kicking back, admiring the staircase," I told him. He looked happy to see me. I felt he was checking up on me to see if I was still around.

"That's cool," he replied, making his way toward the rest room. I wanted to tune into him now. To figure out what was going on in his mind.

We went back out into the bar area, sitting down next to Jason and Bruce at the table. A few minutes later, War sauntered over to the bar and sat down on one of the stools. I watched him for a moment, concentrating. Bruce started talking then, interrupting my thought process. I waited for him to finish, but he never did.

His sentences all ran together without a pause in between. He blabbed on and on about psycho-intelligent concepts that I didn't feel in the least like grasping: those kind of theoretical philosophical discussions that could last for hours—or even days. I didn't *have* hours or days. The bar would be closing soon and War would be leaving. How could this be happening?! I tried moving to another table to escape the psychobabble. He followed. I tried talking to Jason and Krisstopher, but they were too busy watching people. I wanted to watch people too! Why wouldn't he leave me alone? I didn't want to be rude and tell him to shut up because I just couldn't handle his depth of character right now. He might not understand and take it the wrong way. But my head was pounding and I felt dizzy from listening to him while still trying to tune in to War. I felt he had a mental straw and was sucking away at my brain, draining the energy right out of it. Like a spiritual vampire.

And then the lights came on, blinding everyone. The Reptile Haus was closing. My heart sank as people began filing out the door. I watched War finish up his beer, then followed Jason and Krisstopher out into the parking lot, Bruce shuffling behind me. It was pouring rain outside. Within seconds we were all drenched. I turned around to take one last look at War. Where was he? There he was, walking out the door now, about twenty feet behind us and looking straight at me. I tried playing it cool.

[131]"I'm *melll-ting*. I'm *melll-ting!*" I cried, mimicking the Wicked Witch of the West from *The Wizard of Oz*. And I was. For my beautiful War.

"If anyone wants ta hang out and party at my house, they can!" he called out suddenly.

"Jason, let's see what War's doing. You wanna go back to *his* house?" I asked excitedly.

"No… that's *lame*, man. He's probably just going to have a couple of *girls* over or something," he answered, my heart sinking. Disappointed, I followed them to the back of the parking lot and the four of us piled in his little car once more, Bruce squeezing into the front seat. I felt sorry for him. Being so big, he was literally squished in between the seat and the dashboard. To make matters worse, the sunroof was leaking majorly, and buckets of water dumped on his head while Jason laughed hysterically at his dilemma. It was kind of funny. Even Krisstopher and I had to laugh. We handed him some towels that were in the back seat and he tried plugging up the leak. After about ten minutes, however, they were sopped. He and Jason kept wringing them out. Needless to say, he was not a happy camper.

We stopped at the legendary Heavenly Burgers, where I tasted my first heavenly hamburger along with a root beer float. Then we pulled up in front of the huge wall mural on the side of the building next door.

"Check this out," Jason said excitedly, pointing at it. It was an old advertisement for beer, featuring a medieval scene complete with a castle and some elves.

"Wow, how cool!" I breathed, mesmerized by the elves standing outside the castle drinking little bottles of magic brew. They seemed alive, their beady little eyes sparkling at us. Jason turned on The Mythical Micro Dots and the voice of Elliot Spell hissed and slithered like a charming snake while layered waves of celestial keyboards and tribal drums entranced us all.

Soon enough, however, I was bored with the wall. I wanted to know what War was doing. If only I could be with him right now! The windshield served as a large looking glass for me. I concentrated for a moment, staring into it. At once he appeared, looking rather sinister. It seemed he was in a dungeon-like room, the thin streams of water on the windshield transforming into cobwebs hanging from the ceiling. I was next to him, that sensual evil feeling enveloping me once more as I watched us embrace. A slab of cement, like an altar, stood before us. And then I was climbing up on the altar—

The windshield wipers flew up suddenly, ruining my picture.

"Jason! I'm trying to scry!" I snapped.

"Aren't you looking at the wall? Isn't it cool?"

No, I wasn't looking at *the wall*.

\* \* \*

*Into the fiery abyss*
*You built this city of pain...*
*A power that knows no shame*

We played again. A small pub in Detroit. This time we were actually listed in the *Urban News* beforehand. As with the last show, I sang my heart out to War, knowing he could hear me. The spell he had me under was evident, as he occupied a place in nearly all of the lyrics I wrote. Sweat on my face, my eyebrows knitted together in determination mixed with angst, I sang of his power. His lust. His addiction. His infernal end. My words poured over the audience, piercing the realm of the spirit— and I hoped, piercing his soul.

Oddly enough, we'd opened up for a magician. This time the show had gone rather well, except for when Krisstopher's bass cut out halfway through one of the songs. We just kept playing like nothing happened and finished the song. Shortly after I announced we were having technical difficulties, it cut on again and everything was fine. When we finished our set, some guys from the band Kissed in Her Diary came over to our table to tell us they thought we were really good.

\* \* \*

I got this brilliant excuse to see War again. I mentioned to Krisstopher that he could probably get us some acid. I had the next day off and Krisstopher didn't have to work until the afternoon, so it was the perfect opportunity to trip. I just hoped War would be able to score for us or else I wouldn't be able to see him.

I called him up and he told us to meet him in a bank parking lot in Ann Arbor. So Krisstopher and I set out into the wintry night, nervous excitement welling within me the closer we got to War's stomping grounds. When we reached the bank parking lot, we sat in the [132]Volvo with the heat on, blasting Priesthood and twirling the stuffed pirate doll with the plastic face that hung by a noose from the rearview mirror. War arrived about ten minutes later, and after rolling down the window and talking with him for a brief moment, we followed him past town and down back roads until we pulled up in front of an old, two-story house.

The three of us climbed the outside staircase to an apartment on the second floor, War making sure I didn't slip on any ice. He had on another leather now, and my favorite tall black boots. He knocked on the door and a hippie girl dressed in baggy overalls and bright socks answered, greeting him happily.

"Hey War! How ya doing? Come on in."

"Hey, what's up, Megan? This is Martyr and her boyfriend uh—Krisstopher."

She smiled and said hello as we followed her into the living room, where her friends were all sitting around listening to Don Avin or something.

"Man, you guys like all those oldies, huh?" War laughed.

"This isn't *oldies*. This is the classic rock station," she replied.

"Yeah, well *whatever*. I can't get into that stuff, ya know what I'm sayin'? Hey, I didn't know you wore glasses."

Megan sat down on the couch now. "Yeah... sometimes. I just felt like bummin' around tonight."

I stared at her admiringly. I didn't dare wear my glasses in public. It was a self-conscious thing I had going, probably from grade school when they used to call me Four Eyes. Now I only wore contact lenses when I was around people. I liked how Megan didn't care about trying to impress anyone—she just did her own thing.

She handed me three squares of acid with yellow suns on them, telling us we had to take at least a hit and a half each since it was kind of weak. War didn't want any. He didn't do acid—it wasn't his thing, he said. Krisstopher and I went into the bathroom with some scissors to cut the third hit in half. After a couple of minutes, War was knocking on the door. "Martyr, you alright?" he called.

I opened the door then, and we came out. "Yeah, I was just going to the bathroom," I told him.

We sat down in the living room with everybody and smoked a joint while Megan handed us some literature promoting the legalization of marijuana. All I remember reading is that supposedly Ben Franklin used to get baked, though I had a hard time believing it. Then we talked for a little while. Her friends were all mellow and sociable.

After a while War got up, announcing that we were taking off. We thanked her and said good-bye to everyone, then followed him outside into the brisk night, trudging through the snow to bypass the icy driveway. Our red [133]Volvo looked so lonely parked beside the curb in the silent street, its windows iced up. It was so red it appeared to be bleeding. Krisstopher and I climbed inside and I rolled down the driver side window so I could see out of it.

War leaned over, peering in at me. "Well, you guys takin' off?" His pink hair was incredibly pink—like someone just dumped a bucket of paint on his head. I thought he looked kind of like a clown now as he stood looking into my eyes. Not like [134]Bozo, with a big red ball on his nose or anything. But just like… a sad clown in a leather jacket, hiding behind his disguise.

Krisstopher sat beside me in the passenger seat, clinging to the boom box for dear life (acid without music was simply forbidden). It dawned on me then that I was starting to fry—really hard. And we didn't have anywhere to go.

"Man, I just thought of something," I told them.

"What?" Krisstopher asked.

"We're frying, man. I can't drive right now. Where are we gonna go?"

"Oh yeah… you're right. That's a good question," he agreed in a spaced-out tone. He couldn't drive either since he didn't have a Michigan driver's license. Besides, I wouldn't have wanted him to even if he could—not in *his* condition. We sat quietly for a moment, thinking.

"You guys can hang out at *my* place for a while," War offered.

"Really?!" I was ecstatic. "You sure you don't mind?"

"No, man. I like the company. The only thing is, we gotta be kind of quiet cuz my parents are sleeping and junk. But it's cool. They don't mind people hangin' out as long as we keep the noise to a minimal, ya know what I'm sayin'?"

I followed him back to his house, relieved that the roads weren't icy. Driving in the winter was bad enough, let alone driving and tripping. After a paranoid journey, we made it safely into the subdivision, parking in front of his house. I stood shivering while we waited for him to open the garage door for us, then he led us through the kitchen and upstairs into his brother's old room, Fairy yipping at our heals the whole time while he said his usual, "Fairy, shut up!" After she growled a few times and yipped a few more, he put her in his parents' room and closed the door again. I swore that dog did not like me for some reason.

185

I sat on the floor in the bedroom, just like the first time I'd met War. The blue shag carpeting looked tall and scraggly, like a [135]Smurf forest. I raked my hand through it, watching the pattern it made while War sat on the bed and lit a cigarette. I could see where the roots of his hair were growing out, creating a two-toned effect: pink with a thick stripe of brown-black towards the top. "Your hair looks sooo cool," I told him, staring at it with fascination.

"Yeah?" he smiled. That faint, quiet smile. It always tugged at my heart.

Krisstopher sat silently beside me. He'd brought in the boom box and was searching through our CDs. The cold had drained our batteries while we were at Megan's, but luckily we'd brought along the power adapter. He plugged it in, setting the player down on a nearby table and restarting Priesthood.

The three of us conversed here and there about different things. Then suddenly the music emerged from the background as if demanding to be heard. I stopped talking and listened. A slightly uneasy feeling stirred inside me as the instruments worked themselves into a frenzy of pure hatred, releasing negative energy into the air. The singer spewed forth vomitous declarations of abhorrence. They lashed out like knives in my ear, then wrapped around my soul like a lasso, tighter... tighter... as he continued inadvertently rattling off the names of those on his hate list while using profanity at the same time: *Curse the president! Curse the pope! Curse the church! Curse God! Curse Jesus—*"

"Shut it off! Shut it off—it's *evil!*" I screeched, crawling frantically over to the table and pushing the stop button. I yanked the CD out of the player. "Did you hear what he *said?*"

I'd never heard Jordy Allenson sing those lyrics before about God. The back of the disc caught my interest now as I held it in my hand. I tilted it from side to side, bouncing the light off it to produce a glistening, rainbow effect. Then, after studying my reflection for a few moments, I relaxed my eyes and gazed deep into the mirrored surface.

At once, War's face appeared, followed by his whole figure. I stared, entranced; feeling his eyes pleasantly burning into my skin as he sat on the bed watching me, while at the same time seeing his eyes watching me through the disc. And then with a flicker he changed, transforming into the Devil himself. A heavy, oppressive darkness like nothing I'd ever felt before squeezed my heart in its fist. I let out a short, sharp scream; a bolt of terror ripping through me, and whipped the CD across the room.

"Martyr! What's wrong?" Krisstopher asked, startled.

I apologized to War for my loud outburst, telling them of the evil figure I'd seen.

"Wow," Krisstopher responded. War didn't say much. He lit up a joint and passed it around, probably to calm me down. I popped our band demo into the player, hoping he would notice, and we talked some more. But he didn't seem impressed by the music. Maybe he didn't know it was us. Pretty soon, he mentioned he was hungry and asked if we wanted to grab something to eat.

Downstairs in the kitchen, he offered that we could stay the night since I was still in no condition to drive, so I called my mom and told her we were staying at a friend's and wouldn't be home until the morning. Afterwards, we all stood against the cupboards, talking for a minute while he poured us some pop.

He mentioned something about how he'd always been *different*. The teachers in school were aware that he was a *strange child*—unlike other children. "Yeah, I used to draw weird pictures on the desk. I drew one once of a boy and girl with graphic body parts and antennas stickin' out of their heads. *Ya know what I'm sayin'?*" he asked, staring at me with those intense eyes as if I was supposed to read between the lines.

Antennas sticking out of their heads... Martians? No... antennas... a boy and a girl... oh! I got it. Psychic powers. *Yes, War, I know what you're saying.*

We climbed inside his freezing cold car. As usual, I was underdressed for the weather. Beneath my unzipped leather I wore a tight, shoulderless spandex top and black spandex pants with slits down the sides. My motto: fashion first. I might freeze to death, but at least I'd look good when they found me.

"Here, let me get ya a blanket," he said now as he watched my teeth chatter. Stepping outside once again, he opened the trunk, returning with a green wool blanket. "I always carry one with me—you should too. Ya never know when ya might break down or somethin', ya know what I'm sayin'?" He spread the blanket over my legs, tucking the sides in snugly around them. "There, that'll warm you up."

I thanked him profusely while Krisstopher sat in silence, probably on a journey somewhere far, far away.

We drove down the road a little way. War turned his head to check on me. "Ya warm now?"

*Melting, War. Simply melting.* "Yeah, I'm great—thanks."

About the only thing open at two a.m. was the drive-thru at Heavenly Burgers. He ordered a bowl of chili and something else and we returned to his house, this time heading into the basement where he now resided. Dank and musty, it had a real gloomy feel to it. Down here, War seemed separated from all living.

A large, rectangular table held boxes of spikes, studs, buckles and leather strips. He showed us his leather crafting tools and a couple of the thick, black belts he was finishing up. I was amazed at his talent. Like his jacket, the belts were works of art. He sold them at The Darkroom whenever he needed quick cash.

The Darkroom was a popular store specializing in punk/gothic/alternative attire, occult jewelry, and leather/fetish wear. Located in a wealthy suburban area, it was the talk of the town. Other shop owners complained about the live adult window displays which drew attention away from their stores as gawking shoppers concentrated on scantily dressed models carrying *curious* artifacts.

I discovered the place shortly after it first opened, when it was a tiny hole in the wall. I think Sybil introduced me to it; she knew all the cool hangouts. We'd gone inside, staring intently at the long blond haired lady that worked there with the black and blue bruises up and down her arms and legs. We wondered what happened to her.

I ended up buying a yellow jacket made out of what seemed like some sort of crinkly, soft but durable waxed paper. On the back, someone drew a bunch of Egyptian hieroglyphics in permanent marker—pictures of deities and stuff. The owner Kevin, a thin, pale guy with semi-long hair and little round glasses, explained that the jacket had just arrived from New York where it appeared in a fashion show.

I went there again a couple of years later with my friend Gordy, an old punk rocker who's pictured in the Pit on the back of a Negative

Advance album. Gordy and I bought tickets from Kevin then to see The Square Jerks. The year was 1985, and they were playing in Detroit.

Through the years, The Darkroom expanded, developing more of a punk rock image as it featured retail fashion from England and New York. I started going on a regular basis to purchase tight black clothing and avant-garde shoes.

War hung out at the store a lot since a few of his friends worked there, one of them being Kevin. He'd even modeled for a couple of the store's ads in the *Urban News* (that's how he got the leather briefs Jamie filmed him in). Funny what a small world it was; groups of people intricately woven together like links in a chain.

Shifting my eyes away from the rectangular worktable now, I noticed an old white sheet hanging from the ceiling in the corner of the basement. We followed War over to the other side of it, to his niche in the shadows. His new room consisted of a couch bed, his record player, a huge stack of records with some loose ones lying around here and there on the floor, a crumpled-up shirt and pair of white socks, some magazines and a newspaper, a photo album, a few empty beer bottles and a dirty plate, a filled ashtray, and a packet of [136]Panda Soy Sauce.

We all talked a little more, then after a while War, who'd tried staying awake with us for the duration of the trip, started shutting down; his eyelids refusing to stay open any longer. Pulling off his T-shirt to reveal a skinny bare chest and a silver hoop through one of his nipples, he whipped the shirt in the corner of the room near his boots and stretched out on the bed. When we got tired, he said, we could crash out on the couch near the stairwell.

Krisstopher immediately took him up on the offer, slumbering over to the old couch and sprawling out on it. In a matter of seconds, he was softly snoring. Still amped from the LSD, I tiptoed quietly around the basement, feeling awkward to be the only one stirring in the house. Once again, I looked at the table containing leather stuff: the various sizes of studs and spikes, the hole cutters, the black dye, the buckles… I wished War would make *me* something—a piece of his artwork that I could cherish forever, crafted by his beautiful hands.

It was hard to sleep. I lie down on top of Krisstopher since there was no room to lie beside him. The musty dusty smell of the couch stung my nostrils, and Krisstopher's black army jacket felt coarse against my face. My own clothes now seemed unbearably tight and itchy, the spandex strangling my circulation. I squirmed to get comfortable, finally giving up on the possibility, and closed my eyes. The usual acid visions filled my head: fragments of pictures and colors flashing at the speed of light. I imagined War on the other side of the hanging sheet, his eyes closed. Was he sleeping yet? I hoped he dreamed of me.

"Richard!" Pause. "Richard!"

Half asleep, I raised my head groggily to see War's mom standing at the top of the stairs peering down at me. Daylight shone behind her figure, attempting to make its way into the shadows of the basement. Uuugg... was it morning already? Under her sharp gaze I suddenly felt awkward, delinquent. I buried my head in Krisstopher's chest and closed my eyes once more.

After about ten minutes, she sent her husband down. I sensed him staring at us as he slowly walked by. "Richard, wake up! You've got that appointment today. Richard!"

"Huh?" War grumbled sleepily. "Okay, okay—I'm up."

His dad went back upstairs. A few moments later, I heard War stirring around, then the click of the lighter. Man, that's what I needed. A cigarette. I shook Krisstopher now. "Wake up, Krisstopher. We gotta get going. Where are the cigarettes?" Pulling them out of his pocket, I started over toward War, stopping right before I got to the sheet. "Hey War, are you *decent*, man? I mean, can I come have a cigarette with you?"

We all had a smoke and then followed him upstairs. Sheepishly, I asked his parents if I could use their bathroom. I felt awkward for staying all night partying at their house, and of course, I had a case of next day acid paranoia—when you feel like everybody and their brother knows you fried the night before. Authority figures are especially hard to deal with during this time.

War offered us something to eat but we politely refused, telling him we'd just grab a coffee on the way since everybody seemed to be in a hurry that morning. He had some kind of appointment, and Krisstopher had to get ready for work. He said he'd follow us to make sure we got on the right freeway. I thanked his parents then for letting us stay, and we left.

After stopping at [137]McDonald's for coffee, he instructed me prior to leaving the parking lot where the entrance of the freeway was. But now, as the road was about to branch off in three different directions, I realized I hadn't even heard what he'd said. I'd been so busy concentrating on him, not to mention majorly spaced out from lack of sleep coupled with a faint trace still remaining of the LSD, that I'd totally bypassed everything he told me.

*Man, which way should I go?* I had to make a decision—fast. I wanted to look cool—like I knew what I was doing. Panicking, I strained to remember his directions, but couldn't. Ugghh! Why didn't I pay attention? I *hated* when I did that!

Once again, it seemed he perceived my thoughts, instantly speeding up beside me and pointing to the route I should take. I waved and shouted thank you. He made a thumbs-up gesture and gave me that same sad smile as he looked at me one last time before I merged onto the freeway. Just as the old saying goes, the look was worth a thousand words. *Hey, I'm taking care of you*, it said. *Hey, I love you.*

Later that afternoon as I lie in bed, Krisstopher at work, I thought of that look again. My heart was both happy and hurting as I tried to fathom where all of this was leading. I thought of how nice War was to me, and of how he always took care of me. Sometimes it felt like I was going out with *him* rather than Krisstopher just from the way he acted.

But even with all the supernatural signs that seemed to accompany our strange relationship, I still wondered deep within… was he *really* my eternal soul mate? Or was it all in my mind? I just didn't know.

The closet door caught my eye now with its simulated wood grain pattern. It seemed perfect for scrying. *How does War really feel about me?* I thought as I concentrated, relaxing my eyes and staring deep into it. There was a sudden flicker of movement as if something entered the wood, and then to my amazement, a huge picture of War's face emerged. It wasn't just a picture, but more of a ghostly, life-like image, as if he was actually there in visible astral form inside the door. He looked at me with his shining eyes—the same look he'd given me earlier that morning with the same faint trace of a smile.

191

But now a tear trickled out of one eye, gliding onto his cheek. One sad, lonely tear. I followed its movement down his face, where letters instantly formed beneath it. They spelled:

TRUE LOVE

An arrow pierced my heart at that moment, seeming to confirm something deep within me. And then I broke down and cried.

## VII.

### THE QUEEN OF PENTACLES AND OTHER STORIES

WE WERE IN THE BEDROOM, frying again. Jesus Smith was sounding really good to me. Normally, he and his band were a bit too pop to suit my taste. I guess the music just had to grow on me a little.

I was [138]Pebbles Flintstone. Krisstopher started calling me Pebbles because my dyed red hair was pulled back on my head like her, minus the dinosaur bone. And with my short blue slip and skimpy bandeau top, I did sort of resemble the teenage version of her. But I was missing the leopard print—and [139]Bamm Bamm. I guessed Krisstopher could pass for Bamm Bamm. All he needed was a club.

After lying on the bed for a while, staring at the promotional Jesus Smith poster Krisstopher got while working at the music store, I decided to look in my ball. But I couldn't see anything pertinent tonight. Krisstopher, on the other hand, who lay beside me, was getting a crystal-clear picture in it. Strange, because he wasn't much of a scryer. He specialized more in tarot readings.

He told me he could see the two of us sitting down in chairs in a room, and a cloaked wizard sitting between us. Next, the wizard had a hand on both of us, bashing us together and then pulling us apart. He said he thought the wizard was War, causing us to hurt one another as he tried tearing us apart.

Yes, we were being torn apart, and there were a number of reasons why. War was certainly a major factor, but besides him, we just couldn't exist in harmony anymore. We argued about everything, it seemed. We became distant, barely communicating with one another. I was in constant fear over who captivated him in the work place when I wasn't around. A car dropped him off one night by the side of our garage and sped away before I could see who was driving. I'd wondered why he hadn't called me to come pick him up. I was sure some girl probably gave him a ride home.

And being in a band with him was putting an even greater strain on our relationship. I tried keeping up with him in the songwriting department so as not to have him capitalize on the singing (the deal was, whoever wrote the song got to sing it). But he was extremely competitive; something he must have picked up being an only, love-starved child. He'd stated once that he always had to be the center of attention in a room full of people. Well, his spotlight mentality was really getting to me. We'd just gotten our songs down and now he wanted to spend time learning a bunch of new ones—*his* new ones.

But things weren't going too good for Beastulust. Not too soon after our gig at the pub with the magician, we started experiencing problems. Hazael called off practice a few times simply because he didn't feel like coming. He'd suddenly fallen into a massive state of depression. He couldn't tell us the reason why, because he wasn't sure himself. All he could tell us was that he didn't know what he wanted to do with his life— or even if he wanted to be in the band anymore. I didn't believe what I was hearing! We were just starting to get some recognition, and we had our set down now to a tee. What did he mean, *he didn't know what he wanted to do with his life?* This was hardly the time for an identity crisis!

Finally, he managed to show up for practices once more. Then Fiend's attendance began to waver. He arrived late on a regular basis, and pretty soon he didn't bother coming at all. We found out he had a little cocaine problem.

Krisstopher suggested that we put the band thing on hold for a while. He wanted to go back to New Hampshire—alone. He made the excuse that he needed to see his mother, as well as to take care of some juvenile violations he'd never bothered to clear (apparently there was a warrant out for his arrest). When I expressed to him that I was worried he was going to go there and forget all about me, he reassured me that it would only be for a little while. He said he needed some space, just until he had time to think about everything.

It was plain to see that neither one of us was happy anymore. It seemed we were growing apart beyond repair. I couldn't help but feel defeated. Part of me was tired of trying to make our relationship work. But the other part of me, besides knowing I would miss him a great deal (after all, we'd been through so much together), really could not accept the fact that I'd left my husband for a soul mate who was now reneging on his promises. I felt deceived, like I was in a terrible nightmare of my past choices from which I could not awake. My heart hurt. My pride hurt. All the pain I put Craig through, all the people I told that Krisstopher was my soul mate... ahhhhhh! I was screaming inside now. What was happening to us?

We had one final band discussion over dinner at a family restaurant. I sat glumly, wondering how the three of them could eat at a time like this. They were happy—smiling, laughing, joking...

It was the end of the world for me. Not only was I losing Krisstopher, my best friend and boyfriend, but I was losing my dream—a dream that I'd kept alive for so long. I'd watched it become a reality only to have it vanish into thin air. I didn't want to let it go; it was an accomplishment for me—especially since Jim told me before that I'd never make it as a singer or in a band. And although there was always the opportunity to form a new band, we were *the* band. The perfect goth conglomeration.

Tears welled up in my eyes as we discussed the future. Hazael had a couple of musical projects he wanted to work on with friends. Fiend wanted to lay low for a while; he was still trying to sort out things with his girlfriend. Their relationship had been on the rocks ever since we'd first met him.

"C'mon, don't be so down!" he said cheerily, staring at me from across the table while munching on a French fry saturated in ketchup.

"Martyr's really sad. She thinks everything's falling apart," Krisstopher explained.

"Look, we can always get back together later. We're just tak'n a little break right now, that's all."

"Yeah right," I grumbled sarcastically.

"We can still keep in touch," Hazael offered.

I felt sick. Just great that everyone had places to go and people to see. But I was left here with nothing. Husbandless. Boyfriendless. Bandless. What would I do now? What was left for me?

* * *

"You're going to meet The Queen of Pentacles. I *know* you are," I told Krisstopher. How could I get in the holiday spirit? Christmas didn't mean anything to me now that he was leaving.

"I doubt it. Besides, if I do, I'll be prepared. There's nothing to worry about."

We sat on the floor in my mom's living room, smoking cigarettes and opening our presents early—having our own Christmas together since he wouldn't be around for the real one. We'd bought most of the gifts at the thrift store and made the rest; he was saving up for the trip home and I had a lot of family to shop for.

He held up the ankh patch that I'd hand-sewn for his leather jacket. "Wow Martyr, you *made* this? It's so cool. Thanks, man."

"You're welcome. I'm glad you like it." I opened another gift, smiling as I pulled it out of the box. "Cool! This is an *awesome* candle."

"It's a *magic goddess* candle, empowered especially for you—to help you when you do your spells."

"I *love* it. Thank you so much." I hugged him, kissing him on the lips. "I can't believe you're leaving. Won't you change your mind?"

"No. I can't. But it won't be for long. You'll see. I just really have to get my life straightened out. I'm tired of being a screw-up. I want to get these violations out of the way and start fresh."

"You're really going to turn yourself in as soon as you get there? Because if you put it off, you know you'll never do it."

"Yeah, I know. But first I'm going to visit my mom for a little bit, and hang with my friends. Because as soon as I turn myself in, I'll be going to jail for a while."

"How long, do you think?"

"I don't know. A few months, maybe. Hopefully by turning myself in, I'll get a lighter sentence."

"Man, I'm going to miss you."

"I know. I'll miss you too, Martyr." He pecked me on the lips now. "But don't worry, Sweets. I'll send for you just as soon as I get settled. I promise."

My mom and I dropped him off at the bus station the following week. I cried all the way home.

Christmas came and went. Then New Year's. Life stayed pretty much the same for me—boring. I couldn't bear going downstairs into the band room anymore. I hated the emptiness. The desolation of it all.

I could still see Hazael by the fireplace, banging away on his drums, that extraordinary mind of his working overtime to provide just the right mood. And Fiend over by the bar, fingers flying up and down the guitar strings while skillfully switching his effects pedal to create eerie exotic sounds. Krisstopher in between the both of them, thunking on his monster bass with perfect bliss. And me by the door near the wall, hands—and even an occasional chin—dancing on both keyboards, absorbing the energy of our magic. The magic of our energy. Man, how I missed us!

I recalled the times I sang my heart out, nose running from the cold and lips half frozen because our unfinished basement wasn't heated. And the times I glanced at the leaky water stained walls to see War's name appear as I poured out all of my angst over him into the microphone. Into my keyboards. Into his soul.

There hung our set, written on poster board with magic marker and still taped to the wall by the fireplace. Stephen had something to say about it one day back in the summer when he came down to the basement to talk to Krisstopher and I. He claimed the names of the songs were evil, especially the one entitled *Jesus' Sex Patrol*. Krisstopher gave him the same explanation he'd given me when I hadn't wanted to sing the rather blasphemous chorus line, which also happened to be the title of the song: it was about a child-molesting priest his friend had fallen victim to. It had nothing to do with Jesus, per se—just perverts who claimed to be godly men.

Stephen, however, didn't seem satisfied with his explanation. He looked at both of us with concern, mentioning something about how he was now a *Christian*, to which I vehemently spat out, "Man, I bet I'm

197

a better *Christian* than *you* are! Don't tell me about God! I know what I'm doing!"

He then brought up the witchcraft and serving other gods, telling me that it was in direct opposition to Christianity. I defended myself by telling him I believed in God, to which he responded that [140]the devils also *believed in God*, but they weren't going to heaven. Finally, he left off preaching to us after asking us to please consider *something or other*. Something about God again. Yeah, whatever.

I took a look around the band room now, at Fiend's effects pedal and rack mount, Hazael's partial drum kit, and my keyboards. Parts of us. My eyes then rested on the big signpost Krisstopher stole from the side of the road. He'd ripped the sign off it and spray-painted the post an awesome black and red cracked faux marble design. We then stuck our mascot on top: a black plaster cherub with a skull for a head. At shows, we hung wrought iron candleholders from chains to the sides of the post and lit candles in them.

Farewell to Beastulust. Krisstopher had suggested the name for our band. It was a line from one of his earlier twisted poems, right before I met him. I think he wrote it about Liza or something. I had to admit, he wrote some good songs. *Funeral* happened to be my favorite. And we *did* sound good when we sang together—like Valiant and Genevieve of Christian Corpse, like Ross and Evol of Phantom Experiment. But alas, all good things must come to an end.

There stood my keyboard case, propped up against the wall with the silver duct tape letters he'd cut out to spell:

BEASTIE

That had been the night of the disaster show in Hamtramck with my buddy Uncle Kurt.

Yep, four *Beasties*. And then there were none.

* * *

Something was wrong. Definitely wrong. I sensed it. Krisstopher had been calling me a couple of times a week. Now he called for a couple of minutes every two weeks. Not only that, but his whole demeanor was different. He was sketchy. Vague. He mentioned some new friends he'd been partying with lately—one whose name came up just a little *too much* to suit my taste: *Tanya* this. *Tanya* that. Sean and *Tanya*. *Tanya* and me. Who was Tanya?

Oh, just *some* girl that lived next door to Sean, some guy he met. Hmmm…

I whipped out my tarots. The Queen of Pentacles. Temptation. The Lovers. Ughhh! Was I just reading into this, or was it true? Had the trial finally occurred, and had he flunked it miserably? No… it couldn't be. I was probably making something out of nothing.

It was late in the afternoon, and I sat on the bedroom floor doing spread after spread after spread with the cards. Had he? Had he actually…?

Next, I scryed for a while in my ball until the word SEX appeared. Did he have sexual relations with Tanya? Was she The Queen of Pentacles? I was literally exhausted from the uncertainty. Or was it the truth that wore me out?

I closed my eyes, trying to think. No, trying *not* to think. Trying to relax. Zenith was playing on the stereo. For the most part, they'd been background music until suddenly a verse leaped out in the song, confirming what I thought I already knew.

*"THE STARS HAVE PREDICTED, I'VE SEEN IT ON THE WALL. YOU WILL BREAK MY HEART, UNFAITHFUL SOUL."*

Face in hands, I burst into tears. The prophecy was fulfilled: my soul mate dishonored me. He failed the trial. He gave in to the temptation. It seemed angels had whispered the words to my heart, which now lie bleeding. Three swords had pierced it this bleak afternoon. Just as the cards predicted, Prince Krisstopher, The Knight of Swords, had chosen vice over virtue.

The sun sunk further into the afternoon as I sat staring ahead into nothingness, an old Sex Guns song running through my head. *"I wear a vacant stare. Cuz I don't care. Vacant!"*

Yes, that's how I felt. *Vacancy.* Rooms for rent. Come on in. I'll put you up for the night, a week—maybe even a couple of months…or years. But you'll always end up checking out. And I'll be empty again.

Suddenly I wanted to deny it was true. Was Nathan Hash right? Was it *"all in my head?"* Maybe I should call and find out. Maybe once I talked to Krisstopher he'd be able to explain it away—all my fears, my doubts. I picked up the phone now, dialing through to New Hampshire.

"Sam? It's me, Martyr. Is Krisstopher around?"

"Oh, hi Mahta. No, he's out with some friends, I think."

"Well… maybe you can help me, Sam. Do you know what's going on with him lately?" I asked, desperation in my voice. "I mean, I haven't heard from him in a while. It seems he's always out partying. He used to call me a lot. Now he barely calls at all. And he keeps mentioning some *Tanya* girl. Do you know anything about her? Because I have a really bad feeling that he cheated on me with her."

Silence for a moment. Two moments. Three moments. Uh oh.

She sighed. "Okay Mahta, I can't lie to you." Silence again. I saw the axe waiting to fall. "Krisstopha has been hanging around with Tanya—a lot…" Pause. "And last night, I came home from wuhk to find her cah parked in front. This mohning when I got up to go to the bathroom, her keys were still lying on the counta. She… spent the night."

I burst into tears now, the swords twisting a little deeper into my heart.

"That juhk! I told him he better call you and tell you. It really ticks me off that I have to do the duhty wuhk for him. But I like you, Mahta— and I'm not going to sit heeya and pretend nothing happened."

"Thank you, Sam," I sobbed. "I appreciate that. It's like, I already knew. I just had this horrible feeling today that wouldn't go away. But I didn't want to believe it, you know?" I took a deep breath then, trying to regain my composure. "Sam? Can you tell me one more thing?"

"Hmmm?"

"This Tanya chick—what does she look like? I just really need to know."

Another moment of silence. *Was she prettier than me?* I wondered.

"She's a dog, pretty much. She wehs little round glasses and she's got dahk, shoulda-length hair. I don't know—she's just kind of blah. *Plain* looking, ya know? You're much prettya, Mahta. I can guarantee it. I think Krisstopha's pretty *stupid* if you ask me."

*Glasses? She wears glasses? And all this time I didn't think men liked glasses on women!* I mean, obviously Krisstopher knew I wore glasses, but I didn't dare wear them out in public. I don't recollect now if I ever wore them in private with him, either, although I'd worn them with Craig.

About an hour later, Krisstopher called. At first he tried playing it cool, telling me that Sam wanted him to call for some reason, like he didn't know why. When I told him I already knew he cheated on me with The Queen of Pentacles, he broke down and told me the whole story.

Apparently Tanya had an interest in magic, too. She also owned a deck of tarot cards. A few days prior, she asked him to do a tarot spread for her. When The Queen of Pentacles appeared as her significator card, she explained to him that it had *always* been her card. He told her then, about the infamous prophecy that evolved around it.

And then last night, they'd gone to the bar with another old friend of his, who also happened to be an ex-girlfriend—who wasn't? The three of them got pretty lit, and of course, the conversation turned to sex. Tanya started bragging about her reputation in town with the *menfolk*. Krisstopher just had to see if she held her weight in gold.

"How *could* you?" I bawled. "You knew this might happen! You were warned beforehand. And you promised—you promised you would pass the trial with flying colors."

"Yeah, but I got sick of you always condemning me for doing something I hadn't even *done* yet. I figured I might as well do it and at least get some enjoyment out of it if I was going to get reamed for it anyway."

"Stop! Can't you see you're *hurting me*?" I screamed. "How can you sit there and tell me you *enjoyed* it? Oh God, this can't be happening. Oh God—" I sobbed uncontrollably now.

"Martyr..."

"I can't believe you did this to me."

"Martyr... look. I didn't enjoy it. I swear. You're the one for me, and I see that now. I *love* you. Please, you've got to believe me. I'm telling the truth."

"Just leave me alone for now. I need time to think about things," I told him.

I took a long, hot bath, still crying the whole time in the tub. I felt like sinking down into the water, never to emerge again. This was a nightmare. My whole life was a nightmare.

At work, I moped around endlessly while Ian tried cheering me up after hearing the news. Jason and I weren't speaking, so I didn't bother telling him about it. We'd gotten into an argument one day and still hadn't resolved it. As far as I was concerned, our friendship was history. He was never there when I needed him—only when he needed me. So I really had no one to talk to—no one to confide in. Jamie was doing her own thing now and it was clear to see that we'd grown apart over the years. Who could I trust anymore?

Valentine's Day arrived. Krisstopher sent me a huge package filled with candy, leather roses, and a cool zebra striped bikini. He also included a card with a poem explaining how he'd gone through a dark night of the soul and could see clearly again. He told me I was his fairy princess, and to prove it, he got a tattoo on his arm of a fairy with long hair resembling me.

Slowly, my heart was softening again. Very slowly.

* * *

Things were at a standstill for me. I was in a state of mournful reflection. I'd recently turned down a proposition from Randy's cousin Mark who was now married, and whom I'd thought about throughout my entire wedding ceremony and even up until I moved to Florida. He and I went out to the bar to have some drinks and talk about old times, and though both of us were stone-faced drunk and it easily could have happened, I somehow didn't want it anymore.

I'd even put War on the back burner for a time. I wasn't sure why. I was just completely confused about everything and everyone who'd come into my life. So many relationships, old and new; their purpose unclear. Funny how each one of them had some small part of me. I was scattered about everywhere, my heart a five-hundred-piece jigsaw puzzle that I wished they'd all put back together again.

I bought some new glasses. *Little round ones.* And I even wore them out in public, sometimes for two or three days before I changed over to my contacts. A customer at work said he couldn't figure me out: one minute I looked like a gothic seductress, in black fishnet tights and miniskirts; the next I looked like a Dead Head, in ponchos and tie-dye with my little round glasses. Funny how Tanya helped me to see that four eyes *were* cool. Oh, the sick, twisted irony of it all!

I also purchased a bunch of weed and smoked out every night after work. I'd light a slew of incense and boil a bunch of herbs in my makeshift cauldron to cover up the smell so my mom wouldn't know. Then I'd scrunch down in the small closet in Jim's room and shut the door, inhaling smoke through Krisstopher's home-made metal pipe with the dented screen. Afterward, the hard wood floor felt comfortable and I actually could appreciate the music of The Thankful Dead. Now I knew why Camron and Jasmine always played this stuff when they were high.

The first time I'd traipsed through their bedroom to go to the bathroom and heard the jazzy bluesy folky hippie nonsense, I thought they were joking around. "What's this crap?" I laughed.

"Man, dude, this is The Thankful Dead," Jasmine whispered, as if their very name was sacred.

"The *who*?"

"Man, you've never heard of The Thankful Dead? Dude, they're awesome. They're so wicked."

"Man, they lag!"

I'd gone out into the living room then, lying back down on the futon bed and telling Krisstopher that Jasmine and Camron were listening to some *stupid* music in the bedroom.

But now, I had to admit the band had grown on me. Yes, even I, the Queen of Goth, had developed a fondness for The Thankful Dead. I supposed I was a closet Dead Head. Perhaps it was the gypsy attack I was having; another new kick that might last several more weeks—or several more months. It was hard to tell with me. Like Krisstopher said, I was a chameleon—always changing colors.

In the bedroom floor, I anointed myself with Sister Witch Salve and closed my eyes, hoping to fly. Consecrated stones lay all around me, with some resting on specific pressure points related to my astral body: my forehead, my heart, and my abdomen. I could feel my chakras opening. They were small doors to my inner self, expanding wider and wider. A burning frenzy of passion filled them now.

I wanted to uncoil the [141]kundalini serpent at the base of my spine— to feel its sexual power. The books said once you learned how to master the serpent, you could enter the realm of the spirit and have astral sex, which meant, sexual relations on other planes of existence. But you had to be very careful: those working with chakras and kundalini could experience side effects, which varied depending on the person. Confusion, depression, loss of relationships, suicidal inclinations, and *internal bleeding* were some of them.

Krisstopher had been working with chakras until one of his eyes got really red (almost like it was bleeding). It lasted for about a week. He laid off the chakras for a while and it went away.

\* \* \*

I'd written a short play inspired by a book Krisstopher bought me describing the dark paths one inevitably encounters on his or her spiritual journey: the trials, or temptations to do evil instead of good. It claimed that the spiritual person, at one time or another, experiences a night or nights in which he is temporarily blinded, unable to see the light clearly. It is at this time that temptation overwhelms him. He is weak. He is vulnerable to the evil.

Yes, yes. That was me. First War, now… Fiend? What on earth was going on? Fiend was gaining a greater bearing than I'd imagined possible lately. In the play, I portrayed him as Hermes the Hunter, chasing his prey—me. He was Kernunnos the god of passion and lust, and I was the object of his desire. Fire burned, burned, burned. And I found myself happy to be in it—to be the sacrifice on his altar of magic. Maybe then I would learn what he wanted to teach me.

The pathworking books I was studying claimed that The Devil card, number fifteen, had to be journeyed at some point in one's life, as did all the other cards, or paths. But it was nothing to be afraid of: one had to plummet the very depths of darkness in order to gain true spiritual enlightenment. It would only serve to make the neophyte stronger in his or her spirituality, as often, the very thing we are afraid of is the thing we need to face in order to grow. *A leap into the blackest abyss*, with no assurance of what lies ahead of us, is often necessary, they claimed.

Although The Devil card didn't appear in my tarot spreads concerning Fiend as frequently as it did for those concerning War, I still believed he was involved in something underhanded judging from the literature he read. He'd recently brought over a magazine entitled *Magic and the Netherworld*. There was something evil about this, too, but I couldn't pinpoint exactly what it was.

I called him one afternoon to let him know that Krisstopher finally failed his trial with The Queen of Pentacles. He said he'd expected as much, letting me know that Krisstopher didn't really love me like he thought he did.

I felt I would go insane with grief. I kept picturing my Prince—my Knight of Swords—with The Queen of Poodles, and it was more than I could bear. I wanted to rip her head off. I wanted to curse her. I wanted to… try and be positive and forgive her, realizing my own [142]karma had come back to me. I'd cheated on *Craig*, after all.

∗ ∗ ∗

My friend Joe cheered me up. I hadn't seen him in a long time—not since I introduced him to Krisstopher awhile back and we all had lunch together, discussing midi technology. He was pretty hip on computers, explaining the various options available for sampling sounds and dumping them into my [143]Yamaha since my [144]Kawaii was an older model and not midi compatible.

I'd met him four or five years earlier outside of [145]7-Eleven one night, which was the happening place to be on the weekends for prospective partygoers. There in the parking lot, endless opportunities awaited anxious and intoxicated teenagers, three of them being Shelly, Elyse, and me.

Joe pulled up in his bad little truck, all shiny and black, and inside were two gorgeous guys from England with thick cockney accents that made Sid Vicious sound like David Niven. They were over here in the

States through some Camp USA program, working toward their dream: to go to California where all the babes were, or *birds* as they called them.

Anyway, I saw a lot of Joe back then. He was always hanging with the English hunks, and so was every girl in town. We acted like a bunch of stupid groupies—and they didn't even have a band.

The two of us went out for coffee a lot in those days. We talked about life, about our current flames—about anything and everything one can possibly think of when amped on [146]Columbia's finest, "hand-picked by Juan Valdez." And now tonight, we were going to relive old times.

It was good to see him again. He picked me up at work and we headed over to The Villa Restaurant by my mom's. On the way there, I whipped out my pipe and some weed. I needed to wind down.

"Do you mind?" I asked.

"Uhh… no—go right ahead. But I don't want any. I don't do that stuff anymore," he answered, rolling down his window a bit.

"Oh, well *I* do. In fact, I can't get enough of it," I admitted, packing some of the herb in the bowl. "It helps me relax, you know?"

"Yeah, well I quit all that—the drinking, the drugs… I don't need it anymore,"

"That's cool." I inhaled, holding the itching, burning smoke in my lungs for a minute.

"Man, I can show you how to get high without drugs," he offered. "You like acid? I can show you how to feel like you're tripping when you're totally straight."

Cough, cough, cough. "Oh really?" Cough, cough, cough. "How, man?"

"*God*, man. I get so high with God that it feels like I'm on drugs."

"Yeah, well I believe in God. I'm into white magic, though."

"I'm talking about *Christ*. About knowing Jesus Christ."

"Yeah, well I believe *all* paths lead to God. You've got your way—and that's cool for you. But I've got my way. And this white magic stuff is the best thing that's ever happened to me. I feel so spiritual, like I've never felt before. My dad was into it, you know. I'm just completing the circle—picking up where he left off."

We sat in the restaurant now, downing coffee and talking about our relationships. I told him about Krisstopher cheating on me. He was very sympathetic. Then he mentioned some girl from Japan he'd been seeing for a while. She'd recently gone back to her country. He missed her a lot. Apparently they were pretty serious, but her parents didn't approve of their relationship.

"Y'know, all of a sudden I've got all these coffee engagements," I said. "At first I didn't really have anyone to hang out with, and now all these people are showing up in my life. I'm going tomorrow night for coffee with some guy I met at work. His name is Dave. He asked me if we had some Whorehouse Flower CD or something, and then we ended up having a two-hour long conversation in the store. He's really weird though."

"What do you mean by *weird?*"

"I don't know. He's just into some strange stuff. He's got these books he wants to show me that he's going to bring with him tomorrow. He said he thinks I'll like them. But he mentioned something about *Satanism*. Weird man. Yet, if he is a Satanist, he's the nicest one I've ever met, you know?"

Actually, I'd only met one other professed Satanist, Billy Monohan. He went to my high school, and in tenth grade, he used to brag about how he worshiped the Devil. Then one day, he came to class and told us about a dream he'd had the night before: God and the Devil each had a hold of one of his arms, and were pulling him in two different directions, like a tug-of-war. He said he'd never been so scared when he thought the Devil was going to win. But he didn't. God did. From that moment on, he was no longer a Satanist.

Joe looked concerned now. "Well, I'd just be careful. I know you're a smart lady and I don't mean to tell you what to do, but you don't know this Dave guy. He could be a mass murderer for all you know. And I'm kind of like your big brother looking out for you, you know what I mean?"

I smiled. "Yeah, I know. And I appreciate it. But I'm sure he's harmless. My friends Jason and Ian think he's a nutcase, though. I think it's just because he looks kind of sinister. He's kind of short and has all these tattoos up and down his arms of tarot cards and stuff. And he's got these little dark beady eyes and these thick eyebrows that are always knit together. But he reminds me of Harry Ross—I don't know what it is. And it's like we're on the same wavelength and we just met. I can't really explain it, but he has a lot of the same views I do about life and stuff. And both of us have been totally screwed over by our soul mates. It's like, we just want to spiritually advance and become masters at magic so we can help ourselves and others."

"Do you like this guy? I mean, are you romantically interested in him?"

"No, not at all. He's not my type. I mean, I'm not attracted to him in that way. But you've got to understand—Krisstopher was like my best friend. We did everything together and we were both interested in spiritual things. Now that he's gone, I don't have anyone like that who can relate to me. It's like I lost my only friend—well not my *only* friend, but you know what I mean. I just feel such a great loss. And I don't know what's going on with our relationship right now. I don't know if I can ever trust him again."

\* \* \*

Dave sat across from me in the booth, both of us grinning stupidly like two kindergartners meeting for the first time.

"So… this is cool, man. I'm glad we're here, you know?" he offered.

"Yeah," I smiled shyly. "I was really looking forward to it myself. I needed to hang out with someone and talk."

The waitress brought our coffees and we generously creamed and sugared them. I had a feeling Dave liked me. I was usually right whenever I had these kinds of feelings. I just hoped he'd understand if I only wanted to be friends.

He told me a little bit more now about his girlfriend breaking up with him. He'd already discussed it somewhat in the music store the other night when he'd stayed for nearly two hours talking to me. And I told him about Krisstopher and Tanya—the whole Queen of Pentacles story complete with personal footnotes. Both of us agreed we wanted a totally spiritual relationship with someone. But it wasn't easy finding people who wanted the same thing.

"Oh—I brought those books," he said now, taking them out of his army backpack. "This one is *really* good." He pointed to a book entitled:

[147]*The Satanic Bible.* Flipping through the pages, he showed me a picture of the author, a sinister looking bald-headed guy. "Satanism isn't really bad like people portray it," he explained. "All it consists of is doing whatever you want to do. This book talks about how it's just a free will thing—you make your own rules."

"Yeah, well I'm not into that stuff," I told him, taking another sip of my coffee. "I prefer *white* magic."

"But Satanism isn't black magic. It's just making up your own laws. People think it's about dressing up all scary and sacrificing animals and stuff—but Satanists are really peaceable people. They just want to do their own thing. Just because they don't like the rules the church tries slapping on them, they're labeled Satanists. But what if Satan is the good guy and God is actually the bad guy—did you ever think of that? Cuz I've wondered that sometimes."

"Yeah… I guess I've thought it would be pretty bizarre if that's how it was all along and nobody knew it."

"So seriously—look at this book. I think it will change your mind about Satanism."

I didn't know why, but I did not want to read the book. I felt really strange about it. "I told you, man, I'm not interested. It's just not my cup of tea, you know? I mean, that's cool if that's the path you're on and stuff, but—hey, what's that other book about? Wicca?"

"Oh, yeah. This is a cool one too. I figured you'd like it. There's some really cool artwork in here, see?" He skimmed through the pages, picking a few drawings out to show me. In one drawing, some naked witches were pictured with a half-goat/ half-man, also naked. It looked like they were about to have intercourse with him. There was something weird about this book, too, judging from the drawings. But I'd look it over anyway since it had to do with witchcraft.

"Yeah, I'll leave them both with you and you can check them out for a while," he told me now.

"Thanks, man. Yeah, but you can keep the Satanism one and just let me borrow the other one."

"Well, I'll leave it with you *anyway.* Just in case you change your mind."

We went back to my house later to talk and listen to some tunes. Up in Jim's room, he opened the book again to show me a picture of Sammy Davis Jr. hanging out with the author, La Vey, who founded the Church of Satan on the East Coast. "Yeah, Sammy was a member of the Church of Satan, though he claimed to be a Jew."

I stared at the picture in disbelief. Not Sammy! Not the guy with the glass eye that made me crack up when I watched the [148]Archie Bunker Show. Not the guy who sang that candy song when I was a kid that used to always make me hungry every time I heard it. Bummer.

\* \* \*

Jason and I resolved our argument at work on Saint Patrick's Day. No, we hadn't had any green beer—yet. But we just suddenly missed each other immensely. I didn't know what it was. Some mushy feeling came over both of us at the same time and we started hugging and spewing forth apologies. The green beer came afterward—when we got off work. We went to the Irish pub two doors down and had a couple. Then when they closed, we stopped at Perring Drugs and bought some whiskey and [149]Coke (his favorite).

We sat in the bedroom and drank and talked. But suddenly I just wanted to go to sleep. All I could think about was Krisstopher and Tanya. I took small sips from my glass, starting to hate the taste. Jason kept urging me to drink faster, but I didn't feel like it. Depression was setting in again.

"C'mon, I bet I can get more smashed than you," he dared.

"I bet you can too," I agreed. I just wasn't up for the challenge. I missed Krisstopher.

"C'mon, Martyr. What's wrong with you? You used to love to drink!"

He was right. I used to love to drink. But lately that kind of buzz didn't interest me. When I drank, I got depressed, easily angered, and sleepy. Now I just wanted weed and acid: thinking drugs. I liked the spiritual high they gave me. And I liked how they helped get me to Wonderland.

We called Krisstopher. He was happy we did. He said he wished he could be there partying with us. Then he said he really missed me... and loved me.

* * *

Black Hymn was playing soon at a metal bar in Detroit. Jason and I thought we'd drop some acid and check out Ian's singing. A good glam metal laugh was what we both needed.

I was sure that Ian and I shared another life together. Even the cards said so. But it hadn't been very significant. Not like I wished. I had a crush on him that I just couldn't help. I had a crush on a lot of people. Soul ties. And I didn't even know for sure what it was that drew me to them—or him. At work, he was usually cranky. He'd yell at me and get me in a bad mood, then instantly become happy once he projected his bad attitude onto me. I don't think he even knew he was doing it—like it was a subconscious habit he developed. He spent the remainder of the time being nice to me then, cracking jokes to try and get me *un*mad at him. It drove me absolutely batty.

Meanwhile, I was still on my gypsy kick. I'd probably been one in a prior life, caravanning around with a bunch of dark haired, dark eyed men—ruffians who stole my heart with their reveling and their sweet serenades. We'd gone from town to town reading fortunes—and making a fortune off of people's misfortune. I got this revelation that Ian and I had been gypsies together. Certainly he seemed the part with his dark flowing hair and roving eyes, his stormy temper.

Just starting to feel a little trace of the fry, Jason and I arrived at the bar now where his band was playing. I was decked out in my gypsy punk conglomeration: a long flowing skirt, spandex top, and vintage costume vest accented by my painted biker leather and thigh high suede boots. The metal heads were walking around, dressed in leathers and attitudes. I felt they were eyeing us funny. I didn't know why they would be—hadn't they ever heard of Stacie Hicks? It wasn't like we looked bizarre or anything. I mean, we were in the same arena they were as far as I was concerned—none of us fit in with the real world's fashion force to begin with. But whatever. Maybe I was just being overly sensitive.

"Is it my imagination, or is everybody looking at us funny?" Jason suddenly asked.

"You noticed too?"

We both started cracking up. Suddenly Ian walked on stage, belting out low guttural tones that took us both by surprise while the rest of the band conducted a fast-paced dirge that shook the floor. Either this was some really good acid, or Black Hymn was a lot better than we'd thought.

I smiled now, watching him on stage: a big bad Ian storming around defiantly—his alter ego. Who would have guessed that I could make this same Ian blush by telling him he had a cute little freckle on the tip of his earlobe? Or that he loved to hear [150]William Shatner (Captain Kirk) sing *Lucy in the Sky with Diamonds*? No, right now he looked like he ate little children for dinner. Well, maybe not *that* sadistic. But let's just say he looked quite impressive. And I was quite impressed.

But much to our disappointment, he talked to us for about two minutes after the show and then split to hang with his friends. We left the building, trying to find a good excuse for why we'd just been blown off. Maybe he had to get back and help break down the band equipment. Maybe he was just tired after the set. Maybe he was a complete jerk, totally rude, absolutely inconsiderate to the fact that two friends of his from work drove all the way down to this stinking dive bar in the middle of a gang neighborhood to see his pitiful alter ego. Or maybe he didn't consider us *friends of his*. Hmmm...

We climbed in Jason's car and sat in the parking lot for a while, where we stared at some weird billboard across the street that had no explanation on it whatsoever—just a bald-headed science fiction type guy with a bunch of weird symbols and letters and numbers where his face should have been. Jason told me he'd seen it before, and it even looked like that *without* drugs. There was no logo—no tangible message to grasp from this bizarre advertisement. Or was there? We continued staring at it for a long time...

Outside on the brick wall of the bar, someone had spray-painted:

## THE LEATHER GYPSIES

I knew it. Another sign concerning my past life with Ian. Needless to say, I spent the rest of the night attempting to plug into him while Jason and I tripped out together.

On the way home from the bar, we noticed a yard crammed full of cement figurines in what seemed like the middle of nowhere. We pulled over, Jason shining his headlights on them, and gazed silently at their enchanted beauty. Greek goddesses, gnomes, cherubs...

Suddenly a police car pulled up beside us and a [151]Boss Hogg-looking man—a smokey—a state trooper—peered over at us suspiciously through his rolled down window. I thought for a moment that I was in a [152]*Dukes of Hazzard* episode. "What are you folks doin'?" he asked.

"We were just... looking at the statues," Jason replied a little nervously.

*"Just... lookin' at the statues*, huh?" he echoed, a hint of sarcasm in his voice.

"Yep," we both nodded, trying to look him right in the eye.

Silence.

More silence.

"Well, this here's *private property.*"

Oops.

"Okay. Yeah, sorry... we didn't know."

"Where are you two headed?" he asked, still suspicious.

"Uh... back to White Lake. We just came from watching a friend's band play," Jason replied hurriedly.

"*White Lake*, huh? Well, you're a long way from *White Lake*, aren't you?"

"Yeah, uh... we took a wrong turn somewhere. Can you tell us how to get back on the freeway from here?"

To our relief, [153]Boss Hogg gave us directions and let us off the hook. We pulled out onto the road, wiping the sweat off our brow.

"Man, how the *crud* did we get out here anyway?" Jason laughed.

"I have nooo idea."

"You wanna know something, Martyr? That was really weird."

"Yep. I agree with you one hundred percent."

213

Later, we parked by the lake near my house while I soaked up the energy in Spirit's song, *Mystic Man*. That was it, maybe: Ian wasn't aware of his power. It had to be unlocked. But I could teach him...

The night began fading into the morning. We watched in awe as the moon became a silvery-white yoyo in the sky, gliding up and down on a string.

After hanging out in the bedroom for a while staring into the mirrored surface of my agate stone, Jason crashed out on the bed. I sat on the floor doing tarot readings—trying desperately to make the cards tell me Ian had a romantic interest in me. But they wouldn't.

\* \* \*

On Ian's birthday, I bought him a necklace with a malachite stone for healing, since he had a problem with a reoccurring pain in his leg. Then Jason and I went next-door to the Christian bookstore to get him a card, crossing out 'God' in every sentence and replacing it with *Satan*—for a joke, since Ian always called me Satan. And, because it was quite amusing.

I'd felt kind of funny going into the Christian store. It was too *peaceful* or something, like we were in a library, even though there was music playing in the background. We stood around and laughed as we read the cards while the guy at the cash register just kind of eyed us curiously.

Ian was both shocked and amazed when he found out we'd actually gone into the bible store next door. Nor could he believe we crossed out God on the card we gave him.

"Dude, I can't believe you guys *did* this," he kept saying in a real serious tone, a bewildered half-smile on his face.

I made him another card, too, about him being one of my soul mates.

\* \* \*

Fiend. He called one night to ask if I wanted to go to the bar with him. When he arrived at my mom's, he handed me three sandalwood incense sticks: a small present, he said. I wondered what he'd done to them. Maybe he'd put a spell on them to win my love. This kind of intrigued me. Perhaps I even half-hoped he had. Why not? It made for fun in the grand scheme of my twisted life.

For some reason unbeknownst to me, we ended up at a local top forty music bar not far from my mom's house. Fiend said he thought it was supposed to be alternative night. Yeah, it was *alternative* alright—and it was my alternative to leave. We stayed for about forty-five minutes—I think he was waiting for a friend—and then he disappeared into the restroom. When he returned, he suddenly asked if I wanted to go someplace else. Maybe he picked up some coke or something while he was in there, who knew? So we headed over to Machine, an industrial bar downtown.

I should have known when he kept buying me shots of Yagenheister at Machine that he was up to something. And I suppose I *did* know. Before going in the place, we'd sat in the parking lot and talked about perfect love. He'd asked me how did I know that the perfect love I'd been casting spells for *according to the freewill of the universe* might not be him? He'd been putting out similar spells, he claimed. So how did I know we weren't perfect for each other? Because I didn't feel it in my heart, that's why. Yet... after what Krisstopher had done, I needed to feel attractive again. To boost my self-esteem.

And so... as night turned into morning and the thick waft of sandalwood assaulted my nostrils, I gave another piece of myself away, feeling sick afterward. *There, Krisstopher. I got you back. I hurt you like you hurt me.* And in the process, I hurt myself as well. I couldn't stand the smell of sandalwood after that. I couldn't stand myself.

When I told Krisstopher what I did, he said he'd had a feeling I was going to get together with Fiend. "I understand that you felt you had to get back at me. I mean, it hurts, but I understand why you did what you did. I guess I had it coming."

\* \* \*

Dave came over a lot. We visited health food/New Age shops, we exchanged music... and when he came into the store one day, Ian in his usual cranky mood, I told him I wanted so bad just to walk out and leave Ian without help for the rest of the evening.

"Why don't you?" he asked.

*Yeah, why don't I?* "See ya later. I'm out of here!" I called, waving to Ian and Jason, who stood in the back of the store surrounded by unopened boxes of tapes and CDs, mouths gaping open.

"What do you mean, you're out of here?" Ian asked, wide-eyed and half-smiling as if he hoped I was playing some kind of cruel joke on him.

"I quit."

As much as I felt bad about leaving Jason with a major shipment to put on the shelves, I was relieved to be through with Ian the Roving Eyed Leather Gypsy [154]Dr. Jekyll and Mr. Hyde soul mate. A little sad… but yet, happy. It was quite liberating to stand up for myself for once in my life. Like a breath of fresh air.

Dave suggested I put in an application at the veterinarian's office where his mom worked. They needed a receptionist, and besides working with cool animals, I'd get six dollars an hour—more than I'd ever gotten in my life. Of course, he put in a good word for me and I got the job. I was scheduled to start in another week.

But I was feeling really smothered lately where he was concerned. It seemed he always dropped by unexpectedly, usually when I was on the phone with Krisstopher. I needed some space. Krisstopher didn't like the idea of me hanging around him either, especially when I told him that I thought Dave liked me.

"Look, Martyr, why don't you move out here with me?" he suggested. "I can find us an apartment, and I've got a good job now. Kyle got me a job working at the Inn—doing street soliciting for vacation ownership. It pays good commission. And we can start all over."

"I don't know, Krisstopher. I mean, Dave just got me into a vet's clinic—you know how I love animals. I'll be making six dollars an hour—more than I've ever made. I can't just up and tell his mom now that I don't want the job after they already went to all this trouble. Besides, how do I know it's going to work out for us even if we *do* start over? How do I know I can trust you again?"

I was skeptical. Still, I missed him immensely. The security, the friendship, the warm body to snuggle up to at night… What did I have here, anyway? Things were getting weirder by the day. Besides, I liked starting over; I always had. Going to a new place, seeing and doing new things… a way of escape.

"I love you, Martyr. Just give me a second chance. I promise I won't let you down." Krisstopher urged now.

I was silent for a moment. "Let me think about it, okay? I mean, I'm pretty sure I want to—I miss you so much. But, just let me think about it."

I broke out the I Ching a couple of hours later. It was a special oracle to be used only on occasions of great need, according to its instructions. Well, this *was* a great need. After all, it was detrimental that I get an answer as to whether or not I should move to New Hampshire, because my decision would completely alter the course of things—forever. Never would I be able to regain this moment again. Whatever path I chose would keep me from the one I didn't choose. And even if I turned to take the other path once more, it would never be exactly the same as it would have been had I taken it in the first place, because circumstances would have changed by that time.

…AS ALL LIFE IS IN CONSTANT MOTION.

*Should I move to New Hampshire to be with Krisstopher again?* I asked the oracle now. I carefully tossed the inscribed gold coins while concentrating hard on my question. Next, I looked up their landing pattern in the appropriate diagram and read the answer assigned to it. And there it was. The oracle stated that it would be beneficial for me to [155]*take a trip and see a wise man.*

I called Krisstopher and told him to start looking for an apartment for us. I would indeed take a trip; travel the miles to be with my Prince and Knight of Swords once more.

* * *

"You're going to regret you ever did this," Fiend stated rather nastily. I'd never seen him get this way before. He came to pick up the rest of his band equipment, which was still sitting in the basement.

"No I'm not," I told him defiantly, then added, "What are you going to do, *curse* me or something?"

"You wait and see. I'm telling you, you're going to wish you never left."

I sensed he was hurt. I hadn't meant to use him—well—it wasn't like he hadn't used *me*, anyway. Both of us were simply caught up in the passion of the moment, on the rebound after being degraded by our lovers. We weren't *perfect* for each other. We were just lonely.

I called Dave's mom at the vet and told her I was moving out of state, apologizing for any inconvenience I might have caused. Dave was bummed when he heard the news. "Man, I was just starting to get to know you and stuff. I'm gonna miss hanging out with you."

Soon after that, Hazael came over to pick up the rest of his drums, hugging me good-bye. The practice room was now completely empty, with no trace left of Beastulust save for the candle wax and burn holes in the carpeting.

THE END.

 VIII. NEW BEGINNINGS

Mᴏᴍ ᴀɴᴅ ʜᴇʀ ᴛᴡᴏ ꜰʀɪᴇɴᴅꜱ saw me off on the train. They all waved good-bye sadly, Mom with tears dripping down her face. It broke my heart.

Our red [156]Volvo had long since bit the dust; I'd been getting rides to and from work for the past couple months. Now I would have to get used to walking everywhere once I got to New Hampshire, but at least Krisstopher had found an apartment close to town.

Beneath my thick leather jacket, Zain squirmed around anxiously, claws digging through my blouse and into my skin while I winced in pain. Pushing around with his head, he struggled to break free of the zippered confines and come up into open air. I reached inside with my hands to pet him and calm him down.

"Stop it, Zain!" I whispered.

Animals weren't allowed on the train. I took a peek now inside the small box beside me, where the two anoles scampered back and forth, frightened by all the motion. It was going to be a long trip. I only hoped I could pull it off without someone discovering I'd smuggled three reptiles on board.

I would have to board two other trains plus a bus before arriving in Boston where Krisstopher was meeting me. I had so much luggage it was pathetic. Even the baggage guys avoided me after a while, because every time I reboarded, they had to help me carry a bunch of heavy stuff; and I had no idea I was supposed to tip them as a result. At least my mom had agreed to ship my [157]Yamaha later when we got settled in our apartment, since it didn't have a carrying case like my [158]Kawaii.

Twenty-one hours lapsed. Sweating profusely from the thick leather and long, black knit shawl I had on beneath it to conceal the length of Zain's tail; nauseated from the stench of porta-johns and ripe from no shower, I arrived at the train station in Boston. I was about thirty minutes late since we'd been delayed slightly during one of the boarding times.

I sat down at one of the tables and unzipped my jacket halfway. Instantly, Zain popped his head out. After getting a dose of the fresh air, he soon went berserk; violently writhing and twisting until I took him completely out and let him soak up the light of day. I set him down on the floor, holding onto his leash so he wouldn't get away.

"*So that's* what you had in there," a passenger from the train commented, a surprised look on his face. "I knew you had some kind of animal or something because you kept looking inside your coat the whole trip."

A couple of kids came to have a look now. I answered their questions and then asked the guy what time it was. Krisstopher was over an hour late.

Fear suddenly welled up within me. What if he never showed up and I was stuck at the train station? Maybe he couldn't get a ride. Or maybe he'd changed his mind…

"Martyr!" a familiar voice called.

I turned to see him bolting toward me, and hardly recognized him. It had only been about four months, but it seemed years. His hair wasn't short and spiked anymore. He'd cut it just before leaving, and already it had grown out from behind the ears and the bangs were a little wavy. He'd dyed it back to his natural color: a light brown. Still, he looked great.

He stared at me, amazed. "Wow… it seems strange seeing you. You look so *different*. I mean, you look great, but it seems like it's been such a long time."

"Yeah, I know what you mean. I barely recognized you at first, but you look great, too."

He wrapped his arms around me and we kissed for a while, blocking out the rest of the world. Afterward, he reached over to pet our iguana. "Hi Zainy."

I showed him the two anoles, which he also greeted, and then he looked around in astonishment. "I can't believe you carried all of this stuff with you," he laughed. We hauled it outside and loaded it into Kyle's car, then headed off down the highway.

Kyle and I briefly met the last time I'd been in New Hampshire. He stared at me now through the rear-view mirror, his wife Morgan in the passenger seat beside him. Krisstopher had known him ever since he was about thirteen. Back in their drug days they got into a lot of trouble together; breaking in places and stealing stuff, vandalizing, running from the cops... I guess it was *still* their drug days, but now they kept a low profile, a little older and wiser.

Kyle had always been a Don Juan, sly as a fox with the ladies. Krisstopher told me stories about the two of them growing up—how he used to get all the girls. All he had to do was look at them or something. They went crazy for him and Krisstopher could never figure out just what he had that they were so attracted to.

"It's like he's got some kind of *power* over women, and I don't know what it is," he confessed.

I could see that he was a smooth one with the little sexual innuendoes he made—the looks, the gestures. I supposed there was a certain snake-like charm about him. He was normal enough looking—rather preppie, actually. For some reason he reminded me of a blond headed golfer I'd seen on TV: with the polo shirts, the sweaters tied over his shoulders, the khakis and pastel slacks... the only thing he was missing was the club. But he had those large hazel eyes though, and like Ryan, he knew how to stare sadly at a girl and melt her hard heart into butter; or like War, set her body on fire with one long, lustful glance into her soul. Still, it didn't work with me, because I didn't want it to.

Morgan lit up a bowl and passed it to me. She seemed a lot more sociable than the last time I met her. She looked different, too. No longer pregnant, her long, sandy-blond hair was now cut short and vogue, her wire framed glasses replaced by contacts. She wore an ankle-length tie-dye sundress and a pair of [159]Birkenstock sandals. I started to take a drag off the bowl, then stopped. "Uhh... what about the baby?"

Their little girl, maybe less than a year old, sat in the kiddy car seat next to me, screaming and crying.

"It's okay, go ahead," she assured me, waving her hand. "It won't bother her."

Kyle turned on the radio, his blond head whipping around to have a look at his daughter in the back seat. "Brea! Breaaa!" he crooned. "Listen, it's your favorite—The Thankful Dead." He bobbed his head up and down to the music. Brea stopped crying.

"No way! She likes The Thankful Dead?" I asked, amazed.

"Oh, yeah!" Morgan smiled. "She *loves* The Thankful Dead."

I took a hit off the pipe, holding it in my lungs, and turned to stare at the child. She was a cute baby—you could definitely tell she was theirs. Her short curly locks were blond also, her chubby cheeks red and patchy from her last outburst.

I tried imagining what it would be like to have a kid. I liked kids, but... naahh, I definitely didn't want any. When I'd been with Craig, I used to cry whenever I saw babies in the mall. A sort of maternal instinct would wash over me and I'd suddenly want one really bad. But not now. I exhaled, somehow feeling it wasn't a good idea to smoke out in front of Brea, and then passed the bowl to Krisstopher, who was sitting on the other side of me by the window.

I turned to study Morgan again. She seemed so confident, so at peace with herself. I knew it had to be hard. Kyle wasn't exactly the fatherly type, after all. I guess before meeting him, she'd been the girl everyone desired at parties: smart, pretty, wealthy parents... Then he came along, winning her over with his usual suave demeanor. But he was a playboy.

We pulled into the state park to take a walk. Krisstopher and I went off by ourselves, getting lost in the forest for a while. We laughed and galloped around through the maze of trees, high as kites; in love all over again.

That night, we stayed at Renny and Sam's while Krisstopher's references checked out for the apartment. I woke up the next morning in the shelter of his arms. After about an hour, we finally got up to shower while he raved about tofu and alfalfa sprout sandwiches with hummus dressing at a New Age shop in town that I was absolutely going to love. He was right. I loved it.

The store sold everything from literature on holistic healing and aromatherapy to hand crafted jewelry and healthy food. And the tofu sandwich was out of this world. Though by itself, tofu tasted pretty much like a sponge soaked in water, here they sautéed it in honey and spices to give it a light, delicate flavor. The Silver Moon quickly became our favorite place to eat since both of us were now vegetarians. We were making an effort to be more health conscious in order to aid our spirituality. So many New Agers were either vegans or vegetarians. It seemed the thing to do. I'd even quit smoking again. I found I had more energy as a result, and it felt good to be able to breathe once more.

Dean, our new landlord, owned a small TV repair shop further down the street. We stopped in to get the key and discuss some minor details, Krisstopher introducing me, then headed over to see our apartment; about a twenty-minute walk outside of town.

Located upstairs in a house that was probably about a hundred or more years old and had been sectioned off into four separate flats, the apartment consisted of three rooms: a kitchen/dining area, a bedroom, and a bathroom. I liked how the sun streamed in through the kitchen window that overlooked the main road, cheering up our new little home. The bedroom windows let in a lot of light as well, a pleasant change after spending most of my time in Jim's gloomy room.

Sharon let us borrow some of her furniture, which was stored in a friend's barn somewhere since she'd been committed to a nursing home due to her worsening condition. We took her kitchen table and chairs, placing them beneath the window about ten feet in front of the sink and cupboards; and her old couch, which we stuck against the opposite wall next to the entrance leading to the bedroom. A homemade bookcase of bricks and wooden boards furnished the adjoining wall, where we displayed all of our occult literature. Why hide it? We figured anyone and everyone interested should have an opportunity to be enlightened. Adjacent to the entrance of our apartment, a narrow hallway led into a tiny bathroom consisting of a toilet, sink, and metal shower stall: not a good place to be if you suffered from claustrophobia.

The majority of our move completed, we spent the following day walking around town visiting people while I surveyed my new surroundings. Krisstopher pointed out the various shops, like the rock and mineral store where we could buy crystals and other stones for a decent price, and the vogue/hippie-style clothing store Morgan worked at part time.

"Oh, and Tanya works there at Deadquarters," he mentioned rather casually. Instant anger rose within me at the mention of her name. Why did he have to bring *her* up?

"I want to see what she looks like," I told him indignantly, marching toward the small head shop. "I'm going to go in there and tell her she better never mess with my boyfriend again or I'll waste her!"

"I don't know if she's working today or not."

"Hi, Mahta!" Felician's boyfriend Klay yelled now as he passed by on his bicycle.

"Hey!" I waved. It felt good to be noticed by one of Krisstopher's friends, especially when I barely knew him. The last time I'd seen him was about a year and a half ago at Derek's party.

We walked in the door of the Dead Head/biker shop. The aroma of jasmine incense filled my nostrils. Heading over to a rack of [160]Harley Davidson tank tops, I skimmed through them while glancing around anxiously for a chick fitting Sam's description.

"She's over there—in the back," Krisstopher whispered.

A girl in tiny oval glasses with bangs and shoulder length, dark hair tied back in a ponytail stood behind the far counter where all the pipes and bongs were. *This* was Tanya? She was so… normal.

Suddenly, however, my plans to confront her were replaced by a shy awkwardness, a quiet humiliation. A… fear? I shrunk behind another rack of clothes, peering nervously at her for a split second, then quickly hurried out the door.

"I thought you were going to say something to her," Krisstopher challenged as we left the parking lot and merged onto the sidewalk once more.

"I couldn't. I—"

"Well, you shouldn't go in there and run out. It looks *stupid* when you do that!"

I felt horrible now, like I wimped out. Lingering in front of one of the shops for a moment, I debated on what I should do.

He started walking again. "Come on."

No, I couldn't. I had to say *something*. How could I just let this slide? I pulled off my sweater to reveal my small halter top and tattoo. It was a little cold, but who cared? I wanted to look tough. I wanted to scare her.

"Martyr, where are you going?"

"I'm going back in there," I told him.

This time, he waited just outside the door. I stormed over to the back counter, wanting to rip Tanya's head off but feeling strongly intimidated for some reason.

"Yeah, I wanna see one of those pipes there," I told her, attempting to sound threatening.

"Which one?" she asked, unaffected.

"That one there—with the *skulls*," I pointed, as if that was going to scare her. Why couldn't I bring myself to look her in the eye? I just couldn't. I felt the heat rush to my face as I stood there examining the pipe, blushing while she stared at me. Still looking down, I handed it back to her. "Thanks," I said gruffly, then turned and walked out the door. *Thanks?! I thanked her?* Uhhh, I wanted to kick myself in the head! I was just too puking polite to be mean to her, even though she seduced my boyfriend. Why *her*? Sam was right. She *was* a plain Jane. What on *earth* did he see in her?

Krisstopher didn't really say anything this time. I was glad. He probably thought I threatened her, since he'd been unable to see what actually occurred.

We walked over to Klay's apartment where he and Renny and Derek were hanging out in the living room. Derek lit up a joint and we all smoked out while I listened to them talk, remaining quiet for the most part. My heart felt heavy, like a brick was just dropped on it. All I could think about was Tanya. Klay looked pretty cute as I watched him joke and laugh with Renny. *Really* cute, actually. I just hated Krisstopher at the moment.

The next afternoon as I was busy putting things away in our apartment and getting the place in order, Krisstopher walked in the door with a tall, big boned metal head. He was over six feet in height and a trifle bit overweight, though not much. His blond hair was long and straight, tied back in a ponytail, and he wore a backwards baseball cap, some black jeans, a T-shirt, and tennis shoes.

"Martyr, this is Sean."

"Hi Sean," I greeted cheerily. "How's it going?"

The man looked at me coldly, unresponsive. His blue eyes were like sheets of steel. Immediately I felt something grab me inside and tell me this guy was bad news. His whole presence seemed threatening, though I wasn't sure why.

After our initial introduction, Sean pretty much ignored me, sitting at the kitchen table and focusing solely on Krisstopher while talking as if I didn't exist. I tried getting his attention by looking directly at him whenever I spoke, but he stared right passed me, uninterested in what I had to say.

Soon the two of them left for town again, Krisstopher returning to work, and I was by myself once more, wondering why his friend seemed to have a bad attitude toward me. Apparently he was the Sean that lived next door to Tanya—the one Krisstopher spoke so much about whenever he'd called me in Michigan. They partied together many times in the four months we were apart. Just what he saw in the guy I couldn't fathom. There was nothing inherently good about him that I could detect. But then, I was a little more discerning than Krisstopher when it came to these kinds of things.

\* \* \*

For some odd reason, Krisstopher woke up one morning with the left side of his face all saggy, like it had collapsed or something. His eye was drooping, the lid swollen, and one side of his mouth was contorted as well. Renny thought maybe he'd had some kind of stroke or something. He picked us up and gave us a ride to the nearby hospital. The doctor said it was a rare case—some kind of palsy—and he had no idea what caused it. Thankfully it was treatable, and after about three or four days, Krisstopher's face was back to normal. I couldn't help but wonder if Fiend had something to do with the whole ordeal.

Shortly after that, Kyle hired me for a telemarketing job in the evenings with him and Krisstopher, and at Krisstopher's suggestion, hired Sean as well. We worked in a small upstairs office at the town's Inn. There, we called people and presented to them a free stay complete with dinner in exchange for a supposed "one hour" tour in which highly competitive sales people tried persuading them to buy into vacation ownership at various resorts across the country. Vacation ownership wasn't a bad thing for those who could afford it. In the long run, it was a money saver for people who vacationed often. But for others who only wanted their free stay and dinner, first they had to endure some aggressive sales tactics without giving in to the pressure to buy.

Kyle and Krisstopher also worked during the day doing the same thing, walking the streets in town and handing out brochures to tourists on shopping sprees. This was known as *street soliciting*, though by law, they only had a certain amount of space allotted to them before they overstepped their bounds and received a ticket.

Before going to work our first night, we followed Kyle out behind one of the buildings and he got us high, thinking it would help us relax more. The weed was so potent, however, that I relaxed a little too much. All I found myself wanting to do was stare at the wall. Every muscle in my body felt like [161]Jell-O. Every thought I had was utterly profound, except the thought of conversing with people, which launched me into hyperspace paranoia. I was sure the prospective buyers would be able to detect the fact that I was stoned. Besides, who could carry on an intelligible conversation at this point, anyway, when my tongue felt like a piece of lunchmeat?

Kyle and Krisstopher, on the other hand, picked up the phone and began their pitch seemingly with ease. Sean only hesitated for a moment or two, then quickly switched over to sales mode, raising the receiver to his ear and dialing a number off one of the vacation giveaway cards retrieved from a box at the mall.

I examined him as he sat next to me, his long legs cramped up beneath the little desk. At least he was somewhat decent acting tonight, probably because he was baked. His thick New England accent made me break out in a smile as he tried pronouncing somebody's clearly ethnic last name. I concentrated on it for a moment, then listened to the drone of all three of their voices put together as they slowly lulled me into lethargy.

"Look alive there, will ya Martyr?" Kyle piped energetically, startling me. He hung up the receiver, studying me with inquisitive eyes while at the same time grinning at my predicament. *You are baked like a potato,* his look seemed to read.

He acted like he just drank a pot of coffee and took some smart pills or something. He was the only guy I knew that could smoke mass quantities of weed until it was coming out of his ears and yet still remain completely professional, almost as if it didn't faze him at all. Of course, he'd grown up with a joint in his mouth. How odd to think that his father used to sell marijuana to him and his friends. I tried picturing my mom handing me dime and quarter bags full of weed:

*"Here you go, honey. Bake your brains out. Oh, and don't forget to put on a jacket—it's cold out there."*

Krisstopher told me that Kyle's dad used to have big Thanksgiving bashes. People came from everywhere to taste his famous turkey stuffed with marijuana dressing. It was the highlight of the holiday.

Sean was on his fourth phone call now while I stared dumbly at the cue sheet in front of me. I tried psyching myself up, listening to how easily Kyle and Krisstopher rolled through the whole spiel; Kyle sounding completely alert and sharp as a tack, and Krisstopher not too bad himself considering his condition.

The fact was, I hated sales. I always had. My very first job at a clothing store in the mall was based on commission, and I despised how I had to tackle customers as soon as they walked in the door and persuade them to buy this or that. I was simply not a pushy person. Nor an assertive person, for that matter. But this job was a piece of cake: good hours, good drugs, no jerk of a boss screaming over my shoulder... why couldn't I bring myself to pick up the phone and dial it? I was just too nervous. Too embarrassed.

"Come onnn, Martyr, it's easy," Kyle assured me, sensing my reluctance. "Look, this is all you have to do." He leaned back in the chair, stretching his legs out on the desk to reveal his khaki slacks and brown leather boat shoes, and dialed the phone. "Hello, is this Mr. Bromley? Mr. Bromley, how are you?" he asked casually, as if he'd known the guy for years. "This is Kyle from the River Mountain Inn in New Hampshire. You've been selected to win a free stay for two at our plush resort, complete with a twenty-five dollar dinner certificate at our elegant restaurant..." He blabbed on and on with confidence while I watched in amazement as he made the Inn sound like the Taj Mahal. "You can go then? Great. You're going to love it. I'll put you and your wife down for the eighteenth of May. That's on a Saturday—so be sure and mark your calendar. Okay, I'll see you then, Mr. Bromley. Good-bye." He hung up the phone and smiled proudly at me. "See, nothing to it. You just have to be a good con artist, that's all."

"I feel bad lying to these people," I objected.

"But you're not really *lying*. I mean, they *are* getting a good deal: a free night's stay in our Inn with dinner. They can come here and ski, or shop in town... it's a package worth over one hundred and twenty-five dollars. Who *cares* if they have to drive five hours to get here? At least they can get away for a while. What's so bad about that?"

True, the Inn wasn't a shack or anything. But it wasn't quite as lavish as he made it out to be. And true, it was a free getaway. They even had packages for two or three days as well. Still, the tour took a lot of time—sometimes up to *four hours* depending on the couple's responses—and again, the sales people were *highly aggressive*, to put it lightly.

I listened to Sean beside me now. "Oh, you wouldn't be intarested? But suh, it's not a scam, it's—suh? Are you thaa? Suh?" He hung up the phone and turned to me with a huge grin on his face. "I guess he wasn't intarested."

I managed to make about five or six calls in the two and a half hours we were there, though they were all rejections or future callbacks because the prospective buyers weren't home.

After work, Krisstopher and I planned on tripping together. It was my hope that we could have a reunion celebration: a romantic and magical night rediscovering each other. With moving in our apartment and working and everything else going on, we hadn't really spent a lot of time alone since I'd arrived. And after four months apart, I felt like we had a lot to catch up on.

We left the Inn, Kyle waving good-bye, and walked down the dimly lit street a distance where Sean handed Krisstopher the little squares of paper. Excitement welled within me as I thought of how much fun we'd have. All I wanted was to be close to him right now—to be consumed by his presence like I was when we first met.

"Hey, you wanna hang out and fry with me and Martyr?" he suddenly asked. My body stiffened as I awaited Sean's reply.

"Yeah, shuh. I'll be ovuh in a little while."

Horrified, my heart sank within me. How *could* he? Sean didn't even like me to begin with, and I'd told Krisstopher that before. Why did he want to waste the evening hanging out with *him* as opposed to getting close to *me* once again? We walked back to the apartment while I poured out my complaint the whole way.

"The guy has an attitude problem—I don't like him at all. He's been hanging around with us ever since I got here, practically. Can't you and I just hang out for once—*alone?* Don't you want to spend time with me? I've only been here a little over a *week* so far."

"I'm sorry. I didn't know it was going to bother you. I just figured it would be cool to party with someone else, too."

"Yeah? Well, when will we be able to be alone? The guy never leaves."

"Look, we'll just hang out for a while with him and then tell him we wanna go to bed or something. I'm sure it won't be a big deal."

I didn't like how Sean stuck to Krisstopher like glue. Didn't he have any other friends? He was really cramping my style. And what was wrong with hanging out with just me? Why did there always have to be a third party involved in order for Krisstopher to have fun?

I thought of Camron and Jasmine in Florida. I used to get so envious of their relationship—of how they were off in their own little world, completely satisfied with each other and needing no one else. They took walks together at two in the morning, picking weird flowers and weeds that looked like they came from another planet, returning again with huge smiles on their faces—all over each other like teenagers in love for the first time. I'd lie on the futon and listen to them giggling in the bedroom, having the time of their life, while Krisstopher snored beside me. I could only wish I had someone so absorbed with me. How was it that they were always together, and yet it seemed they still couldn't get enough of each other?

Sean came over about forty-five minutes after we got to the apartment. I made it a point to strike up a conversation with him, figuring I'd give it one more try. If he was tripping with us, I might as well make the best of it. Otherwise, I'd ruin my own trip worrying about it all night.

Krisstopher was showing him some of the songs he wrote. He seemed pretty interested in them, so I thought he might like to read a few of mine. I handed him the pieces of paper and he looked them over a minute. But he said nothing. I knew they were good. I knew I was a good writer. But he said absolutely nothing. He just nodded and started telling us about how he was writing a book based on the [162]Arthurian Legend: King Arthur, Guenivere, Sir Lancelot, etc., etc. It wasn't until I showed an interest in his project that he started warming up to me, talking on and on about it while I made comments like, "Wow." "Great." "Sounds cool."

Yeah, the story of my life. Give my energy to the leeches. Let them suck me dry, demanding my constant praise and attention while they offer me nothing in return. The Energy Leeches. The Selfish Energy Leeches.

*"Suck suck suck. Thank you Paula, for replenishing me. That's just what I needed—a little self-esteem. By the way, you're looking a little pale. Are you feeling alright? Well, I must be going. Good-bye."*

Of course, I was too gullible to understand this at the time. I simply repressed the pain like I'd done with all of life's blows so far, too weak to fight back. Too naive to know how.

After a while, we ended up heading back to Sean's place where he said he had some stuff to drink. The acid was terribly weak, and since he was twice the size of Krisstopher or me, most likely did nil for him. That's probably why he felt he needed to get intoxicated.

It was about a forty-five-minute walk from town to the trailer park where he lived, so altogether it took us a little over an hour. The sky was bright with stars. We followed the dark, winding road scarcely inhabited by cars. Only every once in a while did headlights emerge from a distance and grow closer as one whirred toward us and then quickly passed, the peaceful silence of the night and the quiet humming of various insects enveloping us once more.

I carried a flashlight in my hand, which I twirled around, making circular patterns in the fields. I felt so free out there with no one around us. I must have been talking rather loudly—it seemed maybe I was shouting or making some weird noise or something—because Sean told me to be quiet. I didn't see what the big deal was. It wasn't like there were any houses in sight or anything, and I hardly thought we'd be arrested for disturbing the peace—unless the frogs and crickets reported us. Maybe I was just getting on his nerves. He and Krisstopher talked about something or other while I thought for a moment on War. What was *he* doing? I wondered.

We finally arrived at a patch of woods with a small oak sign that read:

PINE FOREST TRAILER PARK

As we took the entranceway into the clearing surrounded by trees, I felt something was a little strange, but I couldn't place my finger on it. A weird... presence?

We came upon some trailers, and Sean pointed out Tanya's to me. It stuck out like an ugly monument against the blackness of the night. I stared at it for a while, bitterness welling up within me once more as thoughts of Krisstopher hanging out there with her flooded my mind. The lights were off. Sean said she'd gone somewhere for the weekend.

About twenty feet to the right of her trailer was his trailer. We followed him up the steps and into the door. He switched on the fluorescent light above the sink in the kitchen, then a small lamp in the living room. I looked around curiously while Krisstopher plopped down on the couch. Not bad for a guy's place—nice and neat, and kind of plain. A few books on a shelf, a small stereo, a chair, and a couch with an Aztec throw over it made up the majority of furnishings. The only thing that really stuck out in my mind there was the Metal Coffin poster on the wall which pictured the band's rotting skull logo smiling evilly at me. Beneath the skull were the numbers 666.

Sean grabbed a pint of whiskey out of his cupboard and sat down in the chair. I was bored... even a little sleepy. Totally unusual for me when enjoying an LSD experience. Probably because I really wasn't enjoying this one. I supposed it was better than nothing, but it was clear to see that there wasn't much left of the night and my hope of being alone with Krisstopher had long since vanished. I wasn't even getting any visuals to entertain me.

I looked out the window then, admiring the view—nothing but pure forest: pine trees, branches strewn here and there, and dried needles covering the ground. The only bummer about having a backyard like this was the black bears, but Sean hadn't seen any yet, he said.

Krisstopher and I had a pretty nice backyard too. It eventually led to a narrow path through the woods that sloped down a hill—a rather steep journey best traveled, I discovered, by sliding on my butt until I reached the bottom. There, it merged into a wild field beside the river that went on for miles. We would spend many days in the future perched atop the jagged rocks along the bank of the river, listening to the rushing water and chirping birds.

"Well, it's getting late. I guess Martyr and I should be going." Krisstopher told him now.

"Alright. I'll walk you guys back tuh yuh place," he replied. How utterly absurd, since then he was going to have to walk all the way back to *his* place again! But whatever.

As I suspected, he ended up crashing out at our apartment. When I woke up the next afternoon, I put on my new glasses. As if sensing my insecurity, Sean made a comment about them being *coke bottle glasses*. I knew they weren't. I'd spent extra money to get them *rolled*: a process that involved smoothing down the thick part. Actually, they were probably the thinnest, most attractive pair of glasses I'd ever owned. But still it hurt. It hurt that he tried shattering my confidence once more, just like he had with the songs I wrote. Why was it always praises for Krisstopher and cut downs for me? Was the guy *gay* or something? On our walk home earlier that morning, he'd mentioned something terrible about being molested by his grandmother. Maybe he had a thing against women now.

\* \* \*

We received some housewarming gifts from Derek and Renny. They were spiritual housewarming gifts, and I was sure they were sent from the gods and goddesses to let us know we were on the right path.

Renny gave us a huge illustrated comic wall poster of a beautiful, red headed warrior woman. I liked to think she was me in a greater sense, like maybe my alter ego or something, or at least what I was striving to become. Dressed in a white body suit with armor, she knelt down on her knees. In one of her hands, she held a huge [163]sword; in the other, a [164]shield shaped like the [165]sun. The bottom of the poster read:

[166]CHRISTOS STRATIOTES

I wondered what that translated as. *Christos* seemed to have something to do with Christ, but I didn't know what *Stratiotes* meant. I used to get baked and stare at the poster, picturing myself as the warrior woman: well-armed and ready for battle, strong and afraid of nothing. A *spiritual* warrior.

Then there was the little artificial tree in the miniature whiskey bottle that Derek had contributed. At the moment, I was reading about the Jewish Qabalah, which spoke of the Tree of Life and its various paths and spheres traveled by the neophyte on his spiritual journey. The little tree served as a reminder for me, a confirmation that I was headed in the right direction. I set it on our bookshelf, one of my favorite spots in the whole apartment.

The shelf was a little piece of my father's library; a small section of spiritual wisdom to be had by anyone who took the time to browse through it. Sean skimmed through a couple of its books one night after passing around his pipe a few times. He asked us some questions then—a lot of questions, actually—though I can't remember what they were. I just know they were all witchcraft related. I answered him ninety percent of the time, even though he seemed curious to hear Krisstopher's stance on things. After a while, he directed the questions solely at me since Krisstopher was busy looking for something in the bedroom on the other side of the hanging blanket and I was willing to blab freely about my spirituality. That's about the time that I noticed a change in Sean as far as his interest in me was concerned. From that point on, he paid extra special attention to me. He made it a point to include me in the conversation whenever the three of us were together.

We all continued to work telemarketing in the evenings. I even received a bonus check for thirty-five dollars because one of the couples I called actually showed up to take the tour. But I still hated the job. The only thing I looked forward to was getting stoned beforehand.

On the way to the Inn one evening, we took a walk by the old railroad tracks and had a look at all the deserted railway cars lined up alongside them. A historical train station offered tours of the town to anyone interested. As we climbed inside one of the cars, Krisstopher told us the story of how he'd been stoned out of his gourd once and decided to have a showdown with the train. Needless to say, the train won. Apparently he'd stood on the railroad tracks until the last possible minute, but his timing was a little off. The train hit the side of him and sent him flying through the air and crashing to the ground where he was knocked out cold. Luckily for him, it had only been going thirty miles per hour, and so he recovered virtually unharmed except for some cuts and bruises and a minor concussion.

Venturing further along the tracks, the three of us then sat down for a moment on a grassy hill amidst a small forest of trees that led down to the river. Sean doused himself with bug spray after explaining to Krisstopher which one not to use because it made men sterile, then we got up and moved along.

"Heera," he now said, handing me a flower he'd picked.

"For me?" I asked, surprised. I took it from him, studying it closely. It was the strangest flower I'd ever seen. Though nothing was particularly extraordinary about the outside of the flower, it's soft petals white and round, it was the inside of the flower that amazed me. As I stared into the heart of it, I noticed a tiny [167]pentagram within its delicate design— not just a mere star, but a star with lines threaded through it exactly like the famous witch's symbol. "Wow! Thanks!" I gasped with childlike amazement.

He smiled assuredly. "I *knew* you'd like it." It seemed he, too, was aware of the pentagram just from the way he was staring at me now— like it was an inside joke that only the two of us knew. He appeared to be conveying something spiritual to me, as if wanting me to observe his knowledge of… witchcraft? No, maybe I was just imagining things. But I did get the slight feeling that he might be romantically interested in me.

Was Krisstopher mad that he'd given me the flower? I glanced over at him, but he seemed unaffected, as if he hadn't even noticed at all. I was glad, because I felt a little awkward.

"What's in here?" I asked, stopping in front of a large shed containing a somewhat tall and spacious open storage compartment beneath it. Inside the compartment, decorated panels and pieces of wooden furniture were carelessly stacked one upon another.

"Oh, these are stage props. See, that's the play house right over there where they put on all the plays," Krisstopher explained.

"Isn't that a coffin?"

We followed Sean's finger toward a large Celtic cross tacked onto a life sized, blue, vampire-like coffin.

"Wow! Check it out!" Krisstopher exclaimed excitedly.

"Oh man, it's so cool! Totally gothic!" I chimed in.

"Why don't you take it home with you? It would look good in yuh apahtment." Sean suggested now, his long arms folded and a smirk on his face.

"No… we can't. What if they need this?" I objected.

"Martyr, this stuff looks like it hasn't been touched in years. Look at all the cobwebs." Krisstopher argued. "Besides, if these were their good props, they wouldn't leave them out in the open like this. They'd put them in the shed. Look at how some of this stuff is all warped—like it got rained on or something. I bet they'd never even miss this if we took it.

"Krisstapha's right," Sean agreed. "And I'll help you cahry it home if you want. We can come back and get it latuh when it's dahk."

The perfect piece of furniture to compliment any goth's apartment. I couldn't wait. "Yeah, I want to *sleep* in it," I beamed.

So later that night, they walked me home and then went back and got the coffin, which was heavier than it looked. After taking the shortcut through the meadow alongside the river and up the steep, wooded trail to our house, they banged their way upstairs with it and into our apartment, setting it in the corner of our bedroom near the bed. To our surprise, the inside was even padded with satin, just like the real thing. I fancied Peter Morphine would have had a smile of approval on his pale skeletal face, maybe even singing a round of *Bram Stoker is Dead* in honor of the occasion.

* * *

Tanya. I pretty much wanted to kill her. Krisstopher and I were standing in the little information booth on the street where he and Kyle and some others worked during the day. There they passed out River Mountain Inn pamphlets and dinner certificates to those requesting information on the town or the shops.

"Hi *Krisstopher*," a girl's voice called flirtingly.

"Who's that?" I whipped my head around to see the girl walking further down the street, waving at him.

"That's Tanya," he answered, waving back.

I hadn't recognized her for a moment. She looked different now that she was out in the sunlight and not hidden behind a large counter. Sam was right: she was nothing special. She walked half hunched over—kind of dumpy, with a grandma-looking matching shorts and top outfit.

Within an instant I was out of the booth and onto the street, where I growled, "Whore!" at the top of my lungs in my death metal voice. She kept walking, but I knew she heard me. I couldn't believe the wench had the audacity to say hi to him right in front of me.

"Martyr! She *just said hi*," he scolded now.

How could he be so stupid? The woman was deliberately upsetting me. Her motives were plain to see, especially to a person like me, who was anything but clueless when it came to picking up on other people's vibes. Krisstopher on the other hand...

After stewing a minute, I walked by myself over to the back parking lot where Deadquarters was located. Tanya was sitting outside of the store in a lawn chair, eating her lunch. One of the tattoo artist/biker guys that worked at the shop next door stood nearby, talking to her. Krisstopher had introduced me to him earlier; Russ had given him his fairy tattoo. I'd shown him my Anubis jackal, and he commented that he used to have one just like it, pointing to an area of skin on his upper arm now covered by a larger, more colorful design.

"Why'd you cover it up?" I asked, disappointed.

"Oh. I did that back in my Christian days," he explained.

"Your *Christian* days?"

He was silent, refusing to expound on what he meant.

As I approached the tattoo shop now, he looked over at me, nodding hello. I waved, leaning against the window and glaring at The Queen while he told her bye and took off on his [168]Harley. She sat quietly, eating her take-out food and ignoring me. Then after about five minutes, she got up and went inside. I hoped she finally got the hint.

* * *

I quit telemarketing. Sam got me a real job working as a sales clerk at Jentanno, the clothing outlet she managed. Oddly enough, Felician was the assistant manager. So here we were again, the three of us, just like at Derek's.

Sam was really impressive. I found it hard to believe that she was my age and managed her own retail store. But she was very intelligent. She ran it perfectly; not too hard-nosed but definitely not slack, either. Working together kindled our friendship, whereas before, we'd only been acquaintances. Different as the two of us were, I really liked her. I guess I acknowledged her as sort of a big sister looking out for me or something. She just had a good, sensible head on her shoulders that made me feel safe to be with her.

I think the greatest thing about our friendship was the fact that she believed in me. I didn't feel as insecure around her. She always made me feel I was capable of handling any problem that came up—like I was competent—as opposed to other people who saw my weak spots and preyed upon them. And she wasn't two-faced like most women I knew. I respected her a great deal.

Felician, however, was harder to get to know. She rarely talked, and made sure to keep up her invisible fence which prevented people from walking all over her lawn. She strutted around with her head held high and a look of perpetual indignation on her face. Everything she said was very impersonal, very surface. Yet again, there was that tough girl image that I admired—that street-smart attitude. She never left herself open for attack, refusing to trust anyone. I wished I could be like that, instead of wearing my heart on my sleeve and getting slaughtered for it every time. But she rarely smiled. It seemed she was an extremely lonely person because she feared taking chances. She shut people out, and in the process, she shut herself out from any real companionship. Did she ever get *personal* with anyone? I wondered.

And what did she think of me? Sometimes I felt she hated me for going out with Krisstopher, whom she spoke fondly of whenever mentioning their adolescent years and growing up together. I believe Krisstopher said he was the first person she'd ever had a sexual encounter with. Perhaps that's why I sensed some slight aloofness on her part. I was sure he still held a special place in her heart.

She'd had a party recently at her apartment during which time she took me into the bedroom and read me some of her poetry. For Felician, this was a major breakthrough. But she was drunk, so it was probably easier for her to let down her wall. I got a little uptight, however, when I discovered that most of the poems were ones she'd written about Krisstopher years before. Didn't she have any others, or was he always the main topic of her prose?

\* \* \*

I'd had enough. Inside Deadquarters, I stormed toward Tanya now. "Uh, Tanya? Can I meet you after work? I'd like to have a word with you." Maybe she wasn't quite understanding that Krisstopher was *off limits* to her. Maybe I needed to *make* her understand.

"I have something to do after work. I can't," she answered, smiling sweetly.

"Well, when's a good time for you then? Because I really need to talk to you," I insisted, looking her in the eyes for the first time. Scary, but she sort of looked pretty today. "How about if I come over to your house?" I continued. "I know where you live."

"Okay. You can come over tomorrow. I'll be home then."

"What time?"

"Five thirty."

\* \* \*

239

I borrowed Krisstopher's mountain bike and pedaled the half hour it took to get to Tanya's trailer.

*I'll just tell her she better lay off him,* I reasoned now as I climbed off the bike and approached her front door. *I'll explain to her that it's not cool to flirt with other people's boyfriends, and then if she doesn't get the hint, I'll have to bash her head in.* Knock knock knock. I waited. And waited. No answer, so I rapped on the door harder this time.

Silence...

Silence...

More silence.

The shades on the windows were pulled, and no sound was coming from inside. I felt my face redden as I realized I'd been had—I biked all the way over there for nothing. Tanya lied to me, having no intention of meeting me for a little talk. Embarrassed, I knocked on Sean's door. Maybe I'd just see if he knew where she was.

"Hello Mahta," he greeted, surprised. "What brings *you* heera?"

He held the door open for me and I stepped into the kitchen, sputtering angrily about how I was supposed to meet Tanya at her place for a *little talk* and she wasn't home.

He smirked. "Well of cohss she's not home. She's not *stupid*, Mahta. Do you really think she's going tuh wait around tuh get huh butt kicked? No, she's smahta than that. Instead, she's going tuh tick you off by making you come all the way down heera fuh nothing. I saw huh leave a couple of ahhs ago. I think she was going tuh Massachusetts fuh the weekend."

"Well, that's it. I can see I'm going have to do something more *drastic* so she'll get the hint."

"You wanna put a note on huh doora and let huh know you stopped by? I've got some paypa," he grinned.

"Yeah. That would be great. I think I will."

Outside now, Sean taped the note to her door while I stood nearby, tracing pentagrams in the dirt with a stick. The note was a bit threatening, with a reminder that I'd stopped by and didn't appreciate biking all the way over there for nothing. I'd drawn some pentagrams on it, and Sean had added an upside down cross and *666*, or something to that effect.

Then we went back inside his place and had some coffee with cream and vanilla extract.

\* \* \*

A few days later, Sean came over while Krisstopher was at work. I sensed he was really starting to like me—a lot. He brought me a bird's nest that he'd found somewhere, and a beautiful blue jay feather; the biggest and most detailed one I'd ever seen. I was flattered, especially since we'd gotten off to such a bad start.

It was at this point that I started viewing him as a confidant. The things Krisstopher didn't like to discuss about spirituality, he did. So I told him all about myself—my hopes, my dreams, my childhood, and my desire to pick up where my father had left off concerning his journey into the Occult at a younger age. I believed my father was somehow telling me to carry on: to unlock all the mysteries he had failed to discover. He paved the path for me with his books and experiences. Now I had to travel that path with an expectancy that I would succeed.

As usual, Sean got me stoned and then we sat around and talked, me doing most of the talking while he listened intently, taking it all in. Somehow we got on the subject of witchcraft. I mentioned War, telling him I was sure he was a warlock—a black magician who put a spell on me. He just had a power, I told him, that I'd never sensed before in a man. He offered no reply, but sat quietly at the kitchen table, a smirk on his face.

Then we started talking about tarot cards and how Krisstopher had The Magi Deck, which was magnificently painted. For some reason, I went and got one of the cards from the deck, handing it to him. Just about the time he touched it, I realized what I'd done. As I stated before, one is not to touch another's consecrated objects in witchcraft. By doing so, negative energy can be transmitted through them. Now here he was holding Krisstopher's tarot card.

"Oh no!" I gasped, attempting to grab the card back from him. He broke out in a huge smile.

"Too late," he said deviously, clutching the card tightly in both hands as if to willfully contaminate it with bad vibes.

Later, on the way to town, we passed a dead blue jay on the side of the road. It didn't appear to have been hit by a car since it wasn't flattened or anything, but rather, to have been slaughtered. But maybe not.

He accompanied me to the library to locate a book on Armageddon. I explained to him that I was interested in researching the subject since my dad had talked so much about it. I'd recently had a revelation while lying in bed stoned, staring at a pair of jeans draped over our wardrobe. The cloaked skull patch on the knee resembled the face of a grim reaper. As I peered at it, a thought crossed my mind. *What if [169]Armageddon isn't a physical battle? What if it's a spiritual battle—against the forces of good and evil—taking place right now? And people are being fooled because they're waiting for a physical battle to take place?*

With that, I was anxious to read any material on the subject that I could. I even called my mom and asked her to send me a bible so I could study the book of Revelation, which mentioned it.

After searching the library catalog, I found a book containing the word *Armageddon* in its title. But as I skimmed through its pages, I discovered it was about an old battleship or something, and had nothing to do with the biblical Armageddon at all. Disappointed, I tossed it aside, telling Sean.

"Gee, that's too bad," he commented sarcastically.

As I sat on the couch one day looking out the window, a large, [170]locust type bug landed on the screen with a *thud*. I gazed at him, suddenly taken aback when I noticed he wore a breast of armor on his chest, and had the face of a man, with blond wavy locks and pointy teeth! He smiled at me evilly, like a little demon in disguise. I'd never seen anything like this before without the use of acid or mescaline. Marveling, I moved closer to the screen to examine him more thoroughly. He abruptly flew off, leaving me staring after him in bewilderment.

\* \* \*

I'd had quite a few dreams involving a [171]river lately. I knew it had something to do with my spirituality, but I wasn't quite sure *what* as of yet.

242

Often, I'd take Zain with me to a spot further down the riverbank, where there were more trees and foliage, and not as many sharp rocks. There, I'd tie him to a tree branch. He'd climb to the highest point possible until his leash jerked him back, them puff out his dewlap and soak up the sun, turning a beautiful bright green with hints of turquoise across the top of his head and around his neck.

I sat on a blanket and wrote in my magic journal or read Krisstopher's new Wiccan handbook. There by the *whooshing*, rippling water, it was peaceful. I could think about perfecting my spirituality or dream about who I was in past lives and what I learned in those other times long ago.

Sometimes Krisstopher and Sean came along for a swim, the two of them swinging from vines into the center of the waterway with a splash. Or Sean brought his guitar, playing a romantic ballad while we sat quietly, staring at the sun's shimmering reflection on the river's surface.

Afterward, we walked along the road just outside of town while I scanned the dirt with childlike anticipation for small pieces of metal, stones, or any other objects I could use later to make something with. The objects seemed like treasure to me, glistening in the sun with all the luster of a rare diamond or a milky pearl.

I stooped down excitedly now, picking up a dried-out old piece of rubber with a weird design on it. "Wow! Look at this!" I exclaimed.

Beauty is in the eye of the beholder. And things appear especially beautiful when you've smoked three or four bowls.

\* \* \*

As we slid once more down the steep little path to the field, I admired the tree that jutted out just ahead.

"That's a *beautiful* tree, isn't it?" I asked Krisstopher. I'd been reading a lot about trees lately, and their magical powers. Because they were ancient symbols of nature thought to be wise as a result of their many centuries on the earth, it was suggested that one pay them the necessary homage and reverence they so deserved. "I love that tree. I have a feeling it's very wise," I added. I would have to remember to give it a money offering: silver coins, of course, like the magic books instructed.

Later, as we made our way back up the path again, I admired the tree once more. "I *love* that tree—it's a *magic* tree, don't you think?"

As if in reply, it suddenly smacked me in the forehead, leaving a nice sized red spot for me to remember it by.

"Ouch!!!" I cried, wincing in pain. I suppose it could be argued that I ran into the tree, but I would rather swear that the branch reached out and clobbered me one, [172]as if I was being reprimanded for worshiping it.

"Well, it certainly doesn't look like the tree loves *you*, Martyr," Krisstopher chuckled.

\* \* \*

"What's that book you got thaa, Mahta?" Felician asked as I made my way downstairs at Jentanno to pick up my paycheck.

"It's about witchcraft," I answered proudly, showing her the old cover. I'd checked out the book from the library there in town. So far it was pretty boring; not at all easy to read or understand like the newer books were.

"Oh... so yuhr into *witchcraft*, huh?" she asked. I detected a slight bit of concern in her voice.

"Yeah," I responded, suddenly feeling superior. It didn't matter if I fit in with the *old gang* clique or not. I was still cool, because I had power. *Can't you feel my power, Felician? Aren't you just a little intimidated?*

"*I* used to read books like that," she informed me after a minute. *Used to?*

\* \* \*

We sat on a hill in the dark, listening to Sean strum away on his guitar. I was deep in thought, the music carrying me far off, when suddenly I heard someone whisper my name. I turned my head to see a small [173]jawa-like figure in a black cloak further down the hill next to a tree. Evil suddenly clenched my heart and I let out a shrill scream, scrambling to my feet.

"Martyr, what is it—what's wrong?!" Krisstopher panicked.

"There's something evil—we've gotta get out of here! Come on! Let's go—*c'mon!*" I shouted, tearing up the hill with him right behind me.

Sean calmly rose to his feet, guitar in hand, and followed us onto the road; unaffected. When we were within safe distance, Krisstopher demanded an explanation. I told him of the evil presence I'd felt, and of the figure I'd seen. I *had* seen it, hadn't I? And no, I wasn't on acid.

Sean said nothing. From what I could perceive in the dimly lit night, he appeared to be smiling.

\* \* \*

War was on my mind a lot lately. He'd never really left, though for a while his energy seemed to die down a bit, perhaps because I stopped concentrating so heavily upon him. Now I could feel him strongly again, calling to me. Just think, I'd had the chance—the chance to be his, to go with him to New York—and I'd declined for Krisstopher's sake, only to be mocked by an indignant Queen of Pentacles while The Knight of Swords forever defended her honor.

What might we have had, The Knight of Pentacles and me? What might we *still* have? The story wasn't over yet.

\* \* \*

The river was gentle, unlike some. It held a certain fascination, a certain mystery for me. Especially this part, secluded from kids diving off the bridge and people sitting around smoking cigarettes and wading their feet in the cold water. Here, it seemed like another land all together. Sean had shown me this spot. It was the best spot out of the whole river.

In this place, I could stare up at the tall walls of the precipice overlooking the water. Made of sand, rock, and clay, they resembled the walls of an ancient Egyptian city. I liked how the sun shone bright on portions, making it easier to envision hieroglyphics etched in their surface. Gazing up at them now, I traveled back in time, to when War had been a pharaoh, and I, one of his harem. I'd seen it in the crystal ball: him lying on a narrow divan in a vertical striped garment and headpiece, surrounded by beautiful women poised on their knees, ready to serve him at his beck and call. And there in the midst of them, I recognized myself, peering deep into his eyes with a love none of them could possibly fathom. Nor could I.

This locality of the river was occupied by several small, lengthy sections of sandbars. I walked out to one, setting Zain on a huge branch above a more shallow part of the water that extended to just above my knees, and fastened his leash in place. He seemed agitated at my choice of scenery for some reason, like he didn't prefer his surroundings. Tough—he'd survive. He was probably just in a cranky mood today.

The entire area had a pulse all its own. Every rock, every drop of water, every grain of sand throbbed with a strange energy, like I'd entered an [174]electromagnetic field. A perfect place to cast a spell. I hunted around for a large stick. Tracing War's name in the wet sand, I concentrated hard, sending out a telepathic message... of love.

*Feel me War... how I long for you. Answer me. Answer me.* Then I added aloud, "According to your own free will, of course. For the universal good of all. So mote it be." Pouring water over the name, I washed it away, releasing it to work its power.

Zain was still in a most horrible mood. As I untied his leash and plucked him off the branch now, he sliced my hands with his razor-sharp nails, drawing blood, and smacked me in the face with his tail. It was all I could do to hold him while he writhed and twisted violently all the way home. I wondered just what had gotten into him.

The next week, I returned to the spot with Krisstopher, where we pitched a tent further down along the sandy bank. This time, we left Zain at home with a big bowl of food to keep him content.

After setting up our tent and having a bite to eat, we talked for a while as nighttime quickly approached; then settled in for the evening, the sounds of nature encircling us. Tomorrow we'd have a good portion of the day to savor the beauty and power of this part of the river. As Krisstopher dozed beside me in the sleeping bag, I read for a bit with a small flashlight while bugs buzzed and thumped on the canvas of the tent and an occasional mosquito enjoyed a taste of my blood. Every so often I paused from reading, experiencing a slight tinge of fear. *Something* camped with us in the blackness of the night beneath the glowing moon: something unpleasant.

In the morning, we woke bright and early to enjoy coffee roasted over a small fire and some breakfast. Afterward, I crouched down to go to the bathroom in the sand, clad in my zebra striped bikini. Suddenly I felt uneasy again, like someone was watching me. I looked up toward the cliff but could see nothing—only trees.

Soon enough, the sun jutted out of the clouds, casting warmth upon the section further down from us. We grabbed a blanket and some books and headed over there to bask in its rays.

Surrounded by the amber walls of the cliff, I studied more hieroglyphics in my newly purchased [175]*Egyptian Book of the Dead*. My father had two volumes of the ancient manuscript in hardcover, which my mom kept with her because they were very old and probably worth some money. There had to be *something* in these hieroglyphics—some secret waiting to be discovered. Perhaps many secrets. Though the book described Egyptian burial rites and ceremonial practices, I was sure it contained magical formulae apparent only to the observing eye.

Beside me on the blanket, Krisstopher read [176]*The Tibetan Book of the Dead*. We'd gotten both of them at the New Age bookstore in town, where I'd also purchased my second deck of tarot cards: a High Priestess deck. The owners of the store, husband and wife, were very friendly. I noticed, especially, that the man took quite a liking to Krisstopher, making it a point to talk extensively with him whenever we stopped in. Though I wished he would discuss spiritual matters with me the way he did with Krisstopher, he seemed oblivious to my presence. Krisstopher mentioned he was a little peculiar, though he did agree to read[176] *The Tibetan Book of the Dead* at the man's suggestion.

"Ouch!" I cried now, smacking at a tiny black fly that had just bitten me on the calve. One of the pit falls of New Hampshire: the stupid biting black flies. I even hated the way they were shaped compared to regular flies, kind of square in appearance, with scalloped wings. Just the mere sight of them annoyed me, making me want to catch one between my fingers and pluck his translucent scaled pennons right out of his fuzzy body.

I returned to reading my book. Another one bit me, this time on the thigh. And another, on the back. "Ouch! *Stupid flies!*" I growled, swatting at them violently.

"They're not bothering *me*," Krisstopher stated rather matter-of-factly.

"Ouch! Crap! Well, they're bothering *me*. C'mon, let's go someplace else." By this time, I'd been bitten about six times, and was miserable.

"We just got here, Martyr. Ignore them and they'll go away. It's mind over matter."

Sighing, I tried his suggestion, dismissing them from my thoughts and returning to the page where I left off. A few minutes went by, and then another bite, this time on the cheek. *Okay, mind over matter. These black flies are not biting me. This isn't happening. They don't exist. Think… no black flies. There are no black flies. There are no black—* "OUUUCH! ARRRRGH! That's it, Krisstopher! I'm leaving right now! I can't take it anymore!" I shouted in pain, scrambling to my feet and running toward the tent. I already had four more bites on my face.

Krisstopher got up, shaking out the blanket, and followed me. So did the flies. I was practically in tears now from the stinging welts they left.

"Do you wanna just head back home?" he offered. I nodded my head yes. As we walked home along the wooded trail beside the river, the flies continued biting, refusing to leave until we emerged into the open field behind our house.

Soon after entering the apartment, I got the chills accompanied by a fever.

"Oh my God, Martyr! Look at your face!" Krisstopher exclaimed.

I hurried into the bathroom to have a look in the mirror. My eyelids and the area around my mouth had swelled up considerably now, as had my cheeks. I looked grotesque. In addition, the welts on my neck, arms, and legs had also grown even larger and redder.

The doctor said I'd had an allergic reaction from all the poison in my system caused by the bites. So much for Krisstopher's *mind over matter* mentality.

* * *

It was our anniversary. We'd been together for two years already. I wanted to be alone with Krisstopher tonight, but as usual, he needed more people involved. He'd made plans for us to go out to a bar in

Massachusetts and celebrate with another friend Ron whom he worked with, and his girlfriend GiGi.

I didn't like GiGi, ever since I vibed in on the fact that she was after Krisstopher. As many times as I'd tried being nice and striking up a conversation with her, she always gave me the cold shoulder, sticking her nose up at me like she was too upper class even to breathe the same air that I did. Krisstopher, on the other hand, she treated like a king. I wondered if Ron got the same impression.

This particular evening was no different. She brought along a bunch of her rich, preppie girlfriends, and all night they laughed and joked in their little clique while Krisstopher joined in, forgetting I even existed. I walked aimlessly around the bar so as not to look upset. I had hoped Krisstopher might miss me and come looking for me, but he didn't.

After we ran out of cigarettes (I was now smoking again), I found him with one later and asked where he got it, to which he slurred, "GiGi gave me one. She's been giving them to me all night."

I was livid that he hadn't even considered perhaps *I* might like one. No, this wasn't my idea of an anniversary celebration at all. To make matters worse, he'd also arranged for us to sleep over at GiGi's parents' house. How romantic! The next morning when I awoke to go to the bathroom, I noticed one of GiGi's model portfolio pictures on the washing machine right near the bathroom door. Funny that it happened to be one in which she looked halfway gothic: a black and white of her crouching down in the wintry woods, arrayed in a long, dark coat and brimmed hat similar to mine. I hated it. And I knew she'd placed it there for Krisstopher to see. There wasn't a doubt in my mind.

I wondered just exactly what Krisstopher did when he worked out on the street away from my observation. He told me GiGi stopped by on occasion, supposedly to see Ron, but how did I know? Being the flirt that he was, I only knew one thing: I couldn't trust him.

After that night, we argued a lot—about everything: Tanya, and how he repeatedly stuck up for her; GiGi, and how he flirted with her…

I was so tired of trying to make it work. Why couldn't he just be happy with *me*? Why did other people always have to enter the equation? And why couldn't he *be there* for me? I wasn't sure what I needed, but I knew it was more than he could offer. Couldn't he for once give me the attention I desired? I was so sick of always dishing out emotional support when he couldn't do the same for me.

And then after a big blowout one evening—after screaming and shouting for nearly two hours at each other—he found it easy just to go to sleep though nothing was resolved between us. As I stood in the doorway watching him snore, our conversation echoed in my head.

*"Why don't you just leave Tanya out of this? Why do you have to keep bringing her up?"*

*"Because you* **slept** *with her, that's why! And I'm sick of hearing her name every day. Sean keeps mentioning her, and how can I forget what you've done? I have to look at her ugly face every day—every day I'm reminded!"*

*"Well then, maybe you should move back to your mom's. Maybe this isn't going to work after all."*

Suddenly, I hated the fact that I'd made another terrible mistake by leaving Michigan to be with him once more, suckered in by his promises—promises he never kept.

*"... Start all over again, just the two of us."*

Yeah right. At that moment, I hated him; I wished I'd never met him. I hated what I'd done to Craig. I hated my life. And I hated myself.

Grabbing a butcher knife, I headed for the bathroom. The desperate feeling that washed over me time and again—suicide—came flooding back now. I plopped down in the bathroom floor, meditating on plunging the knife into my heart, then raised the long, sharp blade toward my chest. *You don't want to do this... you don't want to do this, do you? You hate blood, remember? You can't stand the sight of blood!* Cowering, I lowered the knife. *I can't kill myself. What am I going to do?! There's no way out. There's no way out. I can't take it anymore. I can't take it—* "Aaaaah!!" Lifting the knife slightly, I brought it down on my calve with enough pressure to cut, but not enough to sever my limb. "Aaaaah!"— slice. "Aaaaah!"—slice.

Blood squirted out like a gusher as my skin slit apart. I stared in shock. "Oh my God! What have I done? Oh my God!" I screamed, panicking. The cuts were not large, but they were serious. Realization set in and I screamed some more.

Krisstopher came running into the bathroom. When he saw the blood, he yelled, "Martyr, what did you *do?* Oh my God, Martyr!"

I rocked back and forth, sobbing while he grabbed a washcloth and held it on my leg. What was happening to me?

"We're going to have to go to the hospital. You need stitches," he told me now.

"No!" I cried in shock. "I don't want to go to the hospital."

He taped the washcloth to my leg after running it under cold water, then carried me into the bedroom and laid me on the bed.

"Are you hungry? Do you want me to run to the store?" he asked nervously, not sure just what to do for me since I refused to go to the doctor.

"Uh huh," I sobbed, still in shock.

"Okay, don't move—I'll be right back. Here. Watch some TV." He turned the television on and left the room. The door to our apartment shut and I was all alone. I lie there staring blankly at nothing, feeling only numbness.

He returned with some juice and snacks: [177]Sun Chips, one of my favorites, and something else. We ate quietly, watching TV. It felt good to have his attention for once. It felt good after giving him all of mine for so long—praising every song he composed, every poem he wrote, every picture he drew—doting over him while he demanded *more* praise, *more* approval—malnourished as I starved for his love and affection.

My leg was throbbing now. Zain stared down at me from the fisherman's net Renny gave him that was hanging from the ceiling, his huge plastic crab buddy beside him. He looked worried about me.

"It's okay, Zainy," I reassured him. Then I returned to watching TV for a few moments until I had to go to the bathroom. "I gotta go to the bathroom," I told Krisstopher, wincing as I tried moving my leg to get up.

No answer. I looked beside me. He was sleeping.

"Krisstopher," I said louder.

Still no answer.

In pain, I hobbled out of bed, barely able to walk. How could he be sleeping again? Didn't he care about me? Hopping on one leg, I made it down the hallway and into the bathroom, sobbing as I went. Why didn't he care? Why did I feel so *alone?* Cringing, I sat on the toilet seat, examining my leg. The blood was still flowing, seeping through the washcloth. It both frightened and sickened me.

"Oh, God! Why doesn't anyone care? Won't somebody help me? Oh, God! What's *wrong* with me?!" I lie on my back in the hallway just outside the bathroom door now, pounding my fists on the floor, pain shooting through my shinbone. Sunlight streamed in the kitchen window, spilling onto my face. I had to work in a couple of hours. What would I do? We had no car... I couldn't walk. Finally, after I continued wailing for nearly sixty minutes, Krisstopher woke up and made his way into the kitchen.

"Martyr, what's wrong?" he asked sleepily, scratching his head while peering down the hallway at me.

"Why won't you *help* me?" I hissed vehemently. "I have to work in an hour!"

"You'll be okay," he insisted, "it stopped bleeding."

"No it freakin' *hasn't* stopped bleeding. Look!" I was frantic.

"Okay," he responded after examining the blood-soaked cloth, "Sam's got a car. Call her and ask her to take you to the hospital."

"What am I going to tell her? She'll think I'm nuts!"

"I don't know... tell her you fell on some glass or something."

But I couldn't. I found myself telling her the truth. "Sam?" I sobbed over the phone now. "C—can you give me a ride to the hospital? Well, I freaked out last night and c—cut my leg with a—a butcher knife. It's bleeding pretty bad..."

While Sam sat in the hospital waiting room, Krisstopher and I walked toward the nurse's station where they were playing a game of [178]Scrabble.

"What's a three-letter word that starts with—" one of them began, then stopped, disappointed to see us. Ushering us into an examining room, she called for one of the doctors.

I gave *him* the story about the glass. That way, they wouldn't put me in the psychiatric ward. He said the cuts were deep, which explained why my shinbone hurt, but they weren't long. I only received three stitches in one and two in the other.

I hobbled into work later that day, which wasn't far from our apartment. Sam had already told Felician. I could tell by the way she eyed me when I walked in the door.

Later, as the two of us were putting clothes away, she asked me quietly what had happened. When I told her I freaked out and slashed my leg, insisting that she already knew anyway, she claimed Sam only mentioned that I'd had an *accident* and *hurt* my leg. Either way, my willingness to confide in her softened something in her heart, and she let down her wall for a brief moment. "Ya know, Mahta, I've felt like that befuh too. But ya just gotta be strong and not let things like that botha ya," she said quietly. "Yuhr a smaht girl. You'll make it."

"Well thank you, Felician. I really appreciate that," I replied, both amazed and grateful for her concern. She was the only one who bothered to talk about what had occurred—the only one who really seemed to care enough to encourage me at a time when I felt like the world was crashing in on me.

Though I told everyone in town who asked that I fell on some glass, they all knew the real story. No one said anything different to me, but I could tell by the way they looked at me, with eyebrows raised and an "*I know better than that*" expression on their faces. Krisstopher had already blabbed it to Kyle, and I was sure Renny and Klay knew as well. Nothing was ever a secret in Connelly Woods. Everyone here knew everybody else's business. Still, maybe I kind of liked the fact that they knew the real story. Maybe someone would help me. I was crying out for help. Couldn't anyone hear me?

* * *

I decided to see a social worker. Maybe even Sam mentioned it—I'm not sure. There was a small counseling center located in the same building as my birth control clinic. The rates were cheap—anywhere from one dollar to ten dollars depending on my paycheck for the week.

It took me over an hour of continuous uphill pedaling on Krisstopher's mountain bike to get to the center. I arrived for my first visit, out of breath and sweating profusely. A young guy in his late twenties/early thirties greeted me. He was dressed kind of preppie, with short, blond hair and gold wire-rimmed glasses. He escorted me into his office and I plopped down in a blue chair, telling him exactly what was bothering me.

I wasted no time in pouring out my dilemma to him—about how I was afraid something was terribly wrong with me lately, and how weird things were happening to me. It felt good to get some things off my chest, especially my abusive past. He listened attentively, rarely commenting except to ask here and there how I felt about certain incidences I mentioned. I left his office feeling lighter. Hopeful. I was happy to have someone listen for a change without being skeptical or critical.

I returned the next week, surprised when an older stern-faced woman with short, curly brown hair addressed me in the waiting room. Motioning for me to follow her, we entered another office, where she instructed me to have a seat. When I asked her what happened to the guy I saw last week, explaining that I preferred him, she told me they had to let him go because he lacked the *proper credentials,* or something to that effect.

"So I guess you're stuck with *me,*" she said snidely.

I wanted to walk out then. I'd just had one of those feelings of instant dislike upon meeting her. Something told me she was not going to be sympathetic at all. But, I'd give it a try. It was the least I could do after biking all that way.

I started out with my spirituality, explaining that I believed in past lives. My soul mate, Krisstopher, had recently cheated on me, and I couldn't seem to get over it.

She interrupted then. "My sister's into all that spirituality crap. Every morning she does yoga exercises on the living room floor, saying her *mantras* while I sit and laugh at her. She's such a flake."

I continued on, putting in a good word for her sister by stating that magic and spirituality were important things to pursue. Then I confided in her about how hurt I was that Krisstopher cheated on me—and how insecure I felt now because he wouldn't let me forget it. He kept bringing up Tanya's name and acting like she'd done nothing wrong to me, defending her all the time while she purposely tried to split us apart.

"How do you know this Tanya girl isn't *his* soul mate?" she snapped. "Maybe he *liked* cheating on you. Maybe he really loves *her*. How do you know *they're* not supposed to be together? It goes both ways, you know."

I stared in disbelief, unable to respond. I thought counselors were supposed to offer support and encouragement. Who was she helping here anyway—me or *Krisstopher*? By the time I left her office, I was more depressed than when I'd arrived. My heart hurt from the knives she'd stuck into it: her ugly words. I felt sick. And worst of all, I was convinced no one would ever understand me. They didn't care to.

I called and requested another counselor the following week. I couldn't give up so soon. Surely someone could help me. There had to be someone there who could offer suggestions as to what was wrong. Was I really nuts? Had I lost my sanity?

A man with short, wavy brown hair, kind eyes, and a mustache smiled at me. It felt good in his office. More peaceful for some reason, and pleasantly warm. The man was very gentle natured. Very calm. He made me feel calm as I sat, legs crossed, on the other side of his desk.

"So... what seems to be the problem—I mean—what brings you here, Paula?"

Sighing, I told him I was really afraid there was something wrong with me, because I was terribly depressed and all kinds of bizarre things were happening—supernatural things.

"Oh?"

"You see, I'm a pagan—a witch, I mean."

At that, his eyes grew as big as saucers, and a serious look washed over his pale face.

"I've been delving into my subconscious a lot lately. You know, doing meditation-type exercises like our New Age books say to do. And I keep seeing and feeling and hearing these weird things." I then proceeded to tell him of Krisstopher and I and Tanya, and of how Krisstopher never stuck up for me but instead always criticized and hurt me.

He advised that perhaps I should get out of that living situation because it didn't seem to have a positive effect on me. "And as for this *delving into your subconscious,* uh... I'd stay away from that stuff for a while if I were you. Let your mind be clear for a while, because you can really create a lot of problems for yourself doing those kinds of things.

I know you say you're a pagan, but perhaps for a while you should just cool out on all that."

*Cool out on it?* It was my life! How else was I going to advance spiritually?

"But other than that, Paula, I see nothing wrong with you. You sound like an intelligent girl who knows how to analyze her own situations."

"Then I'm not nuts? I'm not *mental?*" I asked, relieved.

"No, of course not," he reassured me. "You've just had a tough life, that's all. If you were nuts, you wouldn't be able to sit here and converse back and forth with me. You wouldn't be able to question your sanity if you were insane. No, I don't see any reason for you to keep coming here. Unless, of course, you feel you need someone to talk to. But I'm confident that you know how to solve your own problems."

*I'm not insane!*

That day, the sun shone brightly as I biked home, a smile on my face for the first time in a long time. And the chirping birds never sounded so sweet.

* * *

While in town one day, Krisstopher and I spotted Sean sitting down in front of a shop with a girl we'd never seen before. He introduced her as Misty, his new girlfriend. I found myself relieved that he had someone else to focus his attention on.

Misty was extremely likable. Thin, fair skinned and freckly, she had long blond hair, pale blue eyes, and delicate features. Right away I had a good feeling about her. I didn't sense any negativity coming from her—no attitude—just a really peaceable, mild-mannered disposition. Good natured, she was always smiling.

Soon, the four of us were hanging around continuously; and this time, I didn't mind. Probably because the tension between Sean and I had ceased, and because I felt Misty was no threat to my relationship with Krisstopher.

She opened up to me right away, showing me some of her artwork, which was very good. We sat on the couch at Sean's while she explained one of the pictures to me. In her church, she said, they believed there was the world, then Heaven and Hell. But in her opinion, the world was Hell; and when we died, we then went to Heaven. Hmmm… interesting. Eve and I had discussed that a few years back; she shared the same opinion. I often felt my life was a living Hell, so I supposed it was possible.

Misty had a lemon yellow [179]Nova that she referred to as her "baby." She drove us down dark winding roads in the evening, Sean passing the bowl to us in the back seat while a Uzziah Sheep tape blared through the speakers. We flew through the air, her dome light blinking on and off in time with the music like a flashing beacon in the night. I thought it was magic, but she claimed there was a short in the fuse.

Unfortunately, going out with Misty hadn't seemed to curb Sean's appetite toward me any. I found myself feeling terrible as he ignored her and directed all his attention my way. If he *did* talk to her, he was usually short-tempered. I winced every time he picked me a flower or gave me a small gift, trying desperately to let her know I wasn't interested in stealing him from her; avoiding him where at all possible and clinging to Krisstopher when we were all together. I began to think perhaps Sean was only using her as a ploy to try and get me jealous. The more time went on, the more my suspicions proved correct.

* * *

I stared at the picture of War that Jamie gave me. Looking into his eyes, I felt myself slipping. Slipping into a dream of how it should be, of how a soul mate should act toward me. He loved me, even if Krisstopher didn't. He would never treat me bad. He would never cheat on me.

"*I have more for you than Krisstopher can offer,*" he seemed to be saying. "*More power. More love. I know you better than he does. I love you more than he can ever love you. I've always loved you.*"

How could I ignore it? How could I possibly pretend it didn't exist, this attraction that carried me away into another world, another plain of existence?

Taking off my necklace now, I dangled the little pewter wizard over his picture, swinging it back and forth like the love spell called for while imagining us together. "Let War come to me: the perfect love. For the good of all… for the good of the universe. According to his own free will, if it is he… let him come to me." I was silent for a moment, then added, "You *will* come to me, War. You *will* come to me. So mote it be."

Tears streamed down my cheeks, hitting the carpet; a silent death. I was so confused about everything. I only knew… that I loved him.

* * *

"Martyr, I think you better sit down. I have some bad news," Krisstopher warned.

I held the receiver in my hand, leaning against the counter by the cash register at Jentanno. "What? What happened?" I asked, panic in my voice.

"Tanya just tried to rent the downstairs apartment. I saw the landlord showing it to her."

"*What?!* That evil *witch!* Does she know we live upstairs?" I felt the blood rush to my head. Clinching my fists, I listened as he explained.

"I don't know… I *assumed* she did. But anyway, I looked out the window and saw her talking to Dean. I couldn't believe it! I thought, *Oh **man!** That's **all** we need is Tanya living downstairs—as if we don't already have enough problems.* But don't worry. When she left, I went down and told Dean that she was a big drug dealer and had a really bad reputation in town. He thanked me for telling him and said he wouldn't rent the place to her.

The woman was the Devil incarnate—she had to be. I couldn't believe that she was still out for blood after all this. What would it take to stop her from interfering in our lives? We were just starting to get semi-close again the last two weeks or so. Why did I always have to be reminded of her? Why did she have to keep stirring up that night in my mind—that horrible night that Krisstopher betrayed me? Why did she have to keep ripping the scab off that healing wound? I wanted to tear my hair out now. No—better yet, I wanted to tear *her* hair out.

* * *

Jason came to visit, making the long drive in his new used car. He was going to stay a week with us and then head over to New York to spend some time with his cousin. It was good to see him. I'd really missed him. He brought along a couple of gifts for us: a gliding eye ball toy that really kicked across the linoleum floor, and a Martian Sex Junkie postcard which featured a painting by the lead singer.

Unfortunately, I had to work most of the time while he and Krisstopher and Sean hung out. And then he ended up splitting sooner than he'd intended after he and I got into an argument over my magic journal, which I'd instructed him not to read.

I woke up one morning to a *crinkle crinkle* sound, and recognized it as pages turning. Tiptoeing to the hanging blanket in our doorway and peeking through it, I discovered him sitting on the couch in the kitchen, reading every secret thought, every intimate detail I'd so painstakingly recorded as he unraveled me before his eyes.

I lost it then, shouting at him and waking Krisstopher up. "How *could* you? I don't believe you, Jason! I told you not to read that—it's private!"

"I was just trying to find out what's wrong with you!" he shouted back.

"What's *wrong* with me?! There's nothing freakin' *wrong* with me except you looking through my personal stuff!"

"Fine, I'm leaving. I'll go to New York early and visit my cousin."

Guilt flooded over me with these words. "No, don't leave," I pleaded. "I was just mad—that's all."

"No, it's okay. I think it's time to leave."

There was nothing wrong with me, was there?

## IX. THE WISE MAN AND THE FOOL

I followed Krisstopher into Deadquarters, the waft of frangipani incense filling my nostrils. We were buying a bong. Mikal was standing at the front counter when we walked through the door. She said hello to me while Krisstopher made his way toward the back of the store, a girl I'd never seen before working behind the display case. It appeared as if Tanya wasn't there. Good. I talked for a brief moment to Mikal, then headed over to a rack of clothes. Skimming through them, I spotted a few tops I'd wear and wished I had the money to buy them.

"Hi Krisstopher!" Tanya suddenly came barging out of the back room, making her way toward him.

"Hi," he answered, while I stared wide-eyed at the two of them.

"Here. You left these in my *back seat*." She handed him some books, glancing my way.

"Oh, thanks a lot. I was wondering where these went."

I could feel Mikal's eyes on me, along with the eyes of the other girl, as they both watched for my reaction. My mouth hung wide open, my face three shades of red—no—crimson. But I couldn't say anything. I was so stunned, I couldn't react at all. Embarrassment swept over me as I realized they probably thought I was afraid of her. Was I? Humiliated, I followed Krisstopher out the door and down the street while Tanya's words ran through my head once more: "*Here. You left these in my* **back seat**."

"I can't believe her! I can't believe she could be so *evil*," I finally growled as we headed out of town.

"What? She didn't do anything to you," he protested.

"Why do you keep sticking up for her? Don't you see she's deliberately trying to upset me? How can you even talk to her after all this?"

We walked on the railroad tracks now. It was starting to sprinkle, droplets of rain spattering the wood here and there.

"I don't think she's done anything to you. There's nothing wrong with telling me *hi*. I can say *hi* to her if I want."

"She deliberately mentioned you left books in her back seat to remind me that she had sex with you, don't you get it?"

"I wanted those books back. I didn't know where I'd left them. She was just returning them."

"She was *trying* to get me upset. That's why she approached you right in front of my face."

"Look, you're not my guard dog, Martyr," he protested angrily.

I couldn't believe my ears. His words tore another piece of my heart. How many more pieces would he take from me before he was satisfied?

"You *like* her, don't you? You wouldn't stick up for her if you didn't. She's hurting me, and you don't care!"

Maybe the female counselor was right. Maybe he really *did* love Tanya more than me.

"You're being ridiculous! She's not *hurting* you. It's all in your head."

*All in my head. All in my head.* My frustration turned into tears as I screamed at him, "Why don't you care about me? I can't believe you—I can't freakin' *believe* you!"

"You know, you're acting like a moron," he replied apathetically.

She was turning him—turning him against me. I didn't know how, but somehow, she was. Closing my eyes tightly, I pictured beating her continuously into a pulp, every punch producing an overwhelming feeling of satisfaction within me. Yes… that was it. That was the answer to this problem.

"I'm going to beat the crap out of her! I'm going to beat the *living crap* out of her!" I halted on the tracks, glaring at him.

"Go ahead. See if I care. I'm going home." He turned and started walking, leaving me standing there in the rain, which had changed into a steady drizzle. By the time I reached Deadquarters, I was wet and shivering. Just one more reason to waste Tanya.

I paced back and forth in the side parking lot by the employee entrance, waiting for her to get off work. Pretty soon I sat down on one of the cement parking dividers and watched the raindrops hit the puddles with a splash. I reminded myself that I'd tried being peaceable with her, but she didn't want to smooth things over. She was out for blood. What else could I do? I had to retain some shred of dignity. Krisstopher had already stripped most of it from me, and I certainly wasn't going to let *her* take the rest. The thing was, I just couldn't think about what I was doing or else I'd have second thoughts. I'd just have to pounce on her before she could talk her way out of it. There was no question that when I got mad enough, I had the strength of ten horses. It took a lot to get me to that point—but when I got there, look out! Gary Edmonds could tell you about the time I whaled on him in fourth grade after reaching that point. He even commented to me fourteen years later of how he still remembered being beat up by a girl.

I stared at the door now, wondering if perhaps someone warned Tanya that I was waiting for her. Or maybe there was a hidden window I didn't know about and she could see me sitting in the rain, anticipating my revenge. I'd spotted her car in the parking lot, so I knew she was still there. I knew she never worked late. It would only be a matter of time before she had to come outside; she couldn't hide forever. No, this time, she wasn't going to run away like the last time she ditched me at her house.

About twenty-five minutes passed when I heard the sound of a car pull up in front of the building, and then its door shut. Next thing I knew, Sean was standing there staring down at me, his arms crossed and a huge grin plastered across his face. "So, yuh gonna kick Tanya's butt, huh?" he asked, sitting next to me on the divider.

"Yeah, I am. I'm sick of her crap! How'd you know?"

"I just know these things."

"No, seriously. How'd you know? Did Krisstopher tell you or something?"

"Yeah. Misty and I stopped ovuh tuh see if you guys wanted tuh pahty with us tonight, and he told me you wuh heera waiting fuh Tanya tuh get off wuhk. You know Mahta, yuh making a big mistake."

"What do you mean? The chick is an evil slut! I've got to do *something*. She needs to be taught a lesson."

"Yeah, but yuh going about it all wrong. Yuh going to get yuh butt thrown in jail. Believe me, Tanya won't hesitate tuh prosecute you. She plays duhty. And that's not what you want—that's not going tuh solve anything."

I stared at him, tears in my eyes. He got up and motioned for me to follow him. "Come on. Let's take a walk ovuh heera fuh a minute."

We headed down the railroad tracks until the store was out of sight, then he turned to face me. "Krisstapha doesn't love you, Mahta—not like he thinks he does. If he did, he nevuh would have cheated on you tuh begin with."

I was silent as his words cut like knives into my heart.

"Krisstapha's stupid," he continued. "He doesn't realize what he has. Thaa ah things about you that he doesn't appreciate."

"Like what?"

"Like what's in heera," he pointed to his head, "and what's in *heera*," then pointed to his heart.

"Well, thank you," I said, a little puzzled as to what he was getting at.

"You see, they can take evuhrything from you, Mahta. But they can't take what's in *heera*." Again, he pointed to his heart. "No one can steal that from you. Do you undastand?"

I nodded slowly, wondering what this had to do with anything.

"Now look, don't even give that ugly wench the time of day. Don't even waste yuh time on huh. I've got two hits of acid fuh you if you want them. We can fry tonight and you can fuhget all about huh."

"I don't have any money to buy two hits," I told him sadly. Yes, acid sounded like a great idea. Just what I needed to escape the pain of reality.

"Mahta, thaa *free*. You don't have tuh buy any. It's on me."

"Really?" A smile broke out on my face now.

"So you going tuh pahty with us then and fuhget this sleaze?"

"Yeah! Thanks a lot. And… Sean? Thanks for talking to me."

"Shuh. Anytime. Can I have a hug?" He stretched out his long arms, waiting.

"Yeah." I fell into them and he wrapped them around me, kissing me on top of the head.

"Can I have a kiss?" he asked next.

"Yeah—on the *cheek*," I replied sarcastically, realizing where he was going.

"I just thought I'd ask," he chuckled.

"Hey, what about Krisstopher?" I broke free from his hold. "Do you have enough acid for him?"

"Yeah... we'll go back tuh the house and get him."

I said hello to Misty then, who'd been waiting the whole time in front of Deadquarters, and climbed in the back seat of her Flying Lemon. She seemed different tonight; reserved, and perhaps a little sad.

After hanging out at the apartment for a while with Krisstopher, we all headed to the Inn to shoot some pool, taking the acid just before leaving. It was still raining, pounding down on the roof of the [180]Nova as Misty turned out of the driveway and onto the road. I stared blankly at the windshield wipers as they *whooshed* back and forth. Sean turned on some weird stuff he'd recorded off the *Dr. Deranged* show—some song about the Holy Grail. The music was wacky; the singing sounding kind of like a mixture of [181]King Arthur, the [182]Lucky Charms Leprechaun, and a British version of [183]The Chipmunks.

I had no idea at the time just what the [184]Holy Grail was, other than the partial title of a [185]Monty Python movie. And I'd never heard of *Dr. Deranged*, who, as his name suggested, delighted in playing deranged music guaranteed to open the minds of listeners everywhere while bending the confines of their reality. All I knew was, it was the most bizarre thing I'd ever heard.

Suddenly my ears were drawn to a particular verse being sung. I listened as once again that other realm opened up, and War communicated to me via the lyrical content of the song, sending me yet another message. My eyes grew wide as I heard something about his sword being *"big, sharp, and mighty"* ([186]King Arthur singing), and Krisstopher's being *"little, wimpy, and puny"* (the [187]Lucky Charms Leprechaun voice singing, with backup vocals from [188]The Chipmunks

British Invasion). Laughter piped in the background at this last declaration, while I stared in disbelief at what I'd just perceived. It was an innuendo directed at Krisstopher—in more than one way.

Misty and Sean snickered now, Sean turning around to look at me from the passenger seat while grinning profusely. I sensed he was somehow in on this parable.

We arrived at the Inn and went downstairs to the recreation room where the pool table sat. After choosing our sticks and chalking up, the games began. As usual, I was far from billiard mastery, unable to hit a single ball in the pocket.

"Come on, *think*, Mahta," Sean instructed. "Yuh not *concentrating*." He stared at me now, confident that I could read between the lines. I knew he meant I should use creative visualization coupled with magic power to persuade the ball, but I just couldn't for some reason. He was making me too nervous.

"*Feel* it," Misty suggested.

"I'm trying. I—"

Sean came round the table then, wrapping his arms around me and showing me the proper way to hold the stick and shoot. I was getting really weird vibes from him. The whole episode seemed more like a game of seduction than pool. And somehow, War was present in the room with us though I didn't know how I knew this. He was trying to teach me his ancient skill of *sex magic,* and he was using Sean as a medium—the two of them were connected. I was sure they were in a powerful coven together, like the man Jade told me about who had extraordinary mental telepathy.

I managed to finally shoot a couple of balls in the pocket, but I was happy when the game ended and Sean suggested we go back to his place.

Misty dropped us off, telling us good-bye. She hadn't taken any of the acid. She was tired, she said, and not in the mood to fry. The three of us went inside the trailer, Sean dimming the lights and popping a cassette into the stereo, and Krisstopher heading to the bathroom. I sat quietly on the couch, watching as next Sean began lighting candles throughout the room. He lit one and then paused, cocking his head as if listening for instructions. Then he set it down on the table and lit another.

Eerie, ethereal music suddenly emerged from the background while a man's seductive voice beckoned and moaned. He spoke of *"knowing you in a dream."* I perceived War was using this song, as well, to explain our tie together—our series of past lives. The lyrics spoke of his desperation, his yearning, to be with me forever. Electric waves of passion rippled through my body as I listened to my soul mate serenade me: my eternal soul mate I couldn't be with because I was light and he was... dark?

Suddenly, as if reading my mind, the man's voice changed from passionate to malicious while he warned me of something I didn't know about him. *"But there's an **evil** side of me!"* he hissed.

I grew frightened upon hearing these words. I didn't want to believe it. Was War really evil—was he really with the Devil? And was evil really so bad? What *was* evil, anyway? A word? A feeling? An action?

My eyes followed Sean as he approached the wall about twenty feet in front of where I sat. On it hung a small shelf with more candles. He lit them, taking great pains to arrange them just the right way; then satisfied, stepped out of my view. I stared at the candles, my eyes instantly drawn to the flickering flames, which leapt and danced like wild spirits in a frenzy of lust. Flicker... flicker... flicker... flicker... higher and higher and higher and higher and POOF! A life sized, three-dimensional hologram of War's face suddenly materialized behind the shelf, his pink hair on fire, yet not burning. He stared at me with dark, enticing eyes, each one encapsulating a small flame.

Emotion overwhelmed me as I continued to stare, mesmerized, and even a little afraid. I hadn't seen him in such a long time, and here he was, life-like and not just a picture. How did he do it? How could he make himself appear before me? Wonder gave way to rationalization now: *No, this isn't really happening. This is just the drug distorting reality.* Yet, never had I experienced anything like this. It was more than just a trip. It seemed to be occurring in the spirit world as well as on the material plane. What was different about this LSD Sean had given me? I continued to stare incredulously at the hologram. *Is this real? No, it can't be... it can't—*

*"Martyr, it's me, War. This is **really happening**. I'm **really** here."*

He just read my mind again! That same strong connection we'd always had. Yes, I knew now that it *was* him.

Krisstopher walked into the living room at that moment and the image disappeared.

"Let's go fuh a walk," Sean suggested. "I want tuh show you guys something."

Krisstopher shrugged, following him toward the door. I stared at the wall for a few seconds more, wanting War to return again. I didn't want to go for a walk. I wanted to stay right there with him.

"Come on, Mahta!" Sean called.

I got up from the couch and walked toward the kitchen, where he pointed to a poster tacked to the back of the door. It was a photograph of a river, and beneath it, the words:

[189]RIVER OF FIRE

I wondered where the river was—in New Hampshire, or some other state? The water was actually flaming before my eyes. I stared at the shape of the river, puzzled.

"Do you get it?" Sean asked me, smiling evilly.

"Yeah, it looks kind of like a phallic symbol to me," I told him.

"A *phallic* symbol?!" he half-laughed. "*No*, Mahta!"

Shaking his head, he opened the door and the three of us walked outside into the cool night air. It was late August; the evenings were beginning to get a little chilly. Shivering, I tried adjusting to my new surroundings, which was like emerging from my mother's womb into cold, harsh reality as we left the warmth of Sean's trailer far behind. I shoved my hands into the pockets of my leather while glancing up at the stars. It seemed there were so many in this part of the country, with no city lights to dim their appearance. We reached the shrouded entrance to the trailer park and stepped through it, turning left onto the road. I reminded myself that War was still with me, though I couldn't feel him at that particular moment. He was hovering in the air. Somewhere.

We walked a little way down the road and then turned left again, surrounded by trees as we stepped onto a small wooded path. Suddenly, the sides dropped away and the path began to float, hovering in infinite space. I looked around as the stars and constellations twinkled from every direction, fearing what would happen if I fell over the side. I would most certainly plunge into orbit, lost forever. And yet, a heavy, oppressive force boxed me in so that I *couldn't* fall; a wall—pressing, pressing, until I felt I would smother. I was trapped. "You guys, what's going on?" I seemed to ask. "I don't like this!"

"It's okay. Weh heera now," Sean seemed to reply.

We stepped off the path and into a small clearing; a short, black wrought iron fence before us. As we climbed over it, I spotted a little hill up ahead with tombstones. We were in an old cemetery in the middle of the woods.

"Wow, look!" I pointed. To my amazement, a circle of greenish-white light hovered in midair atop the hill. I recognized it to be a magic circle. Although magic circles are composed of energy, and invisible to the human eye since they exist on the spiritual plane, I could see this one clearly; the greenish-white color being the energy it was comprised of. I knew what I must do.

Running up the hill now, I set out to enter the circle. I felt War wanted me to, as a sort of initiation. Krisstopher tore off after me. I wasn't sure if he could also see the circle or if he was just following me. He and I never shared the same trip, so it was more likely that he was only coming along for the ride.

"*No*, Krisstapha!" Sean yelled angrily. "You stay heera and let *Mahta* go!"

Shrugging, he obeyed, making his way back down the hill and then wandering off in the dark somewhere amidst the rows and rows of tombstones.

I reached the top, breaking through the circle to stand in the middle of it. With my head held upright (one), my feet apart (plus two), and my arms outstretched (plus two), I used my body to signify the *five*-pointed star, or [190]witch's pentagram. Sean stood at the bottom of the hill, arms folded and a satisfied smile on his face, as if I'd done exactly what I was supposed to do. Looking to my left, I noticed two huge, black marble tombstones. They represented War and me.

Stepping outside the circle, I walked over and placed my hands on them. They were hot—so hot they nearly burnt my skin. The night air was too cool for them to still be heated from the sun, so I knew it must be energy I was feeling. But what kind of energy? Energy from the dead?

I felt strongly that I should lie down on my back between them, so I sprawled out on the grass, closing my eyes and placing my hands on my chest like the Egyptian mummies. Suddenly I heard the [191]buzzing of flies, and then felt them quickly cling to my face, crawling all over it. I swatted at them but they refused to leave, so I rose up and headed back down the hill to where Sean was still waiting for me.

"Heera, let's go sit down," he said.

I walked with him to the outskirts of the cemetery. It got very dark all of a sudden, and I couldn't even see where I was going. We came to a long stone wall about three feet high. He patted the spot beside him and I felt my way over to it, pulling myself up onto the cold ledge. Dangling my legs over the wall, I stared straight ahead into the blackness, the two of us quiet for a while. I thought of what just occurred on the hill. Was it in fact some sort of initiation?

"How do you like this place?" he spoke then.

"It's cool," I replied. Funny how I could see him sitting next to me even though I couldn't see him. It was pitch black out, yet it was as if I could see him with spiritual eyes—like more of an *inner vision* than outer sight—and it felt so natural somehow, like I'd been doing it all my life. I grew quiet again; I wasn't in the mood to talk. Where was War? Concentrating, I tried tuning in to him.

"You know, you and Krisstapha ah the only ones who know about this place," he continued, "well—*you*, I mean." He gestured toward Krisstopher's general direction, hinting that he wasn't aware of what was going on like I was.

Off in the distance, I could hear him whooping and hollering about something. I wasn't alarmed though. I knew he was only tripping out on hallucinations. Later, he told me he'd been chased by the [192]Headless Horseman.

I went back to concentrating again, attempting thought transference with War. *Where are you, my Knight of Pentacles? My beautiful warlock? I know you're—*

"This hasn't happened since 1910," Sean interrupted once more.

Man, I wished he'd be quiet! What on *earth* was he talking about, anyway? *What* happened in 1910? Certainly it was nothing he'd experienced *personally*, because that would make him over eighty years old—if not closer to a hundred. Or maybe even… immortal? No… of course not, so then…

*"Sell your soul."* A small, fleeting thought—so small, so fleeting, that it barely had time to register.

Silent, I pondered anything significant occurring in 1910, but realized I was clueless about the whole time period since History class was when I used to catch up on my sleep. Oh well. He was probably just acid babbling anyway.

"Crap! I lost my ciguhrettes. Whaa ah my ciguhrettes?" He made a half-effort to find them, briefly patting the wall between us.

"Your cigarettes?" I asked. Like a puppet on a string, I was off the wall and standing on the ground faster than I could give it any thought. Walking further ahead in the heavy blackness, I suddenly turned to face the stone partition once more, and to my amazement, placed my hands directly on the lost pack of cigarettes; though I couldn't see a thing. "Here you go," I said, handing them to him. *Wow, how did I know right where they were at?*

"Don't you find that intaresting that you knew right whaa they wuh even though you couldn't see them?" he asked me now. "That's what I meant when I said thaa ah things about you that Krisstapha just doesn't appreciate. He doesn't *undastand*."

I knew then, that he was referring to my [193]psychic abilities. I could hardly believe I'd been able to home in on the cigarettes without actually seeing them. I was proud of myself. Yes, I must be spiritually progressing, because it seemed I had more power now.

He lit a cigarette and stood up. "I want tuh show you anotha place." Cupping his hands around his mouth he yelled, "Come on, Kris! Let's go!"

I heard the approaching thump of footsteps jogging on grassy ground, and then Krisstopher appeared before us, breathing heavily. "Whoaaaa," was all he could say, then he let out a half-laugh as if to make light of something disturbing. He seemed relieved to catch up with us once more. I suspected Lucy had taken him on one of her more *frightful* adventures.

We were about to head deeper into the woods when suddenly War called my name. Instinctively, I glanced up at the sky, where I saw a

[194]staircase ascending into the clouds. It was the stairway to Heaven. Another voice spoke then; a voice I'd never heard before. As quickly as it spoke, I forgot what it said.

I followed Sean and Krisstopher into the woods, wrestling twigs and branches. Two orange-yellow dots were shining just up ahead. As we drew nearer, I realized they were the eyes of a huge mother raccoon. Sean mentioned something about her attacking us because of her babies, and the next thing I knew we were running, me screaming the whole way until we finally exited the woods into another clearing.

"It's okay, Mahta," he assured me once we entered the clearing, "she's not chasing us."

"Phhhew," I sighed, my heart pounding against my chest while he laughed.

We'd come out along a cliff overlooking the river. It wasn't a huge cliff, like in Hawaii or anything, but it was pretty steep, most assuredly promising to kill anyone who fancied jumping off it. If the height didn't do it, the huge, scraggly rocks jutting out of the water below would.

A little further down from where we stood, just around the corner, was a restaurant much talked about by Kyle and Krisstopher as it somehow tied in with their juvenile adventures, though I can't remember how. It was appropriately titled: *Cliff River* Restaurant.

Suddenly Sean started running full force toward the cliff. "Come on!" he called. "Follow me!"

Like mindless puppets, Krisstopher and I raced behind him in the darkness, clueless as to where we were headed.

He stopped abruptly. "You guys!" he scolded in disbelief.

"Huh?" We halted, puzzled.

Realizing we hadn't understood, he bolted towards the cliff once more. "Come on! Follow me!"

In blind trust, we bolted after him again, me giggling at this silly little game.

"Stop!" he commanded, [195]halting just on the edge and dangling one foot over. "You guys wanna run off the cliff? Go ahead!"

*The Cliff?* Staring out over the precipice, I heard the rushing of the river's current below, though I could see nothing but blackness.

Krisstopher and I stepped back a little, realizing what we almost did. For a minute, it frightened me that Sean had even thought to play such a cruel joke on us. What would have happened had we kept going? Didn't he realize we weren't in the state of mind for such jokes?

*"Look."*

I followed his finger now as he pointed downward. At once, the ground opened up before my eyes and I saw a [196]pit of slithering [197]snakes. Millions of voices screamed out [198]in torment, echoing in my ears. I knew it was Hell.

"And all fuh [199]five hundred dolluhs," he offered with the finesse of a used car salesman. It seemed he could actually see what I was seeing— the pit, the snakes…

Krisstopher, on the other hand, had focused his attention elsewhere; standing a few feet away from us.

I continued staring downward at the black abyss, horrified. Was it possible that Sean was having the same trip as me—a *user shared* hallucination? And what did he mean, *five hundred dollars?*

*"Martyr…"* War called again.

*War, is that you?*

*"Martyr, I'm here. Come with me Martyr. I'm here."*

*Where? Where are you?*

He sounded like he was calling from the bottom of the abyss! What did he mean, *come with him?* Was he trying to tell me he was a Satan worshiper who wanted me to join him on the dark side? Or was he in Hell? Had War… died?

*"Come and be with me, Martyr,"* he crooned.

I looked at the bright flashing lights now, on the horizon just beyond Hell, yet somehow still in Hell. There, it seemed more pleasant. There, it seemed… kind of like a past life. Like another dimension in time being opened, ready to escort me through its doors.

*"Join me, Martyr,"* War continued to plead. *"Join me…"*

*How can I join you? How?*

*"Jump, Martyr. Jump!"*

*Jump?* I stepped back a few feet, preparing myself for the dive.

*"Yes, jump—go ahead! Join me."*

*I can be with him—forever. I can be with him....* The urge was so strong, I could hardly control it. I backed up about ten more feet, fists clenched and one foot in front of the other, adrenaline rushing through my veins as I prepared to take a running jump off the cliff into oblivion. One, two, three—

*"Don't jump,"* a logical thought said. *"You might die. You don't know what's out there."*

I pictured myself for a second, plummeting to my death; hitting jagged rocks below and being swallowed up by the river. I shuddered as I actually felt my skull crack open on the rocks, felt the water rush into my lungs.

And then another vivid scenario of me falling... falling... falling... plunging into outer darkness: into... Hell. An unbearable feeling ripped through me at this last thought, a terror so great that I could not even fathom it. As War continued to call, it took all of my might to suppress the urge which sought to control me. I shook myself out of the trance and walked back toward Krisstopher and Sean again.

We all sat down, dangling our feet over the edge. Silent, I tried collecting my thoughts. Just what exactly was going on? There was something strange about this whole night. The force—the energy— was unbelievable. My mind drifted to War once more. Why was his power so intense tonight? Surely it wasn't just the acid; I'd taken acid when I'd been present with him and never experienced his spell to this degree. Why, tonight, was he so near—nearer than he'd ever been? Concentrating, I tried to feel him again, to discern what he wanted me to do.

"I'm just [200]the taxi drivuh," Sean blurted out. "I just take people heera. It's up tuh them tuh decide."

Take people *where?* Decide *what?* I was really starting to get annoyed. I wanted to connect with War. Why couldn't Sean just leave me alone? He was beginning to remind me of Bruce, babbling on instead of just letting go and *feeling* the acid. I didn't answer, but slipped back into my alter-trance again, like slipping into an old, comfortable sweater.

"Well?" he asked expectantly.

*Arghhh!* Well *what?* What did this guy *want* from me? My head was pounding, like someone was using it for a bass drum. Boom boom boom boom—the strychnine was taking its toll.

He pointed out toward the horizon. "Look ovuh thaa."

Suddenly I could see the river clearly, its gray foamy waves hissing a threat as they writhed and twisted. And then a huge, greenish-white inverted [201]triangle appeared along the vicinity of the river, encompassing the whole area where Krisstopher and I had camped before. It was composed of the same energy as the magic circle in the cemetery.

"Hey, that's where we were camping a couple of weeks ago!" I said incredulously, my eyes fixed on the triangle. What did it mean?

"Now you know why you wuh attacked by black [202]flies," he informed me rather fiendishly.

No, I didn't know. What was he getting at?

I looked up at the sky, where two silverfish jumped in the starry infinitude. Two fish. Two souls. I thought of War. I loved him. Forever. My father flashed across my mind. I felt he wanted this somehow. My growth, my enlightenment. I must continue the spiritual quest, using the tools he gave me.

"Well?" Sean asked once more.

"Well *what?*" I finally replied.

Krisstopher remained silent. I couldn't really see him. He was just a blurry blob in my peripheral vision, out of the picture like he had been all evening. He didn't seem to mind though. It was how he always tripped. Alone. Disconnected from me.

"IF YOU DON'T KNOW, THEN LET'S GO!" Sean exploded angrily, releasing negative energy in the air as he stood up.

What in the world had gotten him so upset? I wondered. "Wait—" Startled by his outburst, I racked my brain to come up with the answer he desired while he paced back and forth impatiently. How could I appease him? What did he want from me?

Suddenly, a little voice inside me said, *"He wants you to sell your soul."*

*What? Sell my soul? Impossible!* I rationalized now. How absurd, how utterly ridiculous! Where on earth had I come up with such a notion? *It must be the acid—distorting my thinking.*

"Well?" He sat down next to me again, waiting. He was obviously in a hurry. I felt I was under great pressure to answer him immediately or who knew what would happen? But answer him what? I knew I had to say something fast or else he'd want to go and the whole trip would be ruined. A thought popped in my head then. It seemed so silly, I broke out in a smile, wondering if I should say it.

*"Hurry, hurry. Say something,"* another thought urged.

*Okay, okay.* I opened my mouth, and suddenly the words came tumbling out as if they had a mind of their own. "As long as I don't have to eat dead bodies," I heard myself tell him.

*"Ughhhh, what did you just **say?!**"* another part of me—the rational part—cringed, horrified.

I half-smiled at the little joke. Surely he would wonder what the heck I was talking about. He'd at least have to give me credit for my creativity. And who knew? Maybe it would lighten him up a bit.

He grinned now, a big wide grin that stretched from ear to ear.

"Fine," he snickered evilly, "*I'll* eat all the dead bodies. Come on, let's go." He seemed completely satisfied with my answer.

Perplexed, I continued to sit for a moment, my inner eye absorbing the outline of his face against the night—the outline of the trees behind him which before had seemed full and beautiful, but now were scraggly and ugly. They just died.

Then we got up, Krisstopher also rising to his feet, and followed the cliff around towards the restaurant which had long since closed for the evening. Just beyond the restaurant, we passed in front of a big [203]house where the [204]lights were on in the [205]windows upstairs. It was here that I sensed War strongly once more. Pausing, I glanced upward toward one of the windows, and immediately a [206]gift-wrapped present amidst a tidal wave of blood came flowing out of it toward me. Then it vanished, another spiritual vision rather than an outward hallucination. I continued staring up at the window. He was in that room. I sensed he was there.

"Come on, Mahta!" Sean called, prying me away from my thoughts. I hurried to catch up with him and Krisstopher, and we returned to his trailer.

275

In the living room now, he stared at me from the nearby chair as I sat, legs curled up, on his couch. The first traces of daylight spilled through the sides of the curtain. Krisstopher had gone to the bathroom and we were alone.

"Well? How do you feel?" he asked.

I turned toward him in the fading darkness; watched his head spin around and his face transform into a mummified corpse which quickly rotted away. After a moment I answered, "Tired. I've gotta work in a few more hours and I have a *smashing* headache."

He raised his eyebrows. "Is that *all?*" It seemed from the tone of his voice that he was hinting at something I'd forgotten, but I was too exhausted to play any more mind games.

"Yeah, that's *all*. Why, how *should* I feel?"

He looked at me sadly, shaking his head in disappointment. Obviously, I hadn't said the magic words this time in order to satisfy him. Oh well. Who cared? All I wanted to do was go home and sleep.

## A BLACK HEART

*Elohim*
*The blackbird sings*
*Outside my window*
*Now let him in*

I SLIPPED THE CD INTO the jam box and stepped into the shower. The water pelted on my skin while I screamed out the lyrics with Nathan Hash. It was my favorite Devotion and Missiles song, and after what happened last night at Sean's, it described perfectly the way I felt about War. "Your eyes, your smile, your hair, your clothes. I'm mesmerized... by your SOUL!" *Hear me now, War. You are winning. I want to join you. I don't care anymore what it takes. I only know I want to be with you. I'm insane with lust for you. I can't live without you.*

I dragged myself to work after about two hours of sleep, the sun blinding me as I made my way down the road to the clothing store, stopping just outside the door to scoop up a bright pink feather lying on the ground. Pink. The color of War's hair. He'd sent it to me, hadn't he?

As Sam and I folded clothes on the sale tables outside, I filled her in on my trip with Sean: how he'd taken us to the cemetery, and how I'd seen Hell. She commented that she thought Sean was strange, and she didn't like the guy for some reason. But she didn't say much about Hell. I sensed she wasn't taking it too seriously.

Next, I discovered a yarmulke/kippah—one of those little black caps that Jewish men wear—lying in the aisle between two racks of clothes. Inside was an inscription:

From the Wedding of... (So and So)

I was sure, once again, War had sent it—to convey to me that he and I would be married someday.

Later that week, a bride accidentally left her veil behind, which was attached to a hair comb. I took this as a confirmation that I would, in fact, become his bride.

* * *

I instinctively knew Sean was standing behind me. I hadn't heard him walk in the store. I hadn't seen him. But I felt him staring into my back now. I felt him unmistakably. "Hi Sean," I said without turning around. I continued folding the jeans on the shelf.

"How did you know it was me?" he asked, amused, though he already knew the answer.

"I don't know. I just knew." With that, I reeled around to face him.

He pointed to the sheet of sizing letters in my hand. "May I have an *M* please?"

"Uh, yeah. Sure. Here." Puzzled, I peeled off one of the round stickers and handed it to him. Though it stood for *Medium,* something told me he wanted it to stand for *Martyr.* I wondered what he intended to do with it.

"Thank you vahry much," he grinned. "I'll see you latuh." He turned around and walked out the door, leaving me to worry if perhaps I shouldn't have given it to him.

My connection with him intensified after that night at the cliff. I was able to home in on him with remarkable accuracy, even though I wasn't trying to.

As Krisstopher and I walked to the store one evening, I noticed a series of flat stones etched with pentagrams lying in the road every few feet. Then, as we neared town, I sensed his presence strongly and immediately my eyes were drawn to where he was standing at a pay phone.

This sort of thing happened quite often, where I felt him and instantly located him without having to look around or second-guess. Like a magnet, I was pulled to him without ever having to think about it. Unlike my connection with War, I didn't have to try and tune in to Sean: I was automatically tuned in. It required no effort whatsoever on my part.

He took us to another cemetery shortly after that. Misty came with us this time. After I finished staring at two marble pillars that reminded me of [207]Jachin and Boaz, the dividers between good and evil on the Tree of Life, he urged me to come take a walk through the various aisles of graves. The moon was nearly full. I noticed a bizarre rainbow surrounding it; an energy I'd never seen before. It was a brisk night. I breathed in the fresh air, traipsing around happily. This cemetery had a much lighter feel to it. It didn't seem dark or threatening in any way like the other one.

The first grave I came across had a marble chalice on the tombstone. "Look!" I pointed in awe. "It's a [208]cup." For some reason, I really liked the cup. It reminded me of my tarot deck, which contained cups instead of hearts for one of the suits. They signified love.

"Uh huh."

He and I had somehow ended up alone again while Krisstopher and Misty roamed further ahead.

"Come on," he said, urging me onward once more. I didn't see what the big hurry was, but whatever. I caught up with him in the aisle for a moment and then dashed off ahead, stopping randomly at another grave. Again, a huge cup adorned the headstone.

"Here's another one!" I stared at it for a moment, then went on.

He'd walked a few rows over and was waiting for me. As I approached him now, I paused, deciding which grave I wanted to visit next. He watched me quietly. I got the feeling that I should find one that had another cup on it. Where was it? Making my choice, I bolted over to the tombstone, staring at it anxiously. Yes, there it was, another cup! He seemed pleased at my accuracy. Good, I passed one more test. War would be proud.

* * *

Black birds. Crows. Ravens. They captivated me. It all started when I heard the song at Sean's that night. In thick Irish brogue, a man's deep voice sang of finding "his blackbird." He was referring to a lost lover, and I knew War was sending me a message through the song. Strangely enough, the name of the band was Charming Warlock.

It was after hearing the song that black birds and crows began popping up everywhere—especially crows. I frequently dealt cards from my tarot deck containing their pictures, and in the mornings, the huge scavenger birds gathered outside our bedroom window, cawing us awake. They *did* hold a certain mystery, it seemed.

I recalled the one on the clothesline in the basement years before, wondering now just what it signified. Had it been a mere bird—or as I'd heard tell of [209]Don Juan claiming in his bizarre magical experiences to have actually turned into one—a *soul* taking on the form of a bird?

Just the fact that crows were black and flew through the air reminded me of witchcraft anyway. And with their dark brooding eyes and ominous appearance, they tied in perfectly with the hidden world of the Occult—hidden, that is, to those unable to perceive it.

If War could be any bird, I was sure he would be a crow. Dark eyes. Sinister, yet intriguing. A scavenger flying through time and space, combing the earth—for his black bird.

At work, I'd take the boxes out to the dumpster, then pause as two or three large crows gathered in the parking lot behind the store, cawing loudly while peering at me; not a bit intimidated by my presence. I looked forward to seeing them every day. They seemed to understand me somehow.

Recently, I wrote a song—one verse, actually—which I sang faithfully because it had such a nice ring to it. Of course, it was about War and his beautiful, irresistible power:

*Elohim*
*The black bird sings*
*Outside my [210]window*
*Now let him in*

I'd gotten the name *Elohim* from Crowley's book, [211]*Magick*. It was the name of a powerful force governing the universe. I liked the sound of it, and for some reason, it gave me the impression I was addressing something very important whenever I spoke it.

As I stood in the bathroom one day, washing my hands in the sink, I started singing the song. "Elohi-i-im..." I began.

"HA HA HA!" boomed a mighty voice, seeming to come from a million light years away, yet somehow so close to me—so large to me in my apartment then—that I felt like a match stick in a little doll house compared to it. The voice was so exceedingly great that it made me quake, weakening my knees and frightening me half to death.

Screaming, I bolted out of the bathroom and took a running jump onto the bed where Krisstopher was quietly reading a book.

"What?!" he asked, startled.

"I heard this voice when I was singing Elohim," I gasped excitedly, "and it was *so big, so loud, so powerful,* that I feel like a match stick in a dollhouse compared to it!"

"Hmmm. That's nice," he replied, going back to his book.

Frustrated, I punched the pillow. "Man, I *hate* when you don't get excited for me over my spiritual experiences! It's like you're jealous or something!"

"I'm sorry, Martyr," he responded apathetically, "but I just don't understand. I didn't hear the voice. I don't know what to tell you."

The gap between us widened with each passing day. Why couldn't he understand anything spiritual I talked about? We were supposed to be soul mates! He used to be interested in all the supernatural things. We said we were going to grow and learn magic together, and now he barely studied the Occult. He didn't even really want to talk about it anymore.

\* \* \*

Felician's birthday was tomorrow. Although we weren't the closest of friends, I felt like giving her a gift for some reason, so I decided to make her something.

Sean and Misty stopped by as I was constructing the clay heart. Krisstopher was at work; he'd recently gotten a job at a music store in the mall. Sean suggested that we go back to his place and hang out. He said he'd try and get some acid for us.

"I've got to finish this heart for Felician," I told him.

"Bring it with you."

"But I have to find a crystal to go in the middle of it."

"I've got some crystals at the trailer," Misty offered. "You can have one of those if you want."

I guessed I could take one of hers. It wasn't like Felician would be using it for magic or anything, and even if it did have Misty's energy in it, I could always consecrate it. "Okay," I agreed, "I'll go with you guys."

Sean found some acid and we took it. I sat on the couch at his place, sifting through Misty's crystals. After finding one I liked, I shoved a portion of it snugly into the top of the clay heart while I waited for the LSD to take effect. "Okay, I'm ready to bake it," I said, holding my creation up to show them.

"Uh… I don't have an oven," Sean told me.

"What? I've gotta get this in the oven before it dries. Man, what am I going to do?"

"No problem. My *friend* has an oven. Heera." He reached for the heart. I handed it over to him a little reluctantly, though I wasn't sure why.

"Will you make sure you take it out in about twenty minutes? I don't want to ruin it."

"Don't wuhry. *Fred* will take *good caah* of it." He leaned out his living room window now and called his neighbor, Fred. A man in a red and black plaid shirt with short, curly brown hair and suspicious looking eyes came to the window in the next trailer over. Strangely enough, Fred's trailer was located where Tanya's trailer should have been.

"Hey, can you stick this in yuh oven fuh my friend Mahta?" Sean asked. He stretched his arm out the window, handing the heart to Fred, who nodded silently and took it from him. Funny, but Tanya's trailer wasn't close enough to where two people could reach out their windows to each other. "Oh, and Fred? Make shuh you cook it *real nice*. It's fuh Felician the tramp," he added maliciously. Fred smiled sadistically and nodded again, then ducked out of sight.

"Sean!" I protested.

"Well, it's true. She's a duhty rotten tramp."

"You're not going to burn it, are you?" I asked worriedly.

"Don't wuhry, Mahta. Fred will take good caah of it," he assured me.

The acid turned out to be a dead hit. I tried to hide my disappointment as we sat around and talked, waiting for the heart to finish baking. Krisstopher called, mad that we'd taken off without him, and complaining that it was late and I should come home. We argued a few minutes and I told him I'd come home when I felt like it. Then Sean suggested he could come over and hang out with us, but he said he was just going to go to bed—it was too late to party now. *Whatever*, I thought. It felt good to get away from the apartment for a while. I wasn't about to come home to another fight.

There was a tap on the window, then, and Sean opened it, reaching out to grab the heart from Fred. "Oh, dahn. I guess he cooked it too long," he smirked, handing it to me. The heart was completely scorched, black as a piece of coal and all bubbly and shriveled.

"You said he wouldn't burn it!" I complained angrily.

"Well, I guess he tuhned the oven up a little too high. Suhves the wench right."

"*Now* what am I going to do?"

"Yuh'll think of something."

I was sure Fred had deliberately burned the heart, but there was nothing I could do about it. I had to make the best of it since I didn't really have any money to buy Felician anything and I'd planned on giving her the gift the next day. Holding it in my hand, I mused on how to find beauty in the ugly black sculpture. I asked Sean for a piece of paper and quickly jotted down my thoughts.

Gazing on the hardened black heart with the crystal emerging from the top center of it now, I thought of a ray of light shining through the dark and likened Felician to this light, overcoming the trials and difficulties in her life; piercing through the pain, the evil. Satisfied with the analogy, I decided the heart had turned out even better than if I had painted it like I planned, because now it had greater spiritual meaning behind it. Once again, I'd found beauty in ugliness. And I had to admit, I was quite proud of myself for doing so.

Misty had fallen asleep on the couch, and Sean motioned for me to follow him into the kitchen area. "Let's take a walk," he whispered when I neared the door where he was standing.

"Shouldn't we wake Misty up?"

"No. Let huh sleep. Let's just you and I go."

"But it's cold out there. I didn't bring my jacket or anything."

"Heera, waa huh coat," he suggested, pointing to her favorite blue jean jacket with the red bandanna pinned to the sleeve.

"No, man. I can't do that. She might get mad."

"She's not going tuh caah," he insisted.

"Won't she get jealous if you and I go off alone?" I asked worriedly. "I mean, I don't want her to think we're doing something."

"Don't wuhry. She's not going to caah. Besides, we'll be back befuh she wakes up. I just want to go get some fresh aarah, that's all."

I slipped on the jacket now, feeling a little awkward, and we headed out the door. The next thing I knew, we were sitting on the cliff again, our legs dangling over the side. He pulled out his pipe and we took a couple of drags off it, though I could tell there was barely any weed in it and we were mostly smoking resin. I stared up at the starry sky, breathing in the brisk night air. Beyond the river, the faint flashing of headlights lit up the horizon for a second as cars traveled the winding road.

We got on the subject of witchcraft again, and I proceeded to tell him about Fiend, and how secretive and mysterious he was. I hinted to the fact that perhaps Fiend was involved in a coven, and asked if he knew him. He was, after all, involved in something strange himself. I knew it wasn't impossible for the two of them to have crossed paths, especially after all the people that had crossed my own path in the small world.

He commented that he didn't know him, to which I then changed the subject, rattling on about how I wanted more power—like the power to astral project as my father had. I mentioned again that I was carrying on in his footsteps, completing the spiritual circle where he'd left off before he died. Suddenly, I felt a tinge of fear—like I shouldn't be out there alone with Sean, and it wouldn't take much for him to push me right off the cliff. But I didn't want to act afraid, so I babbled on, ignoring it.

He grabbed my hand then, pulling me up off the ground. "Come on, let's go ovuh heera," he said sweetly.

I followed him, talking some more and not even really noticing where we were headed; just tagging along blindly. "I wrote this really cool song about *Elohim*," I told him excitedly. [212]"Crowley talks about Elohim, and when I sang it the other day, I heard this loud, powerful laughter that made me feel like a match stick in a doll house, you know what I'm saying? It was sooo gigantic, and I felt so small—"

"Yeah? How's the song go? Sing it."

"I can't sing it right now. I feel embarrassed."

"Go ahead, sing it."

We were at the black wrought iron fence again, with one foot over it, ready to climb into the cemetery. The fear returned. I shook it off. *Nonsense. I've hung around Sean alone before...* "Okay, it goes— eh hem—Elohi-i-im... the black bird sings... outside my window... now let—"

"Martyr!" Krisstopher's voice called, startling me. "Martyr, are you out here?!"

I started to respond, but Sean grabbed me, cupping his hand over my mouth. "*Sshhh!* Don't ansuh. He'll leave."

"Sean! Martyr!" Misty's voice shouted now. I wriggled free and ran forward.

"Over here, Krisstopher! Over here, you guys!" I called back anxiously. Relief flooded through me as they crunched through the twigs to where we were standing. It scared me that Sean hadn't wanted Krisstopher to find me—that he'd covered my mouth so I wouldn't answer. I wondered what he'd planned on doing once we climbed the fence.

"Do you know what *time* it is?" Krisstopher asked sternly. "What are you guys doing out here? I was worried about you."

I responded angrily to him then, about how if he cared about me, he would *something or other*, blah blah blah.

Misty didn't say much. She just kind of stood with her arms folded and glared at me. I tried explaining to her that it wasn't what it looked like—that Sean and I had only been talking—but for the first time since

285

I'd known her, she was miffed. "Can I please have my jacket back?" she asked coldly.

"Oh—sure." Sheepishly, I pulled it off and handed it to her. "I'm sorry... I was just cold and Sean thought it would be alright if I wore it. I guess I should have asked you, but you were sleeping and I thought we'd be right back."

That was the last time I ever saw Sean and Misty together.

* * *

Felician was plastered, sprawled out on the couch after drinking most of her birthday away. I handed her the heart on a leather cord with the little inscription card attached to it.

"Oh... phthanks, Mahta. What is it, a neckphlace?" she slurred, raising up halfway and putting it over her head.

"Yeah, or uh... you could hang it up someplace in your apartment. It's kind of like a decoration, you know? I made it."

"You made it? It's beauuuutifluhl. Phthanks a lot, Mahta."

She was definitely in no condition to hold a decent conversation, so Krisstopher and I left after about ten minutes of watching her crash out while Klay briefed us on her eventful day.

* * *

I was now Assistant Manager at Jentanno. It happened in the blink of an eye, when Sam and Felician got in an argument and Felician threatened to walk out.

Sam asked for the store keys then, which were attached to a little plastic hook on her belt loop. She handed them over, and they were then placed in my hands. "Mahta, congratulations. You are now assistant manaja of Jentanno."

Felician's face clouded over.

"*Me?*" I asked uneasily.

"Uh huh," Sam replied, giving her a spiteful look.

I felt awkward. Felician's anger permeated the atmosphere in waves so thick I could have cut them with a knife. She stormed out of the store, never setting foot in there again except to get her last paycheck.

Now I had to learn how to close out two registers and work with big numbers—did Sam know I hated math? But I got to wear the cool plastic hook with the keys on *my* jeans. I kind of liked how the keys jingled when I walked, giving me a sense of authority. I had to admit, for one of the first times in my life, I felt important. What I didn't like, however, was the increase in hours and the *salary pay*, which meant whether I worked twenty hours or fifty hours, I still got the same amount every two weeks.

Sean came in the store shortly after that to check out my new position. He smirked when he saw the keys dangling from my belt loop. We talked for a minute, and then he asked if I had any jeans about a size eleven or so, and which jeans would I recommend for his fiancée Mara?

"Fiancée?" I asked doubtfully. "Is Mara the girl you went out with for four years or so back in Mass?"

"Yeah. She'll be heera in a few days and weh getting mahreed."

It seemed a little odd to me that he and Misty had just split up and now he was marrying someone else—all in the span of about three weeks—but whatever. He had a tendency to lie, so I figured I'd take it with a grain of salt.

"Cool. Yeah, sure. Bring her in and I'll fix her up," I said cheerfully. "I can probably get her a discount."

He returned about three or four days later with a big boned brunette who was sullen and reserved. Hardly the attitude of a bride to be, I thought, unless she was being dragged to the altar at gunpoint. I smiled at her and said hello.

"Hi," she mumbled, her face expressionless. She seemed timid and afraid. I wondered if she'd been abused or something.

Sean was as sweet as pie to her, putting his arm around her and pecking her on the cheek, calling her *honey*. But she looked worn out and withdrawn. She hurriedly found a couple pairs of jeans, anxious to leave the store.

A few days later, I got a phone call from Sean in the late afternoon. He told me he and Mara had just gotten married and wanted to go out and celebrate with us. I had a suspicion he was lying through his teeth, using the whole thing as a ploy to try and get me jealous.

He'd told Krisstopher not too long before Mara's coming that he could easily take me away from him, just like [213]Sir Lancelot took Guenivere away from King Arthur. Krisstopher then accused me of having a fling behind his back. I assured him that Sean was lying, and that I had no feelings whatsoever for him. It was then that I realized my assumptions about Sean were correct: he was trying desperately to win my affection.

Prior to Mara's arrival, he claimed to have sold his book on Arthurian legend he'd talked about previously. Supposedly the publishing company gave him a royalty check for twenty thousand to start out with. So now he had money to buy Mara's ring and pay for the wedding. But something wasn't setting right with me. Mara had also written a story along the same lines. I'd read a few pages of it prior to meeting her and thought it was great.

Perhaps Sean really hadn't written a book at all, and was just using *her* idea to impress people. None-the-less, I played along with it, congratulating him. I seriously doubted he had twenty thousand dollars stashed away from a book sale, but I did wonder how it was that he never worked yet still managed to pay his rent and have a steady supply of weed on hand. As far as I knew, except for the telemarketing he did for about three weeks, he hadn't worked since I'd moved there.

As I talked with him on the phone now, he told me he and Mara got married down by the river somewhere. I didn't bother to ask him the details. Quite frankly, I wanted to save him any embarrassment that would occur when I caught him in a lie. Strange that only a few weeks before, Krisstopher and I had been discussing *handfasting*, a type of Wiccan marriage between two witches. We thought of doing it, and I'd mentioned to Sean that I'd like him to play the part of the priest and marry us, to which he smirked. Now all of a sudden *he* was married. There was a chance he'd done handfasting as well, which didn't require any certificate of authenticity since it was a private agreement between two witches, but I doubted it.

When I asked him on the phone why he'd gotten married so suddenly to this woman, he replied, "Well, if you can't have the best, Mahta—if you can't have what you really want—you settle fuh something else."

I knew he was referring to the fact that he was unable to have *me*.

"Awww, that's sweet. Thanks," I told him.

"*Sweet*, huh?" he said with irritation.

The four of us went out to a nice restaurant in town that evening to celebrate. Mara *did* have a ring on. I didn't examine it closely, but it could have been a wedding ring for all I knew, or just one of those imitation diamonds to make it *look* like a wedding ring. Who knew? At least she was a little more cheerful this time, though still not very talkative. Either Krisstopher or I mentioned Sean's book on Arthurian legend then, to which she immediately grew suspicious. "*I'm* writing a book on Arthurian times," she corrected.

Sean squirmed a little in his seat. "Yeah, I know honey, but this is a *diffuhrent* book weh talking about that *I* wrote."

Feeling sorry for him—or maybe just uncomfortable about the whole situation—I changed the subject to get him off the hook. But the worry lines that suddenly collected on Mara's forehead remained the rest of the evening.

The next time we saw Sean in town, she wasn't with him. When I asked where she was, he told me that she'd gone back to Massachusetts to finish packing some stuff and prepare for the move into the house they were getting soon. She'd be there a couple of months, he said, while all the necessary arrangements were made.

"Oh, I see," I grinned, thoroughly convinced he was lying to me.

* * *

Krisstopher called me at work to tell me he was in jail. Apparently the cops had barged right into the music store at the mall and hauled him away in front of everyone. They'd been tipped off by an anonymous source that he had a warrant out for his arrest. Mysteriously enough, as he was being escorted out of the store, he said Tanya suddenly appeared to witness the whole thing.

Sean phoned right after that to inform me he'd been in Tanya's trailer racking up her phone bill (he had a spare key since the two of them used to live together), where he saw a sheet of paper with a list of things to do on it, one of which was to *turn Krisstopher in*. He suggested she probably wanted to get revenge on him where I was concerned.

Whatever the case, luckily Krisstopher got a good court appointed attorney, and ended up only having to spend a week in a correctional facility, as well as make payments toward a large fine.

The first night he stayed at the facility, I got a phone call from Sean around eight o'clock in the evening.

"So, yuh alone tuhnight, huh?" he asked in a somewhat menacing tone.

"Yeah, so? Krisstopher will be back soon."

I wasn't about to let him scare me. We talked some more about Tanya and what a ruthless wench she was, and then I mentioned that my plan for the evening was to crash out early since I was tired.

"Alright, I'll see you latuh then. Oh, and Mahta?"

"Yeah?"

"*Sweet dreams*," he hissed evilly, "ha ha ha."

I hung up the phone. "Ooooh, I'm *scared*, Sean," I said aloud, shaking my head in disgust at his attempt to frighten me. Shortly after that, I went to bed, falling fast asleep.

At about midnight, my eyes suddenly opened. Beside my head on the pillow sat a black form resembling a tarantula, about six inches high and made up of tiny, visible molecules. As I stared at it, the form disintegrated into the air.

On automatic impulse, I jumped to my feet and ran to the window, jerking up the shade. As I peered through the rain at the empty street below, my eyes instinctively fell on Sean, who was passing directly in front of the house at that same instance, his guitar slung over his shoulder; staring straight ahead. Except for his tall figure trudging through the night, the road was dark and deserted. A chill raced up my spine. I knew he'd paid me a bedside visit.

## XI.

A SHADE OF GRAY

*Ah, but power corrupts*
*Even the purest intents*
*A consuming thirst*
*That cannot be quenched*

It was time to put an end to her insolence. No more could I tolerate her sick little game. White would be a deeper shade of gray now, as I wrote my incantations for the night's ritual.

I decided to include the use of those [214] deific names Crowley made mention of, since I couldn't seem to shake them from my spirit lately. As I scratched them earnestly onto the paper: *Elohim, Adonai,* a sense of wrongdoing washed over me. I recall apologetic thoughts and grumbles of rebuttal; to whom, I know not.

Outside, next to the cross marking the spot of our dear departed anole, Kerridwen, I buried the glass jar of urine. It was meant to be a protective talisman, though admittedly, I allowed a few dark thoughts toward my adversary Tanya to penetrate the jar's exterior. This was merely a self-defense tactic, I told myself.

Then back upstairs, I put away my little Book of Shadows until nightfall had its way. Uncertainty gnawed me in the meantime like a persistent maggot. Was this *really* what I wanted to do? What about bad karma? I definitely didn't want any of this stuff coming back to me. Still,

I was only taking measures to protect myself. Tanya had to be stopped before she caused us any more harm.

\* \* \*

A little bit of green eyeshadow seemed appropriate for the occasion. This accomplished, I put on my black brimmed 'Dead Raiser hat,' as I liked to call it, similar to the ones The Field of Fallen Angels wore on their *Dead Raiser* release. The hat gave me the appearance of a gothic cowgirl dressed for an evening of grave digging.

Next, I slipped on the knitted black shawl with fringes which I liked to think was owned by an old generational witch. I'd purchased it from the thrift store, and it had a white tag sewn to the inside that read BAKER in permanent marker. I pictured Mrs. Baker to be some scraggly, white haired old woman: a grandmother to the Craft.

Krisstopher and I were now ready. Together, we set off on foot for the long walk to our chosen place of ritual. Tonight we were trying something different. There seemed to be a great deal of energy surrounding Sean's little playground: the old cemetery near the cliff. I thought it quite fitting that we go there.

We tromped off further down the road, the flickering lights of town fading behind us as we emerged into thick blackness. Both of us were silent except for occasional small talk. I believe we were each carefully weighing out the plans for the evening in our hearts and minds, while the butterflies did backflips in our stomachs.

The stillness of the night broke with the sound of an approaching car, its motor growing louder and louder as it came round the corner and then slowed to a stop right beside us. To my utter dismay, Tanya poked her head out the window.

"Where are you going, Krisstopher? You're not going over toward *my* place for any reason, are you?" she asked, as if knowing our plans. She peered over at me, her tiny little spectacles sitting indignantly upon her pointed nose. In the passenger seat, I could just glimpse the shadowy figure of a male with short hair. He sat in complete silence.

My heart pounded violently now, my breath coming out in sharp gasps as anger seized hold of me.

"Well, hello Tanya. You're looking just as *ugly* as ever tonight," Krisstopher commented. I felt the slightest bit of satisfaction pour over me, even though I knew he never would have said such a thing had she not turned him into the police.

"Tch," she exclaimed, "what did I ever do to *you?*"

"Oh, nothing, you wench! You only got me arrested, that's all."

"I don't know what you're talking about. If I were you, I'd thank Sean for that. *He's* the one who probably did it, not me!"

"Oh yeah, right. You're such a *liar,* Tanya!"

The rest of the conversation was a blur to me, except to say they exchanged a few choice words, and then she turned the car around and headed in the opposite direction; the sound of the motor soon replaced by the chorus of crickets and the occasional burp of a bullfrog.

Any doubts I had were now replaced with determination to rip that quirky boldness right out of her heart—to teach her a lesson about messing with other people's lives and emotions.

As we reached the black wrought iron fence surrounding the tombstones, however, I felt my hesitation return. A threatening silence loomed over the cemetery; a heavy, oppressive fog invisible to the natural eye.

"Come on," Krisstopher whispered urgently, stepping over the fence. He glanced around nervously.

Pulling a black candle for negativity out of the paper bag, I lit it. Though there was not so much as a delicate breeze to shake a leaf, the candle suddenly went out with a dense *poof,* as if the unseen finger of an angel had snuffed it. "Krisstopher, the candle just went out for no reason!" I said excitedly.

Uneasy, he took another look around. "I don't think we should go through with this."

"We *have* to." I lit the candle again. Once more, the flame instantly died. This time, I was sure it was no coincidence.

"I don't have a good feeling about this. I think we should just go," he protested.

"No!" I responded stubbornly. "We have to go through with this to teach her a lesson. I'll just light it again." I flicked my lighter a third time, then stopped as a loud banging noise started in the clearing beyond the small patch of woods, just near the cliff. "What's that?" I asked cautiously.

We listened for a moment and then he whispered excitedly, "Martyr, those are black bears! They're searching through the dumpster at Cliff River."

"How do you know?"

"Trust me, I've seen them in there before. They always ransack the dumpsters for food. Listen to how *loud* that is. That's not a person making that noise!"

We listened, frozen, as they slammed and banged, slammed and banged.

"I hope they don't smell us," he continued. "Don't even move or they might sense us over here. Do you know what to do if one starts chasing you? You have to run from side-to-side because bears can't run zigzag. And if you have to—climb a tree, because they can't climb trees, okay?"

My adrenaline was pumping now as fear swept over me. "I don't know *how* to climb a tree," I whimpered.

Suddenly the banging stopped, replaced by a rustling sound in the woods beside us.

"They're coming this way! We've got to make a run for it!" he cried, grabbing our paper bag full of stuff.

I felt my life flash before my eyes in the blackness. "Oh God! Oh God, help us!" I sobbed, tears streaming down my cheeks as I thought of my flesh being ripped apart while I was eaten alive by bears, unable to see a thing.

"Come on—now!" He grabbed my hand, the rustling no more than twenty feet away, it seemed. We bolted over the fence and tore off down the narrow trail to the dirt road. After running awhile, we realized the bears weren't following and stopped to catch our breath.

"Phhhew! That was a close one," he sighed with relief, lighting a cigarette. We began walking again.

"Alright, we'll just have to go somewhere else," I responded resolutely. Though we'd just escaped a perilous situation only minutes before, I chose to ignore the omens warning us not to continue. My heart was still as hard as a rock where Tanya was concerned.

"No, Martyr. I really think this is not the time to do the spell."

"Not the time?! You just *like* her, that's all! That's why you don't want to do the spell. It has nothing to do with *timing*."

"Look, something is telling us not to go through with this, and I'm not going through with it," he stated firmly.

"Fine, then I'll go by myself. She's not getting out of this. And you *do* like her—I *know* you do!"

"No I don't!" he argued. "I'm telling you I—bluhh... ughh—*blahhhp!*" He hunched over and began violently puking for no apparent reason.

I stared in horror, fearing that this was indeed an omen not to continue. We'd had nothing to drink, and there was no reason for him to get sick, especially so suddenly. Unless... the thought of hurting Tanya made him sick because he loved her so much. "You *do* like her. That's why you're getting sick about it," I snapped.

He heaved the last little bit and stood upright again, wiping his mouth with his sleeve. "No... I don't know why I got sick," he said weakly. "I really think something's telling us not to do this."

We walked on in silence while I considered going out by the river in our backyard and performing the spell on my own.

A car passed us then, slamming on its brakes and pulling over to the shoulder of the road. Sean stuck his head out the passenger side window. "Hey, it's Kris and Mahta! You guys want a ride?" We climbed in the car and he introduced us to the driver, a heavyset woman who appeared to be in her mid-thirties with short, curly brown hair. "So what brings you guys out tuh this neck of the neighbuhhood?" he asked as we pulled back onto the road again.

"Oh... we were just taking care of some business," I replied nonchalantly.

"Taking caah of some business, huh?" He turned around in the seat now to stare at the bag of goods I held in my hand along with my Book of Shadows. "What do you got thaa Mahta?"

"Oh... nothing. We were just taking care of some business concerning *Tanya*, if you know what I mean."

"I see," he answered, knowing exactly what I meant.

"Yeah, we went to the cemetery by your place. But we got stopped before we could go through with anything. It was really strange."

He grinned at me, his eyebrows lifted in silent amusement. "Well of *cohss* you got stopped. I told you, that's *my* stomping ground ovuh thaa. You should know that, Mahta."

What did he mean, *his* stomping ground? I wondered. A thought crossed my mind then, that he was referring to the fact that he performed satanic rituals there. *No. Couldn't be.*

I had a strange dream involving him shortly after that: he was stalking me and I was running from him, trying to hide somewhere so he couldn't find me. I found a table outside beneath a green leafy tree and crawled under it for shelter. Two children appeared: a boy and a girl. They were looking right at me, watching me hide. They chanted, "Sean is the De-vil! Sean is the De-vil!" as if warning me. I woke up suddenly, disturbed by the eerie dream.

\* \* \*

Jentanno was closing down. No wonder they kept having so many sales. As the discounts went from fifteen to twenty-five to fifty percent off everything in the store, Sam warned me that she had a feeling they were going out of business. She took me aside to tell me of her suspicions one day, suggesting that I look for another job in my spare time. They'd tried keeping her in the dark about it, but she was smart. She knew the signs: the steady decrease in numbers followed by the continual sales, and the series of phone calls with special instructions she'd gotten lately from the home office. "Keep this between you and me, Mahta. Because weh going to need all the help we can get," she advised.

\* \* \*

Opening my Book of Shadows, I turned to the page where I'd written out the spell we were going to perform against Tanya before getting stopped. The apartment was quiet. Krisstopher was at work and I was all alone, ready to finish where we'd left off.

But as I stared at the spell now, an uncomfortable feeling washed over me—a feeling that reminded me of all the bad omens Krisstopher and I experienced that night—an indication that it was wrong to curse

Tanya. Wrong? *Wrong?!* Why was it that she could play as dirty as was humanly possible, and yet get away with it? And why did I always get *stopped?* All my life I'd been held back from retaliating when people should have got what was coming to them.

Just like when Suzan threw sand in my eyes and down my throat one time, and then challenged me with a garden hoe. But just as Jim finished showing me how to fight her with the handle of a rake (the actual rake part was missing and we didn't have anything else comparable in the shed), my mom called me into the house, forbidding me to go through with it. She told me I should go apologize to Suzan (?????), who only laughed in my face and threatened me again.

Well, I was tired of being the nice girl. Tired of people abusing me both mentally and physically. In Tanya's case, I'd given her more than enough chances. No, I wasn't going to listen to that small voice tugging away at the seat of my conscience like a little dog grabbing me by the seat of my pants. No, this time, *I* was in control. And nothing was going to stop me.

Making the necessary preparations, I said my alignments to the gods and goddesses, then lit the black candle and began reading the spell, starting with the names Elohim and Adonai. "Curse everything she does. When she takes a shower, let the water scald her—let her not be able to shut it off. Let her face break out. Curse her sexual relationships. [215]Curse her... *crotch.* Let no man want to touch her again..." I drifted off, then added, "Until she learns. Just for a *little* while," to justify the guilt I suddenly felt. Finished, I sat in silence while thoughts of bad karma filled my head. Did I really want to hurt her? Yes... no... well—it was too late now. "After all, it *is* for the good of the universe—it's for my own protection and the protection of Krisstopher, that no further harm come to us through her," I sputtered in defense.

[216]Crowley was right. There *was* no white magic, was there? One always inevitably used it for a selfish means at *some* point, whether or not he chose to admit it. Well, it wasn't like I did it all the time. I'd probably never do it again...

\* \* \*

297

It was pouring rain outside. Krisstopher and I were snuggled safe and sound in bed, propped up on pillows watching TV. We'd just finished smoking some weed Kyle sold us, and I felt warm and fuzzy; spaced out and perfectly content. Until my stomach started to growl. I looked over at Krisstopher. "Hey, I'm hungry, aren't you?" My mouth tasted like a big cotton ball.

"Yeah. How about a little snack?" he yawned lazily.

They sold [217]Little Debbie cakes at the gas station in town, four for a dollar. We always ate those whenever we got the munchies after smoking pot.

"Yeah! Little Debbie cakes!" I sang out excitedly. The [218]brownies, the oatmeal pies, the spice cakes... I could hardly contain myself now.

"You want me to go get us some?" he asked, yawning again.

"Yeah, hon. Thanks." Satisfied, I fixed my eyes on the TV set, returning to the program.

"On second thought, I *always* bike to the store. I think it's *your* turn."

"Huh?" I peeled my eyes off the screen, looking at him once more.

"I said, it's *your* turn. I'm tired of always being the one to make the snack run."

I listened to the sound of the rain pounding violently on the roof and beating against the windows. "Come on, Krisstopher. Please..." I coaxed sweetly.

He remained obstinate. "No, no. I really think *you* should go, Martyr. It'll be good for you to get out of the house for a while. And it'll only take a few minutes."

Just how bad *did* I want [219]Little Debbie cakes, anyway? Maybe I could do without them. "But you know I *hate* mountain bikes—and the seat's too high up for me to reach the peddles," I argued. (It seems maybe he had a different mountain bike when I uttered this protest—like the other one was stolen—or he'd raised the seat. I can't remember now).

"It's not that hard, Martyr! Just stand up on it and peddle. You've done it before. Come on..."

Okay. What was the big deal? It would only take me about fifteen minutes. I was a big girl. I could handle it. But as I started to get up now, I got this feeling—this awful gut feeling—that I shouldn't go. I didn't know why. All I knew was, it was a strong feeling.

"So you'll go then? Thanks, sweetie!" he said, planting a big kiss on my cheek.

Oh, why not? What did I have to be afraid of, anyway? I was a witch—nothing was going to hurt *me!* Making my way down the wooden staircase and out the door, I approached Krisstopher's soaking wet bike on the front lawn. That feeling again—like someone was watching me. An evil in the air... was Sean lurking nearby? I glanced around nervously, but it was dark outside and I couldn't see anything; just the bushes.

Whistling, I climbed on the bike, standing up on the pedals and pushing down hard to get off the lawn and onto the road. *Whoever, whatever* was there, I wasn't going to act afraid. No way. I continued pedaling to the store, the feeling lifting the closer I got to town. It was probably only my imagination.

As I picked out the snacks and paid for them, I realized Krisstopher was right: it felt good to get out of the house for a while, even though I was *drenched.* It gave me a sense of accomplishment—that I'd finally done something on my own. The more I grew dependent in a relationship, the harder it was to go off without the person because I felt self-conscious and insecure—like I was missing the other half of me. It made me unsure of myself and I didn't like that.

Carefully avoiding the crossbar as I climbed on the bike again, I thought of War. He wasn't afraid to be alone. He always tromped around with such confidence. I loved his tough, *I don't care* attitude. I guess I even felt a small part of him inside me now as I pedaled back to the house, telling myself, *There's nothing to be afraid of. There's nothing to be afraid of.* A sense of relief flooded over me as I reached the front lawn once more, looking like a drowned rat. I broke out in a smile. I'd done it! *See, there was nothing to be afrai—*

The bike suddenly hit something—a rock, a piece of wood—something. My feet slipped off the wet pedals, landing me on the metal crossbar with a SMACK! *—right between the legs.* Stinging, burning, excruciating pain like I never felt in my life surged through me. The bike tipped over and I was on the ground. I started to get up when *AAAAAHHH!* Sharp, stabbing sensation in the crotch. *Can't move. AAAAHHHH!!!*

My breath coming out in short, sharp gasps now, I used my arms to pull myself to the door, slithering like a snake. As I tried reaching for the doorknob, pain shot through me again, causing me to lose my breath altogether for a moment. I sobbed loudly, hot tears pouring down my cheeks. Somehow, I managed to open the door far enough to squeeze through, and groped blindly for the bottom of the stairs. "Krisstopher! AAAAHHHH! *Krisstopher!*"

The door to our apartment opened and Krisstopher appeared at the top of the staircase. "Martyr, what's wrong? Martyr?!" He hurried to meet me.

"I fell on the stupid crossbar! AAAAHHHHH! I can't move. It stings! It *stings!*" I wailed loudly.

"Okay, it's okay. Calm down. Here, let me carry you." He scooped me up in his arms and carried me up the stairs and back into the apartment, laying me down gently on the bed.

About fifteen minutes later, two medics came upstairs with a stretcher, one of them staring curiously at our Wiccan books in the corner of the room. "What happened, Ma'am?" he asked.

"Bike accident. I fell on the crossbar—*really hard,* if you know what I mean," I strained through more short, sharp gasps.

"Ouch! Well, you're in good hands. Don't worry," the other one soothed.

They carefully hoisted me onto the stretcher and I was hauled away to the nearby hospital, where pain killers were prescribed for three or four days along with ice packs for the extensive swelling. I limped for a week.

Upon finding out, Sean seemed pleasantly amused. Had *he* caused this to happen? I wondered. I was really starting to dislike him again. The past few times he'd come over, he somehow succeeded in starting an argument between Krisstopher and I. Then once we were at each other's throat, he left with a satisfied smile on his face, as if he'd accomplished his purpose.

I began to realize that he was a mastermind when it came to manipulation. He crawled inside people's heads—found out their insecurities, their fears—and then preyed upon them to get his own way. He wanted desperately to break Krisstopher and I apart so he could have a chance with me, and he'd stop at nothing to do it.

This became crystal clear to me one day as the three of us were strolling down the street. Sean knew that Krisstopher and I competed with each other when it came to music. I'd expressed to him before that Krisstopher always bragged about his stuff—always had to have the last say when it came to writing songs. And deep down inside, I had a complex—a fear that I just wasn't good enough on my keyboards. I'd never taken piano lessons—a major setback—yet in six years I'd taught myself a lot. Even Jason had said, concerning a few popular goth bands that had their own record labels, that he thought I was much better on keys than them. And Fiend loved the way I played. So did Bruce; he raved about our band to everyone he knew, passing out tapes to them.

Sean brought up the band now. "Yeah, I really like that one song *you* did, Kris. What's it called, *Buhning Flesh* or something?"

"Yeah, thanks. It *is* pretty cool, isn't it?" he gloated.

"Uh huh. You know, I really think you could go somewaa with yuh music. I mean, you need tuh be on a recuhd label. I could see you packing stadiums and stuff."

"*Really?* Thanks, man. Yeah... I guess I could, couldn't I?" He was all smiles. I could see his head, a round balloon growing bigger... and bigger... and bigger... as Sean blew more hot air into it.

"Hey, what about *me?* I'm part of the band too," I reminded them.

"Yeah, but you *lag*, Mahta. You can't play keybohds wuth crap," Sean laughed.

"That's not true," I defended, my heart sinking within me. "I sound just as good as all these other bands—and I don't even use samples. I play with both hands."

Krisstopher said nothing for a minute. I'd hoped he'd stick up for his girlfriend, but no, the next time he opened his mouth, it was only to glorify himself. "Yeah, I guess I *am* pretty good, huh?"

I felt sick suddenly. Sick and angry. All my life people put me down, and now it was no different. Even my boyfriend couldn't stick up for me. Well I had news for him: Beastulust wouldn't be Beastulust without my keyboards—the eerie sounds I'd programmed into them, the amazing bass part I did with my left hand while playing the guitar part with my right. I had a unique style of playing, and I knew it. I was great at playing by ear too. In the past, I'd scored among the top students in the school district for tonality. Okay, so maybe there was room for improvement where my musical talent was concerned, but Krisstopher was no exception either.

For instance, I clearly sang way better than him, receiving compliments on my voice. In contrast, some people remarked to me that he couldn't carry a tune. The truth was, he wasn't too bad once he warmed up a bit, but he definitely needed more practice in the vocal arena. So how dare him think he was something without *me!* And as for Sean...

I glared at him angrily. I hated him. He was demented. *Evil.* I wished we'd never met him. I should have known from that very first day when I sensed he was no good. Why hadn't I gone with my gut feeling—my intuition? Probably because I had no choice: Krisstopher had about as much discernment as a doorknob, and how could I have avoided Sean when he took such a liking to him?

I stomped upstairs now and into our apartment, storming into the bathroom and slamming the door behind me. After closing the lid on the toilet seat, I plopped down on it and burst into tears. I could hear the two of them at the kitchen table, talking and laughing as if I didn't exist. I had to get out of here. I had to get out of this place. It was making me crazy. Where could I go? Didn't *anyone* care?

I thought of War. Surely *he* cared. Surely it mattered to *him* if I lived or died. Of course it did. He was my soul mate, and he loved me. I recalled all the messages he'd sent me—all the times he'd reached out to me. If he was so evil, then why was he always there for me spiritually when I needed him? *He* would have stuck up for me just now had he been present. I *know* he would have.

"Mahta! What's wrong?" Sean called, faking concern.

"What are you doing in there, Martyr? Come out here and talk to us!" Krisstopher chimed in, playing dumb and innocent.

I trudged out of the bathroom, yelling at them for a few minutes about their insensitivity, and then we all went down by the river. It was almost fall, and the leaves were withering and dropping off the trees. We sat on the rocks, watching the water's current ripple and flow.

Suddenly the crows cawed out to me, *"War, War! War, War!"* They stood perched atop the trees, watching from their posts like heralds announcing the coming of a new day. A new day...

"I feel him all around," I said now.

"Feel *who?*" Krisstopher asked.

Why not tell him? Why not hurt him like he always hurt me?

*"War,"* I responded. "I don't know what it is, but I know I need to leave here... to find out what's going on with him."

He and Sean remained silent after that.

* * *

Krisstopher fell asleep one late afternoon. I tiptoed out of the apartment, climbing on his bike and heading into town. Who cared about the crossbar? I needed to call War. I couldn't take it anymore, this not knowing what was going on. Forget the telepathic signs—I needed to hear his voice in my *ear.*

Entering town, I spotted Sean standing outside the party store on the corner, not far from one of the pay phones. Crud. How could I get past him?

"Hey Mahta! Whaa ah you going?" he called suspiciously.

The leer on his face told me he already had a good idea. No, maybe not. But what could I do? I didn't want to look like I was hiding anything, or he would surely tell Krisstopher. I stopped the bike in front of him now. "I was just going to... call War and see how he's doing," I replied, trying to sound as casual as I possibly could. "I haven't talked to him in a while, and I really need to talk to him." I turned the bike around to head off toward the phone booth behind one of the stores.

"I see. Well, let me come with you."

*No, don't you dare come with me.*

"You can use my calling cahd," he added. "Heera." He handed me the plastic card. I took it, thanking him, and wondered if he was going to relay this to Krisstopher. Probably. "I'm supposed tuh help you in any way that I can," he informed me.

"Huh?" I asked, giving him a strange look.

"I said, I'm supposed tuh help you in any way that I can. Since I'm yuh teachuh, I mean."

Who told him that? War? I was confused by what he meant. Shrugging my shoulders, I asked him how to use the card. After punching in the numbers, I waited nervously while the phone rang in my ear. One ring. Two rings. Three—

"Hello?" War's familiar nasal tone voice sounded on the other end of the receiver.

*It's him. It's actually him.* My knees weakened. "Hi... War?"

"Yeah, who's this?"

"It's me, Martyr. How are you?"

"Oh. Hi Martyr," he said, sounding about as unenthusiastic as a person can get. "I'm alright. Where are ya, anyway?"

"I'm in New Hampshire. I live here now... with Krisstopher. But I just wanted to call and see how you're doing." His apathy hurt me, but I tried not to let it show.

He asked a couple of general questions, but I could tell from the tone of his voice that he could care less if I answered them or not. I pictured him thinking, *"Let's see. How fast can I get rid of her? I'll just ask a few questions to sound halfway interested since she's calling long-distance, and then hang up."* "Well, uh, I hate to cut it short, but I gotta go. I got some *girls* over, if ya know what I mean," he told me now.

*Girls over?! What does he mean he has girls over?!* My heart broke. *How can he do this to me? I thought he loved me!* "Oh, yeah—sure. No problem," I answered, playing it cool. "Nice talking to you. Take care."

"Uh... yeah. You too. Thanks for callin'. Bye."

I listened to the dial tone for a minute, tears welling up in my eyes. *How can this be? How can he just ditch me like this, after all the signs? After all the omens? After all the—*

"Well? What did he have to say?" Sean asked, his arms folded and an amused look on his face.

He knew, didn't he? Of course he did! I couldn't hide anything from him. He was like a termite chewing through the walls of my mind— nothing was safe from him.

"He said he has girls over," I answered quietly.

"Hmm," he nodded, as if to say, *I told you so.*

"I just don't understand it. How could he do all of this stuff in the spiritual realm and then blow me off in the physical? What kind of *mind game* is he playing?"

He was silent as I handed him back his card.

*Mind game... that was it! He was merely playing a mind game because he was hurt. I'd hurt him when I turned him down for Krisstopher. Now he was getting even.*

"Here, how much do I owe you—is six dollars enough? No—here, have eight instead," I said, handing him the money. I started to get on the bike again and head for home. I just wanted to be alone. To cry. To get angry. My heart felt like it had been ripped out of my chest and thrown to the ground to be stomped on. I felt sick. And Krisstopher would be waking up soon, if he wasn't already awake. How would I hide the truth from him when it was written all over my face that I was heartbroken?

"Mahta. Heera. Sit down fuh a minute, will you?" Sean said. He plopped down beside a tree near the gas station.

I paused. It was getting dark outside. "No, Sean. I've really gotta get home. Krisstopher will be waking up soon, and he doesn't know I'm gone. He'll wonder where I'm at." Why couldn't he just leave me alone? I needed to be alone. Alone...

"This will only take a minute. I promise," he persisted, patting the dirt beside him.

I set the bike down on the ground but continued to stand, babbling on. "I just don't understand it. I thought War was a *warlock*. I thought he had *magic power*. I thought—"

"Mahta, *look*," he interrupted, staring straight at me while pointing behind him at the tree trunk. I followed his thumb to the glowing greenish-white heart hovering in front of the trunk about six inches above his head. It didn't occur to me that he'd *made* it appear, or that I wasn't on any drugs this time but could still see it. No, I was too wrapped up in War.

"Uh huh," I responded vacantly. "But why is War *doing* all this to me? What's going on? I'm so confused..."

He sighed. "Mahta, please sit down. I have something I need tuh tell you."

I dropped to the ground beside him, growing quiet. He pulled out his little wooden pipe, packing the weed firmly with his fingers, and lit it. Inhaling, he passed it to me. I took a hit, holding it in for a few moments. "Yeah?" I finally responded, exhaling. Just what I needed. I needed to relax. Too much confusion going on. I couldn't let go of War. I couldn't let go that easily. Not after all the supernatural stuff that happened. No, he was my soul mate. And besides, he *said* he was evil. He *warned* me that there was an evil side of him—I'd heard it in the song. That's what all this was about! I was merely seeing the evil side of him—the side that liked to mess with my head.

"You know, Mahta…" Sean began, then stopped.

"Yeah?" I had a feeling I already knew what he was going to say. He was going to proposition me, wasn't he? Now that War was out of the picture.

"I don't know how tuh say this."

"Just say it."

"Okay. I really like you, Mahta. I mean, fuh *moh* than a friend. I'd like tuh have a relationship with you. A *real* relationship, though. Not like you and Krisstapha have. He doesn't know how tuh treat you. But you could move in with *me*. I've got this house now, and we could live thaa…"

*And live happily ever after, right Sean?* No, I wasn't that stupid. I saw how he treated his girlfriends, and quite frankly, it scared me. Quite frankly, *he* scared me. I was partly afraid of him, and partly disgusted by his sordidness. How could I answer him? What could I say? All I could do to get out of this one was lie. "Ohhh, that's sweet. Well, thank you very much, Sean. I like you too. I mean, you're *attractive* and everything. I wouldn't mind going out with you." He actually *was* attractive to a certain degree, though not to me. He just wasn't my type; especially not with his malicious personality. And I definitely did not want to go out with him. "But I've got Krisstopher," I continued, "and now I've got this whole War thing that I need to sort through, you know? So I hope you understand when I say we can still be friends."

"Yeah, shuh," he replied, shoving his pipe back in his pocket as if to say, *'No more weed for you if I can't get anything out of the deal.'* "Just don't tell Kris about this, okay?" he added. "Promise me yuh'll keep it between me and you."

"Okay, I promise." Good. Now I could go home. Now I could cry on the way there. Or was I too high to cry?

"Where *were* you?" Krisstopher mumbled sleepily as I came in and lie beside him on the bed. The room was dark. He'd been napping all this time. I paused for a moment before answering, debating on what to tell him. It looked like honesty was the best policy in this situation, especially since I didn't doubt Sean would probably mention something later to him about the phone call.

"I went to call War. Just wanted to see how he was doing," I said, trying to sound nonchalant.

"Oh. And how is he?" he asked.

"He's alright. He had some friends over and stuff. Anyway, we only talked for about five minutes. Sean came with me. He let me use his calling card. You're not mad, are you? Because I figured I'd just be honest rather than hide it from you." There. It was all out on the table. I never *was* very good at keeping anything inside.

"No. I'm not mad."

He rarely got mad anyway. I wondered what he was thinking now, as we lie in the dark. I would have given anything to get inside his head at that moment. My guess was that he was perturbed, but as usual, blew it off with ease.

\* \* \*

Shutting my eyes tightly, I strained to concentrate, to have a vision of War. Where was he? Why couldn't I see him? I needed to see his face. Suddenly, an image appeared in my mind—a man, who looked exactly like the pictures I'd seen of Jesus Christ. Yes, I was sure it was Jesus Christ. He stared at me lovingly, his hands cupped to his chest. All at once, he unclasped them, releasing a beautiful white [220]dove which fluttered toward me. Somewhat startled, I opened my eyes, pondering what this could mean.

\* \* \*

307

We were discussing Sean. Renny was over, and I was telling him and Krisstopher about the dream I had: the children chanting that Sean was the Devil. "I really think it was a warning, you know? I really think we should stay away from Sean, Krisstopher. There's something evil about him."

"You're nuts, Martyr. There's nothing wrong with Sean." Krisstopher protested.

"How can you say that? Don't you see the guy is a liar? He manipulates people to get his own way."

"He does *not*," he argued. "He's a cool guy."

"A *cool guy?*" I asked in disbelief. "Alright. I wasn't going to tell you this because he made me promise not to, but I think you need to know. He made a pass at me—I mean, he propositioned me to be his girlfriend—to live with him in some house he claims he's got."

"He did *not*, Martyr! You're *full* of it. You know what it is? You *wish* he made a pass at you, because secretly, you like him. But he didn't. He doesn't like you Martyr. It's all in your head."

I threw my hands up in the air. "I can't believe you, Krisstopher. How could you be so dumb? Wake up! Sean is trying to take me away from you. Every time he comes over he starts an argument between us. Don't you see it? Open your eyes, Krisstopher!"

I was furious. Furious that he could suggest such a thing—that I *wished* Sean liked me! How could he accuse me of lying to him? How could he not believe me when I told him Sean put the moves on me?

Renny interjected, seeing I was too upset to continue. "Listen to Mahta, Kris. The guy is bad news. He's a *juhk*. A leech. Mahta's *smaht*. She knows what she's talkin' about. I've seen the guy in action. He's no good. And *thaa's* talk goin' around town that he might be a *nahk*. Stay away from him, dude. *Sehriously*."

As usual, Krisstopher listened to anyone but me. Renny persuaded him to cut all ties with Sean. Funny how I'd told him that from the beginning.

* * *

I wanted to be like Liza. To make the bed float in the air. How could I keep Krisstopher entertained? Well, Kernunnos *was* the god of passion, so I'd just ask him to intervene on my behalf. I put out a spell for sex magic, whipping up a batch of the deity's signature incense oil and anointing myself with it while asking him to grant me more power.

Wow. Now I'd seen War's face so clear in my mind, like he was inside my head; his image transparent like a ghost, staring at me with those black eyes while I lie with Krisstopher. I didn't feel I was having relations with Krisstopher; I felt I was having relations with War. It was an airy feeling, similar to a magic carpet ride. At least, if I could ride a magic carpet, I gathered the experience would be quite similar.

# XII. THE DESCENT

*Deeper, deeper*
*Into the caverns, the midst*
*My guide leads the way*
*A cloaked figure, though I can't see his face*

DEAN OFFERED US THE BIGGER apartment downstairs—the one Tanya tried to rent. We were elated. It was like a bungalow; with a small basement, kitchen, big living room, additional room off the living room, and upstairs with a cute little bathroom and huge bedroom. After living in our small efficiency apartment, this place seemed like a mansion to us.

Yet upon walking into it the first day to check it out, a dismal, fearful kind of feeling gripped me. I wasn't sure why. And while Krisstopher was at work the following day and I started moving some of our stuff into the place, that same feeling returned. Fear. Like something wasn't right. Like someone was… watching me.

Krisstopher said he thought maybe the couple that lived there prior to us were involved in the Craft. I remembered their windows being filled with stones and crystals along the tops and on the ledges. The man invited him in once to have a look at the place just before they moved out. He was a nice guy, Krisstopher said, but he felt some vibes upon walking in that indicated he and his wife had a connection to the spirit world.

310

The apartment had a personality all its own. That's what I admired about old houses. Each one was unique, with its individual secrets to discover, unlike some newer homes that used the same blueprint; sometimes it seemed there was nothing to tell them apart other than the address number.

In our living room, a built-in, mint green wall hutch extended to the ceiling. Most likely it was designed for storing fine china dishes since the room was large enough for a section to be used as a dining area. I'd always enjoyed little nooks and crannies and cubbyholes where I could store items and knick-knacks, so the unusual looking hutch quickly became one of my favorite attractions. Adjacent to it, a crooked doorway with an extended ledge, also mint green, led to the carpeted staircase.

I placed our kitchen table and chairs directly across from the hutch, beneath the window facing the small seafood pub next door. To the right of the hutch, in front of the wall near the doorway, sat Sharon's old beat up couch, clad in an afghan to conceal the ugly plaid color.

On the far side of the living room, by the entrance to the kitchen, stood a refrigerator. The kitchen was too small to fit it. A little further to the left of the refrigerator, a door led to an additional room off the house that required a large, exterior kerosene tank beneath one of its windows in order to heat it. The room was very spacious, longer than it was wide. We decided it would be perfect for a band room and practice space, since it was located far enough away from the other apartments in the house to keep the sound muffled. The only set-back was that the room was freezing cold with no heat, and just plain cold *with* heat. Still, if we dressed warm enough, it wasn't too far off from the temperature in my mom's basement.

To the right of the refrigerator was the kitchen, admittedly the smallest one I'd ever seen. But it was quaint. A large ceramic sink displayed plenteous open shelving just above it for storing pots, pans, and dishes. Directly facing the sink stood a small stove with a skinny pantry to the right of it for food and other items. On the other side of the stove, a white wooden door led to the basement.

Small and dark, the basement was more like a cellar, providing insufficient space for a tall person to fully stand up. Its floor was a combination of dirt and rough concrete; its walls gray bricks suggesting a dismal, cheerless mood. About twenty feet to the right of the stairs stood the water tank.

Beyond it, toward the far wall in the back, sat an enormous red furnace that supplied heat to all the apartments. Both of us agreed that the ominous furnace looked scary for some reason. In fact, the whole basement reminded me of the kind you see in a horror flick; when some guy slaughters his family and hides them down there for twenty years.

The safest place in the whole apartment, I felt, was upstairs in the bedroom. There, elevated far above the murky depths of the furnace room, I didn't feel so threatened.

The bedroom was huge, with a sloped ceiling and two large windows on either side, one of which overlooked the mountains far in the background. It was on that wall that we set up Zain's territory, nailing a long shelf into it for his hot rock and hanging his fisherman's net/hammock from the ceiling in front of it. Then Krisstopher found some large, dried out branches and made him a jungle gym. His favorite place from noon until early evening was sitting on one of the branches that crossed directly in front of the window, where he basked in the warmth of the sun and stared out over the scenic horizon with one eye, the other eye watching us to make sure everything was okay in our little world. Our bed and TV were located just across from him on the other side of the room.

Besides being spacious, our bedroom was nice and warm. Old fashioned, accordion style heat registers pumped steam into the air, creating a moist and toasty environment that reminded me of a rain forest. Zain liked it too. He seemed more at ease here than he had been anywhere else.

Out in the hallway, an open linen closet with white shelves faced our bedroom door. Following the wooden banister about twenty feet to the left was the small bathroom: the most interesting one I'd ever seen.

Two rectangular half-windows at the top of its front wall over-looked the stairwell and could be slanted open to let out steam. Beside the toilet, a large, wide, pole-like water pipe extended from the ceiling all the way down into the basement. In front of the pipe, next to Zain's litter box, was the shower stall. There was even a little electric heater built right into the wall beside it for warming up the room so it wouldn't be cold after taking showers in the wintertime. I loved it. Because of its uniqueness, the bathroom was probably my second favorite room in the whole house.

I was proud to say I'd successfully potty trained our little green friend. Every morning after eating, Zain climbed down from the shelf via the jungle gym, crawled out of the bedroom and down the hallway into the bathroom, and deposited his goods in a box filled with cat litter facing the toilet. My efforts had not been in vain. Kyle even had to watch one day, as he found it hard to believe we had a potty-trained iguana. Afterward, we clapped and lauded our smart pet, saying, "Good boy, Zainy. That's a good boy," to which he held his head up high like he was filled with pride. It was really weird. In so many ways, he seemed almost human, as even one of Krisstopher's friends, Tony, had commented.

Always after his morning potty routine, he'd hop onto the cardboard box we'd decorated with lizard and frog wrapping paper beneath the hallway window in front of the stairs, and stare out at another picturesque view of the mountains for about five or ten minutes. Then he'd mosey back into the bedroom again, up the branches and onto the shelf to sit on his hot rock while his food digested.

I cast my first magic circle since moving in on the living room floor, just in front of the mint green hutch. It was evening time, and Krisstopher was upstairs watching TV. I stood in the middle of the room for a minute, looking around at our new place. As my eyes shifted toward the kitchen, I suddenly got a bad feeling. I felt something evil lurking in there, just like I had at times in my mom's house. I shook off the feeling, then. No, I was not going to allow myself to be fearful. I had the power within me to control these kinds of situations. I was, after all, familiar with the spirit world. I'd been experiencing it all my life.

With my goddess [221]athame, a two-edged metal object resembling a knife, I cut the air, drawing an invisible [222]circle of energy around me for protection. Next, I said my alignments to the deities, then stated my petition before them: a petition for greater psychic awareness—greater power to divine and discern spiritual matters. Afterwards, as I stood staring into my crystal ball, a loud male voice, human yet animalistic in tone, hissed, *"You're a **witch**, aren't you?"*

I jumped, frightened, and looked around. The voice sounded as if it was right next to me, yet no one was there. Stiffening, I stood guard in case it spoke again.

Silence.

*No, this didn't just happen. I must be imagining it.* I went back to looking in my crystal ball, ignoring the voice.

*"Witch!"* it hissed again, still beside me.

A chill raced up my spine, then. I knew I had to get away from the entity. Something told me it was evil. So I hurriedly collected my circle and started toward the stairwell. It followed me. I broke into a trot on the stairs as footsteps sounded behind me. Suddenly, the entity reached out and touched my back, sending an electric charge through my body. Screaming bloody murder, I tripped and landed on my stomach halfway up the staircase.

Krisstopher bolted out of the bedroom. "What, Martyr?! What's wrong?"

"There's something following me!" I sobbed. "It asked me if I was a witch, and when I tried to get away from it, it chased me up the stairs!"

"There's nothing there, Martyr," he soothed.

"I'm telling you, I *felt* it. There was something chasing me!"

I know he wanted desperately to believe I wasn't mentally ill—that I had in fact felt an invisible force behind my back. But logic seemed to tell him I'd only imagined it. He looked skeptical now as he helped me up the stairs and into the bedroom.

\* \* \*

We had some really weird utility men in our town. The gas men came over to take a look at the propane tank in the spare room so we could find out about getting some heat in there. I asked one of them how much he thought it would cost, and he gave me a really disgusted look. "I don't know," he snapped. "We can't just *look in our crystal ball* or anything." I sensed he'd glimpsed mine sitting on the mint green wall hutch.

Then the electric guy came by. He was real nervous acting; a short, thin, brown haired man with beady eyes and a thick mustache. Oddly enough, I found him snooping around the house outside a few days after our electricity had already been transferred over.

As I was telling our new landlord Mott about it: a round, jovial man who came in for a beer every now and then, the electric guy suddenly appeared alongside the house, seemingly out of nowhere. "Hey! How'd *you* get here?" I asked, surprised. I hoped he hadn't heard me tell Mott he was weird.

"I'm *magic*," he retorted sarcastically.

Maybe it was just me, but I sensed these people didn't like witches much. I felt like I was in a Samuel Cooper play, about to be burned at the stake.

Even Misty seemed a little tense. She'd popped in one day with her new male friend to smoke a bowl with us, apparently no longer bitter over the Sean incident. As she looked around our living room, she shuddered. We had gargoyles and feathers, stones and crystals, a gold plastic toy replica of an exorcist cross hanging on the band room door, and our altars set up in either corner.

She reached over and picked up an old book lying on my altar that I'd transported from my father's library. It had weird symbols on the cover and something about the practice of magic in its title. The subtitle then read:

## GOD APPROVES

"We used to burn books like this at our church," she commented.

"*Burn* them? Why? There's nothing wrong with this book. It was my father's and he was a very spiritual man," I assured her.

She didn't look too convinced, placing the book back down and staring at her hands with horror like she'd just touched a rotten corpse or something.

It was odd that my friend Charles had also commented on the same book years earlier when we were in my father's library looking through all his stuff. "Was your father a Satan worshiper?" he'd asked after skimming through its pages.

"What?! A *Satan worshiper?!*" I gasped. "No! My father was a very spiritual man. Why?"

"I don't know… I just get a bad feeling about this book—" he glanced around him nervously now, *"and* this room. I've gotta get out of here!" He hurried out into the hallway, explaining as we reached the dining room that he'd felt an evil presence all of a sudden, like someone was watching him.

Later, while he was in the bathroom, he said he heard a low voice laughing at him through the fan—and Charles never did drugs; he only drank occasionally.

"See," I told Misty now, picking up the book and showing her the cover once more, "it says right here that *God approves.*"

She stared at me, as if knowing something I didn't.

\* \* \*

As of late, the visions of War in my crystal ball were somehow different. He appeared more animated looking, and often a large 'S' was scrawled in the background.

Occasionally, a [223]silver hook resembling an anchor was pictured piercing his nostrils, or was located near his face, as if to show an association with him in some way. I developed a fascination for arrows due to the fact that the tip of the hook reminded me of one. I began signing my name MARTYR with arrows pointing downward on the 'M' and 'Y', as well as drawing them on some of the words in my poems. Always, they pointed in the [224]downward direction.

\* \* \*

Happy Sam Hain: The Festival of the Dead. Every witch's favorite holiday, when the vortex to the spirit world opens wide, flooding this realm with unseen forces. Around the globe, covens meet to combine their power on this important night: Halloween.

The Starving Dog music was blaring, *"The Gift of God: Scum!"*

Candles were lit everywhere in the living room as Krisstopher and I scurried around trying to get ready for the party that evening at Kyle and Morgan's. Sam pounded on the door now. She was going with us.

"Hey, Sam! Happy Sam Hain! What do you think of our pad?" I shouted over the music as I let her into the living room.

"Wow, it's big!"

I quickly gave her the grand tour and then we went upstairs to put our costumes on. She was a black cat, I was Cleopatra to the best I could manage with limited materials, and Krisstopher was 'a skull guy,' as he put it. He'd painted his face with glow-in-the-dark, tribal, death makeup. I had to admit, he looked evil.

Kyle and Morgan's was pretty happening. Their apartment had a similar bungalow set-up like ours did, and people were packed in like sardines—along the walls, on the furniture, on the stairs, in the kitchen... The pungent aroma of marijuana wafted through the air, perfume to my nostrils. I stood in the back of the room, breathing it in. Kyle's dad squeezed past me in an old, evil wizard mask, nodding as he went. What was *his* story, anyway? I wondered.

Then Renny suggested we go over to *so and so's* party, whoever *they* were. Judging from the car ride, it was a sure bet they lived in another state. Maybe even another country.

When we got there, a few metal heads were sitting around plastered—about ten altogether. Most of them hadn't dressed up. And they seemed too far gone to be sociable. I sighed. What a wasted trip. At least at Kyle's the vibes were stronger. But by the time Krisstopher and Renny realized this and we drove all the way back to Kyle's, most of the people had cleared out. Yay. Happy Halloween.

Krisstopher was pretty much toast. Unfortunately, I was still sober—and only half-baked. I didn't feel like drinking. I wanted acid, but none was available. And I couldn't feel War *anywhere*. It was like I had a mental block of some kind over me. It bummed me out. Where *was* he? Why had he left me hanging like this?

I sat on the couch, long faced, making idle conversation with Morgan and Sam; watching Krisstopher and Kyle and Renny throw pumpkins in front of cars in the street, then run inside, laughing. This was Sam Hain, The Festival of the Dead. I needed something more entertaining than this. I needed *power*.

* * *

Jentanno closed down in November, giving me a nice little bonus on my last paycheck, as they did Sam, for sticking it out long enough for them to say adios.

Renny and Sam then split for Colorado not long after that; he finally got accepted into that chef school he'd been dreaming about. Before they left, I gave Sam a protective charm I made for her journey. Then on the way to Colorado while she was following Renny in her new sports car, the back windshield mysteriously blew in, shattering into a million pieces. Luckily she wasn't hurt.

I missed her. Who would I have girl talks with now? We used to hang out in the basement at Jentanno and discuss all kinds of things. We'd complain about our boyfriends if they were acting like jerks, or gossip about the women they slept with. Sometimes we'd discuss religion, and how stupid Christianity was.

She told me that Renny's parents constantly tried cramming Christianity down their throats whenever they went over there for dinner—especially his dad. I could relate perfectly, sharing with her about Stephen having his *little talk* with us in the basement. Why didn't these Christians just leave people alone? It seemed they always had to interfere with their little pamphlets and their preaching, while they tried to get everyone to believe the way *they* did.

I remember Jamie and I ran into a few of them on the street once. They tried talking to us about their religion, [225]assuming we were "lost" because we had shaved heads and dressed punk. So I snarled at them that I was Catholic, pointing to the cross hanging in my ear next to the silver skull. How *dare* them assume I needed to be "saved"—whatever that meant!

Another time, one of them—a lady—handed me a laminated card that resembled a thin, plastic credit card. But when I read it, it said:

JESUS SAVES

So I ripped it in half and threw it at her, using a few choice words while yelling that I didn't want her Jesus Saves card!

Then in the mall, a preppy guy approached us, talking to Dayne, Jamie, Stacie, and I about God and Jesus. Again, he assumed we hated life because of the way we were dressed. We asked him why he concluded that because we weren't wearing a yellow polo shirt like him, we were negative and hateful. I can't remember what he said, but I had to admit, he was the nicest Christian I'd ever met. Something seemed different about him. He was so happy and peaceful acting.

Anyway, now that Sam was gone, I really didn't have anyone to hang out with and talk about these kinds of things. Except Krisstopher. Though he was my best friend, unfortunately there were many things I couldn't share with him, especially if they *involved* him! How could I tell him the things he did that I hated? He already knew most of them, and he wasn't doing anything to change. How could I tell him that War would never do any of these kinds of things to hurt me? Or *would* he? I remembered, then, the phone call I'd made to him a couple months back, and how he told me he had to let me go because he had girls over. My heart sank again.

* * *

I got a call from Dave; my mom gave him our number. He was living out in California, distributing tapes of Beastlulust to people. Everyone thought we were great, he said. He then asked us to consider moving out there where we could get better publicity. "You guys need a guitar player, right? I was thinking I'd love to play your stuff. It's *awesome* stuff, man—I mean, really *phenomenal*. I'd really dig playing it. Ask Krisstopher what he thinks."

I covered the receiver with the palm of my hand, relaying the message to Krisstopher.

"Tell him we're not moving out there," he replied snottily, "and we don't need a guitar player. Tony's going to be playing guitar for us."

"He is?" I whispered.

"Just tell the guy to get lost," he said loudly.

"Sshhh! Krisstopher!" I scolded. "Uhhh... Dave? I guess his friend Tony's going to be recording some stuff with us. But man, I really appreciate you passing out our tape to people. That's really cool of you. Alright. Yeah, you take care too. Thanks for calling. Bye." I hung up the phone, yelling at Krisstopher. "The guy's promoting our band in California! The least you can do is be nice to him!"

Apparently Tony was back in town. He'd been in Florida for a while. He and Krisstopher shared many fond memories. Like when they used to melt girls' hearts because he looked like John Von Joli and Krisstopher looked like Billie Ideal. They had no problem finding dates back then.

And of course, they'd also been in a band together—thrash metal. Tony was an excellent guitar player. Like Ingmay Halsteen, he played real classical stuff, his fingers shredding up and down the strings, weaving intricate ballads with complex chord progressions. Amazingly enough—other than a few lessons here and there—he'd taught himself for the most part, spending hours and hours practicing along to rock albums.

He came over to the apartment clad in a biker leather, dark jeans, and black high-tops; his guitar case in hand. The last time I saw him we were living at Sharon's. He'd put on some weight, but he was still the same old Tony: dark, wavy, heavy metal style hair—shortened a bit now—brown eyes, and a somewhat large boned nose (though not as big as War's). He was a fairly handsome man. And for a metal head, he had a really good attitude: friendly, easy-going, not stuck on himself like some of the others I'd met. "Martyr! What's up, sweetie?" he asked, hugging me and giving me a peck on the cheek.

It was good to see him. For a while, after his girlfriend of three years (Shane), broke up with him, he went into a massive state of depression; he wouldn't eat or talk to anyone, and stayed in his room in bed. His mom took him to a psychologist and he was put on Roenack. He said taking the stuff screwed him up even more than he already was. "Don't ever let anyone put you on that stuff, Martyr," he advised. "It just makes you feel suicidal. It really messes with your head."

Great. Just what I needed.

Eventually, he quit taking the prescription and moved to Florida for a while with some surfer friends to get his head straight again and forget about Shane. "Remember how I used to hassle you about wearing combat boots with a skirt, Martyr? Well, I met a girl out there, and she reminds me of you. She wears combat boots with skirts, too. And now I *love* that look!" he laughed. He definitely seemed more cheerful than I'd ever seen him. I was happy for him.

In contrast, as he got a chance to hang around me and Krisstopher for an extensive period of time, he noticed there'd been a change in *me* for the worst. "Why are you always in a bad mood lately, Martyr? What's wrong with you? You're just not yourself," he asked one day as I lie sprawled out on the couch.

He was right. There *was* something wrong with me: I hated my life. I felt unhappy unless we had weed. Kyle and Derek were getting great weed now—stuff that was out of this world. Kyle claimed he had a friend who worked for the government, who was selling it to him as part of an experiment. Of course, I didn't believe him, but whatever. Who cared where he got it? The important thing was, he *got* it! Anymore, it seemed, I'd grown as addicted to it as I once had to cigarettes (I'd quit smoking again). It was more of a mental addiction than anything else; a codependence to fantasy. It brought me closer to the spirit world. Not that I necessarily needed it to be transported there, because I'd been making the trip ever since I was very young. But I felt so much more in tune with that other plane of existence when I was high. The power seemed greater at work for some reason. Magnified. And since Krisstopher provided virtually no companionship for me lately, I visited my friends in that world more often, just like I had when I was a little girl. They offered me comfort. Solace. Companionship. And... love?

Krisstopher wrote about three more songs in their entirety. Tony had no problem laying down guitar riffs on the fourtrack for them, but I just wasn't in the mood to participate. I couldn't connect with Krisstopher anymore. I couldn't connect with his music. Every sound I tried on my keyboard didn't seem to fit, and he wasn't happy with anything that *remotely* fit, anyway. I found myself getting angry. I hated how he always had to run the whole show. Ever since Sean complimented him that day, his ego was out of control.

But what about *my* stuff? I'd composed a great song recently. Funny how the words just came flooding into my head one day as I sat on the couch in the upstairs apartment. I couldn't even write as fast as they were coming. The lyrics centered around a girl named *Blasphemet* who was involved in witchcraft, written from the perspective of a man named [226]*Balaam.*

When we moved downstairs, I put them to music one dreamy, dismal afternoon. The shades were pulled, with just a glimpse of light pouring in through the window over the kitchen table. Krisstopher's big bass amp stood against the wall next to the refrigerator, and I'd carried my keyboard into the living room where it was warmer since we didn't have the propane tank hooked up in the band room yet.

On the couch, I hit the lowest key with one finger, surprised to hear the whispered word, *"Lucifer"* in one of my newly programmed voices. I paused for a moment, then hit it again. *"Lucifer!"* it sounded a second time, clear as a bell. Yes, I *had* heard right. Wow. I touched my hands to the keys and started to play. An energy suddenly rushed through me as a weight pushed down on my fingers, guiding them effortlessly over the keyboard. To my amazement, though I'd never taken piano lessons, the keyboard sounded like an old haunted piano with chords I hadn't exacted upon until now.

I opened my mouth to sing, startled when my voice came out four octaves lower, sounding like a sexually alluring *male* voice. Balaam was pronounced [227]Baa*lim,* with a slightly evil hiss to his name. It seemed he was actually singing and playing the song *through* me, as if I was a [228]medium.

And then the room came alive, the water pipe which descended from the upstairs bathroom cling clanging a gypsy accompaniment on pots and pans while the old-fashioned heat registers wheezed and moaned in unison, as if I had invisible band members helping me perform this ghostly melody. All at once, the floor began to shake, vibrating beneath me like I'd summoned a sleeping Abaddon from his pit—and somehow, I knew it was connected to that fiery furnace directly below me. Krisstopher's bass amp suddenly turned itself up three notches to echo out my ballad of darkness.

I finished the song, spellbound. As the last note reverberated, vanishing into thin air, a low, evil voice laughed, *"HA HA HA! Very good!"* I jumped, looking around the living room to see who was there. *"What's the matter, are you **scared?**"* it sneered.

\* \* \*

322

The ocean. As far as I could see, dark foamy waves... hissing their magic charm in my ear. The ivory moon loomed overhead. What if I just walked into the water and kept on going? Something about water lately...

That river dream I'd had: all my tarot cards sinking beneath the water, hitting rock bottom while I stood staring down at them from a small boat I was in. What did it mean?

But no, I knew better than to plunge into the ocean. Though the feeling overwhelmed me for a moment, I hated sharks. And I wasn't a good swimmer, anyway. I couldn't even go under water without plugging my nose. Tony and Krisstopher stood further down on the beach, tossing stones at the angry whitecaps. Good. I just wanted to be alone. I was feeling War again.

A motor sounded in the distance, and then a truck drove round the bin, slowing down to a near stop just up the incline as if watching me now. I turned my head to stare up at it for a moment. *War?* It drove off. Why was I feeling him so powerfully again, here in this place?

\* \* \*

The urge for acid kind of fizzled out for me. Maybe it had something to do with Mad Marv, I don't know. I'd seen him wandering the streets on numerous occasions. Then one day, Kyle called him over to our table as the three of us sat in the bar. "Listen to this guy talk," he whispered to me as Marv started toward us. "He blew his mind doing too many hits of acid—he's a total mental case."

He sat down beside me while I studied him. His face pale and worn, he appeared to be in his early forties, with (of all things) *pink* hair—though not cool pink like War's, but *stupid* pink—like he was a little too old to be wearing such a ridiculous hairdo, and it didn't match the rest of his outfit anyway.

"So Marv, how's it goin'?" Kyle folded his hands together and leaned over the table a little now, flashing him a big grin.

"There was a white room," he replied somberly.

"A white room?"

"Did *you* see it too? I saw it, and in the hallway down at the bottom... the bottom a... yeah. It was red. And the light was white. Look at the bird in the sky—the door was red. It was red."

"Really, Marv?" Krisstopher interjected, looking over at me with amusement.

"And, and... a very large dove. A very large... he was there. I took them all there when it was time."

Would I end up like Marv if I kept doing acid? Horrified, I listened to him babble on until finally Kyle sent him on his way.

\* \* \*

Another omen? The septic system for the entire house backed up—in our kitchen sink. All of our dishes were covered with fecal material. The smell was unbearable. I was sure I'd die before the plumber got there.

He was a sympathetic man—and a tall man, unable to stand up straight in our scary cellar/basement. For some reason, I found him to be a comfort. Probably because unlike the utility men, he didn't shun me on account of my witchcraft decorations. And I sensed he wasn't afraid of me, either, while they had seemed nervous and fidgety. Yeah, this guy was different. Really down to earth. Really at peace. He advised me to either heavily bleach the dishes or toss them out and get new ones. The latter seemed the better plan to me.

So Tony, Krisstopher, and I set out for a kitchen import shop, purchasing a nice collection of gothic dishware: black, of course. *Something* to be happy about, anyway.

**XIII.** DARK NIGHTS OF THE SOUL

*O, how I heard him*
*He called to me*
*On the wings of a dream...*

WINTER ARRIVED; THE HILLS, FORESTS, and winding roads blanketed once more in a quilt of brilliant white. Though the winters were beautiful here in New Hampshire, I found them to be quite boring, probably because I didn't partake in any snow sports like the rest of the town. About the only snow sports for me was walking to Derek's apartment to get more weed—and those occasional trips to the laundry mat or grocery store. But since we'd purchased a little pale blue [229]Dodge Omni from someone in the *Auto Trader's* paper, we didn't walk to those places anymore.

The [230]Omni cost us eight hundred dollars, just like the [231]Volvo had. We test-drove it for about five minutes, just far enough down the road to decide we wanted it—no "ifs," "ands," or "buts." Who cared what the speedometer read? We didn't even look. Were there any problems with it? Well, it got us down the road, didn't it? Then it was a keeper! The owner agreed to accept payments, too, so we were definitely not passing this one up!

Now that we had wheels, we could visit people we rarely saw anymore, like Kyle and Morgan. They'd recently moved out of town

325

and into a condo about twenty minutes away. Morgan's mom was leasing it to them.

Brea was getting so big, walking now and everything! She headed right over to me as I sat in their living room holding a joint in my hand that Kyle had passed my way, as if the smell of it had sparked her curiosity. She stood beaming at me while I tried hiding the joint, whisking the air with my hand to direct the smoke away from her.

"It's alright. You don't have to do that," Morgan told me from across the room.

"Yeah, but what if she gets high?" I asked, worried.

"Nah, she's not going to get high," Kyle protested. "Besides, she's used to this. We do it all the time."

I shrugged, putting the joint to my lips. Suddenly the door opened and Morgan's mom jetted into the room. "Uh oh!" I exclaimed, trying to hide it again.

"It's okay, Martyr," Morgan laughed. "My mom doesn't care."

Wow... being able to do drugs right in front of your mother. How bizarre! "I'm glad to hear *that!*" I said, breathing a sigh of relief. Passing the joint to Krisstopher now, I leaned back in the chair, listening to Morgan and her mom talk about decorating Brea's room. The TV droned on in the background, Krisstopher and Kyle staring blankly at it.

"Martyr! Come see this lamp my mom did for Brea!" Morgan called.

I got up lazily and followed them into Brea's bedroom. "Wow, you made this?" I asked admiringly. Her mom nodded her head proudly. The little lampshade had stars and moons painted on it, while two fairies perched at the base. "Those are beautiful fairies," I told her, smiling.

"*Angels!*" she corrected firmly. "Those are *angels.*" Her tone suggested she didn't wish to call attention to the realm of magic.

I thought of the Wiccan guy who owned the occult bookstore back in Michigan that I nearly got hired at—that is, until he found out how freely I discussed the Craft. He too had tried concealing it. "*Metaphysical,*" he corrected quickly. "I don't prefer to use the term *occult*, due to the fact that we had a brick thrown in our window some years back because of it." He went on to comment that I *looked* like a Wiccan, with all my black clothing and silver rings. Apparently he didn't want to suggest such a look to the public. He said his employees all dressed like normal, everyday people.

Later, I found out that he and all of his employees met in an actual coven after hours. That explained why he asked me if I minded "*working late after the store closed*" in a real secretive tone of voice. I'd been too naive at the time to understand that he meant doing magical/sexual things with coven members.

"Oh yeah, sure! I don't mind working late. I just *love* books!" I told him eagerly. I didn't get the job. He claimed my birth chart wasn't compatible, or something to that effect.

Then I ran across a friend of a girl that actually worked at the store for a time, so I heard what kind of *late hours* she was required to put in. I thank God now that I didn't get the job. I'd wondered why I always got an eerie vibe upon entering the store, as did other people I took there. Something was attempting to warn me of the place, despite the fact that I too was a witch.

So what was the big deal about *fairies*, anyway? And incidentally, they *were* fairies. I gave Morgan and her mom a strange look now.

"Yeah, Martyr. They're *angels*," she laughed a little nervously.

Hmmm...

* * *

Priesthood was coming in concert. They happened to be one of Krisstopher's favorite bands, and in the industrial arena, I guessed they were mine too—even though their latest release kind of gave me the creeps. Sean picked up the cassette tape awhile back for Krisstopher, which featured a strange magical formula on it that was supposedly taken from something written by [232]Aleister Crowley.

The tape contained songs like *Psalm 666*, which featured a distorted, demonic sounding sample of a girl saying, "Christ has come into my heart."

Though the band had come a long way since their new wave days, it seemed with each album they got a little more satanic, totally cutting down God, Jesus, the Holy Ghost, and the Bible. At times, I couldn't even bear to listen to them—I'd constantly hear something else scary

I never heard before, and it would freak me out so bad that I'd have to turn the tape off, just like over at War's when I heard Jordy Allenson scream out blasphemies at the end of *Stigma*.

But I couldn't wait to go to their concert. They were playing in Boston, Mass, so Krisstopher had the idea that we could cruise on over to Salem the following day and visit the [233]Witch Museum. I looked forward to doing this even more than the concert. Now I could finally pay tribute to all those poor, innocent victims who died as a result of the witchcraft trials. The road trip would serve as a vacation get-a-way; just the two of us. Krisstopher mentioned maybe then we could grow close again.

We left Zain with a bunch of food and headed off, purchasing a quarter bag of weed for the journey. How come the pot just kept getting better and better? It didn't even take much anymore to get me stoned—a couple of nice sized bong hits and I was lethargic for hours. It was almost as good as LSD, though the high was more of a spiritual one, it seemed. Rather than hallucinating on tangible objects, I merely *perceived* things in my mind's eye to an incredibly strong degree, like having *inner* spiritual visions.

Krisstopher packed a bowl now as we drove out of town and onto the interstate. That distinguishable aroma filled my nostrils, making my mouth water as I anticipated the high. For the last few months, it smelled exactly like Assault Ant and Roach Killer. It had a different look, too. A shiny powder covered the moist green clumps.

Derek was our main supplier since Sean was out of the picture. Right after we'd moved into the downstairs apartment, the lady whose house Sean had been living in called us—the one that had been driving the car the night he offered Krisstopher and I a ride after the bear scare. Somehow she'd gotten our number and wanted to warn me to stay away from him. They'd been seeing each other, she said. Then she found out he was a *nark:* meaning, he worked undercover for the cops, which probably explained why he had about three different aliases he went by.

That was about the time the bizarre pot scare began. Apparently some big wigs from the FBI were supposed to be coming into town to bust all the higher ups in the drug ring. How this information was obtained was beyond me. But word was going around that people like

Kyle and Derek, who'd been busted before, now cooperated with the cops by working undercover in order to get the charges dropped against them. Even Kyle himself had bragged about how it was no big deal. He told us if we got busted for possession, all we had to do was agree to work with the feds, turning in a few names of people we didn't like, and everything would be cool.

For a while, no one had weed. There was a drought in the town, and even throughout most of the state. I went into massive withdrawals, despite what *The Guide to Getting High* claimed in one of their articles: that marijuana causes absolutely no harm to the brain and is not *addictive.*

"I want some freakin' weeed!" I screamed at Krisstopher, tears streaming down my cheeks. "I've gotta have some weeed!" I felt anxious and shaky, like when I quit smoking cigarettes and my body craved the nicotine. I needed to smell it, taste it, feel it—yes, most of all, to *feel* that incredible high.

*Boston, Mass:*

Plenty baked, we entered the gymnasium in our painted leathers, my black brimmed Dead Raiser hat adorned with a silky blue scarf picturing demon cats.

"Man, there's some really *different* looking people here," a plain clothed jock commented as he passed by, eyeing us with interest.

From the second level, we stared down over the railing at the death metal band below, the singer growling, low and distorted, something about the "Ice Man." The *Ice Man?* Now why did I have a feeling he meant the Devil? —although he might have been referring to a crystal meth dealer or user. I decided after watching the band for about five minutes that they were evil. They gave me the creeps. Looking around with curiosity, I noticed a few people from Connelly Woods, though I didn't personally know them. Friends of friends. And then the Satan worshipers left the stage and Krisstopher motioned for me to follow him. We made our way down to floor level, scoping out the bleachers for a good spot.

Jordy Allenson appeared on stage in his cowboy hat with the rest of the band, and within minutes, the ripping drums, distorted guitars, and foreboding bass began, followed by various sampled voices on keyboard.

I sat in a hypnotic stupor beside Krisstopher, watching as clusters of mismatched, zombified teenagers bashed into one another in front of the stage as if they were out for blood. I sensed their apparent rebellion on more than just a physical level. It seemed the very forces of darkness were present at this show, while they danced around blindly, unaware.

Huge wall-to-wall TV screens depicted pictures flashing faster than one could fully comprehend, as if subliminally brainwashing the audience, while a sampled voice repeatedly declared, "*Novus ordo seclorum!*" which is Latin for: "New order of the ages," or *New world order.*

Allenson stretched his arms out wide then, and hung his head, rolling his eyes as he mocked Jesus being crucified. Behind him on the screen, a huge shadow of a cross appeared, and the song *Puppet* began. For the first time, I understood what it was about, gasping as the realization of their intent became crystal clear: supposedly Jesus was just a puppet mastered by the establishment—an empty, lifeless dummy who came to die for our sins. My eyes were then drawn to the large [234]goat's head skull attached to the microphone stand. I knew it was meant to represent Satan.

Suddenly I felt War. He was here, but where? Looking around me at the crowd on the bleachers, I strained hard to find him, but with no luck. Presently I gazed up at the balcony. There! Wearing a bandanna, he stood in the shadows, staring directly down at me. For a long time, the two of us continued to make eye contact. Then the battle began.

"*Evil,*" he hissed in my thoughts.

The sounds of the instruments echoed him like backup vocals. "*Evil,*" they crooned.

*No, good,* I replied through thought transference, still staring.

"*No, evil,*" he argued, again the instruments chiming in.

*No, good. Good. Good.*

"*Evil. Evil. Evil.*"

*Stop it! Good... good... good.* Energy drained from me as I sought to make him understand—to make him see that darkness was not the way.

And then... he turned his head just as the stage lights flickered across his face, revealing a side profile devoid of a large nose—it wasn't War! *What kind of mind game is this?*

At that moment, a sampled voice from an old movie about drug addicts crackled through the gymnasium. They'd edited it to make it sound distorted, lowering it a few octaves. It even sounded similar to War's nasal toned, lagging voice. *"You can't trust a $^{235}$mainliner,"* it warned. A large hypodermic needle filled with serum appeared on the screen then.

\* \* \*

We drove around for about an hour after the show, looking for a place to stay. Finally, we pulled over at some motel with an Aztec bird painted on the sign. I sensed War was leading us there.

He appeared in my head *that* night, too, riding on the wings of a dream in electric white flashes, using Krisstopher's body as a vehicle so he could experience me.

*Salem, Mass:*

We headed for the much talked about town, the snow falling in large, brilliant white flakes as we merged onto the expressway. All around us was a fluffy wonderland, cars *whooshing* by cautiously in the trails others had left before them. Everything looked so beautiful. A delicate powder covered the once naked branches, glistening in the sunlight.

As we entered Salem, the first thing I noticed was the little witch on a broom emblem painted on the side of every cop car as they promoted the town's history. I had no idea it was such a commercial thing. Krisstopher informed me that they'd been doing it for years. I marveled that they prided themselves in it.

"Wow, we should move *here*," I said excitedly. And then as we drove right past the museum, it seemed our car went under a great, black cloud. The atmosphere around us suddenly changed from light and warm to dark and cold, though not on a natural level.

I scanned the area for a place to park, noticing an old, white haired man in a blue windbreaker walking just up ahead on the sidewalk. He appeared almost animalistic in stature, his back slightly bowed like a jackal waiting to pounce. As we approached him, a voice suddenly hissed, *"Look—now!"* though only I could hear it. I turned my head toward him just as we passed by, his head also turning at that exact moment and his eyes glaring insanely into mine, a flash of light shooting out of them. He smiled evilly, his teeth white and jagged, ready to rip apart the flesh of his prey.

"Did you see that guy?" I asked Krisstopher now. I wondered why I'd been instructed to tune in to him—why we'd connected.

We parked the car and walked out to the dock in the harbor. Gulls loomed in the sky above, shrieking a warning as they revealed the dark secrets of the old historic town; if only we could understand their cries.

Leaving the ocean, we strolled the sidewalk along which were scattered various shops, all of them advertising palm reading, tarot cards, and other methods of divination. I was surprised to see the town actually promoted such things rather than discouraged them. But as we stopped occasionally to peer into the store windows, I got an uneasy feeling.

We turned down one of the old red brick side streets now, where a sign on another shop caught my eye. It pictured a large black crow, as well as an astrological symbol depicting one of the planets.

"Look, Krisstopher—a *crow*," I whispered.

"Wow. I wonder what kind of shop that is," he responded.

"I don't know. Let's see."

We started to walk toward it when a group of young adults huddled in the street drew our attention. They appeared to be around our age, maybe even a little younger. Dressed in black, they were all pale as ghosts—and not from applying makeup like I used to do to purposely achieve that effect—it was their natural skin color. Their eyes were cold and lifeless, while their faces held a certain darkness in them that I'd never seen before. Though I recognized them to be goths, it occurred to me that they weren't *trying* to be. They didn't have to *try* and look the part, because they *were* the part. They were the epitome of what gothic *was*—the darkness that we deliberately mimicked and fashioned ourselves after. But to them, it was more than just dress; it was a way of life. I could tell… by the incredibly evil vibes they gave off. They weren't *playing* spooky. They *were* spooky. They continued to huddle on the corner near the store, staring over at Krisstopher and I and whispering, one of them wearing a black cloak with a hood drawn up over her head.

Then Krisstopher suggested we venture back toward the museum since the exhibit would be starting soon. We left them standing there, still watching us.

[236]A lady took our tickets and escorted us into a dark room, shining a flashlight on one of the benches against the wall and instructing us to sit down until enough tourists arrived to begin. Eventually more people filed in, taking their appointed seats, and she closed the door, welcoming us to the museum. She began expounding upon Salem's history. As she talked, a glowing red circle resembling a ceremonial magic circle suddenly appeared on the floor in the center of the room. Whoever constructed the circle most assuredly had this intention in mind when they designed it. Some people got up to look at it now, and I felt impressed to go also. I heard a voice tell me to do so. Krisstopher followed me.

Inside the circle, where witches stand, were listed all the names of the men and women who died in the witchcraft trials. As I stared at the names, I noticed a magic rune accompanied them. It occurred to me then, that the museum knew more about the Craft than I had assumed. Though I thought the tour consisted merely of historical facts devoid of any knowledge concerning actual Wiccan practices, on the contrary, it was quite *informative* of these practices. In fact, it seemed to condone them rather than admonish against them.

As others took their seats again, I continued standing beside the circle, awaiting further instructions. The tour had already begun, and everyone else was now seated, including Krisstopher. Hearing no voice and suddenly feeling awkward to be the only one still standing, I slowly made my way back to the bench, sitting beside him. He was fully engrossed in the exhibit.

[237]As the story unfolded, I focused on the servant girl who brought back a book of spells from her ancestors who practiced voodoo. I'd read a play once in college involving this historical account of the trials, so I

was somewhat familiar with it, though I'd forgotten most of the details until they were re-introduced to me now.

[238]The servant girl had shown the book to the householder's daughters, and they'd read some of its contents aloud. Now they were starting to act strange. Their parents and relatives were noticing a change in their behavior. Moody and withdrawn, they stared off into space as if under the Devil's spell.

Immediately I compared myself to them, a glimpse of realization hitting me as Tony's words came flooding back to my mind: *"Why are you always in a bad mood lately, Martyr? What's wrong with you? You're just not yourself."*

And Jason's: *"I was just trying to find out what's wrong with you!"*

And Krisstopher's: *"Man, Martyr, what's **wrong** with you? I can't talk to you lately. You're always staring off into space like you're in your own little world. Why are you so depressed and withdrawn?"*

"That sounds like *me*," I whispered nervously, growing more fearful by the moment.

"Uh huh," Krisstopher mumbled, though I doubted he even knew what I was talking about; he was too absorbed in the story.

[239]Next, the girls were doing bizarre things, such as barking like dogs. It seemed they were possessed with demons. My heart skipped a beat as panic swept over me. *Man, what if that happens to **me**? I hope I don't get like that!* But as the narration continued, my fears gradually dissolved—or at least, were put on the back burner.

When the tour ended, we browsed around in the souvenir/gift shop which was actually an occult store selling all kinds of witchcraft paraphernalia. Krisstopher and I were elated.

"Oh, *wow*, Krisstopher! Let's get something, okay?" I asked excitedly. I was thrilled that witches were accepted and approved of in this town. Yes, it *would* be a good idea to move here where we could meet and commune with others who shared our beliefs. We could even open our own business, doing tarot and crystal ball readings. Of course, as Krisstopher had stated, the cost of living in Salem was higher due to the fact that it was such a tourist trap. But hey, we could save up. It would be worth it.

A book on the shelf suddenly caught my eye. It was about Dianic worship, and pictured a woman lifting up her arms to the moon. As I stared at the cover, the voice that had been talking to me now returned. *"Go over there. Pick it up,"* it instructed.

*Pick it up? Really?* I obeyed, walking over to the shelf and picking up the book. Immediately an energy shot through my hand, slightly shocking me.

*"Buy it. Buy the book,"* it instructed again.

Dazed, I walked over to Krisstopher, still carrying it in my hand. "I have to get this book, Krisstopher. Something is telling me to get this book."

"Alright," he shrugged, looking at the blown glass witchballs in the display case. At one time, fishermen used the balls as buoys. Jasmine used to have a few hanging in her living room. Apparently they received the name *witchball* because they floated on water when tied in nets, just as witches supposedly did when tied up and thrown into the water during witch trials.

"Oh, *wow,* Krisstopher. *Witch*balls! Can I get one of these too?"

"But you already have a crystal ball."

"Yeah, I know. But I want one of these because the energy will be greater since it came from the actual [240]Witch Museum," I explained.

So we purchased two witchballs. He picked out a green one, and mine was, of course, *pink*. On the way home, I drove with mine in my lap to charge it with some of my energy. As I rubbed my hand over it, I felt with my goddess (or index) finger the indentation at the top where the glass had been blown. There was a sharp edge sticking out that hadn't been sanded.

*"Run your finger over that again,"* the voice suddenly spoke. I obeyed, feeling the jagged edge once more with my forefinger. *"Now cut yourself."*

*Huh?*

*"Cut yourself. It will be a type of [241]covenant between you and War,"* it explained.

I hesitated for a moment, then pressed down a little harder on the edge of the glass, though still not quite hard enough to puncture my skin. Did I really want to do this? I hated blood. It made me sick to look at it. Whenever I'd cut myself by accident in the past, I always got real dizzy and felt like I was going to throw up. And exactly what would happen if I *did* cut myself? What would that mean—something *bad*? No… I didn't have a good feeling about this at all.

"*Well, what are you waiting for?*" the voice prodded.

I removed my finger from the indentation now. *I can't.*

I sensed whatever was speaking on behalf of War was very disappointed.

\* \* \*

The book on Dianic worship proved to be very interesting. It contained useful stories from various witches worldwide. Strange, but I'd read something in it about a *monkey* named Pan appearing to an Asian woman as she sat meditating. It reminded me of what Jade had relayed to me that night at the apartment about the monkey appearing in her bedroom when she was totally sober. In this particular account, the monkey was associated with [242]disorder and pandemonium, which helped one get in tune with his or her inner self and achieve harmonial balance. One thing in the book that really stuck out at me, though, was the book's dedication to a high-ranking warlock who died of a terrible disease. I remember thinking, *If he had so much power, then why wasn't he able to heal himself? Why weren't the deities able to heal him?*

\* \* \*

"*Emily sits with her crystal*
*Telling the future today*
*Emily sits with her tarot cards*
*Demons get in the way*
*And it rains, and it rains*"

—The Nuns of Grace

We'd just picked up the long-awaited Nuns of Grace release. It featured all of my favorite songs plus a bunch of other ones I'd never heard before, and included bonus prints from their previous EPs, which I hung in our living room and kitchen. The cover pictured their famous pentagram symbol with a woman's veiled head in the center, and a title that read:

## NAIVETE' WANDERS BY ACCIDENT

As I examined it now, I wondered if they meant that naiveté wandered into *witchcraft* by accident. Hmmm... what *did* they mean? Judging from the song *Emily,* which spoke of divination and demons, it appeared as if they could very well be referring to witchcraft.

At any rate, I was elated to finally have the new release. Andrew William Elder was my favorite singer of all time. Something about his low, haunting voice stirred my soul. I certainly envied the woman who dated him. Imagine having someone like that serenade you! Although I had to admit, the guy from The Field of Fallen Angels rated a close second for mesmerizing voices.

The very first time I ever heard a Nuns of Grace song, Andrew's voice along with the dark, sensual music immediately put me under a spell. From that minute on, I was hooked. I think I related to Andrew in a lot of ways. He was always raving about lust and magic. Some woman always had a clutch on his heart. Or soul. Or both. Probably another reason I was so intoxicated with the band: I'd always been a sucker for those mystical, alluring love songs.

In the mornings, after I drove Krisstopher to work at the restaurant located inside the Inn, I'd pick up a newspaper so I could hunt for jobs later; then come home and pop in the CD, taking red skull bong hits in the hallway (I didn't want to irritate Zain with the smoke). Afterwards, I'd lie across the bed in our room while the heaters wheezed, pumping warm steam into the air; and listen to that deep, romantic voice while writing poetry or painting.

I'd written a really heartfelt poem to War recently—kind of a sequel to the *Elohim* song. In it, I likened him to a blackbird trying to enter the window of my soul. It spoke of time and space and good and evil—I was quite impressed with it. Of course, whenever I baked out, I found it easier to write anyway, because the words and ideas flowed into my mind without much effort on my part. Still, they were from my heart, as I'd been meditating on these types of revelations for quite some time.

I even cried while writing the poem, making sure to let a few teardrops fall onto the page to seal my message of yearning. And then I mailed it off to him.

I was presently working on a painting as well. Krisstopher and I bought a couple of small canvases, and I'd started a picture of War in his leather; a type of sad clown with pink hair, holding [243]three pink balloons. Finishing up The Ace of Spades pin on his jacket now, I concentrated on his lock: that sacred lock he wore around his neck that I so wished I held the key to.

Zain snorted, watching me from his roost above. Lately, he'd been a little uneasy. I wasn't quite sure why. Whenever I communicated to him concerning War, he seemed less than happy about the whole thing, like he knew something I didn't. Maybe he was jealous. I'd heard that animals of the opposite sex oftentimes grow very attached to their owners, even viewing them as mates. It just seemed he was extra sensitive lately, and always on guard.

Of course, things had been *less than normal* around here, and getting weirder by the moment! Like that incident in the hallway the other day: I'd just gotten out of the shower and was headed over to the linen closet when I felt a weight in the atmosphere—a change in air-pressure that told me something was moving toward my general direction. But when I turned my head to the left toward the bathroom again, I could see nothing. And then a crabby old voice sputtered, *"Move out of my way!"*

That's when I saw the old man with the top hat, his body a transparent color, flash across my mind. He pushed me aside rather rudely and headed right for the wall, disappearing into it. Needless to say, it frightened me half to death that such a thing had occurred.

And how could I explain these types of experiences to Krisstopher? How in the world could I explain something that wasn't really *there* in the physical realm? I knew he thought I was nuts. I couldn't say that I blamed him, yet it was so frustrating not having anyone who could understand just what I was going through.

He was currently in the process of looking up psychiatrists in the phone book—he wasn't quite sure what else to do. Admittedly, I *did* look insane. A *paranoid schizophrenic* is probably what many doctors would classify me as—with acute cases of *dementia*. But no, no. It was that *other world*. That spiritual world that only spiritually minded people could perceive. Those who were too practically minded missed it altogether as they plowed through the daily grind of ordinary life, completely unaware. It was so aggravating to try and make these kinds of people see it *differently*.

But maybe there was someone who *would* understand. I'd called the New Age bookstore we frequently visited, incidentally named the *Jumping Over the Edge* Store, and gotten the number to a highly recommended psychic channeler. Surely *she* was familiar with these types of paranormal occurrences. They said she channeled angels who gave her advice when dealing with the problems of others. So I made an appointment with her. She was coming to our house next week. I could hardly wait. In the meantime, I carefully thought on all the questions I needed answers to. Granted, I only had an hour since I couldn't afford to give her more than fifty bucks, but that should be sufficient time for most of what I was dealing with, anyway.

\* \* \*

Had War gotten my letter? I wondered.

A couple of times Krisstopher and I were in bed together, and it was just like I wanted—just like Liza was able to do—the two of us flying through space. And then I sensed War so powerfully again—Krisstopher's body began to feel like his body as he appeared in my mind, that dark sultry stare of his burning a hole through my soul.

But it got a little strange—even a little scary—when Krisstopher started to grunt and growl like an animal, his tongue turning long and pointy in my mouth like a goat's tongue, his body growing unusually hairy to the touch. I wondered if perhaps it was only my imagination, until he mentioned he'd experienced similar things on *his* end. I knew then, that War was indeed into black sex magic. Sensual, but bestial. And it frightened me. How could he come between us like that? There was only one explanation: he had to be astral projecting.

Was it possible for someone to be so evil and yet still have pure love towards me? If he did whatever he wanted to get his own way, would he also *hurt me* to do so? I didn't want to think about it. It ruined my fairy tale romance. Blew it to bits.

I sat in the upstairs hallway now, staring at the picture of him Jamie had given me, my crystal ball nearby. I remembered how he always made sure I was safe and warm, always held my hand to keep me from tripping over rocks and slipping on ice. That first day we met, when his eyes locked with mine, my heart locked with his. That power between us... I couldn't let it go. No—I *wouldn't* let it go. I would hold onto it for dear life. It seemed the only reality I had left. A tear streamed down my cheek. *You're so beautiful*, I thought, looking deep into his eyes, deep into his soul. *You told me I was the chosen one. You told me I was the woman for you. Where are you? I can't feel you. I'm supposed to be your Princess of Pentacles!*

Suddenly a glowing figure appeared in the ball—in the form of a wizard looking man—though he was all energy. The only thing I could really determine was his black cloak. He beckoned to me, urging me to reach out and touch the ball right where his finger was pointed at me. Slowly, dreamily, I moved my hand toward the rounded glass, touching my fingertip to his. At once, [244]volts of electricity surged painfully through my body, sending me flying backwards on my back. Dazed, I lie on the floor, unsure of what had happened.

\* \* \*

We'd just come back from Mass, where we'd eaten at an incredible Indian restaurant with beautiful paintings of Hindu lovers, the males with big noses and dark eyes like War. The food was out of this world: basmati rice with peas and almonds and cloves, tandoori chicken with curry, and homemade cheese with spinach and yogurt sauce. The spices mixed with the healthy vegetables gave us a natural high. Of course, we were high to begin with, but that was beside the point.

I waited now for the psychic channeler. She was due to arrive any minute. Pacing the floor, I watched Krisstopher in the band room as he plugged in the fourtrack and set up to record some songs. I'd requested that he disappear for a bit while I covered some personal issues with the channeler.

A small sports car pulled up and a woman climbed out of it dressed in a long wool coat, knit cap, glasses, and wavy brown hair. She clutched a large bottle of spring water in one hand and a leather carryall bag in the other. I was a little surprised by her appearance. I guess I'd been expecting someone from the movies: you know, a staunch, grave faced old woman with a tight bun in her white hair; wearing a long, black crepe dress with an enormous, flashy brooch pinned to its high collar. I held the door open and she stepped into the living room. "Hi, I'm Marie," she smiled, extending her hand.

"Hi Marie, I'm Martyr," I smiled back, shaking it.

She removed her coat and hat and plopped down on the couch, lifting a pad of paper and a pen from her bag. I took a seat beside her while she told me a little about herself. She'd recently moved from New Mexico, where all sorts of bizarre things were happening to her there. She said she thought the energy level in the place was just too intense. Apparently many New Agers resided in the state, so that particular part of the earth was a virtual magnet of power.

We talked a little about confusion and being dazed out, a concern I had. She informed me that oftentimes after meditation, if she forgot to close her lotus petal (a New Age term for the subconscious mind or sixth sense), she attracted all sorts of confusion and negative energy to herself, even getting in car accidents because she wasn't focused.

She'd always been gifted in the area of contacting the spirit realm, although sometimes it got to be more of a hindrance than a help. For instance, if she wanted to get a good night's sleep, it was nearly impossible since the spirits, or *angels* as she called them, woke her up at all hours to perform light shows in the air with glowing stars and things. She'd plead with them to let her go back to sleep, but they wouldn't listen.

It was reassuring to know that like me, she experienced similar manifestations. Of course, I'd met people along the way who either believed in or witnessed firsthand the supernatural. But I hadn't run into any as of late, so it was a positive reinforcement for me.

I confided in her now, of the things that were taking place, especially since we'd moved into this apartment. I wondered if perhaps it was haunted or plagued by evil spirits. I'd even had a dream as a child involving a basement similar to this one. In the dream, I'd been running from an evil, furry animal-looking creature, unable to go anywhere as it continued to gain on me.

I'd always been aware of another world, I explained, ever since I was very young. Unlike other children I knew, I had an ability to contact this other world quite easily, as my father had paved the way for me.

What I didn't realize at the time I told her this, however, was that I'd been gifted with prophetic abilities at birth, which is why it was so easy for me to discern this other realm. Nonetheless, despite my being born with a prophetic gifting, it's a fact that children are naturally more cognizant of the spiritual world anyway, until they are either convinced by their parents or other grownups that they are only imagining things and it's not real, or until they shut down their ability due to fear and lack of understanding.

So perhaps in addition to the doors my father opened for me by dabbling in the Occult, there was also the factor that he believed in the spirit realm and never denied its existence to me, which could help explain why I still had childlike faith to perceive it when many other children and adults I knew did not.

I went on then, to tell Marie of War and his magic power—of how I was sure he was my soul mate—my *eternal* soul mate. Would I be with him? Why wasn't it happening if we were meant to be together?

She shut her eyes, calling on the angels to give her the answers I needed. As they spoke to her (though I couldn't hear them), she hurriedly jotted down their replies on paper. Then turning to me, she first addressed the issue concerning War. "You and War are definitely soul mates," she assured me, "and you *will* be together in the future. However, it might not be like you think. The angels don't think you'll be together forever. But you do have something to work out with him."

My heart sank within me. *No. I have to be with him forever. I have to. He's my eternal soul mate.*

She then confirmed the fact that I had a spiritual gift, maybe even channeling of spirits as she did, but I first had to learn how to use it properly. There was an entity in my house as I'd suspected, she informed me, and it was merely trying to teach me how to utilize this power of mine: not necessarily an evil entity, but a *teacher*. I should listen to it.

I thanked her for the information, still a little sad and disturbed about War. As she got up to leave, she mentioned that she'd seen an apparition of a *black cat* in our kitchen. War! He was here—somewhere.

\* \* \*

Another beautiful gray morning. A couple of hits in the hallway, and now I lie on the bed staring out the window as the first traces of light began chasing the shadows away.

*"On a crimson altar, I'll sacrifice my love to you..."* the singer of England at Witching Hour promised, a sample from an old Dracula movie sounding in the background. I thought of War flying in my window to stand beside me—that look in his eyes while taking me in his arms—thirsty... for my blood.

Maybe it wasn't such a bad thing after all. *Blood*, I mean. Elizabeth Royce made it sound so romantic. Dark but sensual. Evil but beautiful. Her books on vampires sold millions because they glamorized that other world of darkness. I found them to be enticingly sexual. Like War.

And then there was [245]Aleister Crowley, who'd recommended reading Bram Stoker's [246]*Dracula* for its legendary account of vampires. Apparently he held some credence to its tale. I was in the middle of the book now, but found the new remake of the movie to be much more exciting. We'd seen it a few weeks ago at the theater. It was a smash. Whoever wrote the screenplay definitely had knowledge of witchcraft and reincarnation. In fact, they were the central themes of the movie:

[247]Count Dracula, a religious man who went to war with others upholding supposedly Christian beliefs, returns to find his beloved wife committed suicide by *jumping off a cliff* after hearing false news of his death. He then vows to get even, selling his soul in order to get revenge. His goal is to look for his once wife and forever true love, whom he finds in another life occupying another body. Despite his love for her, however, he has carnivorous sexual desires and an unquenchable thirst for blood due to the evil he has vowed himself to.

I found the similarities to be quite amazing: Dracula looking for the woman he once shared a life with—his *true love*. War telling me he wasn't just looking for any woman, but a special woman—his *true love*. It was fate.

"*But your prayers are helpless now...*" Andrew William Elder informed me in a song.

*No. They aren't helpless. I'll win War over to the good. There has to be a way.*

\* \* \*

That smell. That unmistakable smell. *Assault* marijuana. Where was it? I rolled down the driver's side window, taking a big whiff. Yes, it was definitely the stuff. But where—

My eyes caught sight, then, of a wooden sign amidst a section of pine trees to my left. It read:

GOVERNMENT EXPERIMENTAL FOREST

Whoa. Maybe Kyle wasn't lying after all.

\* \* \*

Clad in our wool army berets and leathers, we snuck round the corner and through the alley, peering cautiously in every direction. Since the Fed scare, we were a lot more prudent about our trips to Derek's. Krisstopher rapped on the door now as I stood shivering in the cold night air. After a moment Derek opened, motioning silently for us to come in. We stood before him in the living room, two military popsicles.

"It's Kris and Mahta. I like yuh hats." He disappeared into the back bedroom, returning with his scale. As we sat on bar stools at the counter facing the kitchen, he weighed out a quarter bag for us.

I whipped out the tarot card I'd brought for him. He had a collection of Jokers, which he'd shown me last time we were over. I thought it only fitting that he have the coolest one of all: The *Fool* card from one of my tarot decks. Since I had other decks, I wouldn't miss it too badly. And I made sure to cleanse it of all energy before giving it to him.

He stared at it now—a little strangely, I noticed. "Uh... thanks," he said, forcing a half-smile. I had a feeling he could have done without it.

The next time we dropped in, he was extremely talkative, this time showing us his eyeball ring collection, which he proudly brought out from the bedroom in a wooden, padded jewelry drawer. As Krisstopher and I admired the various rings, we somehow got on the subject of the Masters of Rock concert Derek had seen a couple of years back, which featured many popular metal bands.

"Yeah, when I was standing in line, this guy was passing out some weihd little booklet. I thought it was kind of cool, so I kept mine. You wanna see?" he asked, seeming to address the question more at me.

"Yeah, sure," I told him. He returned from the blanketed doorway of his bedroom with a small pamphlet, handing it to me now as he sat back down. It pictured the Devil's face on the front cover. "Whoa... scary..." I commented, thinking some Satan worshiper had given it to him.

"Uh huh. But what gets me is what's inside. Go ahead. Open it up," he urged. I peered inside at the little message, which mentioned something about the Devil only having a short time on the earth, and his mission was to win as many souls as possible. It ended with something like,

ARE YOU JUST ONE MORE DROP OF BLOOD IN HIS BATH?

"Whoa... that last line kinda reminds me of *me*," I said worriedly. "I wonder if that's why all this weird stuff is happening to me lately, you know what I mean?"

"Uh *huh*," he said, shaking his head yes and peering directly into my eyes as if he knew exactly what I meant—as if I got the message he was trying to relay to me.

\* \* \*

"Hi, War? It's me, Martyr. Yeah. I'm still in New Hampshire. I was just wondering if you got my letter. Yeah? Well, I know. You keep telling me you don't understand what I'm talking about, but I was trying to explain that we're soul mates. And according to the Tree of Life and yin and yang, there must be two opposing forces in everything—in all of nature. So I think I'm realizing that I'm the positive and you're the negative. I'm the good and you're the evil. But it's okay—I think maybe it's *supposed* to be that way."

At least this time he was a little warmer to me. And no girls over, either.

\* \* \*

Krisstopher set the jam box in the back seat and we headed off down the road, My Days With The Happy Death Klan blasting, "*I thrive on drugs. I thrive on drugs. I'm the bad habit.*"

We were off on another *bake trip,* as we liked to call them—a ride on the winding back roads while we smoked a couple bowls and admired nature. It seemed the more I drove around in this never-ending snow, the more I actually came to like it—maybe even love it. Something about the icy cold snow now that really appealed to me. As we made our way through the forest trails, I even saw a few *ice men* of my own: little black creatures against the bright white background; not really visible in a physical sense; but in my mind, as clear as day. They resembled little elves or gnomes, though having the consistency of shadows. Every once in a while they peered at me from behind a tree, or scurried across the path just before us.

"*Black birds! It's a highway war. I'll spend eternity, forever loaded,*" the song continued.

I looked beside me at Krisstopher, who stared out the window. What was happening to us? We rarely talked anymore. Part of me still loved him immensely. I mean, we'd always been in our own little world—just the two of us (whenever he allowed it). People commented on how much alike we were. We seemed so close, they said. His jokes, his laughter, his companionship, his handsome face and beautiful blue eyes, his arms holding me tight at night... he was such a big part of me now. What would I ever do if I had to leave him? The thought was a reoccurring one as of late. I felt it might be a reality soon enough.

And yes, I still found myself incredibly jealous of any woman who frequented his conversation. Did I really have a right to be after all I'd said about War? Nonetheless, it was *he* who'd told me from the start—although not until *after* I left my husband for him—that he wanted to be *free:* that love should be free and open, not tied down. And of course, that had been right after I'd discovered him flirting in the kitchen with some girl at our first Halloween party together, his arms around her. Maybe from then on, I'd secretly resented him. All I knew was, it hurt.

But he was my soul mate, alright. We were two peas in a pod. Oh, the silly little intricate webs we wove, consumed with thoughts and emotions for any halfway attractive person setting foot in our lives—so many of them dangling from a fine silken thread while we made our rounds, deciding which one we wanted to toy with next—which one we wanted to suck the life out of. Was that *karma?* Was that the whole purpose of human relationships?

Now there was Deena at the Inn. I noticed Krisstopher spoke a lot of her. Too much for my liking. And how could I hate her? She was a nice girl; a cute little death metal head with long, wavy brown hair. She played the guitar too—right up his alley—though she lived with her boyfriend Marty. We'd been over there a few times to party, often playing that evil video board game that I loved because one of the characters was a dead witch. Yes, I had to admit, the two of them would probably make a good pair.

And there was also the waitress at the restaurant where he worked that reminded us both of Felician. She looked a lot like her, and definitely acted similar—the tough girl image and all. He told her all about my weird experiences in our apartment, and she commented to me that she'd had similar ones herself. Yeah, Krisstopher talked a lot about *her* too. But what could I say about it? It seemed only a matter of time before we fell apart beyond repair. And my heart hurt.

I noticed as of late that Kyle was really putting the moves on me. He'd flash me a tongue here and there when no one was looking, or give me the eye. He even bought me a couple of drinks the other night at the restaurant—Long Island Iced Teas—before I gave him a ride home. I sensed he would have liked me to loosen up, but I made sure not to reach that point. I found myself feeling more sorry for Morgan every day as I wondered if she had any idea about his lust problem (not that I had room to talk after what I'd done to Craig). But she was smart, and probably very aware of it.

Funny how she and Deena and I had something in common: all of us heard voices, especially when we were high, since it was easier to tune in to them then. Still, I don't think they understood to what extent *I* was hearing them. But then, they weren't involved in witchcraft to the extent that I was, either. I knew Morgan embraced a lot of New Age philosophies: holistic healing, meditation and yoga, etc. And I was sure Deena delved into some occult stuff, too, judging from the death metal music she listened to (which sounded like a bunch of angry, screaming demons) and the types of games she and Marty had lying around. But I doubted that either she or Morgan had gone quite as far as I had when it came to exploring the supernatural realm.

\* \* \*

I lie on the floor in Zain's territory, my back against the ivory colored carpeting, my arms stretched out over my head. The sun tried shining through the window above me, while Krisstopher took a late afternoon nap on the bed across the room. In the background, the television set flickered, the sound turned all the way down.

I closed my eyes for a moment, concentrating on the wheezing heat registers: *Eeeeeeee! Sssssssss! Eeeeeeee! Oooooooaaaahhheeeeee sssssss!* Then I opened them once again to see Zain staring down at me from his hot rock on the shelf. Lately, it seemed I detected a hint of terror in his watchful eye.

Squirming restlessly, I crossed one of my legs and sighed. I was in a sullen mood today. It seemed my hope was fading where War and I were concerned, as I began to wonder if we'd ever be together in the physical. What if I was wrong about everything? What if he *didn't* love me? Maybe he'd been telling the truth when he said he didn't know anything about witchcraft. Maybe he wasn't my soul mate after all. A terrible, sinking feeling clutched my heart as I fathomed this last thought.

Suddenly, an invisible presence rushed toward me, hovering just above my body, and War's familiar voice sounded. *"Martyr, it's me, War.*

*I'm astral projecting."* It was him! He'd heard my thoughts—just when I was ready to give up.

I spoke to him in my mind now. *War? What's going on? Why—*

"*Sshh! Just listen,"* he prodded gently. It was so good to hear his voice! I hadn't actually heard it in the spiritual realm since that night at the cliff, though I knew he'd transferred thoughts to me.

I could feel him lightly breathing on me now, just inches away from my stomach, though still invisible to my eyes. I imagined his soul hovering above me while his body lie at home in bed, eyes shut in concentration as he projected himself to me. Then it was true! He *did* know all about sex magic. Maybe he was going to teach me how to astral project too, and we could have astral sex on the spiritual plane—just our souls meshing together.

"*Close your eyes,"* he commanded.

I did as he wished. Presently, I began to feel a tingly sensation on my skin as if I was being lightly licked. Warm rays of ecstasy rippled through me. Finally. It was going to happen, wasn't it? We'd never contacted physically before. But now it would be something much more—even more than the visions of him while his soul had used Krisstopher's body to experience me. After a few moments, the tingling moved up to my lips. He was kissing me very softly. But I had my mouth closed. I wasn't sure why—I guess I was a little afraid.

"*Open your mouth, Martyr,"* he whispered. I hesitated for a split second, then parted my lips slightly. At once, a tidal wave of negative energy flooded the atmosphere around me, and I felt a great wickedness such as I'd never experienced before—*ever.* A heavy force, similar to a vacuum-like suction, pushed against my lips as if trying to enter my mouth. I squirmed a little, panicking. "*Sit still! It's okay, Martyr. Let it happen,"* he instructed.

But something deep inside me cried, *"No! Don't let it in—it's evil!"* With that, I let out a short, sharp scream; closing my mouth and yanking myself up off the floor. "This isn't happening. This isn't happening," I whispered, pacing back and forth while clutching my head in my hands.

"*You should have let me in!"* the voice scolded angrily, no longer sounding like War. Now it sounded like the animalistic voice I'd heard in the living room that time before being chased up the stairs.

*No, I'm afraid!*
I blocked it out, fearful to continue further contact with it. I wasn't
sure anymore that it was War. I wasn't sure *what* it was.

\* \* \*

Renny had given us a book for Christmas about witchcraft and
sorcery. He thought that since we were witches, we'd love it. But as
far as I knew, neither of us had touched it yet; it'd been lying around
for awhile. Finally, I felt motivated to pick it up. [248]Skimming through
its pages, I read about witches and their Sabbaths, a time when the
Devil often appeared in the form of a goat to them. They'd have sexual
intercourse with him and his demons. My face paled as I read this.
I examined a picture of one of the witches with the hairy goat devil.
Immediately I thought of Krisstopher—of the entity that came between
us while we were having sex—the pointy tongue I felt and the hairy fur;
the animalistic grunts and growls.

I flipped through a couple of more pages, reading about early cases
of demonic possession in the church, in which the demons entered
the person by way of an orifice, or opening, in the body. Most of the
victims claimed that the demonic spirit entered in through their *mouth*.
Frightened, I let out a cry; my hands shaking, my heart beating fast.
Something had tried entering *my* mouth—had it been a demon?!

I went on to read of one man's experience with demons. He claimed
they were chasing him, and he couldn't seem to get rid of them. He'd
tried potions of garlic and other herbal remedies, but with no success.
On the proceeding page, he'd drawn pictures of what each demon
looked like, with their names listed below them. Curious, I examined
his drawings.

As I looked over most of the demons, which appeared very bestial, I
suddenly stopped, paralyzed with fear when my eyes landed on the only
human looking one of them all. It was War!—the animated War I'd seen
recently. The resemblance was uncanny! He had longish hair, dark eyes,
a rather large nose, luscious lips, and an extremely seductive look on
his face. He was bare-chested, riding on some sort of dragonous beast
whose tail was an [249]arrow pointed downward. Within the same picture,

scrawled in smoke, was a large 'S' which I assumed represented Satan. The demon's name was [250]Ashteroth. He was a demon who partook in sexual pleasures.

When Krisstopher came home that evening, I tried relaying all this to him. Excited, I sputtered out all the things I'd read while he stared blankly at me, dumbfounded. I remember that as I was speaking, the lights suddenly flashed on and off in our bedroom. When I'd finished, he didn't know what to say. I knew he didn't believe me. I knew he thought I was nuts. What was I going to do? These demons were after me, and I had nowhere to turn.

A few days later, a verse in a Christian Corpse song caught my attention. I'd never really heard the lyrics before, though I'd listened to the song at least a hundred times. I shivered as Ross Willing sang, *"SLEEP WITH THE DEVIL, THE PRICE YOU MUST PAY... SWEET LADY, FOR TRUE LOVE, THE PRICE YOU MUST PAY."*

\* \* \*

Liza had been in town recently, though Krisstopher swore he didn't hook up with her or anything. He'd seen her mom in the bar one night as he was working the restaurant section. She told him Liza was staying with her for a few days and was really messed up—mental and emotional problems, I guess. She had Zain (her kid) with her.

Anyway, her mom had been in the bar a couple of times so far. Krisstopher informed me that he sensed she was flirting with him somewhat—just what I needed to hear! Tonight he'd come home and changed, then took off to her place. She'd invited him over for a few drinks.

The woman was in her early fifties, at least, though I had to admit, she wore it well. I couldn't believe she was putting the moves on Krisstopher. Didn't she have anyone her own age to get with? Of course, Krisstopher reassured me that he was only going there to have a few drinks and reminisce about old times. That is, if he was telling the truth. Maybe he was going there to resurrect the flying bed experience with Liza. Or maybe he was with someone else entirely and had only used the Liza and her mother thing for an excuse. Who knew where he really was?

I only knew that he was *somewhere* with *someone,* just when I needed him most.

I was so scared. Everything in my world had suddenly grown so dark, so out of control. Or had it? Maybe it was all in my head. I couldn't tell anymore what was real and what wasn't. Who could I talk to? Who could help me?

After crying for a good half hour, I pulled out my runes, which to my dismay seemed to indicate that if I committed suicide, I would have joy. I could then go into another life and start all over again. I could escape everything here that was plaguing me. Everything. *Yes. That's what I'll do then,* I decided as I scooped up the little stones and put them back in their cloth pouch, *but how?* I was too chicken to stab myself; I'd already had a bad experience with that. I didn't know how to hang myself. Then an idea came to me.

In the bathroom, I rummaged through the medicine cabinet. [251]*Nyquil,* [252]*Tylenol,* [253]*Sudafed… what's this?* My eyes landed on a prescription bottle. Grabbing it, I carefully examined the label. Painkillers for Krisstopher, probably from when he hurt his back or something. There were a good fifteen or so still in the bottle. Plenty enough to kill me. I took a deep breath now. Did I really want to do this? Cupping my hand, I poured out about six and popped them into my mouth, washing them down with water. The realization hit me then that I might actually die. But surely six wasn't a whole lot. Enough to demand attention, to hurt myself a little… a cry for help, maybe. If I really wanted to die, I could take more.

As was always the case when I had a suicidal notion, I knew somewhere deep within me that I shouldn't do it. And I never had enough guts to do it, anyway, so I always made sure I slightly missed the mark. Still, I had no idea what these pills were. Hopefully six wasn't a lethal amount. Or hopefully it was. I didn't know what I wanted. I guess part of me wanted to die and part of me didn't. The part that said, *I can't cope with this anymore, and no one understands*—that part wanted to die. But then there was another part deep down inside me which told me it was not the answer to my problems—the nagging uncertainty of just where I'd go if I actually went through with it. Would I wake up with no more problems? Or would I wake up with *eternal* problems?

I pondered death now, as I went back into the bedroom and lie across the bed. "If I die, Zainy, I'll miss you," I told him, hot tears streaming down my cheeks. He stared down at me sadly as if he understood exactly what I said. Of course he did. He was my animal familiar.

I wondered if War would miss me. Probably not.

After about fifteen or twenty minutes, I heard the front door open and Krisstopher came up the stairs.

"I took some pills," I told him, "and I don't care. I'm going to die."

"You *what?!*" he asked, his face turning white as a ghost. "*What* pills? Martyr, *what* pills?"

"Don't worry about it. You don't care anyway."

"Come on, we're going to the hospital!"

"No, I don't want to go to the hospital."

"We're *going to the hospital.* Do you realize what a *stupid* thing you've done?! Now, come on!" he cried, yanking me off the bed in desperation.

"You don't care about me," I sobbed. "That's why you're sleeping around on me."

"*What?!* Martyr, I didn't do anything tonight. We just had a couple drinks. Now what pills did you take? Tell me—*quick!*"

"They're in the medicine cabinet," I mumbled.

He returned with the bottle in his hand. "Are these them? Are these the ones?!"

"Uh huh."

"Come on! They're going to have to pump your stomach or something."

In the hospital, I lie on the hard examining table, waiting for the doctor. I *accidentally* took too many—that was my excuse to the nurse. They didn't have to pump my stomach. They just gave me some other medication to repel the painkillers and induce vomiting. I spent the rest of the night in the bathroom throwing up until there was nothing left in my system to throw up. Then I had dry heaves.

# XIV. DARKEST BEFORE THE DAWN

STEPHEN CALLED ME AFTER THAT. He'd found out from my mom, who'd found out from Krisstopher, that I'd tried killing myself.

"Stephen, I'm scared! The Devil's after me! I've got these things chasing me up the stairs and trying to climb inside my mouth. I feel like I'm losing my mind!"

"Well, it's Satan, Paula. What do you expect when you've been messing with all that witchcraft stuff?"

"But what am I going to do? I'm afraid!"

"Alright, you've tried all your gods and goddesses. It doesn't look like they've done too much for you. Now why don't you try Jesus? Why don't you try reading the Bible?"

"I can't. I can't understand the Bible. It's boring."

"Look, just skip past all the generational lineages—you know, the 'he begat he begat' stuff—and read something else. Eventually, God will supply the understanding for you."

"I don't know… I'll think about it."

"Do you have a bible?"

"Yeah, Mom mailed me one a couple of months back. It's *your* old one, actually."

\* \* \*

"Hey, sis. Are you feeling better?"

"Yeah, I'm okay."

"So have you been reading the Bible?"

"Well, I started to, but then I found a [254]Mormon bible some guy gave me when I worked at the record store. It's easier to read, and it's got really cool pictures in it. I've also been studying [255]*The Lost Teachings of Jesus*—about how he was into magic and stuff."

"Uhhh... I wouldn't be reading those things if I were you. They're not quite the same thing as the Bible."

"What do you mean?"

"Um... just stick to the Bible. You have to know the truth before you can recognize the counterfeit. Trust me. I'm your brother. I wouldn't steer you wrong, okay?"

"Okay."

So I picked up the King James Bible one morning after being frightened again. I'd seen the word SIN etched in the bedroom carpet. That's when I sat on the bed and opened the cover, slowly flipping through the pages. Stopping, I read one of the passages. It spoke of the city of Ephesus in the Roman province of Asia, and how all of Ephesus and most of Asia worshipped the great goddess Diana. My eyes widened. I didn't know Diana was in the Bible! The apostle Paul was telling the city, and especially those who made silver shrines for Diana, that there weren't any gods made with hands. I read some other things, too, but I couldn't really remember what.

That night as I slept, I tossed and turned; a spiritual war taking place: good against evil. I could hear a voice within me—deep down in my spirit—dictating bible scriptures, while something else cringed with fear, unable to tolerate the torture.

When I awoke the next morning, it seemed a [256]great weight had been lifted off me. I felt lighter. And happier. I went downstairs, pressing play on the jam box atop the fridge. A Christian Corpse song blared, *"Satan, be! Satan, be! Satan, be! Satan, be... cast out."* Hurriedly I turned it off, understanding for the first time who it glorified—understanding the evil intent behind it.

* * *

Zain's whipping tail and bobbing head let me know that there was something in the room again. From up on the shelf, he snorted and arched his back, cracking his tail some more.

"What, Zainy? What is it?" I asked. But I could feel it too. It was all around me—and I felt like other people sensed it as well.

I'd been in the grocery store a few days before when a woman passing by, upon seeing me, made several sweeping motions with her arms as if slicing the air to clear negative energy, while mumbling something under her breath. It made me wonder if she was praying or something—rebuking the evil.

I decided I would purchase a rosary from the Jumping Over the Edge store. It was all I could think of, since it seemed to repel the evil when I was younger. In the store now, I held the light green beads in my hand. The sight of the shiny silver cross somehow comforted me. I picked out a black rosary for Krisstopher and took them both up to the register. "I think I'm starting to get into Jesus," I told the female clerk.

"Well, he *was* a great prophet," she smiled, but something told me he was much more than that.

Back home in the shadows of the living room, I lit the candles and the black raven incense I'd bought to ward off evil. Then I clutched the rosary in my hand, knelt down, and prayed—to God.

I'd read a section about church in the [257]book Renny got us, and what certain symbols came to represent throughout the church age. After tracing a picture of the bleeding heart of Mary, I made it into a two-sided mobile, stuffing it with some herbs the guy who'd been chased by demons used and sewing it together. I hung it in the kitchen as a protective talisman, right near the basement door.

The large, plastic exorcist cross on the band room door scared me lately. I got a really piercing, evil pang in my heart whenever I looked at it, [258]maybe because it reminded me of the demon possessed girl in the movie. So I wrapped some artificial roses around it to give it a less threatening appearance.

\* \* \*

I still didn't have a job yet. I'd put in some applications, and even gone to a few interviews, but with no success. I wanted to continue working in retail, as an assistant manager if possible, though I was getting to the point where I'd take anything. I was surprised that even the motels and ski lodges hadn't called me, as busy as they were this time of year.

Krisstopher was still waiting tables at the restaurant. Every day he got to see Deena, who worked the front desk at the Inn, and Kyle, who still managed telemarketing and street soliciting; as well as some of his other friends there in town.

Meanwhile, I sat home alone in the dismal confines of my reality. In a way it was good though, because I had plenty of time to think, and some positive changes were taking place as a result.

I decided to quit smoking pot. It was really beginning to mess with me—bad. Every time I smoked it, I grew ice cold, my body became partially paralyzed, and I got a sharp, stabbing pain in my head. Then I heard a big POP! and felt a bunch of fluid running around in my brain. It scared me to death. But I was really having a difficult time quitting. Kyle kept dropping by with a nice big joint to smoke. Funny how for a couple of weeks, I'd been jonesing for weed really bad and it was nowhere to be found, and now that I wanted to quit, it was everywhere!

I'd asked Krisstopher not to smoke it in the apartment because I was trying hard to quit. I was really afraid that if I didn't, something terrible would happen. But he argued that it was *his* apartment too, and he wasn't about to be restricted from smoking pot in his own apartment.

Lately, he was more like my worst enemy than my friend. He hated the rosary I bought him, accusing me of turning into a *Holy Roller* like my brother. "I don't even *know* you anymore, Martyr," he snapped.

Kyle held the joint out to me now. I could smell the pesticide aroma, my mouth beginning to water as my body anticipated the high associated with it. "Come onnnn, Martyrrr… have a hit. You *know* you want to," he coaxed.

"But I've got this stuff popping in my head and this fluid running around and—"

"Naaahh… it's *all in your mind*. You're fine," he reassured me. "Now come onnn…"

*Go on, take a hit. What's one hit going to do? Just one...* I snatched it from him and took a long drag, hating myself for giving in.

Later, Krisstopher and I lie on the bed upstairs watching TV. He got up to go to the bathroom while I continued to stare at the boring news guy, scrying behind him in the backdrop scenery. Suddenly, the room began to shake like we were having an earthquake. No, it wasn't the room. It was... me? But I wasn't shaking on the outside. What was happening? Now something was pulling on me—not on my *physical* body, but on my astral body—on my *soul.*

*"We're going to kill you!"* an [259]Exorcist sounding voice hissed, swearing at me. The demons yanked some more on me, my skin a big sleeping bag crumpling around me as they lifted me further out of it. Screaming bloody murder, I groped for the Bible on the nightstand next to me. Frantically opening it, I cried out for God to help me while attempting to read scriptures.

At once, I heard a voice bellow, *"Leave her—now!"* Immediately the evil presence left me. I was sure an angel had rescued me. Krisstopher came running in the room then, a frightened look in his eyes as he hurried to my side.

"It's okay," I sobbed, "it's gone. I opened the Bible... and it's gone."

\* \* \*

We dropped by Marty and Deena's to see what they were up to. Deena had mentioned to Krisstopher earlier that they were renting a movie and we should stop by. As we sat down on the couch now, she put in [260]*Jacob's Ladder.* We'd just finished smoking a couple of bowls, and that lethargic feeling was kicking in. I yawned and stretched out my legs, sitting on my hands for heat as the customary chills attacked me once more.

[261]Somewhere in Vietnam, an experimental drug was being given to soldiers to see if it would make them fight better. After smoking the joint, the American soldiers were having bad reactions—clutching their heads, having seizures, etc. My stomach turned watching them. To my recollection, it seems one guy started convulsing, then fell down, bashing his head against the ground until blood gushed out.

I felt extremely nauseous now, my face turning white as a ghost and little beads of sweat breaking out on my brow. My head was hurting bad again, just like the guys in the movie. *Experimental pot. Experimental pot,* was all I kept thinking. "Come on, Krisstopher! Let's *go!*" I suddenly burst out, jumping up from the couch.

"Huh?"

"I can't watch this movie—it's making me sick. Let's *go!*" I was already at the door, the reality of the movie producing a terror in me that I wanted to get rid of as soon as possible. Groping for the handle, I couldn't wait to get outside in the cool air—to forget I'd ever watched that horrid scene.

He shrugged, following me while mumbling apologies to Marty and Deena. "She's sick, man. Sorry."

\* \* \*

Something told me not to smoke it. I'd dropped Krisstopher off at work again, and it was that morning routine that I missed. The skull bong hits. *One* wouldn't hurt me, would it? Or maybe two? As I inhaled deeply, the water crackling in the reservoir, it seemed I literally sucked something up into my brain. Immediately I felt a sharp pain in my head, almost as if something had entered it! Ignoring the pain, I put the bong down and went into the room to put on some music. *Music.* That's what I needed.

But after about ten minutes, I turned into a solid block of ice. My hands were almost blue in color, and a million thoughts were rushing through my head all at once. I could feel myself losing consciousness, like going into a coma with my eyes open. I screamed out, trying to move. My body was completely numb; it felt like a dead weight. "God, help me!" I cried out.

*"If you do not quit smoking pot, you will become mentally retarded,"* a voice within me seemed to say. I believe God was speaking to me.

My father once told me about a place he delivered mail to—a group home for people who blew their mind on drugs. He said they couldn't even go to the bathroom by themselves, they were so brain dead.

I was able to move again. *Thank God. Thank God.* Stumbling to my feet, I limped out into the hallway. "I've got to do something. I've got to do something. Stay awake. Stay awake," I muttered frantically.

My keyboard—that was it! I'd play my keyboard, and everything would be okay. Tripping down the stairs, I fumbled around for it in the shadows, barely able to pick it up and carry it back to the room.

I set it down on the carpet and turned it on, attempting to play. To my horror, my hands were like [262]Jell-O. I couldn't move my fingers at all. They dragged sloppily over the keys. "Oh my God, *help* me! I can't even play. I can't even play... what's happened?" I sobbed.

A voice said, "*If you quit smoking pot, you will play keyboards better than you've ever played before.*"

"Okay, okay! I'm *sorry!*" I wailed. "I'll quit smoking pot, I promise!" The feeling in my fingers soon returned.

\* \* \*

I knew what I had to do. I had to move back home—to my mom's. It was the only way I could withstand the temptation. This place was killing me. I had to get out before it was too late. And I'd see Stephen too. He could help me. I broke the news to Krisstopher that I was leaving, explaining why.

"Okay. I understand," he said coolly. "You've got to do what's best for you."

But I had a feeling he didn't really believe I'd go. I always brought up leaving whenever things weren't going well between us. He probably assumed this time was no different.

So many changes were taking place within me. I could feel them happening, and it just seemed so right.

Recently, I'd written Jesus a letter and stuck it in my God Box. It was an apology for serving other gods and goddesses—for sinning against him. The weird thing was, nobody told me to do it, but I felt I should do it. I guess I wanted to, even. I remember crying as I read it aloud to him. I was really sorry I hurt him.

It seemed I'd [263]lost my ability to divine. Whenever I did tarot spreads, I couldn't even make out the cards anymore. Though I'd stopped saying my alignments to the deities and said them to Jesus now, the cards were so ambiguous, like one big tangled mass of confusion.

My crystal ball was even worse. I was still using the clear one since the pink witchball didn't work as well for some reason. But now when I peered into it, I only saw ugly, alien-looking demon creatures with jagged fangs. They stared at me evilly, devil fish trapped inside a fish bowl. No matter how many times I attempted to scry, they were the only vision obtainable—like they'd been there all along and I was just now recognizing them for what they truly were. Then I read something in the Bible about how witches, sorcerers, fortunetellers, astrologers, and mediums are all an abomination to God. He doesn't want anyone to practice these things, and they're cursed if they do. That explained why I was seeing demons: because scrying is associated with the Devil.

Shortly after that, I wrote War a long letter explaining that I was no longer a witch and that I was getting into Jesus. I included a poem: something about how I was *digging in a cemetery and found faith, and hope, and love.* At the close of the letter, I mentioned that I was moving back to Michigan soon and hoped to see him again.

Next I wrote Joe, sharing similar news with him about my decision to leave witchcraft and follow Jesus. I told him that evil spirits were chasing me and I was afraid. He and his mother wrote me back, including a protective prayer, Psalm 91, for me to read whenever I was fearful.

Meanwhile, Kyle had a new nickname for me: *Polly Purebred,* ever since he'd heard of my religious conversion. I carried my bible around sometimes for protection, and mentioned to Misty and Deena that I was no longer a pagan. Everyone in town was pretty shocked—including me. The time drew near for me to leave. Jason called and I told him the good news. He was happy that he'd be seeing me again, though bummed for Krisstopher.

My mom sent me some birthday money to help cover the trip home. I was able to buy a small jam box for the ride since Krisstopher was keeping the other one, plus some new clothes at a church thrift sale for really cheap—cheaper than I'd ever seen. I'd been wanting a different winter coat and boots; I didn't feel like wearing my old stuff anymore. The transformation I was undergoing on the inside was manifesting on the outside, though I didn't really understand it. I was naturally gravitating away from the really dark gothic look, and I didn't quite know yet how to maintain a balance in my appearance. So... new clothes... for a new season in my life. It was strange, but somehow I knew [264]God had provided the money for me to get everything I needed. There wasn't a question in my mind.

Krisstopher was starting to show his true feelings; he told me he didn't want me to leave. But I knew I had to or else I'd just fall back into the same lifestyle again, and it was a dead-end road. Though talking about it with him made me sad, part of me was happy—happier than I'd ever been. For the first time in my life, I felt I had a future. Something to look forward to. Something to live for.

Fortunately, Sam and Renny called from Colorado. Renny helped me plan a route home. He told Krisstopher exactly what to highlight on the map for me so I wouldn't take any unexpected turns and get lost. Sam offered support, which was just what I needed at that moment.

And then the day came. I collected all of my stuff together: clothes, books, etc., and Zain, and loaded up the [265]Omni. I agreed with Krisstopher to pay the rest of the money we owed on it so long as I could have it. It was lightly snowing outside when I drove into town, swinging by the restaurant to say good-bye to him.

"Well, I guess you're really doing this, huh Martyr?" he said, looking at me now with his hands shoved in his pockets.

It was finally starting to sink in for both of us. For a minute we were silent, then I spoke. "Well, uh... I've gotta get going." Instinctively, we hugged and kissed one another. But there was a wall between us this time. I purposely put it there.

"Be careful."

"I will."

He watched as I got into the car. "Bye Zainy. I'll miss you," he called, waving to our little green pet monster perched atop a pile of junk in the back seat. It was a sad moment for both of us. Yet I knew deep down it was the right thing to do. I waved one last final good-bye, heading off down the street, a piece of my heart remaining behind with him.

Once I got on the freeway just outside of Boston, Zain moved up from his spot near the window of the hatch, crawling into the front seat with me. "Awww, do you miss me Zainy?" I asked sweetly.

Suddenly the hatch unfastened, blowing open, and a bunch of my clothes and stuff got sucked out onto the road. I realized, then, that if Zain hadn't moved, he would have been history; and I am sure that an angel prompted him into the front seat, lest my heart should break at his death and cause me to turn back.

The ride home was a challenging one, as unseen forces seemed to be warring against me—trying to stop me from completing the journey. But I felt God's presence with me. [266]My rosary hung from the rearview mirror for protection, though later I would take it down after discovering that I didn't need a rosary when I had a God that was much more powerful.

I rode in and out of blizzards, barely able to see in front of me at times and wondering how I managed to stay on the highway. On several occasions, I had to pull over and load up on windshield wiper fluid; I was going through it like water.

Then when I stopped after dark to fill up at a lonely gas station and was ready to head out again, my doors mysteriously locked so I couldn't get back in the car (my keys were still in the ignition). By divine providence, the young gas station attendant happened to have a Slim Jim tool. After helping me open the door, he then tried coaxing me into spending the night with him, but I politely refused and hurried out of there.

I pulled over around midnight, finally locating a motel, and Zain and I crashed there. I was just in the nick of time since I found him half-frozen under the passenger seat, his leash caught on one of the adjusters. In tears, I pulled him out and rushed into the room, sticking him under my sweater until his hot rock warmed up. He survived.

For the first time in a long time, I lie alone in bed that night, hot tears streaming down my cheeks as I looked with uncertainty to the future. Everything was happening so fast that my head was spinning. I missed Krisstopher already, and I was really cold. I wished he could hold me. Then it felt like somebody *was* holding me, though not so much in the *physical* sense. I just felt a wave of peace wash over me, like God was telling me everything would be alright.

As I stared up at the ceiling, the whirring of the heater somewhere off in the background, I felt the sudden urge to pray for War. I don't remember exactly what I said. I just know I prayed for him that night in the little motel room somewhere outside of New York.

The next morning, I rose bright and early before the break of dawn. As I got ready at the bathroom counter, I told Zain excitedly, "We're going to see War again!" But tears streamed down my cheeks as I continued to think of Krisstopher, the uncertainty of just where I was headed washing over me once more. As if comforting me now, Zain suddenly took a running jump, landing on my leg and climbing all the way up onto my shoulder. If iguanas could give hugs, I guess that would be how. I pressed my face to his head for a moment. "Can I have a kiss, Zainy?" I asked. He flicked out his tiny tongue and I licked it. It was just our little way of displaying affection for one another.

The Ohio turnpike was long and boring, but at least there was no chance of getting lost on it. When I finally reached Toledo, it was around two in the afternoon. The car started to chug and sputter. I could tell it was ready to die at any minute, so I revved the gas super hard and maybe even said a prayer. Three times it did that, and three times I mashed the pedal to the floor. Finally it quit.

I made it to Michigan in one piece, thank God. As I pulled into the parking lot of the grocery store where my mom worked, I breathed a sigh of relief. I was happy to be home. I kind of missed this place. I snuck up to the meat counter where Mom had just finished waiting on a customer.

"This is my daughter!" she told her coworkers excitedly. I could tell she was overjoyed to see me once more.

After giving her a big hug and talking for a while, she gave me the house keys and I went home to start unloading my stuff, setting up Zain first in his old spot on the clothes shoot in Jim's room. "Well, this is your new home," I told him, having a look around the place.

Then I raided the refrigerator, overwhelmed at the sight of all the food in it, and ate the corned beef and cheese my mom told me about. Afterwards, I had a look in the cupboards, excited when I discovered they were stocked full of all kinds of yummy stuff I'd forgotten existed.

It felt weird being back home again. After living in our apartment for so long, everything seemed different. I'd have to get used to the smell of my new surroundings, which wasn't bad—kind of like a combination of [267]Lemon Pledge and food—and the new layout: no staircase in the living room, no basement in the kitchen (though that suited me just fine—what was it about basements, anyway?)

But as I stared at my new sleeping arrangement, the sadness returned. I thought of Krisstopher hundreds of miles away. *No,* I shook it off, *I have to start over.*

The next morning, Jason gave me directions to the office building where he worked selling concert tickets, and I applied for a job. Afterwards, I spent the rest of the day visiting with my mom's friends. Later that evening, I felt the urge to call War. I had to find out where we stood now. Seated at the snack bar in the kitchen, I dialed his number, my hands shaking and butterflies in my stomach. "War?"

To my surprise, he seemed happy to hear from me. I told him I was back in town, and he asked me if I wanted to meet him in about an hour or so at the [268]Greyhound Bus Station in Ypsilanti. He'd decided it was the safest place for me to wait for him, though he advised that I should be careful and talk to no one.

I hung up the phone, jumping up and down for joy, then went into the dining room and knelt on my knees below the Catholic cross hanging on the wall. I thanked Jesus for allowing us to see each other again. I'd prayed for this moment all day.

As usual, War was meticulous with directions. I had no problem finding the bus station at all. Inside, I waited alone on a bench facing the window, dressed in my new purple crushed velvet coat and black knee-high vinyl boots. I was the only one in the place. A car pulled up next to the window then, and a dark-haired War peered inside at me, pushing open the passenger door as I made my way out onto the sidewalk. I climbed into his [269]Cavalier, unable to believe he was finally sitting beside me in *flesh and blood.*

"Hi," I smiled shyly, giving him a hug.

"Heyyy... what's up?" he replied, pulling back onto the street. Emotion flooded over me at the sound of his voice. "I was thinkin', you just wanna go back to my place and talk? We can listen to records and stuff," he offered.

"Yeah," Pause. "Yeah... that would be fine. I've got so much to tell you. I don't even know where to begin."

In his basement now, I sat on the bed while he sat across from me on the couch. He'd done a little rearranging since the last time I'd been there. But his records were still strewn all over the floor, dirty dishes and takeout bags everywhere; a heap of clothes in the corner, ashtrays overflowing with Carlsboro butts...yeah, War still lived here.

I stared at him curiously. He looked a little different than I'd seen him in my crystal ball for the last year or so. His fingernails had grown horridly long, and of course, the pink hair was history, now a brownish-black—his natural color. He seemed a little older, and a bit worn. But he was still beautiful. He looked at me with those dark eyes of his.

"So... tell me about New Hampshire. I hear you're gettin' into Jesus now or somethin'?"

Yep. He was still beautiful.

I proceeded to explain to him then, about all the weird things that had gone on. The cat, the crows, the different signs; his face appearing to me in a hologram at Sean's, the vision of Hell at the cliff and his voice telling me to jump, the sexual presence between Krisstopher and I, and finally, him astral projecting to me and trying to enter my mouth.

"Martyr, that wasn't *me!*" he said, a bewildered look on his face. For the first time, I believed him. "I told ya, that witchcraft stuff is *bad news.* Didn't I tell ya that?"

"Yeah... but then, if it wasn't *you* doing all those things... then who *was* it?"

"I don't know man. It musta been the Devil or somethin', like ya said earlier."

It was finally starting to hit me that I'd been in delusion this *entire time.* I'd been tricked into believing that War had some kind of magic power.

"But I thought your name was War, for *war*lock," I protested.

"*Nooo!*" he exclaimed. "Martyr, my last name is *Worenshtein,* and they call me *War* for short."

No *wonder* he meant it could be spelled W-A-R or W-O-R!

"Ohhhh!" I laughed. I felt like a complete *fool.* I went on then, to talk about Jesus, and how I was starting to read the Bible. I told him about the night the evil spirits tried pulling me out of my body, and how I opened the Bible and something chased them away.

"Yeah, well I don't know if I believe in God," he told me.

"But I thought you were a Jew," I challenged. "I mean, it's your nationality or whatever."

"Yeah, well my *family's* Jewish. But *I'm* an atheist." Still, he wanted to hear more about Jesus. I feared at first he was going to take me back to the bus station for mentioning my newfound religion so much, but it was quite the contrary. "Hey, ya wanna get somethin' to eat? Then we can talk more about this kinda stuff. I love talkin' about this kinda stuff with ya, but I'm gettin' kind of hungry, ya know?"

"Yeah, sure. Okay."

He drove us to [270]Denny's restaurant. On the way there, he grabbed my hand and held it. I thought for sure I was dreaming. All the time I'd been in New Hampshire involved in witchcraft, he'd wanted nothing to do with me. And now suddenly, the minute I started telling him about Jesus Christ, he liked me all over again.

"I want ya to be my girlfriend," he said now, looking deep into my eyes as I sat across from him in the booth. It reminded me of that first time he'd told me he liked me, on the way to the store to get rolling papers.

"Yeah... I'd like that," I replied dreamily as we held hands over the table. On the far wall in the mirror, the words SOUL MATE magically appeared without me even attempting to scry. Maybe *that's* what it was all along: I first had to come to the good myself before I could win War over to it.

\* \* \*

"It's that anchor! I can't *stand* to look at that anchor! It reminds me of a vision I had in my crystal ball. It reminds me of the *evil!*" I shrieked, panicking.

"But it's just a poster. It won't hurt ya, see?" War answered, pointing at the movie advertisement on his brother's bedroom door.

"It doesn't matter—it's evil. It's *evil!*"

"Okay, ya want me to take it down, hon? I'll take it down." *Rrrrip.* "There."

As I eyed the crumpled-up poster in his hands, the fear left me.

367

"Here. Do you wanna read the Bible? Let's read the Bible," he soothed. "I'll be right back. Let me go find it. I know my parents have one here somewhere. Will ya be okay for a minute?"

I shook my head yes, sitting down on the bed.

"Okay. I'll be right back. I promise."

He returned with a hardcover Jewish version of the Old Testament known as the Tanakh (and also the Torah, although technically the Torah is really the first five books of the Old Testament. Since Jews don't believe that Jesus is the Messiah—or Savior to come—(unless they are Messianic Jews), their bible does not include the New Testament). Sitting down beside me now, he opened the cover and we browsed through the pages.

"What's this? [271]Adonai?" I asked.

"Yeah. It's the Hebrew word for *God,* I guess," he explained. Then in another place, I saw [272]Elohim, also another Hebrew word for God.

"Wow, [273]Aleister Crowley had those in his [274]Magick book."

He didn't comment, but I hadn't really expected him to. He probably didn't even know who Aleister Crowley *was.*

"Here, let's read out loud, okay?" he suggested. "You read some, and then I'll read some."

I stayed with him that night for comfort. But the only thing he did was hold me in his arms.

As I listened to music on my way home the next morning, I realized that the guy from Zenith was referring to divination when he sang about the *stars predicting,* and *seeing it on the wall.* I supposed I'd always known that—I mean—it wasn't too hard to understand his words. Yet, all the time I'd understood them, I hadn't *really understood* them at all. It was almost like I had new ears now, and the implications were strikingly clear: the singer encouraged divination, and divination was evil. It led to spiritual curses. Therefore, I should not condone divination by listening to the tape. So I took it out, tossing it on the floor.

Then I put in a Devotion and Missiles tape. They sounded so good as I plowed through the snow in my little [275]Omni, thinking of War and I and all that had happened in the short time I'd been back. The band never failed to magically transport me to an ethereal fantasyland at the touch of a button… and Nathan Hash's voice was *still* a whispering drip, even without the acid. *"Ride the* [276]*Kundalini Serpent!"* he sang invitingly now. The song was a cheerful one, with a really catchy riff.

"Ride the Kundalini Serpent!" I joined in happily, then stopped abruptly. Wait a minute... kundalini was a *bad* thing! Why hadn't I known that before? It was a way for demons to gain access to your body through the base of the spine. "Uh oh..." Pressing the eject button, I yanked the tape out of the cassette player and tossed it on the floor with the other one.

After pulling over to get gas, I rummaged through the rest of the cassettes to see what else I could listen to. How about... Isis Pearls? No... I guess not. Hmmm. It seemed my selection was getting narrower by the minute.

\* \* \*

"I don't know, hon. I know ya really believe these voices and stuff—I mean, I know ya think they tell ya things. But, I just can't get into it. Something just doesn't set right with me," War told me. We were in the mall, walking arm in arm and watching all the different people pass by us.

"Yeah, but Tzaddi is my magic name—my *secret* name—and the voices *knew* that. They *called* me that." Of course, it hadn't occurred to me at the time of our conversation that I'd also written the name in my Book of Shadows before, so it really wasn't that much of a secret.

We stopped at the flower shop now. "Ya want a rose? I'm gonna get ya a rose."

"No... it's okay. You don't have to do that."

"No, I *wanna* do it. I wanna get ya a rose, okay?"

"Can I help you?" the girl behind the counter smiled.

"Yeah. Can I have one red rose?" he asked her.

I could smell hot buttered popcorn coming from the kiosk next door.

"Would you like some baby's breath with that?"

"Uh... yeah. You can throw some of that in."

I squeezed his arm excitedly. "Thank you *so much,* War. I haven't had anybody give me a flower in a long time." Sean was probably the last one.

"That will be six dollars and fifty cents."

"*Six fifty?!*" I exclaimed. "For *one* rose? Man, that's expensive."

"Don't worry. You're worth it," he told me, putting his arm around me.

"*Awww,* thanks War. That's sweet."

"Here you go." The girl handed him the rose wrapped in pretty tissue paper.

"Thanks." He took it from her and presented it to me. "For my beautiful lady."

"Oh—and don't cut yourself on the thorns," she warned me. "They're sharp."

The rose was gorgeous. Huge and fully blossomed, it was a beautiful dark red color. The dainty sprigs of baby's breath set it off quite nicely.

"Thank you so much—really. I just can't believe how sweet you are. This is such a dream come true," I laughed joyfully, hugging him. He was just what I'd always wanted: a romantic, chivalrous prince. In fact, I'd never met anyone so romantic.

As we got into the car now, I gazed admiringly at the rose once more. Then I looked out the windshield at the beautiful sunset in the distance before starting the engine.

"You *are* my soul mate," I whispered, kissing him.

\* \* \*

Krisstopher called. I was in the middle of getting ready to go to the club with Jason and War. Excited, I explained all the things that God was doing in my life. I now had a spiritual gift, I told him. I could channel angels really well. Whenever I was lost, they'd tell me which way to turn. They gave me all kinds of information, helping me out whenever I needed advice. And I didn't have to be high on drugs to hear them. They were always right there, easy to be heard. They were my friends.

I mentioned that War was over, and that he and Jason and I were getting ready to go to the Metro. He was my boyfriend now, I informed him; we *were* supposed to be together after all.

He said he wanted to kill himself since I'd left. Worried, I put my hand over the receiver and told War.

"He's probably just sayin' that to get ya back," he reassured me.

Returning to our conversation, I urged him to find God for himself because it would change his life. "God will help you get over me, Krisstopher. I promise. He can straighten your whole life out and you can start all over again."

He swore at God then while snarling, "He took you away from me."

With that, I hung up the phone, angry that he'd blasphemed God. After a few moments he called back, apologizing for his behavior. He then asked to speak to War.

"Here, Krisstopher wants to talk to you," I said, handing him the phone. Puzzled, he took it from me.

"What's goin' on, dude?" Pause. "Yeah, I know. Look, I'm sorry things had to work out this way. I mean, I feel really bad and everything. Yeah, I love her. I know… she's a special lady. I'll make sure I take good care of her, okay? Don't worry. She's in good hands. Alright. See ya later, dude—and don't do anything stupid, okay?" He handed the phone back to me and I said good-bye to Krisstopher.

I hurt for him, but I knew this was the best thing for both of us. He'd never gotten this upset before. Fine time to show me how much he cared—now—when it was too late.

Jason arrived and I gave him a big hug. It was so good to see him again. We'd talked a few times since that day he left our apartment, upset over the magic journal issue. It was in the past now, and the two of us were happy to be reunited once more. "Man, Martyr. I can't believe you and War *finally* got together. You've liked him for the longest time!" he commented while War was in the bathroom, probably flossing his teeth again. (Mr. Worenshtein was a dentist. They had so much dental floss and mouthwash in their house that it was unbelievable. I never realized how much crud could collect between a person's teeth until War showed me the benefits of flossing).

"I know, Jason. I can hardly believe it myself. It's like a dream come true."

"And you haven't even been back a whole *week* yet!" he laughed. "Man, I've gotta hand it to you: when you see something you want, you don't stop at *anything* until you get it."

At the club, I danced to The Nuns of Grace while the two of them sat and watched, downing beers. I hadn't really wanted War to drink, but he said he was only having a couple. I'd originally planned on drinking as well, but I got the thought that I shouldn't—the thought that God was going to show me how to get drunk without any alcohol (which he did later as I learned to experience his presence in a deeper way). So, I just danced that night instead. Every time a good song ended and I went to sit down, War grabbed me and started kissing me so hard I could barely breathe.

"Man, you are sooo hot. I see all the guys lookin' at ya," he told me. My lips hurt, but I was truly flattered by all his affection.

He slept in Jim's room that night, and I slept in my old bedroom. Both of us were suddenly evolving into the realization that it was wrong to have sex outside of marriage. Plus, my mom just let me move back in and I didn't want to overstep my boundaries.

Before going to bed, I knelt down on the floor and prayed to God in my mind: *God, I really wish War would ask me to marry him. I love him so much.*

The next morning when I woke up, I went into Jim's room. War was just waking up, too. I climbed onto the bed. He raised up, staring into my eyes. "Ya know, Martyr, I've been thinkin'…" he said now, taking my hands in his.

"Yeah?" I asked dreamily. Perched on my knees, I was lost in his gaze.

"I've been thinkin'… and I want ya to be my wife. Will ya marry me?"

My heart skipped a beat while warm chills of excitement surged through me. It was happening—just like I'd prayed! "Yes!" I responded happily, tears in my eyes as I hugged him tightly. "God answered my prayer! I told him I wished you'd ask me to marry you, and he answered my prayer!" Just like a storybook romance. Maybe they weren't so far from reality after all.

We drove back to his house so he could break the news to his parents. He instructed me to pull over in the school parking lot across from his subdivision while he went and told them. It would just be better if he did it alone, he said. So I parked by the fence near the tennis court, listening to Elliot Spell sing of soul mates and other lives just as two big crows landed in front of my car, a beautiful omen if ever I saw one.

He returned then, climbing inside the car and presenting me with an imitation diamond ring he borrowed from his mother to seal our engagement. "I know it's not much," he apologized, "but at least it's somethin' until I can get some money together to buy one for ya. Here. Let's do it the right way this time." Slipping it on my finger, he asked once more, "Will ya marry me?"

"Yes, War. I will," I replied, elated. He had my heart, my soul... forevermore.

"I've already talked to my dad. I'm pretty sure I can start work back at my uncle's factory again. Then we can save up for an apartment and stuff. And I'm quittin' heroin for good this time. I'll get clean so I can take care of ya—so we can have a family and stuff. But I'm gonna have to start goin' to the meth clinic again."

He could do it; I knew he could. I had faith that he could kick this nasty habit once and for all.

As I stepped into his house now, his mother greeted me with a smile. "Congratulations, Paula! I'm so happy for both of you."

"Yes, congratulations," his dad chimed in.

They stood in the living room staring at me, a dazed look on their faces.

My eyes misted up with tears. "Thank you. Thank you sooo much—for the ring, too. It's beautiful. I'll take good care of it, I promise. But I just want to hug you now, Mrs. Worenshtein. Because you gave birth to War. And he's beautiful. I just love your son soooo much. Thank you for bringing him into the world—thank you *both*." I stared at Mr. Worenshtein now while still hugging his wife. Then I ran over and hugged him.

They gave War some money to take me out to eat. The two of us went to [277]Denny's again. At his recommendation, I ordered [278]country-fried steak, one of his favorite dishes. It was great. We sat next to each other in the booth, laughing, talking, sharing food, and gazing fondly at one another. It was that wonderful time when two people first fall in love and everything is a bed of roses. The snow was whiter. The sun was brighter. Nothing could have rained on our parade at that moment. Nothing.

That evening we went to the movies, seeing [279]*Bram Stoker's Dracula* at my suggestion. The whole time, I kept watching War to see if he was perceiving any of it on a spiritual level, but he appeared to be almost falling asleep during some parts, his eyelids slowly shutting. I think he was happy when it finally ended and he could go out into the lobby and have a cigarette.

Afterwards, he took me to the mall, buying two hazelnut coffees at one of the coffee shops. We walked upstairs to the food court section, where he kept looking around anxiously. He seemed really fidgety and hyperactive. I wondered if he was jonesing for some drugs. Whenever we passed by any guys, he'd look at them proudly, drawing me even closer as if to say, "This is *my* woman, and you can't have her." A couple of punk kids came up to us, passing out a flyer for some show in Imlay City. War introduced me as his *fiancée Paula*. Just the sound of it made my heart pound excitedly. I was still in awe over how fast, how perfectly, everything had happened.

The name *Martyr* was somehow losing its appeal to me; I just decided one day to start calling myself *Paula* again, and War followed suit after that. I think I realized *Martyr* was a tad bit on the sacrilegious side, as was Andy's painting on the back of my leather. War helped me take the painting off with a special dye remover.

I was trying to get in the habit of calling him *Richard*, or *Rich* now, since he wasn't a warlock. That way, I could break the previous mental/ spiritual association I'd attached to his nickname. I think he wanted it that way too, since whenever he called on the phone, he always referred to himself as *Rich*.

\* \* \*

My mom arranged for us to meet Stephen for dinner one evening. She wasn't exactly sure about our sudden engagement, especially since she knew that Rich was a heroin addict, and I tended to live my life by impulse, jumping out of one relationship right into another. I sensed she felt neither of us was mature enough to handle that kind of commitment.

"Honey, I *am* happy for you," she insisted. "But I just think it's kind of sudden. Why don't you talk to your brother about this, okay?"

"So what's this guy look like, anyway?" Stephen asked on the phone now. "Mom mentioned I should be prepared for a shock tonight." He let out a chuckle.

"He might look a little scary to you," I explained, "but you should be used to it by now—I mean, after everything you've seen *me* get into. He's got... a lot of nose rings, and earrings, and uh... some bad stuff tattooed across his knuckles. But he's a sweetheart. He's really actually very *harmless*. And I love him. He might be a little drastic... but I love him, Stephen. So be nice. Don't get all weirded out or anything, okay?"

Jim called from jail after that, and we talked for about ten minutes.

Rich came downstairs, entering the dining room. "Ya think this shirt looks oka—" He stopped in mid-sentence, kneeling down beside me on the floor by the heat vent. "Paula, honey, what's wrong? Why are ya cryin'?"

"I just got off the phone with my brother Jim," I sobbed. "I told him we were going over to Stephen's house tonight for dinner—that he wanted to meet you because you and I were getting married—and he told me that I better not marry you—that he was going to beat the crap out of me if I married you. He acted like a jealous boyfriend or something. I hate him. I freakin' *hate* him! He's hit me before, and I'm afraid!"

He stroked my hair now, kissing away my tears. Then he took me in his arms. "Paula, honey, I won't let him hurt ya—I'll protect ya. No one's gonna hurt ya. I won't let anyone hurt ya."

Relief flooded over me. I knew he meant it. Kneeling there beside me, a look of concern etched across his beautiful face as he stared lovingly into my eyes, this man was *indeed* connected to me—the only man who took pleasure in defending me, just like the night he came running to my rescue thinking Krisstopher had kicked me in the face. In his white long-sleeved dress shirt now, he looked exactly like a prince. My knight in white. I felt safe with him there—safer than I'd ever felt with anybody—except probably my father.

\* \* \*

We sat at the dinner table, an assortment of food before us. Stephen's wife, my sister-in-law, was out of town, so Stephen made the best of what was available in the cupboards: some canned pears, applesauce, bread, macaroni and cheese; and a salad he'd found in the fridge. Richard didn't seem to mind. He ate everything on his plate, even going for seconds.

"Soooo, you're going to marry my sister, huh?" Stephen asked nonchalantly. At least, he *thought* he asked nonchalantly.

"Yeah," Richard answered, putting his arm around me now. "I love her." Our eyes locked for a moment. He set his fork down and we started kissing.

"Eh hmmm," Stephen cleared his throat. "Welllll, that's just great—uh—congratulations."

I stopped suddenly, staring into space. "I just really feel something happened to Lauren. The angels are telling me something happened to her. Is she okay?"

"Well yes, as far as I know..." my mother said, giving me a strange look.

I paused, listening to the voices. "... In her childhood. Yes, something terrible happened to her in her childhood."

Lauren was my niece, Jim's daughter. Stephen gave me a bewildered stare. "What's this? What *angels?*"

"She's got this gift. She can hear spirits," Richard explained.

"Yeah, the angels talk to me. They tell me which way to go when I'm lost, and all sorts of stuff. It's a gift from God."

"I see." He was silent for a few moments. "Well, you guys want to retire to the family room?"

He and my mom cleaned off the table while Richard and I made our way down the three steps to the next level. We plopped on the couch, staring into each other's eyes.

"I love you," I told him dreamily.

"I love you too," he answered, an enraptured look on his face.

After a few minutes, Stephen and my mom joined us, sitting down in chairs while we talked a little about our plans for the future. Richard explained that he was going back to work for his uncle at the factory. We'd get some money together and then get an apartment.

"When do you guys plan on getting married, exactly?" Stephen asked him.

"Uh... we're not really sure. Probably just as soon as I can afford it. I mean, my parents will probably help and stuff. I wanna save up some money for a nicer ring for Paula."

I stared down at my ring with admiration. It fit tighter on my finger since I'd wrapped yarn around the bottom. I loved it—even more than the gold band Craig had bought me—because Richard had given it to me from his heart. He'd proposed to me, the way I'd always dreamed it should be. I never had to beg him to do it. He did it because he wanted to. That meant more to me than the biggest diamond in the world. Besides, I didn't even like diamonds. Not unless *he* liked them. Whatever he picked out was fine by me.

\* \* \*

We were in the hood of Pontiac; to some, a dangerous place. But I'd lived here before with Ryan, and it really wasn't that bad. You just had to know how to act. If you appeared scared, then someone was sure, like a dog, to sense your fear and prey upon it. But if you just went about your business with the mindset that you had a right to be in this place just as much as the next person, then it was just like any other town. Not that you should stand in the middle of a crack neighborhood and ask for trouble—unless, of course, you had no choice because you happened to *live* in the crack neighborhood.

Rich came out of the building now, motioning for me to come in. I turned off the car and followed him back inside. The clinic was small. While he went up to the nurse, who was surrounded by bulletproof glass, I took a seat in one of the beige padded chairs.

"Hi War! Nice to see you again," the nurse smiled.

"Heyyy. How's it goin'? I want ya to meet my fiancée Paula." He pointed over at me now.

I stood up for a moment and waved. "Hi, nice to meet you."

"Nice to meet you, too... Paula, is it?"

"Uh huh," I told her.

"Well, congratulations! When is the wedding?"

"Uh… we're not sure yet," Rich answered. "Probably just as soon as I get some money together."

"Great! Okay War, would you step into the office? I need to weigh you again."

"Uh, yeah. Sure."

He returned after a moment, and she handed him a very small paper cup through the opening in the glass.

"See, this is what it looks like," he said, bringing it over to show me.

I stared at the thick greenish liquid better known as *methadone,* a favorite of heroin addicts suffering from withdrawals because it provides a similar high as the drug, yet is legal. Usually the serum is mixed with orange juice to water down its bitterness, but Rich requested it full strength.

He downed the little cup now, making a funny face. "It tastes kind of gross, but ya know, I'm actually startin' to like it."

The nurse and I laughed.

"Okay, War, we'll see you soon. Take care of yourself," she smiled.

"Alright, man. You too."

* * *

"Ya don't mind if these two girls come over and get high with me, do ya?" Rich asked me now. "They're friends of mine, and I don't get to see them much."

*Yes,* I minded! Were these the *girls* that were with him back in the summer when I called and he had to let me go so quickly?

"I probably won't smoke that much weed, anyway. Just a little…"

I wished he wouldn't smoke any at all. Now that I'd quit, I didn't want to be around the stuff. And I wanted him to get off *all* drugs, not move from one dependency to another.

"No, sure, have them come over. I'd love to meet them," I lied. How could I tell him what I really felt? I didn't want to drive him away.

"Alright. Cool." He went into the kitchen then, picking up the receiver once more. "Yeah, my fiancée says it's cool. Come on over."

The girls arrived about twenty minutes later and he introduced us. For some reason, I sensed a connection existed between he and one of them, like he found her to be attractive. It was the way he looked at her every once in a while. She was pretty: a slender, hippyish girl—kind of natural looking—with long, blond hair.

"I can't believe you're getting married, Rich," her friend exclaimed now.

"Yeah, I know. It's cool though."

The angels were talking again. As I listened, making a comment about what they were saying, the girls looked perplexed. He explained to them that I heard voices, and they told me things.

"What'd you call that again, Paula?"

*"Channeling."*

"Yeah, that's it."

"I have a spiritual gift from God. I can communicate with the angelic realm."

* * *

"Paula, how would you like to go to the bible study I was telling you about and meet a man named Bill Reese? I'm sure he'd really like to meet you. He's heard a lot about you."

"Uh… I don't know, Stephen." I twisted the phone cord between my big toe as I sat on the bed in my old room. I liked sleeping in here much better than in Jim's old room. Too many memories there.

"Well, I'll be honest with you. This gift of channeling you say God gave you—it just doesn't sound to me like it's from God. It sounds *satanic*, Paula."

I felt my blood pressure rise with this last remark. How *dare* him insult my gift! "It's not satanic, Stephen! I told you, the voices help me out. Why would the Devil help me out?"

"Well, then, why did you have to call in sick to work today? You told Mom they were screaming at you and you couldn't hear the teacher, so you weren't able to take that test!"

Ticketec, where Jason worked, recently hired me. I had to take a five-day computer training course as part of my job requirement, passing a written test before going out onto the sales floor to train some more.

During the start of the class, the angels talked to me non-stop. I found it extremely hard to concentrate. On either side of me, others were busy typing away, but I hadn't even heard the instructor give any directions. Looking around nervously, I asked the angels how to get to the next computer window. Angry, demonic voices suddenly screamed at me, calling me all sorts of names as they told me I was insane. Frightened, I looked at the teacher. I could see his mouth move, but I couldn't hear a word he was saying.

"*Get away from her!*" a voice called out. Instantly, the other voices faded away. "*Those were the bad angels—the demons,*" the voice continued soothingly. "*We had to chase them away because they were interfering.*" The voices were nice again. Unfortunately, this went on the entire week: the good angels, the bad angels, the good angels, the bad angels...

Earlier that morning, I awoke with the realization that if I even attempted to take the test, I would surely flunk it. So I called into Ticketec, telling them I was sick and would have to reschedule the test. Though I hated to lie, I knew I couldn't possibly tell them I was hearing voices, lest they think I was insane and I lose my job! To my relief, they were quite sympathetic. They said it would be no problem, although I would have to complete the one-week training course again in order to take the test. Since I hadn't really understood the course to begin with, it was probably better that I go through it once more anyway.

"Paula, all I'm asking is that you come to this bible study once. If you don't like it, then you don't have to return," Stephen continued now. "I just want you to meet Bill Reese. Maybe he could help you understand this better... whether or not you do, in fact, have a gift from God. At least talk to him about it."

"I don't know..."

"Well, just think about it, okay? If you decide you want to go, then give me a call."

Later, when I spoke to Rich on the phone, I explained the whole Ticketec incident to him. I told him my brother wanted me to talk to some guy at his bible study about hearing voices. "He's trying to tell me that I don't have a gift from God. He thinks it's *satanic!*" I sputtered angrily.

"Well, why don't ya at least go and check this guy out?"

"*What?!* Are you *serious?*" I asked in disbelief. "Why are you taking *his* side? Do you think I'm nuts, too?"

"No, man, of course not. I'm just sayin' it couldn't hurt to talk to this guy."

"But it's not satanic. It's a gift from God," I protested.

"I don't know, man. Somethin' about it doesn't sound right to me, either. I'm not sayin' it's wrong. I'm just sayin' it wouldn't hurt to find out what this guy thinks."

Silence.

"Come on, Paula. Listen to your brother. He's helped ya out so far."

Well, he had a point there.

"I'll go with ya, alright?"

Why was it that I absolutely *did not* want to go to this bible study? Why did it seem the hardest thing in the world to do right now? Still, I'd force myself—for his sake. Besides, something seemed to be telling me to swallow my pride and go. "Well… alright. But only if you go with me like you said you would."

\* \* \*

It was dark when we pulled up in front of the travel lodge, but the wall lanterns outside were lit up, as were the numbers on the doors.

"What room number is it?" Rich asked.

"I don't know. I think he said room 101."

Just then, Stephen strolled down the sidewalk in his suit and long wool coat, arriving straight from work. He motioned for us to follow him, waiting while we climbed out of the car, dressed in black and wearing our leathers. I hadn't really felt like wearing mine, but Rich asked me to. He liked the way it looked on me.

"Hi Paula! Hi Richard—or is it *War?* Glad you guys could make it," my brother greeted now, shaking Rich's hand.

"Hi. Either one, I guess. Yeah, thanks for invitin' us," he replied.

Stephen opened the door marked 101 and we followed him inside. The room seemed incredibly bright—and warm. I sensed a good feeling here, though I was a little nervous when about fifteen people turned to stare at us with surprise. "Uh, this is my sister Paula—the one I told you guys about," he explained now, "and this is her fiancé Richard."

"Well, hellooo," a man called cheerily. "Come on in. Make yourselves at home." Tall and white haired, he looked to be in his early sixties, and sat behind a desk facing the others.

"Hi Paula. Hi Richard," some people greeted as we made our way over to the chairs and sat down.

"Paula, Richard... this is Bill Reese," Stephen pointed to the man behind the desk. "He's our bible study teacher."

"So nice to have you here tonight, Paula," Bill smiled. "And that goes for Richard, as well. I understand you two are engaged. Congratulations."

"Thanks."

"So tell me a little about yourself. How did you two meet?"

"Well, I met War through my friend Jamie, and it was love at first sight."

"*War?* Who's *War?*"

"Oh, that's me. My nickname is War. But my real name is Richard."

"Oh, I see. And how'd you get a name like *War,* anyway?"

"Well, my last name is Worenshtein, and my friends just started callin' me War for short."

I noticed a young girl and her brother sitting on the floor, staring at us. They looked a little frightened.

"Okay, well that explains it," Bill chuckled. "I was wondering who Paula fell in love with at first sight when she's supposed to be marrying *you!* It kind of scared me there for a minute."

Everyone laughed.

"Richard, that's quite a pair of boots you have there. Do you ride a motorcycle?"

"Nahh," he smiled, a little embarrassed.

"I *love* his boots. Aren't they cool?" I said dreamily.

Everyone laughed again.

"So anyway—go on, Paula."

"Well, like I said, I met him through my friend Jamie, and it was love at first sight." I looked at Rich now, and he smiled, gazing deep into my eyes. Then he reached for my hand, gently squeezing it. "My crystal ball and my tarot cards told me he was my soul mate. You see, I was a witch, and..." I proceeded to tell them the story while they looked on, amazed.

When I finished, Bill spoke. "Well, thank the good Lord you woke up and realized you were being deceived."

"Uh huh," "That's right," "Praise the Lord," the others agreed.

"Bill, I think Paula has some questions concerning a certain spiritual gift she has," Stephen interjected now.

"Oh?"

"Go ahead, Paula, tell him."

I was silent for a moment, feeling put on the spot.

"Yes, by all means, don't be shy. Tell me about this gift," Bill coaxed gently.

"Well, it all started when a psychic channeler came to my house. She told me she possessed this spiritual ability that she referred to as a *gift of channeling angels.* She asked the angels questions and they answered her. She said sometimes they even woke her up at three or four in the morning to show her things; they actually performed light shows in the air with stars and stuff—though I guess it got to be annoying because they wouldn't let her sleep. She asked them to stop but they wouldn't.

She told me she thought *I* had a spiritual power too, and that it might also be the gift of channeling spirits. But I had to learn how to use it, because it took practice. Like one time, she forgot to close up her lotus petal in her head after meditating, and she got into a car accident because she wasn't properly grounded. She said sometimes if she wasn't focused like that, bad things happened.

So anyways, God has given *me* this gift too. I can hear voices now, and they help me out. When I'm lost, they tell me which way to go, and it's the right way—it's really cool."

"Yeah, but tell him about how they scream at you and you get confused," Stephen prodded. "She even had to cancel a test at work because she couldn't hear what the teacher was saying."

"That was the *only* time," I protested.

"Well, Paula," Bill began, a serious look on his face, "there are nine spiritual gifts listed in the book of Corinthians. I'm afraid channeling spirits isn't one of them—*discerning of spirits* is, but that's altogether different. Now, you say these voices you hear claim to be angels. How do you know they're not demons coming to you *disguised* as angels? That's what demons are: they're fallen angels. The Bible says that [280]Satan himself comes as an *angel* of light, transforming himself into a minister of righteousness. I'm going to read you something from 1 Corinthians in the Bible, chapter 14, verses 32 and 33. Paul is speaking of spiritual gifts now, and how to use them. It reads, *'And the spirits of the prophets are subject unto the prophets,'* which means, the gift doesn't control *you—you* control *it. 'For God is not the author of confusion, but of peace, as in all churches of the saints.'*

You said yourself that the channeler couldn't control when the spirits came to her. They caused her to lose sleep and wouldn't obey her desire for them to leave. That is not something God would do, for he is a gentleman. Also, you stated that she became confused if she wasn't grounded, and got into car accidents and experienced other bad things. God would never cause her to be confused. We just read this in his word. He would never scream at you and interfere with your job, either. Therefore, these voices are not from God. I'm afraid they are demonic spirits pretending to be angels.

Angels don't act like that, Paula, and if they say anything, it lines up with God's word. In the Bible, we see angels did talk with people—but only in certain circumstances when God wanted something to be made known. Because of Jesus' death on the cross, however, we now have a direct line of communication with God, and his Holy Spirit to lead us and guide us. When we are baptized with the Holy Spirit, we learn how to discern the things of God. We can then operate in the spiritual gifts."

As I sat listening to all of this, his words cut into me like knives. Yet, it was a good pain. A pain to better me, somehow. I knew Bill was speaking the truth to me. I just knew it with all my heart. I felt Richard and I were both supposed to be here. Like God was calling us.

I'd told Richard about the night in the motel room on my way back to Michigan when I felt I should pray for him for some reason. He relayed to me that it was the same night he deliberately burned himself all over with cigarettes—the night he got really depressed and considered killing himself.

"Maybe God had you pray for me because he knew I might kill myself," he told me.

384

"Yes. I think you're right," I agreed. God *was* calling us, wasn't he? "The Devil's had a hold on you for a long time, Paula," Bill said now. "He doesn't want to let you go. That's why he's trying to deceive you with this *spiritual gift* thing, to keep you involved in witchcraft and have you think you're serving God. If you would, I'd like you and Richard to stay after the class so I can talk to you a little more about this." He pointed to another man. "Alex, will you stay as well?"

When the class ended, the four of us stayed behind, Bill and Alex reading some scriptures on the sin of witchcraft. Bill explained that all of the occult items in our homes had to go—anything connected to that world. To back it up, he showed us scriptures on [281]burning or destroying evil objects. "Whatever you have, Paula, that you've consecrated to the Devil, you must get rid of immediately. There are evil spirits associated with those objects."

I glanced down at my rings: my goddess ring on my forefinger, and my Isis ring on my middle finger. Yanking them off my hand, I went over and threw them in the garbage can by the door.

"That goes for you too, Richard. Whatever drew you into that world before, you must now leave it behind or it'll drag you back into it."

He had Alex write down some bible scriptures for us to take home and read. Then after the two of them prayed over us, Richard and I knelt down on the floor, [282]repenting of our sins, and [283]asked Jesus to become Lord and Savior of our lives.

"Now Richard, I want you to go home and help Paula get rid of all her occult stuff, okay? And Paula, I want you to do the same for Richard. Then next week, you two need to come back and get filled with the Holy Spirit, because the Devil wants you back very badly. He knows what a witness you'll be for the kingdom of God, and he'll lose many souls because of it."

# XV. ARMAGEDDON

*In the morning, I woke*
*He was gone*
*He took his black cloak*
*And moved on*
*...On the wings of a dream*

I WAS ON MY FOURTH garbage bag now.

"Are they still screaming at ya?" Richard asked.

"Yes. But they're getting farther and farther away."

"*\*%#! Don't throw that out! You \*%#! Nooooo!*" the voices screamed. I felt like Linda Blair.

"What about *this*? Do you think *this* is bad?" I asked, holding up a postcard I purchased at the occult bookstore I'd wanted to work at—the one operated by a coven of witches.

"*No, that's not bad. You can keep that,*" a voice whispered sweetly.

"Yeah, that doesn't look too good either, Paula. Ya better throw that away just to be safe," Richard advised.

"Funny, a voice just told me to keep it. I guess it *must* be bad."

After my fifth garbage bag full of stuff, I looked around. My room was practically empty except for the furniture, my keyboard, my clothes, and Zain. No wonder the Devil had witches consecrate everything. He probably figured the chances of them wanting to get rid of all their material possessions and have nothing would be nil.

I stared at Zain now on the dresser. "Oh, no! What about *Zain?* I consecrated *Zain,* too! He was my animal familiar." My heart sank then, as I thought of burning him. I couldn't do such a thing. It would kill me. Tears welled up in my eyes.

"We'll have to ask Bill. Maybe he can just exorcise him or somethin'," Rich said hopefully.

"Yeah," I brightened up. "Maybe."

I was finally finished. I stared at all the bags, amazed. "Man, I didn't realize I had so much bad stuff."

We couldn't possibly burn everything because of city ordinances, so we took the bags to a dumpster somewhere. I wasn't aware at the time that using commercial dumpsters was also illegal; but God knew my heart's intention and honored it.

"Will ya come home with me now and help me throw out *my* stuff?" Rich asked me on the way back to the house.

"Yeah, sure."

"You can spend the night. I'll call my parents and let them know."

"Alright, let me just check with my mom. I hope it's okay, because I don't want to be alone tonight. I'm scared."

\* \* \*

We sat in the basement now, going through his albums. They were the first things he felt had to go.

"Rich, look at this cover! I can't believe it!"

A big, ugly demon held a little, wimpy looking Jesus in his hands, crushing him.

"Yeah, that's pretty evil, isn't it? Alright, that goes." He threw it aside in the pile. "What do ya think about *this* one, Paula? Ya think *this* is bad?" he asked reluctantly, holding up another album.

"Yeah. Just the name sounds bad."

"No, but these guys aren't satanic," he argued. "They just sing about life and stuff."

"Let me see." I took it from him, turning it over to read the back. "Come on, Rich, look at the names of these songs. They're totally blasphemous."

I knew he liked the album a lot. That's why he didn't want to part with it.

"Yeah... you're right," he said disappointedly, tossing it with the others. He got up now, grabbing a box stashed away in the corner. "I *definitely* have to get rid of *this* stuff." Rummaging through it, he pulled out a couple of hypodermic needles, a blackened spoon, a bong, a crack pipe, and even a small bag of weed.

"Man, I'm so proud of you," I told him, giving him a hug.

"And what about this shirt? Ya think this skull shirt is bad?" he asked.

"I don't know... it looks kind of evil. I mean, skulls represent death, right?"

"Well, I don't know that that's necessarily bad."

"Yeah, but the things I wasn't sure about, I tossed anyway—just like you said, it's better to be safe. I don't know..."

"Alright. I'll get rid of it."

We took about two big bags full of his stuff to the dumpster that night. Then, exhausted, we slept downstairs on the bed; bundled up in a dozen blankets. Again, we did nothing. He just held me safe in his arms and we both fell asleep.

\* \* \*

I let out a scream and sat up in bed, bursting into tears.

Rich woke up, wrapping his arms around me. "Paula, honey, what's wrong?"

"I think I'm possessed," I sobbed. "I had this dream that I wa—I was running down the stairs at my mom's while these d—demons burst out of my stomach, screaming in tongues. Then when I woke up, I felt this heavy force above me, and this sharp pain in my—in my stomach. The demons told me, '*You're possessed. We're in you.*' And I thought of that time when they tried to climb inside my mouth. Maybe they did!" I cried harder now, shaking uncontrollably.

"Paula, honey, nooo. You're not possessed. They're lying to ya." He held me tightly, rocking me back and forth and wiping away my tears. "Look, we'll ask Bill Reese, alright? Don't worry. It was just a bad dream.

Here, let's pray, okay?" He took my hand now, and we knelt down on the bed, bowing our heads. "Jesus, help Paula. Help her not to be afraid. Please protect her and make these demons leave her *now*. Amen."

"Thank you," I sniffled.

He kissed me. "No problem. Hey, ya want some pancakes? How 'bout if I make us some pancakes?"

Pancakes normally made me nauseous. It all stemmed from the time Jim forced me to eat banana pancakes when I had the stomach flu. I told him I was sick, but he didn't listen. He made me eat them anyway, and I threw up all over the place. Ever since then, I hated most things with bananas, and I wasn't fond of pancakes, either. After about five bites, I usually started gagging. But hey, if *he* liked them, then I'd try them again.

He put on a robe, and to my surprise, some plaid bedroom slippers. Then we went upstairs, where he grabbed one of his mom's robes for me to wear. I felt so domesticated, like we'd been married for twenty years or something. It was mid-morning and his parents weren't home. They were working at the dentist office, where Mrs. Worenshtein was her husband's receptionist.

In the kitchen now, he poured a big glass of orange juice and handed it to me, then started making the batter. The sun was shining bright through the sliding glass doors next to the table, casting a warm glow on the room. I stared out into the snowy yard, daydreaming. A few minutes later, he presented me with a plate of three huge, golden pancakes. I smothered them with butter and drenched them with syrup. He sat down at the table with a stack of his own, and we ate. They were the best pancakes I'd ever tasted.

As I continued to look outside at the snow filled backyard, he suggested we collect some of the dead branches strewn about and take them back to my house. I'd expressed I needed to build Zain another tree fort like the one in his old room.

I also needed to go to the fruit market and get a few items for his new reptile diet. While in New Hampshire, he'd developed a large boil near the side of his mouth that the vet had to lance open. Every day for a little over a week, I had to squirt medicine in it with a syringe. The vet told me the boil was probably the result of a vitamin deficiency, since captive iguanas often lose many of the important nutrients and minerals found in their native environment. He gave me a comprehensive feeding schedule created by a reptile specialist, containing a breakdown of all the various foods they required as well as how often to rotate their diet.

Oh yeah! And how could I forget? We'd also found out from the vet that Zain was a *female*. He'd done some sex testing procedure, a painful looking process in which he poked open the fold in the tail with a metal tool to see if it contained testacles or not—kind of like *reptile gynecology*, I guess—and there weren't any testacles.

But I was so used to calling Zain a *he* that it was hard to relate to her as a female iguana now. It seemed to change everything completely, kind of like discovering that your good friend Jack you've hung out with for two years is really *Jackie*. Well, okay... maybe not *that* drastic.

Rich and I took showers and got dressed. Afterwards, as I stood in his brother's bedroom rummaging through my purse, he plopped down on the bed and motioned for me to sit down on the floor beneath him. "Here, let me brush your hair."

*Brush my hair?* I took a seat on the blue carpeting between his skinny legs while he gently brushed the tangles out of my long, wet hair. I thought about how different our relationship was. No one ever wanted to brush my hair before. He was just so *into* me.

He stopped, handing me the brush. "Will ya brush mine now?"

I marveled at the part of him I was coming to know: the softhearted, love starved man who craved affection. Even his hair was soft, like spun silk. I brushed the dark strands, the thin nylon bristles catching on a tangle now. "Oh, I'm sorry. Did I hurt you?"

"Nahh, it's okay. I didn't even feel it."

After a few more strokes, I stopped. "Okay, you're all set." I handed him the brush and went back to rummaging through my purse.

"Y'know, my mom was telling me I should cut my nails. She said they look horrible. What do you think?" He peered down at his fingernails.

*Oh, wow... God answered another prayer. Thank you, God.* "Uh... well, whatever you want."

Why couldn't I just tell him how I felt—that they were long and pointy and yellow and looked like something out of a horror movie? He certainly had no problem expressing his opinion to *me*. But I was just too afraid of hurting his feelings. "I mean, you could always just *trim* them a little… but whatever you want."

So one by one, the dragon lady fingernails fell in the ashtray, little yellow half-moons amidst the cigarette butts. I breathed a sigh of relief as he clipped away. It was nice to see him concerned once more with his outward appearance—not in a vain way, but just in a healthy way. I'd noticed a drastic change in him since the short time I'd stayed in New Hampshire—like he'd really gone downhill. He'd been drug-free for a while—up until the time I met him. And he must have really started using again big time after my move. Strange that personal hygiene and upkeep were usually one of the first things to go among junkies, or drug addicts, like they just didn't care about themselves anymore.

"Paula?"

"Hmmm?" I looked up at him now as he held the medium sized padlock from his choke chain between his fingers.

"I've been thinkin'… do ya want the key to this lock? I mean, it's somethin' I just don't give out to *anyone*, y'know."

*The key? The key?!!!* My heart skipped a beat, and a warm, tingly feeling washed over me. "Really? Oh, Warrr—I mean—Rich! You don't know how much this *means* to me!" I threw my arms around him, kissing him. "I've wanted the key to your heart for a long time now," I explained. "I knew from the very first time I saw that lock around your neck that it meant something spiritual." *Thank you, God. This is a dream come true.*

\* \* \*

In my [284]Omni, we sat in the parking lot of Trace Hardware, staring at each other dreamily. We were about to have my own personal key made, since Rich would also need one to open his lock if he decided to switch chains.

"I can't believe you're mine. I still can't believe it," I told him. "You're just sooo beautiful."

"I am?"

"Yeah, you are."

We kissed for a few moments, then I pulled away so we could get going. He gently pulled me back again and we kissed some more. For some reason, with the sun shining on his face and that dark hair of his and those Jewish features really standing out, he reminded me of Jesus—like I was looking into the face of Jesus or something. I didn't want to kiss him anymore then, because just for that particular moment, it weirded me out.

"Man, it's weird. You look like Jesus right now. I mean, not like you *are,* or anything. But I mean, he *was* a Jew. It's just kind of cool seeing what he might have looked like."

"Wow… really? That's cool."

We got the key made. I held it for a few moments, treasuring it. Finally, I'd opened his heart—the heart he kept barricaded with a facade of punk rock and drugs, and somehow, he'd known I would all along.

*"Y'know, I think you could be the one to help me get off heroin. I think you'd be good for me,"* his words echoed in my mind. Then I stuck the key in my pocket.

* * *

I cut open the small kiwi while he watched, smiling.

"Wow, look at the inside of it! It looks so cool," I said, carving thin slices with the knife.

"Wait until ya taste it. You're gonna love it," he told me.

We'd gone to the fruit market next to the hardware store and picked out some stuff for Zain. That's when Rich told me all about the kiwis. They were on sale, four for a dollar. He said they were great. So we bought eight: four for Zain and me, and four for him to take home with him.

"I think my dad bought a couple once. I'm pretty sure I tried them. But that was a long time ago," I said, biting into a slice after handing one to him. "Yummy. This is delicious!"

"See, I knew you'd like it," he beamed.

"Now, let's see what Zain thinks of his—I mean—*her* new concoction. I have to mix everything together into one big bunch of slop for her."

I plugged in my mom's food processor, throwing some kiwi, kale, and yellow squash into it. Then I went downstairs and grabbed a cup of Fish Chow out of the big ten-pound, stinky bag. It looked kind of like [285]Cocoa Puffs, but reeked like fish. Adding some of that to the vegetable/fruit mixture, I turned on the processor, grinding it into a puree. Afterward, we went upstairs where my mom was busy putting up a shelf for Zain. Rich helped her with it while I sorted out the tree branches we'd brought from his backyard.

We tied the branches together with strips of leather and cloth, creating an iguana jungle gym similar to the one in New Hampshire. Sitting on her hot rock now atop the shelf, Zain looked like a satisfied queen in her palace. I slid the little bowl in front of her, presenting her with the best of pudding cuisine. She stuck her nose in the dish, tasting it, then snorted in disgust, shaking her head back and forth as if to say, *"No, no, lady. You aren't pawning that slop off on me. Sorry."*

"I don't think he digs it," Rich commented.

"*She,*" I corrected. "Zain, eat the food. It's good for you. Besides, I spent a fortune on all this stuff. Fish chow isn't cheap, you know."

*"No way Jose.' Maybe the tackle and bait place has a nice return policy. You should look into it."*

"Oh well. She'll eat it if she gets hungry enough," I sighed.

\* \* \*

"Man, ya wanna hear something really tripped out? When I went to New York that last time, I met this punk kid I used to go to school with. I hadn't seen him in a really long time. He asked me to squat with him in this abandoned building he and a bunch of his friends took over, so I went with him there.

Everything was really secretive, and ya had to know someone to get in. So when we walked inside the place, I just got this really strong feeling—a *bad* feeling, y'know what I'm sayin'? The people seemed really weird actin' to me. I remember lookin' up, and seein' these long, black bags hangin' from the rafters—kind of like *body* bags or somethin'. And the place smelled really funky too, like rotten flesh. Then I glanced over at one of the guys. He had some kind of altar set up or somethin', and on top of it was a real human skull head. Just at that moment, my friend—the guy who took me there—looked at me and said, 'Saaatan, man. Do you get it?' Man, Paula, I've never been so scared in my entire life!"

"So what did you do then?" I asked excitedly.

"I said to the guy, 'Well, man, I gotta be goin' now,' —y'know, real cool and stuff, like I wasn't afraid—like I just had somewhere I had to be. Then I got the crap outta there and headed right for the police station. Now y'know, for *me* to be goin' to the police station, it's gotta be some pretty serious crap, y'know what I'm sayin'? Cuz I could get searched and stuff. But man, I knew I had to turn those guys in. That place was *evil*, man. They were into some *evil* junk. And I swear man, the whole time I walked to the police station, I felt like someone was followin' me—like these eyes were watching me. I kept lookin' back to make sure no one was behind me. I've never been so freaked out in my life!"

"Wow, Rich, that *is* scary. But I believe you. I know that there *are* people out there like that."

"Yeah, they say a certain amount of people disappear every year cuz they're sacrificed to Satan."

\* \* \*

"So then, I started playing this song. I swear, Rich, it was like someone just pressed my hands down on the keys and played it *for* me. And I sang it really *scary* too. Here, listen to it." I turned on my keyboard and began to play *Blasphemet*. Suddenly, I was pulled like a magnet into that other world again, spell bound.

*"Paula, Paula, come out and play! Come back to us, don't run away!"* it called.

The music... it sounded soooo incredibly good. It made me feel so high, like I could do *anything*—be *anyone*. It was my alter ego. A flood of familiar memories swept over me—faces, places, emotions—LOVE, LUST, FANTASY, POWER, IDENTITY *Rrrrushhh*—all at once.

*Music*. It was all I'd known since as far back as I could remember. The comfort of music. It made love to my soul—cradled it and crooned it and stroked it and wooed it and—*wouldn't let it go*. Cling, clang, *click*. Heavy chains locking in place.

"Uh... I don't think you should play that anymore, Paula. It sounds kind of evil," Rich cautioned, a worried look on his face.

"Yeahhh..." I replied distantly, taking my fingers off the keys. *Snap out of it, Paula. SNAP OUT OF IT!* "Yeah... I... guess you're right." [286]I'd been a little mouse, instantly entranced by the sound. Happy to follow it *anywhere.*

[287]THE PIED PIPER PLAYS HIS MUSIC FOR A PRICE
AND IN THE HAUNTING MELODY, LIES THE CHAIN OF HIS DEVICE

HIS GARMENT WAS ARRAYED WITH [288]TABRETS AND PIPES
O LUCIFER, THE ANGEL OF LIGHT
HOW THOU ART FALLEN
TO THE EARTH

THE PIED PIPER WITH HIS MUSIC CAST A SPELL
THE PIED PIPER LED THE CHILDREN INTO HELL

\* \* \*

I took the class over again at Ticketec, this time understanding it. I didn't try to listen to voices. Instead, I paid close attention to the teacher. During the computer training, if I got stuck on something, I silently called upon God for help; and either the teacher or someone sitting beside me assisted me, or I figured it out myself. God always provided a way.

During breaks, a couple of the girls even asked me if I wanted to go down to the cafeteria with them, so I didn't feel so alone in the big place.

When it came time to take the test, I breezed through it. I was relieved to find it was a lot easier than I'd thought. I started work immediately after that, listening in on phone calls with an experienced employee, as all new hires were required to do. The girl turned out to be a Christian, and was surprised when I started talking to her about God and Jesus after noticing a Christian T-shirt she was wearing; she'd assumed I was an unbeliever.

I told her of all the stuff I'd recently come out of: the witchcraft, drugs, scary music, etc., and she was amazed. We often prayed together in the restroom before going on our shift, or whenever I felt the Devil bearing down hard on me. It was nice having someone there who understood—someone to help me fight the spiritual battle.

I was still experiencing great demonic oppression. Sick thoughts repeatedly popped in my head all day at work. I tried putting them out of my mind while attempting to talk to customers at the same time. [289]Where on earth did these thoughts come from? Thoughts of bludgeoning people I didn't even know who walked by my cubicle, or bizarre lesbian thoughts that seemed to come from nowhere, or thoughts of spitting on God and cursing his name—or even having *sex* with God! They frightened me to death. I was beginning to wonder if I wasn't insane after all. Christian Corpse songs played over and over and over again in my mind, revering Satan and blaspheming God and Jesus. I'd close my eyes tight and force them out of my head, trying to think of another song to drown them out.

Each day after battling the forces of evil for five to eight hours at a time, I returned home mentally exhausted, my head pounding like a bass drum and my body weak as if someone had just sucked the life out of me. I'd climb in bed at three or four in the afternoon and sleep until eight or nine at night, or sometimes until I had to get up for work again the next morning.

"Paula, what's wrong?" Rich asked on the phone now.

"I can't *take* it anymore, Rich! I feel like I'm losing my mind. I just can't take it anymore. All these horrible thoughts, and voices that try and speak to me and—" I burst out crying. "I'm going to check myself into a mental institution—Clayton Valley or something. Then I can look out the window and rock back and forth in a chair all day."

"No, Paula. Don't you dare! Listen to me—you are *not* insane. Don't listen to the Devil. He's lyin' to ya. Look, I'm gonna call your brother Stephen, alright? I'm gonna have him call ya, so answer the phone when he calls, okay? Ya promise?"

"Okay," I sniffled.

I hung up the phone and sprawled out on the floor, still crying. After about five minutes, it rang again.

"Paula? What's wrong, sis? Richard just called me and told me you want to commit yourself to a mental institution."

"I can't *take* it anymore, Stephen. These sick thoughts, these voices... I feel like I'm insane."

"No, Paula. You're not insane. You're a very smart woman. The Devil is putting those thoughts in your head. He's trying to make you lose hope and give up. You're better now than you've ever been, and he knows that. He hates you, Paula. You're his worst nightmare because of your powerful testimony you can share with others. He's trying to stop you from doing that—to make you doubt yourself. If you check yourself into a mental institution, they're going to give you a bunch of drugs to sedate you so that you have no will to fight anymore. The Devil will *really* be able to take advantage of you then. Don't do that Paula, alright?"

"Alright."

"You feeling better now?"

"Yeah... thanks."

"Good. I'm glad. Are you coming to bible study on Monday?"

"Yeah. We'll be there."

"Good. I'll see you then, sis. I love you."

"I love you too. Bye." Click.

This really *was* Armageddon, wasn't it? And I really *was* that lady warrior I always wanted to be, fighting against the forces of evil. She didn't look like she was getting her butt kicked on the poster, though. She looked very confident. Very strong. Very self-assured. Would I ever look like that?

I called Rich back. "Rich? Yeah... I'm okay. Thanks a lot for calling my brother. I don't know what I would have done if you hadn't." *Thank you, God, for sending Rich.* An angel in disguise.

\* \* \*

"Rich, quick! Come here!" I stopped The Field of Fallen Angels cassette, pressing rewind.

"Huh?"

He walked briskly into the room to where I knelt down on the floor beside the jam box.

"Listen to this. What does this guy say? Wait, let me find it. Okay. Right... here." I pressed play now at the beginning of the song.

"He said '*The Shrine of Satan*,'" he stated rather matter-of-factly.

"That's what I *thought* he said!" I told him excitedly. "I've never *heard* that before—and I've listened to this tape about two thousand times. It's one of my favorites."

Of course, now that I thought about it, it was the same tape that had the background voices talking real low on a distant track, one of which said, "*Satan will give you power.*" I'd heard it one time as I was just about to fall asleep and everything was nice and quiet, like they'd purposely made it almost subliminal. I mentioned it to Jason and Krisstopher, and then just kind of blew it off, eventually forgetting all about it.

"This tape is going in the garbage—now," I said, grabbing it out of the cassette player and heading downstairs with it.

It hadn't even crossed my mind to go through my music collection the night we threw everything out. But now God was putting it on my heart to do so.

* * *

Monday night rolled around and we headed to the study.

"What are ya gettin' off here for, Paula?" Rich asked as the [290]Omni veered onto the next exit ramp.

"Oh wow! I don't know. It's like, something just turned the steering wheel! Oh no… and look at this traffic. Man, we're going to be late now."

We arrived about twenty minutes late. Bill handed us our own personal bibles that Faith Walk Ministries sponsored for us. They were crisp and new, with stiff black covers. We thanked him and sat down, trying to find the scriptures as he continued where the class had left off in the study of divine healing.

"Okay, if you'll turn to Matthew chapter 4, verse 23."

I groped blindly through the pages. The guy next to me noticed I was lost and helped me get to the gospel of Matthew. I thanked him, turning then to help Richard, but someone had already assisted him.

"Okay, we see here that Jesus went about all Galilee, teaching in their synagogues, and preaching the gospel of the kingdom, and healing all manner of sickness and all manner of disease among the people. *How many* sicknesses did he heal? *Some?*"

"Nooo, *all,*" the class answered.

"That's right. All. [291]God is no respecter of persons. He doesn't do for one what he wouldn't do for the other. Respect of persons is a sin, he says."

I marveled as we read on about people being healed of palsy and blindness, stomach disorders and blood diseases. *Wow. I never knew this stuff was in the Bible,* I thought to myself.

Somehow, [292]with each verse we read, I felt my faith growing and growing while an inner peace filled my mind like nothing I'd ever experienced before.

"Luke chapter 6, verses 17 and 18: here we read that a great multitude of people out of all Judaea and Jerusalem and Tyre and Sidon came to hear him, and to be healed of their diseases. And also they that were vexed—or tormented—with unclean spirits—or demons—and they were healed."

Hope revived when I heard this last scripture. *Those tormented with demons were healed!* And it wasn't at all like [293]*The Exorcist* or anything. No big shiny crosses pointed at people or pressed onto their foreheads while a screaming priest worked himself into a sweat for hours with no success. Jesus cast out the devils *with his word,* and the demons fell at his feet trembling. The disciples merely used *the name of Jesus* when commanding the evil spirits to depart from people, and they left. It was just as simple as that. I was overjoyed.

As the study was ending, I walked up to the desk to talk to Bill, a worried look on my face. "Bill? Can I ask you a question?"

"Why sure, Paula. Shoot away. I'm listening."

"I'm afraid. I had a dream I was running down the stairs while demons burst out of my stomach, screaming in tongues. Then when I woke up, they told me they're *in* me—that I'm *possessed.* I felt a sharp pain in my stomach and... I think I'm possessed." Tears streamed down my cheeks now as I stood trembling.

"You're not possessed, Paula. You're saved. You've given your heart to the Lord Jesus."

"But—"

"Satan is trying to scare you, Paula. The Devil knows you're about to receive the baptism of the Holy Spirit evidenced by speaking in tongues.

That's why he caused you to have that dream—to try and stop you from getting filled. If you get filled with the Holy Ghost, which is the power of God that even [294]Jesus himself had to get filled with while he was here on earth before he could start his ministry, he surely won't be able to have any power over you. The Holy Ghost will be inside you, then, and he won't be able to possess you. But you need to get filled, both you and Richard."

I sighed, relief flooding over me.

"Don't listen to the Devil. He's a liar, and the [295]father of lies, just like Jesus said he was."

Richard came up beside me now, patting me on the back. "See, I told ya he was just lyin' to ya. You're okay."

That night, after everyone left except for Alex and Dale, Bill went over the scriptures on the baptism of the Holy Spirit with Richard and me: its prophecy both in the Old and New Testaments, and its fulfillment in the book of Acts. We learned that the evidence for receiving the baptism (which is separate from water baptism) is [296]speaking in tongues: a heavenly prayer language as the Holy Spirit makes intercession to God using *our* voice but his words. This type of prayer exceeds our language, which is limited, and also bypasses our understanding, so our prayers will be pure and effective. We don't know what to pray in certain situations—especially situations we have no knowledge of unless God reveals something to us—so allowing the Holy Spirit to pray through us not only puts us in touch with God by tuning us into our spirit rather than our flesh, but also assures His perfect will is accomplished through our intercession.

This *prayer language* of tongues is different than *the gift* of tongues, because it is *us speaking to God* as opposed to *God speaking to us*. While the gift of tongues is something the Holy Spirit must initiate upon a person when he chooses to do so, and requires the gift of interpretation to translate what God is speaking through the tongues to people, the prayer language of tongues is something the born-again believer can initiate on his or her own whenever he/she so chooses, and requires no interpretation because it is meant to bypass the understanding and go straight to God.

"But what if I can't speak in tongues?" I asked, worried.

"Paula, it says right here in Luke 11:13 that if our evil—or *earthly* fathers, as the word implies in this particular passage—give good gifts unto their children, how much more will God our heavenly Father give the Holy Spirit to them that ask him? All you have to do is lift your voice after we ask in faith, believing that the Holy Spirit will honor our prayer of faith and will give you the heavenly prayer language. But God is a gentleman. He's not going to pry your mouth open for you against your will. You must show him you are willing to receive the Holy Spirit by doing your part.

Now, God is holy. [297]He says he gives his Holy Spirit to those who obey him. God cannot dwell in darkness, or sin. He's a [298]God of light and righteousness. So before he will come and dwell in your temple—or body—you must first have a clean temple—a clean conscience. Therefore, if you have any sin in you, you must confess it in order to be filled with his Holy Spirit. I'll give you a minute to think about it.

Father, we just ask that you reveal any unconfessed sin to Richard and Paula so that they can confess it and be washed clean by your precious blood. We ask this in the name of your son Jesus, our mediator. Amen. Richard, Paula... if God reveals anything to you, just confess it quietly and we'll move on."

Both of us bowed our heads now, mumbling under our breath. Next, we stood with our eyes closed and our heads directed upward, raising our hands in the air to reverence God and show our willingness to submit to his power.

"Now, I'm going to ask God to fill you with the Holy Ghost. Afterwards, Alex and Dale and I will begin speaking in tongues. I want you and Richard to open your mouths and raise your voice. Don't analyze what you are saying. Just utter the first sound that comes out and the Holy Spirit will take over from there, using your tongues. Okay?"

The prayer finished, the three of them lifted their voices, speaking in tongues. It sounded so incredible, and each one a little different. I opened my mouth then and uttered a sound. The next thing I knew, I was pouring forth a beautiful language I'd never heard before while an incredible feeling of peace washed over me. I listened to myself in awe.

"That's it, Paula. You've got it. Don't be afraid to lift your voice. A little louder now... there you go."

Richard, hearing me, suddenly got filled as well. I heard him speaking in a strange language too—different than mine—as again, each of ours varied. Yet there was nothing eerie or uncomfortable about it. The language, though unnatural, seemed so incredibly *natural*. And I knew for sure it wasn't me making it up, because I'd never been able to roll my tongue before like my friends always tried teaching me (such as in pronouncing Spanish words), and suddenly, it was rolling all by itself!

"Now, you can stop it whenever you want. Remember, *you* control it. It doesn't control *you*," Bill reminded us.

I stopped then, shutting my mouth. Richard stopped also, and then Dale and Alex.

"Praise the Lord! Thank you Father!" Bill rejoiced.

"Yes, thank you Lord," "Praise you Father," Dale and Alex added.

I was still smiling, still in awe. I turned to Richard. He had a similar look of surprise and amazement on his face.

"Remember now, you two can speak in tongues whenever you want—whether you're in the car, in the shower—whatever. Every time you do, you're strengthening your spirit, as you now have a way to walk in the spirit rather than in the flesh. You now have the power of God dwelling inside you. He'll help you to overcome, faster, the things you couldn't overcome in your own will power. Let him give you the strength to grow and mature, and live a victorious life. Congratulations! Oh! And I have a little engagement gift from my wife Kathy for you two. She sends her love." He handed us a box wrapped in pretty flowered paper.

*A gift? We don't even know the lady. Wow.*

"And here's ten dollars. I want you both to go have dessert or something—on me."

We thanked them all and headed out to the car, Richard carrying the gift-wrapped box and me sticking the ten-dollar bill in my purse. It was a chilly night. We climbed into the cold car, yet I don't remember really caring that it was cold. It seemed a nice, snuggly warm blanket, though invisible, had suddenly wrapped around me. And it had. They call him the [299]*Comforter*: the Holy Ghost. Richard unwrapped the gift, pulling out a wooden plaque containing some bible verses from 1 Corinthians chapter 13 about love: *Love is patient. Love is kind. Love is not envious, or boastful, or proud, etc., etc.* Kathy thought that since we were going to be married, it was a good passage to know.

"Well, that was nice of her," I said.

Next, he pulled out a cassette tape. "What's this? Praise and worship?" he asked, puzzled.

"Here, put it in the player, Rich," I told him, pointing to the back seat.

We drove to [300]Big Boy, where we split a [301]hot fudge ice cream cake and drank coffee. As he smoked a cigarette now, we talked about what just happened back at the travel lodge.

"I felt a warm, peaceful feeling. And then I heard myself speaking in tongues, and I couldn't believe it!" I shared with him. "What did you feel?"

"Well, I kinda got a white light in my mind, like a bright, warm light—it's kinda hard to explain."

"Oh yeah, I think I *did* kind of see something sort of flash in my mind now that you mention it."

"Hey, let's try it again," he whispered.

"Alright."

We leaned over the table close to each other and began quietly speaking in tongues.

"Wow. Cool!" I said when we stopped.

He smiled. "Yeah, that *is* pretty cool, isn't it?"

But as I looked at him now, I suddenly felt worried. And I wasn't sure why.

On the way home, we got lost. Everything seemed really different. Neither one of us could recognize any of the roads—or the town, for that matter. It seemed we'd been going round and round in circles for hours.

And then I saw them. We'd just turned right to head down a small rural road, passing a tall white building—like a house of some kind—on the corner. There on the front lawn stood three gigantic white horses, looking more like fire breathing dragons, or possessed Clydesdales. They were as tall as the building, and something about them scared me royally.

"Did you just see that?!" I asked in disbelief. "Those white horses back there? They were huuuge! Did you see how *evil* they looked?"

Was I merely seeing things? I hadn't taken acid in a long time—or any drugs, for that matter. It'd been about three months since I'd smoked pot, which incidentally, Rich informed me sounded like it had been laced with PCP—or Angel Dust—a horse tranquilizer. That explained why I'd been unable to move at times, and was losing consciousness.

"Man, what's goin' *on?* I feel like we're in some kind of *time warp* or somethin'," he remarked despairingly.

"You too? This must be Satan, then. Cuz I feel really weird right now."

"Yeah, me too."

I prayed then, for God to help us, and I finally found a road I recognized. We arrived at my mom's dazed and tired, telling her all about our strange detour. Then we shared with her the good news of our baptism in the Holy Spirit.

"Your aunt spoke in tongues before," she commented.

"Really? Which one?"

"Shirley. She was real religious for a while."

"*Awhile?* What happened?"

"I'm not sure…"

Upstairs in my room, I tried falling asleep, but I wanted Rich to hold me. "Rich, are you going to sleep soon?" I asked. He was sitting up, smoking a cigarette in the dark. I raised myself on one elbow now, noticing he was starting to nod off.

"Huh? Yeah… in a minute. Just let me finish this cigarette."

"But you're starting to fall asleep. Why don't you just put it out before you end up burning the house down?"

My mom used to constantly warn me about smoking in bed. I suddenly got a picture in my mind of Rich starting a fire while we slept and killing us all.

"I'm awake. Really. I won't fall asleep with it. I promise," he insisted, taking a drag off it.

"Alright. If you say so," I sighed, laying my head back down on the pillow and closing my eyes. Within seconds, I was fast asleep.

The next morning, I pushed back the covers to climb out of bed. A half-smoked cigarette rolled onto the mattress, the sides of the paper burnt all the way down and part of the ash still intact.

"What's this?" I asked, picking it up. "Rich, did you leave this cigarette burning last night?" I shook him.

"Hmmm?" He turned the other way, pulling the covers back over him, which was when I caught sight of the large burn hole in the electric blanket. I stared at it, anger brewing within me. How could he be so careless?

"Look at this! Do you realize you could have killed us all? You promised me you wouldn't fall asleep with a cigarette, and you did!" I shouted.

Abruptly he rose up, examining the burn hole. "I'm sorry. Geez."

"Is that all you can say?! My mom bought me this electric blanket for Christmas, and now it's ruined!"

"What do ya want me to say? Man, calm down. You're actin' like a filthy rag this morning."

*Ouch.* That hurt. He'd never called me that before. He'd never called me *any* bad names. I guess I didn't envision that true knights in shining armor did such things. A slap of reality.

We didn't say much after that, but hurriedly got ready. I was taking him to the meth clinic again.

"Look, I'm sorry," I said, turning to him once we were in the car. "I didn't mean to yell at you. It's just that... you *promised* me..."

"It's alright. I forgive you."

Was that *all* he could say after burning my blanket? "Well, shouldn't you say *you're* sorry too?"

"But I already *did*," he replied, looking at me funny. "Okay, I'm sorry *again* for burning a hole in your blanket."

Okay, so I wasn't exactly good at forgiving people—so I had to remind them of what they did over and over—probably something I picked up from my father. But still, I just felt cruddy for some reason, regardless of the whole blanket incident. Why? I didn't know. It was like Rich and I were growing apart, though how I arrived at this conclusion, I really wasn't sure. I just felt some kind of invisible space moving in between us—something that I couldn't explain, because I had no real evidence to support it. It was just a *feeling*.

\* \* \*

My mom and I sat in the living room while I stared at the TV, a horrified expression on my face. What in the world was going on? These people on the talk shows gloated at the audience, bragging about their sex changes and their homosexual lifestyles—as if it was completely normal and acceptable. Wait a minute... I remembered a time not too long ago when it *was* completely normal and acceptable in my eyes—when it was no big deal. But now, now I could see what I couldn't see before. There was an invisible war going on: the enemy taking captive the minds of people and skewing their identity into something other than the way God made them. I could discern the evil spirits at work.

Since becoming a Christian, my eyes were suddenly opened to my surroundings, like I'd been [302]asleep all my life and now I was awake. Like I'd been dead, and now I was alive. I felt like I was on drugs or something, only better. Everything was somehow different in a divine way—like Heaven touched earth and penetrated the barrier between natural and supernatural, revealing the answers to enigmas I never realized existed.

*Thank you, God. Thank you sooo much for saving me. I understand now.* [303]*I was blind, but now I see.*

\* \* \*

What had gotten into Zain? All of a sudden she was mean, constantly whipping her tail at me and arching her back whenever I got close to her. She even hissed at me recently when I reached out to pet her, jolting backward as if I burned her or something.

And she hated Rich, it seemed. Whenever Rich entered the room, she got highly upset, no matter how nice he tried to be to her. I was disappointed. I wanted the two of them to be friends. But then, I wasn't even sure if Zain was *my* friend anymore. Ever since I'd gotten into the Bible and stuff, and especially since I'd been filled with the Holy Spirit, she acted as if she couldn't stand me—like she hated to be in my presence.

\* \* \*

We rented a movie and slept on the couch bed in the family room at Rich's after an eventful day of eating at restaurants: breakfast, lunch, and dinner. It seemed we ate out a lot lately, mainly because his parents gave him money to spend on me. But I suspected it also took the place of heroin and crack for him—something to do to pass the time—another way to feed his flesh. And I supposed that went for me, as well, since I wasn't sexually active now like I used to be. Unfortunately, I'd gained a few pounds due to our daily food binges.

Earlier that day, as we'd sat in the fast food place, Rich suggested we pray over our food. I looked around nervously at all the people devouring their hamburgers, fries, and ice cream floats.

"Well... okay," I said.

He reached for my hands and we bowed our heads and prayed. Afterwards, we both took a quick glance in every direction. A few people were giving us curious stares, but oh well. We hadn't done it to be seen or anything, as God knew.

The movie we rented had a lot of swearing in it. Rich warned me it did, and man, was *he* right—every other word practically. It was the first instance, I think, when swearing actually bothered me. Really strange. As time went on in my new walk with God, I began to realize that [304]profanity is purely satanic in origin—that's why the demons always swore at me. It makes perfect sense, because if it were holy, the demons wouldn't be doing it.

Anyways, the next morning, Rich woke me up to ask if his dad could have the keys to my car. Mr. Worenshtein thought he'd let us sleep in while he took it to the repair shop and got the brakes fixed on it. They'd been squeaking for a while, and since I was driving their son back and forth to get methadone ([305]the Cavalier had long since bit the dust and Rich didn't have a license anyway), he and his wife thought I should have reliable transportation.

"But I don't have the money right now," I mumbled sleepily.

"Don't worry about the money. *They* want to pay for it. It's their way of sayin' thanks."

Later, when the brakes were ready, we took their car and met them at the shop so I could fill out the paperwork and hear all the warranty information.

"Thank you so much," I told them. "I'm very grateful for this—and I'll pay you back."

"No, don't worry about it," his dad smiled. "It's a gift."

"No, really. I'll pay you back just as soon as I get the money."

\* \* \*

"Rich, look what I found. It's my magic journal. I forgot all about this," I said, opening the thick black binder that Jason had secretly delved into the morning we got in an argument. I hadn't noticed it the night I was throwing all my occult items out. He sat beside me on the bed while I pointed to a page. "See, you're in here."

He read a little about the signs and visions of him that I received. "Man, you were into some *messed up stuff,*" he commented, turning the page. Skimming it, he turned to the next one.

"There you are again. Actually, you're in here quite a lot."

About halfway through the journal entries, we came to the incident at the cliff.

"Oh, wow, we've *got* to read this. It's about that time I was telling you when I saw your face on the wall and then you were talking to me at the cliff."

Our eyes affixed to the page now, he read it aloud. Presently, we came to a part that read:

## I THINK I SOLD MY SOUL LAST NIGHT

My face paled and I suddenly felt sick. I'd completely forgotten about the incident. Now it struck me like it never had before as I realized the consequences of my actions. I'd made a pact with the Devil. "Oh my gosh, Rich! *I think I sold my soul!*"

Terror ripped through me as a demonic voice hissed, "*That's right. You sold your soul. You're mine forever now, and there's nothing you can do about it. You're going to Hell!*"

"I can't be saved!" I cried, bursting into tears. "It's too late for me!"

"What?! No, Paula. Nooo!" Rich cradled me in his arms, kissing me on top of the head. "Look, let's call Bill Reese. Maybe he'll know what to do." He took the business card Bill had given him out of his wallet, dialing the number. "Bill? Hi, it's Wa—Richard. Good, thanks. But um, Paula's kind of upset right now. We came across this magic journal she forgot she had, and we were readin' it… then she found out she might have sold her soul. Okay, just a minute." He handed me the phone. "He wants to talk to ya."

Taking it, I briefly explained the story to Bill through sniffles.

"Paula, I want you to take that journal and *burn it,* or *get rid of it,*" he said disgustedly. "The Devil is a liar, and he's trying to scare you. You might have sold your soul, but Jesus bought it back with his blood. Your soul belongs to Jesus now. Don't fear the Devil. You're not to have the [306]spirit of fear, okay? Don't let him get a foothold in your life."

"Okay," I sighed, more relieved than I'd ever been in my whole life. [307]*Jesus bought back my soul! I'm saved! I'm going to Heaven!*

\* \* \*

"Hey Kevin! What's up?" Rich asked as we walked into The Darkroom. He wanted to get some studs for his jacket, and another cross earring; he was wearing his crosses right side up now.

"Hi War. How's it going?" Kevin greeted. He still looked the same, only a little older. Despite the outlandish and exotic clothes his store carried, he always dressed kind of mellow for the most part: in jeans, a T-shirt, and a long-sleeved plaid shirt; clothing indicative of someone no longer concerned with image—at least, as far as the *external* was concerned.

"This is my fiancée Paula."

"Hi," I smiled.

"Hi Paula. Nice to meet you." He shook my hand.

I knew he didn't remember me from before. But then, I looked a lot different now, too.

"I wanna get some small studs," Rich told him, "and that cross right there." He pointed down at the display case to the medium sized cross located next to the yellow and green nail polish and multi-colored hair dyes. I looked around at the various skulls and gargoyles hanging on the walls, and all the bondage stuff, feeling really uncomfortable. Kevin unlocked the back of the case and reached inside, pulling out the cross.

"Yeah, so I'm a *Christian* now," Rich suddenly informed him.

"Ohhh…?" He raised his eyebrows, silent for a moment. After ringing the items up and taking Rich's money, he said, "Well, I'll tell you what, War, why don't you come here for a minute? I need to talk to you."

The two of them disappeared behind the black curtain in the back where Kevin's office was located. I stood in the middle of the store and waited, anxious to go. After about five minutes, they returned.

"Alright, see ya Kevin. Take it easy."

I wondered what had gone on back there. I was afraid to ask, thinking maybe Kevin had slipped him some drugs. Just then, another one of Rich's friends, Spam, walked into the store, still sporting his green mohawk. He was the guy who made the cool medallions. He'd worked at The Darkroom for a long time; Andy and Jamie knew him too. I'd been over his apartment once with Jamie and took down his number so that when I got the money, he could make me a medallion similar to the one he made Bruce. But I never called him. I think I moved to New Hampshire shortly after that.

"Spam, man! Come outside. I wanna talk to ya for a minute."

Shrugging, he followed us out the door and onto the sidewalk as Rich grabbed my hand.

"This is my fiancée Paula."

I nodded a hello, wondering if he remembered me.

Suddenly Spam's long time punk friend and drug companion spewed forth excitedly, "Hey dude, I'm startin' to get into *Jesus* now, man. I'm a born-again Christian!"

I watched as his eyes widened in disbelief and he stood there gawking at Rich.

"And I don't do drugs or anything now, man. I'm serious! This is the best I've ever felt."

Still gawking, he shoved his hands in his pockets nervously. I could tell he was at a loss for words. "That's cool," he finally managed to get out. "I mean… you *look* like you're doin' alright."

Silence…

More silence…

He glanced quickly over at the door, planning his escape. "Well, listen dude, I'll see ya around. I've gotta get back to work."

"Yeah, alright. Good seein' ya, man. Take it easy."

\* \* \*

"But why can't ya just exorcise it?" Rich asked Bill as tears welled up in my eyes.

"I'm sorry," he replied, "but Paula has made the iguana an idol. It has a familiar spirit. God requires that all idols be destroyed."

"You mean, *kill* her? I can't *kill* her!" I protested, horrified.

He paused a moment. "Nooo, I think it'll be okay if you just give it away to someone. The pet won't have the same meaning attached to it for them as it did for you, so the spirit won't affect them in the same way. Paula, God made your iguana. Now he wants to see who you cherish more—*him,* or that animal."

My heart hurt. Zain was like my kid or something. I'd grown so attached to her. *God, this is so hard to do. This hurts me, God. You know how much I love Zain! But, I love you more… so if you require it, then I'll do it.* "Okay," I sighed. "I'll give her away."

\* \* \*

We sat in Rich's parents' car now. He'd picked me up so I could bond with Zain for a while before we said our goodbyes. I was giving her to some friends of his that lived way out in Ortonville.

I'd packed the hot rock, fluorescent light, hammock, food, calcium supplement, and feeding schedule in a box in the back; along with Zainy's friend, Mr. Crab. Unfortunately, we had to trash the big branches we collected from Rich's backyard. After they thawed out in my room, all the bugs came out to say hello, including gross little yellow inchworms—*yech!* Oh well. I would mention to Zain's new owners that all they had to do was pick some branches, preferably in the summer, or buy some from the pet store. As long as Zain had her hot rock and hammock, she could do without the tree fort for a while.

Rich turned on the heat for her and I set her on the dashboard so she'd stay warm. It was still really chilly outside; spring temperatures hadn't arrived yet. Suddenly she lunged at him, landing on his neck as if to convey one last expression of dislike.

"Aaaah! Would ya get her off me, please, so I can drive?"

"Yeah, sure. Sorry." I carefully pried her claws off of his shirt, holding her in my hands now. "Zainy, settle down! That wasn't very nice," I scolded, touching my nose to hers.

Looking her over, I began to feel very sad. Never again would I see her turquoise and green little head, or get sprayed in the face with the salt from her nostrils. Yet, the sadness I felt seemed a lighter degree than what it should have been—like again, a big blanket of comfort was wrapped around my heart, lessening the blows of life.

As we turned down a dirt road, Rich said, "Well, this is it. This is their street."

Already? It seemed we'd just left, and now I could only wish I had more time to spend with my little green friend. As if understanding she would see me no more, she suddenly huddled close to my chest, pressing her head against my cheek. *"Good-bye,"* she seemed to say, *"I'll miss you."*

Tears streamed down my face as I sobbed, "Bye, Zainy. I'm going to miss you. You be a good boy—I mean—*girl*, okay?" I kissed her on the nose as we pulled into the driveway of a little white house. Rich honked the horn and then climbed out to get the stuff in the backseat. I opened the door, wrapping my coat around her to shield her from the cold. A thin, [308]stoner looking guy with dark, shoulder length hair came out of the house to greet us. He introduced himself and we went inside where his girlfriend was waiting. After meeting her, I then recited to both of them Zain's habits and daily care regimen.

The guy took me into the back bedroom to show me where his new iguana would be staying. A dark, spacious closet was set up with long shelves perfect for her hot rock. They were elevated enough to where she wouldn't feel threatened. Above them hung a fluorescent light.

"Yeah, and in the summer, we've got a huge kiddy wading pool that we'll set up in the front yard for her. That's what we did for his other iguanas, and they loved it," the girl told me.

"So you'll take good care of him—I mean, *her*—and sprinkle the calcium supplement on her food every day?"

"Don't worry. Ron is real experienced with iguanas," she assured me. "He's already had a few of them. Zain is in good hands."

As we all stood in the room now, Zain suddenly jumped onto the shoulder of her new owner, as if realizing the time had come to part ways with me.

"Wow, look at that. She just took right to you like she's completely comfortable with this situation," I marveled. "She usually doesn't do that right off the bat."

"See, we're bonding already," he laughed.

"Bye Zainy! Zainy... bye!" I waved. But this time, she wouldn't turn her head to answer my call. She didn't belong to me anymore.

\* \* \*

Jamie phoned me one evening while Rich and I were hanging out at my mom's. The last time we'd talked was right before I left for New Hampshire. Excited to hear from her now, I shared the news of my engagement to Rich. She then relayed to me that she and Andy recently broke up. She was moving to California in a few days and wanted to say good-bye. I invited her over, and the three of us went to The Villa to grab a bite to eat.

As we sat in the booth, she filled us in on what she'd been up to since the last time we talked. I stared at her, wondering what happened. Though her unicorn horn hairdo had long since grown out, she seemed more *masculine* now, like someone gave her a massive shot of testosterone. Her arms were huge from where she'd been weight lifting, and tattooed around one of them was a picture of a bunch of girls in a circle holding hands. The first thing that came to my mind when I saw the tattoo was that she was promoting lesbianism, but I quickly cast down such an assumption. However, as she stretched back in the seat, lifting her arms over her head, I saw that her armpits were hairier than Rich's!

She expressed that she was very bitter toward men, and I wondered if it was due to her break up with Andy. He'd been her first real love, after all. It grieved me to see her react so negatively. I sensed a great hardness in her heart, a callousness I'd never detected before.

Rich and I explained how we ended up getting together to become engaged, and how we were both born-again Christians. I thought she'd be happy since she and Andy tried talking to me about Jesus that time in the car, but instead, she looked rather apathetic, changing the subject.

She mentioned then, that Jonathon was murdered about a year or so back while climbing into his friend's apartment window. Rumor had it that his friend's roommate thought he was a burglar and stabbed him to death.

Tears came to my eyes as I saw him in my mind standing by the lockers at high school, smiling at me in his long johns and sports cup, a hooked walking cane clasped in his hand; then the two of us kissing downstairs in his basement. *He's too young to die... too young to die...* "Ohhh, I wonder where he's *at* right now," I breathed fearfully.

Now that I realized the terrible truth about Hell, the loss I felt for my old punk friend was all the more greater than if I had just thought he went to another life or something. I tried blocking out the image in my mind of him screaming out in darkness, eternally separated from all living; in excruciating torment as he retained all of his senses despite not having a fleshly body to fulfill his desires anymore. Thirsty... in pain... abandoned... and fully aware of the truth he could have embraced, but yet chose to reject—to his infinite demise. As far as I knew, he never accepted Christ as his personal Savior, so there was no blood atonement for his sins.

Jamie changed the subject, then, and I tried not to dwell on it any longer, concentrating instead on what she was saying.

Finally, we finished eating and returned to the house. It was there in my mom's dining room that she suddenly asked if I'd like to see her new *nipple ring*, anxious to lift up her shirt and bare her chest to me. This seemed to confirm my earlier suspicions that cute, lovable Jamie was becoming a [309]*lesbian*. Declining, I hurriedly walked into the kitchen to escape the whole scene, suspecting her motives for showing me were far from innocent. But to my surprise and hurt, Rich took her up on the offer, going into the bathroom with her for a minute and shutting the door to *examine it*.

Jamie presently lives with her female lover, and is now a man.

* * *

Since we'd covered a number of scriptures on divine healing, Rich wanted to take a step of faith and lower his meth dosage, trusting that he would eventually be able to kick it altogether. Bill had shared something with him about [310]a lady who went over to the Far East and helped a bunch of people get off heroin by leading them to the Lord and then to the baptism of the Holy Spirit. So his parents took him to the meth clinic one afternoon like he wanted.

I left straight from work to meet them at the mall in the food court. After hugging them and giving Rich a quick kiss, I ordered something to eat and sat down. We talked for a while about my new job and how I liked it. I noticed Rich was very fidgety. He kept glancing over at the arcade where a lot of the crack addicts hung out. It made me nervous. When I finished my hamburger and fries, he grabbed his leather out of the locker and we said good-bye to his parents, heading out to my car.

On the way to my mom's, he asked me to pull over at one of the mini malls so he could buy me a purse. I told him I really didn't need a purse—I had my fringed, drawstring hippie bag already—but he insisted. So we went into one of the shops and he picked out a little beige square purse, explaining that he was going to dye it black and fix it up really cool for me. Ever since I'd seen that long table downstairs in the basement with all his leather crafts on it, I'd wished he would make me something. Now once more, my wish was coming true—yet another desire of mine that God fulfilled where he was concerned!

"Purses are a little harder than belts. I don't have the right tools to make one from scratch," he informed me after we got back in the car. "But I can at least fix this one up for ya. And no one will have one like it."

"Okay, cool. Thanks," I told him happily. Again, I marveled at how giving he was. He always made me feel so special.

As we turned into my mom's driveway, a middle-aged woman with medium length, curly blond hair pulled up alongside the garage in her red sports car.

"Who's that?" Rich asked curiously.

"Oh! It's Sandy, my brother's girlfriend. Hi Sandy!" I called as we climbed out of the car.

She shut her door and walked over to where we were standing. "Paula! Look at you, you look great! When'd you get back?"

"Thanks! I got back not too long ago. Oh—and this is my fiancé Rich. Rich, this is Sandy, Jim's girlfriend."

"*Fiancé?!*" she asked in astonishment while he shook her hand.

"Yeah. Isn't he *awesome?*" I beamed. "Hey, come on in and I'll tell you all about it."

We went inside the house now, and I explained how Rich and I met, and how we ended up getting together. As she sat at the dining room table listening, I noticed she was staring at me with an amazed look on her face. "Paula," she said once I finished, "I can't believe it. You look so light. It's like a new you."

"*Light?*" I asked, puzzled. "But I'm all dressed in black—I mean, except for this skirt."

"I don't mean your clothes, honey. I'm talking about your face. [311]Light is just *radiating* from your face!"

"Really? Wow! Well, I'm a *Christian* now."

"I know, you mentioned that. And I can really see the change in you. It's a positive one. I'm so happy that you're finally getting your life straightened out, honey."

That evening as Rich and I slept, I suddenly awoke to a heavy weight in the atmosphere above my head, like a million demons hovered over me. And they did. They started screaming at me, "*You *%#! We're going to kill you! You *%#!*"

I felt electric shocks to my spine as they attempted to pull me out of my body. "Noooo!" I winced painfully. I began praying for them, hoping they would feel bad and leave me alone. Beside me Rich slept soundly, oblivious to the attack.

"*She's trying to pray for us,*" one of the demons laughed evilly. "*You stupid *%#! You can't pray for us! We're demons!*"

The painful shocks continued while I cried out in agony, shaking Rich. No movement. "Rich, wake up. Help meeee!" I begged weakly, shaking him again.

"Huh? What's wrong?" he croaked, barely awake.

"The demons—they're trying to get me! They're trying to pull me out of my body! It hurts. It *hurts...*" I moaned.

He wrapped his arms around me, still lying down. "It's okay," he mumbled groggily. "It's okay... let's pray." When he finished, the attack ceased. "You okay now?"

"Yeah. Thanks," I sniffled, squeezing him tightly. "Goodnight."

"Goodnight, hon." He kissed me on the cheek and we fell back asleep.

"Paula? Wake up. Paula?" He was shaking me.

"Hmmm? What?" I opened my eyes to see him sitting up in bed.

"I'm really jonesing for some meth right now."

"It's in the fridge, Rich."

"I know, I know... but I don't wanna take any. I already had some earlier."

"Well, try not to think about it, then."

"I *did* try, but I can't. I feel really restless right now."

"Here, do you want to pray?"

"Yeah."

"Okay." I sat up in bed. "Father God, please help Rich to be able to go back to sleep. Please take away this feeling from him so that he doesn't have to take any more methadone tonight. In Jesus' Name. Amen."

"Thanks."

"You're welcome. Here, will you lie back down with me?"

"Yeah."

I fell asleep again. I'm not sure for how long, because Rich was shaking me once more. "Paula?"

"Yeah?"

"Will you come downstairs with me? I have to get some meth out of the fridge."

\* \* \*

"So it sounds like you were just on a lot of drugs and having some wild hallucinations," Jayna, the owner of Calaviti's Pizzeria, our old official hangout, commented now. She prepared an Italian sub while I sat in the chair next to Elyse, whom I hadn't seen in ages. I hadn't seen any of them in ages, really.

"No, no. It wasn't just the drugs though. I'm telling you, it was Satan. Sometimes I wasn't even *on* drugs, like when the cat talked to me. And this kind of weird stuff has been happening since I was a kid."

"I always found witchcraft fascinating," Elyse said, putting out her cigarette in the ashtray.

"I know you did. You used to tell me you wished you had the power to make people fall off ladders and stuff. That's why I'm telling you it's evil. Don't mess with it."

"Well, I have a book on it. Kind of. And it's more like positive magic."

"No, it's *not positive magic*. That's what they tell you to sucker you into it. The Devil knows some people aren't stupid enough to worship him knowingly. So he devised white magic, which is sugarcoated Satanism. That way, he can still be worshiped under a different guise."

"Hmmm…" Elyse stared at me now.

Jayna didn't look too convinced. She'd moved toward the window in the front of the kitchen, where she was busy spreading out some dough.

"So you're engaged to War?" Elyse asked.

"Yes," I smiled.

"And what about Krisstopher? Was he bummed?"

"Yeah. He wanted to kill himself. It scared me. But I think he's better now. He called the other day and told me he walked into a Catholic church and knelt down and prayed. He calls me every once in a while. Breaking up was the best thing for both of us, really. We were always arguing."

But now that I thought about it, Rich and I were arguing a lot lately, too. It seemed we were being pulled in different directions. [312]Both of us had areas in our lives that God was trying to weed out, and the other one impeded progress in those areas. Where I was strong, he was weak. Where he was strong, I was weak. We were at different levels in our spiritual growth, as God sought to remove the biggest obstacles that stood in the way first before working on the others.

But we were both so messed up. We'd come from similar backgrounds: sex, drugs, rebellion, inner wounds that hadn't healed, suicidal inclinations… We were emotionally needy people, and we depended upon each other way too much. Neither one of us was really whole enough to help the other. I mean, we helped each other *somewhat*—the best we knew how considering the sad fact that we needed help ourselves. It was just a weird situation.

Sometimes, he *smothered* me with affection and I didn't like it. Maybe it was just that I felt he loved my flesh more than my spirit. He didn't seem to want to discuss God as much as I did. He nodded off while I talked with him—although it was probably the meth that made him drowsy—and I felt I was missing something in our relationship. Something I missed in *every* relationship. *What was it?*

I sensed he was looking back on it all, like [313]Lot's wife—looking back on the land he left behind, plenteous with drugs and everything else capable of fulfilling any desire that might arise within him.

Sometimes, when we drove through the town of Ypsilanti, he spoke longingly about the neighborhoods where he used to score. He even took me to one of them, pulling over on the street to stare at a crack house.

"Look, that's where I used to score, man. Right there. In that white house," he whispered, mesmerized.

"Come on, Rich," I urged. "We don't need to be here. Let's go."

He drove off then, pulling back onto the main street. But he was really quiet for a while. I had a feeling he was jonesing bad—contemplating what it would be like again if he just went into that house... The temptation was great for him amidst a town full of users.

To make matters worse, his parents, especially his mom, really discouraged him since he'd become a Christian. Though they both acknowledged a great change in him and were very happy, I think they merely equated the change to him having me in his life, and not to Jesus Christ.

Once, his mother even yelled at him because he told some synagogue friends of hers we ran into at a Chinese restaurant that he was a born-again Christian, and that Jesus Christ was the Messiah.

"Don't you *ever, ever* mention the name of Jesus again around any Jews, do you understand?!" she screamed at him over the phone when he told her what he said to them. She was so loud, I could hear her from where I stood in the kitchen. Rich told me [314]she was afraid they'd be kicked out of the synagogue—looked down upon. Some Jews in the Bible feared the same thing, even though they believed Jesus was the Messiah.

So Rich *did* have it hard. At least my family never tried to discourage me from being a Christian. While my mom wasn't saved, she knew that Jesus Christ had drastically changed my life for the better. She bragged to all her friends that I was a born-again Christian. "Paula has gone from night to day. It's unbelievable what a change I see in her!" she repeatedly told them.

And thankfully, I had Stephen there for support and encouragement, which helped tremendously. I was eternally grateful for his persistence and love, even when I mocked and ridiculed him. Of course, I apologized to him for all those times I called him a *holy roller* and talked bad about him to all my friends. I hadn't been able to recognize then, that his love for me was demonstrated by his willingness to tell me the truth, regardless of how I reacted to it. His love for my soul was more important than the petty worry that he might [315]*offend* me. Instead of tickling my ears with what I wanted to hear while I went merrily on my way to Hell in a handbasket, he loved me enough to tell me what I was doing was wrong, in hopes that I would someday come to terms with this fact and cast aside my pride before it was too late.

Now, *that* was true love—the kind of love Jesus Christ was trying to show me all along: an *unconditional* love for people's souls, not a conditional emotion contingent upon one's selfish desires being met. Jesus willingly laid down his life for me on the cross so that I could be with him forever—even when I was dead in my sins and violently opposed to him. He was beckoning for me to return to him, the Shepherd and Bishop of my soul: my soul mate.

Jim seemed a little taken aback by the new me, but never really said much about it—at least, not until in later years when he mildly persecuted me. Amazingly enough, through the power of prayer, God took away all the bitterness I held in my heart for him. I was able to look at him one bright, sunny morning after newly being saved and realize I still loved him.

However, God also revealed to me that love for a person does not mean we have to subject ourselves to their continual abuse. And if they really loved *us*, they would not hurt us to begin with, because love is desiring what's best for a person—the well-being of body, soul, and spirit. In addition to loving others, we must also love ourselves enough to set limitations on those who would seek to injure or destroy us. Each one of us is God's unique masterpiece. We must seek to preserve the wonderful gift he has given us: the gift of life. We are made in his image, with the potential to carry out the divine plan he specifically has in mind for us. Therefore, if it is in our ability to do so, we must guard our hearts from the people used by Satan to hinder and abort this plan. Although we are to forgive those who have hurt us, [316]we are not obligated to remain in abusive relationships, but rather, to keep emotional and/or geographical distance from them (when possible) if they are unwilling to change. By doing this, we not only protect ourselves from further harm, but also create a safe environment where we can heal from the damage already ensued.

Moreover, I learned that contrary to what humanism teaches, though I was abused, I am not scarred for life. I have turned my life over to Jesus Christ, and his word declares that I am a [317]*new* creature—a *new* creation—and old things have passed away. [318]He heals the broken hearted and binds up their wounds. I don't have to go through life using the fact that I was abused as a crutch to keep me down. I have overcome the abuse, and the pain of it, through his healing. Yes, pain is real. But God's power is also real, and greater than any pain.

\* \* \*

"Maybe we should just forget it! This isn't working," I sobbed.
Silence.
"Look, I'm sorry. I love you, Paula. I wanna make this work," Rich told me now.
"I'm sorry too," I whispered into the receiver.
"It's the Devil. He's tryin' to break us apart."
"Yeah, I think you're right."
We'd been arguing about Hell. Bill had given us some pamphlets a friend of his printed, and one of them was all about Hell. It explained why God had to send people there, though he loved them and wanted them all to accept the sacrifice of His Son and be saved.

Rich said he didn't think a loving God would send people to a place like Hell. Somehow we got into an argument about it, and I just sensed he was starting to turn away from God and Christianity. It scared me, because God was the only thing that had changed my life. He'd brought me out of great darkness and evil. Didn't Rich understand? God was everything, and without Him, we were nothing!

"I wanna see you tonight," he told me now. "I really need to feel close to you again. Why don't you come over, okay?"

"Okay," I agreed, feeling hopeful once more. Maybe everything would be alright. Maybe we just had some things to work out. That was normal in a relationship, wasn't it? I was getting all worried for nothing.

Mrs. Worenshtein answered the door when I arrived, along with Fairy, who was even starting to like me now; probably because she no longer sensed evil spirits around me.

"Are you two going to be alright?" Mrs. Worenshtein asked, a concerned look on her face as we stood in the foyer.

"Yeah. It was just a small argument. I think it's the Devil trying to break us apart," I assured her, giving her a hug.

"Well, okay… you had me worried for a minute."

She really *was* a nice lady. And soon, she'd be my mother-in-law; kind of like a second mom. Wow. She and I were starting to bond a little, too. She was going to teach me how to sew.

"Heyyy," Rich greeted, striding into the living room and giving me a kiss.

"I guess I'll leave you two alone then, so you can work things out." She went upstairs into her bedroom and shut the door. He took me in his arms, holding me for a long time.

"I don't want to break up—I love you," I told him.

"I know you do," he said quietly, kissing me again. "Hey, ya wanna go to Bargain Village? I need to get a few shirts and stuff, and if ya see anything there ya like, I'll buy it for ya."

"Nooo, you don't have to do that. It's okay."

He wanted to drive, so we took his parents' car. He still didn't have a license, though. I cringed as he stuck the jam box between us, blaring hardcore music. It sounded horrible to me now—way *abrasive* for some reason, like a bunch of chaotic noise. I was happy when we reached the thrift store and he shut it off.

Bargain Village was huge, like a department store. Dingy fluorescent lights shown down upon racks and racks of used clothes. I couldn't wait to delve into them. I still had a little money my mom gave me while I waited for my first paycheck to come. They were holding it back because of the pay period.

Rich found a couple of white shirts and a pair of long johns. Then he spotted a thin, black leather jacket he thought would look good on me. At the time, I was wearing the gray tweed coat I'd bought right before leaving New Hampshire. Despite the fact that Rich liked my biker leather with the studs, spikes, and painted sleeves, I rarely wore it anymore.

"Here, try this on. I bet this would look great on you," he said, yanking the jacket off the hanger now. He helped me into it. "Let's see... stand back. Oh yeah, that looks great, man. You look *hot*. Check it out. Here's a mirror."

I *did* like it a lot better than my other leather, although I'd been aiming to get away from the leather look altogether—at least for that particular point in time, until I could find balance in my appearance. I just needed to make a break from the old so I didn't get sucked back into it.

"I'm gonna buy it for ya, okay?"

"No, no... I can buy it, Rich."

"No, let *me* buy it. I wanna. Alright?"

"Okay, wow. Thanks."

\* \* \*

I read the Bible every day. I couldn't get enough of it. I even read it from cover to cover, although so fast that I wasn't sure exactly what I retained of it. That was, until I started talking to people. I opened my mouth, and scriptures I forgot I read suddenly rolled off my tongue, while more flooded into my mind, waiting to be recited. I didn't have to try and memorize them or anything. They just popped up at the right time, precisely when I needed them. And they were always the ones to best fit that particular discussion. It was amazing.

Rich said he was reading his bible here and there too, like when he had to take the bus the other day for something because no one was available to drive him. Meanwhile, Bill gave him quite a few pamphlets on how to witness to Jews and prove Jesus is the Messiah. He greatly desired to share the gospel with his family members.

I'd recently met his grandparents. They lived in his subdivision, just a few houses down from him, and they were sweet old people. His grandmother was so happy to see the change in him. She didn't seem upset that I was a Gentile. She even agreed to teach me Hebrew sometime. I thought it would be neat to learn.

Before Easter, I was going to celebrate the Passover with them. At the time, I wasn't sure exactly what it was, but discovered later that it's an Old Testament feast comparable to the New Testament Communion, portraying a [319]type and shadow of Jesus Christ, the perfect paschal Lamb of atonement whose body was killed and his blood shed to protect us from the destroyer: death.

As I stated before, it was extremely difficult for Rich to believe his family would go to Hell if they didn't accept Jesus as their personal Savior. He really struggled with that a lot. We were in the car one day when he brought it up again.

He'd asked me to turn on the radio, so I skimmed the stations, stopping when I heard somebody preaching. Apparently it was a Christian radio station. Satisfied, I leaned back in the passenger seat to listen. He hurriedly reached over and turned it off. "Can we just not listen to anything right now?" he snapped.

"But I thought you wanted to hear the radio," I protested, shocked.

"Yeah, but I meant classical music or somethin'. Ya know, somethin' relaxin', with no talkin' or anything."

"But Rich, the guy's talking about the Bible and God. I thought you *liked* hearing about that stuff."

I was worried.

"I do, but just not all the time. I'm sick of hearing about all this God stuff right now."

*Sick of hearing about God?* He was *all* I wanted to hear about! If it wasn't for God, I wouldn't even be there. Rich and I wouldn't be together, and I'd probably be somewhere possessed with a demon or something. God was taking away all the darkness from me. He'd changed both our lives. How could Rich be *sick* of him?

I thought back on a previous conversation we'd had right after the two of us got saved. Bill had talked about people who come to Christ and then lose their faith and fall away, going back into the world again and forfeiting their salvation because their [320]sin separates them from God.

"I hope that doesn't happen to me," I'd told Rich shortly after that.

"Oh, I'll *never* lose my faith in God," he said confidently. "There's no way."

"Well, I *hope* I never lose mine," I said not so confidently, and with a tinge of worry in my voice.

And here we were just a short time later, talking in the car again just like then. Only, despite his recent pledge of faith, he was now telling me, in so many words, that he was *sick of God*. I felt nauseous—a terrible, awful, sinking gut feeling that something was wrong.

"But look at what God has done in our lives, Rich! How can you be sick of hearing about him?" I protested.

"I know, I know. But I just need a break for a while, that's all."

I was silent. How did he get to this point? What was going on? How had things changed so *fast?*

"Besides, I have trouble believing a loving God would send anyone to Hell. That would be a totally cruel thing to do. If he loved people so much, then he wouldn't do that."

Oh. So *that's* what was happening. He still didn't want to accept the fact that people get punished for their sins—their wickedness.

"But he [321]loved the whole world so much that he sacrificed His only Son so we could be saved. How would *you* feel if you did that and people just ignored it, like it was no big deal? He gave them a way of salvation. It's *their choice*. He has to punish them if they do whatever they want."

In actuality, people sent *themselves* to Hell.

"Well, my parents are good people. And I know a lot of good people who have really good hearts. Are you sayin' that just because they don't believe in Jesus, they're going to Hell? What about all the good Jewish people out there? You think they're going to Hell?"

I knew God loved the Jews very much, but I knew he also required that they accept Jesus as their Messiah in order to have an atonement for their sins and be saved.

"Well, I was reading in the book of Revelation the other day about Jesus saying that [322]many who say they are Jews are from the synagogue of Satan… and they're going to [323]bow their knee before him on the Day of Judgment."

"That's not true—that's a lie!" he spouted angrily. "There's no way God would do that!"

"Well, that's what it *says*," I told him quietly. I couldn't believe I knew that. I didn't even recall reading it until just then. "I mean, how do you think *I* feel? My family's not saved either, except for Stephen. But I can pray for them and witness to them. I *hope* they come to know Jesus."

"Alright, let's just not talk about this anymore, okay?"

\* \* \*

I pulled into the driveway, exhausted and starved. I'd had a busy day at work. Tickets went on sale for a major concert and the phones rang non-stop. I noticed the time now: six o'clock and Rich wasn't here yet. He said he'd be here at six to have dinner with us.

I could smell the food as I made my way into the garage and up the steps to the kitchen door. Lauren was having dinner with us too. My mom picked her up earlier that day, and she was anxious to meet my new fiancé. I'd bragged all about him to her.

"Well hello, honey. How was work?" my mom asked as I walked into the kitchen.

"Busy. Hey Lauren! How are you, hon? It's good to see you again." I gave my niece a big hug, then turned to my mom again. "Has Rich called or anything?"

"No, he hasn't. And dinner's almost ready."

"Well, maybe he'll be here anytime. He's probably just running a little late," I said hopefully, smiling at Lauren now. At twelve years of age, she was a mature girl who'd seen more than her share of heartache when it came to dysfunctional families. And still, she remained sweet and positive. "Wow, you set the table and everything. Thanks, hon."

"Yes, she's been helping me all day around the house," my mom told me, patting her on the back. "Haven't you, honey?"

"Yep," she smiled.

The phone rang. She dashed over to it, picking it up. "Aunt Paula, it's for you."

"Who is it?" I asked worriedly.

"I think it's your fiancé. His name is *Rich*, right?"

That awful, sinking gut feeling again. "Rich, where *are* you? Dinner's almost ready and we're all waiting for you."

"Sshh, I know. I'm sorry," he whispered.

"Where *are* you?" I asked again.

"I'm in Ann Arbor."

"*Ann Arbor?!* You mean, you haven't even left yet?" The feeling was growing worse. Much worse.

"Look, I got somethin' to tell ya, but I'm afraid to tell ya. I'm afraid you'll get mad at me."

"Just a minute. Let me switch phones." I set down the receiver. "Lauren, will you hang up the phone when I get upstairs?" Hurrying up the staircase now, I grabbed the other phone from off the hanging wall shelf and dragged it into the bathroom. "Okaaay! You can hang it up now!" I called down to her. Then I shut the door and sat on the soft, carpeted floor with my back against the tub. "Alright, Rich? Go ahead."

"Promise ya won't be mad?" he whispered again.

"What did you do? Why are you whispering?"

"Well, I was by myself all day today, and Satan was botherin' me really bad. I couldn't talk to ya cuz you were at work, so… I went and got some crack and smoked it."

"You *what?!*" I shouted, tears coming to my eyes.

"And I can't come over right now. I'm too high."

"Rich, how *could* you?!"

"I knew you were gonna be mad. That's why I didn't wanna tell ya."

"Why didn't you *pray?*" I asked, desperation in my voice.

"I *did* pray. I asked God to help me not to get any. And it didn't work."

427

"Well, God's not going to come down and tie your hands behind your back, Rich. *You made the choice* to get it. God's not going to force you *not* to do something. You should have done something else to get your mind off it, like read the Bible."

I felt incredibly sick. So *this* was where it had all been heading: Rich was looking for an excuse to start using again—that's why he didn't want to hear about the *going to Hell* bit. He'd started drawing away from God so he could satisfy his own selfish desires. Emotion overwhelmed me as the reality of what he'd done hit me now.

"I can't believe you, Rich!" I sobbed. "You promised me you were going to get clean. You said we were going to have a life together and you were going to take care of me. You said you were going to start working again and stuff. And now—look what you've done. It's all ruined. *Ruined!*"

I knew what I had to do. It was painfully clear to me. Almost too painful to bear. And yet, God seemed to be wrapping my heart up in that fuzzy warm blanket again, telling me that it was alright, he'd help me get through it.

"But we still *can* have a life together, Paula. I just smoked some crack, that's all," he reasoned.

That's *all?* "No, Rich. I'm afraid it's too late. You want the drugs more than you want me—*or* God. I'm afraid I'm going to have to break off the engagement… but I still want to be your friend. We just can't have a life together because you refuse to quit using drugs. There's no way."

Click. The phone went dead, and then I listened to the dial tone on the other end for a moment, staring into space with tears in my eyes. *I should call him back.* I dialed his number. It rang about four or five times, then his mom picked up. I explained to her that I just broke off the engagement and Rich hung up on me. "Is he okay?" I asked.

She told me to hold on while she checked. After a minute, I heard her scream, "*No Richard, no!*" Hurried footsteps sounded, and she picked up the phone again. "Paula, he's cutting his arm with a knife! I told him to stop, and he won't stop!"

"Let me talk to him," I told her. I wanted to feel pain for him, but all I could feel was numbness. I hoped he wouldn't do anything stupid, like actually kill himself. He told me before that when he was upset or depressed, he [324]cut or burned himself as a way of releasing the inner pain he felt. I hoped this was only the case now, and that he would stop in a minute.

"Paula, he said he doesn't want to talk to you. I think it's best if you just leave him alone right now, okay?"

"Is he going to be alright?" I asked.

"Yes, I think so. He's calmed down a bit now. But I don't think you should come over or anything. I think you should just let him be."

I finished speaking to her and hung up the phone, then burst into tears, stretching out on the floor and burying my face in the carpet. I cried for about ten minutes. Afterwards, a great peace washed over me. I said a prayer for Rich, then put the phone back on the shelf and went downstairs, explaining what happened to Lauren and my mom.

"I'm afraid you won't get to meet Rich after all," I told Lauren sadly. "I just broke off our engagement."

\* \* \*

When I walked into bible study alone the following Monday, everyone asked where Rich was. I explained to them that he'd gone back to drugs, and that I broke off our engagement. Maybe I should have called him to see if he wanted to attend the study with me, I said. But Bill told me to let him be—that if he was really searching for God and hungry for his word, he'd come back on his own. If he didn't, then I'd know he was more interested in a relationship with me rather than with God.

Just as we were getting ready to start the study, Rich walked in. My heart fluttered at the sight of him. I'd really missed him. He said hello to everyone, flashing me a quick look with those beautiful, dark eyes of his and taking an empty seat near the door. Excitement welled within me now. Maybe he was going to get serious about God after all. Maybe he was truly sorry for what he'd done. But I tried not to look at him. I wanted him to concentrate on the study and not on me.

Afterwards, as I said good-bye to everyone and made my way out to the car, he followed me.

"Heyyy," he said, just as I was ready to get in.

I turned to face him, to look into his big, sad eyes. "Hey," I said coolly.

"Can I have a hug?" He held out his arms. I hugged him stiffly, smelling his leather again, but this time, no spikes poking me in the chin like his last jacket.

"I've… gotta go now," I told him, opening the car door.

"Alright. I'll see ya around, okay?"

"Okay."

I was sad—and angry. Because I had a feeling he only came to the study to try and get *me* back, not God.

\* \* \*

I was lying in bed, trying to go to sleep, but couldn't. Thoughts of Krisstopher flooded my mind. I just got this overwhelming feeling that I should call him in the morning. It was such a strong feeling that it almost hurt.

The next day, I called as soon as I got up. "Krisstopher? It's me, Paula. Are you okay?"

"Hi, Paula! Yeah, I'm okay, why?"

"I don't know… I was just trying to go to sleep last night, and I got this overwhelming feeling that I should call you for some reason. It scared me."

"No," he laughed, "there's nothing to be afraid of. I'm just fine. But thanks for your concern."

He sounded a lot better. Happier. He told me then, as we talked some more, that he knelt down in front of the TV during a [325]Billy Graham Special the night before and gave his heart to the Lord. I was overjoyed! I filled him in on everything that had been happening with me, and how I'd broken off the engagement with Rich.

He expressed that he would like for me to start sending him the Faith Walk studies by mail so he could begin reading them. Since he didn't have a bible, I told him I'd give him Stephen's old one. I mailed the bible and the studies off to him the following afternoon.

A couple of days later, he called me as I was getting ready to go have dinner at Calaviti's. We talked all about God and the things He was doing in our lives. God had made a way for him to go to night school, and he was finally going to get his G.E.D.—something he'd wanted to do for a long time. I found myself missing him immensely, as old memories came flooding back. Now that he was drawing close to God, I was drawing close to him. In the middle of our conversation, the doorbell suddenly rang.

"Hold on for a minute, Krisstopher. Let me see who's at the door," I told him, laying the receiver on the bedroom floor and running downstairs to answer it. To my surprise, Rich stood before me.

"Heyyy, how's it goin'?" he asked.

"Hey, come on in. I was just… getting ready to go eat at Calaviti's— and Krisstopher's on the phone. Come on up to my room, if you want. I'll be done in a minute."

I hurried up the stairs ahead of him, carrying the phone out of my room and into my mom's bedroom, where I closed the door. "Krisstopher, Rich is here," I whispered.

"What's *he* doing there?" he asked, a little perturbed.

"I don't know. But he's waiting for me in the room. I'll call you back after he leaves, okay?"

"I've gotta go to school in a little while," he told me.

"Okay, well then I'll call you back tomorrow, okay? …I love you too, bye."

Rich sat on my bed now, looking around the room. "So what's up?" he asked me.

"Not much. I'm just getting ready to go to Calaviti's to get something to eat."

"Oh."

"You can come if you want," I told him, figuring he wouldn't want to. He'd probably be bored sitting there while I talked to my friends. I knew how antsy he got.

"Alright," he said. "I'll go."

For some reason, I wished he wouldn't. It seemed my heart had grown hardened toward him ever since he dumped God and let me down, too. I sensed he wasn't willing to straighten out: it was just a gut hunch the Holy Spirit was giving me, and it disappointed me. I'd seen such a positive change in him, and we'd gone through so much in such a short time. Now suddenly, he'd thrown it all away for a temporary high. I just couldn't respect that. He never talked any more about that night he stood me up for crack. I knew it would only happen again if I stayed with him; he would drag me down and impede the spiritual progress I'd made. Without God, he would not have the strength to kick his habit—and he clearly did not want God's help.

I guess a part of me had never really gotten over Krisstopher, either. We'd spent three and a half years together, and ties like that didn't break easily.

Then there was the other factor—the factor I wasn't even aware of: that I constantly depended upon someone else to make me happy or make me feel good about myself. I couldn't stand to be alone. All my life, if somebody dumped me, or I dumped him, immediately I had to have a backup relationship for a safety measure. I needed that security blanket of having someone to live for—someone who could give me a sense of self-worth and make me feel valuable... and loved. So like a spiritual whore, I jumped from one *soul mate* to another, instead of trying to find my real [326]soul mate: Jesus Christ. I searched for wholeness in broken humanity. And I never found it, because it couldn't be found.

We drove to Calaviti's, not talking much in the car. When we arrived, I introduced Rich to my friends.

"You're right," Elyse commented after she and I had gone into the back room where they kept the big dough makers, "there *is* something about him that's attractive."

"Yeah, but I broke off our engagement, Elyse," I whispered to her now. "He started the drugs again, and he doesn't want God anymore."

"You mean, you're not engaged?!"

"No. But now *Krisstopher* is a Christian. He got saved a few nights ago, and we've been talking again."

"You're *kidding,* Paula! I swear, your life is like a soap opera," she laughed, shaking her head. After a few minutes she whispered, "So who do you like better now, Rich or Krisstopher?"

"Krisstopher," I answered. Then I went back out to the counter where Rich stood talking to Jayna. We ate and hung around for a while longer, then left.

As soon as we pulled back into my mom's driveway, Rich immediately got out and headed for his car. "See ya later," he called.

This time, he didn't ask for a hug. I felt a pang of guilt mixed with longing for him. Guilt that I didn't want to be close to him anymore. And longing for the days when I was.

* * *

"Yeah, Paula? It's Rich. Listen, I wanna come over tomorrow and pick up my stuff, if that's okay. Y'know, my mom's ring, and the thermos and stuff."

"Alright. Sure. I'll be here."

"I'll probably come around twelve o'clock or so. And uh—I just thought ya might want to know that I don't believe in Jesus anymore. Yeah, my mom had a rabbi stop by the house and talk to me for a while. I think I'm gonna start getting into the Jewish religion."

I couldn't believe my ears. "How *could* you, Rich? You were saved and filled with the Holy Ghost—you spoke in tongues. How could you deny all that now?!" I listened to his pathetic excuses as horror took hold of me. Horror mixed with pure, righteous anger that he let himself believe a lie. "Well, *whatever,* Rich. I feel sorry for you then, if you let go of Jesus *that* easily."

"Oh yeah, and I've gotta confess somethin' to ya," he added. "Y'know the night we threw out all my albums and stuff in the dumpster?"

"Yeah…"

"Well, I had my dad take me to get it all back again a couple of days later."

His words stung my heart. He'd been hiding that from me all this time? I wanted to cry. But regardless, I couldn't look back. I had to keep moving forward. My life had only just begun, and I wasn't letting anyone stand in the way.

# XVI. A NEW DAY

I WAS PLAYING MY KEYBOARD when he walked in the room the next day to get his stuff. It was sitting out on the bed for him: the ring, his mom's thermos, and his blue ski vest.

"Hi. It's all right there," I told him, pointing.

He looked it over. "Uh… do you have my key?" he asked.

I froze, unable to speak. *The key. He wants the key back.* A little pang shot through my heart, piercing the numbness for a moment. "Yeah, sure," I answered, trying to sound cheerful. I got up from the chair, reaching for where it lay on the dresser. "Here you go."

"Thanks. Well… I guess that's everything."

"Yep."

We stood a few feet apart now, facing each other while I stared into his dark eyes one last time.

"I'll see ya around," he told me.

"Alright. Bye."

I sat down at my keyboard again. Abruptly, he turned and walked out of the room, heading downstairs. I could hear my mom say, "Bye Richard. I'm sorry things didn't work out." And then I heard the garage door shut and a few seconds later, the car start. Peering out the window, I watched him drive away.

\* \* \*

"Yeah, uh—Paula?" It felt good to hear his voice. "Yeah, my mom wants her money for the brakes on the car."

*Her* money? His *dad* paid for them, and he told me not to worry about it—that it was a gift! Anger seethed within me now, boiling over like molten lava. Was *this* the only reason he called? "You tell your mother she'll *have* her money—just as soon as I get paid again! I can't believe her!"

I went on to say a few more things about her being *selfish* and *money hungry*, to which he quickly rose to her defense, yelling at me for talking about his mother that way. I yelled back at him, then slammed the phone down in his ear. After standing there for a moment, wondering how someone I'd been so close to only a few weeks before could now be so spiteful, I asked God to forgive me for my outburst.

Admittedly, I'd forgotten all about the money, but what a rude way to bring it up, especially so soon after everything happened. Didn't he and his family care about anything other than material possessions? Were they only concerned about getting their stuff back once a relationship severed? It hurt me that he hadn't even bothered to ask how I was doing, or even to talk to me for a minute—after all we'd been through.

A few days later, I mailed the money to Mr. Worenshtein, with a letter thanking him once again.

* * *

I had my own place now, which I rented in exchange for tending a swimming pool thirty-five hours a week at an apartment complex. The job required cleaning the pool for about three hours with a large, vacuum-like device, and then watching to make sure the swimmers abided by the rules the rest of the day while rinsing out the filters every so often.

I'd handed in my application along with another guy who was an experienced pool cleaner, asking God to please help me get the job if he thought I could handle it. I really wanted that apartment.

"And how about *you*? Have *you* had experience cleaning pools before?" the grounds manager asked me once the other guy left.

"Uhhh… no. But I'm well-rounded. I mean, I usually adapt easily to any job."

I was hired on the spot. Besides working at the apartment complex and at Ticketec, I continued to go to Monday night bible studies, and even started attending a Tuesday night study that Stephen recommended. The study was at someone's house, and there were a lot of warm, friendly people there, along with a really nice guy teaching it who had a way of bringing the bible stories to life as he showed us how to apply them to our own personal situations. When I walked in the first night and Stephen introduced me as his sister, one of the women exclaimed excitedly, "You're the *witch!* We've been praying for you for nearly *two* years now, and here you are! God *is* a miracle worker!"

I was in awe. Needless to say, I felt greatly indebted to all of them for their petitions to God on my behalf, and made sure to thank them, marveling at the extraordinary power of prayer.

\* \* \*

Electric shocks to my spine again. Owwwww. Ahhhhhhhhhhhhh. Incredible pain. I knew I was dreaming, but I couldn't wake up. In the dream, the Devil appeared. He'd disguised himself in the form of a man, but I knew who he was, as evil permeated the air around me. I struggled to escape him—to wake out of the nightmare—but a heavy weight rendered me comatose and paralyzed. Suddenly, I got the idea to call on the name of Jesus in the dream. *"Jesus! Jesus!"*

Within seconds, the spell was broken and I was able to shake myself awake, like emerging to the surface after nearly drowning in the depths of my subconscious mind. I opened my eyes to discover the face of a demon hovering in the air about a foot away from me, made up of purple and red molecules similar to the spider image I'd seen in New Hampshire.

I scrambled to my knees, pointing right at it. [327]"In the name of Jesus Christ, I *rebuke* you!" I shouted. To my relief, it retreated backwards, vanishing into thin air.

\* \* \*

436

I remained in constant contact with Krisstopher, who planned on returning to Michigan just as soon as he earned his G.E.D. certificate and saved up enough money. He wanted to attend bible studies with me and get filled with the Holy Ghost. There was even talk of us getting back together again.

Finally one night, he called to tell me he'd bought a used car and was on his way, due to arrive within the next couple of days. Then the following night, I got another call from him. He was stranded in New York, where his car suddenly broke down from engine knock, unrepairable. Strange that it happened right after he'd *also* discerned something evil in The Field of Fallen Angels tape—something about hating God—and chucked it out the window.

I called Jason, explaining the situation to him, and he agreed to drive me to pick Krisstopher up since the [328]Omni wasn't too reliable at that point. We left late that night, arriving the following afternoon in New York at the motel where Krisstopher was staying.

After attaching the rental cap to the top of Jason's car and loading Krisstopher's stuff in it, the three of us set out for Michigan once more, happy to be together again like old times. While Jason napped in the back seat, surrounded by boxes of clothes and books, Krisstopher took over the steering wheel. We'd only been driving for about thirty minutes, however, when suddenly the car sputtered and died, leaving us stranded on the side of the highway. Apparently the head gasket blew. We all got out to survey our surroundings; and not a building in sight for miles, the two of them leaned against the car glumly as other automobiles sped past us, unconcerned with our plight.

"Don't worry, have *faith,*" I told them cheerfully. "God will help us." I prayed then, and within minutes, a police officer pulled up and asked if we wanted him to call a tow truck. The tow truck arrived about fifteen minutes later, taking us to a small town with a motel. There, Stephen wired us some money. After renting a room, we ate at [329]Pizza Hut and walked around the town, scoping out the shops.

The following afternoon, we bought three bus tickets for Michigan. The bus was due to depart in two more days, so we called the tow truck guy the next morning and arranged for him to pick us up at about two o'clock and drive us to a hotel closer to the station.

Meanwhile, we left Jason's car in the middle of an Amish farm somewhere on the outskirts of New York, where it would be safe until he could save up enough money to come back with his dad later and get it. The tow truck driver knew the Amish people, and thankfully, they agreed to keep it there for a while.

Unfortunately, the rental cap *also* remained behind, costing us about ten dollars a day though we weren't even using it. By the time Jason and his dad picked up the car and brought the cap back to Michigan, we had accrued a very steep amount in fees—much more than I had initially thought when I published the first edition of this testimony, because as I think about it, I believe Jason didn't go back for the car until nearly three months later. Doing the math on this now, it would be closer to a thousand dollars or more that we owed, which explains why my mom said they might want us to sign a lien, and why Krisstopher and I didn't have that kind of money at the time. Either way, the only thing we could do was pray.

We walked into the truck and trailer place, expecting they'd want us to sign a lien until we paid the money. The manager asked us what happened. After we expounded the whole story to him, he told us to forget it, tearing up our bill.

"*Forget it?*" we asked, dumbfounded.

"Yeah. I'm letting you off the hook. Go on, get out of here."

We thanked him profusely and left the store, rejoicing and praising God.

\* \* \*

Krisstopher got filled with the Holy Spirit, and then Bill water baptized the two of us in a pool at the travel lodge. [330]Water baptism symbolizes the inward cleansing that occurs at salvation when a person accepts Christ's sacrificial death and resurrection, and repents of sin.

Though for a while the Devil tried to detain us in some way whenever bible study rolled around—car problems, little unexpected emergencies, etc.—we remained steadfast, refusing to be discouraged. We began growing in the Lord together: attending both studies, and reading our bibles, faithfully.

However, we found ourselves growing apart as far as an intimate relationship was concerned. Although we'd even discussed marriage at one point, many factors came along to complicate matters between us, and we eventually went our separate ways. When last I knew of him, he was married and had a child. But sadly, he'd backslidden in his walk with God. I hope and pray that he returns to the knowledge of the truth that set him free so many years ago. I wish only the best for him.

Throughout the course of five years, I tried contacting War (Richard) a couple of times just to see how he was doing. I felt we parted on very bad terms, and wanted to express to him how sorry I was that things hadn't worked out between us, as well as to communicate to him that I'd grown and matured a lot in my walk with Jesus. But I always got the answering machine whenever I called his house, with his mother's voice saying no one was home. Though I hoped maybe he'd call back, he never did.

Then for a while, I forgot all about him as I pressed on in my spirituality. That's not to say I wiped out his existence, but rather, I put that part of my past behind me so I could get on with my life.

In the summer of 1997, however, I began to really wonder about him again, and to pray heavily for him, in hopes that he would come to terms with his separation from God and pursue his salvation once more.

Right before Thanksgiving that same year, Jason called me. I hadn't heard from him in a while. I'd been in the middle of reviewing my original version of this story, which I'd written shortly after I broke off the engagement. I'd just come to the part about Rich and I getting together when the phone rang and Jason's voice greeted me on the other end. It was nearly two o'clock in the morning, and I had to get up for work at six thirty. But I just felt I should answer the phone rather than let the machine get it.

As usual, Jason and I talked for about two and a half hours, primarily because we hadn't seen each other in a long time and had to catch up on things. Noticing now that it was four-thirty, I stated that I better wrap things up and get to bed, and of course, continued talking anyway. "Yeah, I was just going over my story—the part about War and me," I told him. I continued on the subject of War, expressing that I hoped he'd cleaned up his act.

"Uhh… I guess you haven't heard, then."

"Heard *what?*" Fear swept over me now.

"Well, Paula… I'm afraid I have some bad news."

"No, Jason! *Nooo…*" I whimpered.

"Yep, I'm afraid so," he sighed.

"You mean, he's… *dead?*"

He sighed again. "I didn't want to be the one to break it to you, but when you kept talking like nothing had happened, I knew you didn't know yet."

"Noooo," I sobbed, "noooo… how?" But I feared I already knew the answer to my question. It was suicide, wasn't it?

"He [331]killed himself," Jason replied regrettably. "I heard he jumped off his roof or something."

I didn't go into work that day. I spent the next few hours crying after calling Mrs. Worenshtein and confirming her son's death. I asked her if he'd jumped off the roof, and she told me she didn't want to discuss it. I knew then, that the information Jason heard was probably correct. Finally, I cried myself to sleep.

A few hours later, the phone rang, waking me out of my dreams into harsh, cold reality once more. *War's DEAD!*

Little had I known earlier that summer when I'd been praying for him, and even when I'd started running down the street after someone who resembled him shouting, "War! War!" —he'd been dead already for three months.

Apparently, he met a girl after we broke up—a junkie like him. For three years they dated off and on, scoring heroin and other drugs whenever and wherever they could. Friends of his said I wouldn't have wanted to know him then. They said he'd changed drastically for the worst.

Both he and his girlfriend Michelle were miserable. They wanted to kick the habit but felt they couldn't. So they made a pact to kill themselves through carbon monoxide poisoning, sitting in a running car parked in an enclosed garage. When Rich's parents discovered him, he was unconscious, though still alive. Michelle wasn't so fortunate. Apparently after Rich passed out, she went around to the back of the car and stuck her mouth right up to the exhaust pipe. They found her lying beneath it, dead.

Rumor has it that Rich told all his friends God gave him a second chance. He cleaned up, leaving his punk rock image behind and quitting the drugs. Someone said that he promised God that if he ever fell away again, he'd kill himself. Someone else said, though, that he was just so depressed without Michelle that he couldn't take it; I guess he kept a vigil burning by her picture at all times, even when he wasn't home.

After a year or so, he started using again. Not long after that, he attempted another suicide. His parents received a call that he was in the hospital suffering from a fractured skull and severe brain damage after falling, (or jumping), from the roof of their home. Someone took him to the hospital, though no one knows who. He was on life support for a few days, but the doctors advised that if he *did* live, he would be a vegetable for the rest of his life. So on a dismal day in May, Mr. and Mrs. Worenshtein pulled the plug on the life support system and their beautiful son died.

The sickening part of this whole story is that all of the signs and omens concerning War and his final destiny came to pass. The reason being, that once he turned back from serving Christ and joined himself to the evil world again, [332]the prince of this world, the Devil, then had full authority over his life.

*But he wasn't in witchcraft like you were, Paula!* perhaps some of you might be thinking.

Well, according to God's word, [333]REBELLION IS AS THE SIN OF WITCHCRAFT. There's really no distinction between the two. If you are not with God, then you are with the Devil. If you are not *for* God, then you are *against* God, and he cannot have a place in your life because you have separated yourself from his fellowship, from his blessings, and from his protection.

I urge you to consider this fact: [334]the main principle in Satanism as acknowledged by Anton LaVey, founder of the Church of Satan in California, is the doctrine of *free will;* first expressed by Aleister Crowley, a renowned Satanist and black magician as well as a freemason and member of the Golden Dawn, when he stated, [335]"DO WHAT *THOU WILT* IS THE WHOLE OF THE LAW." In simpler terms, without the

Old English articles, it means: "DO WHAT *YOU WILL* IS THE WHOLE [OR ONLY] LAW." In other words, *you* make your own law. The only law that exists is the law *you* decide for yourself.

It is certainly true that we all, as God's creation, are given a free will choice to make our own decisions. A loving Creator would have it no other way, because as most of you know, you cannot force another person to love you. Neither does God force us to love or obey him. It has to be our conscious, free will choice. However, when we seek to do our own will rather than God's will, we become instruments of *self*ishness, no matter how we try to justify it!

Satanists have argued that doing what one wills originally was designed with the *good of all* in mind. How can this be, when one is serving *self?* How can one have the good of *all* in mind when he is only focused on *one* person: himself? And how can he fulfill a *higher purpose* when he is concentrated on one goal: feeding the desires of his own carnality, or *lower* self—when he is merely focused on what *he wills* to do and not on what might be better for God and others to have him to do?

Satan, before his fall from heaven, made these [336]five statements: "I WILL *ascend* into heaven. I WILL exalt my throne *above* the stars of God. I WILL sit *also* upon the mount of the congregation, in the sides of the north. I WILL *ascend above* the heights of the clouds. I WILL be *like* the most High," to which God cast him down for his rebellion and pride, because he went about to do *his own will,* and to try and be, as the fifth statement declares, *like the most High:* God.

Isn't that just what New Age teaches: *I* am God? *I* have the power? *I* can do it all myself—do whatever *I* want—do it *my* way?

So you see, it doesn't take a bubbling cauldron, magic spell, look into one's crystal ball, or drink of blood to be a witch or Satanist. [337]All it requires is selfishness on your part to do whatever your heart desires, no matter what God says about it, no matter what the cost.

Jesus, when here on earth, declared: "For I came down from heaven, not to do mine own will, but the will of him that sent me." (John 6:38) So while the angel Lucifer chose to live for himself, Jesus the Son chose to live for the Father God.

Well, as this story nears an end, I want to assure you that God worked all things out for my good. Today, I am happily married to a handsome, wonderful, spiritual man God chose for me—who is also my partner in ministry.

But at the time of this testimony's original publication, I deeply mourned the loss of War, and wondered time and again what would have happened had he chosen a different path. Would we still be together? I don't know.

Or... would my future have included Krisstopher, had we both grown more in spiritual things, healed from our brokenness, and quit seeking fulfillment in everything else and everyone else but God? Again, I don't know.

What I do know is this: until I learned to make Jesus Christ my love above all others, I went from one relationship to the next, seeking something that could never be found. In the process, I hurt a lot of people along the way, and it saddens me to think of them now (like Craig, for instance, who really deserved better than the person I was at that time). Only when I turned away from the spirit of whoredoms and returned to my Love of Loves—the One I'd been created for—did I discover contentment.

So for those of you searching for true love, it is found first and foremost in the God/man Jesus Christ, who conquered death so we could live forever with him. He defied time and space to seek after us, becoming one of us, to prove his love for us. He desires for each and every one of us to live eternally with him, in perfect marital bliss.

No other love compares to his love, because he loves us perfectly as no other person can, and he completes us as no other soul can. Without him, we are missing the piece that makes us whole. Each of us has a void in our spirit—an emptiness that will never be satisfied until we fill it with him. We can try filling it with the temporary pleasures of this life, but soon, we find we are again dissatisfied; and so once more, seek comfort in a lesser lover. While people and things can give us momentary happiness, they will never give us the inner peace we are truly longing for—a peace that surpasses all understanding. Yeshua/Jesus is that peace. He is the answer to our deepest heart's cry. He is the Eternal Flame to which we are drawn, if only we will allow ourselves to be drawn!

> The LORD hath appeared of old unto me, saying, Yea, I have loved thee with an everlasting love: therefore with lovingkindness have I drawn thee. (Jeremiah 31:3)

> And I, if I be lifted up from the earth, will draw all men unto me. (John 12:32)

As War can now testify, our life here on earth is but a vapor, and what matters most is not the here and now, but the ever after. The Bible admonishes,

> For what is a man profited, if he shall gain the whole world, and lose his own soul? or what shall a man give in exchange for his soul? (Matthew 16:26)

We only have one life to live, and we must live it wisely. There will be no second, third, fourth, or ninth chance—no unresolved karma to perfect in a reincarnated body, as Satan would have us believe. We are accountable right here, right now, and the decisions we make in this life will affect our eternity. Scripture warns:

> … it is appointed unto men *once* to die, but after this the judgment… (Hebrews 9:27)

When we die, we will go to either Heaven or Hell. And for those of us who go to Heaven, Christ tells us in his Word that we will not marry nor be given in marriage: but will be like the angels in Heaven (Mark 12:25). We will not have an eternal soulmate, except for One—the Lover of Our Soul—the Great I Am: who was, is, and always will be. He is Elohim, expressed in three persons: God the Father, God the Son, and God the Holy Spirit. To him, and him alone, will we be married.

> Let us be glad and rejoice, and give honour to him: for the marriage of the Lamb is come, and his wife hath made herself ready.

> And to her was granted that she should be arrayed in fine linen, clean and white: for the fine linen is the righteousness of saints.

> And he saith unto me, Write, Blessed are they which are called unto the marriage supper of the Lamb… (Revelation 19:7-9)

If you would like to partake in the marriage supper of the Lamb Jesus by accepting him into your life today, say this simple heartfelt prayer, and he will gladly embrace you with open arms; revealing his great love to you:

> **Father God, I have sinned against you. Please forgive me for all of my sins. I believe Jesus Christ is God the Son, who came in the flesh to die for my sins and wash them away with his blood. I believe he resurrected, and lives forevermore. I want him to be Lord and Savior of my life. Come into my heart, Jesus. Satisfy the deepest longings of my soul. Help me live for you and not for myself. Amen.**

… I found him whom my soul loveth:
I held him, and would not let him go…
(Song of Solomon 3:4)

# SHADOWPLAY

O, the inner beauty
Every flower meant for me
An offering to a wise old tree
I am One, the Force is me

Mother Nature, hear my spell
Diana, bless me very well
Cast the circle, close my eyes
Clutch the crystal, visualize

Take me to another life
Where is my soul mate, Prince of Knives?
A karmic bond we must fulfill
According to our own freewill

O, the tear-stained beauty
The silence of a cemetery
But yet, I feel them close to me
Like Yin and Yang, so mote it be!

The raven sings, he calls your name
I see you in the windowpane
Is this the Universal Scheme
Qabalistic path, or distant dream?

The Sun, the Moon, the Star of hope
The mixed-up World, kaleidoscope
Love your brother and kill your mind
Here are the blind, leading the blind

Where is the Light? It disappeared
Nothing but pain and emptiness here
Deities, please, why do you hide?
The runes say "Joy—commit suicide"

I turned to the East, I summoned the West
The Bible, my last hope of rest
No more past life visions inside the glass
Just pictures of demons surrounding me fast

Where's psychic protection?
It seems like damnation
This isn't White Magic
It's the glamour of Satan

And woe! To acknowledge I've stood on a cliff
A footstep away from the Blackest Abyss
And O! To receive the real gift of sight
To finally distinguish the Dark from the Light

All the works of diviners, a secret delusion
Just works of the One God, in blind confusion
Like calling on *Elohim* when casting a spell
My child, you cannot mix Heaven and Hell

The true mystery lies in the Doctrine of Purity
Not tarots and runes, which are Evil's Obscurity
Within us the power of God is the key:
The Holy Spirit which helps us to finally see

O, for the lost soul
Of Aleister Crowley
And where is your wisdom
O, Golden Dawn?
Aren't you just really the Devil's pawn?

Yes, I know I have finally discovered the Light
For, the Devil's disciples now put up a fight
The chains that once bound me
Now loose from around me
And spirits, once worshiped
Now the cause of my plight

Poor Lucifer, you've lost your hold on me
Through the blood of Christ Jesus, I'm finally free
Salvation for eternity
Salvation from insanity

You see, I've been to Hell and back
No sphere can win the Narrow Path
For O, the Devil is so unkind
I thought myself wise, I was losing my mind

In the Shadows, a child can play
And cast a glance at Danger's Way
But woe! To the child now of age
Who pays no heed to the Father's adage

For, a slap on the wrist is no longer the hire
His punishment lies in the Lake of Fire

# SCRIPTURES FORBIDDING THE OCCULT AND WITCHCRAFT

*Old Testament:*

Thou shalt not suffer a witch to live. (Exodus 22:18)

Note: This was an Old Testament command to take the life of a witch so that his/her evil would not spread to the sanctified nation of Israel, who well knew the commandments of their God, being taught them from a very young age. Now, however, we are under the grace of Jesus Christ, and we do not *kill* witches; we are to let God deal with them. However, in a spiritual sense, if they do not repent of their sins and accept Jesus Christ as their Savior, they will not be *suffered to live*, but will spend eternity in Hell.

There shall not be found among you any one that maketh his son or his daughter to pass through the fire [as a sacrifice to other gods], or that useth divination, or an observer of times [astrology], or an enchanter, or a witch,

Or a charmer, or a consulter [channeler, medium] with familiar spirits [demons], or a wizard, or a necromancer [one who contacts and/or has relations with the dead].

For all that do these things are an abomination unto the Lord: and because of these abominations the Lord thy God doth drive them [the pagans] out from before thee. (Deuteronomy 18:10-12)

And the soul that turneth after such as have familiar spirits, and after wizards, to go a whoring after them, I will even set my face against that soul, and will cut him off from among his people. (Leviticus 20:6)

A man also or a woman that hath a familiar spirit, or that is a wizard, shall surely be put to death: they shall stone them with stones: their blood shall be upon them. (Leviticus 20:27)

Note: Another Old Testament command that is no longer in effect in the physical sense of death. Again, God is the one who inflicts the punishment—not man. (See first scripture under this section for more detail).

So Saul died for his transgression which he committed against the Lord, even against the word of the Lord, which he kept not, and also for asking counsel of one that had a familiar spirit, to enquire of it;

And enquired not of the Lord; therefore he slew him, and turned the kingdom unto David the son of Jesse. (1 Chronicles 10:13,14)

Stand now with thine enchantments, and with the multitude of thy sorceries, wherein thou hast laboured from thy youth; if so be thou shalt be able to profit, if so be thou mayest prevail.

Thou art wearied in the multitude of thy counsels. Let now the astrologers, the stargazers, the monthly prognosticators, stand up, and save thee from these things that shall come upon thee.

Behold, they shall be as stubble; the fire shall burn them; they shall not deliver themselves from the power of the flame... (Isaiah 47:12-14)

For thus sayeth the Lord of hosts, the God of Israel; Let not your prophets and your diviners, that be in the midst of you, deceive you, neither hearken to your dreams which ye cause to be dreamed.

For they prophesy falsely unto you in my name: I have not sent them, saith the Lord. (Jeremiah 29:8,9)

The children gather wood, and the fathers kindle the fire, and the women knead their dough, to make cakes to the queen of heaven [goddess], and to pour out drink offerings unto other gods, that they may provoke me to anger. (Jeremiah 7:18)

But they are altogether brutish and foolish: the stock [tree—when worshiped, sticks, wooden idol] is a doctrine of vanities. (Jeremiah 10:8)

Because your fathers have forsaken me, saith the Lord, and have walked after other gods, and have served them, and have worshiped them, and have forsaken me, and have not kept my law;

And ye have done worse than your fathers... (Jeremiah 16:11,12)

Shall a man make gods unto himself, and they are no gods? (Jeremiah 16:20)

Therefore hearken not ye to your prophets, nor to your diviners, nor to your dreamers, nor to your enchanters, nor to your sorcerers... (Jeremiah 27:9)

But they hearkened not, nor inclined their ear to turn from their wickedness, to burn no incense unto other gods. (Jeremiah 44:5)

But we will certainly do whatsoever goeth forth out of our own mouth, to burn incense unto the queen of heaven, and to pour out drink offerings unto her, as we have done, we, and our fathers, our kings, our princes, in the cities of Judah, and in the streets of Jerusalem... (Jeremiah 44:17)

And Ahaziah fell down through a lattice in his upper chamber that was in Samaria, and was sick: and he sent messengers, and said unto them, Go, enquire of Baal-ze-bub [Beelzebub, or Satan] the god of Ekron whether I shall recover of this disease. And he said unto him, Thus saith the Lord,

Forasmuch as thou hast sent messengers to enquire of Baal-ze-bub the god of Ekron, is it not because there is no God in Israel to enquire of his word? therefore thou shalt not come down off that bed on which thou art gone up, but shalt surely die.

So he died according to the word of the Lord which Elijah had spoken ... (2 Kings 1:2,16,17)

Their sorrows shall be multiplied that hasten after another god: their drink offerings of blood will I not offer, nor take up their names into my lips. (Psalm 16:4)

Their idols are silver and gold, the work of men's hands.

They have mouths, but they speak not: eyes have they, but they see not:

They have ears, but they hear not: noses have they, but they smell not:

They have hands, but they handle not: feet have they, but they walk not: neither speak they through their throat.

They that make them are like unto them; so is every one that trusteth in them. (Psalm 115:4-8)

They made a calf in Horeb, and worshiped the molten image.

Thus they changed their glory [God] into the similitude of an ox that eateth grass.

They forgot their saviour, which had done great things in Egypt. (Psalm 106:19-21)

Then the lords of the Philistines gathered them together for to offer a great sacrifice unto Dagon their god, and to rejoice: for they said, Our god hath delivered Samson our enemy into our hand. (Judges 16:23)

When the Philistines took the ark of God, they brought it into the house of Dagon, and set it by Dagon.

And when they of Ashdod arose early on the morrow, behold, Dagon was fallen upon his face to the earth before the ark of the Lord. And they took Dagon, and set him in his place again.

And when they arose early on the morrow morning, behold, Dagon was fallen upon his face to the ground before the ark of the Lord; and the head of Dagon and both the palms of his hands were cut off upon the threshold; only the stump of Dagon was left to him.

Therefore neither the priests of Dagon, nor any that come into Dagon's house, tread on the threshold of Dagon in Ashdod unto this day. (1 Samuel 5:2-5)

For rebellion is as the sin of witchcraft, and stubbornness is as iniquity and idolatry. (1 Samuel 15:23)

*New Testament:*

And when they had gone through the isle unto Paphos, they found a certain sorcerer, a false prophet, a Jew, whose name was Bar-Jesus [not to be confused with Jesus]:

Which was with the deputy of the country, Sergius Paulus, a prudent man; who called for Barnabus and Saul, and desired to hear the word of God.

But Elymas the sorcerer (for so is his name by interpretation) withstood them, seeking to turn away the deputy from the faith. Then Saul, (who also is called Paul,) filled with the Holy Ghost, set his eyes on him,

And said, O full of all subtilty and all mischief, thou child of the devil, thou enemy of all righteousness, wilt thou not cease to pervert the right ways of the Lord?

And now, behold, the hand of the Lord is upon thee, and thou shalt be blind, not seeing the sun for a season. And immediately there fell upon him a mist, and a darkness; and he went about seeking some to lead him by the hand. (Acts 13:6-11)

And upon a set day Herod, arrayed in royal apparel, sat upon his throne, and made an oration unto them.

And the people gave a shout, saying, It is the voice of a god, and not of a man.

And immediately the angel of the Lord smote him, because he gave not God the glory: and he was eaten of worms, and gave up the ghost [died]. (Acts 12:21-23)

Then certain of the vagabond Jews, exorcists, took upon them to call over them which had evil spirits the name of the Lord Jesus, saying, We adjure you by Jesus whom Paul preacheth. And the evil spirit answered and said, Jesus I know, and Paul I know; but who are ye?

And the man in whom the evil spirit was leaped on them, and overcame them, and prevailed against them, so that they fled out of that house naked and wounded. (Acts 19:13,15,16)

Moreover ye see and hear, that not alone at Ephesus, but almost throughout all Asia, this Paul hath persuaded and turned away much people, saying that they be no gods, which are made with hands:

So that not only this our craft is in danger to be set at nought; but also that the temple of the great goddess Diana should be despised, and her magnificence should be destroyed, whom all Asia and the world worshippeth. (Acts 19:26,27)

And it came to pass, as we went to prayer, a certain damsel possessed with a spirit of divination met us, which brought her masters much gain by soothsaying.

The same followed Paul and us, and cried, saying, These men are the servants of the most high God, which shew unto us the way of salvation.

And this did she many days. But Paul, being grieved, turned and said to the spirit, I command thee in the name of Jesus Christ to come out of her. And he came out the same hour.

And when her masters saw that the hope of their gains was gone, they caught Paul and Silas, and drew them into the marketplace unto the rulers. (Acts 16:16-19)

# COMMANDS TO DESTROY ALL IDOLS/OCCULT PARAPHERNALIA

*Old Testament:*

The graven images of their gods shall ye burn with fire: thou shalt not desire the silver or gold that is on them, nor take it unto thee, lest thou be snared therein: for it is an abomination to the LORD thy God.

Neither shalt thou bring an abomination into thine house, lest thou be a cursed thing like it: but thou shalt utterly detest it, and thou shalt utterly abhor it; for it is a cursed thing. (Deuteronomy 7:25,26)

But thus shall ye deal with them; ye shall destroy their altars, and break down their images, and cut down their groves, and burn their graven images with fire. (Deuteronomy 7:5)

And I took your sin, the calf which ye had made, and burnt it with fire, and stamped it, and ground it very small, even until it was as small as dust: and I cast the dust thereof into the brook that descended out of the mount. (Deuteronomy 9:21)

And he brought out the grove from the house of the Lord, without Jerusalem, unto the brook Kidron, and stamped it small to powder, and cast the powder thereof upon the graves of the children of the people.

And he defiled Topheth, which is in the valley of the children of Hinnom, that no man might make his son or his daughter to pass through the fire to Molech [a god].

And he took away the horses that the kings of Judah had given to the sun, at the entering in of the house of the Lord, by the chamber of Nathanmelech the chamberlain, which was in the suburbs, and burned the chariots of the sun with fire.

And the altars that were on the top of the upper chamber of Ahaz, which the kings of Judah had made, and the altars which Manasseh had made in the two courts of the house of the Lord, did the king beat down, and brake them down from thence, and cast the dust of them into the brook Kidron.

And the high places that were before Jerusalem, which were on the right hand of the mount of corruption, which Solomon the king of Israel had builded for Ashtoreth the abomination of the Zidonians, and for Chemosh the abomination of the Moabites, for Milcom the abomination of the children of Ammon, did the king defile.

And he brake in pieces the images, and cut down the groves [Pagan places of worship], and filled their places with the bones of men.

Moreover the altar that was at Beth-el, and the high place which Jeroboam the son of Nebat, who made Israel to sin, had made, both that altar and the high place he brake down, and burned the high place, and stamped it small to powder, and burned the grove. (2 Kings 23:6,10-15)

And they brought forth the images out of the house of Baal, and burned them.

And they brake down the image of Baal, and brake down the house of Baal, and made it a draught house unto this day. (2 Kings 10:26,27)

### New Testament:

Many of them also, which used curious arts brought their books together, and burned them before all men: and they counted the price of them, and found it fifty thousand pieces of silver. (Acts 19:19)

# SUGGESTED READING MATERIAL

*The Beautiful Side of Evil;* Michaelsen, Johanna; © April 1984; Harvest House Publishers:
The true story of a woman assisting a psychic surgeon who operates on people through demonic power, and how she is led to the saving knowledge of Jesus Christ.

*Heaven Rejoices;* Park, Irene; (Formerly titled *The Witch That Switched);* © June 1996; Whitaker Distributors:
The true story of an ex-priestess of a satanic coven and how she comes to know Jesus Christ as her Lord and Savior.

*A Soul for Sale;* Kornacki, Carol; © 2010; A& A Books www. carolkornacki.org:
The similar true story of a drug addict/witch with a severely abusive background who sells her soul.

# ENDNOTES

1   Air: signifies the spirit world, and also Satan's realm:

Wherein in time past ye walked according to the course of this world, according to the prince of the power of air, the spirit that now worketh in the children of disobedience. (Ephesians 2:2)

2   Ladder: symbolic of spiritual ascension. Also symbolic of Jesus Christ, the mediator (or repairer of the breach [gap]) between man and God. He came to restore a spiritual relationship between people and their Creator, so they could have direct contact with the Almighty God once more, whereas before they were separated from him because of sins:

And he [Jacob] dreamed, and behold a ladder set up on the earth, and the top of it reached to heaven: and behold the angels of God ascending and descending on it. (Genesis 28:12)

And he [Jesus] saith unto him, Verily, verily, I say unto you, Hereafter ye shall see heaven open, and the angels of God ascending and descending upon the Son of man [Jesus]. (John 1:51)

3   *New England Town:* unpublished work © August 1978 by Paul Platonas.

4   *The Dance of the Veils:* unpublished work © March 1979 by Paul Platonas.

5   There shall not be found among you...

...A charmer, or a consulter with familiar spirits, or a wizard, or a necromancer.

For all that do these things are an abomination unto the Lord: and because of these abominations, the Lord thy God doth drive them out from before thee. (Deuteronomy 18:10-12)

6   There shall not be found among you...

...A charmer, or a consulter with familiar spirits, or a wizard, or a necromancer.

463

For all that do these things are an abomination unto the Lord: and because of these abominations, the Lord thy God doth drive them out from before thee. (Deuteronomy 18:10-12)

7    Mrs. Beasley © 1967-1974 by Mattel.

8    The Devil is the prince of the power of air (Ephesians 2:2). See endnote 1 under *Air*.

9    Chinese Checkers © Cardinal Industries, Inc., No. 178.

10   *Sleeping Beauty:* Walt Disney's *Sleeping Beauty* © July 1997 by Walt Disney Staff; Mouse Works; ISBN: 1570827311.

11   There shall not be found among you...

     ...A charmer, or a consulter with familiar spirits, or a wizard, or a necromancer.

For all that do these things are an abomination unto the Lord: and because of these abominations, the Lord thy God doth drive them out from before thee. (Deuteronomy 18:10-12)

12   Our Fathers and Hail Marys: God does not want us to pray repetitious prayers. He wants us to talk to Him as we would talk to our earthly father, *pouring out the concerns of our hearts* to Him. Jesus told his disciples, when instructing them on how to pray,

     But when ye pray, use not vain repetitions, as the heathen do: for they think they shall be heard for their much speaking.

     Be not therefore like unto them: for your Father knoweth what things ye have need of before ye ask him. (Matthew 6:7,8)

     Psalm 62:8 tells us:

     Trust in him at all times; ye people, *pour out your heart before him:* God is a refuge for us. Selah.

13   *Amityville Horror* © by Jay Anson; ASIN: 0671727397; Out of print.

14   Like Father, Like Daughter: I was beginning to follow in my father's footsteps. I inherited the sins of my father because I *chose* to hate God and love deceit and unrighteousness:

     Thou shalt not bow down thyself to them [other gods or graven images], nor serve them: for I the Lord thy God am a jealous God, visiting the iniquity of the fathers upon the children unto the third and fourth generation of them that hate me. (Deuteronomy 5:9)

15   ™Andre' Cold Duck: © Andre' Champagne Cellars.

16   Bleeding: Many biblical covenants were sealed with blood. When God established the marriage covenant between man and woman, he ordained that it be sealed with the shedding of blood during consummation [or intercourse], as the two become *one flesh*.

17   Mrs. Beasley © by Mattel.

18   *Alice in Wonderland:* taken from *Lewis Carroll: The Complete Illustrated Works* © October 1995; (Reprint edition) by Lewis Carroll; Illustrated by John Tenniel; Grammercy; ISBN: 0517147815.

19   ®™ *I Love Lucy* © CBS Inc.

20   Homosexuality and Lesbianism are forbidden by God:

Thou shalt not lie with mankind, as with womankind: it is abomination. (Leviticus 18:22)

For this cause, God gave them up unto vile affections: for even their women did change the natural use into that which is against nature:

And likewise also the men, leaving the natural use of the woman, burned in their lust one toward another; men with men working that which is unseemly, and receiving in themselves that recompense of their error which was meet [due]. (Romans 1:26, 27)

Then the Lord rained upon Sodom [where the gay men were] and upon Gomorrah brimstone and fire from the Lord out of heaven;

And he overthrew those cities, and all the plain, and all the inhabitants of the cities, and that which grew upon the ground. (Genesis 19:24, 25)

21   Wicca, adapted from the Old English word *wicca*, meaning: sorcerer, and *wiccian*, meaning: to cast a spell; is said to have been created by a man named Gerald Gardner back in the late 1800's or early 1900's. Also said to have taken a part in its origin are world-renowned black magician and mason Aleister Crowley, anthropologist Dr. Margaret Murray, and authors Robert Graves and Charles Godfrey Leland.

However, it has been around long before that. The Bible defines witches as those who whisper spells, practice enchantments and/or necromancy, consult familiar spirits, worship objects of nature or created things, adhere to astrology, and commit idolatry. Also, biblical scripture compares rebellion to the sin of witchcraft. Participation in an actual coven is not required in order to be a witch.

Some information on Wicca obtained from the Internet article, *Wicca: The New Religious Movement* © John McNair; Original date unknown.

22　Monarch ™ © Ford Motor Company.

23　Ibid.

24　Jacuzzi ®™ © Jacuzzi Inc.

25　Eor, Christopher Robin, and Tigger referenced from *The Complete Tales of Winnie the Pooh* © October 1996 (reprint edition) by A Milne; with Ernest H. Shepard as illustrator; Penguin, USA; ISBN: 0525457232.

26　*Happy Days* © 1974 by Gary Marshall and Paramount Pictures Productions.

27　*The Brady Bunch* © 1965 by Sherwood Schwartz, © 1969 by Paramount Pictures Productions.

28　Sodomy: The only way males can perform sexual intercourse. The word derives from *Sodom,* the land that was destroyed with fire and brimstone by God because of its sexual perverseness. God had sent two male angels to Sodom to rescue Lot, the only righteous man in the city, and his family; before God pronounced judgment against the people. When the homosexual men in the city, or the *Sodomites,* saw the angels going into Lot's house, they knocked on the door and commanded that Lot send the men [angels] out to them so that they could know them *intimately:*

And they called unto Lot, and said unto him, Where are the men which came in to thee this night? bring them out unto us, that we may *know* them [have sexual relationship with].

And Lot went out at the door unto them, and shut the door after him, And said, I pray you, brethren, do not so wickedly. (Genesis 19:5-7)

God's Word Says Sodomites Shall Not Go To Heaven:

Know ye not that the unrighteous shall not inherit the kingdom of God? Be not deceived: neither fornicators, nor idolaters, nor adulterers, nor effeminate [homosexuals], nor abusers of themselves with mankind [sodomites, as it translates],

...shall inherit the kingdom of God. (1 Corinthians 6:9, 10)

God's Word Says Sodomites/Homosexuals Can Be Redeemed

Homosexuals can be redeemed when they repent and change their lifestyle. God created them with a *nature to like the opposite sex,* and he can restore them once more:

...Nor effeminate [homosexuals], nor abusers of themselves with mankind [sodomites, as it translates],

...shall inherit the kingdom of God.

And such **were** some of you: but ye are washed, but ye are sanctified, but ye are justified in the name of the Lord Jesus, and by the Spirit of our God. (1 Corinthians 6:9-11)

For this cause God gave them up unto vile affections: for even their women did change the natural use into that which is **against nature.**

And likewise also the men, **leaving the natural use** of the woman, burned in their lust one toward another; men with men working that which is unseemly, and receiving in themselves that recompence of their error which was meet. (Romans 1:26, 27)

Translations from: *Strong's Exhaustive Concordance of the Bible* by James Strong; S.T.D., LL.D., 1890; public domain.

29   Cross dressing (or wearing clothes of the opposite sex with the motivation or intent of trying to identify with its gender) is forbidden by God in scripture:

The woman shall not wear that which pertaineth unto a man, neither shall a man put on a woman's garment: for all that do so are abomination unto the Lord thy God. (Deuteronomy 22:5)

Note: this scriptural command does *not* include wearing unisex clothes such as modern day blue jeans or tennis shoes, provided a person stays within their sexual boundaries. Please realize that in biblical times, men and women *both* wore robes, but there was still a distinction between the robes to differentiate a person's gender.

Today, wearing a husband's comfy T-shirt is *not* crossdressing, as long as you are not trying to look like or identify with a man, therefore dishonoring the gender God gave you. Again, some clothes are gender neutral and do not cross the line. The heart motive is what we must always examine.

30  Whitman's Sampler of assorted candies © Whitman's Candies Inc.

31  Korg keyboards © Korg USA Inc.

32  Levi Jeans © Levi Strauss Co.

33  The *Hunchback of Notre Dame* © 1923 by Madacy Entertainment; ASIN: 6304819293. Hunchback played by Lon Chaney.

34  ™Sam Hain and Glenn Danzig.

35  Baby Alive © by Kenner.

36  It is interesting that Jezebel was a woman who practiced witchcraft in the Old Testament, as well as a female personification of all false prophecy in the *Church* (also personified as a female, i.e. the *bride* of Christ; or Zion, New Jerusalem, Israel—which are referred to as *shes* and *hers*. All are portrayed as females, though speaking of *one collective body* of believers). Therefore, Jezebel is the false counterfeit bride of Christ operating under a spirit of witchcraft.

And it came to pass, when Joram saw Jehu, that he said, Is it peace, Jehu? And he answered, What peace, so long as the whoredoms of thy mother Jezebel and her witchcrafts are so many? (2 Kings 9:22)

Notwithstanding I have a few things against thee, because thou sufferest that woman Jezebel, which calleth herself a prophetess, to teach and to seduce my servants to *commit fornication*, and to eat *things sacrificed to idols* [spiritual whoredoms and blasphemies]. (Revelation 2:20)

For other female personifications, see the King James Bible under Nahum 3:4,7 (referring to the city of Ninevah as a mistress of *witchcraft* and *whoredom*), Jeremiah 3:7,8,10 (referring to Israel as a woman, and to Judah as her sister), and Revelation 12:1-5 (referring to both natural and spiritual Israel as a woman clothed with the sun and moon, and a crown of twelve stars on her head).

37 X: This is often the symbol of an antichrist, though an exception would be the "X" in the shortened form: Merry Xmas, where the English X is the transliterated letter for the first Greek letter in Christos, meaning Christ.

38 *The 700 Club* © by Pat Robertson/© the Christian Broadcasting Network, Inc.

39 Kentucky Fried Chicken © KFC Corporation.

40 *Cleopatra* © 1963 by Twentieth Century Fox; Produced by Walter Wanger; Directed by Joseph Mankiewicz.

Starring Elizabeth Taylor as Cleopatra.

41 *A Clockwork Orange* © 1971 Warner Bros./Hawk Films; Produced and directed by Stanley Kubrick. Based on the novel *A Clockwork Orange* © 1962 by Anthony Burgess.

42 For this cause God gave them up unto vile affections: for even their women did change the natural use into that which is against nature:

And likewise also the men, leaving the natural use of the woman, burned in their lust one toward another; men with men working that which is unseemly, and receiving in themselves that recompense of their error which was meet [due]. (Romans 1:26,27)

Note: Jesus stated that whoever looks on a woman to lust after her has committed adultery with her already in his heart. Though I never committed the physical act of lesbianism, because I entertained it in my heart, it was still sin. I was, in essence, a lesbian (or at least, bisexual), at heart. Jesus also taught that sin starts in the heart (or mind). (Matthew 5:28/Matthew 15:19,20)

43 *The Addams Family:* based on cartoon characters created by Charles Addams; © 1964 by Filmways Television Productions, Inc./Orion Television Syndication; © 1964 (Distr.) Worldvision Home Video, Inc.; Exec. Prod. David Levy; Prod. Nat Perrin; Assoc Prod. Herbert W. Browar; Direc. Ruby Levitt.

Morticia Addams originally played by Carolyn Jones. Gomez Addams originally played by John Astin.

44 Ibid.

45 Ibid.

46 Nissan © Nissan cars; Japan.

47 Southern Comfort © the Southern Comfort Company.

48   Disney ™ © Disney (Walt Disney Studios).

49   It is true that drugs open one up to the spiritual world of Satan and his sorceries. The word *sorcery* in the Greek translates to: *pharmakeia* (compare pharmacy). See endnote 92 under *The use of drugs in witchcraft* for source of reference.

Translation of *sorcery* borrowed from: *Strong's Exhaustive Concordance of the Bible* by James Strong; S.T.D., LL.D., 1890; public domain.

50   Nissan © Nissan cars; Japan.

51   Jack Daniels © Jack Daniels Distillery; Lem Motlow, prop.

52   Cokes: © Coca-Cola Corporation.

53   Mountain Dews: © the Pepsi Cola Corporation.

54   Committed adultery:

Neither shalt thou commit adultery. (Deuteronomy 5:18)

Neither shalt thou desire thy neighbor's wife… (Deuteronomy 5:21)

For by means of a whorish woman a man is brought to a piece of bread: and the adulteress will hunt for the precious life. (Proverbs 6:26)

Ye have heard that it was said by them of old time, Thou shalt not commit adultery:

But I say unto you, That whosoever looketh on a woman to lust after her hath committed adultery with her already in his heart. (Matthew 5:27,28)

55   Underworld: a world under the earth, or *Hades*. In the Bible, Hades is another name for Hell, and is said to be located somewhere under the earth.

56   In the time of Moses, when he was sent by God to confront Pharaoh to release the Jews, God performed plagues through his hand and the hand of his brother Aaron (using a rod, etc.) as punishment for Pharaoh's stubbornness. The Egyptian magicians were able to duplicate some of the plagues with their magic powers, but when they could no longer do so because God forbid them, they told Pharaoh that truly it was because the plague was *the finger of God*, and could not be matched:

Then Pharaoh also called the wise men and the sorcerers: now the magicians of Egypt, they also did in like manner with their enchantments.

For they cast down every man his rod, and they became serpents: but Aaron's rod *swallowed up their rods.* (Exodus 7:11,12)

...for Aaron stretched out his hand with his rod, and smote the dust of the earth, and it became lice in man, and in beast; all the dust of the land became lice throughout all the land of Egypt.

And the magicians did so with their enchantments to bring forth lice, but they could not: so there were lice upon man, and upon beast.

Then the magicians said unto Pharaoh, *This is the finger of God:* and Pharaoh's heart was hardened, and he hearkened not unto them; as the Lord had said. (Exodus 8:17-19)

57   There are no past lives. This is simply a lie created by Satan to convince people that they can do whatever they want to in this life because they'll have many other lives in which to perfect their spirituality. The Bible states:

...It is appointed unto men *once* to die, but after this the judgment. (Hebrews 9:27)

58   Though saved believers will be together in heaven, as Jesus states they will all be one in him and in the Father God; he also tells us that they will not marry or be given in marriage there. They will be like the angels in heaven, who have no need for such an earthly form of love. The love in heaven will surpass any human form of emotion we are accustomed to. We will have no need of marriage and sexual relationships there.

That they all may be *one;* as thou, Father, art in me, and I in thee, that they also may be *one* in us: that the world may believe that thou hast sent me. (John 17:21)

Jesus answered and said unto them, Ye do err, not knowing the scriptures, nor the power of God. For in the resurrection they neither marry, nor are given in marriage, but are as the angels of God in heaven. (Matthew 22:29, 30)

59   Kahlua © The Kahlua Co., Mexico; Distributed by Hiram Walker and Sons.

60   Coke © the Coca-Cola Corporation.

61   The *Rocky Horror Picture Show* © 1975 by Twentieth Century Fox; ASIN: 6305076650.

62  Big Bad Wolf: borrowed from the fairytale of *Little Red Riding Hood* by Brothers Jacob Ludwig Carl, Jacob W. and Wilhelm K. Grimm; a reprint edition is now available: © September 1987 (Reprint edition) Illustrated by Trina Schart Hyman; Holiday House; ISBN: 0823406539.

63  *Little Red Riding Hood:* ibid.

64  There is no disease that God cannot cure:

Bless the Lord, O my soul, and forget not all his benefits:

Who forgiveth all thine iniquities; who healeth all thy diseases. (Psalm 103:2,3)

And Jesus went about all the cities and villages… healing every sickness and every disease among the people. (Matthew 9:35)

65  Nissan © Nissan cars; Japan.

66  Johnny Walker Red ™ © Johnny Walker Red Scotch and Schieffetin and Somerset Co., Distributors.

67  Doc Martens Airwair boots ™ Dr. Martens © by Dr. Klaus Maertens; © R. Griggs & Company.

68  *National Geographic* TV series © National Geographic Society.

69  Captain Morgan's Spiced Rum © Captain Morgan Rum Co.

70  Thou shalt not steal. (Exodus 20:15)

Let him that stole steal no more: but rather let him labour, working with his hands the thing which is good, that he may have to give to him that needeth. (Ephesians 4:28)

71  Yamaha keyboards © Yamaha Corporation of America

72  Yamaha keyboards: ibid.

73  Korg keyboards © Korg USA Inc.

74  Cross with an X through it: see endnote 37 under *X*.

75  Alignments/declaring and invoking/honoring: These are all counterfeits of things God calls His people to do. When Christians declare God's power and honor His name, they align themselves, or become one, with Him.

Psalm 22:3 tells us that God inhabits the praises of his people. By praising Him, they invoke His power.

Jesus instructed the disciples in Matthew 6:9, when they asked him to teach them how to pray, that they should pray according to this *manner,* (or format): First and foremost, *Our Father, who art in heaven* (acknowledge His lordship and majesty), *hallowed* (sacred) *be thy name.* In other words, for effective prayer, give God the honor due His name; for once again, He inhabits the praises of His people. Note, also, that another aspect of aligning oneself with God is desiring *His* will, and being *holy* as He is holy. See 1 John 5:14,15; James 4:3; 1 Peter 1:16; Leviticus 11:44 in the *King James Bible.*

76   Stated my need: Spells, a counterfeit of prayer, also call for one to state, or make known, his request to the deities. Philippians 4:6 tells us:

Be careful [or anxious] for nothing; but in everything by prayer and supplication with thanksgiving let your requests be made known unto God.

77   Considered it done: Spells, taking an element of God's truth and twisting it, are said to work when one considers them already done, though they might not have manifested yet in the physical. This is a counterfeit of a biblical principle known as *faith:* believing in something that isn't always visible or tangible to us at the time. Having faith for the thing we ask moves God to bring it about. Jesus said:

Have faith in God. For verily, I say unto you, That whosoever shall say unto this mountain, Be thou removed, and be thou cast into the sea; and shall not doubt in his heart, but shall believe that those things which he saith shall come to pass; *he shall have whatsoever he saith.*

Therefore I say unto you, What things soever ye desire when ye pray, believe that ye receive them, *and ye shall have them.* (Mark 11:22-24)

The Bible tells us that God *calls the things that be not as though they were* (Romans 4:17). That is how He made all of His creation, by *speaking it into existence through His word:*

And God *said,* Let there be light: *and there was light.* (Genesis 1:3)

God's word was, and is, Jesus Christ:

In the beginning was the Word, and the Word was with God, and the Word *was* God.

The same was in the beginning *with* God.

All things were made by him; and without him was not any thing made that was made.

And the Word was made flesh [Jesus Christ], and dwelt among us, (and we beheld his glory, the glory as of the only begotten of the Father) [or God's only Son] full of grace and truth. (John 1:1-3, 14)

78   "So mote it be" is a counterfeit of the biblical declaration: *amen*, which means: *so be it.*

79   Docs: Airwair boots ™ Dr. Martens © by Dr. Klaus Maertens; © R. Griggs & Company.

80   Ibid.

81   Volvo stationwagon © AB Volvo Car Corp.

82   Volvo stationwagon © AB Volvo Car Corp.

83   YMCA: © Young Men's Christian Association.

84   Marshall amps © Jim Marshall/Marshall Amplification.

85   Peavey microphones © Peavey Electronics Corporation.

86   Animal *familiar:*

There shall not be found among you ...

... A charmer, or a consulter with familiar spirits...

For all that do these things are an abomination unto the Lord: and because of these abominations the Lord thy God doth drive them out from before thee. (Deuteronomy 18:10-12)

And the soul that turneth after such as have familiar spirits, and after wizards, to go a whoring after them, I will even set my face against that soul, and will cut him off from among his people. (Leviticus 20:6)

A man also or woman that hath a familiar spirit, or that is a wizard, shall surely be put to death: they shall stone them with stones: their blood shall be upon them. (Leviticus 20:27)

Note: death to those with familiar spirits was a strict, Old Testament law for the Jew whose God was the Holy One of Israel, and who knew better than to contaminate himself with the idol gods and occult practices of other nations.

Today, however, as a result of Jesus' sacrificial death, ALL are given a chance to come to God, because He is *longsuffering*, not desiring that anyone should perish. He wishes for *all* to come to repentance through Christ (2 Peter 3:9); though many, by their own choice, will not. (Matthew 7:13,14; John 14:6)

87  Kernunnos/Pan: the horned goat god of witches in his dual aspect. Several witches teach that Satan is a Judeo-Christian adaptation of this positive goat god.

However, it is also a known fact among many witches—especially those in higher degrees—that sexual intercourse occurs between witches and demons, or Satan. Many ancient drawings depict this intercourse with a goat/man during witch's Sabbaths or High (though not holy) Days. Furthermore, people who have been redeemed from satanic covens and ritual abuse have testified that this is true, and many have had to be delivered from these demons after becoming possessed with them. Though Satan is not flesh and blood, he is a spirit, and therefore can inhabit and/or make contact with fleshly bodies.

See text in chapter XIII regarding: *goat's tongue/hairy body,* and also *[War's] spirit astral projecting (tingly sensation on skin)* for examples.

In the Bible, especially the book of Leviticus, which dates back to approximately 1445 B.C., the word *devils* translates four times in the Hebrew to *sa'ir*, or **goat-demons:** demons having the form of a goat, or satyr.

And they shall no more offer their sacrifices unto *devils* [**goat demons**]; after whom they have gone a whoring. This shall be a statute for ever unto them throughout their generations. (Leviticus 17:7)

The word *sa'ir* can be broken down further to: *shaggy, a he goat, a faun, devil, goat, hairy, satyr,* etc.

It is interesting to note that Lucifer (before becoming Satan), is described in scripture as "the anointed cherub that covereth," whose workmanship of tabrets (drums, rhythm instruments—*timbrels)* and pipes (woodwinds—*socket, groove, hole, pipe)* was prepared *in* him (Ezekiel 28:13,14). He was obviously a living instrument of music, **literally.** Though no one knows in particular just what he looked like in Heaven, Ezekiel described the "cherubim" he saw as "having the likeness of a man, with hands under their wings and the sole of a calf's foot." Each cherub had four faces: the face of a man, the face of a lion, the face of an ox, and the face of an eagle (Ezekiel 1:5-10). Speculating then, perhaps Lucifer had the face of a goat, as he also was a cherub and held a prominent position as worship leader in Heaven. Or perhaps his appearance was changed to that of a goat after his fall.

Similarly, John the Revelator described "four beasts" who worship around the throne of God continuously as: "each one having six wings, and each full of eyes in front and back." The first creature he saw was like a lion, the second creature like an ox, the third creature like a man, and the fourth creature like an eagle (Revelation 4:6-11).

Information on the word *goat-demons* obtained from *Vines Complete Expository Dictionary of Old and New Testament Words* ©1985 (a derivative work) by W.E. Vine, with Merrill F. Unger and William White, Jr.; Thomas Nelson Publishers; ISBN: 0-8407-7559-8.

Translation for the word *devils (sa'ir)* obtained from *Strong's Exhaustive Concordance of the Bible* by James Strong; S.T.D., LL.D., 1890; public domain.

Jesus, in the New Testament, compares goats to evil people (sinners) who refuse to follow him:

And before him [Jesus] shall be gathered all nations: and he shall separate them one from another, as a shepherd divideth his sheep from the goats:

And he shall set the sheep on his right hand, but the goats on the left. Then shall the King [Jesus] say unto them on his right hand, Come, ye blessed of my Father, inherit the kingdom prepared for you from the foundation of the world:

Then shall he say also unto them on the left hand, Depart *from me, ye cursed, into everlasting fire, prepared for the devil and his angels.* (Matthew 25:32-34;41)

88   Sids: meaning, the late Sid Vicious of the Sex Pistols, one of the first punk rock bands to come into existence.

89   Dixie Cup © Hugh Moore and the Dixie Cup Company.

90   Budweiser beer © Anheuser Busch, Inc.

91   Chevrolet Cavalier™ © General Motors.

92   The use of drugs in witchcraft/spiritism: *Pharmakeia,* the Greek word from which *pharmacy* derives, translates to *magic, sorcery, witchcraft.*

From: *Thayer's Greek-English Lexicon of the New Testament* © March 1994 (21ˢᵗ Reprint edition) by Joseph Henry Thayer, D.D.; Baker Books, a division of Baker Book House Company; ISBN: 0-8010-8838-0.

Adapted from *Strong's Exhaustive Concordance of the Bible* by James Strong; S.T.D., LL.D., 1890; public domain.

93   7-Eleven Convenience Stores © Southland Corporation.

94   Chevrolet Cavalier ™ © General Motors.

95   Budweiser beer, Est. 1876; © Anheuser-Bush, Inc.

96   Zig Zag Cigarette Papers © the Zig Zag Company and Braunstein Freres; Est. 1888; France; Distr. by North Atlantic Operating Co., Inc; Louisville, KY.

97   Oldsmobile ™ © General Motors.

98   Possibly relayed from *The Teachings of Don Juan: A Yaqui Way of Knowledge* by Carlos Castaneda; © June 1985 (Reissue edition); Mass Market Paperback; Pocket Books; ISBN: 0671600419.

99   Swarm of flies: see endnote 202 under *Flies.*

100  *Pieta* © by Michelangelo.

101  Aleister Crowley: Aleister Crowley, a world renowned black magician, was involved with the Golden Dawn organization for a while, as well as with the Masonic Temple. See endnote 114 under *Golden Dawn* for more info.

102  *Magick In Theory And Practice* © by Aleister Crowley; Castle Publications; Out of print.

103  Korg keyboards © Korg USA Inc.

104  Denny's Restaurant franchise © Syndicated.

105  Korg keyboards © Korg USA Inc.

Note: great keyboards—just don't let iguanas poop on them.

106  Kawaii keyboards © Kawai America Corporation.

107  Korg keyboards © Korg USA Inc.

108  Castle: Supposed to house my prince War, the castle was symbolic of the temple (the house, or dwelling, of his soul) i.e. his human body, or even his whole being—body, soul and spirit. The broken-down castle signified self-neglect, both spiritually and physically:

He that hath no rule over his own spirit is like a city that is broken down, and without walls. (Proverbs 25:28)

I went by the field of the slothful, and by the vineyard of the man void of understanding;

And lo, it was all grown over with thorns, and nettles had covered the face thereof, and the stone wall thereof was broken down. (Proverbs 24:30, 31)

By much slothfulness the building decayeth; and through idleness of hands the house droppeth through. (Ecclesiastes 10:18)

109 Though spelled differently, Emmanuel (as it is spelled in the New Testament of the Bible) is another name for Jesus Christ. It means: *God with us*. Little did I know that the Devil was singing through me, confessing the weakness of Jesus Christ as deity.

Behold, a virgin shall be with child, and shall bring forth a son, and they shall call his name Emmanuel, which being interpreted is, God with us. (Matthew 1:23)

110 Cokes: Coca-Cola © the Coca-Cola Corporation.

111 Heinekins: Heinekin beer; Heinekin Brouwerijen B.V.; Amsterdam, Holland; Est. 1873; © Heinekin USA Inc.

112 From *Magick In Theory And Practice* © by Aleister Crowley; Castle Publications; Out of Print.

113 *Magick in Theory and Practice;* ibid.

114 The Golden Dawn is an organization embracing new age/witchcraft theology and practice. It was originally founded by three Freemasons: Drs. William Woodman, William Westcott, and Samuel Mathers in 1887. Though it denies being a religion, this organization and all its various sects practice idol worship; and though it claims to even be "progressing toward Christianity," its members pray to other gods, therefore violating the First Commandment of the Bible: *Thou shalt have no other gods before me* (Exodus 20:3); as well as violating Jesus' doctrine, the very foundation of Christianity, which states: I [Jesus] am *the* way (not *a* way), *the* truth and *the* life, and no man can come unto the Father, but by *me*. (John 14:6)

Interestingly enough, Lucifer's name, before his fall from heaven, meant *Son of the Morning*, a very similar title as *The Golden Dawn*.

Aleister Crowley, a world renowned black magician, was involved with the Golden Dawn organization for a while, as well as with the Masonic Temple.

The Masonic Temple, The Golden Dawn, and the Illuminati are very similar in both origin and practice. The Freemasons, as noted in *Morals and Dogma* (a Masonic handbook) © Albert Pike (out of print to the best of my knowledge), go by the title *Luciferians*. They believe, (as it is eventually revealed to the higher degree initiates), that Lucifer is really the great architect (or creator), and not God. However, they keep this hidden to the lower degree members, which are encouraged to worship at every altar, acknowledging all religions and paying homage to all 'gods.'

Note that Crowley attained a very high degree with the masons, and was well aware of their Satan worship, as even he himself carried a calling card which read: *666 The Beast.*

Information on the founders/sects of this organization and its denial to being a religion obtained from *The Golden Dawn FAQ and Resource Lists* © 1993-1998 Steven R. Cranmer of Harvard Edu.

115 Aliens: demons who pretend to be ascended masters. Though they are, in fact, higher life forms as far as their supernatural abilities go, they are in no way superior in their spirituality since they are fallen angels reserved for the final day of darkness and Hell. However, they succeed in tricking many people with their lying signs and wonders, and are able to *transform* themselves into such alien-looking creatures with ease, if so desired.

And no marvel; for Satan himself is *transformed* into an angel of light (or seemingly, spiritual en*light*enment).

Therefore it is no great thing if his ministers also be transformed as the ministers of righteousness (appearing to be spiritually *right* and possessing truth*)*; whose end shall be according to their works. (2 Corinthians 11: 14, 15)

116 Groom with black hair: just as tarot cards are twisted truths stolen from the Bible, so this crystal ball vision was biblically symbolic, as well. (The Devil delights in taking an element of God's truth and perverting it). The groom symbolizes a type of Jesus Christ as he is portrayed in the Song of Solomon, married to the worldwide church of believers.

(Denoting the handsomeness of the bridegroom):

His head is as the most fine gold, his locks are bushy and black as a raven. (Song of Solomon 5:11)

It can also be speculated that God was attempting to reach my spirit with truth amidst the counterfeit, as He can speak through any means He chooses (although He does not always condone the means He chooses). He will try to get His point across even in the most negative of circumstances, simply because that is all He has to work with at the time.

117 Chalice, or cup: symbolic of the new covenant Jesus Christ established with his blood.

(Note that many biblical covenants were shed with blood):

After the same manner also he [Jesus] took the cup, when he had supped, saying, This cup is the new testament in my blood (figuratively, not literally); this do ye, as oft as ye drink it in remembrance of me. (1 Corinthians 11:25)

I will take the cup of salvation, and call upon the name of the Lord. (Psalm 116:13)

118 Bride: symbolic representation of the *Church,* or *body* of believers:

For I am jealous over you with godly jealousy; for I have *espoused* you to one husband [God/Jesus], that I may present you as a *chaste virgin* [spiritually pure, holy] to Christ. (2 Corinthians 11:2)

Let us be glad and rejoice, and give honour to him: for the marriage of the Lamb [Christ] is come, and his *wife* hath made herself ready.

And to her was granted that she should be arrayed in fine linen, *clean* and *white;* for the fine linen is the righteousness of saints [sanctified, holy, ones, i.e. believers]. (Revelation 19:7,8)

And I John saw the holy city, New Jerusalem [consisting of the Church of believers] coming down from heaven, prepared as a bride adorned for her husband. (Revelation 21:2)

119 Coke: © the Coca-Cola Corporation.

120 Crystals/rainbow: another natural type of something spiritual in God's kingdom, the crystal and the rainbow are symbolic of the Holy Spirit (*Shekinah glory*) and the realm of heaven:

And the likeness of the firmament (heaven) upon the heads of the living creature was as the colour of the terrible (awesome) crystal, stretched forth over their heads above.

As the appearance of the bow that is in the cloud in the day of rain, so was the appearance of the brightness round about. This was the appearance of the likeness of the *glory of the Lord.* And when I saw it, I fell upon my face, and I heard a voice of one that spake. (Ezekiel 1:22,28)

121 Glowing man in white: a type of Jesus:

And above the firmament that was over their heads was the likeness of a throne, as the appearance of a sapphire stone: and upon the likeness of the throne was the likeness as of the appearance of a man upon it.

And I saw as the colour of amber, as the appearance of fire round about within it, from the appearance of his loins even upward, and from the appearance of his loins even downward, I saw as it were the appearance of fire, and it had brightness round about. (Ezekiel 1:26,27)

And in the midst of the seven candlesticks one like unto the Son of man [Jesus], clothed with a garment down to the foot, and girt about the paps with a golden girdle.

His head and his hairs were white like wool, as white as snow; and his eyes were as a flame of fire;

And his feet like unto fine brass, as if they burned in a furnace; and his voice as the sound of many waters.

And he had in his right hand seven stars: and out of his mouth went a sharp twoedged sword: and his countenance was as the sun shineth in his strength. (Revelation 1:13-16)

122 Stretched out his arms: symbolic of a spiritual calling, an invitation:

Because I have called, and ye refused; I have stretched out my hand, and no man regarded. (Proverbs 1:24)

But to Israel he saith, All day long I have stretched forth my hands unto a disobedient and gainsaying people. (Romans 10:21)

O Jerusalem, Jerusalem, thou that killest the prophets, and stonest them which are sent unto thee, how often would I have gathered thy children together, even as a hen gathereth her chickens *under her wings* [stretching out her wings to embrace them], and ye would not! (Matthew 23:37)

123 Possibly taken from *The Teachings of Don Juan: A Yaqui Way of Knowledge* by Carlos Castaneda © June 1985 (Reissue edition); Mass Market Paperback; Pocket Books; ISBN: 0671600419.

124 Kleenex brand tissue © Kimberly Clark Corporation.

125 Tree: another one of Satan's counterfeits taken from the Bible, the tree is symbolic of Jesus Christ:

In the garden of Eden:

And out of the ground made the Lord God to grow every tree that is pleasant to the sight, and good for food; the tree of life also in the midst of the garden, and the tree of knowledge of good and evil. (Genesis 2:9)

In the life of mankind:

I [Jesus] am the vine, ye are the branches: He that abideth in me, and I in him, the same bringeth forth much fruit: for without me ye can do nothing.

If a man abide not in me, he is cast forth as a branch, and is withered; and men gather them, and cast them into the fire and they are burned (symbolic of Hell's torment). (John 15:5,6)

In New Jerusalem:

In the midst of the street of it, and on either side of the river, was there the tree of life, which bare twelve manner of fruits, and yielded her fruit every month: and the leaves of the tree were for the healing of the nations. (Revelation 22:2)

126 Table: symbolic of the heart in man:

Let not mercy and truth forsake thee: bind them about thy neck; write them upon the table of thine *heart*. (Proverbs 3:3)

The sin of Judah is written with a pen of iron, and with the point of a diamond: it is graven upon the table of their *heart*, and upon the horns of your altars. (Jeremiah 17:1)

Forasmuch as ye are manifestly declared to be the epistle of Christ ministered by us, written not with ink, but with the Spirit of the living God; not in tables of stone, but in fleshly tables of the *heart.* (2 Corinthians 3:3)

127 Big black book: counterfeit of the law of God, and/or the Bible:

For when Moses had spoken every precept to all the people according to the law, he took the blood of calves and of goats, with water, and scarlet wool, and hyssop, and sprinkled both the book, and all the people. (Hebrews 9:19)

This book of *the law* shall not depart out of thy mouth; but thou shalt meditate therein day and night, that thou mayest observe to do according to all that is written therein: for then thou shalt make thy way prosperous, and then thou shalt have good success. (Joshua 1:8)

128 Snake (or serpent): symbolic of Satan as he first appeared in the garden of Eden, coiled in a tree. Note that Satan is a changeling, and is also able to work through animate agents:

Now the serpent was more subtil than any beast of the field which the Lord God had made. And he said unto the woman, Yeah, hath God said, Ye shall not eat of every tree of the garden?

For God doth know that in the day ye eat thereof, then your eyes shall be opened, and ye shall be as gods, knowing good and evil. (Genesis 3:1,5)

And he laid hold on the dragon, that serpent, which is the *Devil,* and *Satan,* and bound him a thousand years. (Revelation 20:2)

129 According to Satan, I could only gain true wisdom by letting him *bite* me!

130 This indicated that my animal was being inhabited by a familiar spirit, or *demon.*

131 Borrowed from *The Wizard of Oz* © 1939 (Theatrical Release) by MGM/ United Artists Studios; *The Wizard of Oz* © August 22, 1997 (DVD) by MGM/ Home Video. Based on characters created by Lyman Frank Baum in May of 1898.

The Wicked Witch of the West originally played by Margaret Hamilton.

132 Volvo stationwagon © AB Volvo Car Corp.

133 Volvo stationwagon © AB Volvo Car Corp.

134 *Bozo the Clown* © Syndicated, by Larry Harmon.

135 *The Smurfs* © Peyo/IMPS and Hanna/Barbera.

136 (Panda) Soy Sauce: Kari-out Co. Soy Sauce © Kari-out Co.; Tarrytown, NY.

137 McDonald's Restaurant © McDonald's Corporation.

138 Pebbles Flintstone: taken from the animated series *The Flintstones* © September 30, 1960 Hanna-Barbera Productions, with characters originally illustrated by Dan Gordon and designed by Ed Benedict.

139 Bamm Bamm: ibid.

140 Thou believest that there is one God; thou doest well: the devils also believe, and tremble. (James 2:19)

141 Kundalini serpent: reference is made once again to a serpent, or snake. The kundalini serpent is an Eastern term for the sexual energy chakra residing in the tailbone area, at the base of the spine. When uncoiled, it is said to give a person greater sexual pleasure and control. The kundalini serpent also correlates to the Tree of Life in the Qabalah. Note the shocking similarities:

In the Bible:

Adam and Eve, the Tree of Life in the middle of the garden, and the serpent (or Satan).

In New Age/Witchcraft:

Man and woman, the Tree of Life (a spiritual tree *within* one's inner being), and the kundalini serpent.

The kundalini serpent is simply another guise for Satan.

142 Karma: a counterfeit of a biblical principle known as sowing and reaping.

Be not deceived; God is not mocked: for whatsoever a man soweth, that shall he also reap. (Galatians 6:7)

Who [God] will render to every man according to his deeds:

Tribulation and anguish, upon every soul of man that doeth evil, of the Jew first, and also of the Gentile;

But glory, honour, and peace, to every man that worketh good, to the Jew first, and also to the Gentile. (Romans 2:6,9,10)

143 Yamaha keyboards © Yamaha Corporation of America.

144 Kawaii keyboards © Kawaii America Corporation.

145 7-Eleven Convenience Stores © Southland Corporation.

146 Borrowed from Cafe de Columbia Coffee; Juan Valdez ® © National Federation of Coffee Growers of Columbia.

147 *The Satanic Bible* © June 1989 (Mass Market Paperback Reissue edition) by Anton S. LaVey/La Vey; Avon; ISBN: 0380015390.

148 The Archie Bunker Show: *All in the Family* © Columbia Pictures Television. Also Bud Yorkin Productions and Norman Lear/Tandem Productions.

149 Coke © The Coca-Cola Corporation.

150 William Shatner: *Lucy in the Sky with Diamonds* (John Lennon/Paul McCartney) from *Golden Throats 4: Celebrities Butcher The Beatles* P & © 1997 Rhino Entertainment Company; from *The Transformed Man* P & ©1968 by William Shatner; Decca #DL-75073.

*Star Trek* and Captain Kirk are ™ © of CBS Studios, Inc.

151 Boss Hogg: from *Dukes of Hazzard* © 1979-1985 by Bros. Television and Lou Step Productions. Based on the movie *The Moonrunners* © 1975 by Gy Waldron.

J.D. (Boss) Hogg played by Sorrell Booke.

152 *Dukes of Hazzard*; ibid.

153 Boss Hogg: from *Dukes of Hazzard*; ibid.

154 *Dr. Jekyll and Mr. Hyde* © June 1991(Reprint) by R.L. Stevenson; Oxford University Press; ISBN: 0194216616.

155 Take a trip and see a wise man: See chapter nine, entitled *The Wise Man And The Fool*.

156 Volvo stationwagon © AB Volvo Car Corp.

157 Yamaha keyboards © Yamaha Corporation of America.

158 Kawaii keyboards © Kawaii Corporation of America.

159 Birkenstock sandals © Johann Adam Birkenstock; © Birkenstock Footprint Sandals, Inc. and Margot Fraser.

160 Harley Davidson © Harley-Davidson Inc.

161 Jell-O © Kraft Foods, Inc.

162 Arthurian legend: most stories are adapted from both history and folklore, including an older work entitled *Le Morte D'Arthur* by Sir Thomas Malory. There is a reprint edition of this original work available from the Penguin English Library; © July 1981 (Reprint edition); edited by Janet Cowen; Viking Press; ISBN: 0140430431.

Note: all deal with the myth surrounding an English King, Arthur, and some of the more popular stories involve witchcraft (the Ladies of the Lake, the Witch in the Wood), sorcery (Merlin, the King's advisor and friend), and adultery (the Queen, Guenivere, has an affair with Sir Lancelot the Knight), etc.

Note also: *Guenivere* is spelled about five different ways depending on what version of the legend you are reading, and Merlin is often spelled *Merlyn*.

163 Sword: symbolic of the Word of God.

And take the helmet of salvation, and the sword of the Spirit, which is the *word of God*. (Ephesians 6:17)

164 Shield: symbolic of faith, which protects believers, or Christians, from the fiery darts of the Devil. Note: a *believer* in Christ is one who *follows*, or *obeys* Christ, and not just pays mere credence, or lip service to.

Above all taking the shield of *faith*, wherewith ye shall be able to quench all the fiery darts of the wicked. (Ephesians 6:16)

165 Sun: symbolic of Jesus, who is compared to the sun because of his shining splendor.

Note the play on words: sun/son.

But unto you that fear my name shall the Sun of righteousness arise [Jesus, the righteous, arose from the dead] with healing in his wings. (Malachi 4:2)

For the Lord God is a sun and a shield: the Lord will give grace and glory: no good thing will he withhold from them that walk uprightly. (Psalm 84:11)

And the city [New Jerusalem] had no need of the sun, neither of the moon, to shine in it: for the glory of God did lighten it, and the Lamb [Christ] is the light thereof. (Revelation 21:23)

Note Christ shining as the *sun*.

166  Christos Stratiotes: Greek for *Christ Warrior*.

167  Pentagram: see text on *pentagram* in chapter four for details.

This is the same symbol as the inverted pentagram of Satan in next drawing below, but—*disguised* to fool people.

The Wiccans still worship the goat devil by constructing this upright pentagram, but instead of calling him Baphomet, they call him *Kernunnos* or *Pan*.

Note the pentagram's resemblance to the masonry symbols (below): both the *inverted* pentagram, which is a symbol of *Baphomet* the goat devil (or Satan); and the compass, or architectural type "A" often seen on the outside of their buildings which is supposed to represent the tool of the "great architect" (they call him "God"—but they secretly know him as Lucifer). There are many books and informative articles one can read about the Freemasons, the all-seeing eye of Horus (or Lucifer), the capstone (or cornerstone), etc.

Note also that Satanist Aleister Crowley was a member of the Masonic Temple.

168  Harley-Davidson motorcycles © Harley-Davidson Inc.

169  Armageddon: I was thinking of the true battle between good and evil taking place in the spirit realm, which is a biblical reality. The book of Revelation describes the battle of Armageddon. However, End Times eschatology (or teaching) defers among believers. Some people uphold that Armageddon is a physical battle occurring at the end of the world. Others believe it is both a physical and a spiritual battle. While still others believe it is only a spiritual

battle, and that Revelation is a symbolic book where everything is happening on a spiritual level only—using natural symbols.

170 Locust:

And he opened the bottomless pit, and there arose a smoke out of the pit, as the smoke of a great furnace; and the sun and the air were darkened by reason of the smoke of the pit.

And there came out of the smoke locusts upon the earth: and unto them was given power, as the scorpions of the earth have power.

And the shapes of the locusts were like unto horses prepared unto battle; and on their heads as it were crowns of gold, and their faces were as the faces of men.

And they had hair as the hair of women, and their teeth were as the teeth of lions.

And they had breastplates, as it were breastplates of iron; and the sound of their wings was as the sound of chariots of many horses running to battle.

And they had tails like unto scorpions, and there were stings in their tails: and their power was to hurt men five months.

And they had a king over them which is the angel of the bottomless pit whose name in the Hebrew tongue is Abaddon [translates to *Destruction*], but in the Greek tongue hath his name Apollyon [translates to *Destroyer*]. (Revelation 9:2, 3, 7-11)

Translations for *Abaddon* and *Apollyon* from *The Thayer's Greek-English Lexicon of the New Testament* by Joseph H. Thayer; copyright 1977 Baker Books.

171 River: symbolic of the Holy Spirit; and also of the washing, or spiritual rebirth of one who confesses his/her sins and accepts Jesus as his/her Savior.

He that believeth on me [Jesus], as the scripture hath said, out of his belly [the midst of him—his spirit] shall flow rivers of living water.

But this spake he of the *Spirit*, which they that believe on him should receive: for the *Holy Ghost* was not yet given; because that Jesus was not yet glorified [had not yet died and ascended to heaven]. (John 7:38, 39)

And he showed me a pure river of water of life, clear as crystal, proceeding out of the throne of God and of the Lamb. (Revelation 22:1)

Not by works of righteousness which we have done [previous to our spiritual conversion], but according to his mercy he saved us, by the *washing* of regeneration, and renewing of the *Holy Ghost.* (Titus 3:5)

172 And it came to pass, through the lightness of her whoredom, that she defiled the land, and committed adultery [spiritually] with stones and with *stocks* [*trees,* as it translates]. (Jeremiah 3:9)

Saying to a *stock* [tree], Thou art my father; and to a stone, Thou hast brought me forth: for they have turned their back unto me, and not their face: but in the time of their trouble they will say, Arise, and save us.

But where are thy gods that thou hast made thee? let them arise, if they can save thee in the time of thy trouble... (Jeremiah 2:27,28)

Translation borrowed from: *Strong's Exhaustive Concordance of the Bible* by James Strong; S.T.D., LL.D., 1890; public domain.

173 Jawa: A small, cloaked creature with glowing yellow eyes from the Star Wars film series; somewhat resembling the Grim Reaper. TM & © Lucasfilm Ltd. All Rights Reserved.

174 Electromagnetic field: see text concerning *triangle* in chapter nine, as well as its corresponding endnote.

175 *The Egyptian Book of the Dead* © June 1967 by E.A. Wallis Budge; Peter Smith Pub.; ISBN: 0844617644.

176 *The Tibetan Book of the Dead* © June 1974 (3rd edition) by W.Y. Evans-Wentz (Editor); Oxford Univ. Pr. (Trade); ISBN: 0195002237.

177 Sun Chips: Frito Lay Inc.; © Recot, Inc.

178 Scrabble ™ © Milton Bradley.

179 Chevrolet Nova ™ © General Motors.

180 Chevrolet Nova ™ © General Motors.

181 King Arthur: see endnote 162 under *Arthurian legend.*

182 The Lucky Charms guy: Lucky the Leprechaun, a.k.a. L.C. Leprechaun for Lucky Charms cereal © General Mills.

183 The Chipmunks: introduced in 1958 by Ross Bagdasarian as *Alvin and the Chipmunks,* and later brought to TV as *The Chipmunks* © 1961 © 1983.

184 Holy Grail: symbolic of the New Testament communion in Christ's blood, this is said to have been the same cup, or chalice, he used at the Last Supper.

185 *Monty Python and the Holy Grail* © 1975 Columbia/Tri Star Studios; Directed by Terry Gilliam. ASIN: 6302293553.

186 King Arthur: see endnote 162 under *Arthurian legend.*

187 The Lucky Charms guy: Lucky the Leprechaun, a.k.a. L.C. Leprechaun for Lucky Charms cereal © General Mills.

188 The Chipmunks: introduced in 1958 by Ross Bagdasarian as *Alvin and the Chipmunks,* and later brought to TV as *The Chipmunks* © 1961 © 1983.

189 River of Fire: symbolic of the *Lake of Fire,* or *Gehenna,* the second death and final *Hell:* Sean was trying to hint to me that he was into Satanism, but I didn't understand.

And the devil that deceived them was cast into the lake of fire and brimstone, where the beast and the false prophet are, and shall be tormented day and night for ever and ever. (Revelation 20:10)

Notice: the Devil will be tormented, not the *tormentor!*

Please note also: there are four words for *Hell:*

1.Hades (Greek) = a temporary abode of departed souls, including a previous compartment for the righteous before Christ took them to Heaven with him (they could not ascend until Christ died and washed the sin from their conscience, since the previous animal sacrifices required by God under the Old Testament Law could only provide a temporary *covering* for their sin, but not wash it away). The compartment the Old Testament Saints stayed in while waiting for Christ to die was known as *Abraham's bosom* (See Luke 16:22-31). Now, however, *righteous* souls go directly to Heaven when they die; just as the wicked go directly to Hell.

2.Sheol (Hebrew) = a form of the Greek word *Hades.* A conscious existence after natural death in which the wicked suffer, and at one time the righteous (before Jesus' death) waited in paradise (a temporary holding place) for him to die for their sins and then come and take them to Heaven. Sheol was typically referred to as *the grave* underneath the ground, or *death.*

3.Tartarus (Greek) = a pit of darkness (spiritual darkness) where the wicked angels, or demons, are reserved until the Day of Judgment. In my opinion, they are only reserved in the *mind* of God, however, and are not really in Hell at this moment, as the Bible tells us they were thrown out of Heaven and now *walk the earth* seeking souls for their destruction. It would be the same as you or me buying a ticket to ride a train and because of this, having reservations to our destination, but not *there yet* as we haven't actually boarded the train. The Devil and wicked angels are reserved in everlasting chains until the Day of Judgment, when they will be cast into the Lake of Fire. (See 2 Peter 2:4 and Jude 6)

4.Gehenna (Greek) = the *permanent* abode of everlasting torture for the Devil, demons, and all those who refuse to accept Christ as their personal Savior, thus separating themselves from God.

Some translations of the word *Hell* obtained from the *Vines Complete Expository Dictionary of Old and New Testament Words* © 1985 (a derivative work) by W.E. Vine, with Merrill F. Unger and William White, Jr.; Thomas Nelson Publishers; ISBN: 0-8407-7559-8.

190 Witch's pentagram: see endnote 167 under *pentagram,* and text in chapters IV. and IX.

191 Buzzing of flies: see beginning text of chapter VI, as well as endnote 202 under *Flies.*

192 The Headless Horseman: from *The Legend of Sleepy Hollow* by Washington Irving © January 1997 (Reprint edition); Troll Communications; ISBN: 0893753483.

193 Psychic abilities/power: the Devil has power, and can perform miracles. However, the price for such power is severe demonic oppression, possibly possession, insanity, and loss of one's soul.

Even him whose coming is after the working of Satan with all power and signs and lying wonders.

And with all deceivableness of unrighteousness in them that perish; because they received not the love of the truth, that they might be saved.

And for this cause God shall send them strong delusion, that they should believe a lie;

That they all might be damned who believed not the truth, but had pleasure in unrighteousness. (2 Thessalonians 2:9-12)

For they are the spirits of devils, working miracles, which go forth unto the kings of the earth and of the whole world, to gather them to the battle of that great day of God Almighty. (Revelation 16:14)

Note: God gives believers the Holy Spirit, who can gift people with *words of knowledge* (to supernaturally know something past or present), *words of wisdom* (to supernaturally know something future), *prophecy*, and *discernment of spirits*. These are some of the abilities Satan counterfeits. Please also note that many psychics, or those with paranormal abilities, have been gifted by their Creator God, but are using their giftings on the wrong side by tapping into the spirit realm illegally, without the authority of Christ, thereby receiving their knowledge from Satan and his demons.

194 Staircase, or stairway to heaven: Symbolic of Jesus Christ, as the mediator between man and God, restoring contact with our heavenly Father once more. See endnote 2 under *ladder*.

It is he [God] that buildeth his *stories* [translates *steps, stairs, to ascend, to go up*] in the heaven, and hath founded his troop in the earth; he that calleth for the waters of the sea, and poureth them out upon the face of the earth: The Lord is his name. (Amos 9:6)

Translation from: *Strong's Exhaustive Concordance of the Bible* by James Strong; S.T.D., LL.D., 1890.; public domain.

195 The Fool card: This card (though modified slightly from its original version in this endnote description, but still retaining the essential elements needed to make the author's point), depicts a man with closed eyes, standing with one foot over a cliff, ready to step off, unbeknownst to him, into the abyss of spiritual darkness. A hand is tugging him by the seat of his pants, symbolic of the little *tugging* in the seat of our conscience that often seeks to be heard, or felt.

The Fool signifies one who is spiritually blind, or foolish:

The fool has said in his heart, There is no God. They are corrupt, they have done abominable works, there is none that doeth good. (Psalm 14:1)

Let them alone: they be blind leaders of the blind. And if the blind lead the blind, both shall *fall into the ditch* (or spiritual darkness). (Matthew 15:14)

Though in its positive aspect, The Fool card is said to signify one who takes a leap into the unknown to gain true spiritual wisdom, let it be known that leaping into the darkness of the Occult is *not* the way to gain spiritual wisdom, but rather, demonic oppression and/or possession, and insanity.

196 Pit: symbolic of Hell, or spiritual darkness. The Devil is reserved in the mind of God to be cast into Hell on the Day of Judgment. Until then, he walks the earth with his demons, seeking souls to take with him.

He brought me up also out of an horrible pit, out of the miry clay, and set my feet upon a rock, and established my goings. (Psalm 40:2)

And he laid hold on the dragon, that old serpent, which is the Devil and Satan, and bound him a thousand years (which can also mean *unknown or unlimited amount of time*, according to some Greek scholars).

[Note that eschatology (or End Times Teaching/Interpretation) defers among bible scholars].

… And cast him into the bottomless pit, and shut him up, and set a seal upon him, that he should deceive the nations no more till the thousand years should be fulfilled: and after that he must be loosed a little season. (Revelation 20:2,3)

197 Snakes: commonly symbolic of the Devil and evil. See endnote 128 under *snake*.

198 In torment:

And in hell he (the certain rich man) lift up his eyes, being in torments, and seeth Abraham afar off, and Lazarus in his bosom.

And he cried and said, Father Abraham, have mercy on me, and send Lazarus, that he may dip the tip of his finger in water and cool my tongue; for I am tormented in this flame. (Luke 16:23,24)

199 Five hundred dollars: charging a *price*—symbolic of *selling* something. Also note that FIVE is the number of "I will" statements that Satan made before his fall from Heaven (Isaiah 14:12-15), as well as the number of points on a witch's and Satanist's pentagram. In the New Testament, FIVE signifies ministry, and Satan also has a ministry trying to recruit souls for Hell; because he will

be burning in the Lake of Fire, and wants to take as many souls with him as he can.

200 The taxi driver on the road of life:

The *highway* [road] of the upright is to depart from evil: he that keepeth his way preserveth his soul. (Proverbs 16:17)

201 Triangle: though symbolic of many things, including the biblical trinity of Father, Son, and Holy Spirit, the triangle, when *inverted*, is to witches, Satanists, and Freemasons the sign of the horned god, Kernunnos/Pan, i.e. Baphomet: the Devil. This being, because the two points (on either side) represent his horns, while the point facing downward represents his face; i.e. the shape of a goat's head. Please also note that the triangle right side up in the Occult represents the establishment of the New World Order, or Illuminati. (see the dollar bill, for example), with the all-seeing eye of Horus/Lucifer and the triangle missing the capstone (cornerstone), which represents the false Christ, or Antichrist who is yet to come.

202 **Flies:** Baal-zebub/Beel-zebub, both names for Satan, translate as: *Lord of the Fly* in Hebrew, or *dung-god* in Greek.

Translation from: *Strong's Exhaustive Concordance of the Bible* by James Strong; S.T.D., LL.D., 1890; public domain.

And he said unto him, Thus saith the Lord, Forasmuch as thou hast sent messengers to enquire of Baal-zebub the god of Ekron, is it not because there is no God in Israel to enquire of his word? therefore thou shalt not come down off that bed in which thou art gone up, but shalt surely die. (2 Kings 1:16)

But when the Pharisees heard it, they said, This fellow doth not cast out devils, but by Beelzebub the prince of the devils. (Matthew 12:24)

203 House: symbolic of one's body, both in the physical and spiritual sense. Made by our Creator, we are to live in a way that brings honor to our body, by taking care of it *physically*, and at the same time, nurturing it *spiritually*; seeking the truth that we may live. See also endnote 108 under *Castle.*

204 Light: symbolic of spiritual enlightenment, life, and holiness:

That was the true Light [Jesus], which lighteth every man that cometh into the world. (John 1:9)

Wherefore he saith, Awake thou that sleepest, and arise from the dead [spiritually] and Christ shall give thee light. (Ephesians 5:14)

Ye are the light of the world. A city that is set on a hill cannot be hid.

Let your light so shine before men, that they may see your good works, and glorify your Father which is in heaven. (Matthew 5:14,16)

205 Window: symbolic of the soul:

Behold, when we come into the land, thou [Rahab the harlot] shalt bind this line of scarlet thread (symbolic of Christ's blood) in the window (symbolic of our soul) which thou didst let us down by: and thou shalt bring thy father, and thy mother, and thy brethren, and all thy father's household, home unto thee.

But Joshua had said unto the two men that had spied out the country, Go into the harlot's house, and bring out thence the woman, and all that she hath, as ye sware unto her.

And the young men that were spies went in, and brought out Rahab, and her father, and her mother, and her brethren, and all that she had; and they brought out all her kindred, and left them without the camp of Israel.

And they burnt the city with fire... [type of Judgment Day/Hell]. And Joshua [meaning *Jesus, Savior,* in Greek] *saved* Rahab the harlot [harlot is a type of the world] alive, and her father's household, and all that she had; and she dwelleth in Israel even unto this day; because she hid the messengers, which Joshua sent to spy out Jericho. (Joshua 2:18; 6:22-25)

206 Gift and blood: symbolic of Christ's sacrificial offering to us in order that we may have eternal life.

For the wages of sin is death; but the gift of God is eternal life through Jesus Christ our Lord. (Romans 6:23)

For the life of the flesh is in the blood: and I have given it to you upon the altar to make an atonement for your souls: for it is the blood that maketh an atonement for the soul. (Leviticus 17:11)

In whom we have redemption through his blood, the forgiveness of sins, according to the riches of his grace. (Ephesians 1:7)

207 In the Old Testament, Jachin and Boaz were pillars in the temple of God, symbolic of saints, or believers, who persevere until the end.

And he set up the *pillars* in the porch of the temple: and he set up the right *pillar,* and called the name thereof Jachin (for speed, on the South): and he set up the left *pillar,* and called the name thereof Boaz (for power, on the North). (1 Kings 7:21)

Him that overcometh will I make a *pillar* in the temple of my God, and he shall go no more out: and I will write upon him the name of my God, and the name of the city of my God, which is new Jerusalem, which cometh down out of heaven from my God: and I will write upon him my new name. (Revelation 3:12)

*Speed* and *power* symbolisms referenced from *The Zondervan Pictorial Bible Dictionary* © 1963, 1964, 1967 by Zondervan Publishing House; with General Editor Merrill C. Tenney; ISBN: 0-310-23560-X.

208 Cup: represents salvation/Christ's blood. See endnote 117 under *Chalice* or *Cup.*

I will take the cup of salvation, and call upon the name of the Lord. (Psalm 116:13)

209 Possibly from *The Teachings of Don Juan: A Yaqui Way Of Knowledge* by Carlos Castaneda. © June 1985 (Reissue edition); Mass Market Paperback; Pocket Books; ISBN: 0671600419.

210 Window: symbolic of the soul. See endnote 205 under *Window.*

211 *Magick In Theory And Practice* © by Aleister Crowley; Castle Publications; Out of print.

212 From *Magick In Theory And Practice* © by Aleister Crowley; Castle Publications; Out of print.

213 Sir Lancelot, Guenivere and King Arthur: see endnote 162 under *Arthurian legend.*

214 From *Magick In Theory And Practice* © by Aleister Crowley; Castle Publications; Out of Print.

215 Be not deceived; God is not mocked: for whatsoever a man soweth, that shall he also reap. (Galatians 6:7)

Who [God] will render to every man according to his deeds: Tribulation and anguish, upon every soul of man that doeth evil, of the Jew first, and also of the Gentile;

But glory, honour, and peace, to every man that worketh good, to the Jew first, and also to the Gentile. (Romans 2:6,9,10)

216 From *Magick In Theory And Practice* © by Aleister Crowley; Castle Publications; Out of print.

217 Little Debbie Cakes © McKee Foods Corporation.

218 Brownies, Oatmeal Cream Pies, Spice Cakes: products of Little Debbie; ibid.

219 Little Debbie Cakes © McKee Foods Corporation.

220 Dove: symbolic of the Holy Spirit.

And Jesus, when he was baptized, went up straightway out of the water: and, lo, the heavens were opened unto him, and he saw the Spirit of God descending like a dove, and lighting upon him. (Matthew 3:16)

221 Athame, or two-edged knife: This is merely a counterfeit of God's *word*, which is described as a two-edged sword that believers wield for protection. It is a natural object representing a spiritual principle in the Bible.

And take the helmet of salvation, and the sword of the Spirit, which is the *word of God.* (Ephesians 6:17)

For the *word of God* is quick, and powerful, and sharper than any two-edged sword, piercing even to the dividing asunder of soul and spirit, and is a discerner of the thoughts and intents of the heart. Hebrews 4:12)

And to the angel of the church in Pergamos write; These things saith he [Jesus] which hath the sharp sword with two edges.

Repent; or else I will come unto thee and fight against thee with the sword of *my mouth.* (Revelation 2:12,16)

222 Circle of energy, or magic circle: If one is walking in righteousness according to God's word, and free of sin, he is automatically protected spiritually by

God, who surrounds him. He does not need to draw a circle, because the circle is already there:

As the mountains are round about Jerusalem, so the Lord is round about his people from henceforth even for ever. (Psalm 125:2)

And he answered, Fear not: for they that be with us are more than they that be with them.

And Elisha prayed, and said, Lord, I pray thee, open his eyes, that he may see. And the Lord opened the eyes of the young man; and he saw: and behold, the mountain was full of horses and chariots of fire (angels—see next scripture) round about Elisha. (2 Kings 6:16,17)

The chariots of God are twenty thousand, even *thousands of angels:* the Lord is among them, as in Sinai, the holy place. (Psalm 68:17)

The angel of the Lord encampeth round about them that fear him, and delivereth them. (Psalm 34:7)

223 Silver hook: Satan was using War as bait to hook a fish, or soul—*me.* Note: the fish has long been a symbol of Christianity.

224 Downward direction: Hades, or Hell, the place of lost souls, is said to be located in a shaft somewhere down in the earth. Compare these terms: the *under*world, the *under*ground.

225 Abstain from all appearance of evil. (1 Thessalonians 5:22)

For rebellion *is as* the sin of witchcraft, and stubbornness *is as* iniquity and idolatry. (1 Samuel 15:23)

226 Balaam was a diviner hired to curse the children of Israel, but God wouldn't allow him to:

He sent messengers therefore unto Balaam the son of Beor to Pethor, which is by the river of the land of the children of his people, to call him, saying, Behold, there is a people come out from Egypt: behold, they cover the face of the earth, and they abide over against me:

Come now therefore, I pray thee, _curse_ me this people; for they are too mighty for me: peradventure I shall prevail, that we may smite them... (Numbers 22:5,6)

How shall I curse, whom God hath not cursed? or how shall I defy, whom the LORD hath not defied? (Numbers 23:8)

Behold, I [Balaam] have received commandment to bless: and he [God] hath blessed; and I _cannot reverse it_. (Numbers 23:20)

Surely there is no enchantment against Jacob, neither is there any divination against Israel. (Numbers 23:23)

227 Baalim is a plural form of Baal, a Phoenician god and a form of _Baal-zebub:_

And it came to pass, as soon as Gideon was dead, that the children of Israel turned again, and went a whoring after Baalim, and made Baal-berith their god. (Judges 8:33)

And the children of Israel did evil in the sight of the Lord, and forgat the Lord their God, and served Baalim and the groves. (Judges 3:7)

Translation obtained from _Strong's Exhaustive Concordance of the Bible_ by James Strong; S.T.D., LL.D., 1890; public domain.

228 Medium: One who has a _familiar spirit_ [a demon].

Then said Saul unto his servants, Seek me a woman that hath a familiar spirit, that I may go to her, and enquire of her. And his servants said to him, Behold, there is a woman that hath a familiar spirit at Endor.

And Saul disguised himself, and put on other raiment, and he went, and two men with him, and they came to the woman by night: and he said, I pray thee, divine unto me by the familiar spirit, bring him up, whom I shall name unto thee. (1 Samuel 28:7,8)

229 Dodge Omni © Chrysler Corporation.

230 Ibid.

231 Volvo stationwagon © AB Volvo Car Corp.

232 Aleister Crowley: see endnotes 101, 114.

233 © The Salem Witch Museum; Salem, Massachusetts.

234 Goat's head skull: See endnote 87 under *Kernunnos/Pan*.

235 Mainliner: junkie, heroin addict.

236 Exhibit © The Salem Witch Museum; Salem, Massachusetts.

237 Tour Excerpts of The Salem Witch Museum are taken from *A Guide to the Salem Witchcraft Hysteria of 1692* © June 1984 (Reprint edition) by David C. Brown; ISBN: 0961341505. Notice: I have not borrowed any text or quotations directly from the author of this tour. The story told here is historical fact, and can be found in educational textbooks, where I originally read it in college.

238 Tour Excerpts of The Salem Witch Museum: From *A Guide to the Salem Witchcraft Hysteria of 1692* © June 1984 (Reprint edition) by David C. Brown; ISBN: 0961341505.

Notice: I have not borrowed any text or quotations directly from the author of this tour. The story told here is historical fact, and can be found in educational textbooks, where I originally read it in college.

239 Tour Excerpts; ibid.

240 © The Salem Witch Museum; Salem, Massachusetts.

241 Covenant: compare coven. Most covenants were sealed with blood in the Bible (Leviticus 17:11). The Israelites were required to shed the blood of animals to *cover* (though not remove) their sins (Hebrew 9:18-22; 10:4). Jesus shed his precious blood to *remove* sin completely from the conscience of man and establish a new and better covenant (Hebrews 9:12-14). And the covenant between man and wife is shed with blood (if the woman is a virgin at the time of intercourse) (Deuteronomy 22:15-17, 20, 21).

So Satan also desires the shedding of blood in order that his power over a person be even stronger and more binding. The blood tells him, in the spiritual realm, that he has a covenant with you; you belong to him.

242 Note that God says he is not the author (or creator) of *confusion* (or pandemonium), but of peace (1 Corinthians 14:33). He says that all things should be done decently and *in order* (or orderly) (1 Corinthians 14:40). Therefore, we can conclude that this monkey was really a satanic spirit in disguise, as he promoted the opposite of what God creates and commands. His presence brought confusion rather than peace.

243 Three: in the Bible, it is a number signifying the trinity of God as expressed in three persons: Father, Son, and Holy Spirit. In Satan's kingdom, it represents

the father of lies (Satan), the antichrist, and the unholy, satanic spirit of rebellion/witchcraft. Without realizing it, I was painting an accurate picture of a spiritual principle taking place in War's life. In their negative aspect, the balloons were symbolic of the prince of the power of air (Satan), as well as the lies of that antichrist spirit of rebellion that were controlling his life.

244 Volts of electricity: We are told Satan transforms himself into an angel of light, and Jesus compared him to *lightning*:

And the seventy returned again with joy, saying, Lord, even the devils are subject unto us through thy name.

And he [Jesus] said unto them, I beheld Satan as *lightning* fall from heaven. (Luke 10:17,18)

Incidentally, the very name *Lucifer,* given to the Devil before he sinned and became evil, means *brightness,* or *son of the morning.* This explains why he can transform himself into an angel of *light.*

Please observe, also, the satanic lightning bolt on many satanic music albums, CDs, and logos/cover art. This usually indicates that they have sold their soul to the Devil for musical talent, fame and fortune, as even some will openly admit (though others keep it a secret, because remember: the occult is supposed to be *hidden* or *secret).* There are many great articles, videos, and documentaries that cover this fact in more detail.

245 *Magick In Theory And Practice* © by Aleister Crowley; Castle Publications; Out of Print.

246 *Dracula:* Original edition written in1897 by Bram Stoker.

247 Movie *Bram Stoker's Dracula* © 1992 Columbia/TriStar Pictures; Produced and Directed by Francis Ford Coppola.

Starring Gary Oldman as Dracula, and Winona Ryder as Mina. Based on the 1897 novel entitled *Dracula* by Bram Stoker; Ibid.

248 To the best of my knowledge, although I no longer have the book to refer to, this is from the book formerly titled: *The Illustrated Anthology of Sorcery, Magic and Alchemy* © by Emile Angelo Grillot De Givry; ASIN: 0685706583 (out of print).

Now entitled: *Witchcraft: Magic and Alchemy* © June 1971 by Emile Angelo Grillot De Givry, Grillot De Givry, J. Courtney Locke (Translator), Givry De Grillot; Dover Pubns; ISBN:0486224937.

249 Arrow pointed downward: see endnote 224 under *Downward direction.*

250 Ashteroth/Ashtaroth: god/goddess of the Zidonians, Philistines and Phoenicians, pertaining to love and war:

And the children of Israel did evil again in the sight of the Lord, and served *Baalim,* and Ashtaroth, and the gods of Syria, and the gods of Zidon, and the gods of Moab, and the gods of the children of the Philistines, and forsook the Lord, and served not him. (Judges 10:6)

Note: Often sacrifices to these gods included ritualistic orgies.

Translation from *Strong's Exhaustive Concordance of the Bible* by James Strong; S.T.D., LL.D., 1890; public domain.

251 © Vick's ® Nyquil Distr. by Procter and Gamble.

252 Tylenol © McNeil Consumer Products Company.

253 Sudafed ® Products © Warner-Lambert Company.

254 *The Book of Mormon* © June 1973 (Rev. Edition) by Joseph Smith; Herald Pub. House; ISBN: 0830902732.

255 *The Lost Teachings of Jesus, Volume Two* © March 1, 1989 by Mark L. Prophet, Elizabeth Clare Prophet; Summit Univ. Press; ISBN: 091676673X.

256 Great weight lifted off me: the "monkey on my back" was gone, meaning, the Devil's oppressive chains were being loosed.

257 To the best of my knowledge, though I no longer have the book to refer to, this is from the book formerly titled: *The Illustrated Anthology of Sorcery, Magic and Alchemy* © by Emile Angelo Grillot De Givry; ASIN: 0685706583 (out of print). Now entitled: *Witchcraft: Magic and Alchemy* © June 1971 by Emile Angelo Grillot De Givry, Grillot De Givry, J. Courtney Locke (Translator), Givry De Grillot; Dover Pubns; ISBN:0486224937.

258 *The Exorcist* © 1973 Warner Studios; Directed by William Friedkin. Possessed girl Regan MacNeil played by Linda Blair.

259 *The Exorcist;* ibid.

260 *Jacob's Ladder* © 1990 Artisan Entertainment; Directed by Adrian Lyne.

261 From the movie *Jacob's Ladder;* ibid.

262 Jell-O © Kraft Foods Inc.

263 Lost the ability of divination: The ability to divine comes from Satan. While such divination might come to pass or hold some element of truth, it is only because the Devil possesses a certain degree of knowledge and power. However, God's power is much, much greater. In the Bible, when the apostle of Jesus cast out a spirit of divination from a woman, she lost her supernatural ability.

And it came to pass, as we went to prayer, a certain damsel possessed with a spirit of divination met us, which brought her masters much gain by soothsaying:

The same followed Paul and us, and cried, saying, These men are the servants of God, which shew unto us the way of salvation.

And this did she many days.

But Paul, being grieved, turned and said to the spirit, I command thee in the name of Jesus Christ to come out of her. And he came out the same hour.

And when her masters saw that the hope of their gains was gone, they caught Paul and Silas, and drew them into the marketplace unto the rulers... (Acts 16:16-19)

264 But my God shall supply all your need according to his riches in glory by Christ Jesus. (Philippians 4:19)

265 Dodge Omni © Chrysler Corporation.

266 Worship a graven image of the cross: The Bible states that God is a Spirit, and they that worship him must worship him in spirit and in truth. He is not a rosary or a cross. He is not a statue. He is not a tree, a stone, etc. He is a Spirit, and the Father of Spirits. Therefore, we are to worship *Him* and *Him alone.* Though we cannot (unless granted a holy vision) see Him, we are to pray to *Him*, and not to a graven image. Nowhere in the Bible did followers of God use rosary beads, pray vain repetitions in order to receive forgiveness of sins or obtain favor from God, or worship statues. Only the heathen did such things. Rosaries are modified forms of magic amulets supposed to contain power. Repetitious prayers are modified forms of magic incantations. Statue worship is clearly a violation of the first commandment, as well as a form of idolatry, or witchcraft:

Thou shalt have no other gods before me.

Thou shalt not make unto thee any graven image, or any likeness of anything that is in heaven above, or that is in the earth beneath, or that is in the water under the earth [for the purpose of worshiping it]:

Thou shalt not bow down thyself to them, nor serve them: for I the Lord thy God am a jealous God... (Exodus 20:3-5)

But when ye pray, use not vain repetitions, as the heathen do: for they think they shall be heard for their much speaking. (Matthew 6:7)

Ye worship ye know not what... [said by Jesus to a Samaritan woman who practiced pagan worship along with Judaism]

But the hour cometh, and now is, when the true worshippers shall worship the Father in spirit and in truth: for the Father seeketh such to worship him. God is a Spirit; and they that worship him must worship him in *spirit* and in *truth*. (John 4:22-24)

God is a living Spirit who is able to talk to us in many ways: through thoughts, through other people and circumstances, through visions, dreams, scripture, supernatural experiences, and in a still small voice. But never will any of these ways of communication violate His Word, for His Word of truth remains forever.

267 Lemon Pledge © S.C. Johnson and Son Inc.

268 Greyhound Bus Station © Greyhound Transportation.

269 Chevrolet Cavalier ™ © General Motors.

270 Denny's Restaurant © Syndicated.

271 Adonai: The Hebrew name for God, which translates, *Lord*.

Borrowed from *Strong's Exhaustive Concordance of the Bible* by James Strong; S.T.D., LL.D., 1890; public domain.

272 Elohim/Elohiym: *Plural* form of God, embracing the Trinity of Father, Son and Holy Spirit. Reference: ibid.

273 Aleister Crowley: see endnote 114 under *Golden Dawn*.

274 *Magick In Theory And Practice* © by Aleister Crowley; Castle Publications; Out of print.

275 Dodge Omni © Chrysler Corporation.

276 Kundalini Serpent: reference endnote 141 under *kundalini serpent*.

277 Denny's Restaurant © Syndicated.

278 Country-fried steak: Chicken Fried Steak ™ Denny's Restaurant © Syndicated.

279 Movie *Bram Stoker's Dracula* © 1992 Columbia/TriStar Pictures; Produced and Directed by Francis Ford Coppola.

Starring Gary Oldman as Dracula, and Winona Ryder as Mina.

Based on the 1897 novel entitled *Dracula* by Bram Stoker.

280 And no marvel, for Satan himself is transformed into an angel of light.

Therefore it is no great thing if his ministers also be transformed as the ministers of righteousness; whose end shall be according to their works. (2 Corinthians 11:14,15)

281 See section: *Commands to Destroy All Idols/Occult Paraphernalia* in this book.

282 Repenting of our sins: the first step of salvation.

And that repentance and remission of sins should be preached in his name [Jesus] among all nations, beginning at Jerusalem. (Luke 24:47)

283 Asked Jesus to become our Lord and Savior: the next step.

That if thou shalt confess with thy mouth the Lord Jesus, and shalt believe in thine heart that God hath raised him from the dead, thou shalt be saved.

For with the heart man believeth unto righteousness; and with the mouth confession is made unto salvation. (Romans 10:9,10)

284 Dodge Omni © Chrysler Corporation.

285 Cocoa Puffs cereal © General Mills.

286 Inspired by the story, *The Pied Piper of Hamelin* © by Robert Browning; 1888 Frederick Warne and Co., Ltd.; London. Illustrated by Kate Greenaway.

287 Ibid.

288 Tabrets and pipes: Lucifer was the angel of music in heaven, leading God's choir. Today, he still holds a powerful ministry in music, though it has been corrupted through his fall. *His* music produces feelings of lust, pride, witchcraft/enchantment, anger, rebellion, and anxiety. God's holy and

anointed music (though not always of slow tempo or in traditional, hymnal style), enables spiritual breakthrough and produces spiritual fruit such as joy and peace. It edifies us while ministering the word and presence of God. People have been healed simply by listening to holy, anointed music. When King Saul had an evil spirit oppressing him, David played his anointed music on the harp and the evil spirit left him. (1 Samuel 16:14-23)

Thou [Lucifer] hast been in Eden the garden of God; every precious stone was thy covering, the sardius, topaz, and the diamond, the beryl, the onyx, and the jasper, the sapphire, the emerald, and the carbuncle, and gold: the workmanship of thy tabrets and of thy pipes was prepared *in* thee in the day that thou wast created. (Ezekiel 28:13)

Thy pomp is brought down to the grave, and the noise of thy viols [translates to *lyre or psaltery*]: the worm is spread under thee, and the worms cover thee.

How art thou fallen from heaven, O Lucifer, son of the morning! how art thou cut down to the ground, which didst weaken the nations! (Isaiah 14:11,12)

Psalm 22:3 tells us that God inhabits the praises of his people:

But thou [God] art holy, *O thou that inhabitest the praises* of Israel.

Note: We can conclude that if God inhabits the praises of his people, the Devil also inhabits the music that glorifies *him.*

Translation from *Strong's Exhaustive Concordance of the Bible* by James Strong; S.T.D., LL.D., 1890; public domain.

289 Whether planted in our minds by the Devil and his demons, created by our own imaginations, or triggered by an outward source such as      an object or song with which we have a mental association, thoughts are *not sin* unless we entertain them. Like changing the channel on a television set, we have the power to control our thoughts. The Bible says we are to *bring them into captivity* instead of letting them have free course of our minds. We are instructed to *cast down wrong thinking* that opposes God's truth, and only dwell on positive thoughts that are righteous and pure. Christians are to *put on the mind of Christ,* meaning, to think as *he* would think—on God and His word—so as not to entertain thoughts that would lead them into unrighteousness. Note: sin first comes from *within;* originating in the *heart* of mankind. Sin stems from unrighteous motivation of the heart. (See Matthew 15:19,20 below).

*Casting down* imaginations, and every high thing that exalteth itself against the knowledge of God, and *bringing into captivity* every thought to the obedience of Christ. (2 Corinthians 10:5)

Finally brethren, whatsoever things are true, whatsoever things are honest, whatsoever things are just, whatsoever things are pure, whatsoever things are lovely, whatsoever things are of good report; if there be any virtue, and if there be any praise, think on these things. (Philippians 4:8)

Let this mind be in you, which was also in Christ Jesus. (Philippians 2:5)

...But we have the mind of Christ. (1 Corinthians 2:16)

Wherefore gird up the loins of your mind, be sober, and hope to the end for the grace that is to be brought unto you at the revelation of Jesus Christ. (1 Peter 1:13)

For *out of the heart* proceed evil thoughts, murders, adulteries, fornications, thefts, false witness, blasphemies.

These are the things which defile a man [if entertained]... (Matthew 15:19,20)

290 Dodge Omni © Chrysler Corporation.

291 For there is no respect of persons with God. (Romans 2:11)

But if ye have respect to persons, ye commit sin, and are convinced [convicted] of the law as transgressors. (James 2:9)

292 "With each verse we read, I felt my faith growing and growing." The word of God is the bread of life to our soul. Just as our physical bodies need food in order to thrive and be healthy, so our spiritual bodies need spiritual food in order to live and grow.

So then faith cometh by hearing, and hearing by the word of God. (Romans 10:17)

...The words that I [Jesus] speak unto you, they are spirit, and they are life. (John 6:63)

...That he [God] might make thee to know that man doth not live by bread only, but by every word that proceedeth out of the mouth of the Lord doth man live. (Deuteronomy 8:3)

And Jesus said unto them, I am the bread of life: he that cometh to me shall never hunger, and he that believeth on me shall never thirst. (John 6:35)

293 *The Exorcist* © 1973 Warner Studios; Directed by William Friedkin.

294 Isaiah 11:2; 61:1; (Luke 3:21,22—*After* Jesus was water baptized, he was praying, and received the Holy Ghost); Luke 4:18; Acts 10:38

295 Father of lies:

Ye are of your father the devil, and the lusts of your father ye will do. He was a murderer from the beginning, and abode not in the truth, because there is no truth in him. When he speaketh a lie, he speaketh of his own: for he is a liar, and the father of it. (John 8:44)

296 Speaking in tongues, the evidence of the baptism of the Holy Spirit: it is a supernatural *prayer language*—us speaking to God, as opposed to the *gift of tongues,* which is God speaking to us followed by a *gift of interpretation* so we can know what He is saying. In the Old Testament, God prophesied that He would give rest and refreshing unto his people through the use of another prayer language, or utterance, that would build up their spirits as they pray:

For with stammering lips and another tongue will he [by the Holy Spirit] speak to this people. To whom he said, This is the rest wherewith ye may cause the weary to rest; and this is the refreshing: yet would not hear. (Isaiah 28:12)

This prophecy was fulfilled on the day of Pentecost after Jesus' crucifixion, when the disciples waited like he commanded them, for the promise of the Holy Spirit which they would need in order to minister effectively and mortify [put to death] the sinful deeds of their flesh.

And being assembled together with them, [Jesus] commanded them that they should not depart from Jerusalem, but wait for the promise of the Father, which, saith he, ye have heard of me.

For John truly baptized with water; but ye shall be baptized with the Holy Ghost not many days hence. (Acts 1:4,5)

But ye shall receive power, after that the Holy Ghost is come upon you: and ye shall be witnesses unto me both in Jerusalem, and in all Judaea, and in Samaria, and unto the uttermost part of the earth. (Acts 1:8)

And when the day of Pentecost was fully come, they were all with one accord in one place.

And suddenly there came a sound from heaven as of a rushing mighty wind, and it filled all the house where they were sitting.

And there appeared unto them cloven tongues like as of fire [an indication that the O.T. prophecy was being fulfilled], and it sat upon each of them.

And they were all filled with the Holy Ghost, and began to speak with other tongues as the Spirit gave them utterance. (Acts 2:1-4)

Likewise the Spirit also helpeth our infirmities; for we know not what we should pray for as we ought: but the Spirit itself maketh intercession for us with groanings which cannot be uttered [*uttered naturally or natively,* as the word implies in the context of this verse. It is a language we have not known by nature, unfamiliar to us before this time. Therefore, it is not in our natural makeup to utter such things without God's supernatural power enabling us to do so]. (Romans 8:26)

For if I pray in an *unknown* tongue, my spirit prayeth, but my understanding is unfruitful. (1 Corinthians 14:14)

Note again: the **prayer language** of tongues is not something we will understand because it's a language we don't know or haven't learned; it's coming from the Holy Spirit to our spirit. It can be either an earthly language foreign to us, or a heavenly language (the language of angels), but unlike the **gift** of tongues, it will not be known what we are saying because Holy Spirit is praying to God through us, using a supernatural language that does not need a gift of interpretation. This type of prayer is very effective in the spirit realm, since we don't always know how to pray perfectly for people or situations; but Holy Spirit does.

In summary: the **prayer language of tongues** is something believers can do anytime, anywhere, without needing a prompting from the Holy Spirit, and without needing interpretation.

A **gift of tongues,** on the other hand, is prompted by the Holy Spirit, and will need the gift of interpretation from either the speaker or someone else:

...To another the working of miracles; to another prophecy; to another discerning of spirits; to another *divers kinds of tongues* [or, the gift of tongues]; to another *the interpretation of tongues:*

But all these worketh that one and the selfsame Spirit, dividing to every man severally as he will. (1 Corinthians 12:10,11)

Paul the apostle made the distinction in Church, however, concerning those who were simply using the prayer language of tongues at inappropriate times (as opposed to the gift of tongues), and there was no gift of interpretation following, so no one knew what was being said. Though this would be okay in a corporate prayer setting (everyone praying in tongues), it isn't proper at a church service when it's not orderly and no one can be edified by it because they can't understand what is being communicated. (1 Corinthians 14)

297 And we are his witnesses of these things; and so is also the Holy Ghost, whom God hath given to them that obey him. (Acts 5:32)

298 God of light and righteousness:

God is light, and in him is no darkness at all.

If we say that we have fellowship with him, and walk in darkness, we lie, and do not the truth. (1 John 1:5,6)

Note: from these scriptures, we can conclude that there is no *yin/yang.* In other words, God is not half-light and half-dark. Sin and evil are dark. Righteousness and good are light. The Devil is dark. God is light. He who does God's will is light. He who does the Devil's will is dark.

299 And I will pray the Father, and he shall give you another Comforter, that he may abide with you forever;

Even the Spirit of truth; whom the world cannot receive, because it seeth him not, neither knoweth him: but ye know him; for he dwelleth with you, and •*shall be in* you. (John 14:16,17)

•Note: Here Jesus was speaking of the future indwelling of the Holy Spirit, which would take place on the day of Pentecost when the disciples were baptized with the Holy Spirit. Though they had received the Holy Spirit's regeneration when Jesus breathed life in them and they were born again after being dead in their sins; they were *not* Holy Spirit baptized yet (or filled with the Spirit), because he told them later on to *wait* for the baptism of the Holy Ghost.

And, being assembled together with them, commanded them that they should not depart from Jerusalem, but *wait* for the promise of the Father, which, saith he, ye have heard of me.

For John truly baptized with water; but ye shall be baptized with the Holy Ghost not many days hence. (Acts 1:4,5)

300 Big Boy Restaurant Franchise © Syndicated.

301 Hot fudge ice cream cake ™ © Big Boy Restaurant Franchise; ibid.

302 Wherefore he [God] saith, Awake thou that sleepest, and arise from the dead, and Christ shall give thee light. (Ephesians 5:14)

303 I was blind, but now I see: Borrowed from the song *Amazing Grace* w: John Newton (1725-1807).

304 But now ye also put off all these; anger, wrath, malice, blasphemy, filthy communication out of your mouth. (Colossian 3:8)

Let no corrupt communication proceed out of your mouth, but that which is good to the use of edifying, that it may minister grace unto the hearers. (Ephesians 4:29)

305 Chevrolet *Cavalier* ™ © General Motors.

306 Spirit of fear: Fear is an open door for the Devil to come into our lives. He delights in terror. Look at Halloween, for example

For the thing which I [Job] greatly feared has come upon me, and that which I was afraid of is come unto me. (Job 3:25)

The fear of man bringeth a snare: but whoso putteth his trust in the Lord shall be safe. (Proverbs 29:25)

For God hath not given us the spirit of fear; but of power, and of love, and of a sound mind. (2 Timothy 1:7)

307 Jesus bought back my soul:

The Lord redeemeth the soul of his servants: and none of them that trust in him shall be desolate. (Psalm 34:22)

For great is thy mercy toward me: and thou hast delivered my soul from the lowest hell. (Psalm 86:13)

Forasmuch as ye know that ye were not redeemed with corruptible things, as silver and gold, from your vain conversation received by tradition from your fathers;

But with the precious blood of Christ, as of a lamb without blemish and without spot. (1 Peter 1:18,19)

For ye are bought with a price: therefore glorify God in your body, and in your spirit, which are God's. (1 Corinthians 6:20)

308 Stoner: one who does drugs, or *gets stoned.*

309 For this cause God gave them up unto vile affections: for even their women did change the natural use into that which is against nature:

And likewise also the men, leaving the natural use of the woman, burned in their lust one toward another; men with men working that which is unseemly, and receiving in themselves that recompence of their error which was meet. (Romans 1:26,27)

310 *Chasing the Dragon* © June 1982 by Jackie Pullinger/Jackie Pillinger; Servant Publications; ISBN: 0892831510.

311 They looked unto him [God], and were lightened [translates: *radiant]:* and their faces were not ashamed. (Psalm 34:5)

And after six days Jesus taketh James, and John his brother, and bringeth them into an high mountain

And was transfigured before them: and his face did shine as the sun, and his raiment was white as the light. (Matthew 17:1,2)

And it came to pass when Moses came down from mount Sinai with the two tables of testimony in Moses' hand, when he came down from the mount, that Moses wist not [knew not] that the skin of his face shone while he talked with him [with God].

And when Aaron and all the children of Israel saw Moses, behold, the skin of his face shone: and they were afraid to come nigh him. (Exodus 34:29,30)

...A man's wisdom maketh his face to shine, and the boldness of his face shall be changed. (Ecclesiastes 8:1)

Translation *radiant* from *Strong's Exhaustive Concordance of the Bible* by James Strong; S.T.D., LL.D., 1890; public domain.

312  Since every person is not on the same level spiritually, and each has sins and strongholds that differ one from another, God deals with us all differently. When we come to Him, we are not handed a list of changes to accomplish overnight. But as we grow and mature, He weeds out, by His power working within us, the things that are not profitable in our lives—the things that cause us to stumble. What might be a sin for one person, therefore, is not necessarily a sin for another person, depending on where they are at in their spiritual walk. It only becomes a sin for them once God reveals that a change in that area is required, for James 4:17 says,

Therefore to him that *knoweth* to do good, and doeth it not, to him it is sin.

Of course, before knowing Jesus as our Savior, we already know certain things are sin because our conscience tells us so, but because we are unregenerated and continue on in spiritual darkness, our minds are blinded to those sins, and therefore God must again reveal to us the truth about these things once we turn to him.

313  Lot's wife: Salt is a preservative. Lot's wife turned into a pillar of salt as punishment from the Lord, because she *looked back* with longing on the life she left behind, seeking to preserve it.

And when the morning arose, then the angels hastened Lot, saying, Arise, take thy wife, and thy two daughters, which are here; lest thou be *consumed in the iniquity* of the city.

And it came to pass, when they had brought them forth abroad, that he said, Escape for thy life; *look not behind thee,* neither *stay* thou in all the plain; escape to the mountain, lest thou be consumed.

And he [God] overthrew those cities, and all the plain, and all the inhabitants of the cities, and that which grew upon the ground.

But his wife looked back from behind him, and she became a pillar of salt. (Genesis 19:15,17,25,26)

314 Nevertheless among the chief rulers also many believed on him [Jesus]; but because of the Pharisees they did not confess him, lest they should be put out of the synagogue.

For they loved the praise of men more than the praise of God. (John 12:42,43)

315 God is not politically correct. Jesus was not, and *is* not, politically correct, and his disciples were not, and *should not strive to be,* politically correct. Though the truth offends many, the truth must be told.

God's word says:

Lord, who shall abide in thy tabernacle? who shall dwell in thy holy hill?

He that walketh uprightly, and worketh righteousness, and speaketh the truth in his heart. (Psalm 15:1,2)

The wicked shall be turned into hell, and all the nations that forget God. (Psalm 9:17)

Jesus said:

"...I am the way, the truth, and the life: no man cometh unto the Father, but by me." (John 14:6)

"Blessed are ye, when men shall hate you, and when they shall separate you from their company, and shall reproach you, and cast out your name as evil, for the Son of man's [Jesus'] sake." (Luke 6:22)

Paul said:

"For do I now persuade men, or God? or do I seek to please men? for if I yet pleased men, I should not be the servant of Christ." (Galatians 1:10)

"But as we were allowed of God to be put in trust with the gospel, even so we speak; not as pleasing men, but God, which trieth our hearts.

For neither at any time used we flattering words, as ye know, nor a cloke of covetousness; God is witness.

Nor of men sought we glory, neither of you, nor yet of others, when we might have been burdensome, as the apostles of Christ". (1 Thessalonians 2:4-6)

316 Inspired by *Boundaries: When to Say Yes, When to Say No, To Take Control of Your Life* © 1992 by Henry Cloud and John Townsend; Zondervan Publishing House; ISBN: 0-310-58590-2.

317 Therefore if any man be in Christ, he is a new creature: old things are passed away; behold, all things are become new. (2 Corinthians 5:17)

318 He healeth the broken in heart, and bindeth up their wounds. (Psalm 147:3)

The Spirit of the Lord God is upon me; because the Lord hath anointed me to preach good tidings unto the meek; he hath sent me to bind up the brokenhearted, to proclaim liberty to the captives, and the opening of the prison to them that are bound. (Isaiah 61:1)

319 Passover: a type and shadow of Jesus Christ: The lamb's blood (animal sacrifice to cover sin as in the beginning when God clothed Adam and Eve with animal skins) was smeared on the top and two sides of the door of houses (signifying the trinity of Father, Son and Holy Spirit, and also similar to the beams of a cross); to keep the plague of death from entering in when it slew the Egyptians, or unbelievers, in the land.

Note: God ordained animal sacrifices until the time of Christ's death, because there had to be a sacrifice for sin (blood for blood, life for life—Leviticus 17:11) something to die instead of man, and no man could die for another man's sins because all of mankind had sinned and come short of the glory of God. Animals can't sin, so they were the only substitutional sacrifice that could be offered until the sinless man, Jesus Christ (Yeshua ha Massiach), could die for the sins of the world. Christ never sinned; he was without blemish (or fault).

The Passover lamb had to be without blemish and spot, as Christ was without blemish and spot (without sin, pure):

Old Testament:

Your lamb shall be without blemish, a male of the first year: ye shall take it out from the sheep, or from the goats: (Exodus 12:5)

New Testament Fulfillment:

The next day John seeth Jesus coming unto him, and saith, Behold the Lamb of God, which taketh away the sins of the world. (John 1:29)

Old Testament:

And ye shall keep it up until the fourteenth day of the same month: and *the whole assembly of the congregation of Israel* shall kill it in the evening. (Exodus 12:6)

(Note: The Jews killed Jesus, or had him killed by the hand of the Romans because the Romans had taken away their right to inflict capital punishment).

New Testament Fulfillment:

And it came to pass, when Jesus had finished all these sayings, he said unto his disciples,

Ye know that after two days is the *feast of the passover,* and the Son of man [Jesus] is betrayed to be crucified.

Then *assembled together the chief priests, and the scribes, and the elders of the people [the congregation of Jewish religious leaders],* unto the palace of the high priest, who was called Caiaphas,

And consulted that they might take Jesus by subtilty, and kill him.

But they said, Not on the feast day, lest there should be an uproar among the people (Matthew 26:1-5)

And it was the preparation of the *passover,* and about the sixth hour: and he [Pilate] saith unto the Jews, Behold your King!

But they cried out, Away with him, away with him, crucify him, crucify him...

Then delivered he him therefore unto them to be crucified. And they took Jesus, and led him away. (John 19:14-16)

Old Testament:

And they shall take of the blood, and strike it on the two side posts and on the upper door post of the houses [see endnote 203 under *House;* also see endnote 108 under *Castle]* wherein they shall eat it [the lamb].

And they shall eat the flesh in that night, roast with fire, and unleavened bread; and with bitter herbs they shall eat it. (Exodus 12:7,8)

New Testament Fulfillment:

Jesus said,

"Whoso eateth my flesh and drinketh my blood [not literally, but figuratively: in a *spiritual* sense] ...hath eternal life; and I will raise him up at the last day." (John 6:54)

Old Testament:

For I will pass through the land of Egypt this night, and will smite all the *firstborn in the land of Egypt,* [symbolically this represents those born the first time—*naturally,* rather than the second time—*spiritually,* for Jesus said to see or enter the kingdom of heaven, one must be born *again* (John 3:3-7)], both man and beast; and against all the gods will I execute *judgment:* I am the Lord.

And the blood shall be to you for a token upon the *houses* [symbolically, our temples, or bodies—in the spiritual, physical and material sense] where ye are: and when I see the blood, I will *pass over* you, and the plague [of death] shall not be upon you to destroy you, when I smite the land of Egypt [Egypt is a type, or symbolism, of *sin. God executed judgment against all the gods of Egypt.* God took his people out of sinful Egypt and made them pass over the Red Sea: *Red,* as a type of Christ's blood, and *Sea,* as a type of the washing of water by the word of God (Ephesians 5:25,26), into the Promised Land (Salvation/ Eternal Life). (Exodus 12:12,13)]

New Testament Fulfillment:

Forasmuch then as the children are partakers of flesh and blood, he [Jesus] also himself likewise took part of the same, that through death [the killing of his flesh/shedding of his blood] he might destroy him that had the power of death, that is, the devil.

And deliver them who through fear of death were all their lifetime subject to bondage. (Hebrews 2:14,15)

Forasmuch as ye know that ye were not redeemed with corruptible things... but with the precious blood of Christ, as of a lamb without blemish and without spot. (1 Peter 1:18,19)

And he [Jesus] took bread, and gave thanks, and brake it, and gave unto them, saying, This is my body which is given for you: this do in remembrance of me.

Likewise also the cup after supper, saying, This cup is the new testament in my blood, which is shed for you. (Luke 22:19,20)

Much more then, being now justified by his blood, we shall be saved from wrath [the *judgment* of God] through him. (Romans 5:9)

320 And Jesus said unto her, Neither do I condemn thee: go and sin no more. (John 8:11)

My little children, these things write I unto you, that ye sin not.

And *if* any man sin, we have an advocate with the Father, Jesus Christ the righteous. (1 John 2:1)

Nevertheless, I have somewhat against thee, because thou hast left thy first love [left a relationship with Christ based on intimate knowledge of Him (seeking him in adoration/devotion/prayer) and being familiar with his character as well as obeying his command to live holy lives].

Remember therefore from whence thou art fallen, and repent, and do the first works; or else I will come unto thee quickly, and will remove thy candlestick out of his place, except thou repent. (Revelation 2:4,5)

And Jesus answering said unto them, Suppose ye that these Galilaeans were sinners above all the Galilaeans, because they suffered such things? I tell you, Nay: but except ye repent, ye shall all likewise perish.

Or those eighteen, upon whom the tower in Siloam fell, and slew them, think ye that they were sinners above all men that dwell in Jerusalem?

I tell you, Nay: but except ye repent, ye shall all likewise perish. (Luke 13:2-5)

And being made perfect, he [Jesus] became the author of eternal salvation [eternal security] unto *all them that obey him.* (Hebrews 5:9)

*What is the contrapositive of this statement?*

Jesus is *not* the author of eternal salvation (eternal security) to those who do *not* obey him.

But your iniquities have separated between you and your God, and your sins have hid his face from you, that he will not hear. (Isaiah 59:2)

For which of you, intending to build a tower, sitteth not down first, and counteth the cost, whether he have sufficient to finish it?

Lest haply, after he hath laid the foundation, and is not able to finish it [forsakes it], all that behold it begin to mock him,

Saying, this man began to build, and was not able to finish.

So likewise, whosoever he be of you that forsaketh not all that he hath, he cannot be my disciple. (Luke 14:28-30; 33)

THERE IS A COST TO SALVATION. IT REQUIRES LIVING A HOLY LIFE—PRACTICING RIGHTEOUSNESS AS WE CONTINUE TO BE CONFORMED INTO CHRIST'S IMAGE—AND ENDURING UNTIL THE END. IF A PERSON SINS AND **DOES NOT REPENT OF HIS SIN,** HE IS NO LONGER SAVED, BUT SEPARATED FROM GOD AND ETERNAL LIFE.

321 Loved the whole world: God does not discriminate. He is no respecter of persons, for respect of persons is a sin (James 2:9; Acts 10:34,35). He has given **everyone** an equal chance to come to him, predestinating, or predetermining beforehand, *only* a PLAN by which they can be saved through his Son, Jesus. It is an invitation extending to **all,** but unfortunately, not all will *choose* to accept it. Those who accept it then become the chosen. God predetermined that there would be a people who would accept his Son and be conformed to his image, but he didn't know *who* they were from the beginning of time.

Although he can move men's hearts to accomplish his plans or prophecies (providential government), he does not move their hearts against their will to be saved; they must make the conscious choice. Once they decide to be saved, through free will, they can also change their minds and opt out at any time, to which they would no longer be the chosen and predestined.

For God so loved the world, that he gave his only begotten Son, that **whosoever** believeth in him should not perish, but have everlasting life. (John 3:16)

The Lord is not slack concerning his promise, as some men count slackness; but is longsuffering to us-ward, not willing that **any** should perish, but that **all** should come to repentance. (2 Peter 3:9)

322 Many who say they are Jews: (See Revelation 2:9; Revelation 3:9):

God loves the Jews—they are a people he chose for his very own and he has an everlasting covenant with them—IF… they accept his redemptive plan.

He sent them the ultimate blood sacrifice: Jesus Christ, their Messiah—a sacrifice better than that of animals. Jesus (or Yeshua, in Hebrew) fulfilled over 365 biblical prophecies concerning the coming Messiah. Even the Torah and Tanakh declare the Son of God, and state clearly that redemption and eternal life are found in him. The only way for the Jew to be saved is to accept God's promised Son as the sacrifice for their sins.

And God said, Let **us** make man in **our** image, after **our** likeness [Father, **Son** and Holy Spirit] … (Genesis 1:26)

Who hath ascended up into heaven, or descended? who hath gathered the wind in his fists? who hath bound the waters in a garment? who hath established all the ends of the earth? what is his name, and **what is his son's name**, if thou canst tell? (Proverbs 30:4)

Kiss the Son, lest he be angry, and ye perish from the way, when his wrath is kindled but a little. Blessed are all they that put their trust in him. (Psalm 2:12)

Therefore the Lord himself shall give you a sign; Behold, a virgin shall conceive, and bear a **son,** and shall call his name Immanuel [God with us] (Isaiah 7:14)

For unto us a child is born, unto us **a son is given:** and the government shall be upon his shoulder: **and his name shall be called** Wonderful, Counsellor, **The mighty God, The everlasting Father,** The Prince of Peace. (Isaiah 9:6)

He is despised and rejected of men; a man of sorrows, and acquainted with grief: and we hid as it were our faces from him; he was despised, and we esteemed him not.

Surely he hath borne our griefs, and carried our sorrows: yet we did esteem him stricken, smitten of God, and afflicted.

**But he was wounded for our transgressions, he was bruised for our iniquities:**

the chastisement of our peace was upon him; and with his stripes we are healed.

All we like sheep have gone astray; we have turned every one to his own way; and **the LORD hath laid on him the iniquity of us all.**

He was oppressed, and he was afflicted, yet he opened not his mouth: **he is brought as a lamb to the slaughter,** and as a sheep before her shearers is dumb, so he openeth not his mouth.

He was taken from prison and from judgment: and who shall declare his generation? for he was cut off out of the land of the living: **for the transgression of my people was he stricken.**

And he made his grave with the wicked, and with the rich in his death; because he had done no violence, neither was any deceit in his mouth.

Yet it pleased the LORD to bruise him; he hath put him to grief: **when thou shalt make his soul an offering for sin**... (Isaiah 53:3-10)

The New Testament states that the Jew is no longer a natural one, but a *spiritual* one. Whereas before, circumcision (or the removal of filth from the flesh—the foreskin) set the Jew apart from the Gentile, he is now called to be circumcised in *the heart*, or spirit; removing all sin from his *inward* parts. Sin could not be removed from his inward parts before Christ died to remove sin from the conscience—it could only be removed from *the flesh* (by covering it with the shed blood of animals—who had never sinned as man had). Now however, when one repents of his sins and accepts Jesus as his Lord and Savior, he fulfills the Old Testament command in Jeremiah 4:4, which says,

*Circumcise* yourselves to the Lord, and take away the *foreskins of your heart,* ye men of Judah and inhabitants of Jerusalem: lest my fury come forth like fire, and burn that none can quench it, because of the evil of your doings.

New Testament Parallel:

For he is not a Jew, which is one outwardly; neither is that circumcision, which is outward in the flesh:

But he is a Jew, which is one *inwardly;* and circumcision is that *of the heart,* in the spirit, and not in the *letter* [the letter meaning: the natural, written law apart from true spiritual regeneration]; whose praise is not of men, but of God. (Romans 2:28,29)

Next, the spiritual Jew is called to receive the promised Pentecost, or baptism of the Holy Spirit, to show that God has accepted the sacrifice for his sins (Christ dying *in place of* him), and has come down to fill the temple (his body), with the consuming fire (Holy Spirit, or Shekinah glory) which resides in the temple because the sacrifice is well pleasing to Him.

And suddenly there came a sound from heaven as of a rushing mighty wind, and it filled all the house where they were sitting.

And there appeared unto them cloven tongues like as of fire, and it sat upon each of them [showing the sacrifice of Christ in them was approved].

And they were all filled with the Holy Ghost, and *began to speak with other tongues, as the Spirit gave them utterance.* (Acts 2:1-4)

The Spirit of the living God dwells *within* the saved believer upon baptism of the Holy Ghost (*Ghost* meaning the *Spirit* of God), enabling him to live a victorious life as he is continuously purged of old habits, living out the new spirit man. The Day of Pentecost occurred 50 days after the Passover Feast in the Old Testament, just as in the New Testament, Jesus commanded his disciples to *wait* for the promise of the Father, the Holy Spirit. Fifty days after his blood atonement on the cross (a type of *spiritual* Passover), the disciples gathered at Pentecost and were filled with the consuming fire of God: the Holy Ghost. They then went out as witnesses to Samaria, Judaea, and the uttermost part of the earth, empowered for an effective ministry, as even Jesus himself was baptized with the Holy Spirit before beginning *his* ministry (See John 1:32,33; Acts 10:38; Luke 3:16)

323 Bow their knee: (See Philippians 2:10; Romans 14:11)

324 Cutting/inflicting pain upon one's self is a sign of demonic oppression, or in some cases, demonic *possession*. A person who resorts to such measures is in the clutches of Satan, the great destroyer. I should know, because I *was* such a person! Refer to chapter eight concerning *butcher knife*.

And when he [Jesus] was come out of the ship, immediately there met him out of the tombs a man with an unclean spirit [or demon].

Who had his dwelling among the tombs; and no man could bind him, no, not with chains:

Because that he had been often bound with fetters and chains, and the chains had been plucked asunder by him, and the fetters broken in pieces: neither could any man tame him.

And always, night and day, he was in the mountains, and in the tombs, crying, and cutting himself with stones. (Mark 5:2-5)

325 © Billy Graham Ministries.

326 Soul mate: Though God designed husband and wife to be *help mates* for each other (Genesis 2:18, 22-24), the greatest soul mate one can have is the one who cares the most for his/her soul: Jesus. After all, he loved us while we were yet sinners and blasphemers and haters of God—enough to die for the salvation of our souls.

For ye were as sheep going astray; but are now returned unto the Shepherd and Bishop [over seer] of your souls. (1 Peter 2:25)

For scarcely for a righteous man will one die: yet peradventure for a good man some would even dare to die.

But God commendeth his love toward us in that, while we were yet sinners, Christ died for us. (Romans 5:7,8)

327 And the seventy returned again with joy, saying, Lord, even the devils are subject unto us through thy name. (Luke 10:17)

And these signs shall follow them that believe; In my name shall they cast out devils; they shall speak with new tongues;

They shall take up serpents; and if they drink any deadly thing, it shall not hurt them; they shall lay hands on the sick, and they shall recover. (Mark 16:17,18)

328 Dodge Omni © Chrysler Corporation.

329 Pizza Hut Restaurant © Pizza Hut Incorp.

330 Water baptism is an act that *follows* conversion, for one must first take the necessary steps of salvation. Romans 10:9,10 tell us that *confession of the Lord*

*Jesus with the mouth* and *belief in the heart* that God has raised him from the dead are the steps of salvation:

That if thou shalt *confess with thy mouth* the Lord Jesus, and shalt *believe in thine heart* that God hath raised him from the dead, *thou shalt be saved.*

One must first be a believer in order to be water baptized. Observe the conversation Philip had with the Ethiopian eunuch:

As they went on their way, they came unto a certain water: and the eunuch said, See, here is water; what doth hinder me to be baptized?

And Philip said, If thou believest with all thine heart, thou mayest. And he answered and said, I believe that Jesus Christ is the Son of God.

And he commanded the chariot to stand still: and they went down both into the water, both Philip and the eunuch; and he baptized him. (Acts 8:36-38)

331 Killed himself: The Devil attempts to steal people's souls by influencing them to take their own lives, for then he knows he has gained a soul for Hell—another person who will suffer eternally as *he* will.

The thief [Satan] cometh not but for to steal, and to kill, and to destroy: I [Jesus] am come that they might have life, and that they might have it more abundantly. (John 10:10)

Note: the Devil can't succeed in influencing people to commit suicide, unless, of course, they allow him to. People have a free will to disobey God, resulting in sin and demonic oppression. They also have a choice to turn to God and be free from sin and oppression.

332 The prince of this world is the Devil:

Now is the judgment of this world: now shall the prince of this world be *cast out.* (John 12:31)

And the great dragon was cast out, that old serpent, called the Devil, and Satan, which deceiveth the whole world: he was *cast out* into the earth, and his angels with him. (Revelation 12:9)

333 For rebellion is as the sin of witchcraft, and stubbornness is as iniquity and idolatry... 1 Samuel 15:23)

334 *The Satanic Bible* © June 1989 (Mass Market Paperback Reissue edition) by Anton S. La Vey/LaVey; Avon; ISBN: 0380015390.

335 *Magick In Theory And Practice* © by Aleister Crowley; Castle Publications; Out of print.

336 Satan's five I WILLS: see Isaiah 14:12-14

337 He that committeth sin is of the devil; for the devil sinneth from the beginning. (1 John 3:8)

Prophetic music by GEORGIA PLUME
soundcloud.com/paulagilbert


In Union With God Ministries
inunionwithGod.com

Printed in the United States
By Bookmasters